Temporary Equilibrium
Selected Readings

This is a volume in
ECONOMIC THEORY, ECONOMETRICS,
AND MATHEMATICAL ECONOMICS

Consulting Editor: Karl Shell, Cornell University

A list of recent titles in this series appears at the end of this volume.

Temporary Equilibrium
Selected Readings

Edited by

Jean-Michel Grandmont

*Centre d'Etudes Prospectives d'Economie Mathématique
Appliquées à la Plantification
Paris, France*

ACADEMIC PRESS, INC.
Harcourt Brace Jovanovich, Publishers
Boston   San Diego   New York
Berkeley   London   Sydney
Tokyo   Toronto

ACADEMIC PRESS, INC.
1250 Sixth Avenue, San Diego, CA 92101

United Kingdom Edition published by
ACADEMIC PRESS, INC. (London) Ltd.
24–28 Oval Road, London NW1 7DX

Library of Congress Cataloging-in-Publication Data

Temporary equilibrium.

(Economic theory, econometrics, and mathematical
economics)
    Bibliography: p.
    Includes index.
    1. Equilibrium (Economics)   I. Grandmont, Jean-
Michel.   II. Series.
HB145.T45   1987   339.5   87-1128
ISBN 0-12-295145-X (alk. paper)
ISBN 0-12-295146-8 (pbk. : alk. paper)

Printed in the United States of America
88 89 90 91 9 8 7 6 5 4 3 2 1

Contents

A la mémoire d'André Nataf   ix

Preface   xi

Acknowledgements   xiii

Introduction   xv

I. Temporary Equilibrium : An Overview   1
1. J.M. Grandmont, Temporary general equilibrium theory, *Econometrica* **45** (1977), 535–572.   3
2. J.M. Grandmont, Temporary equilibrium theory: an addendum.   41

II. Decision Making   85
1. J.M. Grandmont, Continuity properties of a von Neumann-Morgenstern utility, *J. Econ. Theory* **4** (1972), 45–57.   87
2. J.S. Jordan, The continuity of optimal dynamic decision rules, *Econometrica* **45** (1977), 1365–1376.   101

III. Competitive Assets Markets   113
1. J.R. Green, Temporary general equilibrium in a sequential trading model with spot and futures transactions, *Econometrica* **41** (1973), 1103–1123.   115
2. O.D. Hart, On the existence of equilibrium in a securities model, *J. Econ. Theory* **9** (1974), 293–311.   137
3. P.J. Hammond, Overlapping expectations and Hart's conditions for equilibrium in a securities model, *J. Econ. Theory* **31** (1983), 170–175.   156

IV. Models of Money   163
1. J.M. Grandmont, On the short-run equilibrium in a monetary economy, *in* "Allocation under Uncertainty: Equilibrium and Optimality", (J Drèze, ed.), pp. 213–228, New York: Macmillan, 1974.   165
2. J.M. Grandmont and Y. Younès, On the role of money and the existence of a monetary equilibrium, *Review of Economic Studies* **39** (1972), 355–372.   181
3. J.M. Grandmont and Y. Younès, On the efficiency of a monetary equilibrium, *Review of Economic Studies* **40** (1973), 149–165.   199

4.   F. Gagey, G. Laroque, and S. Lollivier, Monetary and fiscal poli-
       cies in a general equilibrium model, *J. Econ. Theory* **39** (1986),
       329–357.   217

V.   Deterministic Dynamics   **247**
1.   G. Fuchs and G. Laroque, Dynamics of temporary equilibria and
       expectations, *Econometrica* **44** (1976), 1157–1178.   249
2.   G. Tillmann, Stability in a simple pure consumption loan model,
       J. Econ. Theory **30** (1983), 315–329.   271
3.   G. Fuchs, Is error learning behaviour stabilizing?, *J. Econ. The-
       ory* **20** (1979), 300–317.   286

VI.   Stochastic Processes   **305**
1.   J.M. Grandmont and W. Hildenbrand, Stochastic processes of
       temporary equilibria, *Journal of Mathematical Economics* **1**
       (1974), 247–277.   307
2.   L.E. Blume, New techniques for the study of stochastic equilib-
       rium processes, *Journal of Mathematical Economics* **9** (1982), 61–
       70.   339
3.   S.E. Spear and S. Srivastava, Markov rational expectations equi-
       libria in an overlapping generations model, *J. Econ. Theory* **38**
       (1986), 35–62.
       Corrigendum, *J. Econ. Theory* **39** (1986), 464–466.   349

VII.   Quantity Rationing   **381**
1.   J.P. Benassy, Neo-Keynesian disequilibrium theory in a monetary
       economy, *The Review of Economic Studies* **42** (1975), 503–523. 383
2.   J.M. Grandmont, G. Laroque, and Y. Younès, Equilibrium with
       quantity rationing and recontracting, *J. Econ. Theory* **19** (1978),
       84–102.   404
3.   F. Hahn, On non-Walrasian equilibria, *The Review of Economic
       Studies* **45** (1978), 1–17.   423
4.   D. Gale, A note on conjectural equilibria, *The Review of Eco-
       nomic Studies* **45** (1978), 33–38.   441
5.   O. Hart, A model of imperfect competition with Keynesian fea-
       tures, *Quarterly Journal of Economics* **97** (1982), 109–138.   447

A la mémoire d'André Nataf

Some readers may be surprised to see a book on temporary equilibrium dedicated to the memory of André Nataf. As exemplified by the following sample of his publications, André Nataf is most well known for his work on the theory of choice, demand theory, and on the theory of aggregation.

I wish to pay tribute here to one of his achievements that is perhaps less well known but no less important. André Nataf was one of these economists who worked hard, since the end of World War II, to promote in France the application of formal methods to economics. He chaired, in particular, the CERMAP since its foundation in 1961 by Pierre Massé, which was one of the first sizeable research institutes in France designed to develop the application of mathematical methods to the study of planning and of economics. The institute was to merge in 1969 with the CEPREL, then headed by Jean Benard, to give birth to CEPREMAP. I knew André Nataf as a research associate at CERMAP from 1964 to 1968. The scientist as well as the man was impressive. His natural kindness, his constant care for trying to make abstract theory bear on practical issues, and, above all, his high standards of intellectual honesty, both in his scientific and his personal life, were and still are an example to all of us.

André Nataf died in August, 1968, a few weeks before my arrival as a PhD student in Berkeley, where my interest in temporary equilibrium analysis and, more generally, in providing more precise microeconomic foundations to macroeconomics, began to shape. Formal economic theory and econometrics are by now lively disciplines in France. The personal contribution of André Nataf to this happy development was important. Let the publication of this book be the occasion for all of us to remember him. We owe him much.

Selected Publications of André Nataf

Sur la possibilité de construction de certains macromodèles, *Econometrica* **16** (1948), 232–244.

Remarques et suggestions relatives aux nombres-indices, *Econometrica* **16** (1948), 330–346, with R. Roy.

La causalité dans le théorème du rendement social (abs.), *Econometrica* **18** (1950), 65–67, with M.J. Verhulst.

Remarques sur les fonctions de production (abs.), *Econometrica* **19** (1951), 192.

Etudes de la demande d'importation de certains produits aux Etats-Unis entre les deux guerres, *Cahiers du Séminaire d'Econométrie* **1** (1951), 114–122.

Influence du revenu et de sa distribution sur la demande (abs.), *Econometrica* **20** (1952), 310–311.

L'agrégation dans les théories économiques bien spécifiées (abs.), *Econometrica* **22** (1954), 112.

Aperçu historique sur l'agrégation, *Cahiers du Séminaire d'Econométrie* **4** (1956), 25–36.

Influence des investissements sur l'évolution des prix (abs.), *Ecoometrica* **25** (1957), 479.

Consommation en prix et revenus réels et théorie des choix, *Econometrica* **27** (1959), 329–354, with C. Fourgeaud.

Modèle à prix variables et plans de développement (abs.), *Econometrica* **31** (1963), 264.

Les travaux sur les problèmes de l'agrégation de 1952 à 1962 (abs.), *Econometrica* **32** (1964), 448.

"Théorie des Choix et Fonctions de Demande", Monographies du Centre d'Econométrie, CNRS, Paris, 1964.

Preface

The conventional theory of general economic equilibrium (Arrow, Debreu, and McKenzie) has undergone a significant reappraisal during the seventies which was prompted by the recognition of its essentially static nature. The resulting class of so-called temporary equilibrium models takes into account the fact that markets take place sequentially over time and that economic units may only learn gradually the dynamic laws of their environment. The reappraisal led to major improvements of our understanding of long-standing issues, such as the microeconomic foundations of monetary theory or the choice-theoretic structure of traditional Keynesian macroeconomic models of unemployment.

The collection of articles reproduced in this book provides a synthetic view of the progress made in the last fifteen years in the field. The topics covered include: individual decision-making under uncertainty; the existence of an equilibrium, in the short run, in competitive assets markets; the integration of money and, in particular, of its role as a medium of exchange, into competitive equilibrium theory; the stability of a long-run equilibrium when traders use prespecified learning processes; the study of stochastic processes of short-run equilibria when the economy is subjected to random shocks; and the analysis of short-run equilibria with quantity rationing with temporarily given prices and of their connections with Keynesian macroeconomic models or with the theory of imperfect competition. The book also offers an overview of the field as well as a fairly extensive bibliography.

This collection of readings can be used as the basis of a one semester graduate course in economic theory. It should be a useful tool to students and professional economists interested in the long-standing problem of providing macroeconomic theory with adequate microeconomic foundations.

Jean-Michel Grandmont

Acknowledgements

The author and publisher are grateful to the following publishers and authors for granting permission to reproduce the articles that are included in the present book. Specific thanks are due to:

The Econometric Society for the articles: Dynamics of temporary equilibria and expectations, *Econometrica* **44** (1976), 1157–1178, by G. Fuchs and G. Laroque; Temporary general equilibrium theory, *Econometrica* **45** (1977), 535–572, by J.M. Grandmont; Temporary general equilibrium in a sequential trading model with spot and futures transactions, *Econometrica* **41** (1973), 1103–1123, by J.R. Green; The continuity of optimal dynamical decision rules, *Econometrica* **45** (1977), 1365–1376, by J.S. Jordan.

The Society for Economic Analysis Ltd. for the articles: Neo-Keynesian disequilibrium theory in a monetary economy, *Review of Economic Studies* **42** (1975), 503–523, by J.P. Benassy; A note on conjectural equilibria, *Review of Economic Studies* **45** (1978), 33–38, by D Gale; On the role of money and the existence of a monetary equilibrium, *Review of Economic Studies* **39** (1972), 355–372, by J.M. Grandmont and Y. Younès; On the efficiency of a monetary equilibrium, *Review of Economic Studies* **40** (1973), 149–165, by J.M. Grandmont and Y. Younès; On non-Walrasian equilibria, *Review of Economic Studies* **45** (1978), 1–17, by F.H. Hahn.

Elsevier Science Publishers B.V. (North-Holland) for the articles: New techniques for the study of stochastic equilibrium processes, *Journal of Mathematical Economics* **9** (1982), 61–70, by L.E. Blume; Stochastic processes of temporary equilibria, *Journal of Mathematical Economics* **1** (1974), 247–277, by J.M. Grandmont and W. Hildenbrand.

John Wiley and Sons, Inc. Publishers for the article, A model of imperfect competition with Keynesian features, *Quarterly Journal of Economics* **97** (1982), 109–138, by O.D. Hart.

Macmillan Press Ltd. for the article, On the short-run equilibrium in a monetary economy, *in* "Allocation under Uncertainty: Equilibrium and Optimality", J. Drèze (ed.), pp. 213–228, London: Macmillan, 1974, by J.M. Grandmont.

Academic Press, Inc., for the articles: Is error learning behaviour stabilizing?, *Journal of Economic Theory* **20** (1979), 300–317, by G. Fuchs; Monetary and fiscal policies in a general equilibrium model, *Journal of Economic Theory* **39** (1986), 329–357, by F. Gagey, G. Laroque, and S. Lollivier; Continuity properties of a von Neumann-Morgenstern utility, *Journal of Economic Theory* **4** (1972), 45–57, by J.M. Grandmont; Equilibrium with quantity rationing and recontracting, *Journal of Economic Theory* **19** (1978), 84–102, by J.M. Grandmont, G. Laroque, and Y. Younès; Overlapping expectations and Hart's conditions for equilibrium in a securities model, *Journal of Economic Theory* **31** (1983), 170–175, by P.J. Hammond; On the existence of equilibrium in a securities model, *Journal of Economic Theory* **9** (1974), 293–311, by O.D. Hart; Markov rational expectations equilibria in an overlapping generations model, *Journal of EconomicTheory* **38** (1986), 35–62, by S.E. Spear and S. Srivastava, and the corresponding Corrigendum, *Journal of Economic Theory* **39** (1986), 464–466; Stability in a pure consumption loan model, *Journal of Economic Theory* **30** (1983), 315–329, by G. Tillmann.

The author is most grateful to the editor of the series, Karl Shell, and to the staff of Academic Press, in particular to William Sribney, for their continuous and kind cooperation during the preparation of this book.

Introduction

We have witnessed in the last 15 years major improvements in our understanding of the microeconomic foundations of monetary theory, of macroeconomics, and of the theory of business cycles. The specific contribution of temporary equilibrium theory to this development has been important. This is not a fortuitous coincidence. The conceptual framework of the temporary equilibrium method, as designed long ago by Hicks [12, 13] and the Swedish school (Lindahl [16]), is indeed well adapted to the study of economic dynamics. It describes successfully the sequential unfolding of markets that takes place in actual economies in calendar time and, in particular, takes into account the subtle interplay between expectations of individual traders and actual realizations of economic variables that is so central to the workings of any economic or social system.

Collecting in a convenient book form a few significant articles in the field that have been published in scattered journals or books appears, accordingly, to be a worthy venture. By making more accessible the main ideas and achievements of the temporary equilibrium approach, this volume of readings will contribute, it is hoped, to the diffusion of methods that should be at the heart of the analysis of dynamic economic processes for a long time to come.

It seems unnecessary to review again here an area that has been surveyed already elsewhere. In this respect, the readers will find in the first chapter of the present volume an updated overview with a fairly extensive list of references. What I wish to do, instead, in this introduction is to present briefly, at a fairly informal level, the salient features of the temporary equilibrium method and to discuss its relationships with the notion of an intertemporal equilibrium and with the axiom of self-fulfilling expectations. I argue that the study of dynamic economic processes *necessitates* the use of the temporary equilibrium method or some elaboration of it. The basic point here is the obvious enough but sometimes neglected observation that, in a genuine dynamical economic system, the future *must* be forecast on the basis of the past. We shall see that the temporary equilibrium approach includes self-fulfilling expectations as a particular case. The approach is actually more general since it permits, in principle, incorporation into the analysis of the fact that economic units typically learn only gradually the dynamic laws of their environment, and thus it provides an understanding of how traders may succeed in eventually coordinating their forecasts in decentralized economies. None of these points is novel or very deep, but since they are not, perhaps, understood as widely as they should be, I felt that they needed a little emphasis.

In order to convey these ideas most neatly, I shall look at a simple example. Let us disregard all sources of uncertainty and, working in discrete time, focus on the case where the state of the economy at any date t can be described by a single real number x_t in some feasible set X. Suppose that there are m economic units indexed by $i = 1, ..., m$ and, to simplify matters further, that the equilibrium state at date t is completely determined by the forecasts $x^e_{i,t+1}$ made at the same date by all economic units about the state of the economy in the immediate future, through the functional relationship

$$x_t = f(x^e_{1,t+1}, ..., x^e_{i,t+1}, ..., x^e_{m,t+1}). \tag{1}$$

In this formulation f, a function from X^m into X, describes the outcome of the market equilibrating process in period t, i.e., x_t, for a given "state of expectations". This process may be competitive or the result of any other game-theoretic (non-Walrasian) equilibrium notion. Thus the function f depends on the "fundamental" characteristics of the agents (tastes, endowments, production technologies, and objectives), on the institutional set-up through which they interact, and on the policies followed by governmental agencies. The fact that f is assumed to be independent of t means that these characteristics are constant over time, or, at least, that they evolve according to laws that are themselves constant.

Intertemporal Equilibria with Self-fulfilling Expectations

An equilibrium concept that is routinely employed in this context is that of an intertemporal equilibrium with self-fulfilling expectations. It is defined as a sequence of states $\langle x_t \rangle$ and of forecasts $\langle x^e_{i,t+1} \rangle$ such that the market equilibrium equation (1) is verified and, in addition,

$$x^e_{i,t+1} = x_{t+1} \tag{2}$$

for all i and all dates t. "For all dates" means here for t greater than some initial date, say $t = 0$, or, in some circumstances, for all t varying from $-\infty$ to $+\infty$.

The fact that time appears explicitly as an index in this formulation should not deceive the reader. The above equilibrium concept is inherently static: *all elements of the sequences $\langle x_t \rangle$ and $\langle x^e_{i,t+1} \rangle$ are determined simultaneously* by an outside observer, hence the emphasis on the word "intertemporal" in the definition. All markets, past, present, and future are equilibrated at the same time.

If one tries to give a dynamical (i.e., recursive) interpretation of such an intertemporal equilibrium, one finds that, unfortunately, time goes in the wrong direction. Consider indeed an intertemporal equilibrium $\langle x_t \rangle$, $\langle x^e_{i,t+1} \rangle$, and look at the manner in which an equilibrium is obtained in period t. From (2), the *future* equilibrium state x_{t+1} determines the forecasts made in period t. The market equilibrium equation (1), in turn, determines the corresponding current state x_t. The resulting functional relationship is obtained by eliminating forecasts between (1) and (2):

$$x_t = F(x_{t+1}) \qquad (3)$$

where $F(x)$ is defined as $f(x, ..., x)$. One can thus give a recursive interpretation of an intertemporal equilibrium, but it is one in which at every date the future determines the present, an awkward violation of one of the elementary laws of physics. One might think it would be possible to get around the problem by "inverting" (3) so as to make time go forward. While mathematically correct, this procedure would not work: the crux of the difficulty lies in equation (2), which contradicts the principle that "the future must be forecast on the basis of the past"[1].

Sequences of Temporary Equilibria

The problem we face at this stage is writing down a genuine recursive dynamical system in which markets are actually equilibrated sequentially over time and in which at each date past history determines the current behavior of the traders and, thus, the current equilibrium state. To this end, as the previous discussion makes clear, and whether expectations are self-fulfilling or not, there is *no* other option than appending to the market equilibrium equation (1) a specification of the way in which traders form their forecasts, at each date, on the basis of their information on the current and past states of the economy.

If we assume, for the simplicity of the exposition, that every trader's information at each date t is fully described by the sequence $(x_t, x_{t-1}, ...)$,

---

[1] I cannot resist pointing out that this sentence is quoted from R.E. Lucas, Jr. and T.J. Sargent [18], Introduction, p. xvi.

this means that we have to supplement (1) with forecasting rules of the form[2]

$$x^e_{i,t+1} = \psi_i(x_t, x_{t-1}, \ldots) \tag{4}$$

or all i and t. To keep in line with the stationarity assumptions made up to now, the *expectations functions* ψ_i have been assumed to be constant over time. Note that whatever *a priori* information a trader has on the characteristics of the economy, on governmental policies, i.e., on the relation f, or on the other traders' forecasting rules, it is implicitly embodied in his expectations function.

Using (4), the market equilibrium relation (1) reads

$$x_t = f(\psi_1(x_t, x_{t-1}, \ldots), \ldots, \psi_m(x_t, x_{t-1}, \ldots)) \tag{5}$$

which determines, in principle, the temporary equilibrium state x_t and thus from (4), the current equilibrium forecasts, given the past history $(x_{t-1}, x_{t-2}, \ldots)$. The dynamical evolution of the simple economy under consideration is then described, given the temporary equilibrium map f and the forecasting rules ψ_i, as a sequence of temporary equilibria that unfolds recursively over time.

Self-fulfilling Expectations

Such sequences of temporary equilibria can generate intertemporal equilibria with self-fulfilling expectations under appropriate restrictions on the forecasting rules ψ_i. Assume that every trader has full information about the characteristics of the economy, i.e., knows the market equilibrium relation f and, thus, F. Consider next an arbitrary intertemporal equilibrium with self-fulfilling expectations and the corresponding sequence $\langle \bar{x}_t \rangle$ with t varying from $-\infty$ to $+\infty$. Since the sequence verifies (3), which involves the known map F, a trader observing at date t the time series $(\bar{x}_t, \bar{x}_{t-1}, \ldots)$ may infer that the observed recurrence will be obtained also in the future. To get a determinate forecast from that observation, however, the function F must be invertible. So, assume furthermore that F is monotone, so that it has an inverse F^{-1}, a function from $F(X)$ into X. The forecasting rule of each trader is assumed to obey

---

[2] We assume, for simplicity, that current and past forecasts are not arguments of the forecasting rules. Adding them would not change qualitatively the arguments presented below.

(H) For every sequence $(\bar{x}_t, \bar{x}_{t-1}, \ldots)$ that is part of an intertemporal equilibrium with self-fulfilling expectations,

$$\psi_i(\bar{x}_t, \bar{x}_{t-1}, \ldots) = F^{-1}(\bar{x}_t)$$

If the traders' forecasting rules are restricted in this way, any intertemporal equilibrium with self-fulfilling expectations can be generated as a sequence of temporary equilibria, i.e., as a solution of the dynamical system defined by (4) and (5), along which there are no forecasting errors. The reader will easily verify that the restrictions embodied in (H) are in fact necessary to get that outcome.

Note that to get a determinate sequence of temporary equilibria, it is crucial that the expectations functions in (H) depend actually on *past* states $(\bar{x}_{t-1}, \bar{x}_{t-2}, \ldots)$. If, on the contrary, each ψ_i depended only on x_t and satisfied (H), one would get $\psi_i(x) \equiv F^{-1}(x)$ for all x in $F(X)$ and (5) would become an identity; the temporary equilibrium x_t would be indeterminate in $F(X)$, and this would be true at every date. In fact, as far as the existence and determinateness of the sequence of temporary equilibria arising from (5) is concerned, it is highly recommended to work with expectations functions ψ_i—satisfying (H) if one wishes to get self-fulfilling forecasts—that display little sensitivity to the current state x_t and depend a lot on past history $(x_{t-1}, x_{t-2}, \ldots)$. Indeed, in the limit case where each ψ_i does not depend on x_t, (4) and (5) determine *uniquely* the current temporary equilibrium x_t and the current forecasts, given $(x_{t-1}, x_{t-2}, \ldots)$. Under appropriate differentiability conditions, this feature will be preserved if the elasticity of the expectations functions with respect to the current state x_t is small.[3]

It should be emphasized, finally, that condition (H) does *not* determine a unique forecasting rule. Examples of expectations functions that meet the condition and are independent of the current state are provided by

$$\psi_i(x_t, x_{t-1}, \ldots) \equiv F^{-k}(x_{t+1-k})$$

for an arbitrary $k \geq 2$, where F^{-k} is defined recursively by $F^{-j}(x) = F^{-1}(F^{-j+1}(x))$; but there are many others. The other remark is that the dynamical system obtained by solving (5) for x_t, given past history, may involve more or less long lags, although it is able to generate under assumption (H) the same trajectories as the simpler one-dimensional difference equation $x_{t+1} = F^{-1}(x_t)$.

---

[3] Such inelasticity conditions arise in many contexts when dealing with the existence of a temporary equilibrium with arbitrary prespecified forecasting rules. The previous argument shows that they arise also in the context of self-fulfilling expectations. This should be no surprise since the temporary equilibrium method encompasses self-fulfilling expectations as a particular case.

Learning

Let us summarize our findings. We saw that the notion of an intertemporal equilibrium is intrinsically timeless; in such a concept past, present, and future markets are equilibrated all at the same time. We found next that if one takes time seriously and wishes accordingly to develop a theory in which the market of period t is adjusted before the market of date $t + 1$ actually opens, it is necessary to prespecify a forecasting rule for each trader. The resulting sequence of temporary equilibria could in fact generate any intertemporal equilibrium with self-fulfilling expectations under appropriate (but generally nonunique) restrictions on the forecasting rules.

If we were interested exclusively in self-fulfilling expectations, the preceding argument, while admittedly of some importance from a conceptual viewpoint, would be largely a semantic matter. Confining oneself to self-fulfilling expectations, however, is unduly restrictive. The underlying assumptions, indeed, are extreme. There is first the fact that the map F must be invertible, a condition that is not generally verified in economic models.[4] But, above all, the requirement that all traders know the map F beforehand is exceedingly strong. It would mean, in particular, that all traders are fully informed about the other traders' characteristics, their behavior, the equilibrium mechanisms of the economy, etc.

Self-fulfilling expectations do not come out of heaven but are the *outcome* of a time-consuming learning process. Modelling properly the dynamical evolution of an economy requires, accordingly, specifying not only the internal equilibrium mechanisms of the economy—here equation (1)—but also how each trader learns the dynamics of his environment over time. Now, *any* learning process will generate in the end an expectations function specifying how forecasts are made on the basis of current and past observations. There is no loss of generality, therefore, in the simple case considered here, summarizing the traders' learning processes by the induced forecasting rules ψ_i, as in (4).

In this approach, learning processes and the corresponding expectations functions ψ_i belong to the characteristic data of the economy, on the same level as tastes, endowments, technologies, or governmental policies. As mentioned earlier, expectations functions do, however, incorporate implicitly whatever *a priori* information the traders may have on the fundamental characteristics of the economy or on the other traders' learning processes. This fact has to be kept in mind, of course, when

---

[4] Examples of such noninvertibility can be found, for instance, in Azariadis [1], Azariadis and Guesnerie [2], Benhabib and Day [6], and Grandmont [10]. See also [23].

performing comparative statics (or dynamics) exercises, in particular when evaluating the consequences of policy changes. The possible impacts of such policy changes, not only on the fundamental characteristics of the economy—i.e., on the temporary equilibrium map f—but also on the traders' forecasting rules ψ_i, will have to be carefully taken into account.

The fact that each forecasting rule ψ_i is assumed to be constant over time, as in (4), is compatible with changes of the agents' views about the world, provided that the dynamic rules governing these changes are themselves constant. For instance, trader i may employ a whole class of "models" of his environment, generating forecasting rules of the form

$$x_{i,t+1}^{e} = \psi_i^*(\alpha_t, x_t, x_{t-1}, \ldots)$$

where α_t is some unknown element (describing, e.g., "structural parameters") in some set A. The trader's estimation of α_t at date t, for example, through the application of some more or less complex but *given* statistical procedure, will result in some relation

$$\alpha_t = \alpha(x_t, x_{t-1}, \ldots).$$

Putting together these two relations yields indeed an expectations function as in (4).[5]

In the simple model considered here, the dynamic evolution of the economy will thus be described by a sequence of temporary equilibria verifying (4) and (5) at all dates, where the functions f and ψ_i have been prespecified. The dynamics actually observed by any single economic unit will then result from the interaction of the unknown map f and of the unknown forecasting rules employed by the other traders, which will complicate further the inference problem that has to be solved. Forecasting mistakes will occur presumably for a long time, and it is only in the long run that one may hope to see such mistakes to disappear, if they ever do.

Convergence to self-fulfilling expectations means here convergence of the trajectories $\langle x_t \rangle$ and of the forecasts $\langle x_{i,t+1}^{e} \rangle$ generated by (4) and (5) to a path $\langle \bar{x}_t \rangle$ along which forecasting errors vanish eventually, i.e., such that $|x_t - \bar{x}_t| \to 0$ and $|x_{i,t+1}^{e} - \bar{x}_{t+1}| \to 0$ as $t \to +\infty$. It seems, however, unlikely that such a convergence will actually be obtained if the dynamic structure of the limit path $\langle \bar{x}_t \rangle$ is too complex. The limit path must be regular (repetitive) enough to enable the traders to discover the laws of evolution of their environment.

[5]One may also assume that current and past forecasts belong to the information set of the trader and study "error learning" behavior of the sort that Gerard Fuchs analyzed extensively (See Chapters I and V).

In our simple deterministic context, it appears reasonable to restrict attention to stationary states ($\bar{x}_t = \bar{x}$ with $\bar{x} = F(\bar{x})$) or to periodic solutions of (3) and to analyze under which conditions, in particular on expectations functions, such "long-run equilibria" are stable in the dynamics arising from (5). We shall discuss this question more precisely in Chapter I, but one may note at this stage an interesting fact: taking into account learning on the transition path of the economy may reverse the stability of long-run equilibria, by comparison to the apparent stability one would get from the dynamics associated with self-fulfilling expectations. The intuition behind this result is that the essence of learning is to predict the future from the past, whereas with self-fulfilling expectations, as explained at the beginning of this introduction, it is as if the future determines the present.

As an illustration, consider the case of "naive expectations", $x^e_{i,t+1} = x_{t-1}$. From (5), then, sequences of temporary equilibria are solutions of $x_t = F(x_{t-1})$. A stationary state $\bar{x}$ will be (locally) stable in this dynamics if and only if it is *unstable* in the dynamics with self-fulfilling expectations, $x_{t+1} = F^{-1}(x_t)$, obtained by inverting equation (3) locally around $\bar{x}$. That sort of result extends to more general and plausible learning processes, as we shall see later in Chapter I. It illustrates the importance of incorporating learning in our models to understand the circumstances under which self-fulfilling expectations may or may not be obtained eventually in decentralized economies.

The argument has been conducted in the framework of a one-dimensional deterministic model for the simplicity of the exposition. It should be clear, nevertheless, that the foregoing findings extend qualitatively to multidimensional economies operating under uncertainty. In all cases, if one wishes to represent the dynamic evolution of an economy as a sequence of temporary equilibria, one must make explicit how at each date traders forecast the future on the basis of past observations, and only on that basis, by prespecifying their learning processes or expectations functions. Given such a framework, a number of issues have to be dealt with. First, under which conditions, in particular with regards to expectations functions, does a temporary equilibrium exist, and what are its properties? Second, does the economy under consideration possess long-run equilibria with self-fulfilling expectations (deterministic stationary states or cycles and stationary stochastic processes), and how many of them are there? Third, can we say something about the stability of these long-run equilibria? These are the sort of issues with which most of the papers reproduced in this book are concerned.

Contents

The articles reproduced in this volume are grouped by topics. A previous survey of the field is included in Chapter I. To that item is added a postscriptum, where a few results concerning the stability of a long-run equilibrium, in a deterministic set-up, and the relationships of temporary equilibria with quantity rationing with macroeconomic models of unemployment or with other models of imperfect competition are reviewed. To the postscript is appended an updated bibliography.

Two papers by James Jordan and myself on the microeconomic behavior of an individual trader in a temporary equilibrium framework are reproduced in Chapter II. The third chapter deals with the important problem of the existence of a temporary equilibrium in competitive assets markets. Jerry Green and Oliver Hart analyze this question in the context of futures markets and of markets for financial securities. The article by Peter Hammond clarifies the relationships between these two studies.

The common thread linking the works reproduced in Chapter IV is the integration of money in a general equilibrium framework under perfect competition. The first paper, which I wrote, analyzes the relative roles of real balance and intertemporal substitution effects in guaranteeing that money has a positive value in exchange, in the short run, in a competitive model similar to those that were studied by Don Patinkin in his seminal book [21]. In the next two papers, Yves Younès and I analyze the interaction of the roles of money as a store of value and as a medium of exchange, and of time preference in ensuring a positive value for money in a competitive equilibrium framework. This is achieved by introducing cash-in-advance constraints of the sort that had been advocated earlier by Robert Clower [7] and that have become popular recently in macroeconomics, following the contribution of Robert Lucas, Jr. [17]. The second of these two papers helps clarify the microeconomic foundations of Milton Friedman's theory of optimum cash balances [8, Chapter 1]. The fourth article in Chapter IV by Frederic Gagey, Guy Laroque, and Stephan Lollivier, also uses cash-in-advance constraints to analyze, in particular, the impact of fiscal policies in a competitive overlapping generations model. Papers dealing with more complex monetary institutions like banking and open markets were not included there, as such issues were reviewed elsewhere, e.g., in [9].

The topic of Chapter V is the study of the stability of a long-run stationary equilibrium in a competitive deterministic framework when traders use prespecified learning processes. Gerard Fuchs and Guy Laroque develop methods to tackle this question in the context of an overlapping generations model involving several goods and money. The paper by George Tillmann deals with the same issue in the simpler case of a single good and money, a case in which more definite answers can be obtained. The third paper by Gerard Fuchs shows that error-learning behavior does not generally improve stability.

The paper by Werner Hildenbrand and myself, in Chapter VI, studies stochastic sequences of temporary competitive equilibria when the economy is subjected to random shocks. The next articles by Larry Blume and by Steve Spear and Sanjay Srivastava develop methods to analyze the existence of equilibria with self-fulfilling expectations in such circumstances.

The last chapter of this volume is devoted to the study of the microeconomic foundations of non-Walrasian temporary equilibria in which prices do not necessarily clear markets and in which ex-post compatibility of supplies and demands is achieved through quantity rationing. The first paper by Jean-Pascal Benassy deals with the conditions of existence and the efficiency properties of such an equilibrium when prices are temporarily rigid. In the following paper, Guy Laroque, Yves Younès, and I develop methods to study the properties of such equilibria by means of notions derived from game-theoretic concepts such as the core or the bargaining set.

A widespread misrepresentation of the theory of equilibria with quantity rationing pretends that the approach involves fixed prices and that it leaves accordingly unexplained an important component of the economic system. This misperception is rather difficult to understand, since researchers in the field took pains to show, at a very early stage of development of the theory, how the approach could be integrated into the theory of monopolistic competition and lead to the *joint determination* of prices and quantity rations in such models (see in particular Jean-Pascal Benassy [3], Guy Laroque and Grandmont [11], and Takashi Negishi [20]). The last three papers reproduced inChapter VII deal with this topic. The distinctive feature of Frank Hahn's paper is that he asks whether the agents' perceived demand or supply curves can be in some sense self-fulfilling in such a framework. The answer he gets is unfortunately negative. Douglas Gale's article further clarifies the exact nature of the results obtained by Frank Hahn. The last paper by Oliver Hart addresses the same topic by using the notion of a Cournot equilibrium and further shows that the whole approach is compatible, indeed, with self-fulfilling perceived demand or supply curves, under appropriate restrictions on the relationships between markets. As mentioned earlier, Chapter VII is concerned mostly with the microeconomic foundations of temporary equilibria involving quantity rationing. Little is said there on the implications of this sort of analysis for macroeconomic theories of unemployment.

Such implications are only briefly sketched in Chapter I. On this point, the interested reader might consult, with great benefit, the excellent books of Jean-Pascal Benassy [4,5], Edmond Malinvaud [19], Guy Laroque [15], Takashi Negishi [20], and Pierre Picard [22].

References

1. C. AZARIADIS, Self-fulfilling prophecies, *J. Econ. Theory* **25** (1981), 380–396.
2. C. AZARIADIS and R. GUESNERIE, Sunspots and cycles, *Review of Economic Studies* **53** (1986), 725–737.
3. J.P. BENASSY, The disequilibrium approach to monopolistic price setting and general monopolistic equilibrium, *Rev. Econ. Stud.* **43** (1976), 69–81.
4. J.P. BENASSY, "The Economics of Market Disequilibrium", Academic Press, New York, 1982.
5. J.P. BENASSY, "Macroeconomics: An Introduction to the Non-Walrasian Approach", Academic Press, New York, 1986.
6. J. BENHABIB and R.H. DAY, A characterization of erratic dynamics in the overlapping generations model, *J. Econ. Dynamics and Control* **4** (1982), 37–55.
7. R.W. CLOWER, A reconsideration of the micro-foundations of monetary theory, *Western Economic Journal* **6** (1967), 1–9.
8. M. FRIEDMAN, "The Optimum Quantity of Money and Other Essays", Aldine, Chicago, 1969.
9. J.M. GRANDMONT, "Money and Value", The Econometric Society Monographs 5, Cambridge University Press, Cambridge, 1983.
10. J.M. GRANDMONT, On endogenous competitive business cycles, *Econometrica* **53** (1985), 995–1045.
11. J.M. GRANDMONT and G. LAROQUE, On temporary Keynesian equilibria, *Rev. Econ. Stud.* **43** (1976), 53–67.
12. J. HICKS, "Value and Capital", The Clarendon Press, Oxford, 1939.
13. J. HICKS, "Capital and Growth", The Clarendon Press, Oxford, 1965.
14. J. H. KAREKEN and N. WALLACE (eds.), "Models of Monetary Economies", Federal Reserve Bank of Minneapolis, Minneapolis, 1980.
15. G. LAROQUE, "Fondements de l'Analyse Macroéconomique à Court Terme", Monographies d'Econométrie, CNRS, Paris, 1986.
16. E. LINDAHL, "Theory of Money and Capital", Allen and Unwin, London, 1939.
17. R.E. LUCAS, JR., Equilibrium in a pure currency economy, *Economic Inquiry* **18** (1980), 203–220 (also published in [14]).
18. R.E. LUCAS, JR. and T.J. SARGENT (eds.), "Rational Expectations and Econometric Practice", The University of Minnesota Press, Minneapolis, 1981.
19. E. MALINVAUD, "The Theory of Unemployment Reconsidered", Basil Blackwell, Oxford, 1977.

20. T. NEGISHI, "Microeconomic Foundations of Keynesian Macroeconomics", North Holland, Amsterdam, 1979.

21. D. PATINKIN, "Money, Interest and Prices", 2nd ed., Harper and Row, New York, 1965.

22. P. PICARD, "Théorie du Déséquilibre et Politique Economique", Economica, Paris, 1985.

23. Symposium on nonlinear economic dynamics, *J. Econ. Theory* (Oct., 1986) (also published as J.M. Grandmont (ed.), "Nonlinear Economic Dynamics", Academic Press, New York, 1987).

CHAPTER **I**

Temporary Equilibrium: An Overview

TEMPORARY GENERAL EQUILIBRIUM THEORY[1]

By Jean Michel Grandmont

This paper surveys some recent studies of economies where trading takes place sequentially over time, and where each agent makes decisions at every date in the light of his expectations about his future environment, which are functions of his information on the present and past states of the economy. The paper reviews particularly the issues raised by arbitrage in capital markets, by the consideration of money and banking activities, and by the introduction of production in temporary competitive equilibrium models. A thorough investigation of the logic of temporary equilibrium models with quantity rationing is also offered, as well as a quick review of the study of stochastic processes of temporary equilibria.

1. INTRODUCTION

One of the great achievements of economic theory in the past two decades has been the rigorous construction of the Walrasian theory of value, which is commonly referred to as the "Arrow–Debreu theory" (for a full account of the theory, see Debreu [24], and Arrow and Hahn [2]). In this theory, each commodity is described by its physical characteristics, by its location and its date of availability, and by the state of the environment in which it is available. It is assumed that there is a complete set of futures markets, one for each such "contingent commodity", that transactions are costless, and that adjustments are made only by price movements. In this interpretation, all contracts are made at the beginning of all times, and there are no incentives to reopen the markets later on. Another interpretation of the same formal model, which makes clearer its intertemporal structure, is the following: Let an elementary state of nature at date t be a complete specification of the history of the exogenous environment of the economy up to that date. Then, one can assume that there is a sequence of spot markets, one for each date and each elementary state of nature at that date. The existence of a complete set of futures markets is replaced by the assumption that there are enough institutions (e.g., markets for securities payable in units of account) which enable the economic units to transfer wealth freely over time and across states of nature. The assumption that the agents all face the same price system in the first interpretation means now that they have a common and perfect foresight of future prices and interest rates. While this theory is a very useful framework of reference, its extreme assumptions make it an inadequate tool for representing the world we live in. It is well known that the Arrow–Debreu model

[1] This survey was presented as an invited lecture at the World Meetings of the Econometrics Society held in Toronto, Canada in August, 1975. I wish to thank the discussants, E. Diewert, J. Green, and F. Hahn for their perceptive comments. This work was supported in part by the University of Bonn, by National Science Foundation grant SOC74-11446 at the Institute for Mathematical Studies in the Social Sciences, Stanford University, by National Science Foundation grant SOC73-09142 at Harvard University, and by a France–United States Exchange award from the National Science Foundation. I had stimulating comments from many colleagues while preparing this survey. I wish to thank all of them, and especially J. P. Benassy, R. Clower, J. Drèze, J. R. Green, F. Hahn, W. Heller, G. Laroque, R. Starr, and Y. Younès.

cannot account for active stock markets or money. In the real world, there is no such thing as a complete set of futures markets, nor are there enough institutions enabling the agents to transfer wealth freely over time and across states of nature. The agents have neither a sufficient knowledge of the laws of the economic system nor sufficient computing capabilities to be able to forecast the future accurately. Finally, it is a fact that, in the real world, some adjustments are made by quantity rationing, at least partially and for some time, when there is an excess demand or an excess supply on some market.

These issues have been ignored for a long time by the traditional general equilibrium theory. But they have occupied the front stage of many other parts of economic science. The idea that economic units have imperfect knowledge of their future environment and that, consequently, the future overshadows the present through the agents' expectations, is at the heart of Keynesian thinking and, more generally, of macroeconomics. The study of the formation of expectations is an important topic of theoretical and applied econometrics. Keynesian models represent a major attempt at studying markets where equilibrium is brought about at least partially by quantity adjustments (rationing). Important fields of economic science have thus tended to display divergent developments. Systematic efforts have been made recently by general equilibrium theorists, however, in order to fill this gap and, more importantly, to move closer to economic reality. The idea underlying these works is not new and can be found in the writings of J. Hicks, under the label *temporary equilibrium*. The method was also adopted by Patinkin [**90**] in his remarkable attempt to integrate monetary and value theories. According to this viewpoint, at each date every agent has to make decisions in the light of his expectations about his future environment, which depend upon his information on the state of the economy in the current and past periods. One can then study the state of the market in the current period either by postulating that adjustments are made only by price movements (*temporary competitive equilibrium*), or by assuming that prices are temporarily fixed during the period and that adjustments are made by quantity rationing (*temporary equilibrium with quantity rationing*). The goal of this survey is to appraise the state of the field.

The works using this method took two related but distinct orientations. The first one postulates that exchange takes place sequentially over time, that at each date there is not a complete set of futures markets, but that the agents forecast correctly their future environment. This method was adopted by Hahn [**57**] in his work on transactions costs, and by Radner [**92, 93, 94**, and **95**] in his series of contributions on competitive equilibria under uncertainty in sequence economies. This approach permits the study of some monetary phenomena and of some features of stock markets (Douglas Gale [**36**]). For a comprehensive appraisal of this line of thought, the reader is referred to the excellent survey of Radner [**96**]. The *perfect foresight* approach to the modelling of sequence economies is very useful as a tool for indicative planning or for the description of stationary states, where it appears natural to assume that agents do forecast accurately their future environment. It can also be used to check that an economic proposition does not depend upon people making mistakes. It is surely, however, an improper approach to the modelling of actual economies. By contrast, the approach that I am going to describe in this essay allows economic units to make mistakes when forecasting their future environment. It therefore takes into account a "disequilibrium" phenomenon which appears important in actual economies, which is the fact that at a given date the agents' plans for the future are not coordinated and, hence, may be incompatible.

The recent spurt of interest in formal temporary equilibrium models has been stimulated by a number of earlier studies. Among those which use the temporary competitive equilibrium approach, one can cite the work on productive activities of Morishima [86], with particular emphasis on durable goods, the attempt made by Drandakis [27] to study monetary phenomena by using this approach and the study of temporary competitive equilibrium under certainty of Arrow and Hahn [2]. The first systematic attempt to study temporary competitive equilibrium under uncertainty seems due to Stigum [101 and 102] and Grandmont [39 and 41]. On the other hand, the recent research on temporary equilibria with quantity rationing has been greatly influenced by the reappraisal of Keynesian macroeconomics undertaken by Clower [21], Leijonhufvud [82], Patinkin [90], and more recently by Barro and Grossman [6]. The first systematic studies of quantity rationing in a general equilibrium framework seem to be due to Glustoff [38], to Younès [107, 108, and 109], to Drèze in a paper circulated in 1971 and published in 1975 [30], and more recently to Benassy [7].

The reader will quickly discover that the subject has not yet reached a degree of maturation which permits the statement of the theory in a general and concise way. The researchers were confronted with a new range of issues, some of which had no place in the Arrow–Debreu model and others which were sometimes ignored by macroeconomic theory. The strategy has been, for the most part, to select a few significant issues and to design simple models through which they can be studied. The result of these conceptual experiments is a bewildering variety of models which all use the same method but deal with different specific problems. Consequently, rather than to attempt to summarize the whole literature, I chose to discuss in detail, from a unified viewpoint, a few pieces of research which I found significant, and tried to make clear what lessons one can learn from them and where further progress can be made. The particular choice I made, of course, reflects my own interests and biases, and the works that I have not discussed in full detail should not be discounted. I have supplemented some sections with a short bibliographical note which should enable the interested reader to pursue his own inquiry.

The paper is organized as follows: In Section 2, I develop the basic model of individual decision making which is commonly used in temporary equilibrium models. Section 3 is devoted to the analysis of temporary competitive equilibrium models, where it is postulated that prices move fast enough in each period to equalize supply and demand. I concentrate on the issues raised by the phenomenon of arbitrage in capital markets (Section 3.2), by the introduction of money and banking activities in these models (Section 3.3), and by the study of production

(Section 3.4). I study in Section 4 the logic of temporary equilibrium models with quantity rationing. In Section 5, I review the study of stochastic processes of temporary equilibria, which is still at an early stage of development. Lastly, bibliographical references follow at the end of the paper.

2. INDIVIDUAL DECISION MAKING

The crucial feature of temporary equilibrium models is the fact that the agents have to make decisions at a given moment while ignoring what will be their environment in the future: they must forecast this environment in order to make a choice. Thus a new concept appears in these models compared to the traditional general equilibrium model, that of an *expectation function*, which describes how an agent's forecast of the future depends upon the information he has at a given moment. The aim of this section is to study precisely how this concept enters an individual's decision-making process in temporary equilibrium theory.

2.1. *Basic Framework*

Divide time into discrete periods. Typically, an agent receives *signals* about his environment in every period: these may describe his information about variables which are not controlled by any economic agent (exogeneous "states of nature"), as well as about variables which are controlled by other economic agents, or jointly determined by these two categories of variables (e.g., prices). Let S_t be the set of all possible signals that he may receive at date t; to fix the ideas, I take S_t as a *separable metric space*. The agent's problem is the following one: given the signals received up to date t, and the decisions taken up to the date by the agent, he must choose an *action* a_t in some space A_t. An action will involve a commitment to exchange currently available goods and services. It may also involve commitments to exchange specified quantities of goods and services to be delivered at later dates (forward contracts), as for instance, in the case of inventories of durable goods. Finally, an action will typically involve a commitment to exchange forward contracts entailing the delivery or the receipt, at specified dates, of a particular "commodity", paper money, when the agent decides to hold idle cash balances or to hold securities of various maturity dates, or to borrow. In the sequel, I will take A_t as a separable metric space.

In order to simplify the exposition, I concentrate on a simple case. Consider an agent at date 1. The signals that he received before that date are given, as well as his past actions, and cannot be changed by current decisions or events. I will not mention them explicitly any more.

The agent must choose a *decision rule*, that is, a set of actions, $\alpha(s_1)$, that he will choose in response to any signal, $s_1 \in S_1$. Given s_1, the actions he is allowed to choose may, however, be constrained to lie in some subset, say $\beta_1(s_1)$, of A_1. Since the choice of an action usually involves commitments for future dates, the agent must make precise in his mind what he will do in subsequent periods. Assume for simplicity that our agent is planning only one period ahead. This is by no means essential: the analysis which follows is valid for an arbitrary finite or infinite planning horizon (Chetty and Dasgupta [17], Christiansen [18 and 19], Jordan [75]). Thus the agent must, in addition to a current action, choose a *plan*, which is represented by a measurable function $a_2(\cdot)$ from S_2 into A_2, and which describes the choice $a_2(s_2)$ he intends to make in period 2 if he receives the signal s_2. Again, his choice at date 2 may be constrained to lie in a subset of A_2, which may depend on his current and future environment as well as on the action he currently chooses, say $a_2(s_2) \in \beta_2(s_1, a_1, s_2)$.

The agent must, of course, be aware of the *consequences* of his choices. In order to simplify the exposition, I will let them depend only upon the couple of actions (a_1, a_2), but the reader must keep in mind that these consequences may well depend upon the agent's environment (s_1, s_2) in the two periods. Thus the consequences of the agent's choices are denoted by $\gamma(a_1, a_2)$, an element of the space of consequences C, which again I take as separable metric space. Since the agent typically faces a decision problem under uncertainty, the *preferences* of the agent will not be defined directly on the space of consequences, but rather will be described by a complete preordering $\gtrsim$ on the space of *probability distributions* on C, say $\mathcal{M}(C)$. Although this is not necessary for the presentation of the theory, it is convenient to assume that these preferences satisfy the *expected utility hypothesis*:

ASSUMPTION 1 (*Expected Utility Hypothesis*): *There exists a von Neumann–Morgenstern utility function* $u: C \to R$ *which is continuous, bounded, such that the mapping* $v: \mathcal{M}(C) \to R$ *defined by* $[v(\mu) = \int_C u \, d\mu, \ \mu \in \mathcal{M}(C)]$ *is a representation of the preferences* $\gtrsim$.

In order to complete the description of the model, I must make precise how the agent forecasts the signals that he will receive in the future. This forecast takes the form of a probability distribution on S_2. It may be influenced by all observations made by the agent up to the current period. In particular, it will be influenced by the signal s_1 currently perceived, and in some cases, by the action a_1 chosen by the agent. In order to keep the formal exposition simple, I will single out the dependence on the current signal, and represent it by the agent's *expectation function* ψ which maps S_1 into the space of probability distributions $\mathcal{M}(S_2)$. I shall make the following continuity assumption:

ASSUMPTION 2 (*Continuity Assumption*): *The mapping* $\psi: S_1 \to \mathcal{M}(S_2)$ *is continuous when* $\mathcal{M}(S_2)$ *is endowed with the topology of weak convergence of probability measures.*[2]

The stage is set now to describe how the agent makes his choice. Given $s_1 \in S_1$, each action $a_1 \in A_1$ and each plan $a_2(\cdot)$ determines a *random variable* $\gamma(a_1, a_2(\cdot))$ defined on the space of future environments S_2 endowed with the

---

[2] The concept of weak convergence of probability measures is equivalent to the well-known concept of weak convergence of distribution functions when S_2 is a finite Euclidean space. For a precise definition, see Billingsley [14] and Parthasarathy [89].

subjective probability $\psi(s_1)$, and taking its values in the space of consequences C. This random variable in turn induces a probability distribution on C, say $\mu(s_1, a_1, a_2(\cdot))$. Thus, given s_1, the agent will choose an action a_1 and an associated plan $a_2(\cdot)$ subject to the constraints $a_1 \in \beta_1(s_1)$ and $a_2(s_2) \in \beta_2(s_1, a_1, s_2)$ for every s_2 in S_2, so that the corresponding probability distribution μ is most preferred. If we choose a von Neumann–Morgenstern representation u of the agent's preferences, this amounts to maximizing the expected utility of $\mu(s_1, a_1, a_2(\cdot))$,

$$\int_{S_2} u(\gamma(a_1, a_2(\cdot))) \, d\psi(s_1),$$

subject to the constraints $a_1 \in \beta_1(s_1)$ and $a_2(s_2) \in \beta_2(s_1, a_1, s_2)$ for every s_2 in S_2.

2.2. Ranking of Actions

In the preceding section, the trader's decision problem was viewed as a problem of intertemporal choice. I show now how the choice of a decision rule can be reduced to a single period by using a standard dynamic programming technique.

The signal s_1 being fixed, choose an arbitrary action a_1 in A_1. Assume that the correspondence $\beta_2(s_1, a_1, \cdot)$ from S_2 into A_2 is compact-valued and continuous, and let for every s_2 in S_2, $u^*(s_1, a_1, s_2)$ be the maximum value of $u(\gamma(a_1, a_2))$ when a_2 varies subject to $a_2 \in \beta_2(s_1, a_1, s_2)$. If one defines

$$(1) \qquad v(s_1, a_1) = \int_{S_2} u^*(s_1, a_1, \cdot) \, d\psi(s_1)$$

then $v(s_1, a_1)$ is clearly the *maximum expected utility* that can be achieved if s_1 obtains and if a_1 is chosen in the current period. One can now say that a_1' is *preferred or indifferent* to a_1'' when s_1 is *currently observed if and only if* $v(s_1, a_1') \geqslant v(s_1, a_1'')$.

This definition is justified because, as the reader will easily check, for every s_1, $a_1^* \in \alpha(s_1)$ *if and only if* a_1^* *maximizes* $v(s_1, a_1)$ *when* a_1 *varies subject to* $a_1 \in \beta_1(s_1)$.

It is readily verified that $v(s_1, a_1)$ defines for each s_1 a complete preordering on the space of current actions A_1 which is independent of the particular representation u that we started with, and depends only on the underlying preferences $\gtrsim$ on $\mathcal{M}(C)$.

This dynamic programming technique is useful at least on two counts. First, it allows viewing the agent's choice as the result of a single-period decision problem, and this is useful, in particular, when one attempts to prove the existence of a temporary equilibrium. Second, one must remember that an action a_1 will in general involve a decision to hold cash or to exchange assets of various maturities. The above procedure permits "introducing" money, bonds, and in general assets of various kinds in the utility function $v(s_1, a_1)$, although they may have no intrinsic value. But then current and past prices are also arguments of the utility function v because they influence the trader's expectations. This gives a sound foundation to discuss some issues in monetary theory, e.g., the absence of money illusion, the quantity theory of money, and the like. I shall come back to these points in the section on money.

2.3. *Continuity of a Decision Rule*

The following result gives sufficient conditions for the continuity of the expected utility v defined in (1), and the upper hemicontinuity of the decision rule α in the context of the above two-period model. For a proof of this result, the reader is referred to Grandmont [40] and Sonderman [99] (see also Delbaen [25]). For the case of an arbitrary finite or infinite planning horizon, the most general treatment is due to Jordan [75].

PROPOSITION 1: *Assume that S_t, A_t, and C are separable metric spaces, and that β_1 and β_2 are compact-valued and continuous correspondences. If the preferences $\gtrsim$ on $\mathcal{M}(C)$ satisfy Assumption 1 and if the expectation function ψ satisfies Assumption 2, then, (i) the expected utility $v: S_1 \times A_1 \to R$ defined in (1) is continuous and bounded; (ii) the correspondence $\alpha: S_1 \to A_1$ is compact-valued and upper hemicontinuous.*

2.4. *Generation of Expectations*

It is sometimes claimed (Radner [96]) that, in temporary equilibrium models, the trader's "expectation formation follows some simple rules-of-thumb". It may indeed be the case that the expectation function ψ is the result of a rough guess. I wish now to emphasize the obvious but neglected point that the model is general enough to allow for the use of sophisticated statistical techniques.

Let us start with the assumption that the agent has a "statistical model of the world" in mind, which tells him at every date that the probability distribution of the signal s_{t+1} depends, of course, on the signals received up to date t, but also on some unknown parameter $\theta \in \Theta$. Let $S^t = \Pi_{\tau=0}^t S_\tau$; then the agent's model can be described by the mappings

$$\Pi_0: \Theta \to \mathcal{M}(S_1) \quad \text{and} \quad \Pi_t: \Theta \times S^t \to \mathcal{M}(S_{t+1}), \qquad (t = 1, 2, \ldots).$$

For instance, Θ may be some subset of a finite Euclidean space, as is usual in econometrics. In other contexts, Θ may be taken as the space of all probability distributions on S^T, where T stands for the agent's horizon. In that case, $\Pi_t(\theta, s^t)$ would be the distribution of s_{t+1} conditional upon s^t determined by the probability distribution $\theta \in \mathcal{M}(S^T)$.

The agent thus faces a classical problem of econometrics, that of estimating the unknown parameter θ. This he can do either by using a rule-of-thumb or by using classical statistical techniques. Any definite nonstochastic method, however, will result in an *estimation rule*, represented as a function

$$\varepsilon_t: S^t \to \Theta.$$

The expectation function $\psi_t \colon S^t \to \mathcal{M}(S_{t+1})$ is then given by

$$\psi_t(s^t) = \Pi_t(\varepsilon_t(s^t), s^t) \in \mathcal{M}(S_{t+1}).$$

If the agent is a Bayesian statistician, he may use his posterior probability on Θ at date t, $\gamma(s^t) \in \mathcal{M}(\Theta)$, which depends on the signals s^t, in order to form the expectation function ψ_t:

$$\psi_t(s^t, B) = \int_\Theta \Pi_t(\cdot, s^t, B)\, d\gamma(s^t)$$

for every Borel subset B of S_{t+1}.

I wanted to emphasize that the formation of expectations in temporary equilibrium models may be the result of the application of classical statistical techniques by the agents. In most of the studies I will be reviewing, expectation functions are taken as data of the system upon which assumptions are to be imposed. Whether the agents' use of statistical techniques would, in fact, uphold these assumptions is an open question. This is an area where our ignorance is great, and where further work would be useful.

2.5. *Bibliographical Note*

The dynamic programming technique employed in 2.2 is well known. It was first used in the context of temporary equilibrium theory by Arrow and Hahn [2] for the case of subjectively certain expectations, and by Stigum [102 and 103] in the case of uncertainty. The use of the concept of weak convergence of probability distributions to describe the continuity of the agent's expectations originated in Grandmont [39 and 40]. The most general treatment of the model presented in Sections 2.1–2.3 is due to Jordan [75]. Section 2.5 is adapted from Jordan [76]. The continuity of the decision rule with respect to the expectation function has been investigated by Christiansen [18], and by Christiansen and Majumdar [20].

3. TEMPORARY COMPETITIVE EQUILIBRIUM

One way to look at the evolution of an economic system is to view it as a succession of temporary or short run competitive equilibria. That is, one postulates that, at each date, prices move fast enough to match supply and demand. This is obviously a very restrictive assumption, since it prevents the occurrence of such disequilibrium phenomena as unemployment. Nevertheless although one assumes equilibrium in each period, the economic system displays a disequilibrium feature along a sequence of temporary competitive equilibria which I believe is important: at each date, the *plans* of the agents for the future are not coordinated and thus will be, in general, incompatible. As Hicks [67] emphasized long ago, this is to be contrasted with the perfect foresight approach (Radner [95]), where by definition such a disequilibrium phenomenon cannot occur.

A recurrent problem in temporary competitive equilibrium models is precisely to prove the existence of a price system that matches supply and demand at a given moment. It is clear that some kind of "market equilibrium theorem" is needed here, as it is in the case of static models of general equilibrium (see Section 3.1). We shall see, however, that the distinctive feature of temporary equilibrium models, compared to static ones, is the fact that one has to make meaningful assumptions on the expectations functions of the agents in order to derive the needed properties of the agents' supplies and demands.

I will illustrate that fact in what follows by analyzing a few pieces of research that addressed themselves to that question. The first topic that I will cover is the problem of the existence of an equilibrium in markets for commitments to deliver commodities at future dates, i.e., in forward markets (Section 3.2). Next, I will show how some issues in monetary theory can be handled in the context of these models (Section 3.3). Finally, in Section 3.4, I will review some works which attempted to introduce productive activities in that kind of model.

3.1. Market Equilibrium

There are many versions of the "law of supply and demand" which can be used in this context. Loosely speaking, they all use the same basic argument. Let D be a convex subset of the unit simplex of some finite Euclidean space; D should be interpreted as the set of admissible price systems p of the contracts exchanged in the markets under consideration. To every p in D is associated an aggregate excess demand $\zeta(p)$ for these contracts, which satisfies Walras' Law, $p \cdot \zeta(p) = 0$. Now, if the projection on D of the excess demand vector has the property to point toward the interior of D when prices are near the boundary of D, then by continuity, there should exist p in D such that $0 = \zeta(p)$. Formally, we have the following assumption and lemma:

ASSUMPTION 3: *For every sequence p^k in D which tends to some p in the boundary ∂D of D, and every sequence $z^k \in \zeta(p^k)$, there exists $\bar{p}$ in D such that $\bar{p} \cdot z^k > 0$ for infinity many k.*

LEMMA 1 (Market Equilibrium Lemma): *Let D be an open and convex subset of the unit simplex of R^l. Let $\zeta: D \to R^l$ be a correspondence which is compact and convex-valued, upper hemicontinuous and satisfies Walras' Law, $p \cdot z = 0$ for $z \in \zeta(p)$. Given Assumption 3, there exists p^* in D such that $0 \in \zeta(p^*)$.*

For the sake of completeness, I give a short proof of this statement which is adapted from known arguments (Debreu [23]).

PROOF: Consider an increasing sequence of compact, convex subsets D^k of D such that D is contained in the union of all the D^k. For each k there exists a compact convex set Z^k which contains $\zeta(p)$ for every p in D^k. For any z in Z^k, let $\mu^k(z)$ be the set of prices p of D^k which maximize $p \cdot z$. To each couple (p, z) of $D^k \times Z^k$, associate the set $\mu^k(z) \times \zeta(p)$. This correspondence has a fixed point.

That is, there exists p^k in D^k and $z^k \in \zeta(p^k)$ such that

$$0 = p^k \cdot z^k \geqslant p \cdot z^k, \quad \text{for all } p \text{ in } D^k.$$

It follows that the sequence p^k must be bounded away from the boundary ∂D of D; otherwise, one could contradict Assumption 3. There is thus a subsequence (same notation) such that (p^k) converges to $p^* \in D$ and such that (z^k) converges to $z^* \in \zeta(p^*)$. By continuity, $p \cdot z^* \leqslant 0$ for all p in D. Since D is open, this implies $z^* = 0$, which proves the lemma.

3.2. Arbitrage in Capital Markets

One of the most interesting problems which arise in many temporary equilibrium models is the question of the existence of a competitive equilibrium in futures markets. I have already noted that a trader at a given date will typically exchange contracts that involve the delivery or the receipt of commodities at specified future dates, these commodities being real goods and services in some cases, fiat money in others. In many cases, spot markets will be active at the date of delivery of these commodities. Therefore, there is often the possibility of *arbitrage* on forward markets in these models. In a competitive framework, the set of feasible trades on futures markets is not bounded by the availability of resources at futures dates. It is accordingly not clear beforehand what are the conditions that we must impose on our models to assert the existence of a competitive equilibrium in such markets. An answer to that question has been provided by Green [52 and 53]: *There must be some agreement between the agents' expectations about future spot prices.* As the methods employed by Green seem applicable to a wide variety of temporary equilibrium models, competitive or not, I will spend most of this section analyzing them.

Green [52] studies an exchange economy which extends over two periods, 1 and 2. There are l_1 consumption goods available in period 1, and l_2 in period 2, with $l = l_1 + l_2$. Storage of goods is impossible. When the traders meet in period 1, each of them knows his endowment of currently deliverable commodities. But their endowment of goods available in period 2 is unknown and will be influenced by some random factors, which are left unspecified (actually, Green assumed future endowments to be known with certainty, but this is a straightforward generalization). In period 1 there are l_1 markets for currently deliverable commodities and l_2 markets for contracts for *sure* delivery of the l_2 goods in period 2. Since the forward markets are not complete in the Arrow–Debreu sense, spot markets will be active in period 2, and spot prices at that date will in general differ from prices for forward commitments in period 1. The question is to find conditions ensuring the existence of a competitive equilibrium in period 1.

I first consider a representative consumer in period 1, and show how his decision-making problem fits into the framework described in the previous section. The trader knows his endowment $e_1 \in R_+^{l_1}$ of current goods, and receives a signal $s_1 = (p_1, q_1)$ which consists of the prices $p_1 \in R^{l_1}$ of current goods, and of the prices $q_1 \in R^{l_2}$ of forward purchases of goods to be delivered in period 2. Thus we can take $S_1 = \Delta^l$, the unit simplex of R^l. In period 2, the trader will receive a signal $s_2 = (p_2, e_2)$, where spot prices of goods available in period 2, p_2, belong to the unit simplex Δ^{l_2} of R^{l_2}, and $e_2 \in R^{l_2}_+$ is his future endowment of goods. Thus $S_2 = \Delta^{l_2} \times R^{l_2}_+$. The trader's expectations are as before represented by a map $\psi: S_1 \to \mathcal{M}(S_2)$, which satisfies the continuity assumption (Assumption 2) of Section 2.1.

An action $a_1 = (x_1, b_1)$ to be taken by the trader in period 1 specifies his consumption $x_1 \in R^{l_1}_+$, and his purchases of forward contracts $b_1 \in R^{l_2}$. Unlimited short selling is permitted. Thus $A_1 = R^{l_1}_+ \times R^{l_2}$. In period 2, a trader's action a_2 is simply his consumption at that date. Thus $A_2 = R^{l_2}_+$.

The set of choices open to the trader in period 2, $\beta_2(a_1, s_2)$, depends on $s_2 = (p_2, e_2)$ and the action taken in period 1, $a_1 = (x_1, b_1)$. All actions $a_2 \in A_2$ whose value $p_2 \cdot a_2$ does not exceed the trader's wealth $p_2 \cdot (b_1 + e_2)$ are feasible if the latter is nonnegative; otherwise, the trader is bankrupt and is thus forced to choose a zero consumption bundle:

$$\beta_2(a_1, s_2) = \{a_2 \in A_2 | p_2 \cdot a_2 \leqslant \max(0, p_2 \cdot (b_1 + e_2))\}.$$

As for $\beta_1(s_1)$, it consists of the actions $a_1 = (x_1, b_1)$ whose value $s_1 \cdot a_1$ does not exceed the trader's wealth in period 1, $p_1 \cdot e_1$. In the simplest version of his model, Green makes the simplifying additional assumption, which is by no means essential, that a trader never *plans* to be bankrupt, even with small positive probability, by adding the constraint: $p_2 \cdot (b_1 + e_2) \geqslant 0$ for every (p_2, e_2) in the support of $\psi(s_1)$. I will adopt it here, too. Thus,

$$\beta_1(s_1) = \{a_1 \in A_1 | s_1 \cdot a_1 \leqslant p_1 \cdot e_1 \text{ and } p_2 \cdot (b_1 + e_2) \geqslant 0 \text{ for all}$$
$$s_2 \in \text{supp } \psi(s_1)\}.$$

The consequences of any couple of actions (a_1, a_2) in $A_1 \times A_2$ are described by the corresponding consumption stream (x_1, x_2). Thus $C = R^{l_1}_+ \times R^{l_2}_+$. The trader's preferences are defined on $\mathcal{M}(C)$ as in the central model, and satisfy the following assumption:

ASSUMPTION 4: *The preferences on $\mathcal{M}(C)$ satisfy the expected utility hypothesis (Assumption 1) of 2.1. In addition, any von Neumann–Morgenstern representation u is concave and monotone.*

Therefore, the trader's decision problem is the same as the one described in Section 2. For every s_1 in S_1, one can thus define a set of optimal actions $\alpha(s_1)$, which may be empty, and a set of corresponding excess demands.

$$\zeta(s_1) = \{z | z = (x_1 - e_1, b_1), a_1 = (x_1, b_1) \in \alpha(s_1)\}.$$

I shall make a few assumptions on expectations:

ASSUMPTION 5: *For every $s_1 \in S_1$, $\psi(s_1)$ assigns probability one to the set of $s_2 = (p_2, e_2)$ in S_2 such that $p_2 \gg 0$.*

13

ASSUMPTION 6: *The support of* $\psi(s_1)$ *is independent of* s_1. *Furthermore, the convex hull of the projection of supp* $\psi(s_1)$ *on* Δ^{l_2}, *has a nonempty interior, denoted by* Π.

Assumption 5 rules out expectations of zero prices at date 2. This is warranted, owing to the assumption of monotonic preferences. The first part of Assumption 6, saying that supp $\psi(s_1)$ does not vary with the current signal, is not necessary to carry out the analysis and, indeed, was not postulated by Green, but it greatly simplifies matters without altering the substance of the results. As for the last part of Assumption 6, it simply says that there is genuine uncertainty about future spot prices and excludes linear dependencies in the expectations. It is not a very strong postulate.

Now let D be the set of prices of period 1, $s_1 = (p_1, q_1)$, which are positive, $s_1 \gg 0$, and such that the vector of relative prices for forward contracts, $q_1 / |q_1|$, belongs to Π. Clearly, D is open in Δ^l and convex. More importantly,

PROPOSITION 2: *Under the above assumptions, and if* $e_1 \gg 0$, (i) $\zeta(s_1)$ *is nonempty if and only if* $s_1 \in D$. *The correspondence* ζ *from* D *to* R^l *is compact-valued and upper hemicontinuous.* (ii) *Consider any sequence* s_1^k *in* D *which tends to some* s *in* ∂D, *and any sequence* $z^k \in \zeta(s_1^k)$. *Then* $\bar{s}_1 \cdot z^k$ *diverges to* $+\infty$ *for every* $\bar{s}_1$ *in* D.

Part (i) of this proposition claims that the trader's behavior is defined if and only if prices are positive and $q_1 / |q_1| \in \Pi$. The first part of this statement comes obviously from the assumption of strictly monotone preferences and carries little information. The fact that the vector of relative prices in forward markets must belong to Π is more interesting. Suppose that $q_1 / |q_1|$ does *not* belong to Π. Then unlimited profitable arbitrage is possible. Indeed, since Π is convex and open relatively to Δ^{l_2}, it follows from a well known separation theorem that there exists $\bar{b}$ in R^{l_2}, $\bar{b} \neq 0$, which satisfies $q_1 \cdot \bar{b} = 0$, and is such that $p_2 \cdot \bar{b} \geq 0$ for all (p_2, e_2) in supp $\psi(s_1)$ with *strict* inequality for some (p_2, e_2) in this set. Therefore, any action $a_1 = (x_1, b_1)$ in $\beta_1(s_1)$ must be dominated by the action $(a_1, b_1 + \bar{b}) \in \beta_1(s_1)$, and $\zeta(s_1)$ must be empty. *Conversely,* if $q_1 / |q_1|$ does belong to Π, then any trade in futures markets must involve a loss with positive probability: for every $b \neq 0$ such that $q_1 \cdot b = 0$, there exists (p_2, e_2) in supp $\psi(s_1)$ such that $p_2 \cdot b < 0$. It is then intuitively clear that the set $\beta_1(s_1)$ must be bounded, because any action $a_1 = (x_1, b_1)$ in this set must satisfy $p_2 \cdot (b_1 + e_2) \geq 0$ for every (p_2, e_2) in supp $\psi(s_1)$. Indeed, this fact is easily proved by checking that the asymptotic cone of $\beta_1(s_1)$ is degenerated to $\{0\}$ (see Debreu [24], (8) of 1.9]). Therefore, $\alpha(s_1)$ is nonempty on D and (i) of Proposition 2 is a straightforward consequence of Proposition 1 stated in Section 2.3.

The importance of (ii) of the above proposition is obvious, in view of the market equilibrium lemma of Section 3.1, for it states that an individual trader's excess demand "points toward the interior of D" when prices are near the boundary of D. Suppose that this statement is false. Then one could find a sequence s_1^k in D

tending to some $s_1 \in \partial D$, $z^k \in \zeta(s_1^k)$ and $\bar{s}_1$ in D such that $\bar{s}_1 \cdot z^k$ is bounded above. But it is easily shown that, in such a case, the sequence z^k is itself bounded: the asymptotic cone of the sequence (z^k) in fact reduces to $\{0\}$ by the same kind of argument that was used to show that $\beta_1(s_1)$ is bounded when s_1 belongs to D. One can then assume without loss of generality that z^k converges to z. By continuity, this would imply $z \in \zeta(s_1)$, leading to a contradiction of (1) of the same proposition, since $s_1 \in \partial D$. Therefore, (ii) of Proposition 2 holds.

What remains to be done to prove the existence of an equilibrium in such an economy is now easy. Suppose that there are m traders, $i = 1, \ldots, m$, each of whom satisfies the above assumptions. If for each s_1 in S_1, aggregate excess demand is defined as $\zeta(s_1) = \Sigma_{i=1}^{m} \zeta^i(s_1)$, then an equilibrium is a price system s_1^* such that $0 \in \zeta(s_1^*)$. For each trader, one can define a set Π^i of the unit simplex Δ^{l_2} as in Assumption 6 above. It is clear that, given these assumptions, a *necessary and sufficient* condition for the existence of an equilibrium in this economy is some agreement among traders about the spot prices that will be established in period 2, that is, the following assumption:

ASSUMPTION 7: *The intersection of all Π^i is not empty.*

If, for each trader i, D^i is defined from Π^i as before, and if D is the intersection of all D^i, then Assumption 7 is equivalent to the statement "D is not empty". If D were empty, then aggregate excess demand $\zeta(s_1)$ would be undefined for all prices and an equilibrium could not exist. On the other hand, if $D \neq \varnothing$, the previous proposition implies that an equilibrium exists by a straightforward application of the market equilibrium lemma of Section 3.1.

Green has extended his model in several directions [53]. First, traders can be permitted to plan to be bankrupt with some probability, i.e., to have a negative wealth at some prices at date 2. In that case, one has to introduce extraeconomic penalties for bankruptcy, in order to prevent traders from taking unlimited short positions in the forward markets in period 1 (see also Grandmont [39] on this point). The traders can also be endowed with previously contracted claims and debts when the market of period 1 opens. These traders may then be bankrupt at the equilibrium, and some default rules must be explicitly designed in that case. Despite all these complications, the major conclusion yielded by the simplest model still holds: there must be a substantial overlap of the traders' expectations concerning future spot prices for the existence of an equilibrium in the forward markets. Qualitatively similar results were obtained by Hart [63] in his study of markets for financial securities of the Lintner–Sharpe type.

While this qualitative conclusion seems well established in the context of the above models, much more work has to be done along the lines laid down by Green. In particular, one important feature of the models that were analyzed is the fact that traders plan only one period ahead. It remains to be seen how Assumption 7 looks when the traders do exchange forward commitments maturing at different future dates. The problem has obvious connections with the theory of the *term structure of interest rates*, as Green himself pointed out in a series of examples (Green [51]; see also Younès [109] for further work in that direction). A systematic study of these points would be useful. Another issue where further work is much needed is that of bankruptcy. The treatment by Green [53] of the problem is not entirely satisfactory, since he uses purely mechanical rules to determine whether an agent is bankrupt and the extent of bankruptcy. Ledyard [81], while commenting on Green's model, suggested that the decision to go bankrupt and the extent of default should be chosen by the agents themselves. This suggestion should be further explored. The issue is of importance, since a proper solution of this problem conditions the formulation of any satisfactory study of financial phenomenon.

3.3. *Temporary Competitive Equilibrium with Money*

One interesting feature of temporary equilibrium models is the fact that traders may be allowed to engage in forward contracts involving the delivery or the receipt of a particular commodity, paper money. This will be the case if we allow them to hold idle cash balances, or to borrow, or to save in the form of financial assets. An important problem in that case, which was emphasized ten years ago by Hahn [56], is to prove the existence of a competitive equilibrium where the price of money is positive, although it has no intrinsic value. A beginning of an answer to that problem was given by Grandmont [41], who showed that the temporary equilibrium price of money was positive if the traders expected the price of money to be positive in the future no matter what were the prices currently perceived. This condition was a refinement of an assumption used before by Stigum [102] in his study of a temporary competitive equilibrium model without money. But perhaps the most interesting aspect of this approach is the fact that we can introduce in our models specific agents whose function is to change the available quantity of money by granting loans to the traders (Grandmont and Laroque [45]) or by engaging in open market operations (Grandmont and Laroque [46]). These agents thus perform the functions of banks. It then becomes possible to investigate the impact on the economy of various monetary policies and to study some issues of monetary theory such as the validity of the short run quantity theory of money, as proposed by Patinkin [90], or of the existence of a "liquidity trap".

In order to show more precisely how these questions can be handled by using the temporary equilibrium approach, I will find it convenient to develop the argument within the framework of a model studied by Grandmont and Laroque [46].

The economy under consideration is an exchange economy which extends over an infinite sequence of periods. In each period, the traders can exchange n perishable consumption goods on spot markets, and can save part of their current income in the form of two kinds of assets. One of them is fiat money, which does not bear interest; the other is a perpetuity, i.e., a promise to pay to the bearer one unit of money in every period. In addition, there is an agent, called the central bank, whose task is to manipulate the outstanding stock of money by selling or purchasing perpetuities on the market. The problem is to study the existence and the properties of a temporary equilibrium at a given date, say $t = 1$.

First consider a representative consumer at date 1, and assume that his planning horizon is limited to period 2. This assumption is made only for convenience; the analysis which follows is valid for any finite planning horizon. Note that this assumption does *not* mean that the consumer believes that the economy will cease to exist at the end of his horizon. Indeed, one could conduct the analysis within the framework of an overlapping generation model of the Samuelson type, with newborn agents coming in in each period. This consumer knows his endowment $e_1 \in R^n_+$ of consumption goods as well as his endowment $b_0 \in R^2_+$ of assets, which results from the decisions he took in the periods prior to date 1. The first component b_{01} represents his stock of money (including the interest payments on his stock of perpetuities), the second b_{02}, his stock of perpetuities. He receives a signal $s_1 = (p_1, q_1)$ which consists of the prices of current goods $p_1 \in R^n_+$ and those of the assets $q_1 \in R^2_+$. Thus we can take $S_1 = \Delta^l$, the unit simplex of R^l, where $l = n + 2$. In period 2, the trader will receive a signal $s_2 = (p_2, q_2, e_2)$ where $(p_2, q_2) \in \Delta^l$ represents the prices of goods and assets that will prevail at that time, and $e_2 \in R^n_+$ is his future endowment of goods. Therefore, $S_2 = \Delta^l \times R^n_+$, and the traders' expectations are described as in the central model by a map $\psi : S_1 \to \mathcal{M}(S_2)$ which satisfies the continuity assumption (Assumption 2) of Section 2.1.

The trader's action in every period is represented by $a = (x, b)$ and specifies his consumption $x \in R^n_+$ and the amount $b \in R^2_+$ of assets he wishes to hold until the next period. Hence, $A_1 = A_2 = R^l_+$. The consequences of a couple of actions (a_1, a_2) are represented by the corresponding consumption stream (x_1, x_2). Thus, $C = R^n_+ \times R^n_+$. The trader's preferences are defined on $\mathcal{M}(C)$ as in the central model and satisfy the following assumption:

ASSUMPTION 8: *The preferences on $\mathcal{M}(C)$ satisfy the expected utility hypothesis (Assumption 1) of Section 2.1. Any von Neumann–Morgenstern representation u is concave and monotone.*

The set of choices open to the trader in any period is the set of actions whose values does not exceed his wealth. Thus,

$$\beta_1(s_1) = \{a_1 \in A_1 | p_1 x_1 + q_1 b_1 \leqslant p_1 e_1 + q_1 b_0\}$$
and
$$\beta_2(a_1, s_2) = \{a_2 \in A_2 | p_2 x_2 + q_2 b_2 \leqslant p_2 e_2 + q_1 \tilde{b}_1\}$$

where $\tilde{b}_1 = (b_{11} + b_{12}, b_{12})$ represents the trader's endowment of assets in period 2 after the payment of interest on perpetuities, which is the result of his action $a_1 = (x_1, b_1)$ (remember that a perpetuity yields one unit of money in every period).

The structure of the trader's decision problem is the same as in the central model of Section 2.1. Thus we can define a set of optimal actions $\alpha(s_1)$ for every s_1 in S_1, and a set of corresponding excess demands $\zeta(s_1) = \{z | z = (x_1 - e_1, b_1 - b_0), a_1 = (x_1, b_1) \in \alpha(s_1)\}$.

I shall make the following pair of assumptions on expectations:

ASSUMPTION 9: *For every s_1 in S_1, $\psi(s_1)$ assigns probability one to the set of s_2 in S_2 such that $p_2 \gg 0$.*

ASSUMPTION 10: *For every s_1 in S_1, there exists s_2 in the support of $\psi(s_1)$ such that the price of money q_{21} is positive.*

It is easily verified that, under these assumptions, the set $\zeta(s_1)$ is nonempty if and only if all prices are positive. Indeed, if the price of some consumption good is zero in period 1, the consumer would demand an infinite amount of it, because preferences are monotone. And if the price of money is zero, Assumption 10 makes it profitable for him to hold unlimited amounts of cash. A consequence of this result is the fact that *any temporary equilibrium will always involve a positive price of money.*

Assume that there are m consumers in the economy, indicated by $i = 1, \ldots, m$, each of whom satisfies the above assumptions. One can define for each of them an excess demand correspondence ζ^i taking the interior of the unit simplex int Δ^l into R^l, hence, an aggregate excess demand correspondence $\zeta = \Sigma_{i=1}^m \zeta^i$. Look now at the other agent in the economy, the central bank. Its task is to choose an action $a = (x, b) \in R^l$ which represents its net supply of all commodities. Its operations are restricted to sales or purchases of perpetuities. Thus, for each $s_1 \in S_1$, the set of feasible actions for the bank is:

$$\beta(s_1) = \{a \in R^l | x = 0, q_1 \cdot b = 0\}.$$

The behavior of the bank is described by its *short run monetary policy*, that is, by a relation η which assigns a (possibly empty) subset $\eta(s_1)$ of $\beta(s_1)$ for every price system s_1 in S_1. I will be concerned in particular in what follows with the policy where the bank pegs the interest rate on perpetuities.[3] If the price of assets is $q_1 \gg 0$, this interest rate r is by definition the inverse of the money price of perpetuities, q_{11}/q_{12}. If the bank wishes to peg the interest rate at some level $r \geq 0$, it will try to bring into equilibrium the market for perpetuities at that rate, no matter what the demands or supplies are expressed by the consumers on that market. In other words, the bank's net supply will be completely elastic whenever $rq_{12} = q_{11}$, and undefined otherwise. Formally,

$$\eta_r(s_1) = \beta(s_1) \quad \text{if} \quad rq_{12} = q_{11},$$

$$= \text{the empty set, otherwise.}$$

A *temporary equilibrium corresponding to a monetary policy η* is defined as a price system s_1 in S_1 such that 0 belongs to $\zeta(s_1) - \eta(s_1)$. The following result states that, under our assumptions, the bank can peg the interest rate on perpetuities at any positive level.

THEOREM: *For every $r > 0$, if $\Sigma_{i=1}^m (e_1^i, b_0^i) \gg 0$, the set of equilibrium price systems corresponding to η_r is nonempty and contained in the interior of Δ^l.*

---

[3] Other policies could be considered, as in Grandmont and Laroque [45].

For a proof of this statement, the reader is referred to Grandmont and Laroque [46], whose reasoning can be easily adapted. The line of the argument is to suppose that, given $r > 0$, the market for perpetuities is always in equilibrium. If, at some price system $s_1 \gg 0$ such that $rq_{12} = q_{11}$, the consumers' aggregate excess demand for perpetuities is b_{12}, the corresponding net supply of money of the bank is $(q_{12}b_{12})/q_{11}$. One then reasons only on the markets for consumption goods and money, and seeks to apply the market equilibrium lemma of Section 3.1.

The first important point to note is the fact that we found an equilibrium for every interest rate $r > 0$ which involves a positive price for money. The crucial assumption for this result is Assumption 10: the price of money is positive in equilibrium because people believe it will be positive with some probability in the future. This is a kind of "bootstraps theory", but it makes sense. On the other hand, if we drop Assumption 10, it is still possible to prove the existence of an equilibrium price system s_1, but the latter may involve a zero price of money, which means a breakdown of the crude banking system under investigation. This obviously would be the case if all consumers believed that the price of money will be zero in period 2 with probability one, for every current price system. But less rudimentary examples can be designed, where the equilibrium price of money is zero, for instance in the case where the traders expect with certainty the price system (p_2, q_2) to be equal to the current price system (p_1, q_1) (see, e.g., Grandmont [41] for such an example in the simple case of an exchange economy with outside money).

The foregoing model allows me to discuss on a precise basis the validity of the short run *quantity theory* of money, as proposed by Patinkin [90].[4] In order to do that, it is convenient to change the normalization of prices and to work with monetary price systems: for every s_1 such that the price of money q_{11} is positive, the corresponding monetary price system s_1^* is obtained by dividing all components of s_1 by q_{11}. Assume now that the bank pegs the interest rate at some positive level r, and consider an associated monetary equilibrium price system $s_1^* = (p_1^*, q_1^*)$. It clearly depends upon the characteristic data of the economy at date 1, and in particular on the consumers' endowments of assets (b_0^i). Suppose that we consider a new economy at date 1, which is identical to the previous one, except that the traders' initial assets are multiplied by some positive number λ, $\bar{b}_0^i = \lambda b_0^i$ for all i. Note that this operation *leaves unchanged the equilibrium price systems observed in the periods preceding date* 1. Patinkin claims that, if the bank sets the interest rate at the same value, then the monetary price system $(\lambda p_1^*, q_1^*)$ will be an equilibrium of the new economy. There, all consumers would consume the same amounts of goods, while they would hold a stock of assets multiplied by λ, compared to the equilibrium of the first economy. It is easy to check that this property is not true in general, unless the traders' expectations are *unit elastic* with respect to current prices of goods, which means that expected money prices of goods are multiplied by λ whenever current money prices of goods are multiplied by λ, the current interest rate being constant. Another way to look at the problem

---

[4] This discussion is based upon Grandmont [41].

is to study the agents' preferences. I showed in Section 2.2 that a trader's excess demand $\zeta^i(s_1^*)$ can be viewed as the result of the maximization of the trader's preferences among actions, represented by an expected utility $v^i(a_1, s_1^*)$, on the set of feasible actions $\beta_1^i(s_1^*)$. Thus Patinkin's claim would be valid if v^i was homogeneous of some degree with respect to asset holdings and money prices of goods, i.e., if

$$v^i(x_1, \lambda b_1, \lambda p_1^*, q_1^*) = \lambda^\alpha v^i(x_1, b_1, p_1^*, q_1^*)$$

for every positive λ. Again, this will not be the case in general, unless the traders' expectations are unit elastic.

This condition therefore seems essential for the validity of the short run quantity theory of money as presented by Patinkin. It can be criticized on the grounds that it implies a sensitivity of expected prices with respect to current prices, which appears to be too great in view of the fact that they depend upon past prices as well. There is more, for it involves some logical problems. Indeed, Patinkin claims that his theory is valid for *every* positive λ. Now, if one assumes that expectations are unit elastic for every positive λ, one gets a contradiction to Assumption 10 by letting λ go to infinity. Thus, within the framework of this model, either one assumes that the trader's expectations are unit elastic with respect to current prices of goods, in which case the equilibrium price of money may be zero, and the short run quantity theory of money rests on shaky foundations, or one postulates Assumption 10 in order to guarantee the existence of a monetary equilibrium, in which case the short run quantity theory of money is not in general valid. This argument leaves open, of course, the possibility that the short run quantity theory of money is valid locally around the equilibrium position of the original economy. Also, it does not exclude the possibility of constructing a model ensuring an equilibrium positive price of money where price expectations are unit elastic (see Hool [72]).[5]

Since the above model has a definite Keynesian flavor, it is worthwhile to study whether there exists a *liquidity trap* in this model. The liquidity trap is usually thought of as a special property of the traders' demand for money which is supposed to go to infinity as the interest rate on perpetuities tends to zero or to a low but positive level. It is possible to show that, in some cases, this property is valid when the interest rate on perpetuities goes to zero. Indeed, consider a sequence of price systems s_1^k in int Δ^l which converges to some $s_1 \in \Delta^l$. The corresponding sequence of interest rates r^k, is defined as q_{11}^k / q_{12}^k. If one wishes that the traders' aggregate excess demand for money tends to $+\infty$ when s_1^k tends to s_1, one certainly has to assume that the corresponding sequence q_{11}^k tends to zero. In that case, it can be shown that the sequence $|\zeta(s_1^k)|$ indeed diverges to infinity. Thus one is sure that the demand for money tends to infinity when the limit price system $s_1 = (p_1, q_1)$ satisfies $p_1 \gg 0$, $q_{11} = 0$, and $q_{12} > 0$. Hence, a liquidity trap exists when the money prices of goods and the money price of perpetuities $1/r^k$ go

[5] If the quantity theory is interpreted as a homogeneity property of the stationary states of a money economy, then it can be shown that it is valid under quite general assumptions (Grandmont and Younès [49], and Grandmont and Laroque [44 and 45]).

to infinity at the same speed. But one can no longer assert the existence of such a phenomenon as soon as $p_{1h} = 0$ for some $h = 1, \ldots, n$, or $q_{12} = 0$. This would be the case in particular when money prices of goods remain finite while the interest rate on perpetuities tends to zero. Indeed, it is easy to design nonpathological examples where under these circumstances, the traders' aggregate demand for money is zero along the sequence s_1^k (see Grandmont and Laroque [46]).

Thus, if one interprets the liquidity trap as a property of the traders' aggregate demand for money, one finds that in some cases it holds, while in other cases it does not. But there is another interpretation of the concept of a liquidity trap proposed by Patinkin [90] which allows us to assert neatly its existence in the above model. For every positive interest rate r, the foregoing theorem guarantees the existence of a set of short run equilibrium price systems. Let $\mu(r)$ be the set of corresponding total money stock in the hands of the consumers at these short run equilibria. Patinkin suggested viewing the liquidity trap as a property of the trade-off described by the correspondence μ.

PROPOSITION 3: *Let r^k be a sequence of positive interest rates tending to zero. Under the assumptions of the theorem, if $M^k \in \mu(r^k)$ is a corresponding sequence of short run equilibrium money stocks, then $\lim M^k = +\infty$.*

For a proof of this statement, the reader is referred again to Grandmont and Laroque [46] whose reasoning can be easily adapted. The idea of the argument is simple. If the foregoing statement were not true, one could find a particular sequence r^k tending to zero, and a corresponding sequence of short run equilibrium price systems s_1^k converging to some $s_1 \in \Delta^l$, such that the limit price system s_1 is an equilibrium for $r = 0$. But that would mean that there exists an equilibrium involving a zero price of money, which is impossible in view of Assumption 10. The economic mechanism underlying this result is easy to grasp. When r^k tends to zero, temporary equilibrium prices move in such a way that traders eventually become sellers of at least a part of their initial stock of perpetuities. In order to bring the market for perpetuities into equilibrium, the bank has to create an amount of money which increases without limit when r^k tends to zero.

It should be noted that in this model the phenomenon can occur only when the interest rate tends to zero since, according to the theorem, the bank can drive down the interest rate on perpetuities as low as it desires. If one follows a suggestion made by Younès [109], one can modify the above model so as to make possible the occurrence of a liquidity trap at a positive interest rate. Suppose that the traders are now allowed to borrow at date 1 by issuing perpetuities, that is, b_{12} can be negative. Then it may be profitable for a trader at some price system to engage in arbitrage operations on the market for perpetuities by issuing perpetuities and holding part of the proceeds in the form of cash balances. In particular, if a trader believes that the interest rate r_2 in period 2 will exceed with probability one a positive level $\bar{r}_2$ which is independent of the current price system, he will be willing to supply unlimited amounts of perpetuities at date 1 if the interest rate at that date is low enough. In that case, the bank would be unable to drive down the interest rate on perpetuities below a positive floor $\bar{r}_1$, and this would lead to the occurrence of a liquidity trap, in the sense of the foregoing Proposition 3, when the interest rate r_1 tends to $\bar{r}_1$ from above. This problem has been investigated by Younès [109] in the context of a model involving several periods, but without a bank. It should not be difficult to make precise the argument that I sketched in the framework of the model presented in this section by using the methods of Green, as they were described in Section 3.2.

The example developed in this section demonstrates that the temporary equilibrium method is a powerful tool for analyzing issues of monetary theory. Progress has been made so far by studying simple models usually involving traders who plan one period ahead, a few kinds of financial assets, and one central bank. More work is needed to include less severely limited planning horizons, a wider variety of financial instruments, and financial institutions such as commercial banks. One can hope, then, to study on a precise basis such monetary issues as the term structure of interest rates or the regulation of the money supply by a central bank when there is a commercial banking sector. The approach should also be helpful in studying some problems in international monetary theory (see Grandmont and Kirman [43] for a first step). Finally, more attention should be paid to the study of the role of money as medium of exchange in temporary equilibrium models. This question has been analyzed in sequence economies with perfect foresight by Hahn [57 and 58], Kurz [79], and Starrett [100], among others, by explicitly introducing transactions technologies. The only temporary equilibrium models which explicitly consider the role of money as a medium of exchange are due to Grandmont and Younès [49 and 50], and Hool [70, 71, and 72]; but this was done by introducing a rudimentary constraint of the Clower type [22], which says that the value of an agent's purchases in a given period cannot exceed his initial cash balance plus a fixed proportion of the value of his current sales. This constraint is supposed to reflect the fact that money is used as an intermediary in every exchange, and the difficulty for buyers and sellers to get together during the marketing period. Grandmont and Younès [49] used their model to study the interaction of the functions of money as a store of value and as a medium of exchange, and to reformulate on a precise basis [50] the arguments of the theory of optimal cash balances, as in Friedman [32]. One interesting point in Hool's research (see, e.g., [72]) is that he shows that, by adding a constraint of the Clower type, one can weaken Assumption 10 of this section so as to make it compatible with unit elastic expectations and still get a temporary equilibrium with a positive price of money. This clearly points to the need for the study of the role of money as a medium of exchange in such models by using less rudimentary formulations and introducing transactions technologies.

3.4. *Temporary Equilibrium and Production*

The works that I have reviewed so far were all concerned with the study of pure exchange economies involving consumers trading in an uncertain world in various institutional setups. Although there is still much work to be done in this area in order to reach a general and concise formulation, the studies that I mentioned in the two preceding sections display a striking unity, and one can hope that a convincing synthesis is not too far ahead. The reason for this relative success is the fact, I believe, that there seems to be an agreement among researchers about the nature of the basic economic unit in exchange economies (the consumer) and the kind of motives (objective function) which one can attribute to it. Although there have been a number of attempts to integrate firms in temporary equilibrium models (Morishima [86], whose work has been generalized recently by Diewert [26], Arrow and Hahn [2], Stigum [101, 102, and 103], Sondermann [99], and Grandmont and Laroque [47]), or in the theory of sequences of markets operating under certainty by using the perfect foresight approach (Radner [95] and Douglas Gale [36]), the result is far less impressive. This is because there is much less agreement about the proper modelling of a firm operating in sequence economies with incomplete futures markets. I shall therefore, without being formal, confine myself in this section to a very brief review of the main characteristics of the works which have been done on this topic and to some remarks concerning the main problems that we face.

Let me begin with a few well known remarks. In the Arrow–Debreu model, a firm is viewed as an economic unit whose task is to combine inputs of some commodities to produce other commodities, and which distributes its profits to its shareholders. Under the assumptions of the model, stock markets would be inactive if they were opened and, given a price system, all stockholders of a firm would choose unanimously a production plan which maximized profit if they were asked to do so. This fact allows representation of a firm in the Arrow–Debreu model as an abstract entity, distinct from its stockholders, whose goal it is to maximize profits on its production set. A related point is that, since the consumers can discount their wealth back to the initial date, the pattern of dividend payments over time is a matter of indifference to the shareholders. Consequently, one can think that all profits are distributed at the initial date.

The situation is much more complicated in temporary equilibrium theory. A firm is still, of course, a unit whose task is to combine inputs at some date in order to produce other commodities at the same date and/or at a later date. The description of the technological possibilities of a firm therefore does not differ much from the one given in the Arrow–Debreu model, except that the time structure of the production set may be described more specifically. But what is new is that:

(i) The traders may have different expectations about the profitability of different firms and thus stock markets may be active (Stigum [102 and 103], Arrow and Hahn [2], Sondermann [99], Radner [95], and Douglas Gale [36]).

(ii) The firms face a budget constraint in each period. In order to finance their production plan, they can issue bonds redeemable in money, and/or issue new equity.

(iii) The pattern of dividend payments over time is no longer a matter of indifference to the shareholders.

Therefore, in addition to a production plan, a firm typically has to choose a financial plan and a stream of dividend payments. The strategy adopted by the researchers in the field was to transpose the formulation of the Arrow–Debreu model, and to view a firm as an abstract entity distinct from its stockholders, with expectations and an objective function of its own, the latter being a more or less complicated function of dividend payments (Stigum, Douglas Gale), of profits (Arrow–Hahn, Radner, Sondermann), and even of the firm's asset–debt structure at the end of its planning horizon (Stigum).

If one adopts this strategy, there are two problems which must be squarely faced. The first one is to find conditions ensuring the existence of an equilibrium in the bond market although there is no a priori upper bound on the supply of bonds by a given firm. I am not aware of any satisfactory answer to that problem. Stigum and Arrow and Hahn appear to be the only ones to consider firms which supply bonds to finance their production plans. Stigum avoids the problem by imposing an arbitrary bound on the firms' supply of bonds. Arrow and Hahn do not impose such a bound but ignore uncertainty. It seems, however, that the problem is similar to the one which arises in pure exchange economies when the consumers are allowed to borrow (Grandmont and Laroque [45]) or to sell short on futures markets (Green [52 and 53]), and that the solutions worked out in that case could be adapted to the case of firms. The second problem, which seems more serious, is to find conditions ensuring the existence of an equilibrium in the stock markets although there is no a priori bound on the supply of new equity by a firm. Stigum and Sondermann avoid the problem by imposing an arbitrary bound on the supply of new equity. Douglas Gale, using the perfect foresight approach, does not impose such a bound, but allows by a suitable normalization of shares equilibrium positions where an infinite number of new shares are issued. The problem is more serious, for unlike the issue of bonds, issuing new equity is a *costless* way of financing a production plan. A related point is that if the debt–asset structure of the firm does not appear in its objective function, then a firm will always choose to finance its production plan by issuing new equity instead of bonds as long as the borrowing interest rate is positive. All these problems have barely been touched upon in temporary equilibrium models, as far as I know.

4. TEMPORARY EQUILIBRIUM WITH QUANTITY RATIONING

The temporary competitive equilibrium approach postulates that in each period prices move fast enough to equilibrate supply and demand. Although this viewpoint enables us to study in principle phenomena such as arbitrage in capital markets, money and banking, and stock markets, which were not taken into account in the traditional general equilibrium theory, it does not permit analysis of "disequilibrium" phenomena such as Keynesian unemployment. Following the works of Clower [21], Hicks [68], Leijonhufvud [82], and Patinkin [90], there has been recently a renewed interest in nontâtonnement models (Hahn and Negishi [62]), which allow trade to take place at prices which do not clear the market in the classical sense, and thus provide a sound microeconomic basis for the formal analysis of "disequilibrium" phenomena. In these models, quantitative constraints on trades, as perceived by the agents, play a central role in the analysis in addition to the price system.

A good deal of the progress made in this area has been achieved by the study of a simple and extreme case where prices are temporarily fixed in each period. The structure of these models is the following: At the outset of each trading period, prices are quoted by some agents in the economic system, say by the sellers, in the light of their past observations and of their expectations about the state of the economy in the coming and the future periods. Once these prices are quoted, they cannot change during the trading period. At these prices, the demands and supplies currently expressed by the agents may not be compatible. In that case, equilibrium is achieved by means of quantitative signals perceived by the agents which set bounds to the trades they can make, that is, by a rationing scheme. Once an equilibrium is reached, trading takes place, and the economy moves to the next period. Then prices may be revised by the agents who control them in the light of the new information generated by the last trading period.

These models turn out to be useful tools to analyze some issues which traditionally belong in the realm of macroeconomic theory. In particular, it is possible to reach a temporary equilibrium where there is an excess supply both in the market for the output of the firms and in the labor market, that is, which displays Keynesian unemployment. But these models are able to generate other situations as well; for instance, one in which there is an excess demand for output and an excess supply of labor (stagflation or classical unemployment), or one in which there is an excess demand in both markets (repressed inflation) (see the series of contributions of Barro and Grossman [4, 5, and 6], and the work of Benassy [7 and 8], Malinvaud [83], Negishi [87] and Younès [108]). This equilibrium concept is therefore very useful because it seems to be able to unify macroeconomic theories which appeared as fundamentally distinct beforehand.

The first studies of this concept in a general equilibrium framework seem to be due to Glustoff [38], to Younès [107, 108, and 111], to Drèze in a paper which circulated in 1971 and was published in 1975 [30], and to Benassy [7 and 9]. In what follows, I will discuss in two basic models which are currently used in the field (Drèze [30] and Benassy [9]).

4.1. *Market Equilibrium with Quantity Rationing*

Consider an economy in a given period. There are $l + 1$ goods to be exchanged, indicated by $h = 0, 1, \ldots, l$, good 0 being money. Prices were quoted at the outset of the period and are described by a vector p in the interior of the unit simplex Δ^{l+1} of R^{l+1}. There are m agents indicated by $i = 1, \ldots, m$. The ith agent's set of feasible net trades is denoted Z^i, a subset of R^{l+1}. The ith agent's actual transactions z must belong to Z^i and satisfy the budget constraint $p \cdot z = 0$.

In addition to the quoted price system, a trader perceives for each commodity h other than money quantitative constraints $\underline{z}_h^i \leqslant 0$ and $\bar{z}_h^i \geqslant 0$ that set lower and upper bounds to the amount of commodity h that he can trade. An important assumption of the model is that no constraint is perceived in the case of commodity 0. One reason for this assumption is to avoid trivial equilibria involving no trade, as we shall see below. A particular *interpretation* of the model is that there are l separate trading posts, one for each commodity h other than money, where the traders exchange commodity h against money at the ruling prices. Although these markets are separated, the traders are supposed to trade simultaneously in all of them. Indeed, for every $h \neq 0$, let $t(h)$ be the elementary transaction describing an exchange of one unit of commodity h against $-(p_h/p_0)$ units of money: $t(h)$ is a vector in R^{l+1} which satisfies $t_0(0) = -(p_h/p_0)$, $t_h(h) = 1$, and $t_k(h) = 0$ for $k \neq 0, h$. Then every trade such that $p \cdot z = 0$ can be written $z = \sum_{h=1}^{l} z_h t(h)$, and conversely. In this interpretation, z_h can be viewed as the intensity of the transaction of commodity h for money, and the constraints $\underline{z}_h^i$ and $\bar{z}_h^i$ can be interpreted as constraints on these intensities. Commodity 0 then plays the role of a medium of exchange like demand deposits, and one can imagine that payments at each trading post are made by writing out checks or by making use of a credit card, the only requirement being that a trader's final money balances must satisfy some a priori given constraints embodied in the definition of the feasible set Z^i. While this particular interpretation is suggestive and presumably contains an important element of truth, it is not a logically necessary part of the models that I am going to describe. The choice of the particular commodity for which no constraints are perceived, however, evidently influences in a crucial way the kind of allocations which will be eventually reached.

I first present Drèze's model [30]. Let $s^i = (p, \underline{z}^i, \bar{z}^i)$ be the signal perceived by the ith trader, where $\underline{z}^i \in R^l_-$ and $\bar{z}^i \in R^l_+$. Given this signal, each trader expresses his constrained excess demand, represented by a subset $\zeta(s^i)$ of Z^i. It will be the result of the maximization of the trader's preferences on the set of net trades $z \in Z^i$ which satisfy the budget constraint $p \cdot z = 0$ and the quantitative constraints $\underline{z}_h^i \leq z_h \leq \bar{z}_h^i$, $h \neq 0$. It will, therefore, in general have the property: for each commodity $h \neq 0$, and every z in $\zeta(s^i)$, then $z_h \leq 0$ whenever $\bar{z}_h^i = 0$ and $z_h \geq 0$ whenever $\underline{z}_h^i = 0$. Finally, the trader's preferences will be represented by an expected utility $v^i(z, s^i)$ which is derived by a dynamic programming technique as in (1) of Section 2.2. It depends in general on the signal currently perceived through its influence on the trader's expectations.

DEFINITION: An *equilibrium with quantity rationing* in the sense of Drèze is described by a set of signals $s = (s^i)$ and by net trades $z^i \in \zeta^i(s^i)$ such that: (i) $\sum_{i=1}^m z^i = 0$, and (ii) for each $h \neq 0$, $z_h^i = \bar{z}_h^i$ for some i implies $z_h^j > \underline{z}_h^j$ for all j; and $z_h^i = \underline{z}_h^i$ for some i implies $z_h^j < \bar{z}_h^j$ for all j.

The last condition means that only traders on one side of the market for commodity h may perceive binding constraints, and is quite natural. It must be remarked that the no-trade allocation ($z^i = 0$) would always satisfy these conditions had I allowed constraints $\underline{z}_0^i$ and $\bar{z}_0^i$ on commodity 0: it would suffice to set $\bar{z}_0^i = 0$ and $\bar{z}_h^i = 0$ for every h and i. This is a reason for postulating the absence of such constraints.

At a Drèze equilibrium, a trader is *constrained* in commodity $h \neq 0$, if he can be made better off by relaxing the quantity constraints associated with that commodity, that is, if there exists z in the set $\gamma_h^i = \{z \in Z^i | p \cdot z = 0 \text{ and } \underline{z}_k^i \leq z_k \leq \bar{z}_k^i, k \neq 0, h\}$ such that $v^i(z, s^i) > v^i(z^i, s^i)$. If the v^i's are quasi concave, then condition (ii) implies that all agents who are constrained in commodity h belong to the same side of the market, that is, all their final trades have the same sign. If they are all nonnnegative, for instance, then all these traders would like to buy more of commodity h than they actually do, if they were allowed to do so: there is an excess demand of commodity h. Note that there may be an "equilibrium" on some market h (no constraint on that market is binding) which results from the fact that some traders perceive binding constraints on some other market k different from h. This corresponds to the concept of "effective demand" put forward by Clower [21] and elaborated upon at length by Leijonhufvud [82].

LEMMA 2: *Assume (i) Z^i is closed, convex, bounded below, and $0 \in Z^i$; (ii) v^i is continuous with respect to z and s^i, and quasiconcave with respect to z. Then, there exists a Drèze equilibrium.*

The central idea of the simple proof that I now give can be found in Drèze [30].

PROOF: Choose $\varepsilon > 0$ and define an auxiliary set $Q = \{q \in R^{l+1} | q_o = 1, -\varepsilon \leq q_h \leq \varepsilon, h \neq 0\}$. Define the set of attainable trades as the set of (z^i) such that $z^i \in Z^i$ and $\Sigma_{i=1}^m z^i = 0$. Under the assumptions of Lemma 2, this set is compact. Let λ be a real number so large that for every (z^i) in the set of attainable trades, one has $|z_h^i| < \lambda$ for all i and h. Now, for every i, and $h \neq 0$, consider two arbitrary real-valued functions $\underline{z}_h^i(\cdot)$ and $\bar{z}_h^i(\cdot)$, defined on Q, which are continuous, nonincreasing, and satisfy: $\underline{z}_h^i(q) = -\lambda$ for $q_h \geq 0$, and $\underline{z}_h^i(q) = 0$ if $q_h = -\varepsilon$; $\bar{z}_h^i(q) = \lambda$ if $q_h \leq 0$, and $\bar{z}_h^i(q) = 0$ if $q_h = +\varepsilon$. This defines for each q in Q a signal $s^i(q)$, and thus a correspondence ζ from Q into R^{l+1} by $\zeta(q) = \Sigma_{i=1}^m \zeta^i(s^i(q))$. It is clear that any vector q in Q such that $0 \in \zeta(q)$ defines an equilibrium with quantity rationing. Conversely, any such equilibrium can be obtained in that way by an appropriate choice of the functions $\underline{z}_h^i(\cdot)$ and $\bar{z}_h^i(\cdot)$.

The correspondence ζ is compact-valued and upper hemicontinuous. Thus, there exists a subset Z of R^{l+1} which is compact, convex, and contains $\zeta(q)$ for all q. For each z in Z, let $\mu(z)$ be the set of elements q^* in Q which maximize $q \cdot z$. To every couple (q, z) in $Q \times Z$, associate the set $\mu(z) \times \zeta(q)$. The correspondence so defined has a fixed point, i.e., there is q^* in Q and z^* in $\zeta(q^*)$ such that $q^* \cdot z^* \geq q \cdot z^*$ for all q in Q. Now, if for some $h \neq 0$, $z_h^* > 0$, that would mean $q_h^* = +\varepsilon$, therefore $\bar{z}_h^i(q^*) = 0$, in which case $z_h^* \leq 0$ from assumption (ii) of Lemma 2. A similar reasoning holds when $z_h^* < 0$ for some $h \neq 0$. Thus $z_h^* = 0$ for all commodities h other than money, which implies $z^* = 0$ since $p \cdot z^* = 0$.

Q.E.D.

The structure of this argument makes clear the type of adjustment which takes place implicitly in this economy. There is some "auctioneer" who quotes quantitative constraints $\underline{z}^i$ and $\bar{z}^i$. In response to these constraints, sets of constrained excess demands $\zeta^i(s^i)$ are sent by the traders to the market. If the auctioneer registers, say, an excess demand for some commodity $h \neq 0$, he lowers the upper bounds $\bar{z}_h^i$ imposed upon the traders' purchases. Any fixed point of this tâtonnement in quantity constraints is an equilibrium in the sense of Drèze.

The foregoing definition of an equilibrium does not specify how shortages are distributed among agents. Consequently, there will be many equilibria (in general, a continuum). This fact is reflected in the proof of Lemma 2 by the arbitrary choice of the functions $\underline{z}^i(\cdot)$ and $\bar{z}^i(\cdot)$. In order to get a more specific theory, it is natural to require that the final outcome of the trading process corresponds to a given rationing scheme. It is indeed possible to modify the above definition of an equilibrium, and the proof of Lemma 2, so as to take into account some specific rationing schemes. For instance, a *uniform* rationing requires that all constraints $\underline{z}^i$ and $\bar{z}^i$ not depend upon the trader, and is easily handled by imposing that the functions $\underline{z}^i(\cdot)$ and $\bar{z}^i(\cdot)$ used in the proof of Lemma 2 be independent of i (Drèze [30]). It is equally straightforward to take care of the case where rationing on a market h must occur according to some given order (*queuing*). Suppose, for instance, that this order specifies that trader 1 should be served first if he decides to buy commodity h, trader 2 the second, and so on. This amounts to saying in the definition of an equilibrium, that $z_h^1 = \bar{z}_h^1$ implies $\bar{z}_h^i = 0$ for all $i \geq 2$, $z_h^2 = \bar{z}_h^2$ implies $\bar{z}_h^i = 0$ for all $i \geq 3$, and so on. To prove the existence of an equilibrium corresponding to this rationing scheme, it suffices in the proof of Lemma 2 to impose the following extra conditions on the functions $\bar{z}_h^i(\cdot)$: $\bar{z}_h^1(q) = \lambda$ for $q_h \leq (m-1)\varepsilon/m$, $\bar{z}_h^2(q) = \lambda$ for $q_h \leq (m-2)\varepsilon/m$ and $\bar{z}_h^2(q) = 0$ for $q_h = (m-1)\varepsilon/m$, and so on. I conjecture that any principle of rationing which can be stated in terms which are independent of the traders' excess demands can be handled without much problem by using the methods I described so far. The case where the rationing scheme depends upon trade offers made by the agents which might violate the constraints $\underline{z}_h^i \leq z_h \leq \bar{z}_h^i$, $h \neq 0$, as in the case of proportional rationing, falls outside the scope of Drèze's model, since such trade offers are not considered (a precise formulation of such rationing mechanisms will be given below when I study Benassy's model). It would be interesting to see how Drèze's model must be amended in order to handle such general rationing schemes. It is important to see that the central problem in this approach would be the formulation of a satisfactory theory explaining why, in the light of the quantitative constraints $\underline{z}^i$ and $\bar{z}^i$ which they perceive, the agents would express trade offers differing from those in $\zeta^i(s^i)$.

An alternative and interesting attempt to model an equilibrium with quantity rationing has been implemented by Benassy [7 and 9]. His model is a generalization of the work of Barro and Grossman [4], and of Grossman [54]. Instead of assuming, as Drèze did, that the traders send to the market their constrained demands, he postulates that they send trade offers which may violate the constraints they perceive. These trade offers in turn determine by a rationing mechanism the agents' actual transactions. From these, the traders formulate new offers. An equilibrium is defined by Benassy as a fixed point of this process in the space of trade offers.

More precisely, assume that the ith agent sent to the market a trade offer $\tilde{z}^i \in R^l$ representing his excess demand for each commodity $h \neq 0$. No trade offer is made for money: this corresponds to the idea which I already mentioned that money is used as a medium of exchange or at least acts as a buffer stock. Let $\tilde{z} \in R^{lm}$ be the vector of all trade offers made by the agents. These offers may not be compatible, that is, $\Sigma_{i=1}^m \tilde{z}^i$ may differ from zero. Benassy postulates that there is a rationing scheme associating to $\tilde{z}$ an ex post transaction $z_h^i = F_h^i(\tilde{z})$ for each trader and each commodity $h \neq 0$. This rationing scheme is supposed to satisfy the following natural conditions for every $\tilde{z} \in R^{lm}$ and every $h \neq 0$:

(i) $\Sigma_{i=1}^m F_h^i(\tilde{z}) = 0$.

(ii) $z_h^i \tilde{z}_h^i \geqslant 0$ and $|z_h^i| \leqslant |\tilde{z}_h^i|$, which means that the sign of an agent's transaction cannot be reversed, and that nobody can be forced to exchange more than he wishes.

(iii) The agents on the "short" side of the market realize their plan, that is, $\tilde{z}_h^i(\Sigma_{i=1}^m \tilde{z}_h^i) \leqslant 0$ implies $z_h^i = \tilde{z}_h^i$. This condition is closely related to (ii) of the definition of a Drèze equilibrium above.

The ex post transactions z_h^i, $h \neq 0$, determine the agent's ex post transaction z_0^i in money by $p_0 z_0^i = -\Sigma_{h=1}^l p_h z_h^i$. This gives an ex post trade $z^i \in R^{l+1}$ which satisfies $p \cdot z^i = 0$ and is a function of $\tilde{z}$ alone. Note that there is no guarantee that z^i is feasible, that is, one may have $z^i \notin Z^i$. I shall come back to this point later on.

The comparison of his original offer with his ex post transactions makes a trader perceive subjective quantity constraints $\underline{z}^i \in R^l$ and $\bar{z}^i \in R^l$ on his trades on commodities $h \neq 0$, as in Drèze's model. The perception of these constraints may also be influenced by whatever information the trader has about the other agents' trade offers. As all of this information is a function of $\tilde{z}$ alone, I write $\underline{z}^i = \underline{G}^i(\tilde{z}) \leqslant 0$ and $\bar{z}^i = \bar{G}^i(\tilde{z}) \geqslant 0$. The functions $\underline{G}^i$ and $\bar{G}^i$ are given data of the problem and are assumed to satisfy the following two conditions for every $h \neq 0$ and $\tilde{z} \in R^{lm}$:

(iv) $\underline{G}_h^i(\tilde{z}) \leqslant z_h^i \leqslant \bar{G}_h^i(\tilde{z})$.

(v) $\tilde{z}_h^i > z_h^i$ implies $\bar{G}_h^i(\tilde{z}) = z_h^i$, and $z_h^i > \tilde{z}_h^i$ implies $\underline{G}_h^i(\tilde{z}) = z_h^i$.

In the case where $\tilde{z}_h^i > z_h^i$, for instance, z_h^i must be nonnegative from condition (ii). It is then natural to assume that the trader perceives that he cannot buy more than z_h^i of commodity h. Other conditions were imposed by Benassy but they will not be needed in the sequel.

I turn now to the crucial assumption of Benassy's model which pertains to the determination of the agents' trade offers. In the footsteps of Barro and Grossman [4] and Grossman [54], he assumes that a trader's demand on some market $h \neq 0$ is the result of the maximization of his preferences ignoring the constraints associated with this commodity, but taking into account the constraints perceived on the other markets. More precisely, given the signals received by the agent on the current period, which are a function of $\tilde{z}$ alone, let his preferences among trades $z \in Z^i$ be represented by an expected utility index $v^i(z, \tilde{z})$ which may be derived by a dynamic programming technique as in (1) of Section 2.2. For every $h \neq 0$, look at the hth component of the net trades which maximize v^i with respect to z in the set $\gamma_h^i = \{z \in Z^i | p \cdot z = 0 \text{ and } \underline{z}_k^i \leqslant z_k \leqslant \bar{z}_k^i, k \neq 0, h\}$. They form a subset of the real line $\tilde{\zeta}^i_h(\tilde{z})$. Note that the constraints $\underline{z}^i$ and $\bar{z}^i$ are considered exogenous by the trader in his maximization problem. The operation is repeated for every $h \neq 0$, and the ith agent's set of trade offers $\tilde{\zeta}^i(\tilde{z})$, a subset of R^l, is taken as the product of all $\tilde{\zeta}^i_h(\tilde{z})$. The product of all $\tilde{\zeta}^i(\tilde{z})$, $i = 1, \ldots, m$, is denoted $\tilde{\zeta}(\tilde{z})$. Then Benassy defines an equilibrium as a point $\tilde{z}$ in R^{lm} such that $\tilde{z} \in \tilde{\zeta}(\tilde{z})$.

LEMMA 3: *Assume* (i) Z^i *is closed, convex, bounded below and* $0 \in Z^i$; (ii) *the functions* F^i_h, G^i, *and* $\bar{G}^i$ *are continuous; and* (iii) *the expected utility index* v^i *is continuous in* z *and* $\tilde{z}$, *and quasiconcave in* z. *Then, there exists a Benassy equilibrium.*

The proof of this result is straightforward. Under the stated assumptions, the correspondence $\tilde{\zeta}$ has compact and convex values, is upper hemicontinuous, and its range is contained in a compact, convex subset of R^{lm}. The restriction of $\tilde{\zeta}$ to this set obviously has a fixed point.

Apart from the mere question of existence, an equilibrium must satisfy other conditions. Any equilibrium $\tilde{z}$ determines perceived constraints $\underline{z}^i$ and $\bar{z}^i$, and an ex post trade z^i which satisfies $p \cdot z^i = 0$. A natural requirement is that z^i is feasible, $z^i \in Z^i$, and furthermore that z^i maximizes v^i with respect to z in the set $\gamma^i = \{z \in Z^i | p \cdot z = 0, \underline{z}^i_h \leqslant z_h \leqslant \bar{z}^i_h, h \neq 0\}$. There is nothing in the proposed definition which guarantees these properties. This is due to the fact that the agents' trade offers are formulated in the model independently on each market h, and without taking into account their consequences (final trades). If these two requirements, especially the first, were not met, it is quite likely that the agents would revise the way they formulate their trade offers. To check if these two conditions are satisfied in equilibrium is thus a test of the logical consistency of the model. It turns out that they are satisfied when the v^i are strictly quasiconcave in z, but that this may not be the case otherwise.

LEMMA 4: *Under the assumptions of Lemma 3, at a Benassy equilibrium* $\tilde{z}$, *the final transactions* z^i *belong to* Z^i *and maximize* v^i *with respect to* z *on the set* γ^i, *provided that* v^i *is strictly quasiconcave in* z *for each* i.

PROOF: To prove this result,[6] consider the vector ζ^i which maximizes v^i on γ^i, and choose an $h \neq 0$. First, assume that ζ^i does not maximize v^i on the set γ^i_h. Then, owing to the fact that v^i is quasiconcave, and in view of the definition of $\tilde{z}$, $\tilde{z}^i_h \notin [\underline{z}^i_h, \bar{z}^i_h]$. If, for instance, $\tilde{z}^i_h > \bar{z}^i_h$, then $\zeta^i_h = \bar{z}^i_h$ again from the quasiconcavity of v^i. But condition (v) of the definition of perceived constraints implies then $z^i_h = \bar{z}^i_h$, hence, $\zeta^i_h = z^i_h$. Suppose now that ζ^i does maximize v^i on γ^i_h. Then $\zeta^i_h = \tilde{z}^i_h$ from the strict quasiconcavity of v^i. Conditions (iv) and (v) in turn imply $\tilde{z}^i_h = z^i_h$, in which case $\zeta^i_h = z^i_h$. Therefore, $\zeta^i_h = z^i_h$ for every $h \neq 0$, and it follows from $p \cdot \zeta^i = p \cdot z^i$ that $\zeta^i = z^i$.   Q.E.D.

---

[6] The idea of the proof is due to Benassy.

One can show that the result stated in Lemma 4 is still valid when v^i is not strictly quasiconcave, if the following circumstance occurs: take any ζ^i which maximizes v^i on γ^i; then there is at most one $h \neq 0$ such that ζ^i maximizes v^i on γ^i_h. As the proof of this result is simple, I leave the details to the reader. (*Hint*: the first part of the foregoing proof shows that $\zeta^i_k = z^i_k$ for $k \neq 0, h$. Take any vector $\tilde{\zeta}$ which maximizes v^i on γ^i_h such that $\tilde{\zeta}_h = \tilde{z}^i_h$. Show that $\tilde{\zeta}_k = \zeta^i_k$ for $k \neq 0, h$, and that z^i is a convex combination of ζ^i and $\tilde{\zeta}$.) But the following example shows that when v^i is not strictly concave, z^i may not belong to Z^i if this happy circumstance does not obtain. Assume that there are three commodities ($l = 2$), two traders i and j, and that all prices are equal. Suppose that agent i's feasible set is $Z^i = \{z \mid z + w^i \geqslant 0\}$ where the endowment of money w^i_0 is such that $1 \leqslant w^i_0 < 2$, and his set of most preferred trades in the set of $z \in Z^i$ such that $p \cdot z = 0$ contains the closed segment joining the two trades $(-1, 1, 0)$ and $(-1, 0, 1)$. Assume that the other trader's most preferred trade happens to consist of selling one unit of each commodity 1 and 2. A possible "equilibrium" in the sense of Benassy would be a situation where trader i offers to buy one unit of each commodity 1 and 2, but he cannot afford it! This shows that some Benassy equilibria may not be sensible when the v^i are not strictly quasiconcave. However, a likely conjecture is that, under the assumptions of Lemma 3, there always exists a Benassy equilibrium such that $z^i \in Z^i$ and z^i maximizes v^i on γ^i (approximate each v^i by a sequence of functions which are strictly concave in z, apply Lemma 3 for each element of the sequence, and go to the limit).

The most interesting feature of Benassy's model is the fact that it can handle general rationing schemes, which Drèze's model cannot, at least in its present state. The weak point is, of course, how the agents formulate their trade offers, which is not justified by a satisfactory theory. These trade offers are made independently on each market, without considering their consequences on final transactions. I have already pointed out that this might lead to inconsistencies in some cases. At any rate, since it is in general infeasible for a trader to finance simultaneously his trade offers $\tilde{z}^i$, one should be cautious when using them as a measure of the size of disequilibrium, as is too often done in some studies of the dynamics of such models. All this points to the need for a better theory explaining how traders formulate trade offers in the presence of constraints on their transactions, a fact that I mentioned earlier in connection with Drèze's model. One possible line of attack of this problem is to assume that the agents know the rationing scheme, and that, given the trader offers of the other agents, each trader sends trade offers on all markets so as to maximize the utility of their consequences. This leads to a concept of Nash equilibrium in the space of trade offers (see Benassy [12], Boehm and Levine [16], and Heller and Starr [64]). Still more work on this topic is needed in order to settle the issue.

Drèze's model may be criticized on the ground that it does not generate an exchange of information among traders about the size of the rationing that they experience. On the other hand, in Benassy's model, the trade offers $\tilde{z}^i$ do not appear to be reliable measures of the size of disequilibrium in each market, for the reasons which I already mentioned. Accordingly, it may be argued, the agents who control some prices do not know whether and by how much to change them in the next trading period. The issue seems essential to any dynamic study of the model, where price changes come into play. But the picture is not as bad as it appears, for the models can be amended and applied to situations where such information does exist. The concept of equilibrium, as it stands, tells us who the agents are who are constrained in commodity h. It can be assumed that this information is at least partly available to the other traders, in which case they know that there is a disequilibrium on some market and have information on the number of agents who perceive binding constraints. But more importantly, the traders do have information about the size of the disequilibrium in this model if they know the final trades of the other agents and if we interpret some markets as futures markets (to be precise, the theory presented in the this section would have to be extended, since the Z^i can no longer be assumed bounded below in the presence of futures markets). Indeed, in many cases, a buyer who is prevented from purchasing a commodity in the current period will place an order to get the same commodity at some unspecified later date. To the extent that he makes a downpayment, this can be interpreted as a forward contract of a special type (or a pair of forward contracts: a purchase of the commodity by the buyer with full payment of the price in the current period, and a loan by the seller to the buyer). In such a case, sellers have some information about the size of the excess demand for some commodity by looking at the size of purchases on the corresponding futures market. Other relevant indicators are the level of stocks in the case of durable goods, of leftovers otherwise. In the special case of the labor market, where futures markets typically do not exist, it is safe to assume that a specific agent, the government, pays unemployment benefits which, again, generates information about the size of unemployment. In the light of all this information, the traders would forecast supplies or demands for the future periods, and would make up their mind about possible revisions of the prices they control for the next trading period. This seems to be a realistic way of modelling the flows of information which actually take place in our economies. A difficult but rewarding project would be to study a model along these lines and to look at its dynamic implications. I believe it could provide a sound microeconomic foundation to macroeconomic theory.

4.2. *Bibliographical Note*

The first formal studies of the existence of an equilibrium with quantity rationing are due to Benassy [7 and 9], Drèze [30], Glustoff [38], and Younès [107 and 111]. The presentation made in this section is adapted from Drèze, who considered the more general case where money prices can vary within some given bounds, and from Benassy. Younès also studies the efficiency properties of equilibria with quantity rationing and relates them to the role of money as a medium of exchange, a point which was emphasized by Leijonhufvud. The issue has been further explored by Benassy [10], and Malinvaud and Younès [84 and 85]. A game theoretic analysis of a model of this type appears in Grandmont, Laroque and Younès [48].

These microeconomic disequilibrium models have been used to analyze Keynesian short run unemployment and monopolistic price setting by Benassy [7 and 11], Hahn [60], Iwai [73 and 74], Negishi [87], and Grandmont and Laroque [47]. The last authors in fact compare two versions of the Keynesian model, one which uses essentially the temporary competitive equilibrium approach, but where money wages are rigid downwards, the other where prices of goods and money wages are chosen at the outset of each period by the firms and the workers, respectively. In both instances, the influence of the firms' expectations about future effective demand on the current level of employment is discussed.

5. STOCHASTIC PROCESSES OF TEMPORARY EQUILIBRIA

The distinctive feature of the models I have analyzed so far is the fact that trade takes place sequentially over time, and that the agents make decisions at each date in the light of their current and the past observations. Thus the state of the economic system at each date depends upon past history of the economy. Let the state of the system at any date be described by a set of exogenous variables represented by an element e of some space E, and by a set of variables which are either directly controlled by the economic agents or jointly determined by them, and are represented by an element d of some space D. Then the state $x = (e, d)$ of the system at any date is an element of a subspace X of the product $E \times D$. In the sequel, I will assume that X, E, and D are separable metric spaces, and postulate, without loss of generality, that the projection of X on E and D is precisely E and D, respectively.

Look at the economy at date t. At that time, the history of the system is known and is described by the sequence $x^{t-1} = (x_{t-1}, x_{t-2}, \ldots, x_1)$, of states of the economy in the previous periods back to the first one (I take as given the history of the system prior to that date). Given the current values of the exogenous variables, say $e_t \in E$, the agents interact in current markets within the institutional setup of the economy. Let $x_t = (e_t, d_t) = f_t(e_t, x^{t-1})$ be the equilibrium state which is reached as the result of this interaction. It depends upon e_t and x^{t-1} since the value of these variables may influence both the present situation of the agents and their expectations.

Assume now that the economy is subject to exogenous random shocks so that the exogenous variables form a stochastic process $(e_1, e_2, \ldots)$ defined on a given probability space (Ω, F, P), each random variable e_t taking its values in E. This stochastic process, plus the functions f_t which characterize the laws of motion of the system, induce a new stochastic process $(x_1, x_2, \ldots)$ on the space of states of the economy, which describes its evolution over time and is given by $x_1(\omega) = f_1(e_1(\omega), x^0)$ and $x_t(\omega) = f_t(e_t(\omega), x^{t-1}(\omega))$, where x^0 represents the history of the economy prior to date 1.

An interesting question to ask about this stochastic process is whether it displays some kind of stability such as ergodicity. In some cases, the stochastic process $(x_t, x_{t+1}, \ldots)$ may tend to a stationary stochastic process when t goes to infinity. Along such a stationary stochastic process, in particular, the distribution of the random variable x_t would be constant. Such a stationary process would then represent a *long run equilibrium* of the system. Whether such long run equilibria exist is thus an important question.

These problems are largely unsolved and much work is needed in this area. Some progress has been made in the case where the processes $(e_1, e_2, \ldots)$ and $(x_1, x_2, \ldots)$ are both Markov with stationary transition probabilities, which I describe in Section 5.1. I will then comment briefly on the problems raised by the question of "rational expectations" in this context in Section 5.2.

5.1. *Markov Processes of Temporary Equilibria*

I now make assumptions ensuring that the stochastic process $(x_1, x_2, \ldots)$ is Markov with stationary transition probabilities. This is not a restrictive viewpoint as long as the system has a finite and constant memory. In that case, the analysis which follows is still valid if one properly enlarges the state space; that is, if one defines the "state" of the economy at date t as $x'_t = (x_t, x_{t-1}, \ldots, x_{t-T})$ where T is the longest lag in the system.

I first assume that the stochastic process $(e_1, e_2, \ldots)$ is itself Markov with stationary transition probability ν acting on E. Thus for every e in E and every Borel subset A of E, $\nu(e, A)$ represents the probability that the value of the exogenous variables is in A at date $t+1$ when their value is e at date t. Alternatively, ν can be viewed as a mapping from E into the space of probability measures $\mathcal{M}(E)$ defined on E.

The next step is to assume that the equilibrium state $x_t = (e_t, d_t)$ at date t depends only on the current values of the exogenous variables e_t and on the past state of the economy $x_{t-1} = (e_{t-1}, d_{t-1})$. Thus I write $x_t = f(e_t, x_{t-1})$ where f is invariant over time and is measurable.

It is now intuitively clear that, with these assumptions, the probability law of x_t depends only on the value of x_{t-1}, and that this dependence does not vary over time. One can indeed show that the process $(x_1, x_2, \ldots)$ is Markov with a stationary transition probability Q acting on X which is given by the following relation, for every $x = (e, d) \in X$ and every Borel subset B of X:

$$Q(x, B) = \nu(e, \{e' \in E \mid f(e', x) \in B\})).$$

In this context, a long run equilibrium is characterized by an *invariant measure* of this Markov process, that is, by a measure $\mu^* \in \mathcal{M}(X)$ satisfying:

$$\mu^*(B) = \int_X Q(\cdot, B) \, d\mu^*, \quad \text{for every Borel set } B \text{ of } X.$$

PROPOSITION 4: *Let E, D, and X be separable metric spaces, and endow $\mathcal{M}(E)$ with the topology of weak convergence of probability measures. Assume that the mapping $\nu: E \to \mathcal{M}(E)$ and $f: E \times X \to X$ are continuous. Then, if X is compact, there exists an invariant measure μ^*.*

The proof of this proposition, which follows easily from standard results of the theory of Markov processes, can be found in Grandmont and Hildenbrand [42]. These authors also show that, under the assumptions of the proposition, a little more can be said about the dynamics of the system, but not much. Thus we are still left with the unsolved problem of the dynamic behavior of the system. An interesting line of research would be to find joint properties of the transition probability ν and of the function f leading, say, to the ergodicity of the resulting Markov process on X. One should then try to interpret the properties of the function f in terms of the basic data of the economy such as preferences, expectation formation, and the institutional setup within which the agents interact. The implementation of such a program has not begun so far, to my best knowledge. It turns out, however, that the model described in this section is quite similar to some models which are studied in some areas of other social sciences, such as learning theory (Norman [88], and Theodorescu [106]). These models have been analyzed by mathematicians under the name "random systems with complete connections", but their results do not seem at present applicable to economics.

5.2. Rational Expectations

Consider the model described in Section 5.1, and assume that each agent in the economy perceives at each date a signal s^i which is a function of the state of the economy at that date, $s^i = \sigma^i(x)$, where s^i is an element of a space S^i which describes all signals that the agent can perceive in any period. A key element of the trader's behavior is how he forecasts future signals in function of the signals perceived in the current and previous period. This is summarized by a mapping ψ^i from $S^i \times S^i$ into $\mathcal{M}(S^i)$. Now the function f describing the dynamics of the whole economic system, hence, the resulting transition probability Q on X, evidently depends upon the expectation functions ψ^i of all the agents. This is an example where the way people forecast the future in fact influences it. Thus, to each collection of expectation functions (ψ^i), one can associate a set of invariant measures for the corresponding transition probability Q. Each such invariant measure, together with Q, defines a stationary Markov process which can be interpreted as a long run equilibrium of the system. Along such a stationary Markov process, the probability that a given trader receives a signal in some subset of S^i at some date conditional upon the signals that he perceived in the previous two periods is constant over time. These conditional probabilities may differ significantly from the ψ^i that we started with. The trader is said to have "rational" or "self-fulfilling" expectations when they coincide.

An interesting and, in the context of the models so far described, still open problem is to find properties of the traders' learning process ψ^i which lead to stationary shochastic processes where the traders' expectations are fulfilled in this sense. An obvious way to deal with the problem in the above model is to try to apply a fixed point theorem, since to each collection of ψ^i, one can associate a set of conditional ex post probabilities. I do not think that this approach is very promising, however, since it would provide little information about the kind of learning process the traders should use. It seems that a more interesting approach would be to start with the assumption that the expectation functions ψ^i are generated from the application of classical or Bayesian statistical techniques, as in Section 2.4. Since in that case the traders accumulate information over time, one would lose the Markov property and obtain a time-dependent stochastic process of the type described at the beginning of Section 5. The question to be studied would be whether a particular statistical technique leads asymptotically, as time goes to infinity, to rational expectations in the above sense. To my knowledge, such a problem has not been studied, or even properly formulated in the context of temporary equilibrium models; although some attempts have been made recently in Bayesian settings by Arrow and Green [1] and Kihlstrom and Mirman [78].

5.3. *Bibliographical Note*

The idea of representing a long run equilibrium by a stationary stochastic process is due to Radner [96]. Section 5.1 is adapted from Grandmont and Hildenbrand [42]. Their model is a stochastic version of Samuelson's pure consumption loan model with overlapping generations and outside money, which was studied in the context of a nonstochastic and stationary environment by Grandmont and Laroque [44]. Grandmont and Hildenbrand also show that, when the uncertainty affecting the individual characteristics of the agents can be represented by independent random variables, and when the number of agents is large, macroeconomic observables such as equilibrium prices become nonrandom. Another approach to this problem has been implemented by Younès [110] by looking at prices which equate to zero the expected value of the aggregate excess demand in every period, in the spirit of Hildenbrand [69].

When the exogenous variables are nonrandom and stationary in the model of Section 5.1 ($e_1 = e$ for all t), a stationary state is defined by an element x^* of X such that $x^* = f(e, x^*)$. The existence and efficiency properties of such stationary states have been studied in specific models with particular emphasis on monetary issues by Grandmont and Younès [49 and 50] and by Grandmont and Laroque [44 and 45]. The stability properties of Grandmont and Laroque's model [44] have been investigated by Fuchs and Laroque [34]. Fuchs [33] has recently studied how these stability properties are influenced by changes in the traders' expectation functions ψ^i (structural stability).

Radner [95 and 96], followed by Douglas Gale [36], has proved the existence of an equilibrium of plans, prices and price expectations when the latter are defined as functions indicating for each date-event pair, what the equilibrium price system would be in the corresponding market, and thus has solved the problem of the existence of rational expectations in this context. The problems raised by the approach suggested in Section 5.2 are still open.

CEPREMAP

Manuscript received November, 1975.

REFERENCES

[1] ARROW, K., AND J. R. GREEN: "Notes on Expectations Equilibria in Bayesian Settings," Working Paper, Department of Economics, Stanford University, 1973.

[2] ARROW, K., AND F. H. HAHN: *General Competitive Analysis.* San Francisco: Holden-Day, 1971.

[3] BALCH M., D. McFADDEN, AND S. W. YU (EDS.): *Essays on Economic Behavior under Uncertainty,* Contributions to Economic Analysis. Amsterdam: North-Holland, 1974.

[4] BARRO, R. J., AND H. I. GROSSMAN: "A General Disequilibrium Model of Income and Employment," *American Economic Review,* 61 (1971), 82–93.

[5] ———: "Suppressed Inflation and the Supply Multiplier," *Review of Economic Studies,* 41 (1974), 87–104.

[6] ———: *Money, Employment and Inflation.* Cambridge: Cambridge University Press, 1976.

[7] BENASSY, J. P.: "Disequilibrium Theory," Unpublished Ph.D. Dissertation, University of California, Berkeley, 1973.

[8] ———: "A Neokeynesian Model of Price and Quantity Determination in Disequilibrium," CEPREMAP, to appear in *Equilibrium and Disequilibrium in Economic Theory,* ed. by G. Schwödiauer, Proceedings of a conference held in Vienna, Austria, 1974.

[9] ———: "Neo-keynesian Disequilibrium in a Monetary Economy," *Review of Economic Studies,* 42 (1975), 503–523.

[10] ———: "Disequilibrium Exchange in Barter and Monetary Economies," *Economic Inquiry,* 13 (1975), 131–156.

[11] ———: "The Disequilibrium Approach to Monopolistic Price Setting and General Monopolistic Equilibrium," *Review of Economic Studies,* 43 (1976), 69–81.

[12] ———: "Effective Demand, Quantity Signals and Decision Theory," CEPREMAP, Paris, 1976.

[13] ———: "Regulation of the Wage Profits Conflict and the Unemployment Inflation Dilemma in a Dynamic Disequilibrium Model," to appear in *Economie Appliquée.*

[14] BILLINGSLEY, P.: *Convergence of Probability Measures.* New York: Wiley, 1968.

[15] BLISS, C. P.: "Capital Theory in the Short Run," Department of Economics, University of Essex, 1974.

[16] BOEHM, V., AND J. P. LEVINE: "Temporary Equilibria with Quantity Rationing," CORE Discussion paper no. 7614, Catholic University of Louvain, Belgium, 1976.

[17] CHETTY, V. K., AND D. DASGUPTA: "Temporary Competitive Equilibrium in a Large Monetary Economy with Uncertain Technology and Many Planning Periods," Indian Statistical Institute, Delhi Center, 1975.

[18] CHRISTIANSEN, D. S.: "Some Aspects of the Theory of Short Run Equilibrium," Unpublished Ph.D. Dissertation, Department of Economics, Stanford University, 1974.

[19] ———: "Temporary Equilibrium: A Stochastic Dynamic Programming Approach," Discussion Paper, Department of Economics, University of Rochester, 1975.

[20] CHRISTIANSEN, D. S., AND M. MAJUMDAR: "On Shifting Temporary Equilibrium," Department of Economics, Cornell University, 1974.

[21] CLOWER, R. W.: "The Keynesian Counterrevolution: A Theoretical Appraisal," in *The Theory of Interest Rates,* ed. by F. H. Hahn and Brechling. London: Macmillan, 1965.

[22] ———: "A Reconsideration of the Microfoundations of Monetary Theory," *Western Economic Journal,* 6 (1967), 1–9.

[23] DEBREU, G.: "Market Equilibrium," *Proceedings of the National Academy of Sciences of the U.S.A.,* 42 (1956), 876–878.

[24] ———: *Theory of Value.* New York: Wiley, 1959.

[25] DELBAEN, F.: "Continuity of Expected Utility," in *Allocation Under Uncertainty, Equilibrium, and Optimality,* Proceedings of an I.E.A. Workshop in Economic Theory, Bergen, Norway, 1971, ed. by J. Drèze. London: Macmillan, 1974.

[26] DIEWERT, W. E.: "Walras' Theory of Capital Formation and the Existence of a Temporary Equilibrium," Institute of Mathematical Studies in the Social Sciences, Stanford University, 1972.

[27] DRANDAKIS, E. M.: "On the Competitive Equilibrium in a Monetary Economy," *International Economic Review,* 7 (1966), 304–328.

[28] DRÈZE, J.: "Investment under Private Ownership: Optimality, Equilibrium and Stability," in *Allocation Under Uncertainty, Equilibrium, and Optimality,* Proceedings of an I. E. A. Workshop on Economic Theory, Bergen, Norway, 1971, ed. by J. Drèze. London: Macmillan, 1974.

[29] DRÈZE, J.: *Allocation under Uncertainty, Equilibrium and Optimality*, Proceedings of an I.E.A. Workshop in Economic Theory, Bergen, Norway, 1971. London: Macmillan, 1974.

[30] ———: "Existence of an Equilibrium under Price Rigidity and Quantity Rationing," *International Economic Review*, 16 (1975), 301–320.

[31] FITZROY, F. R.: "A Framework for Temporary Equilibrium," Alfred Weber Institute, University of Heidelberg, 1973.

[32] FRIEDMAN, M.: *The Optimum Quantity of Money and Other Essays*. Chicago: Aldine, 1969.

[33] FUCHS, G.: "Asymptotic Stability of Stationary Temporary Equilibria and Changes in Expectations," Laboratoire d'Econométrie, Ecole Polytechnique, Paris, 1975.

[34] FUCHS, G., AND G. LAROQUE: "Dynamics of Temporary Equilibria and Expectations," Laboratoire d'Econométrie, Ecole Polytechnique, Paris, 1975.

[35] GALE, DAVID: "Pure Exchange Equilibrium of Dynamic Economic Models," *Journal of Economic Theory*, 6 (1973), 12–36.

[36] GALE, DOUGLAS: "Rational Expectations and the Rate of Return," Christ's College, Cambridge, England, 1975.

[37] ———: "Keynesian Equilibrium and the Theory of Income Constrained Processes," Christ's College, Cambridge, England, 1975.

[38] GLUSTOFF, E.: "On the Existence of a Keynesian Equilibrium," *Review of Economic Studies*, 35 (1968), 327–334.

[39] GRANDMONT, J. M.: "On the Temporary Competitive Equilibrium," Unpublished Ph.D. Dissertation, CRMS Working Paper, University of California, Berkeley, 1970.

[40] ———: "Continuity Properties of a von Neumann–Morgenstern Utility," *Journal of Economic Theory*, 4 (1972), 45–57.

[41] ———: "On the Short Run Equilibrium in a Monetary Economy," in *Allocation Under Uncertainty, Equilibrium, and Optimality*, Proceedings of an I.E.A. Workshop in Economic Theory, Bergen, Norway, 1971, ed. by J. Drèze. London: Macmillan, 1974.

[42] GRANDMONT, J. M., AND W. HILDENBRAND: "Stochastic Processes of Temporary Equilibria," *Journal of Mathematical Economics*, 1 (1974), 247–277.

[43] GRANDMONT, J. M., AND A. P. KIRMAN: "Foreign Exchange Markets: A Temporary Equilibrium Approach," CORE discussion paper no. 7308, 1973.

[44] GRANDMONT, J. M., AND G. LAROQUE: "Money in the Pure Consumption Loan Model," *Journal of Economic Theory*, 6 (1973), 382–395.

[45] ———: "On Money and Banking," *Review of Economic Studies*, 42 (1975), 207–236.

[46] ———: "On the Liquidity Trap," *Econometrica*, 44 (1976), 129–135.

[47] ———: "On Keynesian Temporary Equilibria," *Review of Economic Studies*, 43 (1976), 53–67.

[48] GRANDMONT, J. M., G. LAROQUE, AND Y. YOUNÈS: "Disequilibrium Allocations and Recontracting," IMSSS Technical Report, Stanford University, to appear in *Journal of Economic Theory*.

[49] GRANDMONT, J. M., AND Y. YOUNÈS: "On the Role of Money and the Existence of a Monetary Equilibrium," *Review of Economic Studies*, 39 (1972), 355–372.

[50] ———: "On the Efficiency of a Monetary Equilibrium," *Review of Economic Studies*, 40 (1973), 149–165.

[51] GREEN, J. R.: "A Simple General Equilibrium Model of the Term Structure of Interest Rates," Harvard Discussion Paper No. 183, Harvard University, 1971.

[52] ———: "Temporary General Equilibrium in a Sequential Trading Model with Spot and Future Transactions," *Econometrica*, 41 (1973), 1103–1123.

[53] ———: "Preexisting Contacts and Temporary General Equilibrium," in *Essays on Economic Behavior under Uncertainty*, Contributions to Economic Analysis, ed. by M. Balch, D. McFadden, and S. W. Yu. Amsterdam: North-Holland, 1974.

[54] GROSSMAN, H. I.: "Money, Interest and Prices in Market Disequilibrium," *Journal of Political Economy*, 79 (1971), 943–961.

[55] ———: "A Choice-Theoretic Model of an Income Investment Accelerator," *American Economic Review*, 62 (1972), 630–641.

[56] HAHN, F. H.: "On Some Problems of Proving the Existence of an Equilibrium in a Monetary Economy, in *The Theory of Interest Rates*, ed. by F. H. Hahn and Brechling. London: Macmillan, 1965.

[57] ———: "Equilibrium with Transaction Costs," *Econometrica*, 39 (1971), 417–439.

[58] ———: "On Transaction Costs, Inessential Sequence Economies and Money," *Review of Economic Studies*, 40 (1973), 449–461.

[59] HAHN, F. H.: *On the Notion of Equilibrium in Economics*. Cambridge: Cambridge University Press, 1973.
[60] ———: "On Non-Walrasian Equilibria," IMSS Technical Report No. 203, Stanford University, 1976.
[61] HAHN, F. H., AND BRECHLING (EDS.): *The Theory of Interest Rates*. London: Macmillan, 1965.
[62] HAHN, F. H., AND T. NEGISHI: "A Theorem on Non Tâtonnement Stability," *Econometrica*, 30 (1962), 463–469.
[63] HART, O. D.: "On the Existence of Equilibrium in a Securities Model," *Journal of Economic Theory*, 9 (1974), 293–311.
[64] HELLER, W. P., AND R. M. STARR: "Unemployment Equilibrium with Rational Expectations," IMSSS Working Paper No. 66, Stanford University, 1976.
[65] HELPMAN, E., AND J. J. LAFFONT: "On Moral Hazard in General Equilibrium Theory," *Journal of Economic Theory*, 10 (1975), 8–23.
[66] HERKENRATH, U.: "Random Systems with Complete Connections," Unpublished Ph.D. Thesis, University of Bonn, 1975.
[67] HICKS, J.: *Value and Capital*, 2nd ed. Oxford: Clarendon Press, 1946.
[68] ———: *Capital and Growth*. Oxford: Oxford University Press, 1965.
[69] HILDENBRAND, W.: "Random Preferences and Equilibrium Analysis," *Journal of Economic Theory*, 3 (1971), 414–429.
[70] HOOL, B.: "Money, Financial Assets and General Equilibrium in a Sequential Market Economy," Unpublished Ph.D. Dissertation, Department of Economics, University of California, Berkeley, 1974.
[71] ———: "Temporary Walrasian Equilibrium in a Monetary Economy," Social Systems Research Institute, University of Wisconsin, Madison, 1974.
[72] ———: "Money, Expectations and the Existence of a Temporary Equilibrium," SSRI, University of Wisconsin, Madison, 1974. A revised version is forthcoming in *Review of Economic Studies*.
[73] IWAI, K.: "Towards Keynesian Microdynamics of Price, Wage, Sales and Employment," Cowles Discussion Paper, Yale University, 1974.
[74] ———: "The Firm in Uncertain Markets and its Price, Wage and Employment Adjustments," *Review of Economic Studies*, 41 (1974), 257–276.
[75] JORDAN, J. S.: "The Continuity of Optimal Dynamic Decision Rules," Department of Economics, University of Pennsylvania, Philadelphia, 1975.
[76] ———: "Temporary Competitive Equilibrium and the Existence of Self-Fulfilling Expectations," Department of Economics, University of Pennsylvania, Philadelphia, 1975.
[77] KEYNES, J. M.: *The General Theory of Money, Interest and Employment*, 1936.
[78] KIHLSTROM, R. E., AND L. J. MIRMAN: "Information and Market Equilibrium," *The Bell Journal of Economics*, 6 (1975).
[79] KURZ, M.: "Equilibrium in a Finite Sequence of Markets with Transaction Cost," *Econometrica*, 42 (1974), 1–20.
[80] LAFFONT, J. J.: "Optimism and Experts Versus Adverse Selection in a Competitive Economy," *Journal of Economic Theory*, 10 (1975), 284–308.
[81] LEDYARD, J. O.: "On Sequences of Temporary Equilibria" in *Essays on Economic Behavior under Uncertainty*, Contributions to Economic Analysis, ed. by M. Balch, D. McFadden, and S. W. Yu. Amsterdam: North-Holland, 1974.
[82] LEIJONHUFVUD, A.: *On Keynesian Economics and the Economics of Keynes*. Oxford: Oxford University Press, 1968.
[83] MALINVAUD, E.: *The Theory of Unemployment Reconsidered*. Oxford: Basil Blackwell, 1977.
[84] MALINVAUD, E., AND Y. YOUNÈS: "Une Nouvelle Formulation Générale pour l'Etude des Fondements Microéconomiques de la Macroéconomie," INSEE and CEPREMAP, Paris, 1974.
[85] ———: "A New Formulation for the Microeconomic Foundations of Macroeconomics," Paper presented at an IEA Conference on the *Microeconomic Foundations of Macroeconomics*, S'Agaro, Spain, July 1975, to appear in the Proceedings.
[86] MORISHIMA, M.: *Equilibrium, Stability and Growth*. Oxford: Clarendon Press, 1964.
[87] NEGISHI, T.: "Existence of an Under Employment Equilibrium," in *Equilibrium and Disequilibrium in Economic Theory*, Proceedings of a Conference held in Vienna, July, 1974, ed. by G. Schwödiauer. Forthcoming.

[88] NORMAN, M. F.: *Markov Processes and Learning Models*. New York: Academic Press, 1972.
[89] PARTHASARATHY, K.: *Probability Measures on Metric Spaces*. New York: Academic Press, 1967.
[90] PATINKIN, D.: *Money, Interest and Prices*, 2nd ed. New York: Harper and Row, 1965.
[91] POLEMARCHAKIS, H.: "On the Existence and Optimality of Temporary Equilibrium for a Monetary Production Economy," mimeograph, Stanford University, 1975.
[92] RADNER, R.: "Equilibre des Marchés à Terme et au Comptant en Cas d'Incertitude," *Cahiers du Séminaire d'Econométrie*, CNRS, Paris, 1967.
[93] ———: "Competitive Equilibrium under Uncertainty," *Econometrica*, 36 (1968), 31–58.
[94] ———: "Problems in the Theory of Markets under Uncertainty," *American Economic Review* 60 (1970), 454–460.
[95] ———: "Existence of Equilibrium Plans, Prices and Price Expectations in a Sequence of Markets," *Econometrica*, 40 (1972), 289–303.
[96] ———: "Market Equilibrium under Uncertainty: Concepts and Problems," in *Frontiers of Quantitative Analysis*, Vol. II, ed. by M. D. Intriligator and D. A. Hendrick. Amsterdam: North-Holland, 1974.
[97] SAMUELSON, P. A.: "An Exact Consumption Load Model of Interest with or without the Social Contrivance of Money," *Journey of Political Economy*, 66 (1958), 467–482.
[98] SCHWÖDIAUER, G. (ED.): *Equilibrium and Disequilibrium in Economic Theory*, Proceedings of a Conference held in Vienna, July 1974, forthcoming.
[99] SONDERMANN, D.: "Temporary Competitive Equilibrium under Uncertainty," in *Allocation Under Uncertainty, Equilibrium, and Optimality*, Proceedings of an I.E.A. Workshop in Economic Theory, Bergen, Norway, 1971, ed. by J. Drèze. London: Macmillan, 1974.
[100] STARRETT, D.: "Inefficiency and the Demand for Money in a Sequence Economy," *Review of Economic Studies*, 40 (1973), 437–448.
[101] STIGUM, B.: "Entrepreneurial Choice over Time under Conditions of Uncertainty," *International Economic Review*, 10 (1969), 426–442.
[102] ———: "Competitive Equilibria under Uncertainty," *Quarterly Journal of Economics*, 83 (1969), 533–561.
[103] ———: "Resources Allocation under Uncertainty," *International Economic Review*, 13 (1972), 431–459.
[104] ———: "Competitive Resource Allocation over Time under Uncertainty," in *Essays on Economic Behavior under Uncertainty*, Contributions to Economic Analysis, ed. by M. Balch, D. McFadden, and S. W. Yu. Amsterdam: North-Holland, 1974.
[105] SVENSSON, L. E. O.: "Sequences of Temporary Equilibria, Stationary Point Expectations, and Pareto Efficiency," mimeograph, Stockholm School of Economics, 1975.
[106] THEODORESCU, I.: *Random Processes and Learning*. New York: Springer-Verlag, 1969.
[107] YOUNÈS, Y.: "Sur une Notion d'Equilibre Utilisable dans le Cas où les Agents Economiques ne Sont Pas Assurés de la Compatibilité de Leurs Plans," CEPREMAP, Paris, 1970 (revised, 1973).
[108] ———: "Sur les Notions d'Equilibre et de Déséquilibre Utilisées dans les Modèles Décrivant l'Evolution d'une Economie Capitaliste," CEPREMAP, Paris, 1970.
[109] ———: "Intérêt et Monnaie Externe dans une Economie d'Echanges au Comptant en Equilibre Walrasien de Court Terme," CEPREMAP, Paris, 1972 (English version, 1973).
[110] ———: "Monnaie et Motif de Précaution dans une Economie d'Echanges où les Ressources des Agents Sont Aléatoires," CEPREMAP, Paris, 1972.
[111] ———: "On the Role of Money in the Process of Exchange and the Existence of a Non-Walrasian Equilibrium," *Review of Economic Studies*, 42 (1975), 489–501.

Temporary Equilibrium Theory: An Addendum

The purpose of this addendum is to review a few developments that have taken place since the publication of my *Econometrica* survey. I shall focus first on the study of the stability of a long-run equilibrium with self-fulfilling expectations when there is no uncertainty and when traders use prespecified learning processes on the transition path. This part is meant to be an introduction to the articles reproduced in Chapter V. The second part of the addendum is devoted to the analysis of the microeconomic foundations of equilibria with quantity rationing and to a brief review of the implications of the approach for modelling unemployment. The list of references at the end aims at completing that of the previous *Econometrica* survey.

1. Deterministic Dynamics

The problem of assessing the stability of a long-run equilibrium with self-fulfilling expectations when the traders use given learning processes is central to temporary equilibrium analysis. Progress on this issue over the last ten years has been made essentially in discrete time deterministic models, in particular by looking at the stability of a stationary state in competitive overlapping generations models with money. We give here a brief account of these results in the simple case where the state of the economy can be described at each date by a real number.

Assume that the equilibrium state at date t, x_t, is determined by the forecast x_{t+1}^e made at the same date concerning the immediate future[1]

$$x_t = F(x_{t+1}^e) \tag{1.1}$$

where F is a continuously differentiable map from some open interval

---

[1] We assume only for the simplicity of the exposition that all traders have the same forecast. The analysis is not qualitatively modified when one considers forecasts that differ among traders, as in the introduction.

X into the real line. Intertemporal equilibria with self-fulfilling expectations are then described by sequences $\{x_t\}$ satisfying $x_t = F(x_{t+1})$ for all t. We consider a fixed point $\bar{x}$ of F that is locally unique, with $a = F'(\bar{x}) \neq 0$. Then F can be inverted locally near $\bar{x}$; trajectories generated by intertemporal equilibria, in a suitable neighborhood of $\bar{x}$, will obey the difference equation $x_{t+1} = F^{-1}(x_t)$. Thus if $|a| < 1$, the stationary state will appear to be unstable in this perfect foresight dynamics, whereas it will appear to be asymptotically stable if $|a| > 1$.

We wish to analyze how such an apparent stability or instability is modified when we take into account the fact that forecasts are made at each date on the basis of current and past states of the system and that traders may only gradually learn the dynamic laws of their environment. We shall find that if the influence of the present state on forecasts is predominant, the stationary state will be stable in the dynamics with learning. If, as one might expect, forecasts are mainly made on the basis of the past, stability of the stationary state in the dynamics with learning will be typically *reversed*, by comparison to what happens in the dynamics associated with self-fulfilling expectations.

We now assume that the only information available to the traders at t is $(x_t, x_{t-1}, \ldots)$ and postulate that forecasts are made through a fixed expectations function

$$x^e_{t+1} = \psi(x_t, x_{t-1}, \ldots, x_{t-T}) \tag{1.2}$$

where ψ is a continuously differentiable map from X^{T+1} into the real line, and T is a fixed large memory lag. Observations made in the far past, indeed, are likely to have a negligible influence on current forecasts. The impact of such distant observations are accordingly neglected in the foregoing formulation. The assumption should not matter much, since we are concerned with the asymptotic behavior of the system, when t tends to $+\infty$.

Putting together (1.1) and (1.2) yields

$$x_t = F(\psi(x_t, \ldots, x_{t-T})) \tag{1.3}$$

which determines implicitly x_t, given $(x_{t-1}, \ldots, x_{t-T})$. We are interested in assessing whether or not the trajectories generated by the dynamics with learning implicitly defined by (1.3) converge to the stationary state $\bar{x}$.

In this respect, it is only natural to assume that when traders observe a constant sequence they expect the same state to prevail in the future, that is,

$$x = \psi(x, \ldots, x) \qquad \text{for all } x \text{ in } X. \tag{1.4}$$

Clearly, with such an assumption, $\bar{x}$ will be a stationary state of (1.3).

Let c_j denote the partial derivative of ψ with respect to x_{t-j}, evaluated at the constant sequence $(\bar{x}, \ldots, \bar{x})$, for all $j = 0, \ldots, T$. We assume that $1 - ac_0 \neq 0$. In that case, by the implicit function theorem, (1.3) can be solved uniquely in x_t in a suitable neighborhood of the stationary state $\bar{x}$, to yield a (local) difference equation of the form

$$x_t = W(x_{t-1}, \ldots, x_{t-T}) \tag{1.5}$$

where W is continuously differentiable.

The asymptotic stability of the stationary state $\bar{x}$ in the dynamics with learning associated with (1.5) will be governed by the roots of the associated characteristic equation

$$P(\lambda) \equiv \lambda^T - \frac{a}{1 - ac_0} \sum_1^T c_j \lambda^{T-j} = 0.$$

If all the characteristic roots lie inside the unit circle of the complex plane, i.e., satisfy $|\lambda| < 1$, the stationary state is asymptotically stable in the dynamics with learning. If there is a root such that $|\lambda| > 1$, the stationary state is unstable.

The following proposition is a variation, in our simple one-dimensional case, of a result formerly proved by Fuchs and Laroque [97, Theorem 8], which is reproduced in Chapter V.

PROPOSITION 1. *Let α be the maximum of $|\Sigma_1^T c_j z^j|$ for all complex numbers such that $|z| \leqq 1$. Then if*

$$|a|\, \alpha < |1 - ac_0| \tag{1.6}$$

all roots of $P(\lambda) = 0$ lie inside the unit circle.

A direct proof is easy in our case. Suppose that there is a solution of $P(\lambda) = 0$ such that $|\lambda| \geqq 1$. Then

$$1 = \frac{|a|\, |\sum_1^T c_j \lambda^{-j}|}{|1 - ac_0|} \leqq \frac{|a|\, \alpha}{|1 - ac_0|}$$

which proves the proposition. Notice that (1.4) implies $1 - c_0 = \Sigma_1^T c_j$. Thus

$$|1 - c_0| = \left| \sum_1^T c_j \right| \leqq \alpha \leqq \sum_1^T |c_j|. \tag{1.7}$$

The condition (1.6) appearing in the proposition will thus be verified if

$$|a| \sum_1^T |c_j| < |1 - ac_0|. \tag{1.6'}$$

The stability of the stationary state in the dynamics with learning depends accordingly on the parameters a, c_0, and α. The parameter c_0 measures, at the constant sequence $(\bar{x}, ..., \bar{x})$, the influence of the current state on forecasts, while α summarizes the impact of the past. In view of (1.7), however, c_0 and α cannot be chosen completely independently. In the particular case $c_j \geqq 0$ for all j, one has indeed

$$\alpha = 1 - c_0 = \sum_1^T c_j.$$

A first conclusion is immediate. Given the expectations function, and thus c_0 and α, the stationary state $\bar{x}$ will be asymptotically stable in the dynamics with learning if a is close enough to 0. Indeed, all roots of $P(\lambda) = 0$ tend to 0 when a goes to 0, given the c_j. *Thus, everything else being equal, the stationary state will be stable in the dynamics with learning if it is "unstable enough" (if a is close enough to 0) in the dynamics with self-fulfilling expectations.*

We wish to investigate next the influence of the parameters c_0 and α. To this effect, we look at two extreme cases.

Case 1: We consider first the case where the parameter α is close to 0, which means that c_j is small for all $j = 1, ..., T$ and c_0 is near 1. In that case, the current state is almost the sole determinant of the forecast, i.e., $x_{t+1}^e \approx x_t$. But all roots of the characteristic polynomial are then close to 0. *Thus, everything else being equal, the stationary state is asymptotically stable in the dynamics with "learning" if enough weight is attached to the current state when forming forecasts.* The intuition behind this result is easy to grasp by considering the limit case where $x_{t+1}^e = x_t$. Equation (1.3) becomes then $x_t = F(x_t)$. There is no "dynamics" in that case: the system "jumps" to a stationary state and stays there.

Case 2: The preceding case may look rather strained. The essence of learning is indeed to forecast future states on the basis of the entire sequence of current and past states. It is not unreasonable, accordingly, to expect the influence of the current state alone to be small. We consider, therefore, the limit case $c_0 = 0$. Then Proposition 1 tells us that the stationary state is stable in the dynamics with learning if $|a| < 1/\alpha$. From (1.7), we know that $\alpha \geqq 1$ and that $\alpha = 1$ when $c_j \geqq 0$ for j. Thus, *when $c_0 = 0$ and $c_j \geqq 0$ for all j, the condition $|a| < 1$ implies that all solutions of $P(\lambda) = 0$ lie inside the unit circle: the unstability of the stationary* *state in the dynamics with self-fulfilling expectations implies its stability in the dynamics with learning.*[2]

It is interesting to see, still in the limit case $c_0 = 0$, under which circumstances the converse result is true. Remark first that

$$P(1) = 1 - a \sum_1^T c_j = 1 - a.$$

Thus $P(1) = 0$ whenever $a = 1$. If $a > 1$, one has $P(1) < 0$, and thus the equation $P(\lambda) = 0$ has a real root $\lambda > 1$. This conclusion is based on condition (1.4), which says that the traders extrapolate sequences of states that have been constant in the past. A natural extension of this assumption is that traders also extrapolate sequences that alternate between two values

$$y = \psi(x,y,x,y, \ldots), \qquad \text{all } x, y \text{ in } X. \tag{1.8}$$

This condition contains, of course, (1.4) as a particular case, and it is immediate to verify that it implies

$$c_0 + \sum_1^T c_j (-1)^j = -1.$$

If we assume (1.8) and $c_0 = 0$, we get

$$P(-1) = (-1)^T (1 + a).$$

Thus $P(-1) = 0$ when $a = -1$. If $a < -1$, the equation $P(\lambda) = 0$ has a real root $\lambda < -1$. We have thus obtained

PROPOSITION 2. *Assume condition (1.8) and $c_0 = 0$. If all roots of the characteristic polynomial $P(\lambda) = 0$ lie inside the unit circle, then $|a| < 1$; i.e., the stability of the stationary state in the dynamics with learning implies its unstability in the dynamics with self-fulfilling expectations.*

Bibliographical Notes

The foregoing introduction to the stability of a long-run equilibrium is based in part upon the paper by Fuchs and Laroque [97] which is reproduced

---

[2] The result still holds when the condition $c_0 = 0$ is replaced by $c_0 \geq 0$. For then $\alpha = 1 - c_0$, and when $|a| < 1$

$$|a| \alpha = |a| (1 - c_0) < 1 - c_0 < 1 - a c_0$$

and the result follows from proposition 1.

in Chapter V. They study the dynamics of an overlapping generations model involving finitely many nonstorable goods and money in which traders live two periods. By using differential topology techniques, they show how to reduce the problem to something like (1.1) in a suitable neighborhood of a stationary state. The simple case where the state of the economy is one-dimensional and where $T = 1$ is studied from a global viewpoint by Tillmann [253], whose article is also reproduced in Chapter V. Cases where traders employ subjective models of the economy that are revised over time in the light of current and past observations (states and forecasts) have been extensively studied by Fuchs [92–96] within the framework of an overlapping generations model. Extensions of the analysis given in the text, in the one-dimensional case, to the stability of deterministic cycles (periodic solutions of $x_t = F(x_{t+1})$) have been made recently in Grandmont [114] and Grandmont and Laroque [118].

We still know little about the stability of a long-run equilibrium in a deterministic context, when the state of the economy has an arbitrary finite dimension. This is particularly true when some components of the state variable are predetermined at each date (think of the capital stock that is the result of past investment decisions and depreciation). Another area where our ignorance is great and where efforts have to be made is the stability of a long-run equilibrium (a stationary stochastic process), with learning, when the economy operates under uncertainty. In this respect, the recent work that has been done on learning and convergence to self-fulfilling expectations in stochastic linear macroeconomic models should be useful (Bray [43,44]; Bray and Savin [45]; Champsaur [47]; De Canio [59]; Fourgeaud, Gouriéroux, and Pradel [85,86]; Frydman [91]; Gouriéroux, Laffont, and Monfort [108]; and Wickens [265]). A recent paper by M. Woodford [266] also deals with this issue.

2. Equilibria with Quality Rationing

As emphasized earlier on several occasions, a temporary equilibrium need not be Walrasian: the adjustment of the markets at any given time may be achieved through imperfect competition or by applying any non-Walrasian game-theoretic equilibrium notion. One may, in particular, consider cases in which prices are quoted at the outset of each period through monopolistic or oligopolistic competition among (possibly groups of) traders and in which they remain fixed within that period. A temporary equilibrium corresponding to these prices is then obtained by quantity rations that set upper or lower bounds to the traders' transactions. One then gets a *temporary equilibrium with quantity rationing* and momentarily fixed prices, the structure of which has been extensively reviewed in the *Econometrica* survey reproduced above.

Traditional Keynesian macroeconomic models of unemployment have been known for some time to involve temporarily fixed prices, see, e.g., Hicks [147]. Yet, until recently, the choice-theoretic structure of these models was rather unclear. Quantities such as the activity level, investment, had to adjust in the simple version of the Keynesian multiplier or the IS-LM model. Exactly how the adjustment was supposed to take place, in particular the constraints that each trader had to face when optimizing his objective function, the institutional setup through which they were supposed to interact, were not specified. The systematic analysis of temporary equilibrium models with quantity rationing undertaken in the seventies, following the contributions of Clower [53], Patinkin [214], and Solow and Stiglitz [237], led to an important clarification of this issue and unveiled the hidden but central role of quantity signals, as perceived by the traders in addition to the price system, to achieve an equilibrium in such models.

One of the major outcomes of this research program has been to make clear how important is the exchange structure of the economy for Keynesian unemployment equilibria to be obtained—in particular, the fact that financial intermediaries such as money are used in transactions with the consequence that labor is not generally traded directly for output. The exact nature of this lack of coordination between markets (the "effective demand failures" of Leijonhufvud [189]) was unveiled, in particular, through the study of the efficiency properties of temporary equilibria with quantity rationing. A brief and relatively informal review of this issue is presented below as an introduction to Chapter VII, which deals more thoroughly with these topics.

Another outcome of the research program has been the discovery that different types of unemployment could occur or even coexist. Keynesian unemployment is a situation in which firms perceive constraints on their sales because demand is too low. Keynesian policies that increase aggregate demand are then called for, but unemployment may occur with an excess demand on the goods markets. In such a regime, called "classical unemployment" by Malinvaud [195], the source of unemployment is, rather, the low profitability of productive activities. Keynesian policies do not work in that case, and one must resort to "Classical" remedies that restore profits, such as lowering real wages. In that respect, the temporary equilibrium approach achieved a remarkable synthesis, within a unified conceptual framework, between two viewpoints that had appeared beforehand to be quite foreign to one another. This matter is briefly surveyed below. We also review the connections between models of temporary equilibrium with quantity rationing and theories of imperfect competition as an introduction to the papers by Hahn, Gale, and Hart in Chapter VII, which deal more thoroughly with this issue. Finally, the reader will find at the end of the present addendum a fairly extensive list of references on the literature, dealing in particular with "macroeconomic" temporary equilibrium models with quantity rationing, together with some bibliographical notes, to pursue his/her own inquiry.

2.1. Effective Demand Failures

There are clearly unexploited trading opportunities in a situation of Keynesian unemployment. Firms would like to produce more and to employ more labor, but they cannot because demand is too low. Unemployed households would like to work and consume more, but they cannot because the firms' demand for labor is too small. Both parties could apparently by made better off by directly trading labor against output at the going prices and wages. The story that is usually told to justify the persistence of Keynesian unemployment is that such trades are not generally feasible: unemployed workers in the steel industry do not buy their industry's output. The fact is that there are high costs associated with bartering; money is thus used as a medium of exchange in decentralized economies. Therefore, when a firm contemplates the prospect of hiring new workers, the counterpart of the transaction is paying them money wages. The managers of the firm are unwilling to make the move, because they believe that it will not affect the demand for their output and, thus, that they will be unable to get rid of the additional production. Symmetrically, households are unwilling to increase their purchases of the good because, here again, the counterpart of the transaction is money and they do not perceive that such a move may cause the firms' demand for labor to increase. Because exchanges have to be mediated by money, the signals perceived by the parties involved are *effective demands,* and these *fail* to inform them of the available trading opportunities.

As appealing as it is, this "effective demand failures" argument is only heuristic. One of the great merits of the modern temporary equilibrium approach has been to unveil its choice-theoretic foundations, in particular through the study of the efficiency properties of equilibria with quantity rationing at momentarily fixed prices. The reader will find a thorough investigation of this issue in the first two papers reproduced in Chapter VII. I wish to review here some of the main arguments through a diagrammatical analysis of a simple example.

Let us consider an exchange economy involving two goods indexed by $h = 1$, 2 and a constant money stock, and two traders indexed by i, j at a given date called the current period. The institutional setup is the same as in the *Econometrica* survey reproduced above (Section 4). The positive money prices of the two goods, i.e., p_1 and p_2, are supposed to have been quoted by the traders at the outset of the period, as the result of an unspecified process of imperfect competition between them, and to remain momentarily fixed during the current period. There are two "markets," on which traders exchange good h against money at the going price p_h. The net trades of each agent on market h are noted z_{ih}, z_{jh} for $h = 1$, 2 and determine their final money holdings, i.e., m_i and m_j, through the budget constraints

$$\sum_h p_h z_{ih} + m_i = \overline{m}_i \tag{2.1}$$

$$\sum_h p_h z_{jh} + m_j = \overline{m}_j \tag{2.2}$$

in which $\overline{m}_i$ *and* $\overline{m}_j$ stand for initial money holdings. The traders also face other feasibility constraints such as nonnegativity of consumption of money holdings; we shall always assume in the sequel that these are not binding.

The traders' preferences are described by a utility function of the form $V_i(z_{i1}, z_{i2}, m_i)$ and similarly for trader j. These are indirect utility functions that represent the maximum utility that each trader expects to achieve over his planning horizon given the present action, i.e., (z_{i1}, z_{i2}, m_i), and his expectations about the future (prices and quantity rations); see the *Econometrica* survey reproduced above, Section 2.2. Information on past states of the economy and current prices are thus implicit arguments of the utility functions V_i, V_j since they may affect expectations. The possible influence of current quantity signals (rations) on expectations, which would lead to their inclusion as explicit arguments of the utility functions, has been disregarded here for simplicity. Adding them would complicate the exposition but would not alter the qualitative substance of the results. We shall assume in the sequel, without being more explicit, that V_i and V_j are nice "neoclassical" utility functions, displaying monotonicity, strict quasi-concavity, continuous differentiability, etc.

Given the exchange structure, the expression

$$S_i(z_{i1}, z_{i2}) = V_i\left(z_{i1}, z_{i2}, \overline{m}_i - \sum_h p_h z_{ih}\right)$$

represents the utility level of trader i that corresponds to the transactions z_{i1}, z_{i2} on the two markets. This fact allows a simple graphical description of the trader's preferences in the plane (z_{i1}, z_{i2}), as shown in Figure 1.a. There A_i represents the maximum of V_i under the budget constraint (2.1) and the other feasibility (e.g., nonnegativity) constraints, which are assumed

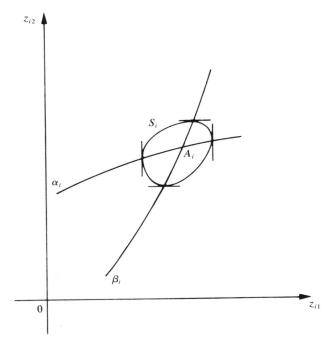

Fig. 1.a

to be nonbinding. This point describes the Walrasian or notional net trades of agent i at the prevailing prices in the absence of quantity rationing. Indifference curves corresponding to $S_i = cte$ are then closed curves near A_i. The curve $A_i \alpha_i$ (resp. $A_i \beta_i$) is the locus of all points of the plane such that the tangent to the corresponding indifference curve is vertical (resp. horizontal). A similar construction can be made for trader j.

This construction permits easy visualization of a temporary equilibrium with quantity rationing, corresponding to the given prices (p_1, p_2). As recalled in the *Econometrica* survey reproduced previously (Section 4), such an equilibrium is brought about by quantity rations perceived by the traders on each market that set upper bounds $d_{ih} \geqq 0$, $d_{jh} \geqq 0$ and lower bounds $s_{ih} \leqq 0$, $s_{jh} \leqq 0$ on their transactions for $h = 1, 2$ with the following properties. Let (z_{i1}, z_{i2}) be the net trade resulting from the maximization of V_i subject to the budget constraint and

$$s_{ih} \leqq z_{ih} \leqq d_{ih}, \qquad h = 1, 2 \tag{2.3}$$

or, equivalently, from the maximization of S_i under (2.3) (here again we omit feasibility constraints such as nonnegativity for simplicity). Let

(z_{j1}, z_{j2}) be the net trade obtained in a similar fashion for trader j. The first requirement is that the net trades should balance

$$z_{i1} + z_{j1} = 0 \quad \text{and} \quad z_{i2} + z_{j2} = 0. \tag{2.4}$$

The corresponding money balances will then satisfy $m_i + m_j = \overline{m}_i + \overline{m}_j$ (Walras law). The other requirement is that only the "long side" of any market may be rationed. That is, for each $h = 1, 2$, if one of the constraints on demand $z_{ih} \leq d_{ih}$ or $z_{jh} \leq d_{jh}$ is binding in the traders' decision-making problem, then the other constraints on the supply side $z_{ih} \geq s_{ih}$ and $z_{jh} \geq s_{jh}$ should not bite; the situation is similar if supply is rationed.

Such an equilibrium leads, therefore, to one of four possible situations depending upon which side of each market is actually rationed, if we disregard borderline cases in which one of the markets is in equilibrium without rationing. In order to duplicate as closely as possible the Keynesian story above, an equilibrium in which supply is rationed on both markets is pictured in Figure 1.b. Notice first that the net trades of the two traders are measured along the same axis, but with reverse orientations: any point of the plane describes a situation in which the agents' net trades balance, i.e., satisfy (2.4). At the equilibrium point K, trader i perceives a binding constraint $z_{i2} \geq s_{i2}$ on his supply of good 2, where

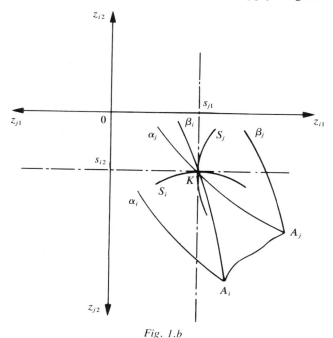

Fig. 1.b

51

s_{i2} is equal to the demand for that good of the other trader. Given that constraint, the optimal choice of trader i is K. Similarly, trader j perceives the binding constraint $z_{j1} \geqq s_{j1}$ on his supply of good 1, where s_{j1} is given by the other trader's demand. Given that constraint, the optimal choice of trader j is also K.

An important issue is knowing whether or not such an equilibrium displays reasonable "efficiency" properties. More precisely, we wish to find under which restrictions on the exchange process it is not possible for the two traders to improve their situation from the equilibrium K by redistributing among themselves goods and money. We may then hope to uncover some of the reasons which explain why such a situation might persist. It is first clear that one should restrict this "recontracting" process to take place at the given prices, for otherwise both traders could generally be made better off. Figure 1.b shows immediately that, even with such a restriction, a temporary equilibrium is generally inefficient. The set of allocations that are efficient at the given prices is described by a curve like A_iA_j in Figure 1.b, along which the associated indifference curves $S_i = cte$ and $S_j = cte$ are tangent and the equilibrium K does not generally belong to this curve. Here, as in a Keynesian unemployment equilibrium, there are trading opportunities that are left unexploited; both traders could be made better off by moving slightly southeast from K. Note that the *phenomenon may occur even when prices are set at their Walrasian equilibrium levels;* it suffices, indeed, to think of the case in which the most preferred points A_i and A_j coincide in Figure 1.b.

The important point to note, however, is that such a move involves a direct trade of good 1 for good 2 or, more precisely, a *simultaneous* exchange on the two markets and, thus, implies an infinite velocity of money when the traders try to move away from K. The argument given earlier to justify the persistence of Keynesian unemployment was that such moves are not generally feasible because, owing to the prohibitive costs associated with bartering, money is the necessary counterpart of any transaction. It suggests that we should restrict the recontracting process to take place on a single market at a time, in the example of Figure 1.b. Indeed, suppose that the two traders try to improve their situation by exchanging good 1 for money at the going prices. If trader i does not perceive the potential effect of this move on the binding ration s_{i2} that he perceives on his supply of good 2, he will not wish to move away from K. The argument is symmetric if the two traders try to exchange good 2 for money.

This example illustrates a result that is general. *A temporary equilibrium with quantity rationing is efficient if one restricts the recontracting process to taking place at the given prices and market by market and if the traders take as given, when trying to improve their situations on a specific market, the quantitative constraints they perceive on the other markets.* This point is studied in a general setup in the article by Laroque, Younès, and myself reproduced in Chapter VII. It is the precise counterpart of the heuristic "effective demand failures" argument that we recalled earlier.

That sort of explanation of the persistence of situations like Keynesian unemployment is of course incomplete, since it leaves unspecified, in particular, how prices are set initially. Yet it shows that any consistent attempt to rationalize the occurrence of such situations through theories that seek to simultaneously explain the determination of prices and of quantities by introducing, for instance, imperfect competition on each market, should involve in some way or another a lack of coordination between markets of the sort that we just discussed. Specifically, any such theory should portray the traders as believing that the actions they may take on a single market have no impact on the quantitative rations they face on the others, a condition which was crucial in the foregoing analysis. Such a belief is, of course, apparently irrational in an economy involving a small number of markets that are strongly related. Looking at "real life" situations suggests, however, a possible way out: hiring new workers in the steel industry will typically affect the demand for steel only indirectly through a very complicated chain, if it influences that specific demand at all. Thus considering a large number of markets that are only weakly "connected" may indeed make the traders' belief approximately rational. The paper by O.D. Hart that is reproduced in Chapter VII and that we shall review briefly below is an excellent illustration of that approach (see also Heller [137]).

Remark. The reader may benefit by pursuing the study of the simple example described in Figure 1.b. Any point of the plane specifies net trades (z_{ih}) and (z_{jh}) that satisfy (2.4). The reader can verify that such an allocation is implementable by choosing appropriate rations (s_{ih}, d_{ih}) and (s_{jh}, d_{jh}), ensuring that (z_{ih}) maximizes the objective function S_i under the constraints

$$s_{ih} \leqq z_{ih} \leqq d_{ih}, \qquad h = 1, 2$$

and, similarly, for trader j. By contrast with the notion of equilibrium employed above, however, the rations are not constrained here to satisfy $s \leqq 0$ or $d \geqq 0$.

Such an allocation is said to be *efficient market-by-market* if and only if it is impossible for each market h to make the two traders better off by exchanging good h for money at the given prices, each agent believing that such a move does not affect the rations he perceives on the other market. It is not difficult to see that under appropriate differentiability conditions, and again ignoring feasibility (nonnegativity) constraints, this efficiency property reads, for each h

$$\frac{\partial S_i}{\partial z_{ih}}(z_{i1},z_{i2}) \frac{\partial S_j}{\partial z_{jh}}(z_{j1},z_{j2}) \geqq 0.$$

The set of points that satisfy this condition is described by the shaded area in Figure 2.

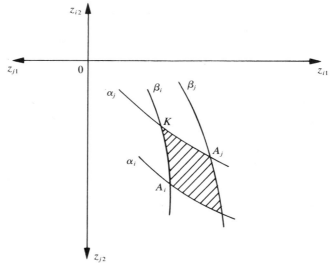

Fig. 2

Let us consider next the following *voluntary exchange* condition which states that no trader should be forced to exchange more than he wishes on any given market. The condition here formally reads, for trader i and for each h

$$z_{ih} \frac{\partial S_i}{\partial z_{ih}}(z_{i1},z_{i2}) \geqq 0$$

and, similarly, for trader j. It is easily verified that the temporary equilibrium represented by the point K is the only allocation of the plane that is efficient market-by-market and satisfies the above voluntary exchange condition. Such a characterization is in fact general as proved by Y. Younès [269]. The analysis of Laroque, Younès, and myself reproduced in Chapter VII shows that the voluntary exchange condition may be viewed as the outcome of the interaction of many traders through a recontracting process that takes place market-by-market at the given prices, each single trader having a negligible influence on the market.

2.2. *Classical and Keynesian Unemployment*

A significant achievement of the temporary equilibrium approach has been in unveiling the central role played by quantity signals in the short-run equilibrating process of traditional Keynesian macroeconomic models and showing, in particular, that different types of unemployment may be obtained. As usual, laying bare the choice-theoretic foundations of this class of macroeconomic models led to a deeper understanding of their conceptual strengths and weaknesses and to a better assessment of where progress can be made. In particular, as we shall see shortly, the temporary equilibrium formulation makes clear how essential is the precise modelling of *expectations formation* in Keynesian models (in fact, in any economic model) in order to evaluate correctly the possible impact of governmental policies—a point which will remind the reader of the celebrated "Lucas critique" [191].

We shall address these issues by looking at a simple but important macroeconomic example that is initially due to R. Barro and H.I. Grossman [15] and to Younès [268] and that has been further elaborated by Benassy, Malinvaud, and a host of others. We consider an economy at a given date (the "current" period) that involves three commodities: a nondurable consumption good, labor, and money. As before, good and labor are exchanged for money on two separate markets at the respective (positive) money prices p and w. It is assumed that p and w are chosen at the outset of the period by the agents who control them through an unspecified process of imperfect competition and that they remain fixed during the current period. There are three traders: a single representative firm, a single representative household, and the "government."

The firm produces (and sells) in the current period the quantity of output $Y \geqq 0$ from $E \geqq 0$ units of labor according to the production function $Y = F(E)$, where F has nice "neoclassical" properties: it is twice continuously differentiable with $F(0) = 0$, $F' > 0$, $F'' < 0$, $\lim_{E \to 0} F'(E) = +\infty$, and $\lim_{E \to \infty} F'(E) = 0$. There are no inventories nor investments. Utilization of current equipment is implicit in this formulation. One may view the above production function as resulting from the use of different equipment ranked by decreasing productivities; the formulation is thus compatible with (variable) idle productive capacities.

Following Malinvaud [195], we assume that the current profit $pY - wE$ is *not* distributed to the household, but rather that it is saved by the firm in the form of a money balance M_f for later distribution. The consequence of this admittedly peculiar assumption is that the marginal propensity to consume out of current profits is zero. This specific assumption is not essential: the qualitative results below would have been the same had we assumed that profits are distributed in the current period and that the marginal propensity to consume out of current wages exceeds the marginal propensity to consume out of current profits.

The household consumes $C \geqq 0$, supplies $L \geqq 0$ units of labor, where L cannot exceed the labor endowment $L^* > 0$; it keeps the money balance $M_c \geqq 0$ for saving purposes and pays the nominal tax T to the government (to be interpreted as a transfer to the household, if negative). The initial money stock is $M_0 > 0$, which includes dividend payments made by the firm at the outset of the period out of past profits. In the sequel, we shall always assume $M_0 - T > 0$, to simplify the exposition[3]. The household's current budget constraint thus reads

$$pC + M_c = wL + M_0 - T.$$

The household's current preferences are described by a utility function $V(C, M_c)$, which does not depend upon labor. As a result, the household's Walrasian labor supply will be constant and equal to L^*. As in the *Econometrica* survey (Section 2.2), and as above in Section 2.1, the function V stands for the maximum utility that the household expects to achieve over their planning horizon, given the current action (C, L, M_c) and their expectations about prices, quantity signals, and the government's actions in the future. As usual, the household's information on the past is an implicit argument of V, in as much as it influences expectations about the future. On the other hand, the given price p and wage w, the variable quantity rations that the household may perceive in the current period, as well as the parameters defining the government's current actions, are not arguments of the objective function V. The implicit underlying assumption here is that the signals perceived by the household in the current period have no influence on their expectations about the future. The reader should keep in mind this observation, as it will be important, in particular, when evaluating the possible impact of the government's policies.

Finally, the government has a fixed target of real public expenditures $G^d > 0$; its actual real expenditures $G \geqq 0$ are financed by taxes and an issue of money ΔM, according to the budget constraint

$$pG = \Delta M + T.$$

---

[3] We assume, to simplify matters, that all taxes are paid by consumers. The analysis would not be modified if the firm also paid taxes to the government.

The compatibility of the traders' *ex post* transactions in the current period is assumed to be achieved through a temporary equilibrium with quantity rationing at the given configuration (p,w). Specifically, the firm will perceive quantitative constraints on the good and the labor markets of the form $Y \leq \overline{Y}$ and $E \leq \overline{E}$; the rations perceived by the household and the government will read $C \leq \overline{C}$, $L \leq \overline{L}$, and $G \leq \overline{G}$, respectively. Each trader will then maximize his or her objective function under these constraints. By definition, the quantity rations are adjusted so as to ensure *firstly* that the resulting transactions balance, i.e., satisfy

$$Y = C + G \qquad \text{and } L = E \tag{2.5}$$

and *secondly,* that only the "long side" of each market is actually rationed. Note that since money balances adjust automatically to the transactions levels on each market through the traders' budget constraints, (2.5) will imply the equality of the demand and the supply of money, i.e., $M_0 + \Delta M = M_c + M_f$ (Walras' law).

If we disregard the borderline cases in which a market is in equilibrium without rationing, a temporary equilibrium may fall into one of the following four possible regimes, depending upon which side of each of the two markets is rationed:

- *Keynesian unemployment,* in which supply is rationed on both markets. Then the firm's output is limited by aggregate demand and the simple Keynesian multiplier model applies.
- *Classical unemployment,* in which supply is rationed on the labor market, whereas demand is rationed on the goods market. Then there is unemployment, and what depresses the activity level is not aggregate demand but rather the low profitability of production. In that case, classical arguments apply.
- *Repressed inflation,* in which demand is rationed on both markets. There is full employment, but excess demand induces inflationary pressures on prices and wages.
- *Underconsumption,* in which the demand for labor is rationed, while supply is rationed on the goods market. This case is degenerate in the simple model under consideration, for then the firm should perceive constraints of the form $Y \leq \overline{Y}$ and $E \leq \overline{E}$ that bite on both markets, which is impossible here since a tight relation between sales and employment was assumed in the firm's production function. This regime would reappear as a nondegenerate case in more realistic models involving several firms (some firms would be constrained in the labor market, while others would be rationed on the goods market, and one would be working inside the aggregate production possibility frontier) and/or inventories.

We focus in the sequel on the two unemployment regimes and present a brief analysis of the way in which quantity rations are supposed to achieve equilibrium in these cases.

To this end, it will be convenient to use the notions of the consumption function and of the private excess supply function which are now described. Consider the household's decision problem of maximizing their objective function V under the budget constraint $pC + M_c = pR$, in which R stands for current "real wealth." Under the usual conditions of continuity and strict quasi-concavity of V, the maximum exists and is unique, leading to an optimum of the form $C = C(p,R)$, $M_c = M_c(p,R)$. It will be assumed in the sequel that the *consumption function* $C(p,R)$ is continuously differentiable and satisfies

$$0 < C_R' < 1 \qquad \text{and} \qquad C_p' < 0. \tag{2.6}$$

The excess supply of the private sector is then defined as follows: let $Y \geqq 0$ be an arbitrary production level that does not exceed *full employment output* $Y^* = F(L^*)$. Next assume that employment adjusts to the corresponding demand for labor $F^{-1}(Y)$. Given the current price and wage and the tax level, the household's consumption is $C(p,R)$, with $R = (wF^{-1}(Y) + M_0 - T)/p$, and the excess supply of the goods of the private sector is equal to

$$S(Y,p,w,T) = Y - C(p,(wF^{-1}(Y) + M_0 - T)/p). \tag{2.7}$$

The *excess supply function* S is similar to the traditional Keynesian saving function (before taxes). It will allow a very simple statement of the results which follow. The reader will immediately verify that

$$0 < S_y' < 1, \qquad S_p' > 0, \qquad S_w' < 0, \qquad S_T' > 0. \tag{2.8}$$

The condition $S_y' > 0$ holds provided that $Y \leqq Y(w/p)$, in which $Y(w/p)$ stands for the activity level that maximizes the profit $pY - wE$, given p and w subject to the sole technological constraint $Y = F(E)$. The reader will note that the inequality $S_w' < 0$ results from the fact that the marginal propensity to consume out of profits was assumed to be zero here. An increase of the wage by Δw, everything else being equal, makes the household's real wealth go up by $\Delta w \, F^{-1}(Y)/p$ and real profits go down by the same amount. The end result is an increase in consumption and thus a decrease in the excess supply of the good. The same qualitative result would have been achieved had we assumed that profits are distributed in the current period and that the marginal propensity to consume out of current wages exceeds the marginal propensity to consume out of current profits. The inequality $S_p' > 0$ is similarly analyzed.

Keynesian Unemployment. We now look at the conditions ensuring the occurrence of a temporary equilibrium with Keynesian unemployment at the given configuration (p, w) and study how quantity rations are adjusted to achieve equilibrium in such a case.

In this regime supply is rationed on both markets. That is, the firm perceives a constraint $Y \leq \overline{Y}$ on its sales, and the household perceives a constraint $L \leq \overline{L}$ on its labor supply, both constraints being binding in equilibrium. The other constraints $E \leq \overline{E}$, $C \leq \overline{C}$, and $G \leq \overline{G}$ are not binding in equilibrium, and we shall disregard them here in order to simplify the exposition (but see the remark below).

We first study the traders' behavior for arbitrary but binding values of the rations $\overline{Y}$ and $\overline{L}$. Consider an arbitrary value of $\overline{Y}$. The firm then seeks to maximize its profit $pY - wE$, subject to the technological constraint $Y = F(E)$ and the additional constraint $Y \leq \overline{Y}$. The fact that the latter constraint is binding means that it prevents the firm from achieving its maximum profit at the given price and wage, i.e.,

$$\overline{Y} < Y(w/p). \tag{2.9}$$

If the ration $\overline{Y}$ satisfies (2.9), the firm will choose the output level $Y = \overline{Y}$, which implies the demand for labour $E = F^{-1}(\overline{Y})$ and the demand for money $M_f = p\overline{Y} - wF^{-1}(\overline{Y})$.

Next consider an arbitrary value of the ration $\overline{L}$. The household then maximizes its utility $V(C, M_c)$ subject to the budget constraint

$$pC + M_c = wL + M_0 - T$$

and the constraints $L \leq L^*$ and $L \leq \overline{L}$. Clearly, the last constraint will bite if and only if

$$\overline{L} < L^*. \tag{2.10}$$

In that case, the household optimal decision will be $L = \overline{L}$ and, in view of the definition of the consumption function,

$$C = C(p, (w\overline{L} + M_0 - T)/p),$$

$$M_c = M_c(p, (w\overline{L} + M_0 - T)/p).$$

We have thus far determined the reactions of the firm and of the household under the assumption that they face the arbitrary but binding constraints $Y \leq \overline{Y}$ and $L \leq \overline{L}$. On the other hand, since the demand for the good is not rationed in equilibrium, the government will achieve its target, i.e., $G = G^d$. Our task now is to find the *equilibrium* values of $\overline{Y}$ and of $\overline{L}$. These are determined by expressing that the two markets clear, i.e., by writing that the resulting actions of traders satisfy (2.5) or, equivalently,

$$\overline{Y} = C(p,(w\overline{L} + M_0 - T)/p) + G^d \quad \text{and} \quad \overline{L} = F^{-1}(\overline{Y}).$$

The equilibrium values of $\overline{Y}$ and $\overline{L}$ must, in addition, satisfy the inequalities (2.9) and (2.10). Equilibrium of the labor market gives $\overline{L}$ as a function of $\overline{Y}$; reporting this value in the goods market equation and in (2.10) yields the system

$$S(\overline{Y},p,w,T) = G^d, \quad \overline{Y} < Y(w/p), \quad \overline{Y} < Y^*. \quad (2.11)$$

A temporary Keynesian unemployment is thus found by solving (2.11) in $\overline{Y}$ and letting $\overline{L} = F^{-1}(\overline{Y})$. Since one has in equilibrium $Y = \overline{Y}$, the first part of (2.11) is similar to the traditional equation $Y = C(Y) + G^d$ or $S(Y) = G^d$, where S is savings, that can be found in elementary macroeconomic textbooks on the Keynesian multiplier. The modern approach, as presented here, shows clearly its choice-theoretic foundations and clarifies the role of quantity rations in the equilibrating process. As a result, a new feature appears here by comparison to the traditional textbook presentation. Not every solution of the equation $S = G^d$ leads to a Keynesian equilibrium; it also has to satisfy the constraints $\overline{Y} < Y(w/p)$ and $\overline{Y} < Y^*$ which express that supply is rationed on the goods market and that there is less than full employment. The system (2.11) will thus have a solution in $\overline{Y}$ only for specific configurations of (p, w) and of the policy parameters (G^d, T).

Finding these configurations is easy. From (2.8), the excess supply function S is increasing with $\overline{Y}$ on the interval $[0, Y(w/p)]$ and is nonpositive at $\overline{Y} = 0$. Thus (2.11) *has a solution, which is then unique, if and only if G^d is less than the value of S when $\overline{Y}$ is equal to the minimum of $Y(w/p)$ and of Y^*.* When $w/p \geq F'(L^*)$, in which case $Y(w/p) \leq Y^*$, this condition reduces to

$$S(Y(w/p), p, w, T) > G^d.$$

Symmetrically, when $F'(L^*) \geq w/p$, in which case $Y^* \leq Y(w/p)$, it reduces to

$$S(Y^*, p, w, T) > G^d.$$

Figure 3 describes the set of configurations (p, w) that satisfy these conditions, given the other characteristics of the model. The equation of the line L_1 is there $F'(L^*) = w/p$. There exists a Keynesian equilibrium corresponding to (p,w) if and only if it lies on the right of the curves L_2 and L_3 of equations:

$$L_2: \quad S(Y(w/p), p, w, T) = G^d, \quad w/p \geq F'(L^*)$$

$$L_3: \quad S(Y^*, p, w, T) = G^d, \quad F'(L^*) \geq w/p.$$

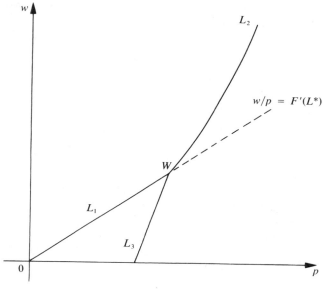

Fig. 3

The reader will verify that, under our assumptions, if these curves intersect, they must do so at a single point (p^*, w^*) which corresponds to the (unique) temporary Walrasian equilibrium of the economy. Figure 3 has been drawn under the assumption that such a Walrasian equilibrium exists.

Remark. The equilibrium values of the nonbinding rations $\overline{E}$, $\overline{C}$, and $\overline{G}$ may be determined through the following procedure. The ration $\overline{E}$ may be set to the Walrasian labor supply, i.e., $\overline{E} = L^*$; it is nonbinding, since in equilibrium $\overline{Y} < Y^*$ and thus $F^{-1}(\overline{Y}) < \overline{E}$. For $\overline{C}$ and $\overline{G}$, we have to specify a rationing scheme on the goods market. If the government is served first, we may set $\overline{G} = \overline{Y}$ and $\overline{C} = \overline{Y} - G^d$. Again, none of these are binding since supply is rationed on the goods market. Note that this procedure of setting the nonbinding constraints independently of the equilibrating process is valid here because we have assumed that current rations do not affect expectations and thus the traders' current objective functions.

Classical Unemployment. We now perform a similar exercise for the case of classical unemployment. In this situation, the labor supply is rationed while demand is rationed on the goods market. Specifically, in equilibrium, the household perceives a binding constraint of the form

$L \leqq L$ on its labor supply; the government and the household perceive, respectively, constraints of the form $G \leqq \overline{G}$ and $C \leqq \overline{C}$ on the goods market, and one of these has to be binding in equilibrium. To fix ideas we shall assume that the government is served first, which implies that the ration $\overline{C}$ is necessarily binding. Here again, we disregard the nonbinding rations $\overline{Y}$ and $\overline{E}$ to simplify the exposition (see the remark below for their determination).

Let us first study the traders' behavior for arbitrary but binding rations $\overline{L}$, $\overline{C}$, and $\overline{G}$. In this regime, the firm perceives no binding constraint. It will choose accordingly its profit maximizing output, i.e., $Y = Y(w/p)$ and the corresponding labor demand $E(w/p) = F^{-1}(Y(w/p))$ and the money demand $M_f = pY(w/p) - wE(w/p)$.

On the other hand, the household will maximize its utility function V under its budget constraint and the additional constraints $L \leqq L^*$, $L \leqq \overline{L}$, and $C \leqq \overline{C}$. Here again, the ration $\overline{L}$ is binding if and only if $\overline{L} < L^*$. Given such a value of $\overline{L}$, the constraint $C \leqq \overline{C}$ will bite if and only if it prevents the household from achieving its most desired consumption, i.e., $C(p,(w\overline{L} + M_0 - T)/p)$. Thus the rations $\overline{L}$ and $\overline{C}$ will be binding if and only if they satisfy

$$\overline{L} < L^* \quad \text{and} \quad \overline{C} < C(p,(w\overline{L} + M_0 - T)/p). \quad (2.12)$$

In that case, the household's optimum choice will be $L = \overline{L}$, $C = \overline{C}$, and $M_c = w\overline{L} + M_0 - T - p\overline{C}$.

Finally, the government perceives the constraint $G \leqq \overline{G}$ on the goods market, which may or may not bite. Its actual expenditures will be then $G = \text{Min}(G^d, \overline{G})$.

The *equilibrium* values of the rations $\overline{L}$, $\overline{C}$, and $\overline{G}$ are found in this case too by expressing that markets must clear. Note that here the activity level and thus employment are determined by the profit maximizing production plan of the firm $Y(w/p)$, $E(w/p)$. What the rations achieve is only to distribute the shortages among the other traders. Equilibrium of the labor market yields $\overline{L} = E(w/p)$. Since the government is served first on the goods market, $\overline{G} = Y(w/p)$; then $\overline{C}$ is what is left of the goods supply after the government has taken its share, i.e., $\overline{C} = Y(w/p) - \text{Min}(G^d, Y(w/p))$.

The equilibrium rations must of course satisfy (2.12). There is unemployment if and only if $\overline{L} = E(w/p) < L^*$ or, equivalently,

$$w/p > F'(L^*). \quad (2.13)$$

Demand is rationed on the goods market if and only if

$$\overline{C} = Y(w/p) - \text{Min}(Y(w/p), G^d) < C(p, (wE(w/p) + M_0 - T)/p)$$

or, equivalently,

$$S(Y(w/p), p, w, T) < G^d \qquad (2.14)$$

Thus *there exists a temporary classical unemployment equilibrium associated with the configuration (p, w) and the policy parameters (G^d, T) if and only if the conditions (2.13) and (2.14) are met.* Given the policy parameters, this corresponds to the region above L_1 and to the left of L_2 in Figure 3.

To sum up this analysis, the economy under consideration may end up in the current period in two different types of unemployment regimes which display quite opposite properties according to which price and wage are quoted initially and which policy parameters are chosen. In a Keynesian equilibrium, what limits the output level is a low aggregate demand for the good. By contrast, what "causes" classical unemployment is the low profitability of production: the real wage is too high. The two types of unemployment may in fact coexist. In the region of Figure 3 that is on the right of L_2 and satisfies $w/p > F'(L^*)$, overall unemployment is measured by $L^* - E$, where Y and $E = F^{-1}(Y)$ denote the equilibrium output and employment levels. Part of the unemployment is indeed "Keynesian"; it is measured by $E(w/p) - E$. But part of it is also "classical", i.e., is due to too high a real wage; that part is measured by $L^* - E(w/p)$.

Remarks.   1. The nonbinding rations $\overline{Y}$ and $\overline{E}$, corresponding to a classical unemployment equilibrium, may be found by setting $\overline{E} = L^*$ and by equating $\overline{Y}$ to the aggregate effective demand of the good

$$\overline{Y} = C(p, (wE(w/p) + M_0 - T)/p) + G^d.$$

2. The reader will verify, by applying the above methods, that the "repressed inflation" regime corresponds in Figure 3 to the region below L_1 and to the left of L_3. The "underconsumption" regime reduces in the present model to the curve L_3.

3. The reader may also study graphically, as above in Section 2.1, the efficiency properties of a temporary equilibrium, given (p, w) and the parameters (G^d, T). Hint: to simplify, assume that the government is not rationed and make the analysis in the plane $C + G^d = Y$, $L = E$ (such a graphical representation of this model can be found, for instance, in Muellbauer and Portes [204]).

Government Policy.   Since the two types of unemployment differ so drastically, one should expect policies aimed at curing unemployment to also be quite different in each case.

In a Keynesian regime, given (p,w) and (G^d,T), the equation that determines equilibrium output is $S(Y,p,w,T) = G^d$ (see (2.11)), which is similar to the traditional macroeconomic textbook equation. One expects, accordingly, the usual Keynesian argument to apply here: aggregate demand should be increased in order to cure unemployment. The equivalent here of the traditional theory goes as follows. Small changes of the parameters ΔG^d, ΔT, Δp, and Δw cause output to adjust according to

$$S'_Y \Delta Y + S'_p \Delta p + S'_w \Delta w + S'_T \Delta T = \Delta G^d. \qquad (2.15)$$

The textbook argument then states that an increase of public expenditures $\Delta G^d > 0$ financed by an additional issue of money ($\Delta T = 0$) must cause output to go up, given the initial price and wage, by an amount $\Delta Y = \Delta G^d / S'_Y > \Delta G^d$: this is the "Keynesian multiplier". Similarly, a decrease of taxes $\Delta T < 0$ should yield $\Delta Y = -(S'_T \Delta T)/S'_Y > 0$. That sort of argument may also be applied to "income policies". For instance, an increase of the prevalent wage $\Delta w > 0$, should make output to go up by $\Delta Y = -(S'_w \Delta w)/S'_Y > 0$, given p, G^d, and T. As noted before, the reason for this result is the fact that the marginal propensity to consume out of current wages exceeds here the marginal propensity to consume out of current profits. The impact of a decrease of the prevalent price $\Delta p < 0$ is similarly analyzed.

The application of this line of reasoning to situations of classical unemployment yields a picture that is quite different. There, policies that increase aggregate demand do not change the output and employment levels, given the initial price and wage, but increase the inflationary pressures in the goods market. What seems to be called for there is an income policy aimed at restoring the profitability of production by lowering the real wage, for instance, by decreasing the nominal wage, given the initial price, or by making the nominal price go up, the initial wage being fixed.

The conclusions of the model seem, therefore, to confirm the traditional textbook diagnosis in the Keynesian case; it yields an additional insight since it shows that policies aimed at increasing employment may depend a lot upon which type of employment actually exists.

This conclusion does not resist, however, a closer examination of the intertemporal choice-theoretic structure of the model and, in particular, of the assumptions made on expectations formation. A moment of reflection should indeed convince the reader that, strictly speaking, *the textbook Keynesian policy evaluations and their counterparts for the case of classical unemployment, as recalled above, apply only to policy moves occurring in the current period (1) that the traders believe to be temporary and (2) that take them by surprise.*

The first conclusion results immediately from the assumptions on the formation of expectations that were explicitly made. We postulated, indeed, that the household's expectations about the future were independent of the signals currently perceived, in particular, of (p,w) and of the current policy parameters (G^d,T). It was this assumption that allowed us to express the household's current consumption as $C(p,R)$, where R is *current* real wealth; the same assumption is in fact made implicitly in traditional elementary Keynesian formulations. As a result, the evaluation coming out of the above model of the consequences of current variations of (G^d,T) is valid only if this variation of the government's policy is thought to be temporary, i.e., to occur only in the current period. By contrast, the model as specified so far has little to say on, or may even give definitely wrong answers to, the problem of assessing the influence of variations of the *time profile* on government policy, for the impact of such variations on the traders' expectations has been entirely neglected. As an example, the household's responses to a current decrease of taxes should be quite different (1) if it knows that the decrease applies only to the current period, or (2) if it knows that it will be followed soon by a move in the opposite direction. Yet the model as specified up to now gives the same evaluation of the consequences of the move in the two cases.

The second point, which claims that policy evaluations through the above model are valid only for moves that are unanticipated by the traders, is a little more subtle but no less important. The foregoing policy evaluations were carried out, as they are in traditional macroeconomic textbooks, under the assumption that the price and/or wage set initially did not respond to current policy moves. That assumption is often justified by the observation that in this class of models "quantities adjust faster than prices". The observation is true, in the sense that a temporary equilibrium is achieved by assumption through quantity rationing in each period, given the price and wage and the policy parameters, but it is besides the point. Although we did not specify the price and wage determination process, we did spell out that these were determined through imperfect competition among the traders at the outset of the period. Whatever the process may be, it is clear that *the anticipation by the traders at the beginning of the period (or even before !) of a variation in the government's current policy should have an effect on the price and wage that are quoted initially.* The absence of any link between the quoted price and wage and the anticipations of the traders about current policy parameters, in the model studied so far, makes it suited only for the analysis of unanticipated policy moves[4]. The same is true of traditional

---

[4] To make things concrete, the reader may consider the efect of a tax variation ΔT in the Keynesian case. If the move is unanticipated, p and w should remain the same and

Keynesian models in which the links between prices and wages and the traders' anticipations about government policy are not explicitly studied.

These shortcomings do not imply, of course, anything wrong in the structure of the models we have discussed so far. The foregoing analysis simply means that the dynamic features of these models, which have been only partially specified, have to be more carefully worked out. It is only when a genuinely dynamic theory of *sequences* of temporary equilibria with rationing is developed, which explains the joint determination of price and quantities from the *intertemporal* maximizing behavior of the agents and from their expectations (which is exactly what temporary equilibrium theory is all about), that a proper evaluation of policy changes can be carried out[5].

2.3   Imperfect Competition

As mentioned earlier several times, models of temporary equilibrium with quantity rationing at given prices must be viewed as a convenient building block of more general models involving the joint determination of prices and quantities through, for instance, imperfect competition. The integration of these two lines of thought was in fact achieved at an early stage of development of the theory.

The principle of the approach is straightforward. If we look at what happens on a given market in a temporary equilibrium with rationing at given prices, the ration perceived, for instance, by a seller on his sales, may be interpreted as a point on the demand curve he faces, corresponding to the price of the commodity under consideration, given the other prices and the actions of the other traders. In order to get a theory of the joint determination of prices and quantities at a given date, it suffices therefore to endow each trader with *perceived demand and/or supply curves* for each commodity, which describe how they think the quantity ration they perceive on a specific market varies with the corresponding price, and to consider a process of imperfect (e.g., monopolistic) competition on each market. This was the approach employed by Benassy [18], Grandmont and Laroque [117], and Negishi [212] following the seminal contribution of Negishi [210].

The approach yields a consistent story of the joint determination of

---

the consequences are those that are described in the text. By contrast, if the variation ΔT is anticipated, it is possible for the traders, given the other assumptions of the model, to change proportionately w and p so as to offset, at least partially, the effect of the anticipated tax variation.

[5]These requirements are not, of course, specific to temporary equilibria with rationing; they are valid for *any* truly dynamic model.

prices and quantities in temporary equilibrium. Yet it suffers from a major drawback. When the traders are endowed with arbitrary subjectively perceived demand and supply curves on each market, almost anything can be rationalized as a temporary equilibrium. A natural question is then whether it is possible to impose the additional requirement that perceived demand or supply curves are in a sense self-fulfilling or "rational", i.e., that they are the true ones. This is the issue studied by Hahn and Gale in two papers reproduced in Chapter VII.

The answer they get is unfortunately negative. The result seems to come from the fact that they assume strong links among markets. All conceivable feedbacks have to be taken into account when formulating true demand or supply functions and, assuming strong interconnections between markets, imposes too many conditions to be satisfied at once. The point should remind the reader of our discussion of the efficient properties of a temporary equilibrium at given prices. We found there that in order to account for the persistence of situations like Keynesian unemployment, we had to postulate that traders believed, in a hypothetical recontracting process, that their actions on a specific market had no consequences on the rations they perceive in the others. We argued that there should be only weak connections between markets in order to make this belief rational. The argument suggests that in the present context one has to also postulate weak connections between markets in order to get a consistent theory of price and quantity determination in temporary equilibrium, through imperfect competition, in which the traders' perceived demand or supply functions are the true ones.

This is the approach taken by Hart in the article reproduced in Chapter VII (see also Heller [137] on this point). Hart considers a simple "macroeconomic" temporary equilibrium model involving one nondurable consumption good, labor, and one "nonreproducible good" that we may interpret as money, in which price and quantities are simultaneously determined at a given date through oligopolistic competition. The consumption good and labor are traded for money on two different markets, as in all models of temporary equilibrium with rationing considered so far. The novel feature here is that Hart postulates the existence of a large number of *spatially distinct* markets for the good, and, similarly, for labor. A large number of identical firms and households are distributed uniformly over these markets. The price of output is determined on each elementary goods market through oligopolistic competition, à la Cournot, between finitely many firms facing a large number of consumers. Similarly, workers are grouped into finitely many syndicates on each elementary labor market, facing a large number of firms. The money wage is then determined, again through Cournot oligopolistic competition among syndicates, each of whom tries to maximize its wage bill. The crucial assumptions made by Hart are that, loosely speaking, (1) if a trader and a firm face each other on an elementary labor market, then they do *not* participate in the same goods market and (2) there are no spillovers between elementary goods markets, nor between labor markets. The main implication is that firms can now predict correctly that what they do on their labor market will have no influence on the households' demand curve for their output. Similarly, households know that their actions on a particular goods market will not affect the demand curve for labor that they face in the specific labor market to which they are allocated. Such a "lack of market coordination" was directly postulated in our analysis of the efficiency properties of a temporary equilibrium at given prices; it is here a consequence of Hart's assumptions on the role of money as a medium of exchange, on the allocation of traders among goods and labor markets, and on the absence of spillovers between goods markets and between labor markets. This feature enables Hart to show the existence of a temporary equilibrium in prices and quantities that may involve Keynesian unemployment, in which each competitor knows the true demand curve on each market in which he participates[6].

Hart's model is a remarkable achievement but is not, evidently, the last word on the topic. Assuming oligopolistic competition on goods markets seems indeed plausible. Postulating that all workers belong to syndicates that compete on labor markets appears, however, to be counterfactual and does not lead to a convincing rationalization of Keynesian unemployment. To make progress, one will have to presumably incorporate other "imperfections" in the *modus operandi* of labor markets, for instance, along the lines of implicit contracts (see Azariadis and Stiglitz [10] and Kahn and Mookherjle [165]) and/or efficiency wages theories (see Akerlof and Yellen [1], Stiglitz [245], and Yellen [267]). The preceding discussions suggest that market coordination failures of the sort we analyzed here should be an important part of the story, no matter which kind of imperfection is chosen. As mentioned earlier, significant progress also has to be made on the description of the intertemporal behavior of the traders involved and on expectations formation. A lot of work still has to be done, but a synthesis along these lines does not appear to be beyond our reach. One may then hope to have a satisfactory solution to the long-standing issue of providing sound microeconomic foundations to Keynesian macroeconomics in a genuinely dynamic setup.

[6] In Hart's framework, traders compete by choosing quantities, and prices adjust so as to clear markets. The reader will note that, nevertheless, equilibrium quantities may be viewed as the outcome of a temporary equilibrium with quantity rationing, given the equilibrium prices.

Bibliography

The following list of references is intended to complete the bibliography of the *Econometrica* survey and to cover fairly extensively the topics dealt with in the present book. The list is rather long, so the following hints might help the reader.

Conditions ensuring the existence of a *temporary equilibrium in competitive asset markets* have been studied, in addition to the papers by Green, Hart, and Hammond reproduced in Chapter III, in particular by Hammond [133], Stahl [241,242], and Werner [264]. *Temporary competitive equilibrium models with money, credit,* etc. are dealt with in particular in two books (Gale [102] and Grandmont [113]). Many of these models use cash-in-advance constraints that have been popular recently in macroeconomics (Lucas [192] and L.E.O. Svensson [249,250]). References on this topic include Bewley [28]; Eichberger [77,79]; Gagey, Laroque, and Lollivier [99]; Hool [155,156]; and Muller and Schweizer [206]. For closely related investigations of the role of money in transactions in a general equilibrium framework, see Diamond [67], Chae [46], and Gale and Hellwig [104]. References to the literature on *stability with learning* were given in Section 1. Interesting contributions to the study of *stochastic processes of temporary equilibria* include, in addition to the papers by Hildenbrand and myself, Blume [34] and Spear and Srivastava [239] that are reproduced in Chapter VI, Hellwig [139] and Knieps [169].

There is a sizable literature on the *microeconomic analysis of temporary equilibria with quantity rationing* that deals with the efficiency properties of such equilibria and/or with their relations with models of imperfect competition, for instance, d'Aspremont, Dos Santos Ferreira, and Gerard-Varet [5], Aumann and Dreze [6], Balasko [11,12,13], Benassy [18,19,20,22,24,27], Bohm [36,37], Bohm, Maskin, Polemarchakis, and Postlewaite [39], Dehez [62], Dehez and Dreze [63], Dreze and Muller [74], Fisher [81,82], Gale [100,101,103], Gary-Bobo [105], Grandmont [110], Grandmont and Laroque [117], Grandmont, Laroque, and Younès [119], Green [120], Greenberg and Muller [122], Hahn [127,128,130,131], Hart [134,135,136], Heller [137], Heller and Starr [138], Honkapohja [150], Kahn and Mookherjee [165], Keiding [167], Kurz [176], van der Laan [177,178], Laroque [181,182,183], Laroque and Polemarchakis [186], Madden [193], Malinvaud and Younès [200], Maskin and Tirole [201], Neary and Roberts [208], Negishi [211,212], Polterovitch [219,220,221], Schulz [227], Silvestre [230,231,232,233], L.G. Svensson [251], L.G. Svensson and Weibull [252], Weddepohl [259,260], Weinrich [263], and Younès [269,271,272,273]. There are also interesting studies of issues in public economics in the presence of rationing (cost-benefit analysis, shadow-pricing, and second best); see, e.g., Dixit [69], Dreze [72], Fourgeaud, Lenclud, and Picard [88,89,90], Guesnerie and Roberts [123], Johansson [161], and Picard [218].

Extensions of the basic *macroeconomic model with quantity rationing* reviewed in Section 2.2 above, in a setting involving productive investment, inventories, and/or bonds that is similar to the IS-LM model, can be found, for instance, in Benassy [24], Bohm [36], Cheffert [49], Danthine and Peytrignet [58], Eichberger [78], Fourgeaud, Lenclud, and Michel [87], Gelpi and Younès [106], Grandmont [115], Green and Laffont [121], Haga [124], Henin [141], Henin and Michel [145], Honkapohja and Ito [153], Hool [157], Malinvaud [197], Michel [203], Muellbauer and Portes [204], and Neary and Stiglitz [209]. There are also many studies of *economic growth with quantity rationing*; see, e.g., d'Autume [7], Azam [9], Henin and Michel [144], Ito [159], Malinvaud [199], Michel [202], and Picard [216,218]. On the application of temporary equilibrium models with rationing to theoretical macroeconomic issues, the reader may consult the surveys or books by d'Autume [7], Benassy [22,27], Dehez [60], Drazen [71], Fitoussi [83], Laroque [185], Malinvaud [195,197], Muellbauer and Portes [204], Negishi [212], Picard [218], and Sneessens [235].

Early references on the study of *open economies* by using these methods include Cuddington [55,56], Dixit [70], Dreze and Modigliani [73], Grandmont [111], Johansson and Lofgren [162], Kenally [168], Neary [207], and Younès [270]. I did not attempt to give a complete list of references on this topic. For an overview of the state of the art in this area, the reader may consult the book by Cuddington, Johansson, and Lofgren [57].

The application of rationing ideas to the analysis of *centrally planned economies* was started independently by Kornai [170] and pursued by him in a series of contributions [171,172,173]. For a review of the theoretical issues in this area and of the empirical results obtained see Charemza and Quandt [48], Howard [158], Portes [222], and Portes and Winter [223].

References to the literature on the *theoretical econometric problems* posed by the presence of quantity rationing in economic models have not been included here. For a review of these issues, see Quandt [224] and Sneessens [235]. Only a few references on the *empirical econometric applications* to Western economies are listed below; see, e.g., Artus, Laroque, and Michel [4], Lambert, Lubrans and Sneessens [180]. For a good survey of recent empirical work, see Laffont [179].

1. G.A. AKERLOF and J. YELLEN, "Efficiency wage models of the labor market," Cambridge University Press, Cambridge and New York, 1986.
2. M. ALEXEEV and D.O. STAHL, II, The influence of black markets on a queue-

rationed centrally planned economy, *Journal of Economic Theory* **35** (1985), 234–250.

3. M. ALLARD, C. BRONSARD, and Y. RICHELLE, Temporary Pareto optimum theory, Working paper, Université de Montréal, 1986.

4. P. ARTUS, G. LAROQUE, and G. MICHEL, Estimation of a quarterly macro-economic model with quantity rationing, *Econometrica* **52** (1984), 1387–1414.

5. C. D'ASPREMONT, R. DOS SANTOS FERRIERA, and L.A. GERARD-VARET, Oligopoly and involuntary unemployment, CORE Discussion Paper, Université Catholique de Louvain, 1984.

6. R.J. AUMANN and J. DREZE, Values of markets with satiation or fixed prices, *Econometrica* **54** (1986), 1271–1318.

7. A. D'AUTUME, "Monnaie, Croissance, et Déséquilibre", Economica, Paris, 1985.

8. A. D'AUTUME and P. MICHEL, Evaluation du capital en présence de contraintes anticipées sur les achats de biens d'investissement, *Annales de l'INSEE* **54** (1984), 101–114.

9. J. P. AZAM, Money, growth, and disequilibrium, *Economica* **50** (1983), 325–335.

10. C. AZARIADIS and J.E. STIGLITZ, Implicit contracts and fixed price equilibria, *Quarterly Journal of Economics* **98** (1983), Suppl., 1–22.

11. Y. BALASKO, Budget-constrained Pareto-efficient allocations, *Journal of Economic Theory* **21** (1979), 359–379.

12. Y. BALASKO, Budget-constrained Pareto-efficient allocations: A dynamic story, *Journal of Economic Theory* **27** (1982), 293–242.

13. Y. BALASKO, Equilibria and efficiency in the fix-price setting, *Journal of Economic Theory* **28** (1982), 113–127.

14. A. BARRERE (ed.), "Keynes aujourd'hui: Théories et politiques", Economica, Paris, 1985. English translation by Cambridge University Press, Cambridge and New York, forthcoming.

15. R.J. BARRO and H.I. GROSSMAN, A general disequilibrium model of income and employment, *American Economic Review* **61** (1971), 82–93.

16. W. BARTLETT and G. WEINRICH, Instability and indexation in a labour managed economy—a general equilibrium quantity rationing approach, Working paper, European University Institute, Florence, 1985.

17. J.P. BENASSY, Regulation of the wage profits conflict and the unemployment inflation dilemma in a dynamic disequilibrium model, *Economie Appliquée* **29** (1976), 409–444.

18. J.P. BENASSY, The disequilibrium approach to monopolistic price setting and general monopolistic equilibrium, *Review of Economic Studies* **43** (1976), 69–81.

19. J.P. BENASSY, A neo-Keynesian model of price and quantity determination in disequilibrium, *in* G. Schwödiauer (ed.) [228], 1977.

20. J.P. BENASSY, On quantity signals and the foundations of effective demand theory, *Scandinavian Journal of Economics* **79** (1977), 147–168. Reprinted *in* S. Strom and L. Werin (eds.) [246], 1978.

21. J.P. BENASSY, Cost and demand inflation revisited: A neo-Keynesian approach, *Economie Appliquée* **31** (1978), 113–133.
22. J.P. BENASSY, "The Economics of Market Disequilibrium", Academic Press, New York, 1982.
23. J.P. BENASSY, The three regimes of the IS-LM model: a non-Walrasian analysis, *European Economic Review* **23** (1983), 1–17.
24. J.P. BENASSY, Tariffs and Pareto optimality in international trade: The case of unemployment, *European Economic Review* **26** (1984), 261–276.
25. J.P. BENASSY, "Macroéconomie et Théorie du Déséquilibre", Dunod, Paris, 1984.
26. J.P. BENASSY, A non-Walrasian model of employment with partial price flexibility and indexation, *in* G. Feiwel (ed.), "Trends in Contemporary Macroeconomics and Distribution", Macmillan, London, 1985.
27. J.P. BENASSY, "Macroeconomics: An Introduction to the Non-Walrasian Approach", Academic Press, New York, 1986.
28. T. BEWLEY, The optimum quantity of money, *in* J.H. Kareken and N. Wallace (eds.) [166], 1980.
29. M.C. BLAD, Exchange of stability in a disequilibrium model, *Journal of Mathematical Economics* **8** (1981), 121–145.
30. M.C. BLAD and C. ZEEMAN, Oscillations between repressed inflation and Keynesian equilibria due to inertia in decision making, *Journal of Economic Theory* **28** (1982), 165–182.
31. O. BLANCHARD and J. SACHS, Anticipations, recessions and policy: An intertemporal disequilibrium model, *Annales de l'INSEE* **47/48** (1982), 117–144.
32. C. BLISS, Capital theory in the short run, in M. Brown, K. Sato, and P. Zarembka (eds.), "Essays in Modern Capital Theory", North Holland Publ., Amsterdam, 1976.
33. C. BLISS, Consistent temporary equilibrium, *in* J.P. Fitoussi (ed.) [83], 1983.
34. L.E. BLUME, New techniques for the study of stochastic equilibrium processes, *Journal of Mathematical Economics* **9** (1982), 61–70.
35. V. BOHM, Disequilibrium dynamics in a simple macroeconomic model, *Journal of Economic Theory* **17** (1978), 179–199.
36. V. BOHM, Quantity rationing vs. IS-LM: A synthesis, Discussion paper, University of Mannheim, 1983.
37. V. BOHM, Fixed prices, rationing, and optimality, CARESS Working paper, University of Pennsylvania, Philadelphia, 1984.
38. V. BOHM and P. LEVINE, Temporary equilibria with quantity rationing, *Review of Economic Studies* **46** (1979), 361–377.
39. V. BOHM, E. MASKIN, H. POLEMARCHAKIS, and A. POSTLEWAITE, Monopolistic quantity rationing, *Quarterly Journal of Economics* **98** (1983), Suppl. 189–197.
40. V. BOHM and H. MULLER, Two examples of equilibria under price rigidities and quantity rationing, *Zeitschrift für Nationalökonomie* **37** (1977), 165–173.

41. C. de Boissieu, A. Parguez, and P. Zagame (eds.), "Economie du Déséquilibre", Economica, Paris, 1977.

42. E.M. Braverman, A production model with disequilibrium prices, *Ekonomika i matematicheskie metody* (1972), 40–64.

43. M.M. Bray, Learning, estimation, and the stability of rational expectations, *Journal of Economic Theory* **26** (1982), 318–339.

44. M.M. Bray, Convergence to rational expectations equilibrium, *in* R. Frydman and E.S. Phelps (eds.), "Individual Forecasting and Aggregate Outcomes", Cambridge University Press, Cambridge and New York, 1983.

45. M.M. Bray and N.E. Savin, Rational expectations equilibria, learning, and model specification, *Econometrica* **54** (1986), 1129–1160.

46. S. Chae, The efficiency and existence of competitive equilibria in a monetary economy with liquidity constraints, mimeo, University of Pennsylvania, Philadelphia, 1984.

47. P. Champsaur, On the stability of rational expectations equilibria, CORE discussion paper, Université Catholique de Louvain, 1983.

48. W. Charemza and R.E. Quandt, Model and estimation of disequilibrium in centrally planned economies, *Review of Economic Studies* **49** (1982), 109–116.

49. J.M. Cheffert, Modèle IS-LM de court terme à fondements microéconomiques, Working paper, Université de Namur, 1983.

50. V.K. Chetty and D. Dasgupta, Temporary competitive equilibrium in a monetary economy with uncertain technology and many planning periods, *Journal of Mathematical Economics* **5** (1978), 23–42.

51. D.S. Christiansen and M. Majumdar, On shifting temporary equilibrium, *Journal of Economic Theory* **16** (1977), 1–9.

52. A. Cigno and B. Hool, Bounded rationality and intertemporal decision making, *Metroeconomica* **331** (1979), 349–366.

53. R.W. Clower, The Keynesian counterrevolution: A theoretical appraisal, *in* F.H. Hahn and F.P.R. Brechling (eds.), "The Theory of Interest Rates", Macmillan, London, 1965.

54. R. Cooper and A. John, Coordinating coordination failures in Keynesian models, Cowles Foundation Discussion Paper, Yale University, 1985.

55. J.T. Cuddington, Fiscal and exchange rate policies in a fix-price trade model with export rationing, *Journal of International Economics* **10** (1980), 319–340.

56. J.T. Cuddington, Import substitution policies: A two-sector, fix-price model, *Review of Economic Studies* **48** (1981), 327–342.

57. J.T. Cuddington, P.O. Johansson, and K.G. Lofgren, "Disequilibrium Macroeconomics in Open Economies", Blackwell, Oxford, 1984.

58. J.P. Danthine and M. Peytrignet, Intégration de l'analyse graphique IS-LM avec la théorie des équilibres à prix fixes: Une note pédagogique, *in* G. Bramoullé and J.P. Giran (eds.), "Eléments d'Analyse du Déséquilibre", Economica, Paris, 1981.

59. S. De Canio, Rational expectations and learning from experience, *Quarterly Journal of Economics* **94** (1979), 47–57.

60. P. DEHEZ, Apports de la théorie de l'équilibre temporaire en analyse macro-économique, *Recherches Economiques de Louvain* **46** (1980), 27–56.
61. P. DEHEZ, Stationary Keynesian equilibria, *European Economic Review* **19** (1982), 245–258.
62. P. DEHEZ, Monopolistic equilibrium and unvoluntary unemployment, *Journal of Economic Theory* **36** (1985), 160–165.
63. P. DEHEZ and J.H. DREZE, On supply constrained equilibria, *Journal of Economic Theory* **33** (1984), 172–182.
64. P. DEHEZ and J.P. FITOUSSI, Equilibres de stagflation et indexation des salaires, Working Paper, OFCE, Paris, 1984.
65. P. DEHEZ and J. JASKOLD-GABSZEWICZ, Saving behavior and disequilibrium analysis, *in* "Systèmes Dynamiques et Modèles Economiques", Editions du CNRS, Paris, 1977.
66. P. DEHEZ and J. JASKOLD-GABSZEWICZ, On disequilibrium savings and public consumption, *Zeitschrift für Nationalökonomie* **39** (1979), 53–61.
67. P. DIAMOND, Money in search equilibrium, *Econometrica* **52** (1984), 1–20.
68. W.E. DIEWERT, Walras's theory of capital formation and the existence of a temporary equilibrium, *in* G. Schwödiauer (ed.) [228], 1977.
69. A. DIXIT, Public finance in a Keynesian temporary equilibrium model, *Journal of Economic Theory* **12** (1976), 242–258.
70. A. DIXIT, The balance of trade in a model of temporary equilibrium with rationing, *Review of Economic Studies* **45** (1978), 393–404.
71. A. DRAZEN, Recent developments in macroeconomic disequilibrium theory, *Econometrica* **48** (1980), 293–306.
72. J.H. DRÈZE, Second best analysis with markets in disequilibrium: Public sector pricing in a Keynesian regime, *in* M. Marchand, P. Pestiau, and H. Tulkens (eds.), "The Performance of Public Enterprise: Concepts and Measurement", North-Holland, Amsterdam, 1984.
73. J.H. DRÈZE and F. MODIGLIANI, The trade-off between real wages and employment in an open economy (Belgium), *European Economic Review* **15** (1981), 1–40.
74. J.H. DRÈZE and H.H. MULLER, Optimality properties of rationing schemes, *Journal of Economic Theory* **23** (1980), 131–149.
75. J.C. ECKALBAR, Stable quantities in fixed-price disequilibrium, *Journal of Economic Theory* **25** (1981), 302–313.
76. J. EICHBERGER, Temporary equilibria with firms and government, Discussion paper, University of Mannheim, 1983.
77. J. EICHBERGER, Temporary equilibrium with bankruptcy, Research report, University of Western Ontario, London, 1984.
78. J. EICHBERGER, Government policy and unemployment, mimeo, Australian National University, Canberra, 1985.
79. J. EICHBERGER, "Geld und Kredit in Einer Okonomie mit festen Preisen", Peter Lang Publ., Frankfurt/Main and New York, 1984.
80. J. EICHBERGER, On the efficacy of fiscal policy, *Annales d'Economie et de Statistique* **3** (1986), 151–168.

81. F.M. Fisher, Quantity constraints, spillovers, and the Hahn process, *Review of Economic Studies* **45** (1978), 19–31.

82. F.M. Fisher, "Disequilibrium Foundations of Equilibrium Economics", Cambridge University Press, London and New York, 1983.

83. J.P. Fitoussi (ed.), "Modern Macroeconomic Theory", Basil Blackwell, Oxford, 1983.

84. M. Fleurbaey, L'équilibre général temporaire et la dynamique de marché, Mémoire DEA N° 39, Université de Paris X-Nanterre, 1985.

85. C. Fourgeaud, C. Gourieroux, and J. Pradel, Rational expectations models and bounded memory, *Econometrica* **53** (1985), 977–986.

86. C. Fourgeaud, C. Gourieroux, and J. Pradel, Learning procedures and convergence to rationality, *Econometrica* **54** (1986), 854–868.

87. C. Fourgeaud, B. Lenclud, and P. Michel, A two-sector model with quantity rationing, *Journal of Economic Theory* **24** (1981), 413–436.

88. C. Fourgeaud, B. Lenclud, and P. Picard, Calcul économique, prix fictifs et contrainte extérieure, *Revue Economique* **35** (1984), 425–445.

89. C. Fourgeaud, B. Lenclud, and P. Picard, Calcul économique et déséquilibres en économie ouverte, *in* P.Y. Hénin, W. Marios, and P. Michel (eds.) [143], 1985.

90. C. Fourgeaud, B. Lenclud, and P. Picard, Shadow prices and public policies in a disequilibrium model of an open economy, *European Economic Review* **30** (1986), 991–1012.

91. R. Frydman, Towards an understanding of market processes: Individual expectations, learning and convergence to rational expectations equilibrium, *American Economic Review* **72** (1982), 652–668.

92. G. Fuchs, Asymptotic stability of stationary temporary equilibria and changes in expectations, *Journal of Economic Theory* **13** (1976), 201–216.

93. G. Fuchs, Formation of expectations: A model in temporary general equilibrium theory, *Journal of Mathematical Economics* **4** (1977), 167–188.

94. G. Fuchs, Dynamic role and evolution of expectations, *in* "Systèmes Dynamiques et Modèles Economiques", Editions du CNRS, Paris, 1977.

95. G. Fuchs, Dynamics of expectations in temporary general equilibrium theory, *Journal of Mathematical Economics* **6** (1979), 229–252.

96. G. Fuchs, Is error learning behaviour stabilizing?, *Journal of Economic Theory* **20** (1979), 300–317.

97. G. Fuchs and G. Laroque, Dynamics of temporary equilibria and expectations, *Econometrica* **44** (1976), 1157–1178.

98. C.A. Futia, Excess supply equilibria, *Journal of Economic Theory* **14** (1977), 200–220.

99. F. Gagey, G. Laroque, and S. Lollivier, Monetary and fiscal policies in a general equilibrium model, *Journal of Economic Theory* **39** (1986), 329–357.

100. D. Gale, A note on conjectural equilibria, *Review of Economic Studies* **45** (1978), 33–38.

101. D. Gale, Large economies with trading uncertainty, *Review of Economic Studies* **46** (1979), 319–338. Correction **48** (1981), 363–364.

102. D. GALE, "Money: In Equilibrium", Cambridge University Press, Cambridge and New York, 1982.

103. D. GALE, "Money: In Disequilibrium", Cambridge University Press, Cambridge and New York, 1983.

104. D. GALE and M. HELLWIG, A general equilibrium model of the transactions demand for money, Working paper, London School of Economics, 1984.

105. R.J. GARY-BOBO, Cournot-Walras and locally consistent equilibria, Working paper, Université de Paris I, Groupe de Mathématiques Economiques, 1986.

106. R.M. GELPI and Y. YOUNÈS, Monnaie et crédit dans une optique d'équilibre non-Walrasien, in "Modèles Monétaires de l'Economie Française", Documentation Française, Paris, 1977.

107. L.A. GERARD-VARET, R. JORDAN, and A.P. KIRMAN, Towards disequilibrium dynamics: A model of temporary equilibria with stochastic quantity rationing, GREQE Discussion paper, EHESS, Université d'Aix-Marseille II, 1986.

108. C. GOURIEROUX, J.J. LAFFONT, and A. MONFORT, Révision adaptative des anticipations et convergence vers les anticipations rationnelles, *Economie Appliquée* **36** (1983), 9–26.

109. C. GOURIEROUX and G. LAROQUE, The aggregation of commodities in quantity rationing models, Working paper, INSEE, Paris, 1983.

110. J.M. GRANDMONT, The logic of the fix-price method, *Scandinavian Journal of Economics* **79** (1977), 169–186. Reprinted in S. Strom and L. Werin (eds.) [246], 1978.

111. J.M. GRANDMONT, Notes on international trade, mimeo, CEPREMAP, Paris, 1981.

112. J.M. GRANDMONT, Temporary general equilibrium theory, in K.J. Arrow and M.D. Intriligator (eds.), "Handbook of Mathematical Economics", Vol. II, North-Holland Publ., Amsterdam, 1982.

113. J.M. GRANDMONT, "Money and Value: A Reconsideration of Classical and Neoclassical Monetary Theories", Cambridge University Press, Cambridge and New York, 1983.

114. J.M. GRANDMONT, On endogenous competitive business cycles, *Econometrica* **53** (1985), 995–1045.

115. J.M. GRANDMONT, Classical and Keynesian unemployment in the IS-LM model in M. de Cecco and J.P. Fitoussi (eds.), "Monetary Theory and Institutions", Macmillan, London, 1986. Spanish version in *Analisis Economico* **3** (1984), 81–113.

116. J.M. GRANDMONT, Stabilizing competitive business cycles, *Journal of Economic Theory* **40** (1986), 57–76.

117. J.M. GRANDMONT and G. LAROQUE, On temporary Keynesian equilibria, *Review of Economic Studies* **43** (1976), 53–67.

118. J.M. GRANDMONT and G. LAROQUE, Stability of cycles and expectations, *Journal of Economic Theory* **40** (1986), 138–151.

119. J.M. GRANDMONT, G. LAROQUE, and Y. YOUNÈS, Equilibrium with quantity rationing and recontracting, *Journal of Economic Theory* **19** (1978), 84–102.

120. J.R. GREEN, On the theory of effective demand, *Economic Journal* **90** (1980), 341–353.

121. J.R. GREEN and J.J. LAFFONT, Disequilibrium dynamics with inventories and anticipatory price-setting, *European Economic Review* **16** (1981), 199–221.

122. J. GREENBERG and H. MULLER, Equilibria under price rigidities and externalities, *in* O. Moeschlin and D. Pollaschke (eds.), "Game Theory and Related Topics", North-Holland Publ., Amsterdam, 1979, 281–309.

123. R. GUESNERIE and K. ROBERTS, Effective policy tools and quantity controls, *Econometrica* **52** (1984), 59–86.

124. H. HAGA, "A Disequilibrium-Equilibrium Model with Money and Bonds", Springer-Verlag, Berlin, 1976.

125. F.H. HAHN, On the foundations of monetary theory, *in* M. Parkin and ·A.R. Nobay (eds.), "Essays in Modern Economics", Longman Group Ltd, Manchester, 1973. Reprinted in F.H. Hahn [129], 1984.

126. F.H. HAHN, Keynesian economics and general equilibrium theory: Reflections on some current debates, *in* G.C. Harcourt (ed.), "The Microeconomic Foundations of Macroeconomics", Macmillan, London, 1977. Reprinted in F.H. Hahn [129], 1984.

127. F.H. HAHN, Exercises in conjectural equilibria, *Scandinavian Journal of Economics* **79** (1977), 210–226. Reprinted in S. Strom and L. Werin (eds.) [246], 1978.

128. F.H. HAHN, On non-Walrasian equilibria, *Review of Economic Studies* **45** (1978), 1–17.

129. F.H. HAHN, "Equilibrium and Macroeconomics", The MIT Press, Cambridge, 1984.

130. F.H. HAHN, On unvoluntary unemployment, Working paper N° 94, University of Cambridge, England, 1986.

131. F.H. HAHN, An exercise in non-Walrasian analysis, *in* W.P. Heller, R.M. Starr, and D.A. Starrett (eds.), "Essays in Honor of Kenneth J. Arrow, Vol. II, Equilibrium Analysis", Cambridge University Press, Cambridge and New York, 1986.

132. P.J. HAMMOND, Overlapping expectations and Hart's conditions for equilibrium in a securities model, *Journal of Economic Theory* **31** (1983), 170–175.

133. P.J. HAMMOND, General asset markets and the existence of temporary Walrasian equilibrium, Working paper, IMSSS, Stanford University, 1983.

134. O.D. HART, A model of imperfect competition with Keynesian features, *Quarterly Journal of Economics* **97** (1982), 109–138.

135. O.D. HART, Economic fluctuations with an imperfectly competitive labour market, *in* J.P. Fitoussi (ed.) [83], 1983.

136. O.D. HART, Imperfect competition in general equilibrium: An overview of recent work, *in* K.J. Arrow and S. Honkapohja (eds.), "Frontiers of Economics", Basil Blackwell, Oxford and New York, 1985.

137. W.P. HELLER, Coordination failure under complete markets with applications to effective demand, *in* W.P. Heller, R.M. Starr, and D.A. Starrett (eds.),

"Essays in Honor of Kenneth J. Arrow, Vol. II, Equilibrium Analysis", Cambridge University Press, Cambridge and New York, 1986.

138. W.P. HELLER and R.M. STARR, Unemployment equilibrium with myopic complete information, *Review of Economic Studies* **46** (1979), 339–359.

139. M.F. HELLWIG, Rational expectations and the Markov property of temporary equilibrium processes, *Journal of Mathematical Economics* **9** (1982), 135–144.

140. P.Y. HÉNIN (ed.), "Etudes sur l'Economie en Déséquilibre", Economica, Paris, 1986.

141. P.Y. HÉNIN, Equilibres avec rationnement dans un modèle macroéconomique avec décision d'investissement endogène, *Economie Appliquée* **34** (1981), 697–728.

142. P.Y. HÉNIN, L'impact macroéconomique d'un choc pétrolier, *Revue Economique* **34** (1983), 865–896.

143. P.Y. HÉNIN, W. MAROIS, and P. MICHEL (eds.), "Déséquilibres en Economie Ouverte", Economica, Paris, 1985.

144. P.Y. HÉNIN and P. MICHEL (eds.), "Croissance et Accumulation en Déséquilibre", Economica, Paris, 1982.

145. P.Y. HÉNIN and P. MICHEL, Une représentation IS-LM des équilibres macroéconomiques avec rationnement, *in* A. Barrère (ed.) [14], 1985.

146. P.Y. HÉNIN and A. ZYLBERBERG, Sur l'efficacité de la politique monétaire dans des modèles de prévisions rationnelles avec ajustement partiel des prix, *Economie Appliquée* **36** (1983), 157–174.

147. J. HICKS, "Capital and Growth", Oxford University Press, London and New York, 1965.

148. K. HILDENBRAND and W. HILDENBRAND, On Keynesian equilibria with unemployment and quantity rationing, *Journal of Economic Theory* **18** (1978), 255–277.

149. S. HONKAPOHJA, On the dynamics of disequilibria in a simple macro model with flexible wages and prices, *in* M. Aoki and A. Marzollo (eds.), "New Trends in Dynamic System Theory and Economics", Academic Press, New York, 1979.

150. S. HONKAPOHJA, A note on monopolistic quantity rationing, *Economic Letters* **6** (1980), 203–210.

151. S. HONKAPOHJA, The employment multiplier after disequilibrium dynamics, *Scandinavian Journal of Economics* **82** (1980), 1–14.

152. S. HONKAPOHJA and J. ITO, Inventory dynamics in a simple disequilibrium model, *Scandinavian Journal of Economics* **82** (1980), 184–198.

153. S. HONKAPOHJA and T. ITO, Stability with regime-switching, *Journal of Economic Theory* **29** (1983), 22–48.

154. S. HONKAPOHJA and T. ITO, On macroeconomic equilibrium with stochastic rationing, *Scandinavian Journal of Economics* **87** (1985), 60–88.

155. B. HOOL, Money, expectations, and the existence of a temporary equilibrium, *Review of Economic Studies* **43** (1976), 439–445.

156. B. HOOL, Liquidity, speculation, and the demand for money, *Journal of Economic Theory* **21** (1979), 73–87.

157. B. Hool, Monetary and fiscal policies in short-run equilibria with rationing, *International Economic Review* 21 (1980), 301–316.

158. D.H. Howard, "The Disequilibrium Model in a Controlled Economy", Lexington Books, New York, 1979.

159. T. Ito, Disequilibrium growth theory, *Journal of Economic Theory* 23 (1980), 380–409.

160. A. Ize, Disequilibrium theories, imperfect competition, and income distribution: A fix-price analysis, *Oxford Economic Papers 36* (1984), 248–258.

161. P.O. Johansson, Cost-benefit rules in general disequilibrium, *Journal of Public Economics* 18 (1982), 121–137.

162. P.O. Johansson and K.G. Lofgren, The effect of tariffs and real wages on employment in a Barro-Grossman model of an open economy, *Scandinavian Journal of Economics* 82 (1980), 167–183.

163. J.S. Jordan, Temporary competitive equilibrium and the existence of self-fulfilling expectations, *Journal of Economic Theory* 12 (1976), 455–471.

164. J.S. Jordan, The continuity of optimal decision rules, *Econometrica* 45 (1977), 1365–1376.

165. C. Kahn and D. Mookherjee, A contracting equilibrium model with Keynesian features, mimeo, Stanford University, 1986.

166. J.H. Kareken and N. Wallace (eds.), "Models of Monetary Economies", Federal Reserve Bank of Minneapolis, Minneapolis, 1980.

167. H. Keiding, Existence of budget constrained Pareto efficient allocations, *Journal of Economic Theory* 24 (1981), 393–397.

168. G.F. Kenally, Some consequences of opening a neo-Keynesian model, *Economic Journal* 93 (1983), 390–410.

169. G. Knieps, Self-fulfilling expectations in stochastic processes of temporary equilibria, *Journal of Economic Theory* 21 (1979), 207–212.

170. J. Kornai, "Anti-Equilibrium", North-Holland Publ., Amsterdam, 1971.

171. J. Kornai, Resource-constrained versus demand-constrained systems, *Econometrica* 47 (1979), 801–820.

172. J. Kornai, "Economics of Shortage", North-Holland Publ., Amsterdam, 1980.

173. J. Kornai, "Growth, Shortage, and Efficiency", Blackwell, Oxford, 1982.

174. J. Kornai and J.W. Weibull, The normal state of the market in a shortage economy: A queue model, *Scandinavian Journal of Economics* 80 (1978), 375–398.

175. J. Kornai and J.W. Weibull, Paternalism, buyers' and sellers' market, *Mathematical Social Sciences* 6 (1983), 153–169.

176. M. Kurz, Unemployment equilibrium in an economy with linked prices, *Journal of Economic Theory* 26 (1982), 100–123.

177. G. van der Laan, Equilibrium under rigid prices with compensation for the consumers, *International Economic Review* 21 (1981), 63–74.

178. G. van der Laan, Supply-constrained fixed price equilibria in monetary economies, *Journal of Mathematical Economics* 13 (1984), 171–188.

179. J.J. Laffont, Fix-price models: A survey of recent empirical work, *in*

K.J. Arrow and S. Honkapohja (eds.), "Frontiers of Economics", Basil Blackwell, Oxford and New York, 1985.

180. J.P. LAMBERT, M. LUBRANS, and H.R. SNEESSENS, Emploi et chômage en France de 1955 à 1982: Un modèle macroéconomique annuel avec rationnement, *Annales de l'INSEE* **55/56** (1984), 39–75.

181. G. LAROQUE, The fixed price equilibria: Some results in local comparative statics, *Econometrica* **46** (1978), 1127–1154.

182. G. LAROQUE, On the dynamics of disequilibrium: A simple remark, *Review of Economic Studies* **45** (1978), 273–278.

183. G. LAROQUE, On the local uniqueness of the fixed price equilibria, *Review of Economic Studies* **48** (1981), 113–129.

184. G. LAROQUE, A comment on stable spillovers among substitutes, *Review of Economic Studies* **48** (1981), 355–361.

185. G. LAROQUE, "Fondements de l'Analyse Macroéconomique à Court Terme", Monographies d'Econométrie, CNRS, Paris, 1986.

186. G. LAROQUE and H. POLEMARCHAKIS, On the structure of the set of fixed-price equilibria, *Journal of Mathematical Economics* **5** (1978), 53–70.

187. D. LAUSSEL, Sentiers de croissance en déséquilibre, in P.Y. Hénin and P. Michel (eds.) [144], 1982.

188. D. LAUSSEL and C. MONTET, Fixed-price equilibria in a two-country model of trade: Existence and comparative statics, *European Economic Review* **22** (1983), 305–330.

189. A. LEIJONHUFVUD, Effective demand failures, *Swedish Journal of Economics* **75** (1973), 27–58.

190. K.G. LOFGREN, The corridor and local stability of the effective excess demand hypothesis: A result, *Scandinavian Journal of Economics* **81** (1979), 30–47.

191. R.E. LUCAS, Jr., Econometric policy evaluation: A critique, in K. Brunner and A.H. Meltzer (eds.), "The Phillips Curve and Labour Markets", North-Holland, Amsterdam, 1976.

192. R.E. LUCAS, Jr., Equilibrium in a pure currency economy, in J.H. Kareken and N. Wallace (eds.) [166], 1980.

193. P.J. MADDEN, Existence of Drèze equilibrium under set-up costs, *Journal of Economic Theory* **33** (1984), 275–288.

194. P. MALGRANGE and P. VILLA, Comportement d'investissement avec coûts d'ajustement et contraintes quantitatives, *Annales de l'INSEE* **53** (1984), 31–60.

195. E. MALINVAUD, "The Theory of Unemployment Reconsidered", Blackwell, Oxford, 1977.

196. E. MALINVAUD, Nouveaux développements de la théorie macroéconomique du chômage, *Revue Economique* **29** (1978), 9–25.

197. E. MALINVAUD, "Profitability and Unemployment", Cambridge University Press, London and New York, 1980.

198. E. MALINVAUD, Macroeconomic rationing of unemployment, in J.P. Fitoussi and E. Malinvaud (eds.), "Unemployment in Western Countries", Macmillan, London, 1980.

199. E. Malinvaud, Notes on growth theory with imperfectly flexible prices, in J.P. Fitoussi (ed.) [83], 1983.
200. E. Malinvaud and Y. Younès, Some new concepts for the microeconomic foundations of macroeconomics, in G. Harcourt (ed.), "The Microeconomic Foundations of Macroeconomics", Macmillan, London, 1977.
201. E. Maskin and J. Tirole, On the efficiency of a fix-price equilibrium, Journal of Economic Theory 32 (1984), 317–327.
202. P. Michel, Trois facteurs de la crise dans un modèle de croissance contrainte, Revue Economique 33 (1982), 807–838.
203. P. Michel, Dynamique de l'accumulation du capital en présence de contraintes de débouchés, Annales d'Economie et de Statistique 2 (1986), 117–146.
204. J. Muellbauer and R. Portes, Macroeconomic models with quantity rationing, Economic Journal 88 (1978), 788–821.
205. H.H. Muller, "Fiscal Policies in a General Equilibirum Model with Persistent Unemployment", Springer-Verlag, Berlin and New York, 1983.
206. H.H. Muller and U. Schweizer, Temporary equilbrium in a money economy, Journal of Economic Theory 19 (1978), 267–286.
207. J.P. Neary, Nontraded goods and the balance of trade in a neo-Keynesian temporary equilibrium, Quarterly Journal of Economics 95 (1980), 403–430.
208. J.P. Neary and K.W.S. Roberts, The theory of household behavior under rationing, European Economic Review 13 (1980), 25–42.
209. J.P. Neary and J.E. Stiglitz, Towards a reconstruction of Keynesian economics: Expectations and constrained equilibria, Quarterly Journal of Economics 98 (1983), Suppl., 199–228.
210. T. Negishi, Monopolistic competition and general equilibrium, Review of Economic Studies 28 (1961), 195–201.
211. T. Negishi, Existence of an underemployment equilibrium, in G. Schwödiauer (ed.) [228], 1977.
212. T. Negishi, "Microeconomic Foundations of Keynesian Macroeconomics", North Holland Publ., Amsterdam, 1979.
213. R.F. Owen, A two country disequilibrium model, Journal of International Economics 18 (1985), 339–355.
214. D. Patinkin, "Money, Interest, and Prices", Harper, New York, 2nd ed., 1965.
215. T. Person and L.E.O. Svensson, Is optimism good in a Keynesian economy?, Economica 50 (1983), 291–300.
216. P. Picard, Inflation and growth in a disequilibrium macroeconomic model, Journal of Economic Theory 30 (1983), 266–295.
217. P. Picard, Choc pétrolier et politique économique: Une analyse de déséquilibre, in P.Y. Hénin, W. Marois and P. Michel (eds.) [143], 1985.
218. P. Picard, "Théorie du Déséquilibre et Politique Economique", Economica, Paris, 1985.
219. V.M. Polterovich, Optimal allocations of commodities under disequilibrium prices, Economics and Mathematical Method 16 (1980), 746–759 (in Russian).

220. V.M. POLTEROVICH, Efficient allocations of commodities under fixed retail prices, in Pekka Sutela (ed.), ''Proceeding of the 5th Finnish-Soviet symposium in economics'', N° 18, Finnish-Soviet Committee on Scientific-Technological Cooperation, Helsinki, 1983.
221. V.M. POLTEROVICH, Equilibrated states and optimal allocations of resources under rigid prices, mimeo, CEMI, USSR Academy of Sciences, Moscow, 1986.
222. R. PORTES, Macroeconomic equilibrium and disequilibrium in centrally planned economies, *Economic Inquiry* **19** (1981), 559–578.
223. R. PORTES and D. WINTER, Disequilibrium estimates for consumption goods markets in centrally planned economies, *Review of Economic Studies* **47** (1980), 137–159.
224. R.E. QUANDT, Econometric disequilibrium models, *Econometric Review* **1** (1982), 1–63.
225. Y. RICHELLE, Essays in temporary equilibrium theory, Thèse de Doctorat, Université de Namur, 1986.
226. U.K. SCHITTKO and B. ECKWERT, A two-country temporary equilibrium model with quantity rationing, *Jahrbeucher für Nationalökonomie und Statistik* **198** (1983), 97–121.
227. N. SCHULZ, On the global uniqueness of fix-price equilibria, *Econometrica* **51** (1983), 47–68.
228. G. SCHWODIAUER (ed.), ''Equilibrium and Disequilibrium in Economic Theory'', Reidel Publ., Boston, 1977.
229. A. SHAH, Keynesian multipliers in temporary equilibrium with consumer credit rationing, *Journal of Economic Theory* **22** (1980), 107–112.
230. J. SILVESTRE, A model of general equilibrium with monopolistic behaviour, *Journal of Economic Theory* **16** (1977), 425–442.
231. J. SILVESTRE, Continua of Hahn-unsatisfactory equilibria, *Economic Letters* **5** (1980), 201–208.
232. J. SILVESTRE, Fix-price analysis of exchange economies, *Journal of Economic Theory* **26** (1980), 28–58.
233. J. SILVESTRE, Fix-price analysis in productive economies, *Journal of Economic Theory* **30** (1983), 401–409.
234. A. SIMONOVITS, Buffer stocks and naïve expectations in a non-Walrasian dynamic macromodel: Stability, cyclicity, and chaos, *Scandinavian Journal of Economics* **84** (1982), 571–581.
235. H.R. SNEESSENS, ''Theory and Estimation of Macroeconomic Rationing Models'', Springer-Verlag, Berlin and New York, 1981.
236. H.R. SNEESSENS, Rationing macroeconomics, a graphical exposition, *European Economic Review* **26** (1984), 187–201.
237. R.M. SOLOW and J.E. STIGLITZ, Output, employment, and wages in the short run, *Quarterly Journal of Economics* **82** (1968), 537–560.
238. D. SONDERMANN, Keynesian unemployment as non-Walrasian equilibria, *in* G.R. Feiwel (ed.), ''Issues in Contemporary Macroeconomics and Distribution'', Macmillan, London, 1985.
239. S.E. SPEAR and S. SRIVASTAVA, Markov rational expectations equilibria in

an overlapping generations model, *Journal of Economic Theory* **38** (1986), 35–62. Corrigendum, **39** (1986), 464–466.

240. D.O. STAHL II, Temporary equilibrium with storable commodities, *Journal of Economic Theory* **42** (1987), 262–274.

241. D.O. STAHL II, Relaxing the sure-solvency conditions in temporary equilibrium models, *Journal of Economic Theory* **37** (1985), 1–18.

242. D.O. STAHL II, Bankruptcy in temporary equilibria forward markets with and without institutional restrictions, *Review of Economic Studies* **52** (1985), 459–471.

243. E. STEIGUM, Keynesian and classical unemployment in an open economy, *Scandinavian Journal of Economics* **82** (1980), 147–166.

244. E. STEIGUM, Capital shortage and classical unemployment, *International Economic Review* **24** (1983), 461–477.

245. J.E. STIGLITZ, Theories of wage rigidity, NBER Working paper 1442, 1984.

246. S. STROM and L. WERIN (eds.), "Topics in Disequilibrium Economics", Macmillan, London, 1978.

247. L.E.O. SVENSSON, Sequences of temporary equilibria, stationary point expectations and Pareto efficiency, *Journal of Economic Theory* **13** (1976), 169–183.

248. L.E.O. SVENSSON, Effective demand and stochastic rationing, *Review of Economic Studies* **47** (1980), 339–355.

249. L.E.O. SVENSSON, Money and asset prices in a cash-in-advance economy, *Journal of Political Economy* **93** (1985), 919–944.

250. L.E.O. SVENSSON, Sticky goods prices, flexible asset prices, monopolistic competition, and monetary policy, *Review of Economic Studies* **53** (1986), 385–405.

251. L.G. SVENSSON, The existence of budget-constrained Pareto-efficient allocations, *Journal of Economic Theory* **32** (1984), 346–350.

252. L.G. SVENSSON and J.W. WEIBULL, Stability and efficiency from a neo-Keynesian viewpoint, *Journal of Economic Dynamics and Control* **7** (1984), 349–362.

253. G. TILLMANN, Stability in a simple pure consumption loan model, *Journal of Economic Theory* **30** (1983), 315–329.

254. G. TILLMANN, Existence and stability of rational expectation-equilibria in a simple overlapping generation model, *Journal of Economic Theory* **36** (1985), 333–351.

255. H.R. VARIAN, On persistent disequilibrium, *Journal of Economic Theory* **10** (1976), 218–227.

256. H.R. VARIAN, Non-Walrasian equilibria, *Econometrica* **45** (1977), 573–590.

257. H.R. VARIAN, The stability of a disequilibrium IS-LM model, *Scandinavian Journal of Economics* **79** (1977), 260–70. Reprinted in S. Strom and L. Werin (eds.) [246], 1978.

258. E.C.H. VEENDORP, Stable spillovers among substitutes, *Review of Economic Studies* **42** (1975), 445–456.

259. C. WEDDEPOHL, Equilibria with rationing in an economy with increasing returns, *Journal of Economic Theory* **26** (1982), 143–163.

260. C. WEDDEPOHL, Fixed price equilibria in a multifirm model, *Journal of Economic Theory* **29** (1983), 95–108.

261. J.W. WEIBULL, A dynamic model of trade frictions and disequilibrium in the housing market, *Scandinavian Journal of Economics* **85** (1983), 373–392.

262. G. WEINRICH, A prototype macroeconomic model with stochastic rationing, CORE Discussion paper, Université Catholique de Louvain, 1983.

263. G. WEINRICH, On the theory of effective demand under stochastic rationing, *Journal of Economic Theory* **34** (1984), 95–115.

264. J. WERNER, Arbitrage and the existence of a competitive equilibrium, Discussion paper, University of Bonn, 1986.

265. M. WICKENS, Are time series forecasts self-falsifying? A study of expectations formation, mimeo, University of Southampton, 1982.

266. M. WOODFORD, Learning to believe in sunspots, mimeo, University of Chicago, 1986.

267. J. YELLEN, Efficiency wage models of unemployment, *American Economic Review Proceedings* **74** (1984), 200–205.

268. Y. YOUNÈS, Sur les notions d'équilibre et de déséquilibre utilisées dans les modèles décrivant l'évolution d'une économie capitaliste, Working paper, CEPREMAP, Paris, 1970.

269. Y. YOUNÈS, On the role of money in the exchange process and the existence of a non-Walrasian equilibrium, *Review of Economic Studies* **42** (1975), 489–501.

270. Y. YOUNÈS, Dévaluation et équilibre avec rationnement, *Economie Appliquée* **31** (1978), 85–112.

271. Y. YOUNÈS, On equilibria with quantity rationing, *in* W. Hildenbrand (ed.), "Advances in Economic Theory", Cambridge University Press, Cambridge and New York, 1982.

272. Y. YOUNÈS, Implementation of plans or contracts and equilibria with rationing, CARESS Working paper, University of Pennsylvania, Philadelphia, 1983.

273. Y. YOUNÈS, General competitive equilibrium with asymmetric information and signalling, CARESS Working paper 8422, University of Pennsylvania, Philadelphia, 1984.

274. A. ZYLBERGERG, Migration equilibrium with price rigidity: The Harris and Todaro model revisited, *Journal of Economic Theory* **37** (1985), 281–309.

CHAPTER **II**

Decision Making

Continuity Properties
of a von Neumann–Morgenstern Utility

Jean-Michel Grandmont

*Centre d'Études Prospectives d'Économie Mathématiques Appliquées à la Planification,
Paris, France*

Received October 23, 1970

1. Introduction

A possible formulation of the problem of a player who must make a decision under uncertainty is the following one. Let Y be the set of all possible *consequences* of the game, and $B(Y)$ be a σ-field of subsets of Y. The player must make a choice among a set P of probability measures defined on the measurable space $(Y, B(Y))$. Each element of P is called a *lottery ticket*.

By assumption, the player's preferences among lottery tickets can be expressed by a binary relation $\succsim^{\ell}$ on P, which is reflexive, transitive, and complete. Any real-valued representation h of the preference relation $\succsim^{\ell}$ is called a *Bernoulli index*. The problem of the existence of such an index has been studied under various assumptions as, for instance, in [13, 19, 10, 4, and 17] and, more recently, in [7, 18, and 8].

It is quite natural to assume that the player also has preferences among sure consequences which can be expressed by a binary relation $\succsim^{c}$ on Y, which is also reflexive, transitive, and complete. An interesting question is to find conditions under which there exists a real-valued representation u of the preferences $\succsim^{c}$ such that the function defined by $h(p) = \int_Y u \, dp$ for every p in P (whenever the integral exists) is a Bernoulli index. Such a representation u is called a *von Neumann–Morgenstern utility*. This problem has also been extensively studied in the literature.

The question of the existence of a *continuous* Bernoulli index and a *continuous* von Neumann–Morgenstern utility, which is of importance in many applications, seems to have received much less attention, except recently in [2, 18], and, to some extent, in [8]. A precise answer to this problem requires a topology both on the set of consequences Y and on the set of lotteries P. The approach which is used here is to start from the assumption that Y is a metric space. The set P is then endowed with

Reprinted from *Journal of Economic Theory* 4 (1972),
45–57, © 1972 by Academic Press, Inc.

the topology of weak convergence of probability measures. It turns out that the study of the existence and continuity of a von Neumann–Morgenstern utility is quite simple (Section 3). The application of this technique to the study of more general decision problems under uncertainty gives apparently new results which are stated in Section 4.

2. DEFINITIONS AND NOTATIONS

Let Y be a metric space, $B(Y)$ its Borel σ-field, i.e., the σ-field generated by its open sets. Let $M(Y)$ be the space of all (countably additive) probability measures defined on the measurable space $(Y, B(Y))$. The space $M(Y)$ is endowed with the topology of weak convergence [15, Chap. 2, Section 6]. In the following, P will denote any (topological) subspace of $M(Y)$. For any element y in Y, p_y will mean the element of $M(Y)$ which assigns probability 1 to the Borel set $\{y\}$. D will be the (topological) subspace of $M(Y)$ defined by $D = \{p \in M(Y) \mid p = p_y \text{ for some } y \text{ in } Y\}$.

In what follows, it will be assumed that a complete preordering is defined on Y or on a subspace P of $M(Y)$. A *preordering* $\gtrsim$ defined on a set X is a binary relation which is reflexive ($x \gtrsim x$ for all x in X) and transitive ($x \gtrsim y$ and $y \gtrsim z$ imply $x \gtrsim z$). The preordering is complete if for any x, y in X, $x \gtrsim y$ or $y \gtrsim x$ is true. The equivalence relation which can be derived from $\gtrsim$ is noted $\sim$: then $x \sim y$ means $x \gtrsim y$ and $y \gtrsim x$. Finally, $x > y$ means that $y \gtrsim x$ is not true. A real-valued function u defined on X is *order-preserving* with respect to the complete preordering $\gtrsim$ if $u(x) \geqslant u(y)$ is equivalent to $x \gtrsim y$.

For any p_1 and p_2 in $M(Y)$ and any real number t in $[0, 1]$, the relation [for any S in $B(Y)$, $p(S) = tp_1(S) + (1 - t)p_2(S)$] defines an element p of $M(Y)$ which is noted $tp_1 + (1 - t)p_2$. A subspace P of $M(Y)$ is *convex* if, for any p_1 and p_2 in P, $tp_1 + (1 - t)p_2$ belongs to P for any real number t in $[0, 1]$. For any sequence $\{p^m, m \geqslant 1\}$ of elements of $M(Y)$ and any sequence of nonnegative real numbers $\{\lambda^m, m \geqslant 1\}$ such that $\sum_1^\infty \lambda^m = 1$, the relation [for any S in $B(Y)$, $p^0(S) = \sum_1^\infty \lambda^m p^m(S)$] defines an element p^0 of $M(Y)$ which is noted $\sum_1^\infty \lambda^m p^m$. A subspace P of $M(Y)$ is *σ-convex* if, for any sequence $\{p^m, m \geqslant 1\}$ of elements of P and any sequence of nonnegative real numbers $\{\lambda^m, m \geqslant 1\}$ such that $\sum_1^\infty \lambda^m = 1$, $p^0 = \sum_1^\infty \lambda^m p^m$ belongs to P. The following result is useful.

LEMMA 1. *If $P \subset M(Y)$ is convex and closed in $M(Y)$, it is σ-convex.*

Proof. Choose $\{p^m \in P, m \geqslant 1\}$ and $\{\lambda^m, m \geqslant 1\}$, $\lambda^m \geqslant 0$, $\sum_1^\infty \lambda^m = 1$. We can assume without loss of generality $\lambda^1 > 0$. Define for all $m \geqslant 1$,

$q^m = \sum_1^m (\lambda^i/(\sum_1^m \lambda^k)) p^i$. Since P is convex, $q^m \in P$. But for all S in $B(Y)$, $\lim q^m(S) = p^0(S)$ where $p^0 = \sum_1^\infty \lambda^m p^m$, which implies [15, Chap. 2, Theorem 6.1] that q^m converges weakly to p^0. Hence, $p^0 \in P$ since P is closed.

Q.E.D.

A real-valued function h defined on a convex (resp. σ-convex) subspace P of $M(Y)$ is *linear* (resp. *σ-linear*) if, for any p_1 and p_2 in P, and any real number t in $[0, 1]$, one has $h(tp_1 + (1 - t)p_2) = th(p_1) + (1 - t)h(p_2)$ (resp. for any sequence $\{p^m, m \geq 1\}$ of elements of P and any sequence of nonnegative real numbers $\{\lambda^m, m \geq 1\}$ such that $\sum_1^\infty \lambda^m = 1$, one has $h(\sum_1^\infty \lambda^m) = \sum_1^\infty \lambda^m h(p^m)$). The following lemma is very useful.

LEMMA 2. *Let h be a real-valued function defined on a σ-convex subspace P of $M(Y)$. If h is continuous and linear, it is σ-linear and bounded on P.*

Proof. (1) h is σ-linear: choose a sequence $\{p^m \in P, m \geq 1\}$ and a sequence $\{\lambda^m, m \geq 1\}$ of nonnegative real numbers such that $\sum_1^\infty \lambda^m = 1$. Since, without loss of generality, $\lambda^1 > 0$, one can define for all $m \geq 1$, $q^m = \sum_1^m (\lambda^i/(\sum_1^m \lambda^k)) p^i$. Since P is convex, $q^m \in P$, and we saw in Lemma 1 that q^m converges weakly to $p^0 = \sum_1^\infty \lambda^m p^m$. Moreover, $p^0 \in P$ since P is σ-convex. Now the linearity of h implies that

$$h(q^m) = \left(1/\left(\sum_1^m \lambda^k\right)\right)\left(\sum_1^m \lambda^i h(p^i)\right)$$

and from the continuity of h, $h(p^0) = \sum_1^\infty \lambda^i h(p^i)$. Therefore, h is σ-linear on P. (2) h is bounded: assume that h is unbounded above, and choose a sequence $\{p^m \in P, m \geq 1\}$ such that $h(p^m) > 2^m$. Then $p^0 = \sum_1^\infty (\frac{1}{2}m) p^m$ belongs to P, and from (1), $h(p^0) = \sum_1^\infty (\frac{1}{2}m) h(p^m)$. But this is impossible since for every m, $\sum_1^m (\frac{1}{2}i) h(p^i) > m$. This contradiction shows that h is bounded above, and a similar reasoning shows that h is bounded below.

Q.E.D.

3. EXISTENCE OF A CONTINUOUS VON NEUMANN–MORGENSTERN UTILITY

Conditions for the existence of a continuous Bernoulli index are first given.

THEOREM 1. *Let Y be a separable metric space. Let $\succsim$ be a complete preordering defined on a subspace P of $M(Y)$. There exists a real-valued continuous function h defined on P which is order-preserving with respect to $\succsim$ if and only if, for any p_0 in P, the sets $\{p \in P \mid p \succsim p_0\}$ and $\{p \in P \mid p_0 \succsim p\}$ are closed in P.*

Proof. If such a function h exists, for any p_0 in P, the set $\{p \in P \mid p \overset{\ell}{\succsim} p_0\}$ is closed in P as the inverse image by the continuous function h of the closed set $\{t \in R \mid t \geqslant h(p_0)\}$ of the real line R. The same reasoning is valid for sets of the form $\{p \in P \mid p_0 \overset{\ell}{\succsim} p\}$. Conversely, $M(Y)$ can be metrized as a separable metric space [15, Chap. 2, Theorem 6.2] and so can P. Hence, P has a countable base of open sets [11, Chap. 4, Theorem 11], and the result follows from [6, Proposition 3].   Q.E.D.

The next step is to find conditions ensuring the existence of a continuous Bernoulli index which is linear.

THEOREM 2. *Let Y be a separable metric space. Let $\overset{\ell}{\succsim}$ be a complete preordering defined on a convex subspace P of $M(Y)$. A set of necessary and sufficient conditions for the existence of a real-valued continuous function h defined on P which is order-preserving with respect to $\overset{\ell}{\succsim}$ and linear is:*

(1) *for any p_0 in P, the sets $\{p \in P \mid p \overset{\ell}{\succsim} p_0\}$ and $\{p \in P \mid p_0 \overset{\ell}{\succsim} p\}$ are closed in P;*

(2) *for any p_1, p_2, and p_3 in P and any real number t in $[0, 1]$, $p_1 \overset{\ell}{\sim} p_2$ implies $t p_1 + (1-t) p_3 \overset{\ell}{\sim} t p_2 + (1-t) p_3$.*

Proof. The existence of a continuous function h implies (1) according to Theorem 1. The fact that the linearity of h implies (2) is straightforward. Let us prove the converse proposition. If $p_1 \overset{\ell}{\sim} p_2$ for any p_1, p_2 in P, any function h defined by $h(p) = t_0$ for all p in P satisfies the requirements. From now on, we shall assume the existence of two elements r_1, r_2 in P such that $r_1 \overset{\ell}{\succ} r_2$. We next show: (a) for any p_1, p_2, p_3 in P, the sets $\{t \in [0, 1] \mid t p_1 + (1-t) p_2 \overset{\ell}{\succsim} p_3\}$ and $\{t \in [0, 1] \mid p_3 \overset{\ell}{\succsim} t p_1 + (1-t) p_2\}$ are closed.

Fix p_1, p_2, p_3 in P and take a sequence t^m in $[0, 1]$ which converges to t^0, such that $p^m = t^m p_1 + (1 - t^m) p_2 \overset{\ell}{\succsim} p_3$. Now p^m converges weakly to $p^0 = t^0 p_1 + (1 - t^0) p_2 \in P$, and this implies that, by continuity, $p^0 \overset{\ell}{\succsim} p_3$. Hence the set $\{t \in [0, 1] \mid t p_1 + (1 - t) p_2 \overset{\ell}{\succsim} p_3\}$ is closed and a similar reasoning shows that the same is true for $\{t \in [0, 1] \mid p_3 \overset{\ell}{\succsim} t p_1 + (1 - t) p_2\}$. This proves (a).

It follows, according to [10, Theorem 8], that there exists a real-valued function h defined on P which is order-preserving with respect to $\overset{\ell}{\succsim}$, and linear. Such a function is constructed in [10] in the following way. For any a, b in P such that $a \overset{\ell}{\succsim} b$, one defines $P_{ab} = \{p \in P \mid a \overset{\ell}{\succsim} p \overset{\ell}{\succsim} b\}$. Then, for any p in P_{ab} there exists a unique element $h_{ab}(p)$ in $[0, 1]$ such that $p \overset{\ell}{\sim} h_{ab}(p) a + (1 - h_{ab}(p)) b$ [10, Theorem 6]. Consider now two fixed elements r_1, r_2 in P such that $r_1 \overset{\ell}{\succ} r_2$. For any p in P, let a, b be two

90

elements of P such that $a \overset{\ell}{\succsim} b$ and p, r_1, r_2 belong to P_{ab}. Then $h(p)$ is defined as $\{h_{ab}(p) - h_{ab}(r_2))/(h_{ab}(r_1) - h_{ab}(r_2))$. According to [10, Theorems 7 and 8], this value does not depend on the particular choice of the couple (a, b) and the function h so defined is order-preserving with respect to $\succsim$ and linear. We have only to show that with our stronger assumptions, this function h is continuous. It is easy to check that, when a and b are fixed with $a \succsim b$, h_{ab} is continuous on P_{ab}. Since $M(Y)$ is metrizable [15, Chap. 2, Theorem 6.2] and $h_{ab}(p) \in [0, 1]$, a compact, it is sufficient [14, Lemma 4.4] to show that the graph of h_{ab} is sequentially closed. Take $p^0 \in P_{ab}$ and a sequence $p^m \in P_{ab}$ converging weakly to p^0. Let $t^m = h_{ab}(p^m)$, and assume that $\lim t^m = t^0$. We wish $t^0 = h_{ab}(p^0)$. According to Theorem 1, there exists a continuous real-valued function g defined on P which is order-preserving with respect to $\overset{\ell}{\succsim}$. Therefore, $g(p^m) = g(t^m a + (1 - t^m) b)$. Since the sequence $(t^m a + (1 - t^m) b)$ converges weakly to $t^0 a + (1 - t^0) b$, in the limit $g(p^0) = g(t^0 a + (1 - t^0) b)$, which shows $t^0 = h_{ab}(p^0)$.

The last step is to prove that h is itself continuous. Fix p^0 in P. Since P is metrizable, it is sufficient to take a sequence $p^m \in P$ which converges weakly to p^0 and to prove $\lim h(p^m) = h(p^0)$. Assume first that there are two elements a, b in P such that $a \overset{\ell}{\succ} p^0 \overset{\ell}{\succ} b$. Then one can choose a and b so that r_1 and r_2 belong to P_{ab} and one can define h relatively to (a, b). For m large enough, one has $a \overset{\ell}{\succ} p^m \overset{\ell}{\succ} b$ and the continuity of h follows from that of h_{ab} on P_{ab}. If for every p in P, one has $p^0 \overset{\ell}{\succsim} p$, one defines h relatively to the couple (p^0, r_2). For m large enough, $p^m \overset{\ell}{\succ} r_2$ and the continuity of h is clear. A similar reasoning is made in the case where $p \overset{\ell}{\succsim} p^0$ for any p in P. This completes the proof.   Q.E.D.

COROLLARY. *Under the assumptions of Theorem 2, if P is σ-convex any Bernoulli index h which is continuous and linear is bounded and σ-linear.*

Proof. This is an immediate consequence of Lemma 2.   Q.E.D.

The question of the existence of a continuous von Neumann–Morgenstern utility is dealt with now. We recall that D is the subspace of $M(Y)$ defined by $\{p \in M(Y) \mid p = p_y \text{ for some } y \text{ in } Y\}$.

THEOREM 3. *Let Y be a separable metric space, completely preordered by $\overset{c}{\succsim}$. Let $\overset{\ell}{\succsim}$ be a complete preordering defined on a σ-convex subspace P of $M(Y)$ such that $D \subset P$. A set of necessary and sufficient conditions for the existence of a real-valued continuous bounded function u defined on Y, order-preserving with respect to $\overset{c}{\succsim}$ such that the function h defined on P by $h(p) = \int_Y u \, dp$ is order-preserving with respect to $\overset{\ell}{\succsim}$ is:*

(1) *for any p_0 in P, the sets $\{p \in P \mid p \overset{\ell}{\gtrsim} p_0\}$ and $\{p \in P \mid p_0 \overset{\ell}{\gtrsim} p\}$ are closed in P;*

(2) *for any p_1, p_2, p_3 in P and any real number t in $[0, 1]$, $p_1 \overset{\ell}{\sim} p_2$ implies $tp_1 + (1 - t) p_3 \overset{\ell}{\sim} tp_2 + (1 - t) p_3$;*

(3) *for any y and y' in Y, $y \overset{c}{\gtrsim} y'$ is equivalent to $p_y \overset{\ell}{\gtrsim} p_{y'}$.*

Proof. (a) The conditions are necessary. Assume that a function u meeting the above requirements exists and let $h(p) = \int_Y u \, dp$. It follows that for any y in Y, $u(y) = h(p_y)$ and (3) is satisfied. In order to prove that h is continuous, take $p^0 \in P$ and a sequence $\{p^m \in P, m \geqslant 1\}$ converging weakly to p^0. Since P is metrizable, it suffices to show $\lim \int_Y u \, dp^m = \int_Y u \, dp^0$. But this is precisely the definition of weak convergence, since u is continuous and bounded [15, Chap. 2, Section 6]. The fact that h is linear is immediate. Therefore, (1) and (2) hold, according to Theorem 2.

(b) The conditions are sufficient. According to Theorem 2 and its corollary, there exists a real-valued function h defined on P which is continuous, bounded, order-preserving, and linear. Define for any y in Y, $u(y) = h(p_y)$. It is clear that u is order-preserving with respect to $\overset{c}{\gtrsim}$ and is bounded. The fact that it is continuous follows immediately from [15, Chap. 2, Lemma 6.1]. It remains to show that for any p in P, $h(p) = \int_Y u \, dp$. Any element p of $M(Y)$ which has a finite support $\{y_1, ..., y_i, ..., y_m\}$ belongs to P since $p = \sum_1^m \lambda_i p_{y_i}$, where λ_i is the probability assigned by p to $\{y_i\}$. Since h is linear, one has:

$$h(p) = \sum_1^m \lambda_i h(p_{y_i}) = \sum_1^m \lambda_i u(y_i) = \int_Y u \, dp.$$

Now, any element p of P is the limit in the topology of weak convergence of a sequence of probability measures $p^m \in P$, each of whom has a finite support [15, Theorems 6.2 and 6.3]. Therefore, for every m, $h(p^m) = \int_Y u \, dp^m$. But $\lim h(p^m) = h(p)$ follows from the continuity of h. Moreover, $\lim \int_Y u \, dp^m = \int_Y u \, dp$ since u is continuous and bounded. Therefore, for any p in P, $h(p) = \int_Y u \, dp$. Q.E.D.

4. CONTINUITY OF AN ACTION'S EXPECTED UTILITY

Let us consider now the player in a more realistic situation. Let X be the set of all possible *actions* available to him. An element x of X specifies all the variables the player controls. On the other hand, the player observes an element t of the set of *observations* T, which specifies all the variables which are beyond his control but are known by him when he makes a decision. The variables which the player does not know at the moment of his choice are described by a point z of the space of *unknown states of nature* Z. The set of all possible *consequences* of the game is denoted as before by Y.

In the remainder of this paper, X, T and Z are assumed to be topological spaces. Furthermore, Z is assumed to be a metric space, $B(Z)$ will denote its Borel σ-field, and $M(Z)$ will be the space of all (countably additive) probability measures defined on $(Z, B(Z))$ endowed with the topology of weak convergence. As before, Y is a metric space, $B(Y)$ is its Borel σ-field, and $M(Y)$ is the space of *lottery tickets* endowed with the topology of weak convergence. The agent's preferences among consequences (resp. lottery tickets) are expressed as before by a complete preordering $\gtrsim$ (resp. $\gtrsim$) defined on Y (resp. $M(Y)$).

It is assumed that the player has definite a priori beliefs concerning the unknown state of nature, which take the form of an element of the space of *expectations* $M(Z)$. The agent may feel that the state of nature which will obtain is stochastically dependent upon the current observation. In addition, he may believe that he is able to exercice a stochastic control on the state of nature through his action. Therefore, the pattern of the player's a priori beliefs is summarized by a mapping ψ taking $X \times T$ into $M(Z)$. The value associated to $(x, t) \in X \times T$ is noted $\psi(x, t)$, and for any A in $B(Z)$, $\psi(x, t, A)$ will mean the probability assigned by the player to the event A when t observed and x is chosen.

It remains to define what will be the consequences of an action $x \in X$ when the state $z \in Z$ obtains. It is clear that these consequences may depend upon the element $t \in T$ which is currently observed. The player is therefore given a mapping φ taking $X \times T \times Z$ into Y, the space of consequences.

By assumption, the player's preferences among actions are expressed by a complete preordering defined on X. These preferences will reflect his more basic preferences among consequences, among lottery tickets, his expectations and the mapping φ. Since the player's expectations depend upon the observation t, it is clear that the preordering on X may also depend on t. We are therefore given *a family of complete preorderings* $\{\gtrsim_t^a ; t \in T\}$. Then $x \gtrsim_t^a x'$ is to be read: when t is observed, the action x' is not preferred to the action x.

The first thing to do is to offer a consistent explanation of these preferences among actions and to show how they are related to the more basic preorderings $\gtrsim^c$ on Y and $\gtrsim^\ell$ on $M(Y)$. This is easy if we make the natural assumption that for any (x, t) in $X \times T$, the function $\hat{\varphi}_{x,t} = \varphi(x, t, \cdot)$ from Z to Y is measurable (this is the case if φ is continuous on $X \times T \times Z$).

For, given $(x, t) \in X \times T$, $\hat{\varphi}_{x,t}$ determines a lottery $\hat{p}$ by [for every S in $B(Y)$, $\hat{p}(S) = \psi(x, t, \hat{\varphi}_{x,t}^{-1}(S))$]. This lottery will be noted $\hat{p}(x, t)$. It is then natural to assume that the family $\{\succsim_t^a ; t \in T\}$ obeys the following simple rule: given any t in T, for any x and x' in X, $x \succsim_t^a x'$ if and only if $\hat{p}(x, t) \succsim^\ell \hat{p}(x', t)$.

In many applications, it is important to have a real-valued representation v of the family of complete preorderings $\{\succsim_t^a ; t \in T\}$ (i.e., given $t \in T$, for any x and x' in X, $v(x, t) \geqslant v(x', t)$ is equivalent to $x \succsim_t^a x'$) which is continuous on $X \times T$. In the remainder of the study, such a function will be called a continuous representation of the family $\{\succsim_t^a ; t \in T\}$. Conditions ensuring the existence of such a representation are examined now. Before we do that, we recall that a topological space satisfies the first axiom of countability if each of its elements has a countable base of neighborhoods.

THEOREM 4. *Let X, T satisfy the first axiom of countability. Let Y and Z be separable metric spaces. Let $\succsim^c$ and $\succsim^\ell$ be complete preorderings defined respectively on Y and $M(Y)$. Assume*:

(1) *for any p_0 in $M(Y)$, the sets $\{p \in M(Y) \mid p \succsim^\ell p_0\}$ and $\{p \in M(Y) \mid p_0 \succsim^\ell p\}$ are closed in $M(Y)$;*

(2) *for any p_1, p_2, p_3 in $M(Y)$ and any real number t in $[0, 1]$, $p_1 \sim^\ell p_2$ implies $tp_1 + (1 - t) p_3 \sim^\ell tp_2 + (1 - t) p_3$;*

(3) *for any y and y' in Y, $y \succsim^c y'$ is equivalent to $p_y \succsim^\ell p_{y'}$;*

(4) *the mappings $\varphi : X \times T \times Z \to Y$ and $\psi : X \times T \to M(Z)$ are continuous*;

then, given t in T, the relation $[x \succsim_t^a x'$ if and only if $\hat{p}(x, t) \succsim^\ell \hat{p}(x', t)]$ defines a complete preordering $\succsim_t^a$ on X. Further, there exists a continuous, bounded real-valued function u defined on Y, order-preserving with respect to $\succsim^c$, such that the function v defined on $X \times T$ by

$$v(x, t) = \int_Z u(\varphi(x, t, \cdot)) \, d\psi(x, t, \cdot)$$

is a continuous representation of the family $\{\succsim_t^a ; t \in T\}$.

Proof. According to Theorem 3, there exists a real-valued function u which is continuous, bounded on Y and is order-preserving with respect to $\succsim^c$, such that $h(p) = \int_Y u \, dp$ is order-preserving with respect to $\succsim^\ell$. The function v defined on $X \times T$ by $v(x, t) = h(\hat{p}(x, t))$ is clearly a representation of the family $\{\succsim_t^a ; t \in T\}$. Now for all (x, t) in $X \times T$,

$$\int_Z u(\varphi(x, t, \cdot)) \, d\psi(x, t, \cdot) = \int_Y u \, d\hat{p}(x, t)$$

holds according to [9, Section 39, Theorem C]. It remains to show that v is continuous on $X \times T$.

Pick (x^0, t^0) in $X \times T$ and choose any sequence $\{(x^m, t^m), m \geqslant 1\}$ of elements of $X \times T$ converging to (x^0, t^0). We wish $\lim v(x^m, t^m) = v(x^0, t^0)$. Now the sequence of continuous real valued functions $u(\varphi(x^m, t^m, \cdot))$ is uniformly bounded and converges continuously to $u(\varphi(x^0, t^0, \cdot))$ on Z (see Section 5 for a definition). Moreover, the sequence $\psi(x^m, t^m)$ converges weakly to $\psi(x^0, t^0)$. Therefore, by Theorem A.3 of Section 5, $\lim v(x^m, t^m) = v(x^0, t^0)$.

Q.E.D.

This theorem justifies a posteriori the title of this section, for $u(y)$ may be interpreted as the "utility" of the consequence y. Then $u(\varphi(x, t, z))$ is the utility of the consequence of the action x when t is observed and z obtains. Therefore $v(x, t)$ may be interpreted as the expected utility of the action x when t is observed.

The above analysis unfortunately may not apply in some economic problems. For we assumed that φ was a function from $X \times T \times Z$ into Y while, in usual economic contexts, the consequences of (x, t, z) are often given by a nonempty subset $\varphi(x, t, z)$ of Y, i.e., φ is a correspondence. When trying to relate the family $\{\gtrsim_t^a ; t \in T\}$ to the preordering $\gtrsim^\ell$, the difficulty is that, given (x, t), the correspondence $\varphi(x, t, \cdot)$ from Z to Y does not seem to induce any probability distribution on the measurable space $(Y, B(Y))$. But there is an easy solution.

Let us call $\beta(x, t)$ the set of all measurable functions g from Z to Y which satisfy $g(z) \in \varphi(x, t, z)$ for all z in Z. Then, any g in $\beta(x, t)$ considered as a random variable defined on the probability space $(Z, B(Z), \psi(x, t))$ induces a probability measure on $(Y, B(Y))$, i.e., a lottery ticket, noted $\hat{p}(x, t, g)$. We shall make assumptions ensuring that $\beta(x, t)$ is nonvoid for all (x, t), and further, that $\hat{p}(x, t, g_1) \overset{\ell}{\sim} \hat{p}(x, t, g_2)$ whenever g_1 and g_2 belong to the same $\beta(x, t)$. On can therefore associate to any (x, t) an induced $\gtrsim^\ell$-equivalence class of $M(Y)$ (instead of a single element when φ is a function), noted $\pi(x, t)$. It is then natural to say that $x \gtrsim_t^a x'$ if and only if $\pi(x, t) \gtrsim^\ell \pi(x', t)$.

It is clear that we must make assumptions on the continuity of the correspondence φ, if we want to find a continuous representation of the family $\{\gtrsim_t^a ; t \in T\}$. To this effect, we recall a few definitions. Let ξ be a correspondence from a topological space L into a topological space N. For any subset G of N, the *strong inverse* of G is $\xi^s(G) = \{\ell \in L \mid \xi(\ell) \subset G\}$ and the *weak inverse* of G is $\xi^w(G) = \{\ell \in L \mid \xi(\ell) \cap G$ is nonempty$\}$. A correspondence ξ is *upper hemicontinuous* (u.h.c.) if $\xi^s(G)$ is open whenever G is open (or equivalently, if $\xi^w(G)$ is closed when G is closed). It is *lower hemicontinous* (l.h.c.) if $\xi^s(G)$ is closed when G is closed (or equivalently, if $\xi^w(G)$ is open when G is open). The correspondence ξ is *closed-valued* if $\xi(\ell)$ is closed in N for all ℓ in L. We can now state our result:

THEOREM 5.   *Let* X, Y, Z, T *be as in Theorem* 4. *Let* $\succsim^c$ *and* $\succsim^\ell$ *be complete preorderings defined on* Y *and* $M(Y)$ *respectively, satisfying* (1), (2), (3) *of Theorem* 4. *Assume:*

(4a)   *The correspondence* $\varphi : X \times T \times Z \to Y$ *is closed-valued, u.h.c. and/or l.h.c.;*

(4b)   *for all* (x, t, z), $y_1 \overset{c}{\sim} y_2$ *holds whenever* y_1 *and* y_2 *belong to* $\varphi(x, t, z)$;

(4c)   *the mapping* $\psi : X \times T \to M(Z)$ *is continous;*

then, if Y *is complete, given* t *in* T, *the relation* $[x \succsim_t^a x'$ *if and only if* $\hat{p}(x, t, g) \succsim^\ell \hat{p}(x', t, g')$ *for some* g *in* $\beta(x, t)$ *and* g' *in* $\beta(x', t)]$ *defines a complete preordering* $\succsim_t^a$ *on* X. *Further, there is a continuous bounded real-valued function* u *defined on* Y, *order-preserving with respect to* $\succsim^c$, *such that the function* v *defined on* $X \times T$ *by*

$$v(x, t) = \int_Z \bar{u}(x, t, \cdot)\, d\psi(x, t, \cdot)$$

(where $\bar{u}(x, t, z) = u(y)$ *for some* y *in* $\varphi(x, t, z)$*) is a continuous representation of the family* $\{\succsim_t^a ; t \in T\}$.

Proof.   We first show

(i) $\beta(x, t)$ is nonempty for all (x, t).
This follows immediately from [12, Section 2, Theorem and Corollary 1].[1]
Next,

(ii)   for all (x, t), $\hat{p}(x, t, g_1) \overset{\ell}{\sim} \hat{p}(x, t, g_2)$ whenever g_1 and g_2 belong to $\beta(x, t)$.

According to Theorem 3, there exists a von Neumann–Morgenstern utjlity u, and (ii) is equivalent to

$$\int_Y u\, d\hat{p}(x, t, g_1) = \int_Y u\, d\hat{p}(x, t, g_2).$$

Applying [9, Section 39, Theorem C] we get for $i = 1, 2$:

$$\int_Y u\, d\hat{p}(x, t, g_i) = \int_Z u(g_i(x, t, \cdot))\, d\psi(x, t, \cdot)$$

Since $u(g_1(x, t, z)) = u(g_2(x, t, z))$ for all z in Z, (ii) follows.

[1] I wish to thank Werner Hildenbrand for this reference.

From (i) and (ii), it is clear that, given t in T, the relation $[x \gtrsim_t^a x'$ if and only if $\hat{p}(x, t, g) \gtrsim^t \hat{p}(x', t, g')$ for some g in $\beta(x, t)$ and g' in $\beta(x', t)]$ defines a complete preordering $\gtrsim_t^a$ on X.

Choose a von Neumann–Morgenstern utility u and define for all (x, t, z), $\bar{u}(x, t, z) = u(y)$ for some y in $\varphi(x, t, z)$. It is easy to check that $\bar{u}$ is a well-defined function and is continuous. In addition, for any g in $\beta(x, t)$ one has $\bar{u}(x, t, z) = u(g(x, t, z))$ for all z. It is therefore clear that the relation

$$v(x, t) = \int_Z \bar{u}(x, t, \cdot) \, d\psi(x, t, \cdot) = \int_Y u \, d\hat{p}(x, t, g)$$

for some g in $\beta(x, t)$ consistently defines a representation v of the family $\{\gtrsim_t^a ; t \in T\}$. One shows easily as in the proof of Theorem 4 that this representation is continuous on $X \times T$.   Q.E.D.

COROLLARY. *Theorem 5 is still valid if Y is not complete but can be imbedded as a topological subspace in a metric space Y^* which is complete and separable.*

Proof. We used completeness only to show that $\beta(x, t)$ is nonvoid for all (x, t). By [12, Section 1, Theorem and Corollary 1], this is still valid under the assumptions of this corollary.   Q.E.D.

5. MATHEMATICAL APPENDIX

Listed here are a few results which are used in the text. In the sequel, Z is a metric space, $B(Z)$ is its Borel σ-field, and $M(Z)$ is the space of all probability measures defined on $(Z, B(Z))$, endowed with the topology of weak convergence.

A family F of real-valued functions defined on Z is *equicontinuous* at $z_0 \in Z$ if for every real number $\delta > 0$, there exists a real number $\eta(\delta, z_0) > 0$ such that $d(z - z_0) < \eta(\delta, z_0)$ implies $| f(z) - f(z_0)| < \delta$ for every f in F, where d is the metric of Z.

A sequence $\{f^m, m \geqslant 1\}$ of real-valued functions defined on Z is said to *converge continuously* to f^0, a real-valued function defined on Z, at z^0 if for every sequence $\{z^m, m \geqslant 1\}$ of elements of Z converging to z^0, one has $\lim f^m(z^m) = f^0(z^0)$ (this implies $\lim f^m(z^0) = f^0(z^0)$). It is easy to show:

THEOREM A.1. *Let $F = \{f^m, m \geqslant 1\}$ be a sequence of real-valued functions defined on the metric space Z, and let $z^0 \in Z$. If*

97

(1) *for all m, f^m is continuous at z^0*;

(2) *the sequence F converges continuously to f^0 at z^0;* ·
the family is equicontinuous at z^0.

The following result can be found in [16]:

THEOREM A.2. *Let Z be a separable metric space and $\{p^m, m \geqslant 1\}$ be a sequence of probability measures belonging to $M(Z)$. Then p^m converges weakly to $p^0 \in M(Z)$ if and only if*

$$\lim_{m \to \infty} \sup_{f \in F} \left| \int_Z f \, dp^m - \int_Z f \, dp^0 \right| = 0$$

for every family F of real-valued functions defined on Z zuch that

(1) *F is uniformly bounded, i.e., there is a real number $M > 0$ such that $|f(z)| \leqslant M$ for all $z \in Z$, $f \in F$;*

(2) *F is equicontinuous at each $z \in Z$.*

Combining Theorems A.1 and A.2 we get

THEOREM A.3. *Let Z be a separable metric space. Let $\{p^m, m \geqslant 1\}$ be a sequence of elements of $M(Z)$ converging weakly to $p^0 \in M(Z)$. Then, for any family $F = \{f^m, m \geqslant 1\}$ of real-valued continuous functions defined on Z such that:*

(1) *F is uniformly bounded;*

(2) *F converges continuously to f^0 at each point z of Z;*

one has $\lim \int_Z f^m \, dp^m = \int_Z f^0 \, dp^0.$

NOTES

Theorems 2 and 3 are well known when no continuity requirement is imposed upon the utility functions: they may be found under various forms in the works quoted in Section 1. The results obtained in [10] show that the condition [for any p_1, p_2, p_3 in P (or $M(Y)$) and any real number t in $[0, 1]$, $p_1 \overset{\ell}{\sim} p_2$ implies $tp_1 + (1 - t) p_3 \overset{\ell}{\sim} tp_2 + (1 - t) p_3$] may be replaced by the weaker one [for any p_1, p_2, p_3, in P (or $M(Y)$), $p_1 \overset{\ell}{\sim} p_2$ implies $\frac{1}{2}p_1 + \frac{1}{2}p_3 \overset{\ell}{\sim} \frac{1}{2}p_2 + \frac{1}{2}p_3$]. A form of Theorem 1 is proved in [18] with other techniques. A form of Theorem 3 has been independently proved by Th. de Montbrial by using the same kind of techniques, when Y is the real line (private communication).

ACKNOWLEDGMENT

I wish to thank Professors Richard Cornwall, Gerard Debreu, and Werner Hildenbrand for many helpful suggestions. They, of course, bear no responsability for any remaining error.

REFERENCES

1. M. ALLAIS, Le comportement de l'homme rationnel devant le risque: critique des postulats de l'école americaine, *Econometrica* **21** (1953), 503–546.
2. K. J. ARROW, "Aspects of the Theory of Risk-bearing," Yrjo Jahsson Lecture Series, Helsinki, 1965.
3. P. BERNOUILLI, Specime theoria novae de mensura sortis, *Commentarii Academiæ Scientarum Imperialis Petropolitanæ*, 1738; Translated in *Econometrica* **22** (1954), 23–46).
4. D. BLACKWELL AND M. A. GIRSHICK, "Theory of Games and Statistical Decisions," John Wiley and Sons, New York, 1954.
5. R. BOWEN, A new proof of a theorem in utility theory, *Internat. Econ. Rev.* **9** (1968), 374.
6. G. DEBREU, Continuity properties of paretian utility, *Internat. Econ. Rev.* **5** (1964), 285–293.
7. P. C. FISHBURN, Bounded expected utility, *Ann. Math. Statist.* **38** (1967), 1054–1060.
8. B. GRODAL AND J. F. MERTENS, "Integral Representation of Utility Functions," Report No. 6823, C.O.R.E., Catholic University of Louvain, 1968.
9. P. R. HALMOS, "Measure Theory," Van Nostrand, Princeton, N. J., 1951.
10. I. N. HERSTEIN AND J. MILNOR, An axiomatic approach to measurable utility, *Econometrica* **21** (1953), 291–297.
11. J. L. KELLEY, "General Topology," Van Nostrand, Princeton, 1955.
12. K. KURATOWSKI AND C. RYLL-NARDZEWSKI, A general theorem on selectors, *Bull. Acad. Polonaise Sci., Série Sci. Math.*, **13** (1965), 397–403.
13. J. MARSCHAK, Rational behavior, uncertain prospects and measurable utility, *Econometrica* **18** (1950), 111–141; Errata, *Ibid.*, 312.
14. H. NIKAIDO, "Convex Structures and Economic Theory," Academic Press, London, New York, 1968.
15. K. R. PARTHASARATHY, "Probability Measures on Metric Spaces," Academic Press, London/New York, 1967.
16. R. RANGA RAO, Relations between weak and uniform convergence of measures with applications, *Ann. Math. Statist.* **33** (1962), 659–680.
17. L. J. SAVAGE, "The Foundations of Statistics," John Wiley and Sons, New York, 1954.
18. K. VIND, "Mean Groupoids," to appear.
19. J. VON NEUMANN AND O. MORGENSTERN, "Theory of Games and Economic Behavior," Princeton University Press, Princeton, 2nd ed., 1947.

Printed in Belgium by the St. Catherine Press Ltd., Tempelhof 37, Bruges

THE CONTINUITY OF OPTIMAL DYNAMIC DECISION RULES

By J. S. Jordan[1]

In recent studies of the temporary competitive equilibrium, agents' current decision correspondences are derived using a standard recursion procedure, which is only applicable when the planning horizon is finite. This paper presents a general derivation of the current decision rule without restrictions on the time horizon or the number of states of the world in any period. It is shown that if utility is continuous in the product topology and if, in each period, expectations and the current constraint correspondence are continuous, then the current decision rule is upper semi-continuous. This result is obtained by associating with each current decision a set of feasible future plans. The expected utility of a current decision is then the expected utility of the best feasible future plan. The feasible future plan correspondence is shown to be continuous and the Maximum Theorem completes the proof.

1. INTRODUCTION

IN STUDIES of the temporary competitive equilibrium, the upper semi-continuity of an agent's current decision correspondence is commonly established by an argument which relies on the backward induction technique of dynamic programming. This procedure, which was used by Stigum [17] in the first proof of the existence of the temporary competitive equilibrium and was refined by Grandmont [9], is only applicable when the planning horizon is finite. This paper extends the continuity theorem of Grandmont to infinite horizon stochastic decision problems.

Section 2 defines the problem and presents a general derivation of the optimal current decision rule. The continuity theorem is stated in Section 3, and several examples are presented in Section 4. The theorem is proved in Section 5, and Section 6 contains some brief references to alternative approaches.

2. DEFINITIONS

2.1 NOTATION: For any topological space X, $\mathscr{B}(X)$ denotes the Borel σ-field of subsets of X, and $\mathscr{M}(X)$ denotes the space of all Borel probability measures on X. The space $\mathscr{M}(X)$ is endowed with the topology of weak convergence. If Y is another topological space, the Borel field $\mathscr{B}(X)$ will often be implicitly identified with the appropriate subfield of $\mathscr{B}(X \times Y)$. The notation $f: X \to Y$ will be used if f is a function, whereas if f is a correspondence, we will write $f: X \longrightarrow Y$. For a correspondence $f: X \longrightarrow Y$, we define the set graph $f = \{(x, y): y \in f(x)\}$.

[1] This paper is an extension of material contained in my Ph.D. dissertation, "Temporary Competitive Equilibrium and the Existence of Self-Fulfilling Expectations," submitted to Northwestern University. The help of the chairman, Professor J. Ledyard, and the other members of my committee, Professors S. Reiter and B. Stigum is gratefully acknowledged. An earlier version was presented to the Third World Congress of the Econometric Society, Toronto, August 25, 1975; and this revision has benefited greatly from detailed comments and criticisms of Professors D. Nachman, F. Shipley, and R. Kertz. Research and typing support was received from NSF grants GS 31346 X and SOC 74-19469, respectively. Any remaining errors are my own.

If $\{X_s: 1 \leq s < \infty\}$ is a family of topological spaces then X denotes the product space $\Pi_{s=1}^{\infty} X_s$ with generic element x. If $t \geq 1$ then X^t denotes the space $\Pi_{s=1}^{t} X_s$ with generic element x^t, and $'X$ denotes the space $\Pi_{s=t+1}^{\infty} X_s$ with generic element $'x$. For $s > t \geq 1$, $'X^s$ denotes the space $\Pi_{s'=t+1}^{s} X_{s'}$ with generic element $'x^s$ and $'\pi^s : 'X \to 'X^s$ is the projection. We will also adopt the following convention: if $t = s$, $Y \times 'X^s = Y$ and $(y, 'x^s) = y$. The indices t and s, and only these indices, will denote time periods.

2.2 DEFINITIONS: For each $1 \leq t \leq \infty$, let X_t be the space of possible states of the world in period t. Let Θ be a topological space and let ψ be a function on Θ to $\mathcal{M}(X)$. For each θ, t, and x^t, let $\psi(\cdot | \theta, x^t)$ be the regular conditional distribution on $'X$ determined by $\psi(\theta)$ given x^t (the existence of such conditional distributions is ensured by assumption A.1 below [**15**, pp. 146–147]). For each t, let $\psi_t : \Theta \times X^t \to \mathcal{M}('X)$ be given by $\psi_t(\theta, x^t) = \psi(\cdot | \theta, x^t)$. The function ψ_t is the tth period *expectation function*. For each θ and x^t, let supp $\psi_t(\theta, x^t)$ denote the support of $\psi_t(\theta, x^t)$. That is, supp $\psi_t(\theta, x^t) = \{'x :$ for every neighborhood U of $'x$, $\psi_t(\theta, x^t)(U) > 0\}$. If $s > t$ we will say $'x^s \in$ supp $\psi_t(\theta, x^t)$ if $'x^s \in '\pi^s$ (supp $\psi_t(\theta, x^t)$).

Let A_t be the space of decisions for period t, and let $b_t : \Theta \times X^t \times A^{t-1} \twoheadrightarrow A_t$ be the tth period *constraint correspondence*. The constraint correspondences are assumed to be related over time by the property that if $a_t \in b_t(\theta, x^t, a^{t-1})$ then $b_{t+1}(\theta, (x^t, x_{t+1}), (a^{t-1}, a_t)) \neq \emptyset$ for all $x_{t+1} \in$ supp $\psi_t(\theta, x^t)$. Finally, let $u : \Theta \times X \times A \to R$ be the *utility function*.

2.3 REMARKS: Examples are given in Section 4. It would be conventional to define a plan as a sequence of functions $\{\delta_t\}_{t \geq 1}$ from $\Theta \times X^t \times A^{t-1}$ to A_t. Ignoring measurability questions for the moment, the functions $\{\delta_t(\theta, \cdot)\}_{t \geq 1}$ combine with $\psi(\theta)$ to determine a joint distribution $\varphi \in \mathcal{M}(X \times A)$. The expected utility of the plan is then given by $\int u(\theta, \cdot) \, d\varphi$, so an optimal plan is one which maximizes expected utility for each θ. Suppose that in period t, the decision maker has observed the sequence of current and past states x^t and has chosen the sequence of past decisions a^{t-1}. Then if $\{\delta_{t'}\}$ is an optimal plan, the functions $\{\delta_{t'}(\theta, (x^t, \cdot), (a^{t-1}, \cdot))\}_{t' > t}$ combine with $\psi_t(\theta, x^t)$ to determine a function φ_t from A_t to $\mathcal{M}('X \times 'A)$, and the current decision $\delta_t(\theta, x^t, a^{t-1})$ maximizes $\int u(\theta, (x^t, \cdot), (a^{t-1}, a_t, \cdot)) \, d\varphi_t(a_t)$ subject to $a_t \in b_t(\theta, x^t, a^{t-1})$. This is the familiar Bellman principle of optimality.

This principle suggests the following approach to the derivation of optimal current decisions. Suppose that in period t, the decision maker chooses a current decision a_t and future decision functions $\{\delta_s\}_{s > t}$ to maximize the above expected utility. Since the functions $\{\delta_s\}_{s > t}$ are evaluated in terms of the probability distribution on $'X \times 'A$ which they determine, it is convenient to suppose that the probability distribution itself is the object of choice. Thus an optimal current decision a_t^0 and future decision rule φ^0 jointly maximize the expected utility $\int u(\theta, (x^t, \cdot), (a^{t-1}, a_t, \cdot)) \, d\varphi$. The current decision is constrained by the correspondence b_t, so it remains to formulate the constraints on the future decision rule.

2.4. DEFINITIONS: For each t, let $e_t: \Theta \times X^t \times A^t \longrightarrow {}^t X \times {}^t A$ be given by $e_t(\theta, x^t, a^t) = \{({}^t x, {}^t a): a_s \in b_s(\theta, (x^t, {}^t x^s), (a^t, {}^t a^{s-1})) \text{ for all } s > t\}$. Let $(Y, \mathcal{B}, \varphi)$ be a probability space and let $\mathcal{B}_1$, $\mathcal{B}_2$, and $\mathcal{B}_3$ be subfields of $\mathcal{B}$. Then $\mathcal{B}_1$ and $\mathcal{B}_2$ are said to be conditionally independent relative to $\mathcal{B}_3$ if for each $E \in \mathcal{B}_1$ and each $F \in \mathcal{B}_2$, $\varphi(E \cap F | \mathcal{B}_3) = \varphi(E | \mathcal{B}_3)\varphi(F | \mathcal{B}_3)$ [6, p. 284].

2.5 FUTURE DECISION RULES: Let $t \geq 1$ and let $(\theta, x^t, a^t) \in \Theta \times X^t \times A^t$. If $\varphi \in \mathcal{M}({}^t X \times {}^t A)$ and (a) for each $E \in \mathcal{B}({}^t X)$, $\varphi(E) = \psi_t(\theta, x^t)(E)$, and (b) for every $s > t$, the σ-fields $\mathcal{B}({}^t A^s)$ and $\mathcal{B}({}^s X)$ are conditionally independent relative to $\mathcal{B}({}^t X^s)$, then φ is called a *future decision rule*. If, in addition, (c) supp $\varphi \subset e_t(\theta, x^t, a^t)$, then φ is said to be *feasible*. For each $(\theta, x^t, a^t) \in \text{graph } b_t$, let $f_t(\theta, x^t, a^t)$ denote the set of feasible future decision rules determined by (θ, x^t, a^t).

2.6 REMARKS: Condition (c) states that future decisions will be in their respective constraint sets with probability one. Condition (b) is an information constraint, requiring that decisions made in period s depend only on states observed up to that time. This interpretation of (b) is made precise in Lemma 2.7 below.

2.7 LEMMA: *Let* $s > t \geq 1$ *and let* $\varphi \in \mathcal{M}({}^t X \times {}^t A)$. *The following statements are equivalent.* (a) *The* σ-fields $\mathcal{B}({}^t A^s)$ *and* $\mathcal{B}({}^s X)$ *are conditionally independent relative to* $\mathcal{B}({}^t X^s)$. (b) *For any* $E \in \mathcal{B}({}^t A^s)$, $\varphi(E | \mathcal{B}({}^t X)) = \varphi(E | \mathcal{B}({}^t X^s))$. (c) *For any* $E \in \mathcal{B}({}^s X)$, $\varphi(E | \mathcal{B}({}^t X^s \times {}^t A^s)) = \varphi(E | \mathcal{B}({}^t X^s))$.

PROOF: The lemma follows from the proof of [6, Theorem 9.7.1, p. 284].

2.8 REMARKS: Statement (b) of Lemma 2.7, combined with condition (a) of 2.5 indicates that a future decision rule φ is determined by $\psi_t(\theta, x^t)$ and the conditional distributions $\varphi_s: {}^t X^s \times {}^t A^{s-1} \to \mathcal{M}(A_s), s > t$. Thus the choice of a future decision rule is equivalent to the choice of a sequence of randomized future decision functions $\{\varphi_s\}_{s>t}$.

2.9 DEFINITIONS: For each $t \geq 1$, let $w_t: \Theta \times X^t \times A^t \times \mathcal{M}({}^t X \times {}^t A) \to R$ be given by $w_t(\theta, x^t, a^t, \varphi) = \int u(\theta, (x^t, \cdot), (a^t, \cdot)) \, d\varphi$. For each t, the *current value function* on graph b_t to the extended real numbers is given by $v_t(\theta, x^t, a^t) = \sup \{w_t(\theta, x^t, a^t, \varphi): \varphi \in f_t(\theta, x^t, a^t)\}$, with the convention that the supremum of the empty set is $-\infty$. The tth period *optimal current decision rule* is the correspondence $d_t: \Theta \times X^t \times A^{t-1} \to \to A_t$ given by $d_t(\theta, x^t, a^{t-1}) = \{a_t^*: a_t^* \text{ maximizes } v_t(\theta, x^t, (a^{t-1}, a_t))\}$ subject to $a_t \in b_t(\theta, x^t, a^{t-1})\}$.

3. THE CONTINUITY THEOREM

3.1 DEFINITIONS: In general, the *effective domain* of a correspondence f on Y into Z, written dom f, is defined by dom $f = \{y \in Y: f(y) \neq \varnothing\}$. If dom f is closed, we will say that f is upper semi-continuous (u.s.c.) if f restricted to dom f is u.s.c. as defined by Berge [1, p. 109]. Also, if dom f is closed, f will be said to be lower semi-continuous (l.s.c.) if f restricted to dom f is l.s.c. as defined by Berge [1, p. 109]. If f is u.s.c. and l.s.c., f is said to be continuous. If f is an extended real valued function on Y, its effective domain is defined by dom $f = \{y \in Y: -\infty < f(y) < \infty\}$, and f is said to be continuous if dom f is closed and f is continuous on dom f.

3.2 ASSUMPTIONS:

(A.1) For all t, X_t is a locally compact Borel subset of a complete separable metric space.

(A.2) For all t, A_t is a locally compact complete separable metric space.

(A.3) For all t, ψ_t has a continuous version.

(A.4) For all t, b_t is continuous.

(A.5) The utility function u is continuous, and for each $\theta \in \Theta$, $u(\theta, \cdot)$ is bounded.

3.3 REMARKS:
Assumption (A.1) insures that for each $(\theta, x') \in \Theta \times X'$, $\psi_t(\theta, x')$ is tight. In most situations of economic interest X_t and A_t are subsets of a finite dimensional Euclidean space and Assumptions (A.1) and (A.2) are not restrictive. From now on ψ_t will denote a continuous version of ψ_t.

3.4 THEOREM:
For each t, (i) v_t is continuous and d_t is u.s.c., and (ii) dom $v_t =$ graph b_t, and dom $d_t =$ dom b_t.

3.5 REMARKS:
Proposition 3.6 below, which is also proved in Section 5, shows that the sequence of optimal current decision rules satisfies the principle of optimality. It is often useful for the current decision rules to be convex valued, and Proposition 3.7 establishes sufficient conditions for this property. The straightforward proof is omitted.

3.6 PROPOSITION:
For each t, let δ_t be a Borel measurable selection from d_t on dom d_t. For each t and each $(\theta, x', a') \in$ graph b_t, if φ^* is the future decision rule determined by (θ, x', a'), $\psi_t(\theta, x')$, and the functions $\{\delta_s\}_{s>t}$, then φ^* maximizes $w_t(\theta, x', a', \varphi)$ subject to $\varphi \in f_t(\theta, x', a')$.

3.7 PROPOSITION:
Suppose that (i) for each t, A_t is a closed convex subset of a finite-dimensional Euclidean space; (ii) for each t, each $(\theta, x') \in \Theta \times X'$, and each $(\bar{a}^{t-1}, \hat{a}^{t-1}) \in A^{t-1} \times A^{t-1}$, if $\bar{a}_t \in b_t(\theta, x', \bar{a}^{t-1})$ and $\hat{a}_t \in b_t(\theta, x^{t-1}, \hat{a}^{t-1})$ and $0 \leq \lambda \leq 1$, then $(\lambda \bar{a}_t + (1-\lambda)\hat{a}_t) \in b_t(\theta, x', [\lambda \bar{a}^{t-1} + (1-\lambda)\hat{a}^{t-1}])$; and (iii) for each $(\theta, x) \in \Theta \times X$, $u(\theta, x, \cdot)$ is concave. Then for each t, v_t is concave and d_t is convex valued.

4. EXAMPLES

4.1 HOUSEHOLD PRODUCTION: Perhaps the most typical example is the problem of allocating commodities between production and consumption in each period to maximize expected utility. For each t, let $A_{1t} = R_+^n$ be the space of inputs to production, let Y_t be a Euclidean space of technology parameters, and let $g_t: Y_t \times A_1^{t-1} \to R_+^n$ be a continuous production function. Let $A_{2t} = R_+^n$ be the tth period consumption space, let $W_t = R_+^n$ be the tth period endowment space, and let Δ_t be the unit simplex of strictly positive prices. Let $A_t = A_{1t} \times A_{2t}$ and let $X_t = W_t \times Y_t \times \Delta_t$. The tth period constraint correspondence is given by $b_t(x^t, a^{t-1}) = \{(a_{1t}, a_{2t}): p_t(a_{1t} + a_{2t}) \leq p_t(w_t + g_t(y_t, a_1^{t-1}))\}$, and assumption (A.4) is satisfied. Let Θ be a space of parametric representations of a subspace of $\mathcal{M}(X)$ such that the function ψ from parameters to distributions satisfies (A.3) (e.g., each θ could describe an autoregressive process in the logarithms of x_t). A bounded continuous von Neuman-Morgenstern utility function on A_1 completes the example. This example is discussed further in [11].

4.2 SHORT-TERM SECURITIES: Suppose that in each period, a consumer can buy or sell short-term securities, each unit of which obligates the seller to pay the buyer one unit of account in the following period. To prevent bankruptcy, the consumer is constrained to sell no more securities than he is certain of being able to redeem without additional sales (refinancing) next period. Let $W_t = R_+^n$ be the tth period endowment space, let $A_{1t} = R$ be the security space, and let $A_{2t} = R_+^n$ be the consumption space. Let $P_t = \{(s_t, p_t) \in R \times \Delta_t : s_t > 0\}$, let $X_t = W_t \times P_t$, and let $A_t = A_{1t} \times A_{2t}$. Given $\psi: \Theta \to \mathcal{M}(X)$, the tth period budget constraint is given by $b_t(\theta, w^t, p^t, a^{t-1}) = \{(a_{1t}, a_{2t}): p_t(a_{2t} - w_t) \leq a_{1t-1} - s_t a_{1t}, \text{ and } a_{1t} + p_{t+1}w_{t+1} \geq 0$ for all $(p_{t+1}, w_{t+1}) \in \text{supp } \psi_t(\theta, w^t, p^t)\}$. Here, as in Green [10], the continuity of b_t requires the continuity of the correspondence supp ψ_t.

Suppose that the constraint against bankruptcy is weakened to allow the consumer to sell all the securities he can eventually redeem, refinancing if necessary. This type of constraint is used in Stigum [18]. This constraint will involve the inner products of infinite sequences of discounted prices and endowments. Since such expressions are not continuous with respect to the product topology, Theorem 3.4 would seem to be inapplicable to this type of problem. However, the following somewhat simpler example indicates that this sort of difficulty is not always fatal.

4.3 VALUE MAXIMIZATION: Suppose that a profit maximizing firm has an infinite planning horizon. In the absence of uncertainty, the firm would choose a technologically feasible sequence of input vectors $\{a_{1t}\}_{t=1}^\infty \subset R_+^n$ and output vectors $\{a_{2t}\}_{t=1}^\infty \subset R_+^n$ to maximize the value $\Sigma_{t=1}^\infty p_t(a_{2t} - a_{1t})$, where $\{p_t\}_{t=1}^\infty$ is the anticipated sequence of prices.

It would be conventional to assume that the input and output sequences are elements of l_∞^n and the price sequence is an element of l_1^n (see for example [13]). Also, to insure the existence of a value maximum for each price sequence, it would be natural to assume that the set of feasible input and output sequences is compact in the weak (l_∞, l_1) topology on l_∞, and thus that there is some $k > 0$ such that for any feasible sequence $\{a_{1t}, a_{2t}\}$, $\|a_{1t}\| < k$ and $\|a_{2t}\| < k$ for all t, where $\| \cdot \|$ denotes the Euclidean norm. Using this assumption, a simple technology model can be constructed as follows. For each t, let $A_{1t} = A_{2t} = \{r \in R_+^n : \|r\| \le k\}$, let Y_t be a Euclidean space of technology parameters, and let $g_t : Y_t \times A_1^{t-1} \to A_{2t}$ be a continuous production function. Then, letting $A_t = A_{1t} \times A_{2t}$, the tth period constraint correspondence is defined by $b_t(y_t, a_1^{t-1}) = \{a_t : a_{1t} \in A_{1t}$ and $a_{2t} = g_t(y_t, a_1^{t-1})\}$. If the firm is uncertain about the technology but anticipates prices perfectly, let $X_t = Y_t$ for each t and let the utility function $u : l_1^n \times A \to R$ be defined by $u(p, a) = \Sigma_{t=1}^{\infty} p_t(a_{2t} - a_{1t})$. Then, because of the compactness assumption, u is continuous when A has the product topology. Given an expectation function $\psi : \Theta \to \mathcal{M}(X)$ which satisfies (A.3), this example can be completed by replacing Θ with $\Theta' = l_1^n \times \Theta$.

Of more interest is the case in which prices are uncertain. In this case let $P_t = R_+^n$ and let $X_t = P_t \times Y_t$ for each t. Then the utility function becomes $u(x, a) = \Sigma_{t=1}^{\infty} p_t(a_{2t} - a_{1t})$, which is not continuous on its effective domain when X has the product topology. However, suppose that the set of possible price sequences is continuously dominated, in the sense that for each θ there is a sequence $p^0(\theta) \in l_1^n$ such that for all $(p, y) \in \text{supp } \psi(\theta)$, $\|p_t\| \le \|p_t^0(\theta)\|$ for all t, and the map $\theta \to p^0(\theta)$ is l_1^n continuous. Then the $\Theta \times P \times Y$ and $\Theta \times l_1^n \times Y$ topologies agree on the set $\{(\theta, x) : x \in \text{supp } \psi(\theta)\}$ and u satisfies Assumption (A.5) on the set $\{(\theta, x) : x \in \text{supp } \psi(\theta)\} \times A$. The proof of 3.4 indicates that the optimal current decision rule d_t is then u.s.c. on $\{(\theta, x') : x' \in \text{supp } \psi(\theta)\} \times A^{t-1}$. If a sequence of realized price sequences $\{p_n\}$ converges in the product topology to a limit p, then for each t, the current information p_n^t converges to p_t. The above assumption serves to guarantee the continuity of expected utility with respect to current information.

4.4 AN INFORMATIONAL DISCONTINUITY: By Assumption (A.3), convergence in the space implies the continuous convergence of all the associated conditional distributions on X. It is thus natural to investigate the continuity of the tth period current decision rule under the weaker assumption:

(A.3') ψ_t has a continuous version.

Unfortunately, this weakening of (A.3) destroys the upper semi-continuity of the correspondence f_t. More specifically, the information condition 2.7(b) is no longer a closed condition. The following economic example indicates that this invalidates the desired result.

We consider a three period horizon problem in which a consumer attempts to allocate a fixed stock of money over time so as to maximize his expected utility of consumption. There is a single commodity available each period and the state of the world in each period is the price of the commodity. For each $t \in \{1, 2, 3\}$, the consumer chooses a current decision $a_t = (a_{1t}, a_{2t}) \in R_+^2$ where a_{1t} denotes the amount of consumption demanded in period t and a_{2t} denotes the amount of money saved in period t. Let the consumer's initial stock of money be one unit. Then b_1 is given by $b_1(x_1) = \{(a_{11}, a_{21}) : x_1 a_{11} + a_{21} \leq 1\}$; b_2 is given by $b_2(x^2, a_1) = \{(a_{12}, a_{22}) : x_2 a_{12} + a_{22} \leq a_{21}\}$; and b_3 is given by $b_3(x^3, a^2) = \{(a_{13}, a_{23}) : x_3 a_{13} + a_{23} \leq a_{22}\}$. The consumer's utility function is given by $u(a^3) = a_{11} + a_{12} + a_{13}$. For $(\theta, x_1) \in [0, 1] \times X_1$, let $\psi_1(\theta, x_1)$ be the distribution which gives probability $1/2$ to the event $(x_2, x_3) = (2, 3)$ and probability $1/2$ to the event $(x_2, x_3) = (2 + \theta, 1)$. Then (A.3′) is satisfied with $t = 1$ but (A.3) is not. In particular, $\psi_2(\cdot, (x_1, 2))$ is discontinuous at $\theta = 0$. Suppose that $4/3 < x_1 < 3/2$. Then if $0 < \theta < 1$, the optimal current decision is

$$d_1(\theta, x_1) = (0, 1)$$

and the optimal future decision rule, φ^*, gives probability $1/2$ to the event $({}^1x, {}^1a) = ((2, 3), (1/2, 0), (0, 0))$ and probability $1/2$ to the event $({}^1x, {}^1a) = ((2 + \theta, 1), (0, 1), (1, 0))$. Then as $\theta \to 0$, $\lim d_1(\theta, x_1) = (0, 1)$ and $\lim \varphi^*$ is the distribution which gives probability $1/2$ to the event $({}^1x, {}^1a) = ((2, 3), (1/2, 0), (0, 0))$ and probability $1/2$ to the event $({}^1x, {}^1a) = ((2, 1), (0, 1), (1, 0))$. However, for this distribution, a_2 and x_3 are not conditionally independent given x^2. At $\theta = 0$, the optimal current decision is

$$d_1(0, x_1) = (1, 0)$$

and the optimal future decision rule gives probability $1/2$ to the event $({}^1x, {}^1a) = ((2, 3), (0, 0), (0, 0))$ and probability $1/2$ to the event $({}^1x, {}^1a) = ((2, 1), (0, 0), (0, 0))$.

This discontinuity is due to the fact that for each $\theta > 0$, x_2 gives perfect information about x_3, but at $\theta = 0$, x_2 gives no information. Thus the continuity of future expectation functions can be interpreted as an informational continuity condition.

5. PROOFS

5.1 LEMMA: *For each t, $\mathrm{dom}\, f_t = \mathrm{graph}\, b_t$.*

PROOF: For each $s > t$ it follows from (A.4) and [16, Theorem 5.1, p. 50] that there exists a Borel measurable function $g_s : \mathrm{dom}\, b_s \to A_s$ such that $g_s(\theta, x^s, a^{s-1}) \in b_s(\theta, x^s, a^{s-1})$. Given $(\theta, x^s, a^{s-1}) \in \mathrm{dom}\, b_s$, for each $s > t$, let $h_s : {}^tX^s \to A_s$ be defined by $h_{t+1}({}^tx^{t+1}) = g_{t+1}[\theta, (x^t, x_{t+1}), a^t]$; $h_{t+2}({}^tx^{t+2}) = g_{t+2}[\theta, (x^t, {}^tx^{t+2}), (a^t, h_{t+1}({}^tx^{t+1}))]$; etc. Let $h({}^tx) = (h_{t+1}({}^tx^{t+1}), h_{t+2}({}^tx^{t+2}), \ldots)$ for all ${}^tx$ such that the right hand side is defined. Letting $S_t(\theta, x^t) = \{{}^tx : x_s \in \mathrm{supp}\, \psi_{s-1}[\theta, (x^t, {}^tx^{s-1})]$ for all $s > t\}$, it follows from the definition of the constraint correspondence that h is defined on $S_t(\theta, x^t)$, and (A.4) can be used to show that h is defined on $cl\, S_t(\theta, x^t)$, where cl denotes closure. A straightforward argument shows that $\mathrm{supp}\, \psi_t(\theta, x^t) \subset cl\, S_t(\theta, x^t)$ so h is defined on $\mathrm{supp}\, \psi_t(\theta, x^t)$.

We can now use h to construct a future decision rule. For any $E \in \mathscr{B}({}^tX)$ and any $F \in \mathscr{B}({}^tA)$, let $\varphi(E \times F) = \psi_t(\theta, x^t)(\{{}^tx : h({}^tx) \in F\})$. It is easily seen that $\varphi \in f_t(\theta, x^t, a^t)$.

5.2 LEMMA: *For each t, f_t is u.s.c.*

PROOF: Let $t \geq 1$ and let $\{\theta_n, x_n^t, a_n^t\}_{n=1}^\infty$ be a sequence in dom f_t converging to some $(\theta, x^t, a^t) \in \Theta \times X^t \times A^t$. It suffices to show that every selection $\{\varphi_n\}$ from $\{f_t(\theta_n, x_n^t, a_n^t)\}$ has a cluster point in $f_t(\theta, x^t, a^t)$. Let $\varepsilon > 0$. Since $\psi_t(\theta_n, x_n^t) \to \psi_t(\theta, x^t)$ by (A.3), it follows from (A.1) and [2, Theorem 8, p. 241] that there exists a compact set $K \subset {}^tX$ such that $\psi_t(\theta_n, x_n^t)(K) > 1 - \varepsilon$ for all n. By (A.4), $b_{t+1}(cl\{\theta_n, x_n^t, a_n^t\}_{n=1}^\infty)$ is compact and by induction we can obtain a compact set $K' \subset {}^tA$ such that if ${}^tx \in K$ and $({}^tx, {}^ta) \in e_t(\{\theta_n, x_n^t, a_n^t\}_{n=1}^\infty)$ then ${}^ta \in K'$. By the feasibility condition 2.5 (c), $\varphi_n(K \times K') = \psi_t(\theta_n, x_n^t)(K)$ for each n, so the selection $\{\varphi_n\}$ is tight and thus has a cluster point $\varphi \in \mathcal{M}({}^tX \times {}^tA)$ [2, p. 37].

It is clear that φ satisfies 2.5(a). Assumption (A.4) implies that e_t has a closed graph, and it follows that φ satisfies 2.5(c). We will complete the proof by showing that φ satisfies 2.7(c). Let $s > t$ and let g be a bounded continuous function on ${}^tX \times {}^tA^s$. Then for each n $\int_{{}^sX} g \, d\varphi_n(\cdot | \mathcal{B}({}^tX^s \times {}^tA^s)) = \int_{{}^sX} g \, d\psi_s(\theta_n, (x_n^t, {}^tx^s))$ for each $({}^tx^s, {}^ta^s) \in {}^tX^s \times {}^tA^s$, and $\{\int_{{}^sX} g \, d\psi_s(\theta_n, (x_n^t, \cdot))\}_{n=1}^\infty$ is an equicontinuous sequence of uniformly bounded functions on ${}^tX^s \times {}^tA^s$ converging pointwise to the function $\int_{{}^sX} g \, d\psi_s(\theta, (x^t, \cdot))$. Therefore by [15, Theorem 6.8, p. 51] $\int_{{}^tX^s \times {}^tA^s}[\int_{{}^sX} g \, d\varphi_n(\cdot | \mathcal{B}({}^tA^s \times {}^tX^s))] \, d\varphi_n \to \int_{{}^tX^s \times {}^tA^s}[\int_{{}^sX} g \, d\psi_s(\theta, (x^t, \cdot))] \, d\varphi$ so $\int_{{}^tX^s \times {}^tA^s}[\int_{{}^sX} g \, d\psi_s(\theta, (x^t, \cdot))] \, d\varphi = \int g \, d\varphi$. Since the function g was chosen arbitrarily, φ satisfies 2.7(c).

5.3 REMARKS: The next step is to prove that f_t is l.s.c. As was noted in 2.8, a feasible future decision rule φ determines for each $s > t$ a randomized decision function which assigns to each $({}^tx^s, {}^ta^{s-1})$ an element of $\mathcal{M}(A_s)$. We will use Lusin's Theorem to show that these functions are continuous on a closed set D with $\varphi(D)$ arbitrarily close to one. Michael's selection theorem is then used to extend these functions continuously to ${}^tX \times {}^tA$, yielding a feasible future decision rule φ' arbitrarily close to φ. The result is then established by showing that f_t is l.s.c. at φ if the randomized decision functions associated with φ are continuous.

5.4 LEMMA: *Let Y be a metric space, let Z be a separable metric space and let $\mu \in \mathcal{M}(Y)$. Let $g: Y \to \mathcal{M}(Z)$ such that for each $E \in \mathcal{B}(Z)$, the function $y \to g(y)(E)$ is $\mathcal{B}(Y)$ measurable. Then for any $\varepsilon > 0$ there exists a closed set $D \subset Y$ such that $\mu(D) > 1 - \varepsilon$ and g is continuous on D.*

PROOF: Since Z is separable, the space $U(Z)$ of bounded uniformly continuous functions on Z is separable. Let $\{h_n\}_{n=1}^\infty$ be a countable dense subset of $U(Z)$. Then the function $\varphi \to \{\int_Z h_n \, d\varphi\}_{n=1}^\infty$ is a homeomorphism between $\mathcal{M}(Z)$ and a convex subset of R^∞ [15, pp. 43–44]. By hypothesis, the function $y \to \int \chi_E \, dg(y)$ is measurable for each $E \in \mathcal{B}(Z)$, so the functions $y \to \int h_n \, dg(y)$ are measurable as the pointwise limit of sums of measurable functions. Then Lusin's Theorem implies that for each n there exists a closed set $D_n \subset Y$ such that $\mu(D_n) > 1 - \varepsilon/2^{n+1}$ and the function $y \to \int h_n \, dg(y)$ is continuous on D_n. Letting $D = \bigcap_{n=1}^{\infty} D_n$ completes the proof.

5.5 LEMMA: *Let Y be a metric space, let Z be a complete separable metric space, and let $g: Y \longrightarrow Z$ be continuous. Let $h: Y \longrightarrow \mathcal{M}(Z)$ be given by $h(y) = \{\varphi : \text{supp } \varphi \subset g(y)\}$. Then h is continuous.*

PROOF: Since dom h = dom g, dom h is closed. To see that h is u.s.c., let $\{y_n\}$ be a sequence in dom h converging to y and let $\{\varphi_n\}$ be a selection from $\{h(y_n)\}$. Since g is u.s.c., $\{\varphi_n\}$ is tight and thus has a cluster point φ, and supp $\varphi \subset g(v)$.

To see that h is l.s.c., let $\{y_n\}$ be sequence in dom h converging to y and let $\varphi \in h(y)$. For each n, let $u_n: Z \longrightarrow g(y_n)$ be given by $u_n(z) = \{z': z'$ minimizes $\rho(z, z')$ subject to $z' \in g(y_n)\}$, where ρ is the metric on Z. Then u_n is u.s.c., so let v_n be a Borel measurable selection from u_n [16, p. 52]. Since g is l.s.c., $v_n(z_n) \to z$ whenever $z_n \to z$ and $z \in g(y)$. For each n, let $\varphi_n \in h(y_n)$ be given by $\varphi_n(E) = \varphi(v_n^{-1}(E))$ for $E \in \mathcal{B}(Z)$. Then $\varphi_n \to \varphi$ by [2, Theorem 5.5, p. 34].

5.6 LEMMA: *Let $t \geq 1$ and let $(\theta, x^t, a^t) \in$ graph b_t. For each $\varphi \in \mathcal{M}('X \times 'A)$ and each $s > t$, let $\varphi_s : 'X^s \times 'A^{s-1} \to \mathcal{M}(A_s)$ be given by $\varphi_s = \varphi(\cdot | \mathcal{B}('X^s \times 'A^{s-1}))$. Let $\mathcal{C} = \{\varphi \in f_t(\theta, x^t, a^t):$ for each $s > t$, φ_s has a continuous version$\}$. Then $\mathcal{C}$ is dense in $f_t(\theta, x^t, a^t)$.*

PROOF: Let $\varphi \in f_t(\theta, x^t, a^t)$ and let $\varepsilon > 0$. For each $s \geq t$, Lemma 5.4 implies the existence of a closed set $D'_s \subset 'X^s \times 'A^{s-1}$ such that $\varphi(D'_s) > 1 - \varepsilon/2^{s+1}$ and φ_s is continuous on D'_s. Let $D_s = D'_s \cap \{('x^s, 'a^{s-1}):$ supp $\varphi_s('x^s, 'a^{s-1}) \subset b_s(\theta, (x^t, 'x^s), (a^t, 'a^{s-1}))\}$. Since b_s is continuous and φ_s is continuous on D'_s, D_s is closed; and since φ is feasible, $\varphi(D'_s) = \varphi(D_s)$.

For each $s > t$, let $h_s : 'X^s \times 'A^{s-1} \longrightarrow \mathcal{M}(A_s)$ be given by $h_s('x^s, 'a^{s-1}) = \{\mu : \text{supp } \mu \subset b_s(\theta, (x^t, 'x^s), (a^t, 'a^{s-1}))\}$. By (A.4) and Lemma 5.5 h_s is continuous for each s. Using the homeomorphism introduced in the proof of Lemma 5.4, one can write $h_s : \text{dom } h_s \longrightarrow R^{\infty}$ and h_s is convex valued. Then it follows from [16, Theorem 1.1, p. 5] and [14, Theorem 1.2, p. 1404] that there exists a continuous extension, φ_s^0, of $\varphi_s | D_s$ to dom h_s such that $\varphi_s^0('x^s, 'a^{s-1}) \in h_s('x^s, 'a^{s-1})$ for all $('x^s, 'a^{s-1}) \in \text{dom } h_s$.

We now extend φ_s^0 to $'X^s \times 'A^{s-1}$. Let $\{K_n\}_{n=1}^{\infty}$ be a nondecreasing sequence of compact subsets of $'X^s \times 'A^{s-1}$ such that $'X^s \times 'A^{s-1} = \bigcup_{n=1}^{\infty} K_n$. For each n let B_n denote the image of K_n under $b_s(\theta, (x^t, \cdot), (a^t, \cdot))$. We can assume that $B_1 \neq \emptyset$. Since b_s is u.s.c., B_n is compact so $h_s(K_n)$ is a compact subset of R^{∞}. Let C_n denote the closed convex hull of $h_s(K_n)$. Then $\varphi_s^0 | (K_1 \cap \text{dom } h_s)$ is a continuous function taking values in C_1 so we can apply [16, Theorem 1.1, p. 5] and [14, Theorem 1.2] again (to the correspondence $h(\cdot) \equiv C_1$) to obtain a continuous extension $\varphi_s^1 : K_1 \to$

C_1. Let the function $\tilde{\varphi}_s^1 : K_1 \cup (K_2 \cap \mathrm{dom}\, h_s) \to C_2$ be given by

$$\tilde{\varphi}_s^1(^tx^s, {}'a^{s-1}) = \begin{cases} \varphi_s^0(^tx^s, {}'a^{s-1}) & \text{if} \quad (^tx^s, {}'a^{s-1}) \in \mathrm{dom}\, h_s, \\ \varphi_s^1(^tx^s, {}'a^{s-1}) & \text{otherwise,} \end{cases}$$

and let $\varphi_s^2 : K_2 \to C_2$ be a continuous extension of $\tilde{\varphi}_s^2$ to K_2. Define the sequence $\{\varphi_s^n\}_{n=1}^\infty$ inductively in this fashion and let φ_s' be the pointwise limit of this sequence. Then φ_s' is the desired extension.

The measure $\psi_t(\theta, x')$ together with the functions $\{\varphi_s'\}_{s>t}$ determine a measure $\varphi' \in C$. Let $D = \bigcap_{s>t}(D_s \times {}^sX \times {}^{s-1}A)$. Then $\varphi(D) > 1 - \varepsilon$ and for all events $E \subset D$, $\varphi'(E) = \varphi(E)$. Therefore if g is a bounded continuous function on $^tX \times {}^tA$, $|\int g\, d\varphi - \int g\, d\varphi'| < 2\varepsilon \sup |g|$, which completes the proof.

5.7 LEMMA: *For each t, f_t is l.s.c.*

PROOF: Let $t \geq 1$, let $\{\theta_n, x_n^t, a_n^t\}_{n=1}^\infty$ be a sequence in $\mathrm{dom}\, f_t$ converging to (θ, x^t, a^t), and let $\varphi \in f_t(\theta, x^t, a^t)$. It suffices to construct a selection $\{\varphi^n\}_{n=1}^\infty$ from $\{f_t(\theta_n, x_n^t, a_n^t)\}_{n=1}^\infty$ such that $\varphi^n \to \varphi$. By Lemma 5.6 we may assume that $\varphi \in \mathscr{C}$.

Let $\hat{\Theta} = \{\theta\} \cup \{\theta_n\}_{n=1}^\infty$. Then $\hat{\Theta}$ is compact so for each $s > t$, $\hat{\Theta} \times X^s \times A^{s-1}$ is paracompact. For each $s > t$, let $g_s : \hat{\Theta} \times X^s \times A^{s-1} \twoheadrightarrow \mathcal{M}(A_s)$ be given by $g_s(\theta, x^s, a^{s-1}) = \{\mu : \mathrm{supp}\, \mu \subset b_s(\theta, x^s, a^{s-1})\}$. By Lemma 5.5 g_s is continuous. Since φ_s is continuous on $\{\theta\} \times \{x^t\} \times {}'X^s \times \{a^t\} \times {}'A^{s-1}$ by assumption, as in the proof of 5.6 we can extend φ_s to a continuous function $\varphi_s' : \hat{\Theta} \times X^s \times A^{s-1} \to \mathcal{M}(A_s)$ such that φ_s' is a selection form g_s on $\mathrm{dom}\, g_s$. For each n, let φ^n be the future decision rule determined by $\psi_t(\theta_n, x_n^t)$ and the functions $\varphi_s'(\theta_n, (x_n^t, \cdot), (a_n^t, \cdot))$, $s > t$. Then by construction, $\varphi^n \in f_t(\theta_n, x_n^t, a_n^t)$ for each n.

It remains to show that $\varphi^n \to \varphi$. Since f_t is u.s.c. the sequence $\{\varphi_n\}$ has a cluster point $\varphi^0 \in f_t(\theta, x^t, a^t)$ so it suffices to check that φ^0 agrees with φ on all finite dimensional subspaces of $^tX \times {}^tA$. Let g be a bounded continuous function on $^tX^s \times {}^tA^s$ for some $s > t$. For each n, $\int g\, d\varphi^n = \int_{tX^s} [\int_{tA^s} g(^tx^s, \cdot)\, d\varphi^n(\cdot \,|\, \mathcal{B}(^tX^s))]\, d\psi_t(\theta_n, x_n^t)$ and the term inside the brackets equals

$$\int_{A_{t+1}} \left[\int_{A_{t+2}} \cdots \left[\int_{A_s} g(^tx^s, (^ta^{s-1}, \cdot))\, d\varphi_s'(\theta_n, (x_n^t, {}^tx^s), (a_n^t, {}^ta^{s-1})) \right] \cdots \right.$$
$$\left. \cdot d\varphi_{t+2}'(\theta_n, (x_n^t, {}^tx^{t+2}), (a_n^t, a_{t+1})) \right]\, d\varphi_{t+1}'(\theta_n, (x_n^t, x_{t+1}), a_n^t).$$

Denoting this term as a function $g^n : {}'X^s \to R$, the sequence $\{g^n\}$ is an equicontinuous sequence of uniformly bounded functions converging pointwise to the function g^0 given by $g^0(^tx^s) = \int_{tA^s} g(^tx^s, \cdot)\, d\varphi(\cdot \,|\, \mathcal{B}(^tX^s))$. Since $\psi_t(\theta_n, x_n^t) \to \psi_t(\theta, x^t)$ it follows from [15, Theorem 6.8, p. 51] that $\int_{tX^s} g^n(\cdot)\, d\psi_t(\theta_n, x_n^t) \to \int_{tX^s} g^0(\cdot)\, d\psi_t(\theta, x^t)$ and thus that $\int g\, d\varphi^n \to \int g\, d\varphi$, completing the proof.

5.8 PROOF OF THEOREM 3.4: For each t, f_t is compact valued by Lemma 5.2 and w_t is continuous so $\mathrm{dom}\, v_t = \mathrm{dom}\, f_t$. Lemma 5.1 then implies that $\mathrm{dom}\, v_t = \mathrm{graph}\, b_t$. Since f_t is continuous by Lemmas 5.2 and 5.7, the Maximum Theorem [1,

p. 116] implies that v_t is continuous and, using (A.3), that dom d_t = dom b_t and d_t is u.s.c. This completes the proof.

5.9 PROOF OF PROPOSITION 3.6: The existence of the functions $\{\delta_t\}$ follows from Theorem 3.4 and [16, p. 52]. Also, for each t, the Maximum Theorem and the continuity of f_t imply that the correspondence $(\theta, x^t, a^t) \rightarrow\rightarrow \{\varphi^0 : \varphi^0$ maximizes $w_t(\theta, x^t, a^t, \varphi)$ subject to $\varphi \in f_t(\theta, x^t, a^t)\}$ is u.s.c., so let h_t be a Borel measurable selection from this correspondence on graph b_t. Given $t \geq 1$ and $(\theta, x^t, a^t) \in$ graph b_t, let $\varphi^0 = h_t(\theta, x^t, a^t)$. Then

$$w_t(\theta, x^t, a^t, \varphi^0) = \int_{X_{t+1} \times A_{t+1}} w_{t+1}(\theta, (x^t, \cdot), (a^t, \cdot), \varphi^0(\cdot | \mathcal{B}(X_{t+1}$$

$$\times A_{t+1}))) \, d\varphi$$

$$\leq \int_{X_{t+1}} w_{t+1}[\theta, (x^t, \cdot), (a^t, \delta_{t+1}(\theta, (x^t, \cdot), a^t)),$$

$$h_{t+1}(\theta, (x_t, \cdot), (a^t, \delta_{t+1}(\theta, (x^t, \cdot), a^t)))] \, d\psi_t(\theta, x^t).$$

For each $s > t$, let φ^s be the future decision rule determined by (θ, x^t, a^t), $\psi_t(\theta, x^t)$, the functions $(\delta_{t+1}, \ldots, \delta_s)$, and h_s. The above inequality shows that $w_t(\theta, x^t, a^t, \varphi^0) \leq w_t(\theta, x^t, a^t, \varphi^s)$ for $s = t+1$, and the inequality for $s > t+1$ follows similarly. The proof is completed by observing that $\lim_{s \to \infty} \varphi^s = \varphi^*$, and $\varphi^* \in f_t(\theta, x^t, a^t)$.

6. BIBLIOGRAPHICAL NOTES

The previous literature that I am aware of can be divided into three lines of approach. In [18] Stigum uses an infinite-dimensional commodity space approach to obtain the continuity of the optimal current decision function in an economic model with finitely many states of the world in each period. Continuity is established with respect to current and past variables while expectations are held constant [18, p. 325]. Although this continuity result per se could be obtained from Theorem 3.4, this would not simplify Stigum's proof of the existence of a sequence of temporary equilibria [18, Theorem 2].

Another method is to solve the finite horizon problem by backward induction and let the length of the horizon increase to infinity. The convergence arguments used in this approach seem to require narrower hypotheses than that of 3.4. However, since this approach treats the current and future decision rules more explicitly, it is easier to obtain additional properties of the current decision rule. For some economic applications and further discussion of this method, see Brock and Mirman [4], Danforth [7], Foley and Hellwig [8], Kennan [12], and Townsend [19].

The third approach is to use Blackwell's discounted dynamic programming theory [3], for the case in which the utility function is of the form $\Sigma_{t=1}^{\infty} \beta^t u(\theta, x_t, a_t)$ for $0 \leq \beta < 1$, and expectations and the constraint correspondences satisfy a

Markov property. In this case, one also obtains the existence of an optimal stationary current decision rule. This method is used by Christiansen [5] in a temporary equilibrium model, and a more general contraction operator analysis is used by Whitt [20, Theorem 2.2, p. 11] in an abstract setting.

University of Minnesota

Manuscript received April 1975; revision received August, 1976

REFERENCES

[1] BERGE, C.: *Topological Spaces.* New York: Macmillan Co., 1963.

[2] BILLINGSLEY, D.: *Convergence of Probability Measures.* New York: John Wiley and Sons, 1968.

[3] BLACKWELL, D.: "Discounted Dynamic Programming," *Annals of Mathematical Statistics,* 36 (1965), 225–235.

[4] BROCK, W., AND L. MIRMAN: "Optimal Economic Growth and Uncertainty," *Journal of Economic Theory,* 4 (1972), 479–513.

[5] CHRISTIANSEN, D.: "Temporary Equilibrium: A Stochastic Dynamic Programming Approach, Part I: The Stationary Case," Discussion Paper No. 75-17, Department of Economics, University of Rochester, August, 1975.

[6] CHUNG, K.: *A Course in Probability Theory.* New York: Harcourt, Brace, and World, Inc., 1968.

[7] DANFORTH, J.: "An Infinite Horizon Model of Search with Quasi-Endogenous Payoffs," in S. Lippman and J. McCall (eds.), *Studies in the Economics of Search.* Amsterdam: North Holland, forthcoming.

[8] FOLEY, D., AND M. HELLWIG: "Asset Management with Trading Uncertainty," *Review of Economic Studies,* 42 (1975), 327–346.

[9] GRANDMONT, J. M.: "On the Short Run Equilibrium in a Monetary Economy," in J. Dreze (ed.), *Allocation Under Uncertainty, Equilibrium and Optimality.* New York: Macmillan Co., 1974.

[10] GREEN, J.: "Temporary General Equilibrium in a Sequential Trading Model with Spot and Future Transactions," *Econometrica,* 41 (1973), 1103–1124.

[11] JORDAN, J.: "Temporary Competitive Equilibrium and the Existence of Self-Fulfilling Expectations," *Journal of Economic Theory,* 12 (1976), 455–471.

[12] KENNAN, J.: "Finite-Horizon and Infinite-Horizon Expected Utility Maximization: A Convergence Theorem," Brown University, mimeo, December, 1974.

[13] MAJUMDAR, M.: "Some General Theorems on Efficiency Prices with an Infinite-Dimensional Commodity Space," *Journal of Economic Theory,* 5 (1972), 1–13.

[14] MICHAEL, E.: "A Selection Theorem," *Proceedings of the American Mathematical Society,* 17 (1966), 1404–1406.

[15] PARTHASARATHY, K. R.: *Probability Measures on Metric Spaces.* New York: Academic Press, 1967.

[16] PARTHASARATHY, T.: *Selection Theorems and Their Applications.* Berlin: Springer-Verlag, 1972.

[17] STIGUM, B.: "Competitive Equilibria Under Uncertainty," *Quarterly Journal of Economics,* 83 (1969), 533–561.

[18] STIGUM, B.: "Competitive Resource Allocation over Time Under Uncertainty," in Balch, M., D. McFadden, and S. Y. Wu (eds.), *Essays on Economic Behaviour Under Uncertainty.* New York: North-Holland/American Elsevier, 1974.

[19] TOWNSEND, R.: "Price Fixing Schemes and Optimal Buffer Stock Policies," Discussion Paper No. 74–48, Center for Economic Research, University of Minnesota, November, 1974.

[20] WHITT, W.: "Approximations of Dynamic Programs," Yale University, mimeo, January, 1976.

CHAPTER III

Competitive Assets Markets

TEMPORARY GENERAL EQUILIBRIUM IN A SEQUENTIAL TRADING MODEL WITH SPOT AND FUTURES TRANSACTIONS

BY JERRY R. GREEN[1]

The existence of an equilibrium is proven for a two-period model in which there are spot transactions and futures transactions in the first period and spot markets in the second period. Prices at that date are viewed with subjective uncertainty by all traders. This introduces the possibility of speculation. Conditions for the existence of a competitive equilibrium include restriction on the nature of price expectations.

1. INTRODUCTION

MODELS OF GENERAL equilibrium have primarily dealt with situations in which prices are announced and decisions taken at an initial point in time. This paper considers the case in which actions are made sequentially and plans may be revised as time progresses.

Economic activity, in the traditional models, consists of carrying out the plans and contracts already made. Further, because these are optimal, if markets were instituted at later dates, no trading would take place: Markets would be unnecessary. In this sense, the institution of "once-and-for-all" trading is self-realizing. If, however, one introduces marketing costs, the appearance of new agents, new commodities, or unanticipated changes in tastes, this self-realization property may fail. Trade would take place, if it were possible. If agents knew about the existence of markets in the future, their plans and actions at the initial date would be changed. This leads to the study of sequential trading, which is a self-realizing institution in the above sense even in cases in which "once-and-for-all" trading is not.

The object of the present paper is to discover the class of cases in which this institutional structure is internally consistent. We shall not treat the more complex possibilities mentioned above. By examining a model in which all markets exist and in which there are no "imperfections," we hope to establish a framework in which they could be studied.

A model of this type has been studied by Grandmont [6]. He assumes the existence of all spot markets at each date. Wealth is transferred between periods by holding money which affords no direct utility. We shall study a system in which trades in all commodities, both present and future, are possible at the initial date, and all future commodities are again tradeable in the future. However, we do not

[1] The author is indebted to G. Debreu and D. Sondermann for helpful discussions, to J. M. Grandmont for an enlightening correspondence, and to a referee. He held a National Science Foundation Postdoctoral Fellowship during the course of this research at the Center for Operations Research and Econometrics, Louvain, Belgium.

consider financial assets of the Grandmont type. Borrowing and lending may occur, nevertheless, by trading commodities deliverable in the future against present ones.

Hahn [8] has treated a sequence of markets economy in the case of certainty. Radner [10] has treated uncertainty in a model somewhat similar to ours. He proves that expectations exist that lead to equilibria at all dates and are consistent with these equilibria, whereas we treat expectations as data of the system. A further difference is that Radner's equilibrium expectations are point forecasts. We shall explicitly rule out this type of belief and shall show that its presence is generally inconsistent with the existence of an equilibrium for our model.

Section 2 describes the model and gives a theorem on the determinateness of optimal individual actions. Section 3 is concerned with further properties of demand correspondences. Section 4 contains the equilibrium theorem. Section 5 gives two examples of the non-existence of equilibrium in cases in which our assumptions fail. A concluding discussion and some open questions are given in Section 6.

The results of this paper are embodied in theorems, lemmas, corollaries, examples, and remarks. They are numbered consecutively within each section. Assumptions and other noteworthy expressions and equations are also numbered consecutively, but their numbers appear in parentheses. Definitions are given in the body of the text. They are not numbered, but the defined term is italicized.

2. THE MODEL AND THE DETERMINATENESS OF INDIVIDUAL BEHAVIOR

In this section we study the behavior of the representative individual in our system. Assumptions made in this section are to be understood, in the sequel, to apply to all individuals.

The relevant span of economic activity covers two periods. Period 1, the present, is the date at which the decisions we study will be taken. Period 2 occurs in the future. There are l_1 commodities in the economy in period 1 and l_2 in period 2. We let $l_1 + l_2 = l$.

In period 1 there are markets for the l_1 currently deliverable commodities and markets for contracts for future delivery of the l_2 commodities of period 2. We assume that storage of commodities is impossible. Thus, even though some of the period 1 commodities may be identical to some of the period 2 commodities, physically, they must be regarded as separate economic entities.

The *endowment* of the individual is $\omega = (\omega^1, \omega^2) \in R^l_+$ where $\omega^1 \in R^{l_1}_+$, $\omega^2 \in R^{l_2}_+$, and both are known with certainty. We assume

(2.1) $\quad \omega \gg 0$.

A *consumption stream*, $x = (x^1, x^2) \in R^l_+$, represents a feasible realization for the individual during the two periods. That is, we assume:

(2.2) The consumption sets are the non-negative orthant of the commodity space each period.

Market prices at date 1 are written $p = (p^1, p^2) \in R^l_+ \setminus \{0\}$, where p^1 is the price vector for current commodities and p^2 is the price vector for future contracts. Since the set of available net trades for each individual is completely determined by the ratios between components of p, we normalize p so that

$$p \in \Delta^l = \{p \in R^l_+ | \Sigma \, p_i = 1\}.$$

An *action* of the individual at date 1 is written $z = (x^1, b)$, where $x^1 \in R^{l_1}_+$ and $b \in R^{l_2}$. We denote by x^1 the first part of the consumption stream that the individual will obtain; b represents the vector of futures contracts traded. If $b_j > 0$, the individual has contracted at time 1 to receive commodity j at time 2, and conversely. At time 2, the market meets again for the l_2 commodities of this period. The endowment of the individual at this time, given that he took the action (x^1, b) at time 1, is $\omega^2 + b$. In general, $\omega^2 + b$ will not be non-negative. It is allowable for an individual to sell contracts for a commodity in excess of his endowment, but he must be prepared to purchase enough of this commodity at time 2 to fulfill his obligations. This is made precise below.

The individual has expectations about the prices he will face at time 2. A price vector at time 2 is written $q \in R^{l_2}_+ \setminus \{0\}$. Since, given an action taken in period 1, the set of trading opportunities is invariant to a change in all prices by the same proportion, we can take

$$q \in \Delta^{l_2} = \{q \in R^{l_2}_+ | \Sigma q_j = 1\}.$$

For every $p \in \Delta^l$, the individual's *subjective beliefs* or *expectations* about $q \in \Delta^{l_2}$ can be summarized by

$$\psi : \Delta^l \to M(\Delta^{l_2}, \mathscr{B}_{\Delta^{l_2}})$$

where $M(\Delta^{l_2}, \mathscr{B}_{\Delta^{l_2}})$ is the set of all probability measures on Δ^{l_2} with its Borel σ-field. Let "int" denote "interior," understood to be taken relative to the manifold $\{q \in R^{l_2} \Sigma \, q_i = 1\}$. We assume

(2.3) (i) for all $p \in \Delta^l$, int co supp $\psi(p) \neq \varnothing$;

(ii) for all $p \in \Delta^l$, $\psi(p) (\text{int } \Delta^{l_2}) = 1$.

This assumption rules out the possibility of point expectations, that is, the situation in which the individual is uncertain about prices, yet "expects" a particular price with certainty, except in the vacuous case $l_2 = 1$. It also implies that no zero price is ever given any positive weight in anyone's expectations. The rationale for this is that they are forecasting future *equilibria* which they know cannot have zero prices since they are insatiable in all commodities themselves.

Strictly speaking, we shall not actually need this assumption in what follows. However, without it, the statement of Theorem 2.1 becomes more complex. (We would have to say that demand is determinate at prices p if and only if $p \gg 0$ and $\bar{p}(p) \in \text{int}_L$ co supp $\psi(p)$, where int_L means the interior of the indicated set relative to the smallest linear manifold L containing it; see below for notation. Similar technical changes would have to be made later in the presentation. On the whole, the increased generality of dropping (2.3) does not seem to be worth it. The spirit of the generalized conditions, that there must be "sufficient" variability of prices for demand to be determinate, remains the same; see Remark 2.8.

We assume that the preferences of the individual can be represented by a von Neumann-Morgenstern utility function, u, on the space of all consumption streams, R^l_+. Further we assume that

$$u : R^l_+ \to R^1$$

satisfies

(2.4a) u is continuous,

(2.4b) u is concave,

(2.4c) u is strictly monotone,

(2.4d) u is bounded

(see Grandmont [5]).

Suppose an individual has taken an action $z = (x^1, b)$ in period 1 and now faces a price system $q \in \Delta^{l_2}$ in period 2. He will choose $x^2 \in R^{l_2}_+$ to solve

$$\max u(x^1, x^2)$$

subject to

$$q \cdot x^2 \leqslant q \cdot (\omega^2 + b).$$

In order for a solution to exist to this problem, it is necessary that $q \cdot (\omega^2 + b) \geqslant 0$ and that $q \gg 0$. If a solution exists, we shall denote the value of the objective function at the optimum by $\phi(x^1, b, q)$. Given (x^1, b), the function $(x^1, b, \cdot)$ is well-defined, continuous and bounded on the set $\{q \in \Delta^{l_2} | q \gg 0, q \cdot (b + \omega^2) \geqslant 0\}$.

The individual then maximizes

$$\int_{\Delta^{l_2}} \phi(x^1, b, q)\psi(p)(dq)$$

subject to $p^1 \cdot x^1 + p^2 \cdot b \leqslant p^1 \cdot \omega^1$.

The set of feasible $(x^1, b) \in R^l$ must be such that the objective function is defined at these points. That is, in addition to the budget constraint, we must have

(2.5) $q \cdot (b + \omega^2) \geqslant 0$ for all $q \in \operatorname{supp} \psi(p)$,

for if this were violated at some q, then it would be violated in a neighborhood of q that is assigned positive weight by $\psi(p)$. Hence, the above integral would not be well-defined. This is formally analogous to the statement that the optimal consumption bundle must lie in the consumption set in standard consumer theory. It is not an assumption on behavior as such. We denote, for all $x^1 \geqslant 0$ and b satisfying (2.5),

$$v(x^1, b, p) = \int_{\Delta^{l_2}} \phi(x^1, b, q)\psi(p)(dq).$$

We call v the *expected utility index*. Let $p \in \Delta^l$, $p = (p^1, p^2)$. If $p^2 \neq 0$, write

$$\tilde{p}(p) = \frac{p^2}{\sum_j p_j^2} \in \Delta^{l_2}.$$

THEOREM 2.1: *A solution to the maximization problem of a trader described as above exists if and only if*

(2.6)   (i) $p \gg 0$,

    (ii) $\tilde{p}(p) \in int\ co\ supp\ \psi(p)$.

Theorem 2.1 is proven in separate parts by Lemmas 2.2–2.6. Lemmas 2.2 and 2.3 prove the sufficiency of (2.6) and Lemmas 2.4–2.6 prove its necessity.

LEMMA 2.2: *Under conditions* (2.6) *the set of feasible actions for the consumer is compact.*

PROOF: Let $p = (p^1, p^2)$ satisfy (2.6); let $B = \{b \in R^{l_2} | q \cdot (b + \omega^2) \geqslant 0$ for all $q \in supp\ \psi(p)\}$; and let $H(x^1) = \{b \in R^{l_2} | p^2 \cdot b \leqslant p^1 \cdot \omega^1 - p^1 \cdot x^1\}$. Thus the set of all feasible actions with prices p is

$$A = \{(x^1, b) | x^1 \geqslant 0, b \in B \cap H(x^1)\}.$$

Let $x^{1k} \to \bar{x}^1$, $b^k \to \bar{b}$, such that $(x^{1k}, b^k) \in A$ for all k. Clearly, $\bar{x}^1 \geqslant 0$ and $\bar{b} \in B$. Also,

$$p^2 \cdot b^k \leqslant p^1 \omega^1 - p^1 x^{1k} \quad \text{for all } k.$$

Taking the limit, we have that $\bar{b} \in H(\bar{x}^1)$. Hence A is closed.

Let $H(0) \equiv H$; $H(x^1) \subseteq H$ for all $x^1 \geqslant 0$.

First we shall show that $B \cap H$ is bounded. Assume not. Then there exists $\langle b^k \rangle$, $k = 1, \ldots$, such that $b^k \in B \cap H$ and $\|b^k\| \equiv \Sigma_j |b_j^k| \to \infty$. Thus there exists j such that $|b_j^k| \to \infty$. Let $J_0^+ = \{j | \{b_j^k\}$ cannot be bounded above$\}$. $J_0^+ \neq \varnothing$, since otherwise we would have $qb^k \to -\infty$ for any $q \gg 0$, and this would contradict $b^k \in B$, for all k. Let $j_1 \in J_0^+$ and let $\langle k_1 \rangle$ index a subsequence $\langle b_{j_1}^{k_1} \rangle$ that is monotone increasing and unbounded. Let $J_1^+ = \{j | b_j^{k_1}$ cannot be bounded above$\}$. If $J_1^+ \neq \{j_1\}$, then let $j_2 \neq j_1, j_2 \in J_1^+$, and let $\langle k_2 \rangle$ be a subsequence of $\langle k_1 \rangle$ such that $\langle b_{j_2}^{k_2} \rangle$ is monotone increasing and unbounded. Continue in this way until obtaining a set $J_m^+ = \{j_1, \ldots, j_m\}$ and a sequence $\langle k_m \rangle$ such that $\langle b_j^{k_m} \rangle$ is monotone increasing and unbounded for all $j \in J_m^+$ and bounded above for all $j \notin J_m^+$.

Let $J_0^- = \{j | b_k^{k_m}$ cannot be bounded below$\}$, $J_0^- \neq \varnothing$ because otherwise $p \cdot b^{k_m} \to +\infty$, contradicting $b^{k_m} \in H$ for all k_m. Let $j_{m+1} \in J_0^-$ and $\langle k_{m+1} \rangle$ be a subsequence of $\langle k_m \rangle$ such that $\langle b_{j_{m+1}}^{k_{m+1}} \rangle$ is monotone decreasing and unbounded. As above, construct $\langle k_{m+2} \rangle, \ldots, \langle k_{m+m'} \rangle$ and $J_1^-, \ldots, J_{m'}^-$ such that $\{b_j^{k_{m+m'}}\}$ is montone decreasing and unbounded for all $j \in J_{m'}^-$ and bounded below for all $j \notin J_{m'}^-$.

Denote the subsequence $\langle k_{m+m'}\rangle$ by $\langle r \rangle$. Thus if $j \in J_m^+$, $b_j^r \to +\infty$, if $j \in J_{m'}^-$, $b_j^r \to -\infty$, and if $j \notin J_m^+ \cup J_m^-$, b_j^r is bounded. Let $B' = \{b \in R^{l_2} | q \cdot b \geqq -q \cdot \omega_2$ for all $q \in$ co supp $\psi(p)\}$. Clearly $B' \subseteq B$. Take $b \in B$ and $q \in$ co supp $\psi(p)$. Then $q = \Sigma \alpha_j q^j$ for some $\{\alpha_j\} \subset [0,1]$ with $\Sigma \alpha_j = 1$ and $q^j \in$ supp $\psi(p)$. Thus $q^j \cdot b \geqq -q^j \cdot \omega^2$ for all j. Combining these inequalities, $q \cdot b \geqq -q \cdot \omega^2$ or $b \in B'$. Hence, $B = B'$.

Since $\tilde{p}(p) \in$ int co supp $\psi(p)$, by assumption, there exists $q \in$ co supp $\psi(p)$ such that $q \gg 0$, and $q_j < \tilde{p}_j(p)$ for all $j \in J_m^+$, $q_j = \tilde{p}_j(p)$ for all $j \in J_m^+ \cup J_{m'}^-$, and $q_j > \tilde{p}_j(p)$ for all $j \in J_{m'}^-$.

Hence $\langle(\tilde{p}(p) - q) \cdot b^r\rangle$ is monotone and diverges to $+\infty$. If $p^2 \cdot b^r \leqq p^1 \cdot \omega^1 - p^1 \cdot x^1 \leqq p^1 \cdot \omega^1$ for all r, then $q \cdot b^r \to -\infty$. Thus $b^r \notin B'$ for r sufficiently large, and as $B' = B$ we have a contradiction. If $q \cdot b^r \geqq -q \cdot \omega^2$ for all r, then $\tilde{p}(p) \cdot b^r \to +\infty$, or $p^2 \cdot b^r \to +\infty$, contradicting $b^r \in H$ for all r. Thus $B \cap H$ is bounded.

Let $\{I | I = p^2 \cdot b$ and $b \in B \cap H\}$ be bounded below by I. If $(x^1, b) \in A$, x^1 must satisfy $p^1 \cdot x^1 \leqq p^1 \cdot \omega^1 - I$ and $x^1 \geqq 0$. Hence, A is contained in the product of two bounded sets. Thus A, the set of all feasible actions with prices p, is compact.

$$Q.E.D.$$

LEMMA 2.3: $v(x^1, b, p)$ is a continuous function of (x^1, b), on the set A of feasible actions at prices p.

PROOF: See Grandmont [5].

LEMMA 2.4: If $p_j^1 = 0$ for some j, then no solution to the individual's maximization problem exists.

PROOF: Let $(x^1, b) \in A$ be such a solution, and let $\tilde{x}_k^1 = x_k^1$ for $k \neq j$ and $\tilde{x}_j^1 > x_j^1$. By strict monotonicity of u, $\phi(\tilde{x}^1, b, q) > \phi(x^1, b, q)$ for all $q \in$ supp $\psi(p)$, $q \gg 0$. Clearly $(\tilde{x}^1, b) \in A$. Hence, (x^1, b) cannot be optimal.

LEMMA 2.5: If $p^2 \neq 0$ and $\tilde{p}(p) \notin$ int co supp $\psi(p)$, then no solution to the individual's maximization problem exists.

PROOF: Let $\Psi = \{y \in R_+^{l_2} | y = \alpha q$ for some $q \in$ co supp $\psi(p)$ and $\alpha \geqq 0\}$. Then Ψ is clearly closed and convex. Further, int co supp $\psi(p) \neq \emptyset$ implies int $\Psi \neq \emptyset$, and the hypothesis of this lemma implies $\tilde{p}(p) \notin$ int Ψ. Thus there exists $z \in R^{l_2}$, $z \neq 0$, such that $\tilde{p}(p) \cdot z = 0$ and $y \cdot z \geqq 0$ for all $y \in \Psi$. In particular $q \cdot z \geqq 0$ for all $q \in$ co supp $\psi(p)$.

Suppose that for all $q \in$ supp $\psi(p)$, $q \cdot z = 0$. Clearly $q \cdot z = 0$ for all $q \in$ co supp $\psi(p)$. Take $\bar{q} \in$ int co supp ψ; $\bar{q} \gg 0$. If z is a vector with all components the same, then $\bar{q} \cdot z \neq 0$ follows from $z \neq 0$. Since this would contradict our assumption, let $z_j > z_{j'}$ for some j, j'. We can then find $\tilde{q} \in$ int co supp $\psi(p)$ near $\bar{q}$ such that $\tilde{q}_j > \bar{q}_j$, $\tilde{q}_{j'} < \bar{q}_{j'}$, and $\tilde{q}_k = \bar{q}_k$ for all other k. Thus either $\bar{q} \cdot z \neq 0$ or $\tilde{q} \cdot z \neq 0$, contradicting $q \cdot z = 0$ for all $q \in$ co supp $\psi(p)$.

Thus there exists $q' \in$ supp $\psi(p)$ such that $q' \cdot z \neq 0$. Let $\bar{N}(q')$ be a closed ball with center q' such that $q \in \bar{N}(q')$ implies $q \cdot z \neq 0$. Suppose $\psi(p)(\bar{N}(q')) = 0$; this would contradict $q' \in \operatorname{supp} \psi(p)$. Let $V = \{q \in \Delta^{l_2} | q \cdot z > 0\}$, and let $\overline{V} = \{q \in V | q \gg 0\}$. Since $\psi(p) (\operatorname{int} \Delta^{l_2}) = 1$, and V contains $\overline{N}(p)$, we have $\psi(p)(\overline{V}) = \psi(p)(V) > 0$.

Suppose now that $(x^1, b) \in A$ is an optimal action, contrary to the conclusion of this lemma. Consider $(x^1, b + z)$. By definition of $\tilde{p}(p)$, $p^2 \cdot (b + z) \leqq p^1 \cdot \omega^1 - p^1 x^1$. By the choice of z, $q \cdot (b + z) \geqq -q \cdot \omega^2$ for all $q \in \operatorname{supp} \psi(p)$. Thus $(x^1, (b + z) \in A$.

It follows from the strict monotonicity of u that $\phi(x^1, b, q) \leqq \phi(x^1, b + z, q)$ for all $q \in \operatorname{supp} \psi(p)$, $q \gg 0$, and that strict inequality holds for $q \in V$. This contradicts the assumption that (x^1, b) is an optimal action. $\hspace{1cm}$ Q.E.D.

LEMMA 2.6: *If $p^2 = 0$, then no solution to the individual's maximization problem exists.*

PROOF: Let $z \gg 0$. If $(x^1, b) \in A$ is an optimal solution, consider $(x^1, b + z)$. Clearly $(x^2, b + z) \in A$ since $p^2 = 0$. Also $\phi(x^1, b + z, q) > \phi(x^1, b, q)$ for all $q \in \operatorname{supp} \psi(p)$, $q \gg 0$. Hence (x^1, b) was not optimal in A. $\hspace{1cm}$ Q.E.D.

REMARK 2.7: The case in which $p_j^2 = 0$ for some j but not $p^2 = 0$ is covered under the conditions of Lemma 2.5. We therefore did not consider this negation of (2.6(i)) separately.

REMARK 2.8: Assumption (2.3) rules out point expectations. If we were to assume that the individual held such expectations (i.e., supp $\psi(p)$ is a single point), it is clear that demand would be determinate only for $p \in \Delta$ such that $\{\tilde{p}(p)\} = \operatorname{supp} \psi(p)$. It is clear that equilibrium in this case could exist only if, for some $p \in \Delta$, every individual held the same beliefs—a most unlikely instance.

We find this conclusion heartening since point expectations mean that the individual is "sure," and this seems contrary to the very spirit of the uncertainty question. In the case considered, in which the uncertainty is genuine, equilibrium will be shown to exist for a much wider class of environments.

3. DEMAND CORRESPONDENCES

We shall now study the dependence of the set of optimal actions on p. Our analysis is for the representative individual and all assumptions made are assumed to apply to all individuals in the economy.

Let $\mathscr{C}(\Delta^{l_2})$ be the class of compact subsets of Δ^{l_2}. Define

$$\sigma : \Delta^l \to \mathscr{C}(\Delta^{l_2})$$

by

$$\sigma(p) = \operatorname{supp} \psi(p).$$

The following two assumptions are made on ψ and σ:

(3.1) $\quad \psi$ is continuous in the weak topology.

(3.2) $\quad \sigma$ is an upper hemi-continuous correspondence.

REMARK 3.1: Assumption (3.1) implies that σ is lower hemi-continuous as follows: Take $\bar{q} \in$ supp $\psi(\bar{p})$. Then if G is a neighborhood of $\bar{q}$, $\psi(\bar{p})(G) > 0$, since otherwise $\Delta^{l_2} \setminus G$ would contain supp $\psi(\bar{p})$. Let $p^k \to \bar{p}$. If σ were not lower hemi-continuous, then there would exist an open neighborhood of $\bar{q}$, $\bar{G}$, such that

$$\bar{G} \cap \text{supp } \psi(p^k) = \varnothing$$

for infinitely many k. Hence, $\psi(p^k)(\bar{G}) = 0$ for infinitely many k. But weak continuity of ψ is equivalent to $\lim_k \inf \psi(p^k)(G) \geqq \psi(\bar{p})(G)$ for all open sets G (see Parthasarathy [9]). Thus $\psi(\bar{p})(\bar{G}) = 0$. This is a contradiction.

Hence, the combination of (3.1) and (3.2) implies

(3.3) σ is a continuous correspondence.

Denote

$$B(p) = \{b \in R^{l_2} | q \cdot (b + \omega^2) \geqq 0 \quad \text{for all } q \in \text{supp } \psi(p)\},$$

$$H(x^1, p) = \{b \in R^{l_2} | p^2 \cdot b \leqslant p^1 \cdot \omega^1 - p^1 \cdot x^1\}, \text{ and}$$

$$A(p) = \{(x^1, b) \in R^l | x^1 \geqq 0, b \in B(p) \cap H(x^1, p)\}.$$

These sets correspond to B, $H(x^1)$, and A of the last section, except that we now consider p to be a variable.

Denote

$$S = \{p \in \Delta^l | p \gg 0, \bar{p}(p) \in \text{int co supp } \psi(p)\}.$$

The result of the last section is that the individual's maximization problem has a solution if and only if $p \in S$.

We now assume

(3.4) S is convex.

REMARK 3.2: This assumption is, of course, a condition on $\psi(\cdot)$. If supp $\psi(\cdot)$ is a constant, it is trivially satisfied. The only role of this assumption is in the proof of Lemma 4.7. Although it may be weakened considerably without affecting 4.7, it may not be done away with altogether; see Remark 4.8 and Example 5.1.

LEMMA 3.3: (i) *The correspondence $A(\cdot)$ is convex-valued, lower hemi-continuous on Δ^l, and has a closed graph*; (ii) *$A(\cdot)$ is compact-valued and upper hemi-continuous on S.*

PROOF: That $A(p)$ is non-empty and convex for all p in Δ^l is obvious. The fact that $A(\cdot)$ has a closed graph follows directly from the lower hemi-continuity of σ; see assumption (3.1) and Remark 3.1. It remains to be shown that:

(i) $A(\cdot)$ is lower hemi-continuous on Δ^l. Let $p \in \Delta^l$ and $z \in A(\bar{p})$. Let $\{p^k\} \in \Delta^l$ be a sequence tending to $\bar{p}$. We wish to find a sequence $\{z^k\} \in A(p^k)$ which tends to z. For any $b \in R^{l_2}$, let $f(b)$ be the minimum of $q \cdot (b + \omega^2)$ when $q \in \Delta^{l_2}$. Then f is a continuous function of b and $f(0) > 0$ since $\omega^2 \gg 0$. Therefore, it is possible to find $\bar{b} \ll 0$ such that $f(\bar{b}) > 0$. Let $\bar{z} = (0, \bar{b})$; choose $0 \leqslant \lambda < 1$, and define $\tilde{z} = (\tilde{x}^1, \tilde{b}) = \lambda z + (1 - \lambda)\bar{z}$. We claim that $\tilde{z} \in A(\bar{p})$ and $\tilde{z} \in A(p^k)$ for k large enough. First, $\bar{p}^2 \cdot \tilde{b} < \bar{p}^1 \cdot \omega^1$, since either $\bar{p}^1 = 0$, in which case $\bar{p}^2 \cdot \tilde{b} < 0$, or $\bar{p}^1 \neq 0$, in which case $\bar{p}^2 \cdot \tilde{b} \leqslant 0 < p^1 \cdot \omega^1$. It follows that

$$\bar{p}^1 \cdot \tilde{x}^1 + \bar{p}^2 \cdot \tilde{b} < \bar{p}^1 \cdot \omega^1.$$

On the other hand, for every $q \in \operatorname{supp} \psi(\bar{p})$,

$$q \cdot (\tilde{b} + \omega^2) \geqslant (1 - \lambda)q \cdot (\bar{b} + \omega^2) \geqslant (1 - \lambda)f(\bar{b}) > 0.$$

Therefore, $\tilde{z} \in A(\bar{p})$. For k large enough, one has

$$p^{1k} \cdot \tilde{x}^1 + p^{2k} \cdot \tilde{b} < p^{1k} \cdot \omega^1.$$

Given $\tilde{b}$, and an arbitrary $p \in \Delta^l$, let $g(p)$ be the minimum of $q \cdot (\tilde{b} + \omega^2)$ when $q \in \operatorname{supp} \psi(p)$. Since $\operatorname{supp} \psi(\cdot)$ is a continuous correspondence, $g(\cdot)$ is continuous on Δ^l. We have $g(\bar{p}) \geqslant (1 - \lambda)f(\bar{b}) > 0$. Therefore, for k large enough,

$$q \cdot (\tilde{b} + \omega^2) \geqslant g(p^k) > 0 \quad \text{for all } q \in \operatorname{supp} \psi(p^k).$$

This shows that $\tilde{z} \in A(p^k)$ for k large enough.

As this is true for any $\lambda < 1$, one can construct a sequence $z^k \in A(p^k)$ which tends to z, as follows. Let λ^n be a sequence $0 \leqslant \lambda^n < 1$ which tends to 1. For any $n \geqslant 1$, let $\bar{z}^n = \lambda^n z + (1 - \lambda^n)\bar{z}$. Consider $k_1 = \min \{\bar{k}|\bar{z}^1 \in A(p^k), \text{ all } k \geqslant \bar{k}\}$, and let $z^k = (0, 0)$ for $k \leqslant k_1$. Then consider $k_2 = \min\{\bar{k}|\bar{k} \geqslant k_1 + 1, \bar{z}^2 \in A(p^k) \text{ for all } k \geqslant \bar{k}\}$, and let $z^k = \bar{z}^1$ for $k_1 \leqslant k < k_2$. Proceed by induction: $k_n = \min \{\bar{k}|\bar{k} \geqslant k_{n-1} + 1, \bar{z}^n \in A(p^k) \text{ for all } k \geqslant \bar{k}\}$, and $z^k = \bar{z}^{n-1}$ for $k_{n-1} \leqslant k < k_n$. The sequence z^k satisfies all requirements. This shows (i) of the lemma.

(ii) $A(\cdot)$ is compact-valued and upper hemi-continuous on S. Let $p^k \in S$ converging to $\bar{p} \in S$. Consider $z^k = (x^k, b^k)$ in $A(p^k)$. It suffices to show that the sequence $\{z^k\}$ is bounded. As $p^{1k} \cdot x^k + p^{2k} \cdot b^k \leqslant p^{1k} \cdot \omega^1$, it is sufficient to show that the sequence $\{b\}^k$ is bounded. Assume that this is not true. One could find a subsequence (retain the same notation) such that $\|b^k\|$ diverges to $+\infty$. One can then proceed as in the proof of Lemma 2.2 to find J^+, J^-, and a subsequence (same notation) such that $b_j^k \to +\infty$ for all $j \in J^+$, $b_j^k \to -\infty$ for all $j \in J^-$, and b_j^k is bounded for $j \notin J^+ \cup J^-$. Certainly, $J^+ \neq \varnothing$, for $\tilde{p}(p^k) \cdot b^k \geqslant -\tilde{p}(p^k) \cdot \omega^2$ for all k, and $\tilde{p}(p^k)$ tends to $\tilde{p}(\bar{p}) \gg 0$. On the other hand, $J^- \neq \varnothing$, since $\tilde{p}(p^k) \cdot b^k \leqslant (p^{1k}/\Sigma_j p_j^{2k}) \cdot \omega^1$ for all k. Since $\tilde{p}(\bar{p}) \in \operatorname{int} \operatorname{co} \operatorname{supp} \psi(\bar{p})$, there exists $\bar{q}$ in $\operatorname{co} \operatorname{supp} \psi(\bar{p})$ such that $\bar{q}_j < \tilde{p}_j(\bar{p})$ for all $j \in J^+$, $\bar{q}_j > \tilde{p}_j(\bar{p})$ for all $j \in J^-$, and $\bar{q}_j = \tilde{p}_j(\bar{p})$ for all $j \notin J^+ \cup J^-$.

Since $\operatorname{co} \operatorname{supp} \psi(\cdot)$ is lower hemi-continuous at $\bar{p}$, there exists a sequence $\{q^k\} \in \operatorname{co} \operatorname{supp} \psi(p^k)$ such that $q^k \to \bar{q}$. Then $(\tilde{p}(p^k) - q^k) \cdot b^k$ diverges to $+\infty$. However, this is impossible, since, for all k:

$$(\tilde{p}(p^k) - q^k) \cdot b^k \leqslant \left(p^{1k} \Big/ \sum_j p_j^{2k} \right) \cdot \omega^1 + q^k \cdot \omega^2. \qquad \textit{Q.E.D.}$$

LEMMA 3.4: (i) If (x^{1k}, b^k, p^k) be such that $(x^{1k}, b^k) \in A(p^k)$ and $p^k \in \Delta^l$ for all k, then (x^{1k}, b^k, p^k) converging to (x^1, b, p) implies $\lim v(x^{1k}, b^k, p^k) = v(x^1, b, p)$. (ii) $v(x^1, b, p)$ is concave in (x^1, b) for all $p \in S$. (iii) $v(x^1, b, p)$ is strictly monotone in (x^1, b) for all $p \in S$.

PROOF: These properties can be shown using the methods of Grandmont [6, Section 3.7, Propositions 1, 2, 3] or Sondermann [11, Lemmas 7.1, 7.2]. We shall not reproduce the proof here. Weak continuity of ψ is necessary for (i), (ii), and (iii) follow from the corresponding properties of u.

The *demand correspondence* is defined for each $p \in S$ as

$$\xi(p) = \{(x^1, b) \in A(p) | v(x^1, b, p) \geqslant v(x^{1'}, b', p) \quad \text{for all } (x^{1'}, b') \in A(p)\}.$$

To shorten the notation slightly we shall write the generic element of $A(p)$ as $z = (x^1, b) \in R^l$.

THEOREM 3.5: Let $p^k \in S$, $p^k \to \bar{p}$, and $\bar{z}^k \in \xi(p^k)$, $\bar{z}^k \to \bar{z} = (\bar{x}^1, \bar{b})$. Then $\bar{z} \in A(\bar{p})$ and $v(\bar{x}^1, \bar{b}, \bar{p}) \geqslant v(x^1, b, \bar{p})$ for all $(x^1, b) \in A(\bar{p})$.

PROOF: Since $A(\cdot)$ has a closed graph, $\bar{z} \in A(\bar{p})$. Let $z \in A(\bar{p})$. Since $A(\cdot)$ is lower hemi-continuous (see Lemma 3.3), there is a sequence $z^k \in A(p^k)$, $z^k \to z$. Now for all k, $v(\bar{z}^k, p^k) \geqslant v(z^k, p^k)$. By (i) of Lemma 3.4, $v(\bar{z}, \bar{p}) \geqslant v(z, \bar{p})$.   Q.E.D.

THEOREM 3.6: (i) $\xi(\cdot)$ is convex and compact-valued and upper hemi-continuous on S. (ii) $p \cdot \xi(p) = p^1 \cdot \omega^1$ for all $p \in S$.

PROOF: The first two parts of (i) follow from the fact that $A(\cdot)$ is convex and compact-valued on S and that $v(\cdot, \cdot, \cdot)$ is continuous and concave in its first two arguments. Since ξ has a closed graph, it is sufficient to show that for any sequences $p^k \in S$ $p^k \to \bar{p} \in S$, $z^k \in \xi(p^k)$, then $\{z^k\}$ is bounded. This follows from the upper hemi-continuity and compact valuedness of $A(\cdot)$ on S.

Part (ii) follows from strict monotonicity of $v(\cdot, \cdot, \cdot)$ in its first two arguments. A proof can be constructed paralleling that of Grandmont [6, Section 3.8, Proposition 1].

LEMMA 3.7: Let A be convex and $N_\varepsilon(a) \subset N_{\varepsilon/2}(A)$ for some a. Then $N_{\varepsilon/2}(a) \subset A$.

PROOF: If not, then there exists x such that $x \in N_{\varepsilon/2}(a)$ and $x \notin A$. Since A is convex, we can find $z \neq 0$ such that $z \cdot x = 0$ and $z \cdot a' < 0$ for all $a' \in A$. Further z can be chosen such that $\Sigma |z_i| = 1$. Since $x \in N_{\varepsilon/2}(a)$, $N_{\varepsilon/2}(x) \subset N_\varepsilon(a)$ and, therefore, by the hypothesis of the lemma, $N_{\varepsilon/2}(x) \subset N_{\varepsilon/2}(A)$. Let $y \in N_{\varepsilon/2}(x)$ such that $z \cdot y = \varepsilon/2$. But for all $\tilde{a} \in N_{\varepsilon/2}(A)$, $z \cdot \tilde{a} < \varepsilon/2$. Hence $y \notin N_{\varepsilon/2}(A)$, contradicting $N_{\varepsilon/2}(x) \subset N_{\varepsilon/2}(A)$.   Q.E.D.

Denote $\bar{\sigma}(p) \equiv \text{co } \sigma(p) \equiv \text{co supp } \psi(p)$.

LEMMA 3.8: S is open in Δ^l.

PROOF: Since $S = \{p \in \Delta^l | p \gg 0\} \cap \{p \in \Delta^l | \tilde{p}(p) \in \text{int } \bar{\sigma}(p)\}$, it suffices to show that the latter set is open. Let $p^* \in \Delta^l$ be such that $\tilde{p}(p^*) \in \text{int } \bar{\sigma}(p)$. Then there exists $\varepsilon > 0$ such that $N_\varepsilon(\tilde{p}(p^*)) \subset \text{int } \bar{\sigma}(p^*) \subset \bar{\sigma}(p^*)$. Since $\tilde{p}(\cdot)$ is continuous, there exists $\delta' > 0$ such that $|p - p^*| < \delta'$ implies $\tilde{p}(p) \in N_{\varepsilon/2}(\tilde{p}(p^*))$. By the triangle inequality we have that $N_{\varepsilon/2}(\tilde{p}(p)) \subset N_\varepsilon(\tilde{p}(p^*))$ and hence

$$N_{\varepsilon/2}(\tilde{p}(p)) \subset \bar{\sigma}(p^*).$$

Since $\sigma(\cdot)$ is lower hemi-continuous, so is $\bar{\sigma}(\cdot)$. Hence, there exists $\delta'' > 0$ such that

$$\bar{\sigma}(p^*) \subset N_{\varepsilon/2}(\bar{\sigma}(p))$$

for $|p - p^*| < \delta''$. Combining the two equations above, $N_{\varepsilon/2}(\tilde{p}(p)) \subset N_{\varepsilon/4}(\bar{\sigma}(p))$ for p such that $|p - p^*| < \min(\delta', \delta'') \equiv \delta$. Since $\bar{\sigma}(p)$ is convex we apply the last lemma, obtaining $N_{\varepsilon/4}(\tilde{p}(p)) \subset \bar{\sigma}(p)$ for $|p - p^*| < \delta$. Thus there is a neighborhood of p^* in $\{p \in \Delta^l | \tilde{p}(p) \in \text{int } \bar{\sigma}(p)\}$.

$$Q.E.D.$$

4. EQUILIBRIUM

The previous sections have studied the theory of individual behavior when the market is known to meet again in the future. We now study the question of existence of an equilibrium for an economy with a finite number, I, of individuals, all of whom behave as above. We denote the index set of all individuals $\mathcal{I} = \{1, \ldots, I\}$ and the generic element of $\mathcal{I}$ by i. Any entity used in the previous sections will now be written with a presuperscript i when it refers to the ith individual. For example, ^iS is the set of prices on which i's demand correspondence, $^i\xi$, is non-empty valued.

Let

$$P = \bigcap_{\mathcal{I}} {}^iS,$$

where P is the set of prices on which everyone's excess demand correspondence is well-defined. We write the *aggregate excess demand correspondence*

$$\zeta: P \to R^l,$$

defined as

$$\zeta(p) = \sum_{\mathcal{I}} {}^i\xi(p) - \left(\sum_{\mathcal{I}} {}^i\omega^1, 0\right).$$

Note that the aggregate excess demand for a currently deliverable commodity j is $\sum {}^i\xi_j(p) - \sum {}^i\omega_j^1$ which corresponds to the usual notion of demand minus supply; and the aggregate excess demand for a futures contract, j, is $\sum {}^i\xi_j(p)$, which is the sum of offers to buy such contracts minus offers to sell them.

An *equilibrium* is an $I + 1$ tuple in $\Delta^l \times R^{ll}$, $(p^*, {}^1z^*, \ldots, {}^Iz^*)$ such that $^iz^* \in {}^i\xi(p^*)$ for all i and

$$\sum_{\mathcal{I}} {}^iz^* = \left(\sum_{\mathcal{I}} {}^i\omega^1, 0\right).$$

In order to have some hope of finding an equilibrium, it is necessary to assume

(4.1) P is non-empty.

That is, there must be some price at which all excess demand correspondences have a non-empty value. Thus (4.1) is a condition on the compatibility of the individual's expectations.

REMARK 4.1: Since ^iS is open and convex for each i, by Lemma 3.8 and assumption (3.4), it follows that P is open and convex, since it is the intersection of a finite number of open, convex sets.

One can construct examples, and we shall present one such in Section 5, such that equilibrium does not exist even under all the assumptions presented thus far. It is therefore necessary to postulate the following:

(4.2)   There exists $C \subseteq \varDelta^{l_2}$ such that (i) C has non-empty interior in $\varDelta^{l_2}$; (ii) for all $p \in \varDelta^l$ and all $i \in \mathscr{I}$, $C \subseteq$ int co supp $^i\psi(p)$.

It is clear that for each $p \in \varDelta^l$ one can find an open set in int co supp $^i\psi(p)$ for all i. Thus the force of assumption (4.2) is to assert that one can choose the same such set for all $p \in \varDelta^l$. We shall say that expectations are *common on C* if (4.2) holds. Intuitively, it means that some futures prices are always given positive weight, irrespective of the current price vector. A further discussion of (4.2) will follow an example of Section 5, in which it fails to hold, all of our other assumptions hold, and there is no equilibrium.

REMARK 4.2: Assumption (4.2) is, of course, a joint condition on all of the $^i\psi(\cdot)$. If each of the supp $^i\psi(\cdot)$ were constant, it would be trivially satisfied. It is interesting to note that (3.4) is also implied by the same condition. One can easily observe that (3.4) and (4.2) are independent, yet both are implied by the same assumption on supp $^i\psi(\cdot)$. This assumption is far too strong, however. We therefore assume (3.4) and (4.2) separately. One can easily verify that there is a wide class of cases in which supp $^i\psi(\cdot)$ are not constant and yet in which (3.4) and (4.2) are both satisfied.

Assumption (4.2) plays two distinct roles in the proof. It is first used to conclude unboundedness of the aggregate excess demand correspondence, as prices go to the boundary of P, from unboundedness of the individual demand correspondences; see Theorem 4.4, Remark 4.5, and Example 4.6.
    The second use is to apply a compactness argument to obtain convergence of a subsequence of fixed points in the existence theorem 4.13. Example 5.2 shows how the proof breaks down, and in fact equilibrium fails to exist, in the absence of this assumption.
    We shall write the closure of P in $\varDelta^l$ as $\bar{P}$.

LEMMA 4.3: *Let* $\{p^k\} \in P$, $p^k \to \bar{p}$, *and* $\bar{p} \in \bar{P} \backslash P$. *Let* $^iz^k \in {}^i\xi(p^k)$ *for all* i. *Then for some* i, $\|{}^iz^k\| \to \infty$.

PROOF: If the lemma were false, $\{\|{}^iz^k\|\}_k$ would lie in a compact set for every i. Hence, a subsequence would converge to $^i\bar{z} = (^i\bar{x}, {}^i\bar{b})$ for every i. Now for some i, $\bar{p} \notin {}^iS$. By (3.5), $^iv(^i\bar{z}, \bar{p}) \geqq {}^iv(z, \bar{p})$ for all $z \in {}^iA(\bar{p})$. This would contradict Theorem 2.1.

$\qquad\qquad\qquad\qquad\qquad\qquad\qquad\qquad\qquad\qquad\qquad\qquad\qquad\qquad$ Q.E.D.

THEOREM 4.4: *Let* $\{p^k\} \subset P$, $p^k \to \bar{p}$, *and* $\bar{p} \in \bar{P} \backslash P$. *Then* $\|\zeta(p^k)\| \to \infty$.

REMARK 4.5: In the theory of general equilibrium with a single market date, this theorem follows immediately from the above lemma since the commodity space is bounded below. In our case, the theorem is proven using the assumption of common expectations (4.2). The following example shows why one may not be able to conclude the theorem from the above lemma in the absence of such an assumption.

EXAMPLE 4.6: Let $l_2 = 2$, and let $I = 2$. Suppose the supports of their expectations are given by

$$\text{supp } {}^1\psi(p) = \{q \in \Delta^2 | q_1 \geqq \tfrac{1}{2}\},$$

$$\text{supp } {}^2\psi(p) = \{q \in \Delta^2 | q_1 \leqq \tfrac{5}{4}\tilde{p}_1(p) - \tfrac{1}{8}\},$$

for all p. Consider a sequence $p^k \to \bar{p}$ such that $\tilde{p}_1(p^k) > \tfrac{1}{2}$ for all k and $\tilde{p}_1(\bar{p}) = \tfrac{1}{2}$. This means that, in the limit, individual 1 is sure (almost sure) that the relative price of future deliverable commodity 1 will be higher at the next market date than at the current market date. He will thus buy futures for this commodity and finance their purchase with sales of the other future. That is $^1b_1^k \to +\infty$ and $^1b_2^k \to -\infty$. But individual 2 believes the opposite. He thinks, in the limit, that long positions in commodity 2 are sure to make unbounded arbitrage profit. Hence $^2b_1^k \to -\infty$ and $^2b_2^k \to +\infty$. Thus although $\|{}^i\xi(p^k)\| \to \infty$ for all i, their speculations might "cancel out," so that we cannot conclude $\|\zeta(p^k)\| \to \infty$. But this example fails to satisfy the assumption that expectations are common on a set with non-empty interior. The only set in $\bigcap_{i=1,2} \text{supp } {}^i\psi(p^k)$ for all k is $\{\tfrac{1}{2}\}$.

We now proceed to a proof of Theorem 4.4.

PROOF OF THEOREM 4.4: Assume that the theorem is false. Then one can find a subsequence (keep the same notation) $z^k = (x^k, b^k) \in \zeta(p^k)$ which converges to $\bar{z}$. We shall derive a contradiction by showing that, for this subsequence, $\|b^k\| \to \infty$. Choose $^iz^k = (^ix^{1k}, {}^ib^k) \in \xi(p^k)$ for every i, such that $\Sigma_i(^iz^k - (^i\omega^1, 0)) = z^k$. For each i, the sequence $\{^ix^{1k}\}_k$ is bounded. This implies, in view of the last lemma, that $\|{}^ib^k\| \to \infty$ for some i.

Let C be such that int $C \neq \varnothing$ and $C \subseteq \text{co supp } {}^i\psi(p^k)$ for all i and k. The existence of such a C follows from assumption (4.2). Let $Y = \{b \in R^{l_2} | q \cdot (b + \omega^2) \geqq 0$ for all $q \in C$}. Since $C \subseteq$ co supp ${}^i\psi(p^k)$, we have $Y \supseteq {}^iB(p^k)$ for all i and k. Let $\tilde{q} \in$ int C and suppose $\tilde{q} \cdot (\tilde{b} + \omega^2) = 0$ for some $\tilde{b} \neq -\omega^2, \tilde{b} \in Y$. Then we can find a q' in C such that $q' \cdot (\tilde{b} + \omega^2) < 0$ since $\tilde{q} \in$ int C. Hence, for all $b \in Y, b \neq -\omega^2$, we have that $\tilde{q} \cdot (b + \omega^2) > 0$. Further $\tilde{q} \in$ int C implies $\tilde{q} \gg 0$. Hence, $\tilde{q} \cdot ({}^ib^k + \omega^2) > 0$ for all ${}^ib^k \in {}^iB(p^k)$ such that ${}^ib^k \neq -\omega^2$. Since $\|{}^ib^k\| \to \infty$ for some i by the last lemma, and $\tilde{q} \gg 0$, $\tilde{q} \cdot ({}^ib^k + {}^i\omega^2) \to \infty$ for this i. Hence, $\tilde{q} \cdot (\Sigma_i ({}^ib^k + {}^i\omega^2)) \to \infty$. Therefore for some j, $\Sigma_i {}^ib^k_j \to \infty$. $\qquad$ Q.E.D.

LEMMA 4.7: *There exists a non-decreasing sequence of sets* $\langle P^n \rangle$, $n = 1, \ldots$, *such that* $P^n \subset P, P = \bigcup_{n=1}^{\infty} P^n$ *and each of the* P^n *is compact, convex, and has non-empty interior.*

PROOF: Since P is open, $P = \bigcup_{k=1}^{\infty} K^k$ where K^k is closed for all k. Let $P^n = \text{co} \bigcup_{k=1}^{n} K^k$. Since P is convex and $\bigcup_{k=1}^{n} K^k \subseteq P$, $P^n \subseteq P$, for all n. Since $\text{co} \bigcup_{k=1}^{n} K^k \supseteq \bigcup_{k=1}^{n} K^k$, $P \subseteq \bigcup_{n=1}^{\infty} P^n$. Clearly P^1 can be chosen to have non-empty interior. Therefore, $\langle P^n \rangle$ has all desired properties. $\qquad$ Q.E.D.

REMARK 4.8: Convexity of each P^n is far more than we shall need in the existence proof. It suffices that each P^n has the fixed point property. For this purpose it would suffice that P be homeomorphic to the interior of the simplex. However, we know of no economically meaningful assumption other than the convexity of each ${}^iS$ that will insure this. In Example 5.1 we show that without convexity of ${}^iS$ one may generate sets P that are not homeomorphic to the interior of the simplex and such that there is no approximating sequence of sets each having the fixed point property. This approximating sequence is necessary for an existence proof along the lines of 4.11, or indeed any other proof involving fixed point theorems of a more general nature than Kakutani's.

LEMMA 4.9: *Let* P^n *be one of the sets whose existence is asserted in the last lemma. Let* $\zeta^n(\cdot)$ *be* $\zeta(\cdot)$ *restricted to the domain* P^n. *Then the range of* $\zeta^n(\cdot)$ *is bounded.*

PROOF: This follows directly from Theorem 3.6 (i) and the proof is therefore omitted.

COROLLARY 4.10: ζ^n *is upper hemi-continuous on* P^n *since the range of* ζ^n *is contained in a compact set.*

THEOREM 4.11: *The economy has an equilibrium.*

PROOF: Let us write $z = (x^1 - \omega, b) \in \zeta(p)$ where $(x^1, b) \in \Sigma^i \xi(p)$ and $\omega = \Sigma^i \omega$. By Lemma 4.9, we can choose $\bar{Z}^n$ to be a compact, convex set containing the range of ζ^n for each n. By this choice of $(P^n, \bar{Z}^n)$, Theorem 3.6, and Corollary 4.10, the conditions necessary for an application of Debreu's result [1] are satisfied. Thus there exists for each n, (p^n, z^n) such that $z^n \in \zeta^n(p^n)$, $p^n \cdot z^n = 0$, and $p \cdot z^n \leqq 0$ for all $p \in P^n$. Since $p^n \in \Delta^l$, there exists a convergent subsequence (retain the index n)

such that $p^n \to p^*$. Suppose $p^* \in \bar{P} \backslash P$. By Theorem 4.4, $\|z^n\| \to \infty$. We shall derive a contradiction by showing that $\langle z^n \rangle$ is bounded.

First it will be shown that b^n is bounded. Let C be the set whose existence is asserted in assumption (4.2). Let $\bar{p}^2 \in$ int C, which is non-empty by this assumption, and let $\bar{p} = (0, \bar{p}^2) \in \Delta^l$.

Hence, $\bar{p} \in {}^i\tilde{S} = \{p \in \Delta^l | \tilde{p}(p) \in$ int co supp ${}^i\psi(p)\}$ for all i. Since ${}^i\tilde{S}$ is open for all i (see the proof of Lemma 3.8), there exists $\bar{p} \gg 0$ such that $\tilde{p}(\bar{p}) = \bar{p}^2$ and $\bar{p} \in {}^iS$ for all i. Then, since $\bar{p} \in P^n$ for sufficiently large n, we have (i) $q \cdot (b^n + \omega^2) \geqslant 0$ for all $q \in C$; and (ii) $\bar{p}^2 \cdot b^n \leqslant \bar{p}^1 \cdot \omega^1 + \bar{p}^2 \cdot \omega^2 \leqslant \Sigma_j \omega_j$. Combining (i) and (ii) and using $\bar{p} \gg 0$, we have shown that $\langle b^n \rangle$ is bounded.

To show that $\langle x^{1n} \rangle$ is bounded, choose $p \gg 0$ in P^1; then $p^1 \cdot x^{1n} \leqslant p^1 \cdot \omega^1 - p^2 \cdot b^n$ for all n, $\langle b^n \rangle$ bounded, and $x^{1n} \geqslant 0$.

Therefore, $\langle z^n \rangle$ is bounded, and this contradiction establishes $p^* \in P$.

By Remark 4.1 (a consequence of Lemma 3.8), P is open. Since ζ has closed graph and z^n remain bounded, there exists a further subsequence converging to $z^* \in \zeta(p^*)$. It remains to be shown only that $z^* = 0$.

Since $p^n \cdot z^n = 0$ for all n, $p^* \cdot z^* = 0$. Suppose $z_j^* > 0$ for some j. Then if $z^* > 0$, $p^* \cdot z^* > 0$ because $p^* \in P$ implies $p^* \gg 0$. Similarly $z^* < 0$, is not possible. If $z_j^* > 0$ for $j \in J^+ \neq \varnothing$, and $z_j^* < 0$ for $j \in J^- \neq \varnothing$, then since P is open, we can find $p \in P$ such that $p \cdot z^* > 0$. But $p \in P^n$ for some n; hence, $p \cdot z^* > 0$ for large n, contradicting $p \cdot z^n \leqslant 0$ for all $p \in P^n$. Thus $z^* = 0$.   Q.E.D.

5. TWO EXAMPLES

EXAMPLE 5.1: This example is constructed to show that, without assumption (3.4), the demand correspondence may be non-empty-valued only on a set, S, which cannot be approximated in the sense of Lemma 4.7 by sets with the fixed-point property.

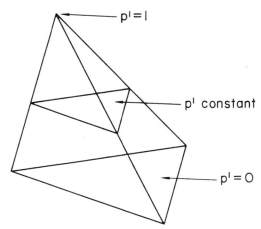

FIGURE 1.

129

Let $l_1 = 1$ and $l_2 = 3$. Then a current price vector may be thought of as a point in the unit tetrahedron (with barycentric coordinates). Let it be oriented, for the purposes of our discussion, such that the vertical axis corresponds to the currently deliverable good.

We may think of the base of the tetrahedron, $\{p \in \varDelta^4 | p^1 = 0\}$, as also representing $\varDelta^3$, the space of prices in period 2.

The example begins by constructing a correspondence between points of $\varDelta^3$ and (barycentric) spheres in $\varDelta^3$ as follows: Consider $\varDelta^3$ and two symmetric subsets, α and β, as shown in Figure 2. The point in the center is $(1/3, 1/3, 1/3)$. Let $\varepsilon > 0$ be fixed.

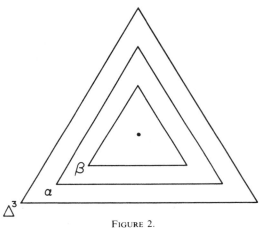

FIGURE 2.

Consider any point, q, between α and the boundary of $\varDelta^3$. Associate to this point an ε-sphere such that q and it are geometrically similar to q and $\varDelta^3$. Clearly all q not on the boundary of $\varDelta^3$ are in the interior of their associated neighborhoods.

For q between α and β construct an image sphere as follows: Let the line from the center point through q cut α and β at a and b, respectively. Let the neighborhood associated with a have "top corner" (say, where q_2 is maximized), c. Let d be the point between a and c defined by

$$\frac{\overline{ad}}{\overline{dc}} = \frac{\overline{aq}}{\overline{qb}},$$

where a line over two letters means the length of the line segment between them.

Let the ε-sphere associated to q be such that q and it are geometrically similar to d and the sphere associated with a. Since d is, by construction, in the interior of this sphere, q will be in the interior of its sphere for all q outside β. It is easy to see that for all q on the boundary of β, q is the "top corner" of its associated sphere, and hence not in its interior. For all q in the interior of β, let this situation persist.

Denote the correspondence thus defined from $\varDelta^3$ to itself by Q. It is clear that Q is continuous.

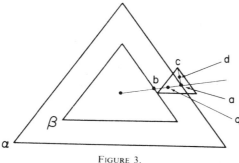

FIGURE 3.

Now consider a point in the tetrahedron, p. Consider the projection of this point in the vertical direction (recall the orientation of Δ^4) into Δ^3. Denote this mapping by $\Pi : \Delta^4 \rightarrow \Delta^3$. Note that this is *not* the projection $\tilde{p}$.

The correspondence from Δ^4 to spheres in Δ^3, which is to be thought of as co supp $\psi(p)$, is defined by $Q(\Pi(p))$. $Q(\Pi(\cdot))$ satisfies all of our assumptions on co supp $\psi(p)$ except (3.4).

We will now show that this mapping gives rise to a set S that is pathological in the sense that it cannot be approximated by sets with the fixed point property. For $p^1 > 0$ but small, the part of the cross-section of the tetrahedron at p^1 fixed that is in S is an annular region close to that between β and the boundary of Δ^3. But the line from $(1, 0, 0, 0)$ to $(0, 1/3, 1/3, 1/3)$ has no points in S, since on this line $\Pi(p) = \tilde{p}(p) = (1/3, 1/3, 1/3)$ and $\Pi(p) \notin$ int $Q(\Pi(p))$; it is the "top corner" of $Q(\Pi(p))$. Hence, S has a torus-like shape, at least near its base.

As yet there are no known properties of the correspondence described above that can account for the pathological behavior of S. Thus we have chosen to adopt (3.4) which is, however, stronger than one actually needs. Nevertheless (3.4) is implied by "supp $\psi(p)$ is constant" and also by "$\tilde{p}(p) \in$ int co supp $\psi(p)$ for all p." However, neither of these is necessary for (3.4); and no assumption sufficient for the approximation of P but weaker than (3.4) with any intuitive economic meaning is known.

EXAMPLE 5.2: This example is to demonstrate that there may be no equilibria in the absence of assumption (4.2). Suppose there are three commodities, two in the future and one at present. To ease the computations (though they will still be too long to present fully herein), let us choose a different normalization of p and q. If $p = (p_1^1, p_1^2, p_2^2)$ and $q = (q_1, q_2)$, let $p_1^1 \equiv 1$ and $q_1 \equiv 1$.

Since $p_1^1 = 0$ is incompatible with determinate demand correspondences, this normalization involves only the assumption that $q_1 = 0$ is never given any positive probability.

Suppose there is only one individual and his utility function is

$$u(x) = \sum_j \log x_j$$

(log is taken to the base e).

In period 2, having already consumed x_1 and having bought contracts b_1 and b_2, the problem faced will be

$$\max \log x_1^2 + \log x_2^2,$$

subject to $x_1^2 + q_2 x_2^2 \leqq b_1 + \omega_1^2 + q_2(b_2 + \omega_2^2)$.

Let the right hand side of the constraint be $W \geqq 0$. Then

$$x_1^2 = \frac{W}{2},$$

$$x_2^2 = \frac{W}{2q_2},$$

is the solution at time 2.

At time 1 the problem is $\max \int u(x)\psi(p)(dq)$, subject to $x_1^1 + p_1^2 b_1 + p_2^2 b_2 \leqq \omega_1^1$, where (x_1^2, x_2^2) in the maximand take the values given above as a function of q_2.

Assume that $\omega_1^1 = \omega_1^2 = \omega_2^2 = 1$ for simplicity. The first order conditions for the above maximization are:

$$0 = \int \frac{-p_1^2}{1 - p_1^2 b_1 - p_2^2 b_2} + \frac{2}{1 + b_1 + q_2(b_2 + 1)} \psi(p)(dq_2),$$

$$0 = \int \frac{-p_2^2}{1 - p_1^2 b_1 - p_2^2 b_2} + \frac{2q_2}{1 + b_1 + q_2(b_2 + 1)} \psi(p)(dq_2),$$

and

$$x_1^2 + p_1^2 b_1 + p_2^2 b_2 = 1.$$

Let us temporarily assume that $\psi(p)$ is the uniform distribution on an interval of q_2 values, say $[\theta_1, \theta_2]$. With this assumption the first-order conditions above can be solved (with considerable algebra) yielding equilibrium values of p_1^2 and p_2^2 as functions of θ_1 and θ_2. These equilibrium functions are denoted $\bar{p}_1^2$ and $\bar{p}_2^2$:

$$\bar{p}_1^2(\theta_1, \theta_2) = \frac{1}{\theta_2 - \theta_1} \log \frac{1 + \theta_2}{1 + \theta_1},$$

$$\bar{p}_2^2(\theta_1, \theta_2) = 2 - \frac{2}{\theta_2 - \theta_1} \log \frac{1 + \theta_2}{1 + \theta_1}.$$

Now suppose that $\psi(p)$ is always a uniform distribution on an interval but that the interval is a function of p. Suppose further that the end-points of the interval are functions only of p_2^2. That is, the interval is

$$[\theta_1(p_2^2), \theta_2(p_2^2)].$$

A temporary equilibrium price system (p_1^{2*}, p_2^{2*}) will be such that

$$p_1^{2*} = \bar{p}_1^2(\theta_1(p_2^{2*}), \theta_2(p_2^{2*})),$$

$$p_2^{2*} = \bar{p}_2^2(\theta_1(p_2^{2*}), \theta_2(p_2^{2*})).$$

We will show that functions $\theta_1(\cdot)$ and $\theta_2(\cdot)$ exist such that these equations (i.e., the second one) can never be satisfied.

Let $\theta_2 - \theta_1 \equiv 1$ and consider a shift in the interval by an amount $d\theta$. It can be shown that

(*) $$\frac{d\bar{p}_2^2}{d\theta} = 2\frac{1}{(1 + \theta_1)(2 + \theta_1)}.$$

Now consider functions $\theta_1(p_2^2), \theta_2(p_2^2)$ such that $\theta_2 \equiv \theta_1 + 1$, $\theta_1 = 1$ for $p_2^2 \in [0, 1 - \log 2]$, and $\theta_1(p_2^2)$ satisfies the differential equation

$$\frac{d\theta_1}{dp_2^2} = \tfrac{1}{2}(2 + 3\theta_1 + \theta_1^2)$$

for $p_2^2 \in [1 - \log 2, \infty)$ with boundary condition $\theta_1(1 - \log 2) = 1$. It is clear that $[\theta_1, \theta_2]$ is a continuous correspondence as a function of p_2^2.

Using equation (*) above,

$$\frac{d\bar{p}_2^2}{dp_2^2} = \frac{2(d\theta/dp_2^2)}{1 + 3\theta_1 + \theta_1^2} = 1$$

for $p_2^2 \in [1 - \log 2, \infty)$. But $\bar{p}_2^2(\theta_1(p_2^2), \theta_2(p_2^2)) = 2 - \log 3/2 > 1 - \log 2$ for $p_2^2 \in [0, 1 - \log 2]$. Thus if p is such that $p_2^2 \leqslant 1 - \log 2$, p cannot be an equilibrium. But if $p_2^2 > 1 - \log 2$, $\bar{p}_2^2 - p_2^2 \equiv 1 + \log 4/3$; hence $\bar{p}_2^2(\theta_1(p_2^2), \theta_2(p_2^2)) \neq p_2^2$ for all $p_2^2 \geqslant 0$, and there can be no equilibrium.

For every value of p_2^2, there is a p_1^2 such that

$$\frac{p_2^2}{p_1^1} \in [\theta_1(p_2^2), \theta_2(p_2^2)].$$

However,

$$\bigcap_{p_2^2 \geqslant 0} [\theta_1(p_2^2), \theta_2(p_2^2)] = \varnothing,$$

so that the example does not satisfy (4.2).

The problem in this example is that the demands cannot be bounded below. If one approximates the set S with sets, P^n, having the fixed-point property (this can be done, but we omit the demonstration), the sequence of $p^n \in P^n$ obtained using the method of Debreu [1] (see Theorem 4.11) will converge to a point in the boundary of S. The associated actions z^n become unbounded. There is no way to contradict this without assumption (4.2). Thus existence cannot be proven using our methods, and it is, in fact, false.

6. CONCLUSION

This section embodies some interpretations of the model, possibilities for extension and generalization, and general remarks that did not seem to fit in elsewhere. These are best introduced by stating our goal of a longer term nature, which is the study of equilibrium theory over time. As a first step in this direction, we choose to begin with the exchange model and perfect competition. That is, all markets available and all individuals behaving as price takers. This is, of course, in the same spirit as the way in which equilibrium theory began in the static case; see Debreu [2]. Reasons for interest in the sequential trading case were given in Section 1.

The principal question is why should one study a case in which all markets exist, no a priori bounds are placed on the volume of trading or the asset positions of the traders, and no financial assets exist (that is, all assets are claims on real goods). With regard to the existence of markets, it is our position that the non-existence of a market is an economic phenomenon, just as is its existence. If a market fails to exist, it is because it is unprofitable to operate, infeasible, or not mutually beneficial. Therefore, rather than place a priori restrictions on the model, we have chosen to consider the "perfect" case, in the belief that generalizations including marketing technologies (as in Foley [4] and Hahn [8] for the certainty case) will produce, as a result of jointly maximizing behavior, a pattern of available markets approximating reality more closely.

Similar remarks apply to financial assets. We hope to show that the introduction of financial assets into the "perfect" exchange model will lead to outcomes that are socially superior in some way. Thus financial assets are a byproduct of socially maximizing behavior. In this way we hope to deduce why certain financial assets are available while others are not, rather than taking the set of such assets as a datum. It may also be possible to deduce normative conclusions about the optimality of a particular structure of active markets and financial assets.

The question of bounds on trading, particularly with regard to claims on future commodities, deserves special attention. As is clear from reading the proof above, difficulties encountered in showing the existence of an equilibrium in the sequential trading model are due principally to the fact that trades are not bounded below. If there were a priori bounds on trading futures contracts, the proof would be much simpler and technical assumptions, in particular (4.2), would be unnecessary. Surely (4.2) is undesirable in the sense that our analysis would be more general without it. Nevertheless, having shown that (4.2) is needed for equilibrium theory to be internally consistent in the "perfect" case is a conclusion of potential descriptive interest. Our institutions in the real world may be thought to have arisen to make the world more orderly, that is to insure that equilibrium exists when otherwise it might not. Thus the phenomenon of collateral loans insures that one does not take an extreme short position in a futures market. Even though such a position may be feasible for an individual (that is in his $A(p)$), his $\psi(p)$ may be quite different from that of the agent (bank, broker) who loans him the necessary funds. This agent requires collateral to guarantee the loan presumably because there is some region of *his* $\psi(p)$ in which his client might otherwise not be solvent, even though in the mind of the client this is unthinkable. Thus, while collateral is an aspect of maximizing behavior, it also serves to restrict the amount of loans possible, that is, to bound the individuals feasible set from below. Thus it may be that the "imperfections" in our world have arisen to protect us from the potential non-existence of equilibrium in a "perfect" world without some of our assumptions.

All of the above mentioned institutional possibilities are open questions that require further study.

Theoretical questions as to the extension of this model involve the consideration of production, and the purchase and sale of commodities by firms over time. This includes investment decisions with uncertain future prices, questions of the choice of durability of inputs, and a host of others. Another important generalization will be to extend this analysis to n-periods instead of only two.

An interpretation of our model in which commodities represent Fisherian "real income" can be applied to interest rate theory. In this way we have extended the results of de Montbrial [3] to the case of uncertainty without point expectations. Several special cases of this theory, emphasizing the differences between comparative static results obtained with this model and in the traditional theories of the term structure of interest rates, are given in Green [7].

A final crucial open question is whether, in a sequential trading model of this type, a temporary equilibrium at one date gives rise to an environment for which a temporary equilibrium exists at the next date.

Harvard University

Manuscript received June, 1972; revision received October, 1972.

REFERENCES

[1] DEBREU, G.: "Market Equilibrium," *Proceedings of the National Academy of Sciences of the USA*, 42 (1956), 876–878.
[2] ———: *Theory of Value.* New York: Wiley, 1959.
[3] DE MONTBRIAL, T.: "Intertemporal General Equilibrium and Interest Rates Theory," Ecole Polytechnique, Paris, mimeographed.
[4] FOLEY, D.: "Economic Equilibrium with Costly Marketing," *Journal of Economic Theory*, 2 (1970), 276–291.
[5] GRANDMONT, J.-M.: "Continuity Properties of a von Neumann-Morgenstern Utility," *Journal of Economic Theory*, 4 (1972), 45–57.
[6] ———: "On the Short-Run Equilibrium in a Monetary Economy," CEPREMAP Discussion Paper, Paris, February, 1971.
[7] GREEN, J.: "A Simple General Equilibrium Model of the Term Structure of Interest Rates," Harvard Institute of Economic Research, Discussion Paper No. 183, Harvard University, Cambridge, Mass., March, 1971.
[8] HAHN, F.: "Equilibrium with Transaction Costs," *Econometrica*, 39 (1971), 417–439.
[9] PARTHASARATHY, K.: *Probability Measures on Metric Spaces.* New York: Academic Press, 1967.
[10] RADNER, R.: "Existence of Equilibrium of Plans, Prices, and Price Expectations in a Sequence of Markets," mimeographed, University of California at Berkeley, February, 1970.
[11] SONDERMANN, D.: "Temporary Competitive Equilibrium under Uncertainty," paper presented at the European Research Conference on Economic Theory, Bergen, Norway, July-August, 1971.

On the Existence of Equilibrium in a Securities Model*

Department of Economics, University of Essex, Wivenhoe Park, Colchester, Essex, England

Received November 5, 1973

1. INTRODUCTION

Since the contributions of Lintner [13] and Sharpe [18] in the mid-1960's, a great deal of research has been done on the analysis of competitive equilibrium in the market for securities. This work has improved our understanding of the way in which security prices are determined, and has also yielded testable conclusions concerning the relationships between equilibrium security prices and investors' attitudes towards risk and forecasts of security returns.

Most of this research has been concerned with an exchange economy in which the types of securities available to investors and the aggregate supplies of securities are taken to be fixed.[1] In the Lintner–Sharpe model, it is further assumed that investors' probability beliefs about security returns are identical, that each investor's expected utility is a function only of the mean and variance of his portfolio return, that there is a riskless security, and that any security may be held in unrestricted positive or negative amounts.[2]

These assumptions may be shown to imply some particularly simple relationships between the equilibrium prices of securities and the means, variances, and covariances of their returns (see Mossin [15]). Lintner [14] has generalized these relationships to the case where investors' probability beliefs differ; more recently, several of the other Lintner–Sharpe assump-

* This article presents material from my doctoral dissertation at Princeton University. I would like to thank Harold Kuhn, Michael Rothschild, a referee, and the editor of this journal for valuable suggestions and criticisms.

[1] Actually, Lintner and Sharpe assume that the supplies of risky securities are fixed, but that there is a riskless security which is supplied perfectly elastically at an exogenously determined interest rate. Mossin [15], however, in his interpretation of the Lintner–Sharpe model, assumes that *all* security supplies are fixed.

[2] In some versions of the Lintner–Sharpe model, it is assumed that the risky securities can be held only in nonnegative amounts. No lower bound is placed on holdings of the riskless security, however.

tions have also been significantly weakened (see Jensen [11] for a survey of the literature).

In deriving these properties of equilibrium prices, it has been assumed that an equilibrium does in fact exist. Surprisingly, no attempt appears to have been made to establish the existence of equilibrium in the basic Lintner–Sharpe model or in more general versions of the model. Yet, the existence of equilibrium is not implied by any of the standard existence theorems (see, for example, Debreu [4]) since these theorems assume that consumption sets (in the present context, the sets of portfolios that investors are permitted to hold) are *bounded* below, whereas the assumption that investors can hold securities in unlimited negative amounts implies that consumption sets are *unbounded* below.

In this paper, we will be concerned with finding conditions for the existence of equilibrium in a very general version of the Lintner–Sharpe model. We will find that an equilibrium does exist if investors' probability beliefs are identical; in fact, all that is required is that investors agree on expected security returns. In the general case where there is disagreement about security returns, however, an equilibrium need not exist.

Suppose, for example, that one investor believes with certainty that security 1 yields a higher return than security 2, and a second investor believes with certainty that security 2 yields a higher return than security 1. Assuming that there are no restrictions on short-selling, if the price of security 1 is less than or equal to the price of security 2, the first investor can engage in profitable arbitrage operations by buying security 1 and selling security 2, and, if the price of security 1 is greater than the price of security 2, the second investor can engage in profitable arbitrage operations by buying security 2 and selling security 1. Hence, no equilibrium exists.

In this example, investors have radically different beliefs about security returns. One would suspect that an equilibrium is more likely to exist if disagreement is somewhat less extreme. This indeed turns out to be the case. In Section 3, necessary conditions and sufficient conditions for the existence of equilibrium in terms of investors' probability beliefs and attitudes towards risk are derived. Roughly speaking, these conditions say that an equilibrium exists as long as there is not "too much" disagreement about security returns. Furthermore, the more risk-averse investors are, the more disagreement is compatible with the existence of equilibrium.

These results are derived without making any of the special assumptions of the Lintner–Sharpe model, such as that utility functions are of the mean-variance type or that riskless borrowing or lending opportunities exist. In addition, investors' probability beliefs about security returns are allowed to depend not only on events occurring before markets open, but also on current security prices. The model does, however, continue to ignore the supply side of the securities market; the types of securities available to investors and the aggregate supplies of securities are assumed to be given. This assumption does not seem an unreasonable one in the short run. Furthermore, in order to account for security supplies in the long run, we would require a more general theory which would explain firms' production decisions under uncertainty. Such a theory lies outside the scope of this paper.

The problem of finding sufficient conditions for the existence of equilibrium when consumption sets are unbounded below has been analyzed in a somewhat different context by Grandmont[6] and Green[8, 9]. Grandmont considers a two-period consumption economy in which there is trading in current commodities in each period and consumers can borrow or lend in units of account in the first period. Green also considers a two-period consumption economy, but assumes that wealth is transferred from one period to the other by buying and selling futures contracts for commodities, rather than by borrowing and lending.

The two-period model presented here is formally very similar to Green's model, with securities taking the place of futures contracts for commodities. The model is less general than Green's, however, in one important respect. Whereas Green assumes that consumers are interested in consumption in both periods, we will assume that investors are interested only in their wealth in the second period. This simplifying assumption permits us to derive sufficient conditions for the existence of equilibrium which are significantly weaker than Green's. In addition, we are able to derive necessary conditions for the existence of equilibrium, whereas neither Grandmont nor Green is concerned with this problem. In general, these necessary conditions are weaker than the sufficient conditions. In the special case where investors' probability beliefs are independent of current security prices, however, the two sets of conditions are equivalent, so that we obtain necessary and sufficient conditions for the existence of equilibrium.

2. THE MODEL

We consider a two-period economy in which trading in securities takes place in the first period and security returns are determined in the second period. The return of a security is to be interpreted as the total value of one unit of the security in the second period, including any dividend payments received. (Returns should therefore not be confused with rates of return.) Returns are unknown in the first period, but investors are assumed to have probabilistic beliefs about them.

Let there be m securities and n investors. For $i = 1,..., m$, $j = 1,..., n$, investor j has a von Neumann–Morgenstern utility function $U_j : R \to R$ and begins the first period with an endowment of $\bar{x}_i^j$ units of security i. We assume that, for all $j = 1,..., n$,

(A.1) U_j is concave;

(A.2) U_j is increasing, that is, $U_j(w_1) > U_j(w_2)$ if $w_1 > w_2$.[3]

Investors are assumed to be interested exclusively in their wealth in the second period and to take no account of the possibility of any further trading after the first period. When trading opens in the first period, each investor selects a portfolio which maximizes his expected utility of second period wealth, given his initial wealth and his forecasts of security returns. These forecasts are assumed to be based on events occurring before the first period and on the security prices ruling in the first period. This formulation allows for the possibility that investors infer information about other investors' forecasts from first period prices, and revise their own forecasts according to this information.

To characterize investors' forecasts more formally, let p_i be the first period price, and r_i the return, of one unit of security i. We will normalize prices so that $p = (p_1 ,..., p_m) \in \Delta = \{p \in R_+^m \mid \sum_{i=1}^m p_i = 1\}$.[4] It will be assumed that security returns are nonnegative, so that

$$r = (r_1 ,..., r_m) \in R_+^m.$$

Let $B(R_+^m)$ be the Borel σ-algebra of R_+^m, that is, the σ-algebra generated by the open subsets of R_+^m, and let $M(R_+^m)$ be the set of probability measures defined on the measurable space $(R_+^m, B(R_+^m))$ (see Parthasarathy [16] for the definition of a probability measure and a measurable space). Then, for $j = 1,..., n$, investor j's probability beliefs concerning second period security returns are assumed to be characterized by a function μ_j which maps Δ into $M(R_+^m)$. That is, for every p in Δ and A in $B(R_+^m)$, $\mu_j(p, A)$ denotes the probability that investor j assigns to the event $r = (r_1 ,..., r_m) \in A$, given that security prices in the first period are p. The dependence of probability beliefs on events occurring before the first period is not made explicit, but is incorporated in the function μ_j.

---

[3] (A.1) and (A.2) imply that U_j is unbounded. As Arrow has pointed out in [1, Chapter 2], the unboundedness of U_j is inconsistent with the usual assumptions about preferences over risky alternatives which are used to justify the existence of a von Neumann–Morgenstern utility function. (A.1) appears to be crucial, however, if we want to prove the existence of equilibrium when there is a finite number of investors.

[4] We will use the following notation. $R_+^m = \{p \in R^m \mid p_i \geqslant 0 \text{ for } i = 1,..., m\}$. Also, if $p \in R^m$, $p \geqslant 0$ means $p_i \geqslant 0$ for $i = 1,..., m$, and $p \gg 0$ means $p_i > 0$ for $i = 1,..., m$.

We make two regularity assumptions about the function μ_j.

(A.3)   There exists a bounded subset C of $R_+{}^m$ such that $\mu_j(p, C) = 1$ for all p in Δ and for each $j = 1,..., n$.

(A.4)   For each $j = 1,..., n$, the function $\mu_j : \Delta \to M(R_+{}^m)$ is continuous in the topology of weak convergence of probability measures.

(A.3) says that each investor believes that security returns lie in a bounded set with probability 1, and that this set can be chosen independently of first period security prices. (A.4) says that probability beliefs depend in a continuous way on first period security prices (see Parthasarathy [16] for a definition of the weak convergence topology).

If investor j holds the portfolio $x = (x_1 ,..., x_m)$, consisting of x_i units of security i, and first period security prices are p, investor j's expected utility is given by $\int U_j(rx)\, d\mu_j(p)$.[5] Define, for each $j = 1,..., n$, the function $V_j : \Delta \times R^m \to R$ by $V_j(p, x) = \int U_j(rx)\, d\mu_j(p)$. U_j is continuous by A.1, so that V_j is well defined. In addition, A.1, A.3, and A.4 imply that V_j is continuous (for a proof, see Grandmont [7, Section 5, Theorem A.3]), and (A.1) implies that V_j is concave in x.

If first period security prices equal p, investor j will choose x so as to maximize $V_j(p, x)$ subject to his budget constraint, $px \leqslant p\bar{x}^j$. It may be the case, however, that investor j is prohibited from holding certain portfolios. For example, there may be institutional or legal constraints which prevent him from holding some securities, or which require him to hold particular securities in nonnegative or nonpositive amounts. Another possibility is that the investor is subject to certain reserve requirements. To allow for these cases, we associate with each investor a feasible set consisting of the portfolios that the investor is permitted to hold. This feasible set is analogous to the consumption set in consumer behavior theory.

Let $X^j \subset R^m$ be investor j's feasible set. We make the following assumptions.

(A.5) X^j is closed and convex for all $j = 1,..., n$.

(A.6)   For each $j = 1,..., n$, there exists $\hat{x}^j \in X^j$ satisfying $\hat{x}^j \ll \bar{x}^j$.

(A.7)   Given $i = 1,..., m$, we may find some j such that X^j has the following property: $x \in X^j \Rightarrow x' \in X^j$ if $x_i' > x_i$ and $x_k' = x_k$ for all $k = 1,..., m, k \neq i$.[6]

(A.8)   Given any $j = 1,..., n, p \in \Delta$, and $x \in X^j$, there exists $\hat{x} \in X^j$ such that $V_j(p, \hat{x}) > V_j(p, x)$.

---

[5] rx denotes the inner product $\sum_{i=1}^{m} r_i x_i$.
[6] x_i is the ith coordinate of x.

OLIVER D. HART

(A.5) and (A.6) are standard assumptions in the consumption context.[7] (A.7) says that, for each security, there is an investor who is permitted to hold that security in unlimited positive amounts. (A.8) is the no "bliss point" assumption. It will be satisfied if each investor believes that some security yields a positive return with positive probability, and is permitted to hold that security in unlimited positive amounts.

In the proof of Theorem 3.3, we will require the further assumption that X^j is the intersection of a finite number of closed half-spaces.

(A.9) For $j = 1,..., n$, X^j has the special form

$$X^j = \{x \in R^m \mid A^j x \geqslant b^j\},$$

where $A^j = \{a^j_{hi}\}$ is an $(H \times m)$ matrix and b^j is an H-vector.

(A.9) is not a very restrictive assumption and allows for all the feasible sets which are normally used in portfolio theory. For example, the sets R^m, R_+^m, and $\{x \in R^m \mid x_i \geqslant 0$ for $i = 1,..., m_1$; $x_i \leqslant 0$ for $i = m_1 + 1,..., m_2$; $x_i = 0$ for $i = m_2 + 1,..., m_3\}$ are all consistent with A.9.

In the consumption context, it is also assumed that X^j is bounded below. We do not make this assumption since we wish to allow for the possibility of unlimited short-selling.

We are now ready to summarize the behavior of an individual investor. Given first period security prices p in Δ, investor j selects x so as to maximize $V_j(p, x)$ subject to $x \in X^j$ and $px \leqslant p\bar{x}^j$.[8]

Equilibrium

We say that $p \in \Delta$ is an equilibrium price vector if there exist $x^1,..., x^n$ such that,

(I)   for each $j = 1,..., n$,

$$x^j \in \{x \in X^j \mid px \leqslant p\bar{x}^j\} \text{ and } V_j(p, x^j) \geqslant V_j(p, x)$$

for all $x \in \{x \in X^j \mid px \leqslant p\bar{x}^j\}$;

(II) $\sum_{j=1}^n x^j = \sum_{j=1}^n \bar{x}^j$.

(I) is the condition that x^j solves investor j's maximization problem at

[7] For a discussion of how A.6 can be relaxed, see Debreu [5].
[8] It might seem more sensible to assume that budget constraints hold with equality in a securities model. It turns out that, under our assumptions, budget constraints do indeed hold with equality in equilibrium.

142

prices p, and (II) is the condition that securities markets clear in the first period.

In defining an equilibrium, we are allowing investors to hold portfolios which yield a negative return with positive probability. If all economic activity ceases in the second period, those investors whose wealth is negative at that stage will presumably go bankrupt. We assume, however, that no bankruptcy provisions are taken into account when portfolio decisions are made, so that $U_j(\bar{r}x^j)$ is investor j's assessment of his utility in the event $r = \bar{r}$, even if $\bar{r}x^j < 0$. For a discussion of models in which bankruptcy is dealt with explicitly, the reader is referred to Arrow and Hahn [2, Chapter 5], Grandmont [6], and Green [9].

An alternative interpretation of the model is that trading in securities reopens in the second period with new endowments given by the equilibrium portfolios of the first period, modified to allow for dividend payments. This process can be repeated in the third and following periods, with no investor ever going bankrupt, as long as the economy continues for an infinite number of periods.

This interpretation is rather unsatisfactory, however, since our assumption that, in the first period, investors are interested exclusively in their second period wealth is not a particularly plausible one if the economy in fact lasts for an infinite number of periods.

3. Conditions for the Existence of Equilibrium

In Section 2, we presented the model and defined a competitive equilibrium. As was noted in the Introduction, however, a competitive equilibrium may well not exist. In this section, we use some partial equilibrium results of Bertsekas [3] to derive necessary conditions and sufficient conditions for the existence of an equilibrium in terms of investors' attitudes towards risk and probability beliefs.

We begin with some definitions. For $j = 1,..., n$, define

$$S_j^+ = \lim_{w \to \infty} \frac{dU_j}{dw}$$

and

$$S_j^- = \lim_{w \to -\infty} \frac{dU_j}{dw} .$$

These limits are well defined since a concave function mapping R into R has a derivative except at a countable number of points. A.1 and A.2 imply that S_j^+ is finite and that S_j^- is finite or $+\infty$.

Define also for $x \in R^m$, $p \in \Delta$, and $j = 1,..., n$,

$$E_x^{+j}(p) = \int_{\{r \mid rx \geqslant 0\}} rx \, d\mu_j(p)$$

and

$$E_x^{-j}(p) = \int_{\{r \mid rx < 0\}} rx \, d\mu_j(p).$$

$E_x^{+j}(p)$ and $E_x^{-j}(p)$ are known as incomplete means. They are well-defined as a result of assumption A.3. $E_x^{+j}(p)$ is the expected value of rx, given that $rx \geqslant 0$, multiplied by the probability that $rx \geqslant 0$ when first period prices are p; $E_x^{-j}(p)$ is the expected value of rx, given that $rx < 0$, multiplied by the probability that $rx < 0$ when first period prices are p. Both expressions are evaluated from the point of view of investor j. Clearly, $E_x^{+j}(p) \geqslant 0$ and $E_x^{-j}(p) \leqslant 0$.

We will also need the concept of a direction of recession of a convex set (see Rockafellar [17] and Bertsekas [3]). Let $X \subset R^m$ be a closed, convex set. $e \in R^m$ is said to be a direction of recession of X if $x + \lambda e \in X$ for every $x \in X$ and $\lambda \geqslant 0$.[9] It is easy to show that, if $x + \lambda e \in X$ for some $x \in X$ and all $\lambda \geqslant 0$, then the same is true for every $x \in X$.

THEOREM 3.1. *If assumptions* (A.1)–(A.3), (A.5), *and* (A.8) *hold and* U_j *is strictly concave for all* $j = 1,..., n$,[10] *a necessary condition for* $\hat{p} \in \Delta$ *to be an equilibrium security price vector is that there do not exist* $e^1,..., e^n$ *satisfying*

(a.1) $\sum_{j=1}^n e^j = 0$;

(a.2) e^j *is a direction of recession of* X^j *and*

$$S_j^+ E_{e^j}^{+j}(\hat{p}) + S_j^- E_{e^j}^{-j}(\hat{p}) \geqslant 0 \qquad \text{for all} \quad j = 1,..., n;$$

(a.3) $\mu_j(\hat{p}, \{r \mid re^j = 0\}) < 1$ *for some* $j = 1,..., n$.

Condition (a.3) says that, for some j, investor j believes that the portfolio e^j yields a nonzero return with positive probability.

It should be noted that in the evaluation of $S_j^+ E_{e^j}^{+j}(\hat{p}) + S_j^- E_{e^j}^{-j}(\hat{p})$ in (a.2), the convention that $\infty \cdot 0 = 0$, $\infty \cdot a = -\infty$ if $a < 0$, $-\infty + a = -\infty$ if a is finite, and $-\infty < 0$ is adopted.

Proof of Theorem 3.1. Let $\hat{p} \in \Delta$ be an equilibrium price vector,

---

[9] Rockafellar defines directions of recession only for $e \neq 0$, whereas, in our definition, 0 is automatically a direction of recession.

[10] Actually, the assumption that U_j is strictly concave is stronger than necessary. All we need assume is that U_j is nonlinear for large positive or negative values of wealth.

$x^1,..., x^n$ equilibrium portfolios, and suppose there exist $e^1,..., e^n$ satisfying conditions (a.1) and (a.2). We will prove that (a.3) cannot hold, which establishes the theorem. The method of proof is to show that if (a.3) does hold, then, for some j and $\lambda \geqslant 0$, the portfolio $(x^j + \lambda e^j)$ is feasible for investor j, satisfies investor j's budget constraint, and is preferred to the portfolio x^j by investor j, which contradicts the fact that $x^1,..., x^n$ are equilibrium portfolios.

We will use the following lemma, which follows directly from Proposition 2 of Bertsekas [3].

LEMMA 1. *Under assumptions (A.1)–(A.3), if $p \in \Delta$ and $x, e \in R^m$, then $V_j(p, x + \lambda e) \geqslant V_j(p, x)$ for all $\lambda \geqslant 0$ if and only if*

$$S_j^+ E_e^{+j}(p) + S_j^- E_e^{-j}(p) \geqslant 0.$$

Lemma 1 and (a.2) imply that

$$V_j(\hat{p}, x^j + \lambda e^j) \geqslant V_j(\hat{p}, x^j) \tag{1}$$

for all $\lambda \geqslant 0$ and $j = 1,..., n$. Suppose that $\hat{p}e^j < 0$ for some j. Then the portfolio $(x^j + e^j)$ costs less than the equilibrium portfolio x^j at prices $\hat{p}$ and, at the same time, gives investor j no less utility than x^j as a result of (1), and is feasible for investor j since e^j is a direction of recession of X^j. From the no "bliss point" assumption (A.8), it follows that there exists a portfolio which is feasible for investor j, which satisfies his budget constraint, and which gives him a *higher* utility than x^j. This contradicts the fact that $x^1,..., x^n$ are equilibrium portfolios at prices $\hat{p}$.

It follows that

$$\hat{p}e^j \geqslant 0 \tag{2}$$

for all $j = 1,..., n$. By condition (a.1), however, $\sum_{j=1}^n \hat{p}e^j = \hat{p} \sum_{j=1}^n e^j = 0$, which, together with (2), implies that $\hat{p}e^j = 0$ for all $j = 1,..., n$. Therefore (1) must hold with equality, that is,

$$V_j(\hat{p}, x^j + \lambda e^j) = V_j(\hat{p}, x^j) \tag{3}$$

for all $\lambda \geqslant 0$ and $j = 1,..., n$, since otherwise investor j would choose the portfolio $(x^j + \lambda e^j)$ instead of the portfolio x^j. However, it is easy to show that, if $\mu_j(\hat{p}, \{r \mid re^j = 0\}) < 1$, then the assumption that U_j is strictly concave implies that $V_j(\hat{p}, x^j + \lambda e^j)$ is strictly concave in λ, which contradicts (3). Therefore, $\mu_j(\hat{p}, \{r \mid re^j = 0\}) = 1$ for all $j = 1,..., n$, and condition (a.3) is contradicted. This proves Theorem 3.1.　　　　Q.E.D.

Necessary conditions for the existence of equilibrium follow directly from Theorem 3.1.

THEOREM 3.2. *If assumptions* (A.1)–(A.3), (A.5), *and* (A.8) *hold and* U_j *is strictly concave for all* $j = 1,..., n$, *a necessary condition for the existence of equilibrium is that for some* $\hat{p} \in \Delta$, *there do not exist* $e^1,..., e^n$ *satisfying conditions* (a.1)–(a.3) *of Theorem 3.1.*

We turn next to sufficient conditions for the existence of equilibrium.

THEOREM 3.3. *Under assumptions* (A.1)–(A.9), *a sufficient condition for the existence of equilibrium is that the following is true for* all $\hat{p} \in \Delta$: *if* $e^1,..., e^n$ *satisfy*

(a.1) $\sum_{j=1}^{n} e^j = 0$

and

(a.2) e^j *is a direction of recession of* X^j *and*

$$S_j^+ E_{e^j}^{+j}(\hat{p}) + S_j^- E_{e^j}^{-j}(\hat{p}) \geqslant 0 \qquad \textit{for all} \quad j = 1,..., n,$$

then

(a.3) $\epsilon > 0$ *can be chosen so that* $\mu_i(p, \{r \mid re^j = 0\}) = 1$ *for all* $i = 1,..., n$ *and for all* $p \in \Delta$ *such that* $\| p - \hat{p} \| < \epsilon$.[11]

(a.3) says that investor j believes that the portfolio e^j yields a zero return with certainty for all price vectors sufficiently close to $\hat{p}$.

Proof of Theorem 3.3. We prove the theorem by considering a sequence of bounded economies converging to the actual unbounded economy. We show that the sufficient condition implies that eventually equilibria of the bounded economies are also equilibria of the actual economy.

Let **E** denote the economy described in Section 2, and let $\mathbf{E}_t$, $t = 1, 2,...$, denote the economy in which there is an added constraint that each investor may hold only portfolios x satisfying $x \geqslant -\mathbf{t}$, where **t** is an m-dimensional vector, each of whose coordinates is t. We confine our attention to $\mathbf{t} \geqslant -\hat{x}^j$ for all $j = 1,..., n$ (see assumption A.6 for a definition of $\hat{x}^j$).

Define the following feasible, budget, and demand sets for the economies **E** and $\mathbf{E}_t$:

$$X_t^j = \{x \in X^j \mid x \geqslant -\mathbf{t}\};$$
$$B^j(p) = \{x \in X^j \mid px \leqslant p\bar{x}^j\};$$
$$B_t^j(p) = \{x \in X_t^j \mid px \leqslant p\bar{x}^j\};$$
$$D^j(p) = \{\hat{x} \in B^j(p) \mid V_j(p, \hat{x}) \geqslant V_j(p, x) \qquad \text{for all} \quad x \in B^j(p)\};$$
$$D_t^j(p) = \{\hat{x} \in B_t^j(p) \mid V_j(p, \hat{x}) \geqslant V_j(p, x) \qquad \text{for all} \quad x \in B_t^j(p)\}.$$

---

[11] $\| \ \|$ denotes the Euclidean norm.

Using the fact V_j is continuous in p and x, we may apply the standard tools of Debreu [4] to show that the bounded economy $\mathbf{E}_t$ has the following property for each t : There exist $p_t \in \Delta$ and $x_t^j \in D_t^j(p_t)$ $(j = 1,..., n)$, such that

$$\sum_{j=1}^{n} x_t^j \leqslant \sum_{j=1}^{n} \bar{x}^j \tag{4}$$

and

$$p_t \left(\sum_{j=1}^{n} x_t^j - \sum_{j=1}^{n} \bar{x}^j \right) = 0. \tag{5}$$

In fact, assumption (A.7) implies that (4) can be strengthened to an equality, so that p_t is an equilibrium price vector for $\mathbf{E}_t$. For, let

$$u = \sum_{j=1}^{n} \bar{x}^j - \sum_{j=1}^{n} x_t^j.$$

Also, for each i, define j_i to be such that investor j_i can hold unlimited amounts of security i (the existence of j_i is guaranteed by A.7). Define the new portfolios $x_t'^1,..., x_t'^n$ by

$$x_t'^{j_i} = x_t^{j_i} + u^i \qquad \text{for} \quad i = 1,..., m$$

and

$$x_t'^j = x_t^j \qquad \text{for} \quad j \neq j_1,..., j_m,$$

where u^i is the vector whose ith coordinate is u_i and whose other coordinates are zero. Since $u \geqslant 0$ and $p_t u = 0$, $x_t'^j \in D_t^j(p_t)$ $(j = 1,..., n)$. Also $\sum_{j=1}^{n} x_t'^j = \sum_{j=1}^{n} \bar{x}^j$, and, hence, $x_t'^1,..., x_t'^n$ are equilibrium portfolios for $\mathbf{E}_t$ at prices p_t .

Proposition 1 states that p_t , as well as being an equilibrium for $\mathbf{E}_t$, is an equilibrium for the unbounded economy $\mathbf{E}$ if the artificial bounds $x \geqslant -t$ are slack for the equilibrium portfolios.

PROPOSITION 1. *Suppose that for some* t, $x_t^j \in D_t^j(p_t)$ $(j = 1,..., n)$, $\sum_{j=1}^{n} x_t^j = \sum_{j=1}^{n} \bar{x}^j$, *and* $x_t^j \gg -\mathbf{t}$ *for all j. Then p_t is an equilibrium price vector for* $\mathbf{E}$ *and the* x_t^j *are the equilibrium portfolios.*

Proof. We need only show that $x_t^j \in D^j(p_t)$ $(j = 1,..., n)$. This follows immediately from the facts that $x_t^j \in D_t^j(p_t)$, $x_t^j > -\mathbf{t}$, X^j convex, and V_j concave in x. Q.E.D.

In view of Proposition 1, we may confine ourselves in the remainder of the proof to the case where, for each t, the constraint $x \geqslant -\mathbf{t}$ is binding for some equilibrium portfolio of $\mathbf{E}_t$. That is, we may assume that, for each t, there exist $p_t \in \Delta$ and x_t^j ($j = 1,..., n$) satisfying

$$x_t^j \in D_t^j(p_t) \qquad (j = 1,..., n), \tag{6}$$

$$\sum_{j=1}^{n} x_t^j = \sum_{j=1}^{n} \bar{x}^j, \tag{7}$$

and

$$x_t^j \not\gg -\mathbf{t} \qquad \text{for some } j. \tag{8}$$

Consider the bounded sequences $\{x_t^j / \sum_{k=1}^{n} \| x_t^k \|\}$ and $\{p_t\}$. Choosing subsequences if necessary, we may assume that $x_t^j / \sum_{k=1}^{n} \| x_t^k \|$ and p_t have limits as $t \to \infty$. Let

$$\lim_{t \to \infty} \frac{x_t^j}{\sum_{k=1}^{n} \| x_t^k \|} = e^j \qquad (j = 1,..., n) \tag{9}$$

and

$$\lim_{t \to \infty} p_t = \hat{p}.$$

The rest of the proof consists of showing that, for large t, $(x_t^1 - e^1),...,$ $(x_t^n - e^n)$ are equilibrium portfolios for the economy $\mathbf{E}_t$ at prices p_t, and that

$$(x_t^j - e^j) > -\mathbf{t} \qquad (j = 1,..., n).$$

The argument of Proposition 1 then establishes that p_t is an equilibrium price vector for the unbounded economy $\mathbf{E}$, and Theorem 3.3 is proved.

Let us show first that $\sum_{j=1}^{n} (x_t^j - e^j) = \sum_{j=1}^{n} \bar{x}^j$. Dividing both sides of (7) by $\sum_{j=1}^{n} \| x_t^j \|$, taking limites as $t \to \infty$, and noting that

$$\lim_{t \to \infty} \sum_{j=1}^{n} \| x_t^j \| \geqslant \lim_{t \to \infty} \max_{j=1,...,n} \| x_t^j \| \geqslant \lim_{t \to \infty} t = \infty$$

by (8), we obtain

$$\sum_{j=1}^{n} e^j = 0. \tag{10}$$

Hence, $\sum_{j=1}^{n} (x_t^j - e^j) = \sum_{j=1}^{n} x_t^j = \sum_{j=1}^{n} \bar{x}^j$ by (7).

It remains to show that $(x_t{}^j - e^j) \in D_t{}^j(p_t)$ $(j = 1,..., n)$ and

$$(x_t{}^j - e^j) > -t \ (j = 1,..., n)$$

for large t. These facts are established in the following three propositions.

PROPOSITION 2. *There exists T_1 such that $V_j(p_t, x_t{}^j - e^j) = V_j(p_t, x_t{}^j)$ for all $t \geqslant T_1$ and $j = 1,..., n$.*

Proof. Since investor j selects the portfolio $x_t{}^j$ at prices p_t in economy E_t when $\hat{x}^j$ [see assumption (A.6)] could have been chosen,

$$V_j(p_t, x_t{}^j) \geqslant V_j(p_t, \hat{x}^j) \qquad (j = 1,..., n).$$

Therefore, since V_j is concave in x, it follows that, for any $\lambda \geqslant 0$ and large t,

$$V_j \left(p_t, \frac{\lambda}{\sum_{k=1}^n \| x_t{}^k \|} x_t{}^j \right)$$

$$\geqslant \frac{\lambda}{\sum_{k=1}^n \| x_t{}^k \|} V_j(p_t, x_t{}^j) + \left(1 - \frac{\lambda}{\sum_{k=1}^n \| x_t{}^k \|} \right) V_j(p_t, 0)$$

$$\geqslant \frac{\lambda}{\sum_{k=1}^n \| x_t{}^k \|} V_j(p_t, \hat{x}^j) + \left(1 - \frac{\lambda}{\sum_{k=1}^n \| x_t{}^k \|} \right) V_j(p_t, 0).$$

Taking limits as $t \to \infty$ and using the fact that $\lim_{t\to\infty} \sum_{k=1}^n \| x_t{}^k \| = \infty$, we obtain

$$V_j(\hat{p}, \lambda e^j) \geqslant V_j(\hat{p}, 0) \qquad (j = 1,..., n). \tag{11}$$

If we now apply Lemma 1, we may deduce from (11) that

$$S_j{}^+ E_{e^j}^{+j}(\hat{p}) + S_j{}^- E_{e^j}^{-j}(\hat{p}) \geqslant 0 \qquad (j = 1,..., n). \tag{12}$$

In addition, since $x_t{}^j \in X^j$, the convexity of X^j implies that for any $\lambda \geqslant 0$, $x \in X^j$, and large t,

$$\left(1 - \frac{\lambda}{\sum_{k=1}^n \| x_t{}^k \|} \right) x + \frac{\lambda}{\sum_{k=1}^n \| x_t{}^k \|} x_t{}^j \in X^j.$$

Taking limits as $t \to \infty$, we obtain

$$x + \lambda e^j \in X^j \qquad (j = 1,..., n), \tag{13}$$

so that e^j is a direction of recession of X^j.

(10) and (12), (13) are respectively conditions (a.1) and (a.2) of Theorem 3.3. Since the sufficient condition holds by assumption, it follows that for some $\epsilon > 0$,

$$\mu_j(p, \{r \mid re^j = 0\}) = 1 \qquad (j = 1,..., n) \tag{14}$$

for all $p \in \Delta$ such that $\| p - \hat{p} \| < \epsilon$. This implies that

$$V_j(p_t, x_t^j - e^j) = V_j(p_t, x_t^j) \qquad (j = 1,..., n)$$

for large t since $\lim_{t \to \infty} p_t = \hat{p}$, $\qquad\qquad$ Q.E.D.

PROPOSITION 3. *There exists T_2 such that*

$$(x_t^j - e^j) \in X^j \tag{15}$$

and

$$(x_t^j - e^j) > -\mathbf{t} \tag{16}$$

for all $t \geqslant T_2$ and $j = 1,..., n$.

Proof. In order to prove (15), we use assumption A.9, that X^j is the intersection of a finite number of closed half-spaces. Since $x_t^j \in X^j$, A.9 implies that

$$A^j x_t^j \geqslant b^j. \tag{17}$$

Dividing both sides by $\sum_{k=1}^n \| x_t^k \|$, taking limits as $t \to \infty$, and using the fact that $\lim_{t \to \infty} \sum_{k=1}^n \| x_t^k \| = \infty$, we obtain

$$A^j e^j \geqslant 0. \tag{18}$$

Suppose now that for some j, $(x_t^j - e^j)$ is not in X^j for large t. Then, choosing a subsequence if necessary, we may assume that

$$\sum_{i=1}^m a_{hi}^j (x_{ti}^j - e_i^{\ j}) < b_h^{\ j} \tag{19}$$

for some h and all t. Dividing both sides of (19) by $\sum_{k=1}^n \| x_t^k \|$ and taking limits, we obtain

$$\sum_{i=1}^m a_{hi}^j e_i^{\ j} \leqslant 0. \tag{20}$$

(18) and (20) imply that

$$\sum_{i=1}^m a_{hi}^j e_i^{\ j} = 0,$$

and, therefore, by (19),

$$\sum_{i=1}^{m} a_{hi}^{j} x_{ti}^{j} < b_{h}^{j},$$

which contradicts (17). This establishes (15).

In order to prove (16), we assume the contrary. Then, choosing a subsequence if necessary, we may assume that for some j,

$$x_{ti}^{j} - e_{i}^{j} \leqslant -t \tag{21}$$

for some i and for all t. Since $x_{t}^{j} \in X_{t}^{j}$,

$$x_{t}^{j} \geqslant -\mathbf{t}, \tag{22}$$

and so (21) implies that

$$e_{i}^{j} \geqslant 0. \tag{23}$$

On the other hand, (21) implies that $x_{ti}^{j} < 0$ for large t, so that

$$e_{i}^{j} = \lim_{t \to \infty} \frac{x_{ti}^{j}}{\sum_{k=1}^{n} \| x_{t}^{k} \|} \leqslant 0. \tag{24}$$

Therefore,

$$e_{i}^{j} = 0, \tag{25}$$

and so, by (21) and (22),

$$x_{ti}^{j} = -t. \tag{26}$$

Using (26), (7) and the fact that $x_{t}^{k} \geqslant -\mathbf{t} \ (k = 1,..., n)$, we obtain

$$e_{i}^{j} = \lim_{t \to \infty} \frac{x_{ti}^{j}}{\sum_{k=1}^{n} \| x_{t}^{k} \|} = \lim_{t \to \infty} \frac{-t}{\sum_{k=1}^{n} \| x_{t}^{k} \|}$$

$$\leqslant \lim_{t \to \infty} \frac{-t}{n(n-1)\| \mathbf{t} \| + n \sum_{k=1}^{n} \| \bar{x}^{k} \|}$$

$$= \lim_{t \to \infty} \frac{-1}{n(n-1) m^{1/2} + n \sum_{k=1}^{n} \| \bar{x}^{k} \|/t}$$

$$< 0,$$

which contradicts (25). Hence (16) is proved.   Q.E.D.

PROPOSITION 4. *There exists T_3 such that $p_t(x_t{}^j - e^j) \leqslant p_t \bar{x}^j$ for all $t \geqslant T_3$ and $j = 1,..., n$.*

Proof. Let $T_3 = \max(T_1, T_2)$ and consider $t \geqslant T_3$. Since $x_t{}^j \in B_t{}^j(p_t)$, we need only show that $p_t e^j \geqslant 0$ for all j. Suppose $p_t e^j < 0$ for some j. Then, since $\sum_{j=1}^{n} p_t e^j = p_t \sum_{j=1}^{n} e^j = 0$ by (10), we can choose j_0 such that $p_t e^{j_0} > 0$. Clearly,

$$p_t(x_t^{j_0} - e^{j_0}) < p_t \bar{x}^{j_0}, \tag{27}$$

and, by Propositions 2 and 3, $(x_t^{j_0} - e^{j_0}) \in D_t^{j_0}(p_t)$. However, as a result of the inequalities in (16) and (27), the no "bliss point" assumption (A.8) implies that there exists a portfolio in $B_t^{j_0}(p_t)$ which is preferred to $(x_t^{j_0} - e^{j_0})$ by invester j_0. This contradicts $(x_t^{j_0} - e^{j_0}) \in D_t^{j_0}(p_t)$. Q.E.D.

We have established that, for large t and all $j = 1,..., n$,

$$(x_t{}^j - e^j) \in D_t{}^j(p_t), \ (x_t{}^j - e^j) > -\mathbf{t},$$

and $\sum_{j=1}^{n} (x_t{}^j - e^j) = \sum_{j=1}^{n} \bar{x}^j$. Proposition 1 therefore implies that, for large t, p_t is an equilibrium price vector for **E**, and Theorem 3.3 is proved. Q.E.D.

Theorems 3.2 and 3.3 are rather unintuitive, and so it might be helpful to apply these theorems to some special cases. Consider first the case where investors are in agreement about expected security returns, that is, for all p in Δ and $x \in R^m$, $\int rx \, d\mu_j(p)$ is independent of j. Then, Theorem 3.3 tells us that an equilibrium exists if no investor is risk-neutral and if the following restriction on probability beliefs holds for all $j = 1,..., n$: For all $\hat{p} \in \Delta$, $\mu_j(\hat{p}, \{r \mid re^j = 0\}) = 1$ implies that $\mu_j(p, \{r \mid re^j = 0\}) = 1$ for $p \in \Delta$ sufficiently close to $\hat{p}$. (This restriction is clearly satisfied if probability beliefs are independent of first period security prices.)

This can be seen as follows. Assume that $e^1,..., e^n$ satisfy conditions (a.1) and (a.2) of Theorem 3.3. Then,

$$0 \leqslant S_j{}^+ E_{e^j}^{+j}(\hat{p}) + S_j{}^- E_{e^j}^{-j}(\hat{p}) \leqslant S_j{}^- E_{e^j}^{+j}(\hat{p}) + S_j{}^- E_{e^j}^{-j}(\hat{p})$$

$$= S_j{}^- \int re^j \, d\mu_j(\hat{p}), \tag{28}$$

the second inequality following from the fact that $0 \leqslant S_j{}^+ < S_j{}^-$ since U_j is concave, increasing, and no investor is risk-neutral. (28) implies that the portfolio e^j has a nonnegative expected return according to investor j.

But, since investors agree on expected returns and $\sum_{j=1}^{n} e^j = 0$ by (a.1), this must mean that each e^j has a zero expected return. Therefore,

$$0 = S_j^+ E_{e^j}^{+j}(\hat{p}) + S_j^- E_{e^j}^{-j}(\hat{p}) = S_j^- E_{e^j}^{+j}(\hat{p}) + S_j^- E_{e^j}^{-j}(\hat{p}), \tag{29}$$

from which it follows that

$$E_{e^j}^{+j}(\hat{p}) = 0. \tag{30}$$

Substituting (30) into (29), we obtain

$$E_{e^j}^{-j}(\hat{p}) = 0, \tag{31}$$

which, together with (30), implies that $\mu_j(\hat{p}, \{r \mid re^j = 0\}) = 1$. Hence, by assumption, $\mu_j(p, \{r \mid re^j = 0\}) = 1$ for $p \in \Delta$ sufficiently close to $\hat{p}$. It follows that condition (a.3) of Theorem 3.3 holds and that an equilibrium exists.

Consider next the case where, for each j, $S_j^+ = 0$ or $S_j^- = \infty$, and assume for simplicity that the returns of the securities are linearly independent for all investors at all prices. Then, the necessary condition of Theorem 3.2 is that for *some* $\hat{p}$ in Δ there does not exist an allocation of portfolios to investors such that the portfolios sum to zero; some investor receives a nonzero portfolio; each investor's portfolio is a direction of recession of his feasible set; and, at prices $\hat{p}$, each investor believes that his portfolio yields a nonnegative return with certainty. On the other hand, the sufficient condition of Theorem 3.3 is that for *every* $\hat{p}$ in Δ there does not exist an allocation of portfolios to investors such that the portfolios sum to zero; some investor receives a nonzero portfolio; each investor's portfolio is a direction of recession of his feasible set; and, at prices $\hat{p}$, each investor believes that his portfolio yields a nonnegative return with certainty.[12]

We see then that an equilibrium exists if investors agree on expected returns and that, if investors are sufficiently risk-averse ($S_j^+ = 0$ or $S_j^- = \infty$), an equilibrium will fail to exist only if there is radical disagreement about security returns. More generally, Theorem 3.3 may be interpreted as saying that an equilibrium exists as long as investors do not disagree "too much" about security returns, and Theorem 3.2 as saying that an equilibrium does not exist if investors *do* disagree "too much." Furthermore, the more risk-averse investors are, the more disagreement is compatible with the existence of equilibrium.

[12] This sufficient condition may be regarded as a general equilibrium version of a partial equilibrium condition obtained by Leland [12] for individual investors.

This last observation may be justified as follows. Note that

$$S_j^{+}E_{e^j}^{+j}(\hat{p}) + S_j^{-}E_{e^j}^{-j}(\hat{p}) \geqslant 0$$

is equivalent to

$$\frac{-E_{e^j}^{-j}(\hat{p})}{E_{e^j}^{+j}(\hat{p})} \leqslant \frac{S_j^{+}}{S_j^{-}}\,.$$

It is clear, therefore, that the higher S_j^{+}/S_j^{-} is, the more likely it is that condition (a.2) of Theorems 3.2 and 3.3 will hold for some e^j. Since Bertsekas [3] has shown that S_j^{+}/S_j^{-} is a measure of risk aversion (the lower S_j^{+}/S_j^{-}, the more risk-averse investor j is), it follows that the more risk-averse investors are, the more likely it is that the necessary conditions and sufficient conditions of Theorems 3.2 and 3.3 will hold. Or, to put it another way, the more risk-averse investors are, the more disagreement about security returns is consistent with the existence of equilibrium.

In general, the sufficient condition of Theorem 3.3 is considerably stronger than the necessary condition of Theorem 3.2. In the special case where probability beliefs about security returns are independent of first period security prices, however, the conditions are equivalent, so that we have necessary and sufficient conditions for the existence of equilibrium.

Finally, it should be noted that the assumption that security returns are nonnegative, which we have made throughout the paper, is inessential. All our results hold in the more general case where returns may be negative, as long as negative security prices are permitted in equilibrium. Theorem 3.3 is proved by imposing the bound $\| x \| \leqslant t$, rather than $x \geqslant -\mathbf{t}$, on $\mathbf{E}$, and applying Theorem 2.4 from Hart and Kuhn [10].

REFERENCES

1. K. J. ARROW, "Essays in the Theory of Risk-Bearing," Markham, Chicago, 1970.
2. K. J. ARROW AND F. H. HAHN, "General Competitive Analysis," Holden–Day, San Francisco, 1971.
3. D. BERTSEKAS, Necessary and sufficient conditions for existence of an optimal portfolio, *J. Econ. Theory* 8 (1974), 235–247.
4. G. DEBREU, "Theory of Value," Wiley, New York, 1959.
5. G. DEBREU, New concepts and techniques for equilibrium analysis, *Int. Econ. Rev.* 3 (1962), 257–273.
6. J.–M. GRANDMONT, On the temporary competitive equilibrium, Working Paper No. 305, Center for Research in Management Science, University of California, Berkeley, August 1970.
7. J.–M. GRANDMONT, Continuity properties of a von Neumann–Morgenstern utility, *J. Econ. Theory* 5 (1972), 45–57.

8. J. R. GREEN, Temporary general equilibrium in a sequential trading model with spot and futures transactions, *Econometrica* **41** (1973), 1103–1124.
9. J. R. GREEN, Pre-existing contracts and temporary general equilibrium, Harvard Institute of Economic Research, Discussion Paper No. 246, June 1972.
10. O. D. HART AND H. W. KUHN, A proof of the existence of equilibrium without the free disposal assumption, Working Paper, Princeton University, October 1973.
11. M. C. JENSEN, Capital markets: Theory and evidence, *Bell J. Econ. Management Sci.* **3** (August 1972), 357–398.
12. H. E. LELAND, On the existence of optimal policies under uncertainty, *J. Econ. Theory* **5** (1972), 35–44.
13. J. LINTNER, The valuation of risk assets and the selection of risky investments in stock portfolios and capital budgets, *Rev. Econ. Statist.* **XLVII** (February 1965), 13–37.
14. J. LINTNER, Security prices, risk, and maximal gains from diversification, *J. Finance* **XX** (December 1965), 587–616.
15. J. MOSSIN, Equilibrium in a capital asset market, *Econometrica* **34** (October 1966), 768–783.
16. K. R. PARTHASARATHY, "Probability Measures on Metric Spaces," Academic Press, New York, 1967.
17. R. T. ROCKAFELLAR, "Convex Analysis," Princeton Univ. Press, Princeton, NJ, 1970.
18. W. F. SHARPE, Capital asset prices: A theory of market equilibrium under conditions of risk, *J. Finance* **XIX** (September 1964), 425–442.

Overlapping Expectations and Hart's Conditions for Equilibrium in a Securities Model*

PETER J. HAMMOND

Economics Department, Stanford University, Stanford, California 94305

Received March 31, 1980; revised March 16, 1982

Hart (*J. Econ. Theory* **9** (1974), 293–311) gave conditions for equilibrium to exist in a securities model where each agent undertakes asset transactions to maximize expected utility of wealth. These conditions rule out agents wanting to undertake unbounded balanced transactions to reach a Pareto superior allocation given their expectations. With mild extra assumptions to make agents unwilling to risk incurring unbounded losses on their portfolios, Hart's conditions become equivalent to an assumption of "overlapping expectations," which is comparable to a much weaker form of Green's "common expectations" (*Econometrica* **41** (1973), 1103–1124). *Journal of Economic Literature* Classification Number 021.

1. INTRODUCTION

Hart [5] presented some interesting conditions for the existence of equilibrium in a securities model in which each agent undertakes asset transactions in order to maximize expected utility of wealth. He rightly claimed that these conditions were significantly weaker than Green's (cf. Green [2, Assumption (4.2), p. 1114]. Elsewhere, I have also shown (Hammond [3, 4]) that Green's assumptions were unnecessarily strong. Here in Section 2 I shall impose some fairly mild extra assumptions on Hart's model which have their parallels in Green's work. I shall then show in Section 3 that Hart's conditions are equivalent to an assumption of "overlapping expectations" which is comparable to a much weakened form of Green's "common expectations."

Let r denote a typical value of the random vector of gross security returns. The condition of "overlapping expectations" effectively requires there to be a particular vector r^* of security returns, the same for all agents, such that, for

* This work was supported by National Science Foundation Grant SES79-24831 at the Institute for Mathematical Studies in the Social Sciences, Stanford University. I am grateful to Oliver Hart and to the referee for helpful comments.

156

any non-zero asset vector e, the events $re > r^*e$ and $re < r^*e$ both occur with positive probability. In fact, in order to $\hat{p}$ to be an equilibrium price vector, it is obviously necessary that $\hat{p}$ itself should have this property of the vector r^*. Otherwise some agent will have expectations for which there exists a non-zero vector of asset transactions $\hat{e}$ which is a source of "easy money" (cf. Leland [8, Assumption X.3, p. 37]) in that it can never lose to hold $\hat{e}$ and it may be profitable. The agent will wish to replicate $\hat{e}$ indefinitely, thus preventing existence of equilibrium. This necessary condition, which I discuss in Section 4, is actually stronger than Hart's necessary condition, and is closer to that of Green.

Section 5 briefly discusses overlapping expectations as a sufficient condition for existence.

2. MODEL AND ADDITIONAL ASSUMPTIONS

I shall follow Hart's [5] model and notation and number his assumptions as he does. Thus, there are agents $j = 1$ to n with von Neumann–Morgenstern utility functions of wealth $U_j(w)$ which are concave (A.1) and increasing (A.2). Agents' expectations concerning the vector r of returns on the m assets are given by the Borel probability measures $\mu_j(p, \cdot)$ on R^m. These expectations are conditioned by the current price vector $p \in \Delta$, where Δ is the unit simplex in R^m_+. Each agent j chooses a portfolio x^j in order to maximize expected utility which is given by:

$$V_j(p, x) := \int_\Delta U_j(rx)\, d\mu_j(p)$$

subject to the budget constraint $px \leqslant p\bar{x}^j$, and to $x \in X^j(p)$, where $X^j(p)$ is the agent's feasible set, which may be conditional on p because the agent's expectations are conditional.

Now the first extra assumption can be stated as follows:

ASSUMPTION 10. *For each agent* $j(j = 1$ *to* $n)$, *either*:

(a) *for each price vector* $p \in \Delta$, $x \in X^j(p)$ *only if* $\mu_j(p, \{r \mid rx \geqslant \underline{w}^j\}) = 1$; *or*

(b) $U'_j(w_1)/U'_j(w_2) \to +\infty$ *as* $w_1 \to +\infty$ *and* $w_2 \to -\infty$.

In part (a), $\underline{w}^j$ *is a minimum wealth constraint. It could in fact also depend on* r.

The second extra assumption is:

ASSUMPTION 11. *For each agent $j(j = 1$ to $n)$, if $x \in X^j(p)$ and if $\mu_j(p, \{r \mid re \geq 0\}) = 1$, then $x + e \in X^j(p)$.*

Note that both (A.10a) and (A.11) are satisfied in the quite plausible case where, for each agent $j(j = 1$ to $n)$:

$$x \Leftrightarrow X^j(p) \Leftrightarrow \mu_j(p, \{r \mid rx \geq \underline{w}^j\}) = 1,$$

i.e., there is a lower limit to each agent's wealth, but no additional constraint on his transactions other than the budget constraint. This is true in Green [2] and Hammond [3, 4], for instance. Assumption 10(b) is mentioned by Hart [5, p. 309] but its full implications were not drawn out.

Let $K_j(p)$ denote the convex cone generated by the support of the probability measure $\mu_j(p)$, and let $C_j(p) := \text{int } K_j(p)$ denote its interior, which is a cone excluding the origin. Given any cone C, let $C^+ := \{e \mid r \in C \Rightarrow re \geq 0\}$ denote the polar cone of C.

The third extra assumption, which closely parallels Green [2, p. 1105, Assumption 2.3(i)], is:

ASSUMPTION 12. *For each agent j ($j = 1$ to n) and all $p \in \Delta$, $C_j(p)$ is non-empty.*

This rules out perfectly autocorrelated assets. In many cases of perfect autocorrelation there is at least one redundant asset, as with the interest rate parity theorem in balance of payments theory and other examples of perfect arbitrage. As Hart [6, Example 1, pp. 427–30] points out, however, there may be perfectly autocorrelated returns with rational expectations even if no asset is redundant.

3. OVERLAPPING EXPECTATIONS

In this section $\hat{p} \in \Delta$ will be a fixed price vector. To save writing, let K_j denote $K_j(\hat{p})$ and let C_j denote $C_j(\hat{p})$.

Making use of A.1, A.2, A.10, A.11 as well as Hart [5, Lemma 1, p. 301] it is easy to see that Hart's necessary condition for $\hat{p}$ to be an equilibrium price vector [5, Theorem 3.1, p. 300] can be written as follows:

If there exist asset transactions e^j ($j = 1$ to n) satisfying (a.1) $\sum_j e^j = 0$ and (a.2') $e^j \in K_j^+$ ($j = 1$ to n) then (a.3) $re^j = 0$ for all $r \in K_j$ ($j = 1$ to n) which implies, because of (A.12), (a.3') $e^j = 0$ ($j = 1$ to n).

The condition rules out the possibility that any asset allocation x^j ($j = 1$ to n) could be improved in a Pareto sense, given agents' expectations, by moving to $x^j + \lambda e^j$ ($j = 1$ to n) for any $\lambda > 0$ (cf. Milne [10]). The following result establishes that under assumption A.12 the condition is equivalent to having *overlapping expectations* at $\hat{p}$ in the sense that $\bigcap_{j=1}^{n} C_j$ or $\bigcap_{j=1}^{n}$ int K_j must be non-empty. Without assumption A.12 of course, $\bigcap_{j=1}^{n} C_j$ could easily be empty at $\hat{p}$.

THEOREM 1. *Under assumption A.12 overlapping expectations are both necessary and sufficient to ensure that* (a.1) *and* (a.2') *imply* (a.3).

Proof. (1) *Sufficiency.* Suppose that e^j ($j = 1$ to n) is a set of asset transactions satisfying (a.1) $\sum_j e^j = 0$ and (a.2') $e^j \in K_j^+$ ($j = 1$ to n). By hypothesis, $\bigcap_j C_j$ is non-empty, and then, for any $r \in \bigcap_j C_j \subseteq \bigcap_j K_j$, it follows that $re^j \geqslant 0$ ($j = 1$ to n). But $\sum_j re^j = 0$ because $\sum_j e^j = 0$. Therefore, for any $r \in \bigcap_j C_j$, $re_j = 0$ ($j = 1$ to n). Since each C_j is an open set, and so therefore is $\bigcap_j C_j$, it follows that $e_j = 0$ ($j = 1$ to n).

(2) *Necessity.* Define $E := \sum_j K_j^+$. Since each K_j^+ is a closed convex cone, so is E. In addition, because $0 \in K_i^+$ ($i = 1$ to n), it follows that $K_j^+ \subseteq E$ ($j = 1$ to n).

(3) Note too that, by Hart's (A.4), for $j = 1$ to n, $K_j \subseteq R_+^m$ and so $R_+^m \subseteq K_j^+$. This implies that $R_+^m \subseteq E$.

(4) Let $-E$ denote the cone $\{e \mid -e \in E\}$. Suppose that $e \in E \cap (-E)$. Then $e = \sum_j e^j$, where $e^j \in K_j^+$ ($j = 1$ to n). And $-e = \sum_j \tilde{e}^j$, where $\tilde{e}^j \in K_j^+$ ($j = 1$ to n). So $0 = e + (-e) = \sum_j (e^j + \tilde{e}^j)$. Also, $re^j \geqslant 0$ and $r\tilde{e}^j \geqslant 0$ for all $r \in K_j$ ($j = 1$ to n).

(5) Therefore $r(e^j + \tilde{e}^j) \geqslant 0$ for all $r \in K_j$ ($j = 1$ to n). It follows that the transactions $e^j + \tilde{e}^j$ ($j = 1$ to n) satisfy (a.1) and (a.2') and so, by hypothesis, they also satisfy (a.3), with $r(e^j + \tilde{e}^j) = 0$ for all $r \in K_j$ ($j = 1$ to n). Therefore $r\tilde{e}^j = -re^j$ ($j = 1$ to n). From (4) it follows that, for $j = 1$ to n, $re^j \geqslant 0$ and $re^j \leqslant 0$ for all $r \in K_j$, so $re^j = 0$ for all $r \in K_j$. But, by A.12, this implies that $e^j = 0$ ($j = 1$ to n), and so $e = 0$. Thus, from (4) we see that $E \cap (-E) = \{0\}$.

(6) It follows that 0 is an extreme point of both the convex cones E and $(-E)$, and so the two non-empty disjoint convex sets $E \backslash \{0\}$ and $\{-E) \backslash \{0\}$ can be strictly separated by hyperplane $r^*e = 0$ through the origin. Thus, there exists $r^* \neq 0$ such that $r^*e > 0$ for all $e \in E \backslash \{0\}$.

(7) Suppose that, for some agent i, $r^* \notin C_i$ ($= $ int K_i). Then, even if r^* is on the boundary of K_i, there exists a hyperplane $r\bar{e}^i = 0$ which separates r^* from the interior of K_i.

(8) Thus, there exists $\bar{e}^i \neq 0$ such that $r^*\bar{e}^i \leqslant 0$ and $r\bar{e}^i \geqslant 0$ for $r \in K_i$.

(9) Therefore $\bar{e}^i \in K_i^+$. Then, however, $\bar{e}^i \in E$ because, from (3), $K_i^+ \subseteq E$. This implies that $\bar{e}^i \in E \backslash \{0\}$ and so, by (6), $r^*\bar{e}^i > 0$, a contradiction of (8). Q.E.D.

4. A STRONGER NECESSARY CONDITION

Following Hart [5, Theorem 3.1, p. 300], a necessary condition for $\hat{p}$ to be an equilibrium price, under assumptions A.1, A.2, A.10, A.11 and A.12, is that $\bigcap_{j=1}^{n} \text{int} \, K_j(\hat{p})$ must be non-empty. However, following Green [2, Lemma 2.5, p. 1108 and Assumption (4.1), p. 1114] it can be seen that $\hat{p} \in \bigcap_{j=1}^{n} \text{int} \, K_j(\hat{p})$ is actually a necessary condition for $\hat{p}$ to be an equilibrium, and, of course, a somewhat stronger necessary condition. The proof, which closely parallels Green's, is given for a more general economy in Hammond [3, 4]. Intuitively, if $\hat{p} \notin \bigcap_{j=1}^{n} \text{int} \, K_j(\hat{p})$, then there exists an agent j and a portfolio e^j with the property that:

$$\hat{p}e^j \leqslant 0, \qquad \mu_j(\hat{p}, \{r \mid re^j \geqslant 0\}) = 1, \qquad \mu_j(\hat{p}, \{r \mid re^j > 0\}) > 0.$$

Then e^j is a source of "easy money" for agent j; it is a non-zero portfolio which agent j will want to replicate indefinitely.

5. A SUFFICIENT CONDITION

It is also possible to demonstrate that having overlapping expectations for every price vector $p \in \Delta$ is sufficient for existence of equilibrium. This is done for a more general economy in Hammond [4]. For Hart's model, we have:

THEOREM 2. *Suppose that* (A.1), (A.2), (A.10), *and* (A.11) *are satisfied, as well as Hart's* (A.4) *and* (A.6), *and that* $\bigcap_{j=1}^{n} \text{int} \, K_j(p)$ *is non-empty for every* $p \in \Delta$. *Then there exists an equilibrium.*

Proof. The proof is similar to that of that [5, Theorem 3.3, pp. 302–8] and is omitted for lack of space. In fact, (A.10), and (A.11) substitute for (A.9) and actually permit a somewhat more direct proof.

It should be noted that Hart's (A.7) and (A.8) follow from my own (A.11) as well as (A.2), and so need not be stated explicitly. Much more remarkably, note that, although $\hat{p} \in \bigcap_{j=1}^{n} \text{int} \, K^j(\hat{p})$ is necessary for $\hat{p}$ to be an equilibrium price vector, the above sufficient condition does not explicitly require this necessary condition to satisfied at any point. Implicitly, it does however, because of the following:

THEOREM 3. *If expectations overlap for every* $p \in \Delta$, *and if* (A.4) *(weak continuity of expectations) is satisfied, then there exists* $\hat{p} \in \Delta$ *such that* $\hat{p} \in \bigcap_{j=1}^{n} \text{int} \, K_j(\hat{p})$.

Proof. Consider any individual j ($j = 1$ to n). Because the measure

$\mu_j(p, \cdot)$ is weakly continuous in p, it follows from Green [2, p. 1110, Remark 3.1] that the support $\operatorname{supp} \mu_j(p, \cdot)$ is a lower hemicontinuous (l.h.c) correspondence from points of Δ to subsets of Δ. So, therefore is $K_j(p)$ because of, for example, Hildenbrand [7, p. 28, Proposition 10]. Whenever $\tilde{p} \in \operatorname{int} K_j(p)$, because K_j is convex valued it follows that $(p, \tilde{p})$ is an interior point (relative to $\Delta \times \Delta$) of the graph of the correspondence K_j (see Hildenbrand [7, p. 35, Problem 6]). So every point of the graph of the correspondence $\operatorname{int} K_j$ is an interior point, which establishes that the graph of $\operatorname{int} K_j$ is open.

Consider the correspondence $C^*(p) := \bigcap_{j=1}^{n} \operatorname{int} K_j(p)$. Its graph is the intersection of the graphs of the correspondences $\operatorname{int} K_j$ ($j = 1$ to n). Therefore since $\operatorname{int} K_j$ has an open graph for each j, so does C^*. The correspondence C^* also has convex non-empty values. It follows from Ky Fan [1, Lemma 4, p. 309] or, more directly from Mas-Colell [9, Theorem 2] that C^* has a fixed point, i.e., there exists $\hat{p} \in \Delta$ such that $\hat{p} \in C^*(\hat{p})$. This is the required $\hat{p}$.   Q.E.D.

REFERENCES

1. K. FAN, A generalization of Tychonoff's fixed point theorem, *Math. Ann.*, **142** (1961), 305–310.
2. J. R. GREEN, Temporary general equilibrium in a sequential trading model with spot and futures transactions, *Econometrica* **41** (1973), 1103–24.
3. P. J. HAMMOND, "General Asset Markets and the Existence of Temporary Walrasian Equilibrium," University of Essex Economics Discussion Paper No. 102, 1977.
4. P. J. HAMMOND, "General Asset Markets, Private Capital Formation, and the Existence of Temporary Walrasian Equilibrium," Stanford University, Institute for Mathematical Studies in the Social Sciences Technical Report (forthcoming), 1983.
5. O. D. HART, On the existence of equilibrium in a securities model, *J. Econ. Theory* **9** (1974), 293–311.
6. O. D. HART, On the optimality of equilibrium when markets are incomplete, *J. Econ. Theory* **11** (1975), 418–443.
7. W. HILDENBRAND, "Core and Equilibria of a Large Economy," Princeton Univ. Press, Princeton N.J., 1974.
8. H. E. LELAND, On the existence of optimal policies under uncertainty, *J. Econ. Theory* **4** (1972), 35–44.
9. A. MAS-COLELL, A selection theorem for open graph correspondences with star-shaped values, *J. Math. Anal. Appl.* **68** (1979), 273–275.
10. F. MILNE, Short-selling, default risk and the existence of equilibrium in a securities model, *Internat. Econ. Rev.* **21** (1979), 255–267.

CHAPTER **IV**

Models of Money

12 On the Short-Run Equilibrium in a Monetary Economy

Jean-Michel Grandmont[1]

CEPREMAP, PARIS

A model of an exchange economy is presented where money is the only asset. It is shown that, under some assumptions, a short-run equilibrium exists if the traders' price expectations do not depend 'too much' on current prices.

I. INTRODUCTION

In order to take into account financial phenomena in a formal model of the economy, it seems worthwhile to consider an abstract world where several successive markets are held, to study the conditions which determine the equilibrium of each market and to find how these equilibria are linked together. This is a very old idea indeed, which underlies almost all economic thinking; it was in particular advanced by J. Hicks in his book *Value and Capital* under the name of 'temporary' equilibrium within a 'week' (see also J. Hicks [17], chapter 6). The same idea is present in the Keynesian theory and Don Patinkin [22] explicitly used this framework in his attempt to integrate money and credit in a general equilibrium theory. In a similar context, the recent work of E. Drandakis [8], R. Radner [23], [24] and B. P. Stigum [26] is in the same spirit.

However, the present state of economic theory in this area is not satisfactory, and there are still many difficulties to be solved before we have a consistent, formal theory of the temporary, or *short-run Walrasian equilibrium* (for a good survey of some of these difficulties, the reader may consult F. H. Hahn [14]). The research which is reported here was intended to make some progress in that direction. The simplified economy which is used to this effect is very similar to the economy which is studied by Don Patinkin in ([22], chapters 2 and 3) or M. Friedman in ([10], chapter 1). As the formal treatment of the model is somewhat technical, it is perhaps useful to give here

[1] I would like to express my deep gratitude to Gérard Debreu for his encouragement throughout this research. I also wish to thank Truman Bewley, Richard Cornwall, Emmanuel Drandakis, Werner Hildenbrand, Henry Lavaill, Thierry de Montbrial and Roy Radner for many helpful suggestions. I am also indebted to Jacques Drèze, Roger Guesnerie, Frank Hahn, Serge-Christophe Kolm and Yves Younes for their comments on an earlier draft. They of course bear no responsibility for any remaining error.

Reprinted from *Allocation under Uncertainty: Equilibrium and Optimality*, J. Drèze, ed. Macmillan, London, 1974, pp. 213–228.

a brief account of the basic structure of the model and of the main results.

We consider an exchange economy where money is the only store of value. Time is divided into an infinite sequence of 'Hicksian' weeks; each week is indicated by an integer t. Markets are held on each 'Monday'; they are of the Walrasian type. All commodities which can be traded on any Monday are either consumption goods or (fiat) money. Consumption goods are perishable and cannot be stored from one week to the next; their number is N. Accordingly, a trader's consumption in the t-th week is noted by q_t, a point of R^N. Further, the consumption goods' *monetary* prices at time t are represented by a price system p_t; all prices considered in this study must be positive (formally, p_t must belong to $P_t = \{p \in R^N | p \gg 0\}$).[1] On the other hand, money has no 'direct' utility but is the only means to store wealth (at no cost) from one market to the next one. Finally, the total stock of money is invariant through time.

As in Patinkin's world, each trader receives on the t-th Monday a real income in kind, which is represented by a consumption bundle ω_t. His stock of money m_{t-1} was carried over from the previous week. The object of the t-th market is to allow for a reallocation of these endowments among traders. One of the objectives of our study is, precisely, to find sufficient conditions ensuring the existence of a short-run market equilibrium at time t.

A preliminary task is obviously to define the traders' behaviour on the t-th Monday. In order to do so, we consider a particular trader and assume that p_t is quoted on the floor of exchange. The consumer must choose his current consumption q_t and the money balances m_t he wishes to carry over until the next market. For the sake of simplicity, we assume that the trader makes plans only for the current week and for the next one. It follows that our trader must forecast next week's prices in order to make his choice. In this expository introduction, we shall take the trader's price expectations as certain (in the text, they will take the form of a probability distribution). They are based upon the consumer's information, which in our model consists only of past price systems and of p_t. Since past price systems are fixed, we shall not mention them and we shall note these price expectations $\psi(p_t)$, an element of P_{t+1}. Now let the consumer's intertemporal preferences at time t be represented by the 'direct' utility function $u(q_t, q_{t+1})$. If we assume that he knows with certainty next week's endowment ω_{t+1}, the trader's problem is to maximise $u(q_t, q_{t+1})$ subject to[2] $p_t.q_t + m_t \leq p_t.\omega_t + m_{t-1}$ and

---

[1] The following notation is used. If p, q belong to R^N, $p \geq q$ means $p_n \geq q_n$ for all n in N, $p > q$ means $p \geq q$ and $p \neq q$, and $p \gg q$ means $p_n > q_n$ for all n.

[2] For all p, q in R^N, $p.q$ denotes the inner product $\Sigma p_n q_n$.

$\psi(p_t) \cdot q_{t+1} \leqq \psi(p_t) \cdot \omega_{t+1} + m_t$, where q_t, q_{t+1}, m_t are unknown. The optimal solution (s) gives us the trader's demand for consumption goods q_t, and money balances m_t, in response to p_t.

This demand can equivalently be obtained by a two-step procedure,[1] which allows us to introduce the concept of the 'indirect' or expected utility of money (a similar two-step procedure will actually be used in the text for the case of stochastic expectations). First, given p_t and for every $(\bar{q}_t, \bar{m}_t)$, choose $\bar{q}_{t+1}$ so as to maximise $u(\bar{q}_t, q_{t+1})$ subject to $\psi(p_t) \cdot (q_{t+1} - \omega_{t+1}) \leqq \bar{m}_t$ with q_{t+1} as unknown. Then define $v(\bar{q}_t, \bar{m}_t, p_t) \equiv u(\bar{q}_t, \bar{q}_{t+1})$. This procedure gives us the expected utility v of the action $(\bar{q}_t, \bar{m}_t)$; this expected utility depends, through price expectations on current prices p_t (and implicitly on past prices). It is clear that the trader's demand in the t-th week is obtained by maximising $v(q_t, m_t, p_t)$ subject to $p_t \cdot q_t + m_t \leqq p_t \cdot \omega_t + m_{t-1}$ with q_t, m_t as unknowns.

This procedure 'introduces money in the utility function' as well as prices, and allows us to discuss an important question: is the expected utility v homogeneous of degree zero with respect to m_t and p_t? In general the answer is no; for instance price expectations may depend only on past prices and not at all on p_t, in which case v does not depend on p_t. On the other hand, this homogeneity property holds if the elasticity of price expectations with respect to current prices is unity, i.e. if $\psi(\lambda p_t) = \lambda \psi(p_t)$ for all positive λ (this condition is in particular satisfied by Patinkin's assumption of static expectations: $\psi(p_t) = p_t$ for all p_t). This is obvious if price expectations are certain; it will be shown in the text that the result is still valid when they are stochastic.

As was stated earlier, the main objective of the study is to find sufficient conditions which ensure the existence of a price system p_t^* which equilibrates demand and supply of all commodities (consumption goods and money) on the t-th Monday. We shall prove an existence theorem when, among other conditions, the traders' price expectations do not depend 'too much' on current prices. It must be noted that this condition is incompatible with the hypothesis of a unitary elasticity of price expectations which was discussed earlier. As a matter of fact, it is easy to construct counter-examples which show that an equilibrium may not exist when $\psi(\lambda p_t) = \lambda \psi(p_t)$ for all λ and p_t. Such a counter-example will be given in the text for the case of static expectations $(\psi(p_t) = p_t$ for all $p_t)$. In that case if $\omega_t = \omega_{t+1}$ for all traders, and if the traders display a preference for present consumption, then the money market *cannot* be in equilibrium (if some other technical conditions are satisfied).

[1] The reader will recognise a standard dynamic programming technique. It was used by B. P. Stigum in a similar context [26].

The remainder of the study is devoted to a precise proof of these heuristic statements in the case of stochastic expectations. The paper is organised as follows. In section II we formally state the main definitions and assumptions. In section III we study the properties of an expected utility index. The traders' demand for consumption goods and money balances is analysed in section IV. The existence of a short-run market equilibrium is established in section V. Finally, conclusions are briefly given in section VI.

In what follows, it is taken for granted that the reader is well acquainted with the techniques which are used in G. Debreu's book *Theory of Value*. In addition, the reader should be familiar with the basic concepts of probability theory. References for additional material will be given in the text. Finally, a mathematical appendix gathers a few results for which no reference could be found.

II. DEFINITIONS AND ASSUMPTIONS

We fix t and focus the attention on the t-th week. There are by assumption K consumers (or traders) each of whom is indicated by an index k which varies from 1 to K. The symbol K will also denote the set $\{1, \dots K\}$.

The set of all consumption bundles available in the j-th week ($j = t, t + 1$) which are admissible for the k-th consumer (his consumption set for the j-th week) is noted Q_{kj}. By assumption, Q_{kj} is equal to R_+^N, for all j (this assumption is inessential). The k-th trader's endowment of real goods at the beginning of the j-th week is noted ω_{kj}, a point of R_+^N. We shall always assume that ω_{kt} and $\omega_{k, t+1}$ are known with certainty by the k-th consumer on the t-th Monday. The k-th consumer's endowment of money at time t is $m_{k, t-1}$, a non-negative real number. The whole endowment is noted $e_{kt} = (\omega_{kt}, m_{k, t-1})$, a point of R_+^{N+1}. We shall make the following assumption. For all k in K,

(a) $\omega_{kj} > 0, \qquad j = t, t + 1.$

An *action* x_{kt} of the k-th trader on the t-th market is a complete description of his consumption q_{kt} (a point of Q_{kt}) in the t-th week and of the money balance m_{kt} (a non-negative real number) he wants to carry over from the current week to the next one. Formally, $x_{kt} = (q_{kt}, m_{kt})$ is an element of the action space $X_{kt} = Q_{kt} \times R_+$. The purpose of this section is to describe the k-th consumer's preferences among actions on the t-th Monday.

We assume for the simplicity of the exposition that the trader makes plans only for the t-th week and the next one. Then, the trader's *intertemporal preferences* at time t are defined on the space of consumption streams $Y_{kt} = Q_{kt} \times Q_{k, t+1}$. A generic element $y_{kt} = (q_{kt}, q_{k, t+1})$ of Y_{kt} describes the trader's consumption at time t and $t+1$. It will be assumed that the trader's intertemporal preferences can be represented by a complete preordering $\gtrsim_{kt}$ defined on Y_{kt}. Then $y \gtrsim_{kt} y'$ is to be read: y is preferred or indifferent to y'. Note that this preference relation can depend upon past consumption. We shall assume for all k:

(b.1) *For all y_0 in Y_{kt}, the sets $\{y \in Y_{kt} | y \gtrsim_{kt} y_0\}$ and $\{y \in Y_{kt} | y_0 \gtrsim_{kt} y\}$ are closed in Y_{kt}.*

(b.2) *For all y, y' in Y_{kt} such that $y \succ y'$, one has $y \succ_{kt} y'$.*

When making his choice on the t-th market, the trader must forecast what his consumption will be in the following week, according to the price system p_{t+1} which will prevail on the next Monday, if he now takes the action $\bar{x}_t = (\bar{q}_t, \bar{m}_t)$ in X_{kt}. Given any $\bar{x}_t$ in X_{kt} and any p_{t+1} in P_{t+1}, let the set of feasible consumption streams $\gamma_{kt}(\bar{x}_t, p_{t+1})$ be defined as the set of elements $y_{kt} = (q_t, q_{t+1})$ of Y_{kt} such that $q_t = \bar{q}_t$ and $p_{t+1} \cdot (q_{t+1} - \omega_{k, t+1}) \leq \bar{m}_t$. Next week's consumption will then be determined by the maximisation of the consumer's preferences $\gtrsim_{kt}$ over $\gamma_{kt}(\bar{x}_t, p_{t+1})$. This procedure gives a set $\phi_{kt}(\bar{x}_t, p_{t+1})$, a subset of Y_{kt}, which is interpreted as the set of *conditional consumption programs* associated with the action $\bar{x}_t$ and the price system p_{t+1}. When $\bar{x}_t$ and p_{t+1} vary, this defines a correspondence ϕ_{kt} from $X_{kt} \times P_{t+1}$ into Y_{kt}. One shows by a standard argument:[1]

Proposition 2.1. The correspondence ϕ_{kt} is nonempty-, compact-valued and u.h.c.[2] on $X_{kt} \times P_{t+1}$.

In order to make a choice at time t, the trader must also forecast next week's equilibrium price system. This forecast will depend upon the consumer's information, which in our model consists only of the sequence of past equilibrium prices and of the price system p_t which is currently quoted. Past prices are fixed in our analysis: we shall omit them. For each p_t in P_t, the trader's forecast will take the form of a probability measure defined on P_{t+1}. Loosely speaking, a forecast is a random variable on R^N which assigns probability one to P_{t+1}. Formally, let $B(P_{t+1})$ be the Borel σ-algebra of P_{t+1}, i.e. the σ-algebra generated by its open subsets. Let $M(P_{t+1})$ be the set of probability measures defined on the measurable space $(P_{t+1},$

---

[1] See G. Debreu ([6], chapter 4) which can be easily adapted.

[2] Let X (resp. Y) be a subspace of R^N (resp. R^M). A correspondence ϕ from X to Y is P-valued if $\phi(x)$ has the property P for all x in X. Further, ϕ is upper hemi-continuous (u.h.c.) on X if for all open sets G of Y, the set $\{x \in X | \phi(x) \subset G\}$ is open in X.

$B(P_{t+1})$) (see K. R. Parthasarathy ([21], p. 1) for a definition). By assumption, the k-th trader's pattern of expectations at time t is given by a mapping ψ_{kt} which takes P_t into $M(P_{t+1})$. Then, for every E in $B(P_{t+1})$, $\psi_{kt}(p_t, E)$ is the probability assigned by the k-th consumer to the Borel set E if p_t is quoted on the t-th market.

We shall use, later on, the 'continuity' of a consumer's expectations. We must therefore introduce a topology on the set $M(P_{t+1})$. We shall choose the usual topology of weak convergence of probability measures (K. R. Parthasarathy ([21], chapter 2, section 6) and make the following assumption. For all k:

(c.1) *The mapping* $\psi_{kt} : P_t \to M(P_{t+1})$ *is continuous.*

We are now able to describe the k-th consumer's *preferences among actions* on the t-th market. These preferences will reflect his tastes, his expectations and his attitude towards risk. Since the trader's expectations may vary according to the price system p_t, his preferences among actions may themselves depend upon it. They will be described by a *family of complete preorderings* $\{\pi_{kt}(p_t) : p_t \in P_t\}$ defined on X_{kt}. Then $x[\pi_{kt}(p_t)] x'$ is to be read: 'the action x is preferred or indifferent to the action x' if p_t is quoted on the t-th market'.

The consumer's preferences will obey the so-called expected utility hypothesis,[1] which is now formally stated:

(d) *There exists a real-valued function* u_{kt} *defined on* Y_{kt} *such that*:
   (i) u_{kt} *is continuous, bounded, concave[2] and order preserving with respect to* $\gtrsim_{kt}$;
   (ii) *if for all* (x_t, p_{t+1}) *in* $X_{kt} \times P_{t+1}$, $u_{kt}(\phi_{kt}(x_t, p_{t+1}))$ *is defined as* $u_{kt}(y)$ *for some* y *in* $\phi_{kt}(x_t, p_{t+1})$, *the real-valued function* v_{kt} *defined on* $X_{kt} \times P_t$ *by* $v_{kt}(x_t, p_t) = \int_{P_{t+1}} u_{kt}(\phi_{kt}(x_t, \cdot)) \, d\psi_{kt}(p_t, \cdot)$ *is for each* p_t *order preserving with respect to* $\pi_{kt}(p_t)$.

We remark that this assumption makes sense. First, $u_{kt}(\phi_{kt}(\cdot, \cdot))$ is a well-defined continuous function according to proposition 2.1. Since it is bounded, the function v_{kt} is well defined. The function u_{kt} is called a *von Neumann–Morgenstern utility* (for short, a von N.–M. utility) and $u_{kt}(y)$ is interpreted as the utility for the k-th consumer on the t-th week of the consumption stream y. Then $u_{kt}(\phi_{kt}(x_t, p_{t+1}))$ is the utility of the conditional consumption program associated with x_t and p_{t+1}, and $v_{kt}(x_t, p_t)$ is the expected utility

---

[1] I greatly benefited from the work of J. Tobin [27] and K. J. Arrow [2].
[2] That is, for all λ in [0, 1], and any y, y' in Y_{kt}, one has $u_{kt}(\lambda y + (1 - \lambda) y') \geqq \lambda u_{kt}(y) + (1 - \lambda) u_{kt}(y')$.

of the action x_t if p_t is quoted on the t-th market. In what follows, such a function v_{kt} will be called an *expected utility index*. Although we wrote the expected utility index as a function of current prices alone, it must be emphasised that this index depends also on the past equilibrium price systems. Finally, the concavity of u_{kt} on Y_{kt} means that the trader is *risk-averse*.

It must be noted that if we start from an *arbitrary* representation u of the preferences $\succsim_{kt}$ and we apply the formula given in (d), we shall not get, in general, a representation of the preordering $\pi_{kt}(p_t)$. What (d) says is that there exists *at least* one representation u of $\succsim_{kt}$ such that this is true (it can then be shown that the representations of $\succsim_{kt}$ which satisfy (d) are determined up to a linear transformation). In short,

Definition 2.2. A trader who satisfies (a), (b.1), (b.2), (c.1) *and* (d) *is called a regular trader.*

III. PROPERTIES OF AN EXPECTED UTILITY INDEX

We consider the k-th (regular) trader at time t. We choose a particular von N.–M. utility u_{kt} and focus the attention on the properties of the expected utility index v_{kt} which is derived from it as in (d). We shall drop the index k when no confusion is possible. We first establish a few technical properties of v_{kt}.

Proposition 3.1. Consider an expected utility index v_t.
(1) v_t *is continuous on* $X_t \times P_t$;
(2) *given p_t in P_t, the function $v_t(., p_t)$ is concave on X_t;*
(3) *given p_t in P_t, for any x and x' such that $x > x'$ one has $v_t(x, p_t) > v_t(x', p_t)$.*

Proof. Assertions (2) and (3) are straightforward. We shall only prove (1). Fix (x^0, p^0) in $X_t \times P_t$ and consider a sequence (x^j, p^j) in $X_t \times P_t$ converging to (x^0, p^0). We wish $\lim v_t(x^j, p^j) = v_t(x^0, p^0)$. Now the sequence of functions $u_t(\phi_t(x^j, .))$ from P_{t+1} to R is uniformly bounded and converges continuously[1] to $u_t(\phi_t(x^0, .))$ on P_{t+1}. In addition, for each j, $u_t(\phi_t(x^j, .))$ is continuous on P_{t+1}. Finally, by (c.1), the sequence $\psi_t(p^j)$ converges weakly to $\psi_t(p^0)$. Therefore, according to [12, section 5, theorem A.3], $\lim v_t(x^j, p^j) = v_t(x^0, p^0)$.
$$Q.E.D.$$
We now turn our attention to the *homogeneity properties* of v_{kt}. Monetary theorists often assume that only 'real' balances enter a

---

[1] A sequence of functions f^j from a subspace Z of R^N to R converges continuously to f^0 on Z if for every z^0 in Z and all sequences z^j converging to z^0, one has $\lim f^j(z^j) = f^0(z^0)$.

typical trader's utility function (or in our terminology his expected utility index). In its most general form (see for instance P. A. Samuelson ([25], pp. 117–24)), this theory asserts that a trader's expected utility index must be homogeneous of degree zero in nominal money holdings and *current* prices. This property is often called 'absence of money illusion'. It should be clear that in our framework, a regular trader will not in general satisfy this requirement. In particular, if there is a lag in the adjustment of a trader's expectations, these expectations – hence the expected utility index – will depend upon past equilibrium price systems, but not on the current one. In this case, the trader suffers from 'money illusion'. But one cannot say that he is inconsistent.

It is interesting to find a condition which implies the above homogeneity property of the expected utility index. We first give some definitions. Fix any positive real number λ. For any subset E of P_{t+1}, the meaning of λE is clear. For any element μ of $M(P_{t+1})$, define the probability measure $\lambda\mu$ of $M(P_{t+1})$ which assigns to any Borel set E of P_{t+1} the probability $\mu((1/\lambda)E)$. Finally for any x: (q, m) in X_t, define λ^*x as $(q, \lambda m)$. With these notations, the property we are looking for is $v_t(\lambda^*x, \lambda p) = v_t(x, p)$ for all positive real numbers λ, any action x in X_t and any price system p in P_t. It is intuitive that such a property will depend upon some kind of 'collinearity' between the trader's expectations and current prices. More precisely, let us consider:

(c.2) *For any* $\lambda > 0$ *and any* p_t *in* P_t, $\psi_{kt}(\lambda p_t) = \lambda\psi_{kt}(p_t)$.

This condition corresponds to the classical assumption of a 'unit elasticity of expectations with respect to current prices'; it is a very strong condition. We get as a particular case the assumption which is made by Don Patinkin in [22]: each trader is sure that p_{t+1} will be equal to p_t (from now on, this case will be called the case of *static expectations*).

Proposition 3.2. Under (c.2), *for any positive real number* λ, *any action* x *in* X_t, *and any* p_t *in* P_t, *one has* $v_t(\lambda^*x, \lambda p_t) = v_t(x, p_t)$ *(i.e. the expected utility index is homogeneous of degree zero with respect to nominal money holdings and current prices).*

Proof. Fix $\lambda > 0$, x in X_t and p in P_t. In order to simplify the notation, let $h(p_{t+1}) = u_t(\phi_t(x, p_{t+1}))$ and $\bar{h}(p_{t+1}) = u_t(\phi_t(\lambda^*x, p_{t+1}))$ for every p_{t+1} in P_{t+1}. It is easy to show that $\phi_t(x, p_{t+1}) = \phi_t(\lambda^*x, \lambda p_{t+1})$ in which case $h(p_{t+1}) = \bar{h}(\lambda p_{t+1})$. Then, the proposition follows immediately from proposition 1, section A.2 of the appendix.

Q.E.D.

Is it true that the homogeneity of the expected utility index implies (c.2)? I have no definite answer to that question. If, however, we consider the case $N = 1$ and if the consumer's expectations are required to be certain (i.e. for each p_t in P_t, the probability measure $\psi_{kt}(p_t)$ is concentrated on a single element of P_{t+1}), it is easy to show that the homogeneity of v_{kt} implies (c.2).

The foregoing analysis suggests that the assumptions of 'static expectations' and of 'absence of money illusion' which Patinkin made in ([22], chapters 2 and 3) are consistent but too specific. On the other hand, our model, which allows for 'money illusion', seems to be in agreement with an idea which was put forward by, for instance, M. Allais [1], P. Cagan [4], or M. Friedman [9], [10]. These authors assume that at any given point in time, the aggregate demand for real money balances depends, among other things, on the expected rate of inflation, which in turn is a function – a weighted average – of current and past actual rates. It is easy to see that such an assumption about the formation of expectations leads to 'money illusion' in the above sense.

Remarks. (1) The 'classical' homogeneity postulate can be interpreted as a proposition dealing with money balances and *expected* prices. One can show that this type of homogeneity holds in our model. We only sketch the argument. Consider a trader at time t and let $\psi \in M(P_{t+1})$ be any probability distribution defined on P_{t+1}. Choose a von N.–M. utility as in (d) and define

$$\bar{v}_t(x_t, \psi) = \int_{P_{t+1}} u_t(\phi_t(x_t, \cdot))d\psi.$$

Then $\bar{v}_t$ can be interpreted as representing the trader's preferences among actions when his price expectations are ψ. By the reasoning of proposition 3.2, one has $\bar{v}_t(x_t, \psi) = \bar{v}_t(\lambda^* x_t, \lambda\psi)$ for all λ.[1]

(2) Another interpretation is that the homogeneity postulate deals with stationary states. This type of homogeneity also holds in our model. We first recall that a trader's expected utility index depends, through his expectations, on past prices: it can be written $v_{kt}(x_t, p_t, p_{t-1}, \dots)$. Now assume that past and current prices are stationary and equal to $p \gg 0$. Assume that the trader expects with certainty in that case p_{t+1} to be equal to p. Looking back at the formula giving v_{kt}, we find that $v_{kt}(x_t, p, p, \dots) = u_{kt}(\phi_{kt}(x_t, p))$. Therefore, trivially, $v_{kt}(\lambda^* x_t, \lambda p, \lambda p, \dots) = v_{kt}(x_t, p, p, \dots)$ holds: v_{kt} is homogeneous of degree zero with respect to m_t and the *stationary sequence* of current and past price systems. Note that this result holds even if price expectations are independent of current prices (for instance if the trader expects with certainty p_{t+1} to be equal to p_{t-1}).

[1] This remark is due to F. Hahn.

IV. DEMAND CORRESPONDENCES

Given p_t in P_t, the k-th (regular) trader must choose an action in his budget set $\beta_{kt}(p_t) = \{x \in X_{kt} | s_t . x \leqq s_t . e_{kt}\}$ (with $s_t = (p_t, 1)$). His gross demand is then as usual given by the satisfaction of the (conditional) preferences $\pi_{kt}(p_t)$ over $\beta_{kt}(p_t)$:

$$\xi_{kt}(p_t) = \{x^* \in \beta_{kt}(p_t) | x^*[\pi_{kt}(p_t)] \ x \text{ for all } x \text{ in } \beta_{kt}(p_t)\}.$$

Here again, it must be emphasised that the consumer's demand depends also on past equilibrium price systems. When p_t varies in P_t, this relation defines a correspondence ξ_{kt} from P_t into X_{kt}. One shows by a standard reasoning:

Proposition 4.1. For any regular trader, the correspondence ξ_{kt} is nonempty-, compact-, convex-valued and u.h.c.. For all p_t in P_t and all x in ξ_{kt}, one has $s_t . (x - e_{kt}) = 0$.

We next study the behaviour of the correspondence ξ_{kt} when the price of the n-th good tends to zero, or when the price level tends to infinity on the t-th market. In the first case, in view of the monotonicity assumption (b.2), it would seem reasonable to expect that the consumer's demand for the n-th good increases indefinitely; in the second case, one would expect that the consumer's demand for money will tend to infinity. Unfortunately, it is easy to show that this may not be the case if no additional restriction is put on the agent's pattern of expectations (see below). In this case, an equilibrium on the t-th market may not exist. We need a new assumption.

(c.3) *The set $\{\psi_{kt}(p_t) | p_t \in P_t\}$ is relatively (weakly) compact.*

Formally, this means that the closure of the above set is a compact subset of $M(P_{t+1})$. This assumption is automatically fulfilled if the k-th trader's expectations are independent of p_t, or if there exists a compact C such that $\psi_{kt}(p_t, C) = 1$ for all p_t in P_t (K. R. Parthasarathy [21], chapter 2, theorem 6.4). These remarks show the economic meaning of the above assumption: although the trader's expectations can depend upon the price system which is currently quoted, the range of variation of these anticipations must not be 'too large' when p_t varies in P_t. Finally, it should be noted that the above condition and (c.2) are incompatible.

Proposition 4.2. Assume that the k-th (regular) trader satisfies (c.3) and $e_{kt} \gg 0$. Consider any sequence p^j in P_t and any sequence $x^j \in \xi_{kt}(p^j)$. If p^j tends to $p^0 \in R_+^N \setminus P_t$, or if $\|p^j\|$ tends to $+\infty$, then $\|x^j\|$ tends to $+\infty$.[1]

[1] For any x in R^N, $\|x\|$ denotes the usual norm of x.

Proof. We omit the index k. Assume that the proposition is false. This means that there exists a subsequence (which can be taken to be equal to the original sequence) such that x^j converges to $x^0 = (q^0, m^0) \in X_t$. One can assume that there exists an element ψ^0 of $M(P_{t+1})$ such that $\psi_t(p^j)$ converges weakly to ψ^0. Choose a von N.–M. utility u_t and let v_t be the corresponding expected utility index. Define a function h on X_t by $h(x) = \int_{P_{t+1}} u_t(\phi_t(x, \cdot)) d\psi^0(\cdot)$. As in proposition 3.1, one shows that for any x in X_t, one has $\lim v_t(x, p^j) = h(x)$ and $\lim v_t(x^j, p^j) = h(x^0)$. In addition, by the Dominated Convergence Theorem [3, A. 28 of the appendix], h is continuous. Finally, as in proposition 3.1, $h(x) > h(x')$ whenever $x > x'$. Let us distinguish the two cases.

$$\text{(i)} \quad \lim p^j = p^0 \in R_+^N \setminus P_t$$

We have $p^0 . q^0 + m^0 \leq p^0 . \omega_t + m_{t-1}$ and $p^0 . \omega_t + m_{t-1} > 0$. It is not difficult to show, as in proposition 4.1, that $h(x^0) \geq h(x)$ for all $x = (q, m)$ in X_t such that $p^0 . q + m \leq p^0 . \omega_t + m_{t-1}$. But this leads to a contradiction, since there exists an index n such that $p_n^0 = 0$.

$$\text{(ii)} \quad \lim \|p^j\| = +\infty$$

We claim that $h(x^0) \geq h(x)$ for all x in X_t such that $x = (q^0, m)$ where m is arbitrary. Fix such an x. Let for all j, $\mu^j = p^j / \|p^j\|$. Since $\|\mu^j\| = 1$, we can assume that μ^j converges to $\mu^0 > 0$. Clearly, $\mu^0 . q^0 \leq \mu^0 . \omega_t$. Now $\mu^0 . \omega_t > 0$ implies that there exists $\bar{q}$ in Q_t such that $\mu^0 . \bar{q} < \mu^0 . \omega_t$. Choose λ in $[0, 1]$ and define $q^\lambda = \lambda \bar{q} + (1 - \lambda) q^0$. Then $x^\lambda = (q^\lambda, m)$ belongs to X_t. We have $\mu^0 . q^\lambda < \mu^0 . \omega_t$, hence for j large enough, $p^j . q^\lambda + m < p^j . \omega_t + m_{t-1}$, which implies $v_t(x^j, p^j) \geq v_t(x^\lambda, p^j)$. In the limit, $h(x^0) \geq h(x^\lambda)$ and when λ tends to zero, $h(x^0) \geq h(x)$. But this leads to a contradiction: if $x = (q^0, m)$ is such that $m > m^0$, then $h(x) > h(x^0)$. This proves the proposition. *Q.E.D.*

We now give an example which shows why an assumption such as (c.3) cannot be avoided. We shall assume, as Patinkin does in [22], that the consumer's expectations are static. In addition, we shall focus the attention on the case $\omega_{kt} = \omega_{k, t+1}$. Finally, we shall assume that the preferences $\succsim_{kt}$ are separable and that the preorderings induced on Q_{kt} and $Q_{k, t+1}$ are identical. Then, the following result says that if the consumer displays a preference for present consumption, he will not keep more than one-half of his stock of money $m_{k, t-1}$. If all traders are of this type, and if the total stock of money is positive, the money market cannot be in equilibrium.

Proposition 4.3. *Consider the k-th (regular) trader and assume:*
(1) $\psi_{kt}(p_t, \{p_t\}) = 1$ *for all* p_t *in* P_t;
(2) $\omega_{kt} = \omega_{k, t+1} = \omega_k$;

(3) *Given q_{t+1} (resp. q_t) in $Q_{k,\,t+1}$ (resp. Q_{kt}), the preordering $\gtrsim_{kt}$ induces a preordering on Q_{kt} (resp. $Q_{k,\,t+1}$) which is independent of q_{t+1} (resp. q_t). The two induced preorderings are identical and are noted $\gtrsim_{kt}{}^*$;*

(4) *for all q_t and q_{t+1} in $R_+{}^N$ with $q_{t+1} >_{kt}{}^* q_t$, one has $(q_{t+1}, q_t) >_{kt} (q_t, q_{t+1})$;*

Then, for every p_t in P_t and every $x_t = (q_t, m_t)$ in $\xi_{kt}(p_t)$, one has $m_t \leq (\frac{1}{2}) m_{k,\,t-1}$.

Proof. We drop the index k. Assume the contrary. Then, for some p_t in P_t, there is an $x_t = (q_t, m_t)$ in $\xi_t(p_t)$ with $m_t > (\frac{1}{2}) m_{t-1}$. Let $y = (q_t, q_{t+1})$ in $\phi_t(x_t, p_t)$. Let u_t be a von N.–M. utility, and let $v_t(x, p_t) = u_t(\phi_t(x, p_t))$ for all x in X_t. Clearly, $v_t(x_t, p_t) = u_t(y)$. Since $p_t \cdot q_t = p_t \cdot \omega + m_{t-1} - m_t$ and $p_t \cdot q_{t+1} = p_t \cdot \omega + m_t$, one has $p_t \cdot q_t < p_t \cdot q_{t+1}$, hence $q_{t+1} >_t{}^* q_t$. Now, let $\bar{q} = (\frac{1}{2})(q_t + q_{t+1})$, $\bar{y} = (\bar{q}, \bar{q})$ and $\bar{m} = (\frac{1}{2}) m_{t-1}$. Consider $\bar{x} = (\bar{q}, \bar{m})$. From $p_t \cdot \bar{q} + \bar{m} = p_t \cdot \omega + m_{t-1}$, it follows that $\bar{x}$ belongs to $\beta_t(p_t)$, hence $v_t(x_t, p_t) \geq v_t(\bar{x}, p_t)$. But $\bar{y}$ belongs to $\gamma_t(\bar{x}, p_t)$ which implies $v_t(\bar{x}, p_t) \geq u_t(\bar{y})$. Now, by (4) and the concavity of u_t, $u_t(\bar{y}) > u_t(y)$. Therefore, $v_t(\bar{x}, p_t) > v_t(x_t, p_t)$. This contradiction completes the proof. Q.E.D.

V. MARKET EQUILIBRIUM

We study the problem of the existence of an equilibrium on the t-th Monday. This study will allow us to test the logical consistency of the model which was presented in the preceding section. We first introduce some definitions.

A *regular economy* E_K is an economy composed of K regular traders. An *allocation* in the t-th week of the regular economy E_K is a K-tuple $x_t = (x_{1t}, \ldots, x_{Kt})$ where x_{kt} belongs to X_{kt} for all k, such that $\sum_k (x_{kt} - e_{kt}) = 0$. An *equilibrium price system* of the t-th market is a price system $p_t{}^*$ of P_t such that there exists an allocation $x_t{}^* = (x_{1t}{}^*, \ldots, x_{Kt}{}^*)$ with $x_{kt}{}^* \in \xi_{kt}(p_t{}^*)$ for all k.

Theorem 5.1. Consider a regular economy at the moment of the t-th market. Assume that for some trader k, (c.3) and $e_{kt} \gg 0$ both hold. Then, there exists an equilibrium price system $p_t{}^*$.

Proof. Define $\bar{S} = \{s = (p, 1) \in R^{N+1} \,|\, p \in R_+{}^N\}$ and $S = \{s \in \bar{S} \,|\, s \gg 0\}$. For every $s = (p, 1)$ in S, define the aggregate excess demand correspondence ζ by $\mathring{\zeta}(s) = \sum_k \xi_{kt}(p) - \left\{ \sum_k e_{kt} \right\}$.

It is easily seen that the correspondence ζ satisfies all the conditions of theorem 1 of section A.1 of the appendix. The result then follows by a standard argument. Q.E.D.

This result says that relative prices and the price level are *jointly* determined, provided the total stock of money is positive. Thus, we reach the same conclusion as Patinkin: the 'classical dichotomy' is invalid in the short run.

The foregoing existence theorem still holds for a regular economy when we assume $\sum\limits_{k} e_{kt} \geqslant 0$ provided that *every* trader satisfies (c.3). The details are left to the reader.[1]

VI. CONCLUSIONS

We have presented a model of an exchange economy where money is the only store of value. We showed that a short-run market equilibrium exists if the traders' price expectations do not depend too much on current prices. This type of result and the methods we used to reach it should be useful for most sophisticated and more realistic models.

We assumed for the simplicity of the exposition that a trader made plans only for the current week and the next one. As a matter of fact it is not difficult to extend the analysis to the case of an arbitrary finite or infinite planning horizon when the traders' expectations are certain.[2] Our results are then still valid. The case of stochastic expectations is more complicated. Its study will probably require the use of stochastic dynamic programming techniques. However, it is likely that the main conclusions of this paper will continue to hold.

This research has been voluntarily restricted to a short–run analysis. The framework which was developed in this paper should, however, be useful for the study of the long-run properties of a monetary economy. The same type of approach should also be useful for the study of an economy with credit. It will then be possible to examine the effect of various monetary policies.

APPENDIX

Section A.1

The following theorem is an extension of a well-known result (see D. Gale [11], H. Nikaido [20], G. Debreu [5] or [6, (1) of 5.6]). A version of it is implicitly contained in L. McKenzie [19] (see also G. Debreu [7, Proposition]). The set $\{1, \ldots, N\}$ is noted N.

---

[1] It should be noted that the assumption of strong monotonicity of preferences (b.2) is essential to our result. An example due to E. Drandakis shows that it might be difficult to weaken this assumption.

[2] For the case of an infinite planning horizon, see [13].

Theorem 1. Let I be a nonempty subset of N and define $\bar{S} = \{p \in R_+^N \mid$
$\sum_{n \in I} p_n = 1\}$. *Let S be any subset of $\bar{S}$ containing $S^0 = \{p \in \bar{S} \mid p \gg 0\}$.*
If $\xi : S \rightarrow R^N$ is a nonempty-valued correspondence whose graph is
closed in $S \times R^N$ and which satisfies:

(a) *ξ is bounded below, i.e., there is an element b of R^N such that*
    for each p in S and all x in $\xi(p)$, one has $x \geq b$;
(b) *for any p in S, $\xi(p)$ is convex and $p . x \leq 0$ for all x in $\xi(p)$;*
(c) *for any sequence $p^j \in S$ such that $\lim p^j = p^0 \in \bar{S} \setminus S$ or $\lim \|p^j\| = +\infty$ and for any sequence $x^j \in \xi(p^j)$, there is an index n in N such that $\overline{\lim} \, x_n^j > 0$;*

then there exists p^* in S and x^* in $\xi(p^*)$ such that $x^* \leq 0$.

Proof. Let S^j be a non-decreasing sequence of nonempty, compact, convex subsets of S^0 such that $S^0 \subset \bigcup_1^\infty S^j$. Then for each j, there is a compact X^j such that $\xi(p) \subset X^j$ for all p in S^j. One shows by a standard argument ([5], for instance) that there exists a p^j in S^j and an x^j in $\xi(p^j)$ such that $p . x^j \leq 0$ holds for all p in S^j.

The sequence x^j is bounded. Thus there is a subsequence (retain the same notation) such that $\lim x^j = x^* \in R^N$. For each p in $\bar{S}$, there is a sequence $\pi^j \in S^j$ such that $p = \lim \pi^j$. Since $\pi^j . x^j \leq 0$, in the limit $p . x^* \leq 0$. This holds for all p in $\bar{S}$, hence $x^* \leq 0$. This shows that the sequence p^j is bounded, for otherwise one could contradict (c). One can therefore assume that the sequence p^j converges to $p^* \in \bar{S}$. But $x^* \leq 0$ and (c) together imply that p^* cannot belong to $\bar{S} \setminus S$. Therefore $p^* \in S$. Finally $x^* \in \xi(p^*)$ since ξ has a closed graph.
$\qquad$ Q.E.D.

Section A.2
Let X be a subspace of R^N which is assumed to be a cone with vertex zero, i.e. if $x \in X$, then $\lambda x \in X$ for all positive real numbers λ. Let $B(X)$ be the Borel σ-algebra of X and $M(X)$ the set of all probability measures defined on the measurable space $(X, B(X))$. For any μ in $M(X)$ and any $\lambda > 0$, define the new element $\lambda \mu$ of $M(X)$ which assigns the probability $\mu((1/\lambda)E)$ to any Borel set E of $B(X)$.

Proposition 1. Let $\lambda > 0$ and consider two real-valued functions h and $\bar{h}$ defined on X such that $h(x) = \bar{h}(\lambda x)$ for all x in X. Choose μ in $M(X)$ and assume that h is μ-integrable. Then:

$$\int_X h d\mu = \int_X \bar{h} d(\lambda \mu)$$

Proof. We only sketch the proof which is elementary. First, it is clearly sufficient to consider only non-negative functions. Second, it is not difficult to show the proposition when h (hence $\bar{h}$) is a simple function. Finally, when h is arbitrary but non-negative, there exists a non-decreasing sequence of non-negative simple functions h^j which converges pointwise to h ([18, (C′) of 5.3]). The sequence $\bar{h}^j$ of simple functions defined by $\bar{h}(x) = h^j((1/\lambda)x)$ is non-decreasing and converges pointwise to $\bar{h}^j$. The result then follows from the Monotone Convergence Theorem ([3], A.26 of the appendix).   *Q.E.D.*

REFERENCES

[1] M. Allais, 'A Restatement of the Quantity Theory of Money', *American Economic Review*, vol. LVI (1966), pp. 1123–57.
[2] K. J. Arrow, *Aspects of the Theory of Risk-Bearing* (Helsinki: Academic Bookstore, 1965).
[3] L. Breiman, *Probability* (Addison-Wesley: Reading (Mass.), 1968).
[4] P. D. Cagan, 'The Monetary Dynamics of Hyperinflation', pp. 25–117 in [9].
[5] G. Debreu, 'Market Equilibrium', *Proceedings of the National Academy of Sciences of the U.S.A.*, vol. XLII (1956), pp. 876–8.
[6] G. Debreu, *Theory of Value* (New York: Wiley, 1959).
[7] G. Debreu, 'Economies with a Finite Set of Equilibria', *Econometrica*, vol. XXXVIII (1970), pp. 387–92; *ibid.*, p. 790.
[8] E. M. Drandakis, 'On the Competitive Equilibrium in a Monetary Economy', *International Economic Review*, vol. VII (1966), pp. 304–28.
[9] M. Friedman (ed.), *Studies in the Quantity Theory of Money* (Chicago: University of Chicago Press, 1956).
[10] M. Friedman, *The Optimum Quantity of Money* (Chicago: Aldine, 1969).
[11] D. Gale, 'The Law of Supply and Demand', *Mathematica Scandinavica*, vol. III (1955), pp. 155–69.
[12] J.-M. Grandmont, 'Continuity Properties of a von Neumann–Morgenstern Utility', *Journal of Economic Theory*, vol. IV (1972), pp. 45–57.
[13] J.-M. Grandmont and Y. Younès, 'On the Role of Money and the Existence of a Monetary Equilibrium', *Review of Economic Studies*, vol. XXXIX, (1972), pp. 799–803.
[14] F. H. Hahn, 'On Some Problems of Proving the Existence of an Equilibrium in a Monetary Economy', pp. 126–35 in [15].
[15] F. H. Hahn and F. P. R. Brechling (eds.), *The Theory of Interest Rates* (London: Macmillan, 1965).
[16] J. R. Hicks, *Value and Capital* (2nd edition) (Oxford: Clarendon Press, 1946).
[17] J. R. Hicks, *Capital and Growth* (New York: Oxford University Press, 1965).
[18] M. Loève, *Probability Theory* (3rd edition) (Princeton: van Nostrand, 1963).
[19] L. S. McKenzie, 'On Equilibrium in Graham's Model of World Trade and Other Competitive Systems', *Econometrica*, vol. XXII (1954), pp. 147–61.
[20] H. Nikaido, 'On the Classical Multilateral Exchange Problem', *Metroeconomica*, vol. VIII (1956), pp. 135–45.
[21] K. R. Parthasarathy, *Probability Measures on Metric Spaces* (New York: Academic Press, 1967).
[22] D. Patinkin, *Money, Interest and Prices* (2nd edition) (New York: Harper and Row, 1965).
[23] R. Radner, 'Equilibre des marchés à terme et au comptant en cas d'incertitude', *Cahiers du Séminaire d'Econométrie*, vol. IX (1966), pp. 35–52.

[24] R. Radner, 'Existence of Equilibrium of Plans, Prices and Price Expectations in a Sequence of Markets', *Econometrica*, vol. XL (1972), pp. 289–303.

[25] P. A. Samuelson, *Foundations of Economic Analysis* (Cambridge: Harvard University Press, 1966).

[26] B. P. Stigum, 'Competitive Equilibria under Uncertainty', *Quarterly Journal of Economics*, vol. LXXXIII (1969), pp. 533–61.

[27] J. Tobin, 'Liquidity Preference as Behaviour Towards Risk', *Review of Economic Studies*, vol. XXV (1958), pp. 65–86.

On the Role of Money and the Existence of a Monetary Equilibrium [1, 2]

JEAN-MICHEL GRANDMONT and YVES YOUNES

CEPREMAP, Paris

Monetary theorists have been criticized (see e.g. F. H. Hahn [9]) for having neglected the " existence problem ", that is the problem of the existence of an equilibrium where money has positive value in exchange. On the other hand, we are reminded by R. W. Clower [4, 5] that one of the weaknesses of contemporary monetary theory is that it primarily considers money as a store of value but does not pay enough attention to its function as an exchange intermediary. One can reasonably expect that the two problems are closely related. We present in this paper an exploratory model which tries to shed some light on these relationships. We shall introduce—in a very crude way—the role of money as a medium of exchange by assuming some " viscosity " in the exchange process, as was suggested by R. W. Clower in [4]. Our main concern will be to establish sufficient conditions for the existence of a monetary equilibrium both in the short run and the long run. We shall also examine the validity of the *Quantity Theory* and of the *classical dichotomy*.[3] The model we shall study is highly abstract and specific. The results and techniques which are developed in this paper should however be useful for the study of more sophisticated and more realistic models.

Without anticipating too much of what will be said in the paper, we can state our major results in a somewhat imprecise way, as follows. First, the evolution of the economy will be viewed as a succession of temporary, or short run equilibria.[4] Specifically, we shall consider an exchange economy where only spot transactions are allowed and where (fiat) money is the only store of value, which is similar to the economy studied by M. Friedman in [7, ch. 1] or Patinkin in [15, ch. 2 and 3]. We shall prove that a *short run monetary equilibrium* always exists in that type of model when, among other conditions, the elasticity of the traders' price expectations with respect to current prices is " small ". This conclusion will be reached by applying the methods of an earlier paper [8]. The theorem is valid even when money has no role to perform as a medium of exchange.

Another problem is the existence of a long run or *stationary market equilibrium*. Since the evolution of the whole economy can be described by a dynamical system, such an equilibrium is defined as a fixed point of this dynamical system. The study of the

[1] *First version received October* 1971; *final version received February* 1972 (*Eds.*).

[2] We benefited from many helpful conversations with R. Guesnerie, S. C. Kolm, J. P. Laffargue, H. Lavaill, J. Ullmo. A preliminary version of this paper was presented at the I.E.A. Workshop in Economic Theory held in Bergen, Norway, Summer 1971. We wish to thank all participants, and especially P. Champsaur, E. Malinvaud, J. Mirrlees and D. Sondermann for their stimulating comments. We are also indebted to the referees for their suggestions. All remaining errors are our own.

[3] It turns out that our model is able to shed some light on some current issues of monetary theory such as the inefficiency of a monetary equilibrium and the " optimum quantity of money " (see M. Friedman [7]). This will be the object of a forthcoming paper. We come back to this point in our conclusion (Section 5).

[4] As a consequence, our theory has all the limitations of that type of models. Unfortunately, no satisfactory model of " general disequilibrium " is as yet available.

181

Reprinted from *The Review of Economic Studies* **39** (1972), 355–372.

existence of a stationary market equilibrium is therefore an important step when we wish to examine the dynamic behaviour of the economy. We shall find that in our model, no stationary monetary equilibrium can exist if money has no role to perform as a medium of exchange. For in that case, every trader wishes to hold zero cash balances in the long run when prices are stable. On the other hand, when money does play a role in the exchange process, a stationary equilibrium will exist only if the traders are willing to hold as an asset (in the long run) the existing stock of money. We shall prove that this is the case when, among other conditions, the traders do not discount future utilities " too much ".

We shall also examine the validity of the *Quantity Theory*. Modern restatements of this theory, as exemplified by the work of G. C. Archibald and R. G. Lipsey [2], M. Allais [1], M. Friedman [7] and P. A. Samuelson [16], lead to a set of propositions dealing with the asymptotic behaviour of the economy as time goes to infinity. In our simple framework, the Quantity Theory can be formulated as follows:

(i) if an individual trader is faced with a price system which is constant through time, his long run demand for consumption goods (resp. nominal cash balances) is homogeneous of degree zero (resp. one) with respect to this price system and is independent of his initial money endowment;

(ii) if the total stock of money is constant through time, the long run Walrasian equilibrium price system of the market is proportional to the stock of money and does not depend on its initial distribution among traders. Further, " real " long run equilibrium quantities are independent of the level of the total stock of money.

We shall find that in our model assertion (i) is always valid. As for assertion (ii), we shall show that it holds trivially, once the existence of a stationary market equilibrium is established.

Finally, we shall study the validity of the *classical dichotomy*. This theory claims that, when looking for stationary equilibria, one can determine separately relative equilibrium prices and equilibrium consumption by studying the real sector alone, ignoring monetary factors. The equilibrium price level and nominal money holdings would then be determined by considering the money sector. We shall show that in our model, this classical dichotomy asymptotically holds when the traders' rates of time preference go to zero.

The remainder of this paper is devoted to a precise proof of these heuristic statements. Before we do that, we shall describe more precisely the abstract economy which will be studied. The economy is composed of a fixed number of traders, who are assumed to live for ever [1] (a trader can be interpreted as a family the population of which is stationary). Time is divided into periods of equal length. Markets are held at the beginning of each period. They are of the Walrasian type, in the sense that prices are free to move in order to match supply and demand. The number of consumption goods available in any period is N. These goods are perishable and cannot be stored from one period to another. On the other hand, (fiat) money has no " direct utility " but serves as the only means to store wealth (at no cost) from one market to the next one. The total stock of money is constant over time.

As in Patinkin's world, each trader receives at the beginning of any period a real income in kind, which is represented by a commodity bundle ω, a point of R^N (ω can be interpreted as the production of the trader or the family). This endowment is constant through time and is known with certainty by the trader concerned. The stock of money a trader owns at the beginning of period t was carried over from the previous period and is denoted $m(t-1)$, a non-negative real number. The object of the tth market is to allow for a reallocation of these endowments among traders. Each trader will have to choose—in a way which will be precisely described in Section 1—his consumption in the current period, $q(t)$, an element of R^N, and the money balances, $m(t)$, he wishes to carry over until the next

---

[1] This assumption is a technical one and makes the mathematical analysis simpler.

market. The tth market will be in (short run) equilibrium if the quoted (monetary) price system $p(t)$, an element of R^N, equilibrates supply and demand for all commodities (consumption goods and money). All price systems which are considered in this study have all their components positive (formally, they belong to the space $P = \{p \in R^N \mid p > > 0\}$).[1]

Money, which is the only asset, is also used in this economy as an exchange intermediary. The role of money as a medium of exchange will be introduced in a very crude way by imposing constraints on transactions. Our starting point will be a suggestion made by R. W. Clower in [4]. His idea was to introduce a constraint saying that in any given period " the total value of goods demanded cannot . . . exceed the amount of money held by the transactor at the outset of the period ". Our specification will be a little more general. We still assume that money is institutionally the necessary counterpart of any transaction; we also assume the existence of constraints saying that a trader will in general be unable to make use of the totality of the proceeds of his current sales when paying for his current purchases. The basic ideas which lie behind these constraints are (i) a trader cannot sell a consumption good and buy another one at the same time, and (ii) a seller must search (or wait) for buyers. As a trader will in general succeed in selling all the quantities he planned to sell only at the end of the marketing period, he will be unable to use all the proceeds before the market ends.[2] This formulation tries to incorporate in the model (as does Clower's specification) an essential feature of monetary economies: demand for goods must be backed by effective money purchasing power (we do, however, ignore an important issue of monetary theory: why do people use money as a medium of exchange?[3] Our approach can nevertheless be viewed as a useful first approximation).

Formally, let us consider a representative trader at the outset of the tth market, and let $p(t)$ be any price system which is currently prevailing. Our trader must choose an action $x(t) = (q(t), m(t))$. Our assumption implies that his choice must satisfy the following requirements. First, $x(t)$ must of course be a non-negative vector in R_+^{N+1}. Second it must satisfy the *budgetary constraint*[4]:

$$p(t) \cdot q(t) + m(t) = p(t) \cdot \omega + m(t-1).$$

Finally, it must satisfy a *transaction constraint*, which we write $q(t) \in \tau(p(t), m(t-1))$. In this notation, $\tau(p, m)$ is a subset of R^N and represents the consumption bundles which are attainable for our trader when his initial money balances are m and when the price system p prevails. In order to simplify the analysis, we specifically require that

$$q \in \tau(p, m) \text{ if and only if } p \cdot (q-\omega)^+ \leqq m + \textstyle\sum_n k_n p_n \cdot (q-\omega)_n^-$$

where $(q-\omega)^+$ and $(q-\omega)^-$ are respectively the trader's net purchases and net sales.[5] The k_n's are exogenously given parameters satisfying $0 \leqq k_n \leqq 1$ for all n, and may vary with the trader. When $k_n = 0$ for all n and all traders, we get Clower's formulation. In the limit case $k_n = 1$ for all n and all traders, the role of money as an exchange intermediary vanishes: the exchange process becomes " frictionless ". In this formulation, money can be considered as a particular capital good which is used as an input in some kind of " production process " (as for instance in E. Malinvaud [13]). Then $\tau(p, m)$ represents the set of outputs (i.e. consumption bundles) which are attainable with the input m when the price system is p. In what follows, we shall assume for the sake of

[1] The following notation is used. If x and y are vectors in R^N, $x \geqq y$ means $x_n \geqq y_n$ for all n; $x > y$ means $x \geqq y$ and $x \neq y$; $x > > y$ means $x_n > y_n$ for all n.

[2] In what follows, these constraints will be considered as a characteristic datum of the economy. This is of course unsatisfactory: a fully articulated theory of money will have to explain " market imperfections " by more fundamental assumptions on transaction costs and so on. Our approach can be viewed as a useful first approximation.

[3] The study of this problem involves the comparison of a barter economy and a monetary economy. This issue has recently received a good deal of attention (see F. H. Hahn [11] and K. C. Sontheimer [17]).

[4] $p \cdot q$ denotes the inner product $\Sigma p_n q_n$.

[5] For any x in R^N, $(x)^+$ is the vector of components $\max (0, x_n)$ for all n. Further $(x)^- = (-x)^+$.

simplicity, that the k_n's are all equal to some k and that the value of this parameter is independent of the trader. This is inessential.[1]

The remainder of the paper is organized as follows. In Section 1, we consider a representative trader and study his short run behaviour in any period, as well as his long run demand for consumption and money balances when he is faced by a constant price system. In Section 2, we consider the economy as a whole. We prove there the existence of a short run market equilibrium (Theorem 2.1), of a stationary market equilibrium (Theorem 2.4), the validity of the Quantity Theory (Proposition 2.3) and the asymptotic validity of the classical dichotomy (Theorem 2.5). We consider in Section 3 the limit case where the traders do not discount future consumption and make use of the " overtaking " criterion. Proofs are gathered in Section 4. Finally, a few closing remarks are given in Section 5.

1. TRADERS

Let us consider a representative trader at the moment of the tth market. His endowment of current consumption goods is ω, his stock of money is $m(t-1) \geqq 0$. We shall assume [2]:

(a) $\qquad\qquad\qquad\qquad \omega > > 0.$

Assume that the price system $p(t) \in P$ prevails. Our trader must choose an action $x(t) = (q(t), m(t))$, in his *budget set*

$$\beta(p(t), m(t-1)) = \{x = (q, m) \in R_+^{N+1} \mid p(t) \cdot q + m = p(t) \cdot \omega + m(t-1) \text{ and } q \in \tau(p(t), m(t-1))\},$$

where the correspondence τ is defined as in the introduction. Our first task is to precisely describe how this choice is made. Clearly, it will depend upon the trader's intertemporal preferences and his expectations about the future.

When making up his mind, the trader must forecast what actions he will take in the next markets. We assume that his planning horizon H is infinite. Accordingly, his *intertemporal preferences* at time t will be defined on the space of *consumption programmes* Y, which is equal to $(R_+^N)^\infty$. A generic element y of Y is described by a countable array $(q(t+h))$, $h = 0, 1, \ldots$, of elements of R_+^N. We shall assume:

(b) *The trader's intertemporal preferences at time t on Y can be represented by the utility function*

$$U(q(t), q(t+1), \ldots) = \sum_0^\infty \delta^h u(q(t+h))$$

where the real valued function u is continuous, bounded, strictly concave and strictly monotone[3] *on R_+^N, and δ is a fixed parameter satisfying $0 < \delta < 1$. The characteristics u and δ are independent of time t.*

The trader has also to forecast the equilibrium price systems in the subsequent periods. We assume that when computing this forecast, our trader takes into account only the price systems $p(t-1), \ldots, p(t-T)$ of the past T periods and the current one $p(t)$. The positive integer T is independent of the particular period t under consideration (one could take $T = +\infty$ without any difficulty). For the sake of simplicity, the trader's forecast is single-valued,[4] i.e. takes the form of a point in the *space of price expectations* P^H (which

---

[1] The whole analysis is valid when the k_{in}'s are allowed to vary with the trader i and the good n. All the changes which are needed in the statement of the results are: (i) $k > 0$ must be read $k_{in} > 0$ for all i and n; (ii) $k = 1$ must read $k_{in} = 1$ for all i and n; (iii) $k < 1$ must read $k_{in} < 1$ for all i and n.

[2] This (very strong) assumption is made in order to simplify the mathematical treatment of the model. As a matter of fact, all the results stated in Sections 2 and 3 are valid, without any change, under the more general assumptions $(a.1)$ $\omega_i \geqq 0$ and $(c.2)$ $\Sigma_i \omega_i > > 0$. The main changes in the proofs are: (i) Lemma 4.1 and Corollary 4.3 are still valid but their proof has to be modified; (ii) the results stated in Lemma 4.5 and Lemma 4.8 (2) are no longer true for individual demands but hold for the *aggregate* demand.

[3] That is, $q' > q''$ implies $u(q') > u(q'')$.

[4] This assumption is, of course, very unrealistic. One could probably replace point expectations by probability distributions, as in [8]. This would, in particular, make assumption $(c.3)$ below less restrictive. We felt, however, that the use of probability distributions would unnecessarily complicate the exposition and the mathematical treatment of the model.

is by definition equal to the product of countably many P. In what follows, P^H is endowed with the product topology).

By assumption, the dependence of the trader's forecast upon current and past prices is stationary and can accordingly be represented by a mapping ψ taking P^{T+1} into P^H which is independent of t. Then, $\psi(p(t), p(t-1), ..., p(t-T))$ describes the trader's forecast when the sequence of current and past price systems is $p(t), ..., p(t-T)$. We shall need the following assumptions:

(c.1) *The mapping* $\psi: P^{T+1} \to P^H$ *is continuous.*

(c.2) *For every p in P, $\psi(p, ..., p) = (p, p, ...)$.*

(c.3) *Given $p(t-1), ..., p(t-T)$ in P, the set $\{\pi \in P^H \mid$ there exists p in P such that $\pi = \psi(p, p(t-1), ..., p(t-T))\}$ lies in a compact subset of P^H.*

The first assumption is of a technical nature. It can be paraphrased as follows. Consider a sequence $p^j(t), ..., p^j(t-T)$ of current and past prices tending to

$$p^0(t) \in P, ..., p^0(t-T) \in P.$$

Let, for any $j \geq 0$, $\psi(p^j(t), ..., p^j(t-T)) = (\pi^j(t+h)) h \geq 1$, where $\pi^j(t+h)$ belongs to P for all $h \geq 1$. Then $(c.1)$ simply means that for any $h \geq 1$, the sequence $\pi^j(t+h)$ tends to $\pi^0(t+h)$. The second assumption means that if prices were constant in the past, the trader expects the price system to keep the same value in the future. The third assumption means that price expectations must not depend "too much" on current prices (this assumption is needed only in order to be sure of the existence of a short run market equilibrium).[1]

We are now able to describe how our trader chooses an action on the tth market. Let $p(t), p(t-1), ..., p(t-T)$ be current and past price systems. Let $\gamma(p(t), ..., p(t-T), m(t-1))$ be the set of all consumption programmes which the trader expects to be feasible in the current period and the next ones. This subset of Y is defined as follows. Consider the trader's price expectations:

$$\psi(p(t), ..., p(t-T)) = (\pi(t+h)), h \geq 1, \text{ where } \pi(t+h) \in P \text{ for all } h \geq 1.$$

Then, a consumption programme $y = (q(t+h)) \in Y$ $(h \geq 0)$ will belong to $\gamma(\cdot)$ if there exist non-negative numbers $m(t+h)(h \geq 0)$ such that:

$$(q(t), m(t)) \in \beta(p(t), m(t-1))$$

$$(q(t+h), m(t+h)) \in \beta(\pi(t+h), m(t+h-1)) \quad (h = 1, 2, ...)$$

where the correspondence β was defined at the beginning of this section. The trader naturally seeks to maximize his utility U over the set $\gamma(\cdot)$. It can be shown (see Section 4) that under our assumptions, there is one and only one maximizer $\bar{y} = (\bar{q}(t+h))(h = 0, 1, ...)$. Define $\bar{m}(t)$ as $m(t-1) - p(t) \cdot (\bar{q}(t) - \omega)$. Clearly, the trader will choose the action

$$\bar{x}(t) = (\bar{q}(t), \bar{m}(t))$$

in the current period. This action depends on current and past prices $p(t), ..., p(t-T)$ and also—through the stock of money $m(t-1)$—on the action $x(t-1) = (q(t-1), m(t-1))$ which the trader took in the previous market. The action $\bar{x}(t)$ will accordingly be denoted

$$\xi(p(t), ..., p(t-T), x(t-1)).$$

When $p(t), ..., p(t-T)$ vary in P and $x(t-1)$ varies in R_+^{N+1}, the procedure defines a mapping ξ from $P^{T+1} \times R_+^{N+1}$ into R_+^{N+1}, which we call the trader's *demand function*.

---

[1] This type of assumption was introduced in an earlier paper [8]. This is a strong assumption, which can hopefully be weakened in further studies. For an example of such a weakening, see *Technical remark* after Lemma 4.5, Section 4. We kept assumption $(c.3)$ as it stands in the text in order to simplify the exposition.

This demand function does not depend on time t. It can be shown that the mapping ξ is continuous (see Section 4, corollary 4.2). For short,

Definition 1.1. *A regular trader is defined by those of his characteristics which are invariant through time* $(u, \omega, \delta, \psi)$ *and satisfies assumptions* (a), (b), $(c.1)$, $(c.2)$ *and* $(c.3)$.

This almost completes the study of the trader's short run behaviour. Before we leave this subject, a comment is in order. Let $x(t) = (q(t), m(t)) = \xi(p(t), ..., p(t-T), x(t-1))$. Then the demand for consumption goods $q(t)$ (resp. for cash balances $m(t)$) is *not* in general homogeneous of degree zero (resp. one) with respect to current prices $p(t)$ and money holdings $m(t-1)$. It is readily seen that this would be the case if the elasticity of price expectations with respect to current prices was unity. This case is ruled out by assumption $(c.3)$.

We now turn our attention to the trader's long run behaviour. Assume that our (regular) trader is faced by a constant price system p of P. The evolution of his demand for consumption goods and cash balances in each period is given by the following recursive system:

$$x(t) = \xi(p, ..., p, x(t-1)).$$

This evolution is entirely determined for $t = 1, 2, ...$, once we know the trader's initial stock of money $m(0)$. A *stationary state corresponding to* p is by definition any element x of R_+^{N+1} which satisfies $x = \xi(p, ..., p, x)$. We shall denote the (may be empty) set of these elements by $\xi^*(p)$. An element x of $\xi^*(p)$ is *stable* if for any $x(0)$ in R_+^{N+1}, the corresponding sequence $x(t)$ converges to x.

The remainder of this section is devoted to the study of the existence and properties of such stationary states. Since part of our analysis will be concerned with the relationship between " real " and " monetary " phenomena, it is convenient to introduce at this stage an imaginary static " real trader " (u, ω) who is associated with our regular trader $(u, \omega, \delta, \psi)$. Then for any p in P, let $\chi^b(p)$ be the (unique) consumption bundle which maximizes $u(q)$ over the set $\{q \in R_+^N \mid p \cdot (q - \omega) \leqq 0\}$ and let $m^b(p)$ be the minimum amount of cash needed to achieve $\chi^b(p)$. As $p \cdot (\chi^b(p) - \omega) = 0$, we have:

$$m^b(p) = \min \{m \mid m \geqq 0, \chi^b(p) \in \tau(p, m)\} = (1-k)p \cdot (\chi^b(p) - \omega)^+.$$

The interest of these concepts will appear in the discussion of our results. First,

Proposition 1.2. *Consider any regular trader* $(u, \omega, \delta, \psi)$. *For any* p *in* P,

(1) $\xi^*(p)$ *is non-empty*;
(2) *if* $x = (q, m)$ *belongs to* $\xi^*(p)$, *then* $(q, \lambda m)$ *belongs to* $\xi^*(\lambda p)$ *for all* $\lambda > 0$;
(3) *for any* $x^* = (q^*, m^*)$ *in* $\xi^*(p)$, *one has*:

    $(3.a)$ $p \cdot (q^* - \omega) = 0$ *and* q^* *maximizes* $u(q)$ *over the set* $\{q \in R_+^N \mid p \cdot (q - \omega) \leqq 0$ *and* $q \in \tau(p, m^*)\}$,
    $(3.b)$ $m^* = \min \{m \mid m \geqq 0, q^* \in \tau(p, m)\} = (1-k)p \cdot (q^* - \omega)^+$,
    $(3.c)$ $u(q^*) \leqq u(\chi^b(p))$ *and* $m^* \leqq m^b(p)$.

The first assertion of this Proposition ensures that stationary states always exist. Assertion (2) says, in effect, that the Quantity Theory holds at the individual level. It should be noted that this conclusion is an immediate consequence of assumption $(c.2)$ and the fact that $\tau(\lambda p, \lambda m) = \tau(p, m)$ for all $\lambda > 0$. Assertion $(3.a)$ is almost evident. What $(3.b)$ says is that the trader will not keep more cash than is needed in order to achieve the stationary consumption q^*: one can therefore say that stationary money balances are held for a " transactions motive ". This amount of cash is $m^* = (1-k)p \cdot (q^* - \omega)^+$. Finally, $(3.c)$ tells us that in a stationary state, the maximum (static) utility level the trader can achieve is given by $u(\chi^b(p))$. In addition, the trader will not keep more cash than $m^b(p)$, which is the minimum needed in order to achieve the consumption bundle $\chi^b(p)$. This again agrees with our common sense.

We must now give an answer to an important question. It is intuitive that the existence of a stationary *market* equilibrium will depend on the traders' willingness to hold in the long run the existing positive stock of money. If we found that for any price system p in P, the traders' stationary cash balances are zero, it would follow that no stationary market equilibrium exists. In view of Proposition 1.2, (3.c), this would be the case for a given p if $m^b(p) = 0$ that is, when $k = 1$ (transactions are fluid) and/or $\chi^b(p) = \omega$ (the agent does not want to trade). If $m^b(p) > 0$ for a given p, it is important to have sufficient conditions which imply that m^* is positive for all $x^* = (q^*, m^*)$ in $\xi^*(p)$. Intuitively, if the trader discounts future consumption very much, his stationary cash balances will be very low and may be zero: in order to have the desired result, the parameter δ should be close enough to unity. This is implied by the following result:

Proposition 1.3. *Consider a real trader (u, ω) and fix p in P.*

(1) *Assume $m^b(p) = 0$. Then for any regular trader $(u, \omega, \delta, \psi)$, the set $\xi^*(p)$ is composed of the unique element $x^* = (\chi^b(p), 0)$. Further x^* is stable.*

(2) *Assume $m^b(p) > 0$. Fix ψ and consider a sequence of regular traders*

$$a_j = (u, \omega, \delta_j, \psi)$$

such that $\lim \delta_j = 1$. Let $\xi_j^*(p)$ be the set of stationary states corresponding to p for the trader a_j. Then for any sequence $x_j \in \xi_j^*(p)$, one has

$$\lim x_j = (\chi^b(p), m^b(p)).$$

The above result also answers the following question: is it possible to determine *separately* stationary consumption and cash balances? In other words, under what conditions is the *classical dichotomy* valid? For a given p, this would be the case if $\xi^*(p)$ reduces to the single point $(\chi^b(p), m^b(p))$. While this is not in general true when $m^b(p) > 0$, Proposition 1.3, (2) tells us that this dichotomy is valid in the limit when δ tends to 1. In that case, one can say that the trader becomes " satiated " in money.

2. MARKET EQUILIBRIUM

We now consider the economy as a whole. By definition a *regular economy* is composed of a fixed number I of regular traders, each of whom is indicated by the index $i = 1, ..., I$. A regular economy is formally defined by its invariants: the number of traders, their characteristics, the parameter k and the total money stock M, and is accordingly noted $E = (I, (u_i), (\omega_i), (\delta_i), (\psi_i), k, M)$. A regular monetary economy is by definition such that $M > 0$. Finally, given any regular economy E, one can define in the usual way a " frictionless " static barter economy $(I, (u_i), (\omega_i))$.

Consider a regular monetary economy E at the beginning of the tth period. Let $p(t-1), ..., p(t-T)$ be the price systems which prevailed in the past T markets. Let $x_i(t-1)$ be the action taken by the ith trader on the previous market. By definition, an *allocation* on the tth market is a I-tuple $x(t) = (x_i(t))$ with $x_i(t) = (q_i(t), m_i(t)) \in R_+^{N+1}$, such that $\sum_i (q_i(t) - \omega_i) = 0$ and $\sum_i m_i(t) = M = \sum_i m_i(t-1)$. Let $\tilde{X}$ be the space of such allocations. A *short run market equilibrium* $(p(t), x(t))$ in the tth market is composed of a price system $p(t)$ of P and an allocation $x(t) = (x_i(t))$ such that $x_i(t) = \xi_i(p(t), p(t-1), ..., p(t-T), x_i(t-1))$ for all i. The following theorem claims that our model is logically consistent.

Theorem 2.1. *Let $E = (I, (u_i), (\omega_i), (\delta_i), (\psi_i), k, M)$ be a regular monetary economy and assume $k > 0$. Given any $p(t-1), ..., p(t-T)$ and any allocation $x(t-1)$, there exists a short run market equilibrium $(p(t), x(t))$ in the tth market.*

It should be emphasized that assumption (c.3) is essential to the theorem. It must be noted that a short run equilibrium exists in this model *even when $k = 1$*, that is, when money is not needed to carry out transactions. In that case, one can say that under the conditions of the theorem, the traders hold money in the short run for some kind of " speculation motive ".[1] We have been unable to cope with the case $k = 0$ (Clower's specification); there is a technical difficulty in that case, for the correspondences $\tau_i(p, m)$ then present a discontinuity when some price goes to zero along with m (for instance $q \in \tau_i(p, 0)$ if and only if $q \leq \omega_i$ when $p \in P$; but if $p_n = 0$, there is no constraint on the component q_n).

Let $W(p(t-1), ..., p(t-T), x(t-1))$ be the set of short run market equilibria corresponding to $p(t-1), ..., p(t-T)$ and $x(t-1)$. Our procedure defines a correspondence W from $P^T \times \tilde{X}$ into $P \times \tilde{X}$. It is now easy to describe the dynamic behaviour of the economy; it obeys the following dynamical system:

$$(p(t), x(t)) \in W(p(t-1), ..., p(t-T), x(t-1)).$$

By definition, a *stationary market equilibrium* of the regular monetary economy E is a fixed point of this dynamical system, i.e. an element (p^*, x^*) of $P \times \tilde{X}$ such that:

$$(p^*, x^*) \in W(p^*, ..., p^*, x^*).$$

Let $W^*(E)$ be the set of these stationary market equilibria. It is easy to get the following equivalent characterization of $W^*(E)$:

Proposition 2.2. *Let* $E = (I, (u_i), (\omega_i), (\delta_i), (\psi_i), k, M)$ *be a regular monetary economy. Consider* p *in* P *and* $x_i = (q_i, m_i)$ *in* R_+^{N+1} *for all* i. *Then* $(p, (x_i))$ *belongs to* $W^*(E)$ *if and only if*:

(1) $x_i = \xi_i(p, ..., p, x_i)$ *for all* i

(2) $\Sigma(q_i - \omega_i) = 0$

(3) $\Sigma m_i = M$.

One must remark on an essential difference between the concepts of a short run and stationary market equilibrium. When we were looking for a short run equilibrium in the tth market, past price systems $p(t-1), ..., p(t-T)$ and the preceding allocation $x(t-1)$, hence the initial distribution $m_i(t-1)$ of the stock M of money, were fixed beforehand: the unknown variables were the current price system $p(t)$ and the current allocation $x(t)$. When we look for a stationary market equilibrium, the stationary sequence of past price systems and the stationary distribution of the money stock M are among the unknown variables of the problem.

It then follows trivially from Proposition 2.2 and the homogeneity properties of $\xi_i^*(p)$ that the Quantity Theory holds:

Proposition 2.3. *Let* $E = (I, (u_i), (\omega_i), (\delta_i), (\psi_i), k, M)$ *be a regular monetary economy. Fix* $\lambda > 0$ *and consider the regular monetary economy* E_λ *obtained from* E *by multiplying the total stock of money* M *by* λ. *Then* $(p^*, (x_i^*))$ *where* $x_i^* = (q_i^*, m_i^*)$, *belongs to* $W^*(E)$ *if and only if* $(\lambda p^*, (q_i^*, \lambda m_i^*))$ *belongs to* $W^*(E_\lambda)$.

An important problem is to find sufficient conditions which imply the existence of such equilibria. There is, however, a technical difficulty, for the sets $\xi_i^*(p)$ are not in general convex. It is well known that non-convexities are " unimportant " when the number of traders is large (e.g. see R. M. Starr [18]). We shall accordingly use a weaker notion of equilibrium. We shall say that $(p^*, (x_i^*))$, where p^* belongs to P and $x_i^* = (q_i^*, m_i^*)$

---

[1] When $k = 1$, and if (c.3) does not hold, the model may have no solution in the short run. Counter-examples can be easily constructed as in [8].

belongs to R_+^{N+1}, is a *stationary market quasi-equilibrium* for the regular monetary economy E if:

(1) $x_i^* \in \xi_i^*(p^*)$ for all traders i, with the exception of *at most* $N-1$ traders for whom $x_i^* \in co\xi_i^*(p^*)$ and $x_i^* \in \beta_i(p^*, m_i^*)(co\xi_i^*(p^*)$ denotes the convex hull of $\xi_i^*(p^*)$);

(2) $\Sigma(q_i^* - \omega_i) = 0$;

(3) $\Sigma m_i^* = M$.

If we look back to Proposition 2.2, we see that this concept is meaningful when the number of traders I is very large compared to the number of goods, for in that case, all the conditions which characterize a " true " equilibrium are satisfied for " almost all " traders. In addition, for all i such that x_i^* does not lie in $\xi_i^*(p^*)$, one must have $x_i^* \in \beta_i(p^*, m_i^*)$, or equivalently, $p^* \cdot (q_i^* - \omega_i) = 0$ and $q_i^* \in \tau_i(p^*, m_i^*)$: the stationary action x_i^* must be feasible for the ith trader.   Finally, such a quasi-equilibrium is identical to a true equilibrium if the sets $\xi_i^*(p^*)$ happen to be convex.[1]   In addition, the equivalent of Proposition 2.3 holds for quasi-equilibria.   We can now state our result:

Theorem 2.4.   *Consider a frictionless barter economy* $(I, (u_i), (\omega_i))$ *and fix* (ψ_i), k *and* $M > 0$.   *Let* C *be the collection of regular monetary economies which have in common the characteristics* I, (u_i), (ω_i), (ψ_i), k *and* M *(each economy in* C *can therefore be indicated by the parameters* (δ_i)*).   Then,*

(1) *If* $k = 1$, $W^*(E)$ *is empty for all economies* E *in* C.

(2) *Assume* $0 < k < 1$ *and* $I > N-1$.   *Assume also that for every* p *in* P, *there is an* i *such that* $\chi_i^b(p) \neq \omega_i$.   *Then there exists a* $\bar{\delta}$, *with* $0 \leq \bar{\delta} < 1$, *such that a stationary market quasi-equilibrium exists for all economies in* C *which satisfy* $\delta_i > \bar{\delta}$ *for all* i.

Part (1) of this theorem agrees with what we expected: if $k = 1$, that is, if money is not actually needed to carry out transactions, no stationary equilibrium can exist since in that case all traders wish to hold zero cash balances when prices are stable (Proposition 1.3, (1)).   Accordingly, $k \neq 1$ is a necessary condition in our model for the existence of a stationary equilibrium.   In addition, it is intuitively clear that we must require that exchange takes place at any equilibrium of the associated static barter economy.   Now, if we look back at the discussion of Proposition 1.3, it becomes apparent that, in order to be sure of the existence of stationary (quasi) equilibrium, we have to impose that the traders' subjective rate of time preference be low enough.   Part (2) of the above theorem makes precise these heuristic statements for the case $0 < k < 1$.   We have been unable to cope with the case $k = 0$ for the reasons presented in the discussion of Theorem 2.1.

We now examine the validity of the *classical dichotomy*.   Indeed, if we look back to Proposition 2.2 we see that there exists some kind of dichotomy between " real " and " monetary " quantities.   For, if we " solve " equations (1) and (2) with the additional requirement [2] $\| p \| = 1$, it is possible to compute (stationary) relative equilibrium prices, equilibrium consumption and " real " equilibrium money holdings.   Then, using the Quantity Theory, we can determine the monetary equilibrium price level and nominal money holdings from equation (3).   This is what P. A. Samuelson claimed in [16] to be the classical dichotomy.   It must be however emphasized that it is conceptually *equivalent* to the Quantity Theory.

This dichotomy does not permit the separate determination of stationary relative prices and equilibrium consumption *ignoring monetary phenomena*.   This would be the case if

---

[1] This concept of quasi-equilibrium is borrowed from R. M. Starr [18]. A more satisfactory treatment would have been to consider a continuum of traders as in R. J. Aumann [3] or W. Hildenbrand [12]. This was outside the scope of this paper.
[2] $\| p \|$ denotes the usual norm of p.

for all $(p^*, (x_i^*))$ in $W^*(E)$, one had $x_i^* = (\chi_i^b(p^*), m_i^b(p^*))$ for all i. We shall say that the *classical dichotomy in the narrow sense* holds if this property is true. In view of Proposition 1.3 *this dichotomy is valid in the limit when the traders' rates of time preference go to zero.*

Theorem 2.5. *Consider a sequence of regular monetary economies*

$$E_j = (I, (u_i), (\omega_i), (\delta_{ij}), (\psi_i), k, M)$$

for $j = 1, 2, \ldots$, *where the characteristics* $I, (u_i), (\omega_i), (\psi_i), k, M$ *are fixed and* $\lim \delta_{ij} = 1$ *for all* i. *Assume that* $0 < k < 1$ *and that for every* p *in* P, *there exists an* i *such that* $\chi_i^b(p) \neq \omega_i$. *Then for any sequence* $(p_j^*, (x_{ij}^*))$ *in* $W^*(E_j)$,

(1) *the sequence* p_j^* *lies in a compact subset of* P;

(2) *any cluster point* $(p_0^*, (x_{i0}^*))$ *of the sequence* $(p_j^*, (x_{ij}^*))$ *is such that*

$$x_{i0}^* = (\chi_i^b(p_0^*), m_i^b(p_0^*)).$$

It should be noted that this limit theorem is also valid for quasi-equilibria.

3. THE LIMIT CASE: NO DISCOUNTING

We study in this section the limit case where the traders do not discount future consumption and make use of the " overtaking " criterion. In view of the preceding sections, both the Quantity Theory and the classical dichotomy in the narrow sense will be valid in that case.

We have to redefine some concepts. Consider a trader at time t. We still assume (a), $(c. 1)$, $(c. 2)$. Now, if $p(t), \ldots, p(t-T)$ are current and past price systems, one defines the set $\gamma(p(t), \ldots, p(t-T), m(t-1))$ of feasible consumption programmes as in Section 1. Our trader will no longer seek to maximize a utility function but will choose any programme $\bar{y} = (\bar{q}(t+h))(h = 0, 1, 2, \ldots)$ in $\gamma(.)$ which " overtakes " any other programme $y = (q(t+h))$ of $\gamma(.)$. That is, $\bar{y}$ will be such that for any y in $\gamma(.)$, there is a S such that for all $s \geq S$:

$$\sum_0^s u(\bar{q}(t+h)) \geq \sum_0^s u(q(t+h))$$

where u is continuous, bounded, strictly concave and strictly monotone. To any programme $\bar{y}$ in $\gamma(.)$ satisfying this requirement, one can associate an action $\bar{x}(t) = (\bar{q}(t), \bar{m}(t))$ where $\bar{m}(t) = m(t-1) - p(t) \cdot (\bar{q}(t) - \omega)$. This gives a (may be empty) set of actions which we note $\xi(p(t), \ldots, p(t-T), x(t-1))$.

We shall, in this section, be concerned only with stationary states. Fix p in P. We shall denote as before by $\xi^*(p)$ the set of actions x^* such that $x^* \in \xi(p, \ldots, p, x^*)$. Then, as expected,

Theorem 3.1. *Consider a trader* (u, ω, ψ) *who satisfies assumptions* (a), $(c.1)$, $(c.2)$ *and uses the " overtaking " criterion. Then for any* p *in* P, *the set* $\xi^*(p)$ *is composed of the unique element* $(\chi_i^b(p), m^b(p))$.

Consider now an economy $E = (I, (u_i), (\omega_i), (\psi_i), k, M)$ composed of I traders who all satisfy the assumptions of the foregoing theorem. We define directly as in Proposition 2.2 the set of stationary market equilibria $W^*(E)$. As we expected, the Quantity Theory and the classical dichotomy hold in that case.

Theorem 3.2. *Consider an economy* $E = (I, (u_i), (\omega_i), (\psi_i), k, M)$ *where all traders satisfy the assumptions of Theorem 3.1, and* $M > 0$. *Then*

(1) $W^*(E)$ *is empty when* $k = 1$.

(2) *Assume that $k<1$ and that for every p in P, there is an i such that $\chi_i^b(p) \neq \omega_i$. Then $W^*(E)$ is non-empty, and $(p^*, (x_i^*))$ belongs to $W^*(E)$ if and only if:*

(α) $x_i^* = (\chi_i^b(p^*), m_i^b(p^*))$;

(β) $\Sigma(\chi_i^b(p^*)-\omega_i) = 0$, *i.e.*, $(p^*, (\chi_i^b(p^*)))$ *is an equilibrium of the associated barter economy*;

(γ) $\Sigma m_i^b(p^*) = M$.

Note that this result is valid also when $k = 0$.

4. PROOFS

Proofs of the results of Sections 1, 2 and 3 are gathered in this section. Due to lack of space, some proofs are only sketched.

4.1. *Proof of Section 1's results*

We first consider an individual regular trader as in Section 1. In what follows, the space of consumption programmes Y will be endowed with the product topology. Then Y is a separable metric space. It is easy to show that the utility function U defined in (b) from Y to R is continuous. In addition, U is clearly strictly concave. It is also straightforward to show that for all p in R_+^N and all $m \geq 0$, the set $\tau(p, m)$ is equal to the set of all q in R_+^N such that for every subset S (may be empty) of N, one has

$$\sum_{n \in S} p_n(q_n-\omega_n)+k \sum_{n \notin S} p_n(q_n-\omega_n) \leq m.$$

Consider the trader at time t. Let $p(t), p(t-1), ..., p(t-T)$ be current and past prices in P and $x(t-1) = (q(t-1), m(t-1))$ in R_+^{N+1}. We now study some properties of the demand function $\xi(p(t), ..., p(t-T), x(t-1))$.

First, choose any countable array $\pi = (\pi_h)(h = 0, 1, ...)$ of prices π_h in the closure $\bar{P}$ of P. Then π is an element of $\bar{P}^H$ where $H = +\infty$, which is endowed with the product topology. Let $m \geq 0$ and define $\bar{\gamma}(\pi, m)$ as the set of elements $y = (q_h)(h \geq 0)$ of Y such that there exist non-negative real numbers $m_h(h = 0, 1, ...)$ with $(q_0, m_0) \in \beta(\pi_0, m)$ and $(q_h, m_h) \in \beta(\pi_h, m_{h-1})$ for all $h \geq 1$. The set $\gamma(p(t), ..., p(t-T), m(t-1))$ defined in Section 1 is equal to $\bar{\gamma}(p(t), \psi(p(t), ..., p(t-T)), m(t-1))$.

Then $y = (q_h)(h \geq 0)$ of Y belongs to $\bar{\gamma}(\pi, m)$ if and only if for any (may be empty) subset S of N, one has

$$\sum_{n \in S} \pi_{hn}(q_{hn}-\omega_n)+k \sum_{n \notin S} \pi_{hn}(q_{hn}-\omega_n) \leq m - A_h$$

for all $h \geq 0$, where $A_0 = 0$ and $A_h = \sum_0^{h-1} \pi_j \cdot (q_j-\omega)$ for $h \geq 1$. Clearly, $\bar{\gamma}(\pi, m)$ is a non-empty, convex set when (π, m) belongs to $\bar{P}^H \times R_+$. If π belongs to P^H, $\bar{\gamma}(\pi, m)$ is a compact subset of Y. For (π, m) in $P^H \times R_+$, let $\eta(\pi, m)$ be the unique element which maximizes U over $\bar{\gamma}(\pi, m)$.

Lemma 4.1. *The function η is continuous on $P^H \times R_+$.*

Proof. In view of [14, Lemma 4.4] which is valid for metric spaces, it is enough to prove that η has a closed graph. Let (π^j, m^j) be a sequence in $P^H \times R_+$ converging to (π^0, m^0), an element of $P^H \times R_+$. Let $y^j = \eta(\pi^j, m^j)$, converging to y^0 in Y. We wish to show $y^0 = \eta(\pi^0, m^0)$. Clearly, y^0 belongs to $\bar{\gamma}(\pi^0, m^0)$. Now let $y = (q_h)$ $(h \geq 0)$ be any element of $\bar{\gamma}(\pi^0, m^0)$. We wish $U(y^0) \geq U(y)$. Fix $0<\lambda \leq 1$ and $\bar{h} \geq 0$. Let

$$\bar{y} = (\bar{q}_h) \ (h \geq 0)$$

191

be defined by $\bar{q}_h = (1-\lambda)q_h$ for $h \leqq \bar{h}$ and $\bar{q}_h = \omega$ for $h > \bar{h}$. Then $\bar{y}$ belongs to $\bar{\gamma}(\pi^j, m^j)$ when j is large, thus $U(y^j) \geqq U(\bar{y})$. In the limit $U(y^0) \geqq U(\bar{y})$. One then shows the desired result by letting λ tend to 0 and $\bar{h}$ to infinity. Q.E.D.

Corollary 4.2. *The demand function ξ is continuous on $P^{T+1} \times R_+^{N+1}$.*

Proof. Given $p(t)$, $p(t-1)$, ..., $p(t-T)$ and $x(t-1) = (q(t-1), m(t-1))$, consider $\eta(p(t), \psi(p(t), ..., p(t-T)), m(t-1))$. This is an element of Y, which we denote $(q(t+h))$, $(h \geqq 0)$. Define $m(t)$ as $m(t-1) - p(t) \cdot (q(t) - \omega)$. Then, by definition,

$$(q(t), m(t)) = \xi(p(t), ..., p(t-T), x(t-1)).$$

Clearly, ξ is continuous. Q.E.D.

As in the proof of Lemma 4.1, one shows:

Corollary 4.3. *Consider a sequence (π^j, m^j) in $P^H \times R_+$ converging to $(\pi^0, m^0) \in \bar{P}^H \times R_+$ with $\pi^0 = (\pi_h^0)$ $(h \geqq 0)$. Assume that $\eta(\pi^j, m^j)$ converges to y^0. Then y^0 maximizes U over the set $\bar{\gamma}(\pi^0, m^0)$ whenever (1) or (2) is true: (1) $m^0 > 0$; (2) $k > 0$ and $\pi_0^0 \cdot \omega > 0$.*

Lemma 4.4. *Choose $\pi = (\pi_h)(h \geqq 0)$ in P^H, $m \geqq 0$ and let $\eta(\pi, m) = (q_h)(h \geqq 0)$. Define recursively m_h for $h \geqq 0$ by $m_h = m_{h-1} - \pi_h \cdot (q_h - \omega)$, with $m_{-1} = m$. Then q_h maximizes u over $\{q \in R_+^N \mid \pi_h \cdot (q - \omega) \leqq m_{h-1} - m_h$ and $q \in \tau(\pi_h, m_{h-1})\}$.*

Proof. Otherwise, there is a q_h' in this set such that $u(q_h') > u(q_h)$. If y' is obtained from y by replacing q_h by q_h', then y' belongs to $\bar{\gamma}(\pi, m)$ and $U(y') > U(y)$, which is impossible. Q.E.D.

Lemma 4.5. *Consider a regular trader at time t. Fix $p(t-1)$, ..., $p(t-T)$ in P and $x(t-1) = (q(t-1), m(t-1))$ in R_+^{N+1}, with $m(t-1) > 0$. Let $p^j(t)$ be a sequence in P which either converges to $p^0(t) \in \bar{P} \backslash P$ or is such that $\| p^j(t) \|$ tends to $+\infty$. Consider*

$$x^j(t) = \xi(p^j(t), p(t-1), ..., p(t-T), x(t-1)).$$

Then, if $k > 0$, $\| x^j(t) \|$ tends to $+\infty$.

Proof. Assume the contrary. This means that one can find a subsequence $x^j = (q^j, m^j)$, which we take equal to the original one, which converges to $x^0 = (q^0, m^0)$. Let

$$\pi^j = (p^j(t), \psi(p^j(t), p(t-1), ..., p(t-T))),$$

an element of P^H, and let $y^j = \eta(\pi^j, m(t-1))$. Since q^j converges to q^0, in view of $(c.3)$, one can assume that y^j converges to some $y^0 \in Y$. Let us distinguish between the two cases. *Case* 1: $p^j(t)$ tends to $p^0(t) \in \bar{P} \backslash P$. Then one can assume without loss of generality that π^j converges to $\pi^0 \in \bar{P}^H$. By Corollary 4.3, y^0 maximizes U over $\bar{\gamma}(\pi^0, m(t-1))$. But this is impossible since one component of p^0 is zero and u is strictly increasing. *Case* 2: $\| p^j(t) \|$ tends to $+\infty$. One can assume that $p^j(t)/\| p^j(t) \|$ converges to some $\mu^0 > 0$. Let $\bar{\pi}^j = (1/\| p^j(t) \|)\pi^j$. Then $\bar{\pi}^j$ converges to $\bar{\pi}^0 = (\mu^0, 0, 0, ...)$. Since

$$y^j = \eta(\bar{\pi}^j, m(t-1)/\| p^j(t) \|),$$

Corollary 4.3 tells us that y^0 maximizes U over $\bar{\gamma}(\bar{\pi}^0, 0)$, which is impossible. One is thus led to a contradiction. Q.E.D.

Technical remark. This is the only place where assumption $(c.3)$ is used. Lemma 4.5 is used only in the proof of Theorem 2.1. The reader will check by himself that Lemma 4.5 is still valid when $(c.3)$ is replaced by the following weaker assumption:

$(c.3$ bis$)$ Given $p(t-1)$, ..., $p(t-T)$ in P and any sequence p^j in P, let

$$\psi(p^j, p(t-1), ..., p(t-T)) = (\pi^j(t+1), \pi^j(t+2), ...) \in P^H.$$

Then,

(i) If p^j tends to $p^0 \in \bar{P}\backslash P$, the sequence $(\pi^j(t+h))(h \geq 1)$ lies in a compact subset of P^H.

(ii) If $\| p^j \|$ tends to $+\infty$, the sequence $\pi^j(t+1)$ lies in a compact subset of P.

We consider now the trader's long run behaviour when he is faced by a constant price system p of P. The proof of Proposition 1.2 will be given after a preliminary Lemma. We first remark that, if $x(t-1) = (q(t-1), m(t-1))$, then $\xi(p, ..., p, x(t-1)) = (q(t), m(t))$ does not actually depend on $q(t-1)$. We can accordingly write $m(t)$ as $\mu(p, m(t-1))$.

Lemma 4.6. *For any $m > m^b(p)$, one has $\mu(p, m) < m$.*

Proof. We first show that given $m > m^b(p)$, there is an $\bar{m} \geq m$ such that $\mu(p, \bar{m}) \leq \bar{m}$. For otherwise, one would have $\mu(p, \bar{m}) > \bar{m}$ for all $\bar{m} \geq m$. Choose such an $\bar{m}$ and let $\bar{x} = {}'(\bar{q}, \bar{m})$ with an arbitrary $\bar{q}$ in R^N_+. Consider $y = (q_h)(h \geq 0)$ which maximizes U over $\gamma(p, ..., p, \bar{m})$ and define $m_h = m_{h-1} - p \cdot (q_h - \omega)$ for $h \geq 0$, with $m_{-1} = \bar{m}$. From the form of the utility function U, we get $m_h = \mu(p, m_{h-1})$, hence $m_h > m_{h-1}$. It follows that $u(q_h) < u(\chi^b(p))$ for all h. Now $y' = (q_h')$ with $q_h' = \chi^b(p)$ for $h \geq 0$ belongs to $\gamma(p, ..., p, \bar{m})$, and $U(y') > U(y)$ which is impossible.

This shows that for any $m > m^b(p)$ there exists an $\bar{m} \geq m$ such that $\mu(p, \bar{m}) \leq \bar{m}$. Now, assume that the Lemma is false. This would mean that we can find $m > m^b(p)$ with $\mu(p, m) \geq m$. Since there is an $\bar{m} \geq m$ such that $\mu(p, \bar{m}) \leq \bar{m}$, and since by Corollary 4.2, μ is continuous, it would follow that there is an $m^* \geq m$ such that $\mu(p, m^*) = m^*$. We now show that this is impossible. Let q^* the element which maximizes u over

$$\{q \in R^N_+ \mid p \cdot (q - \omega) \leq 0 \text{ and } q \in \tau(p, m^*)\}.$$

Clearly, $q^* = \chi^b(p)$. Let $y = (q_h)(h \geq 0)$ be the element which maximizes U over $\gamma(p, ..., p, m^*)$. From the structure of U and Lemma 4.4, $q_h = q^*$ for all $h \geq 0$. Consider now q' which maximizes u over $\{q \in R^N_+ \mid p \cdot (q - \omega) \leq m^* - m^b(p) \text{ and } q \in \tau(p, m^*)\}$. Since $m^* > m^b(p)$, $u(q') > u(q^*)$. Now $y' = (q', q^*, q^*, ...)$ belongs to $\gamma(p, ..., p, m^*)$ and $U(y') > U(y)$, which is impossible. This proves Lemma 4.6.   Q.E.D.

It is now easy to prove Proposition 1.2.

Proof of Proposition 1.2. First, from Lemma 4.4, $x^* = (q^*, m^*)$ belongs to $\xi^*(p)$ if and only if $m^* = \mu(p, m^*)$ and q^* maximizes u over $\{q \in R^N_+ \mid p \cdot (q - \omega) \leq 0$ and $q \in \tau(p, m^*)\}$. Now we know that $\mu(p, 0) \geq 0$ and $\mu(p, m) < m$ for all $m > m^b(p)$ (Lemma 4.6). It follows from the continuity of μ that there is an $m^* \geq m$ such that $\mu(p, m^*) = m^*$. This shows (1). Then (2) is a trivial consequence of $(c.2)$ and $\tau(\lambda p, \lambda m) = \tau(p, m)$ for all $\lambda > 0$. Assertions $(3.a)$ and $(3.c)$ are consequences of Lemma 4.4 and Lemma 4.6. If now $(3.b)$ were false, one would have

$$p \cdot (q^* - \omega)^+ - kp \cdot (q^* - \omega)^- < m^* \leq m^b(p).$$

This would imply $u(q^*) < u(\chi^b(p))$. Let $0 < \lambda < 1$ and $\bar{q} = \lambda q^* - (1 - \lambda)\chi^b(p)$. For λ close enough to 1, $u(\bar{q}) > u(q^*)$, $p \cdot (\bar{q} - \omega) = 0$ and $\bar{q} \in \tau(p, m^*)$, which would contradict $(3.a)$. This proves $(3.b)$ and the proposition. Q.E.D.

We turn now our attention to Proposition 1.3.

Proof of Proposition 1.3. Assertion (1) follows immediately from Proposition 1.2, $(3.b)$ and Lemma 4.6. Assertion (2) is implied by Lemma 4.7, which follows. Q.E.D.

Lemma 4.7. *Fix (u, ω) and ψ, and choose p_0 in P such that $m^b(p_0) > 0$. Consider any sequence of prices p_j in P converging to p_0 and a sequence of regular traders*

$$a_j = (u, \omega, \delta_j, \psi)$$

such that $\lim \delta_j = 1$. Let $\xi^*(p_j)$ be the set of stationary states corresponding to p_j for the trader a_j. Then, for any sequence $x_j \in \xi^*_j(p_j)$, one has $\lim x_j = (\chi^b(p_0), m^b(p_0))$.

Proof. Assume that the result is false. This means that there is an $\varepsilon > 0$ and a subsequence, which we take equal to the original one, $x_j = (q_j, m_j) \in \xi_j^*(p_j)$, which stays at a distance of more than ε from $(\chi^b(p_0), m^b(p_0))$. The sequence q_j is bounded and can be assumed to converge to some q_0, in which case m_j converges to $m_0 = (1 - k)p_0 \cdot (q_0 - \omega)^+$. Clearly q_0 is not equal to $\chi^b(p_0)$. Since $p_0 \cdot (q_0 - \omega) = 0$, this implies $u(\chi^b(p_0)) > u(q_0)$. Now define $A(p, m)$ for any p in P and $m \geq 0$ as $\{q \in R_+^N \mid p \cdot (q - \omega) \leq 0 \text{ and } q \in \tau(p, m.)\}$ For every $j \geq 1$, let q_j' be the element which maximizes u over $A(p_j, m_j + p_j\omega)$. The sequence q_j' is bounded and can be assumed to converge to some q_0'. By a standard continuity argument as in Lemma 4.1, one shows that q_0' maximizes u over $A(p_0, m_0 + p_0\omega)$. Now $y_j = (q_j, q_j, \ldots)$ and $y_j' = (0, q_j', q_j', \ldots)$ belong to $\gamma(p_j, \ldots, p_j, m_j)$. If U_j denotes the intertemporal utility function of trader a_j, $U_j(y_j) \geq U_j(y_j')$ or equivalently

$$(1 - \delta_j)\, u(0) + \delta_j u(q_j') \leq u(q_j).$$

In the limit, $u(q_0') \leq u(q_0)$. But this is impossible. For choose $0 < \lambda < 1$ and define $\bar{q} = \lambda q_0 + (1 - \lambda)\chi^b(p_0)$. For λ close enough to 1, $\bar{q}$ belongs to $A(p_0, m_0 + p_0\omega)$ thus $u(q_0') \geq u(\bar{q})$ and $u(\bar{q}) > u(q_0)$. This shows that $u(q_0') > u(q_0)$. This contradiction completes the proof. Q.E.D.

Finally, we give an intermediary result.

Lemma 4.8. *Consider a regular trader* $(u, \omega, \delta, \psi)$.

(1) *The correspondence* ξ^* *from* P *to* R_+^{N+1} *is non-empty, compact-valued and u.s.c.*[1]

(2) *Assume* $k > 0$, *and let* $p_0 \in \bar{P} \backslash P$, $p_0 \neq 0$. *Then for any sequence* p_j *in* P *converging to* p_0, *and for any sequence* $x_j = (q_j, m_j) \in \xi^*(p_j)$, *one has* $\limsup \| q_j \| = +\infty$.

Proof. (1) is a trivial consequence of Corollary 4.2 and [14, Lemma 4.4]. We now prove (2). Assume that the result is false. One can then find particular sequences p_j and x_j such that q_j converges to some q_0, in which case m_j converges to

$$m_0 = (1 - k)p_0 \cdot (q_0 - \omega)^+.$$

Now, for $j \geq 0$, let $y_j = (q_j, q_j, \ldots) \in Y$ and $\pi_j = (p_j, p_j, \ldots) \in \bar{P}^H$. By definition, $y_j = \eta(\pi_j, m_j)$ for $j \geq 1$. Thus by Corollary 4.3, y_0 maximizes U over $\bar{\gamma}(\pi_0, m_0)$, which is impossible since at least one component of p_0 is zero. Q.E.D.

4.2 *Proof of Section 2's results*

Proof of Theorem 2.1. Consider $S = \{s = (p, 1) \in R^{N+1} \mid p \in P\}$ and for any s in S, let

$$\zeta(s) = \sum_i (\xi_i(p, p(t-1), \ldots, p(t-T), x_i(t-1)) - (\omega_i, m_i(t-1)))$$

be the aggregate excess demand. The function ζ is continuous, bounded below on S. It satisfies $s \cdot \zeta(s) = 0$ for all s in S, and according to Lemma 4.5, $\| \zeta(s_j) \|$ tends to $+\infty$ whenever s_j tends to some s_0 in $\bar{S} \backslash S$ or if $\| s_j \|$ tends to $+\infty$. The desired result then follows by a standard argument (see, e.g. [8, Theorem 1 of the Appendix]). Q.E.D.

Proof of Theorem 2.4. (1) is an immediate consequence of Proposition 1.3, (1). We now prove (2). We first prove:

(i) *under the assumption of Theorem 2.4, (2), there is a* $\bar{\delta}$ *with* $0 \leq \bar{\delta} < 1$ *such that, for every economy in* C *which satisfies* $\delta_i > \bar{\delta}$ *for all* i, *then for any* p *in* P *there exists an* i *such that* $m_i > 0$ *for all* $x_i = (q_i, m_i)$ *in* $\xi_i^*(p)$.

---

[1] A correspondence ξ from a subspace X or R^N into a subspace Y of R^M is P-valued if $\xi(x)$ has the property P for all x in X. Further, ξ is upper semicontinuous (u.s.c.) on X if for all open sets G of Y, the set $\{x \in X \mid \xi(x) \subset G\}$ is open in X.

Assume the contrary. This means that there are I sequences of regular traders $a_{ij} = (u_i, \omega_i, \delta_{ij}, \psi_i)$ with $\lim \delta_{ij} = 1$ for all i, a sequence p_j in P and I sequences

$$x_{ij} = (q_{ij}, m_{ij}) \in \xi_{ij}^*(p_j)$$

such that $m_{ij} = 0$ for all $j \geq 1$ ($\xi_{ij}^*(p_j)$ is the set of stationary states corresponding to p_j for the trader a_{ij}). Since $k < 1$, indeed $q_{ij} = \omega_i$ for all i and $j \geq 1$. From the homogeneity properties of ξ_{ij}^*, one can assume $\| p_j \| = 1$ and thus assume that p_j converges to some p_0. Now if $p_0 > > 0$, from Lemma 4.7, we know that $\lim q_{ij} = \chi_i^b(p_0)$ for all i. This would imply $\chi_i^b(p_0) = \omega_i$ for all i, which is impossible by assumption. On the other hand, if $p_0 \in \bar{P} \backslash P$, one must have by Lemma 4.8, (2), $\lim \sup \| q_{ij} \| = +\infty$, which again is impossible since $q_{ij} = \omega_i$. This contradiction proves (i).

Choose now a $\bar{\delta}$ satisfying (i) and consider an arbitrary economy in C which satisfies $\delta_i > \bar{\delta}$ for all i. We shall show that a stationary market quasi-equilibrium exists for this economy. First define $Q = \{p \in P \mid \Sigma p_n = 1\}$ and for any p in Q, let $\zeta(p)$ be defined as $\sum_i [\text{Proj} \, \xi_i^*(p) - \{\omega_i\}]$, where $\text{Proj} \, \xi_i^*(p) = \{q \in R_+^N \mid \text{there is an } m \geq 0 \text{ such that } (q, m) \in \xi_i^*(p)\}$.

Take now the convex hull of $\zeta(p)$, say co $\zeta(p)$. The correspondence co ζ from Q to R_+^N is non-empty, convex, compact-valued, u.s.c. (Lemma 4.8 and [14, Corollary to Theorem 2.9 and Theorem 4.8]) and bounded below. Further, $p \cdot z = 0$ for all z in co $\zeta(p)$. Finally it is not difficult to show by using Lemma 4.8, (2), that for any p_0 in $\bar{Q} \backslash Q$ and any sequence p_j in Q converging to p_0, one has $\lim \| z_j \| = +\infty$ for all sequences $z_j \in$ co $\zeta(p_j)$. According to a known theorem [8, Theorem 1 of the Appendix], there is a $\bar{p}$ in Q such that $0 \in$ co $\zeta(\bar{p})$. Using a known result [18, Appendix 2, Corollary to Lemma 2], we can say that there are $\bar{q}_i \in R_+^N$ for all i, such that $\Sigma(\bar{q}_i - \omega_i) = 0$ and $\bar{q}_i \in \text{Proj} \, \xi_i^*(\bar{p})$ for all i with the exception of at most $N-1$ traders for which $\bar{q}_i$ belongs to co $(\text{Proj} \, \xi_i^*(\bar{p}))$. If $\bar{q}_i \in \text{Proj} \, \xi_i^*(\bar{p})$, let $\bar{m}_i = (1-k)\bar{p} \cdot (\bar{q}_i - \omega_i)^+$. Then $\bar{x}_i = (\bar{q}_i, \bar{m}_i)$ belongs to $\xi_i^*(\bar{p})$. If $\bar{q}_i$ belongs to co $(\text{Proj} \, \xi_i^*(\bar{p}))$, there exist $N+1$ consumption bundles $q_{ij}(j = 0, ..., N)$ in $\text{Proj} \, \xi_i^*(\bar{p})$ and $N+1$ non-negative numbers λ_{ij} with $\sum_j \lambda_{ij} = 1$. such that $\sum_j \lambda_{ij} q_{ij} = \bar{q}_i$. Let

$$m_{ij} = (1-k)\bar{p} \cdot (q_{ij} - \omega_i)^+.$$

Then (q_{ij}, m_{ij}) belongs to $\xi_i^*(\bar{p})$. Define $\bar{m}_i = \sum_j \lambda_{ij} m_{ij}$. Then $(\bar{q}_i, \bar{m}_i)$ belongs to co $\xi_i^*(\bar{p})$ and to $\beta_i(\bar{p}, \bar{m}_i)$. Now let $\alpha = \sum_i \bar{m}_i$. By (i), we know that $\alpha > 0$. Define $\lambda = M/\alpha > 0$, and consider $p^* = \lambda \bar{p}$, $x_i^* = (q_i^*, m_i^*)$ with $q_i^* = \bar{q}_i$ and $m_i^* = \lambda \bar{m}_i$ for all i. Then $(p^*, (x_i^*))$ is a stationary market quasi-equilibrium. Q.E.D.

Proof of Theorem 2.5. (1) Assume that (1) is false. Then one can find a sequence $(p_j^*, (x_{ij}^*)) \in W^*(E_j)$ such that (i) or (ii) or (iii) holds: (i) p_j^* *tends to* 0. But if $x_{ij}^* = (q_{ij}^*, m_{ij}^*)$, then m_{ij}^* tends to 0 for all i, which is impossible since $\sum_i m_{ij}^* = M$ for all j; (ii) p_j^* *tends to* $p_0 \in \bar{P} \backslash P$, $p_0 \neq 0$. But, applying Lemma 4.8, (2), one should have $\lim \sup \| q_i^* \| = +\infty$, for all i which is impossible, since $\sum_i (q_{ij}^* - \omega_i) = 0$ for all j; (iii) $\| p_j^* \|$ *tends to* $+\infty$. Then $(q_{ij}^*, (m_{ij}^*/\| p_j^* \|))$ belongs to $\xi_{ij}^*(p_j^*/\| p_j^* \|)$ for all i, j, where $\xi_{ij}^*(p)$ is the set of stationary states corresponding to p for the trader $(u_i, \omega_i, \delta_{ij}, \psi_i)$. One can assume that $p_j^*/\| p_j^* \|$ tends to some $\bar{p} > 0$. Certainly, one has $\bar{p} \in P$, for otherwise one could contradict Lemma 4.8, (2) as in case (ii). One can therefore apply Lemma 4.7 and say that

$$m_i^b(\bar{p}) = \lim (m_{ij}^*/\| p_j^* \|) = 0$$

for all i. Since $k < 1$, this implies $\chi_i^b(\bar{p}) = \omega_i$ for all i, which is impossible by assumption. Thus, we are led to a contradiction in all cases, which proves (1). Then (2) follows immediately from Lemma 4.7. Q.E.D.

2 A

4.3. *Proof of Section 3's results*

Proof of Theorem 3.1. First, it is very easy to prove that if x^* belongs to $\xi^*(p)$, then $x^* = (\chi^b(p), m^b(p))$. This is left to the reader. Let now $q^* = \chi^b(p)$, $m^* = m^b(p)$, and $y^* = (q_h^*) \in Y$, $(h \geqq 0)$ where $q_h^* = q^*$ for all h. We must prove that y^* overtakes any other programme $y = (q_h)$ of $\gamma(p, ..., p, m^*)$. Fix such a programme and define m_h for $h \geqq 0$ by $m_h = m_{h-1} - p \cdot (q_h - \omega)$, where $m_{-1} = m^*$. We remark that, by the Kuhn-Tucker Theorem, there exists a positive real number λ such that $u(q) - \lambda p \cdot (q - \omega) \leqq u(q^*)$ for all q in R_+^N. We must consider different cases. *Case* 1: $\lim q_h = q^*$. Then for all h, $p \cdot (q_h - \omega)^+ - kp \cdot (q_h - \omega)^- \leqq m_{h-1}$. As the left-hand side tends to m^*, one gets $m^* \leqq \lim \inf m_h$. Since $y \neq y^*$, there exists an index j such $q_j \neq q^*$, thus an $\varepsilon > 0$ such that $u(q^*) \geqq u(q_j) + \lambda(m_j - m_{j-1}) + \varepsilon$. For all $s > j$,

$$su(q^*) \geqq \sum_0^s u(q_n) + \lambda(m_s - m^*) + \varepsilon.$$

For s large enough,

$$\lambda m_s \geqq \lambda \lim \inf m_h - (\varepsilon/2) \geqq \lambda m^* - (\varepsilon/2).$$

Therefore, $su(q^*) \geqq \sum_0^s u(q_h) + (\varepsilon/2)$ when s is large enough. This shows that y^* overtakes y. *Case* 2: q_h *does not tend to* q^*. In that case, there exists an $\alpha > 0$ and a subsequence j such that $\| q_j - q^* \| \geqq \alpha$. Accordingly, there exists an $\varepsilon > 0$ which depends only on α such that for all these indices j, one has:

$$u(q_j) + \lambda(m_j - m_{j-1}) + \varepsilon \leqq u(q^*).$$

For any $s \geqq 1$,

$$su(q^*) \geqq \sum_0^s u(q_h) + \lambda(m_s - m^*) + \sum_{j \leqq s} \varepsilon.$$

Since $\lambda(m_s - m^*) \geqq -\lambda m^*$, one has $su(q^*) > \sum_0^s u(q_h)$ when s is large enough. Again, y^* overtakes y. Q.E.D.

Then Theorem 3.2 is a straightforward consequence of Theorem 3.1. The proof is left to the reader.

5. CONCLUSIONS

This paper clearly shows that the explicit introduction of the role of money as a medium of exchange is essential to a better theoretical understanding of the workings of a money economy. We introduced in our model this function of money in a very crude and unsatisfactory way. Formal models of the exchange process which would make clear the role of money as an exchange intermediary are urgently needed. They should, of course, be part of a dynamic model of the economy. This must be the subject of further studies.

A less ambitious approach would be to further explore the properties of the model presented in this paper. There are a number of reasons for using this approach. First, the model is simple and easily manageable. More important, this report hopefully demonstrates that by using the model as it stands, one can clarify some basic issues of monetary theory, such as the *Quantity Theory* and the *classical dichotomy*. We shall show in a forthcoming paper that one can make precise in this model some of the arguments which are commonly used in the current controversy about the inefficiency of a monetary equilibrium and the " optimum quantity of money". For instance, one often finds in the literature on the subject (see, e.g., [5], [7] or [16]) the following reasoning. " Along a stationary monetary equilibrium, the traders' marginal utility of real balances is positive if they discount future utilities. On the other hand, the marginal cost of producing real balances (by lowering the price level) is zero. As a result of this discrepancy, a stationary monetary equilibrium is inefficient ". One can make precise this reasoning and show that in this model, a stationary market equilibrium is Pareto inefficient. It turns out that, along a stationary equilibrium, the " dual variable " of a trader's transaction constraint plays the same role as the (rather ambiguous) concept of " marginal utility of real balances ". As we said, these results and a few others will soon be reported in a forthcoming paper.

There are other problems which could be studied with this type of model. Here are a few suggestions for further research.

First, we left untouched the problem of the stability of the system. Even if a stationary market equilibrium exists, it may be unstable. This is a difficult problem. Recent works on monetary growth models show that the stability of a long run equilibrium will crucially depend upon the traders' price expectations.

One can say that in our model stationary money balances are held for a pure " transactions motive ". If we add uncertainty about some " state of nature " which would affect, for instance, the traders' endowments of consumption goods and the characteristics of the exchange process, we would introduce the possibility for the traders to hold money in the long run for " precautionary " and " speculative " motives as well. Prices would not remain constant in the long run: they would be random. Perhaps one could show that under some assumptions they would follow a stationary probability law.

REFERENCES

[1]   Allais, M. " A Restatement of the Quantity Theory of Money ", *American Economic Review*, **56** (1966), 1123-1157.

[2]   Archibald, G. C. and Lipsey, R. G. " Monetary and Value Theory: a Critique of Lange and Patinkin ", *Review of Economic Studies*, **26** (1958), 1-23.

[3]   Aumann, R. J. " Existence of Competitive Equilibria in Markets with a Continuum of Traders ", *Econometrica*, **34** (1966), 1-17.

[4]   Clower, R. W. " A Reconsideration of the Microfoundations of Monetary Theory ", *Western Economic Journal*, **6** (1967), 1-9.

[5]   Clower, R. W. " Is there an Optimal Money Supply? ", *Journal of Finance*, **25** (1970), 425-433.

[6]   Debreu, G. *Theory of Value* (Wiley, 1959).

[7]   Friedman, M. *The Optimum Quantity of Money* (Aldine, 1969).

[8]   Grandmont, J. M. " On the Short run Equilibrium in a Monetary Economy ", CEPREMAP Discussion Paper (February 1971, Paris, to appear).

[9]   Hahn, F. H. " On some Problems of Proving the Existence of an Equilibrium in a Monetary Economy ", in [10].

[10] Hahn, F. H. and Brechling, F. P. R. (Eds.). *The Theory of Interest Rates* (Macmillan, 1965).

[11] Hahn, F. H. " Equilibrium with Transaction Costs ", *Econometrica*, **39** (1971), 417-439.

[12] Hildenbrand, W. " Existence of Equilibria for Economies with Production and a Measure Space of Consumers ", *Econometrica*, **38** (1970), 608-623.

[13] Malinvaud, E.   " Capital Accumulation and Efficient Allocation of Resources ",
Econometrica, **21** (1953), 233-268.

[14] Nikaido, H.   *Convex Structures and Economic Theory* (Academic Press, 1968).

[15] Patinkin, D.   *Money, Interest and Prices* (Harper and Row, 2nd Ed., 1965).

[16] Samuelson, P. A.   " What Classical and Neo-Classical Monetary Theory Really
Was ", *Canadian Journal of Economics*, **1** (1968), 1-15.

[17] Sontheimer, K. C.   " On the Determination of Money Prices " (mimeographed,
October 1970).

[18] Starr, R. M.   " Quasi-Equilibria in Markets with Non-Convex Preferences ",
Econometrica, **37** (1969), 25-38.

On the Efficiency of a Monetary Equilibrium [1, 2]

JEAN-MICHEL GRANDMONT and YVES YOUNES
CEPREMAP, Paris

The purpose of this paper is to study some problems which are related to the recent controversy about the inefficiency of a monetary equilibrium and the so-called " *Optimum Quantity of Money* ". First, we would like to make more precise an argument which is commonly used in the literature when " proving " the inefficiency of a (stationary) monetary equilibrium (see, e.g. R. W. Clower [1], M. Friedman [3], H. G. Johnson [8, 9], P. A. Samuelson [16, 17]). This argument can be paraphrased as follows. " In a stationary monetary equilibrium, traders' marginal utility (or yield) of real balances must be positive if the traders discount the future. On the other hand, it costs nothing to provide an extra unit of real cash balances at the level of the whole society: it suffices to lower the price level slightly. As a result of this discrepancy between marginal utility and marginal cost of real balances, a stationary monetary equilibrium is inefficient when traders discount the future ". While this argument is an intuitively appealing shortcut, it seems desirable to make it a bit more precise, for the concept of " marginal utility of real balances " is rather ambiguous. The need for greater precision can be best illustrated by the fact that some writers on the subject have tried to " explain " the gap between the private and social cost of real balances by the existence of hypothetical and ill-defined " externalities " (see, e.g. M. Friedman [3], H. G. Johnson [9]). Secondly, we would like to study a proposition put forward by M. Friedman [3] and others: when the traders discount the future in the same way, it is possible to induce a (properly chosen) steady decrease of the total money stock by imposing lump sum taxes on traders so that, in the long run, any steady market equilibrium is efficient. In addition, some economists claim that an *alternative* way to achieve the same result would be to pay a (properly chosen) nominal rate of interest on cash balances (see, e.g., H. G. Johnson [9], S. C. Kolm [11, 12]). This is the third issue we shall attempt to clarify in this paper.

We shall conduct the analysis within the framework of a very specific and crude model. This research should accordingly be considered as a first step. We believe that this investigation should however, provide useful guide-lines for the formulation and the study of more realistic models. The model we shall use represents an exchange economy where only spot transactions are allowed and where (fiat) money is the only store of value and medium of exchange. We have already used this model in an earlier paper [5] in order to (hopefully) clarify some of the basic issues in monetary economics such as the *Quantity Theory* and the *Classical Dichotomy*. It is similar to a model studied by Patinkin [15, chs. 2 and 3] and to the simplest model presented by M. Friedman in [3, ch. 1]. As we have already discussed the model at length in [5], we shall limit ourselves to a short presentation of its basic features.

The economy is composed of a fixed number of traders (or families) who are assumed to live for ever and have an infinite planning horizon. Markets are held at discrete and

[1] *Received March* 1972 (*Eds.*).
[2] We are deeply indebted to J. Mirlees, who suggested this research. We also would like to thank P. Champsaur, L. Gevers, C. Henry, S. C. Kolm, J. J. Laffont, P. Laroque, E. Malinvaud and J. C. Milleron for their comments and suggestions. All remaining errors are our own.

A—40/2

Reprinted from *The Review of Economic Studies* **40** (1973), 149–165.

equal intervals of time. Consumption goods available in each period are perishable and cannot be stored from one period to another. As in Patinkin's world, each trader receives at the beginning of each market a real income in kind which is represented by a bundle of consumption goods (this real income can be interpreted as the trader's production). We take it as exogenously given and constant over time. On the other hand (fiat) money has no direct utility but is the only store of value. In addition, the role of money as an exchange intermediary is introduced (in a very crude way) by assuming that money is the necessary counterpart of any purchase or sale of a consumption good and by imposing *a priori* restrictions on transactions. These constraints on transactions express the following assumptions. During each marketing period, sellers (resp. buyers) must look for buyers (resp. sellers) in order to make transactions. As all transactions cannot be made simultaneously, a trader will in general be unable to use all the proceeds of his current sales in order to pay for his current purchases. In this formulation, money is a capital good which is used as an input in the exchange process. Finally, we shall assume that every trader seeks to maximize an intertemporal utility function of the " Ramsey type ":

$$\sum_{h=0}^{h=\infty} \delta^h u(q(t+h)),$$

where $q(t+h)$ denotes consumption at time $t+h$ and δ is a parameter satisfying $0 < \delta < 1$.[1] The analysis will concentrate on steady-state market equilibria of this economy, in which all " real " magnitudes are constant over time.[2]

All the definitions and assumptions we need in this paper are formally stated in Section 1. We consider in Section 2 the *laissez-faire* case (there are no tax payments nor interest payments, so that the total money stock is constant over time). We shall prove rigorously that a stationary market equilibrium is in general Pareto inefficient when traders discount the future. In the process, we shall (hopefully) make more precise the reasoning which we outlined at the beginning of this introduction. As expected, the " dual variables " of the traders' transaction constraints play the role of the traders' " marginal utility of real balances ". In Section 3, we turn to the case where the government induces a steady decrease of the money stock by imposing lump sum taxes (to be paid in money), the distribution of these taxes among traders being fixed once and for all, as in M. Friedman [3, ch. 1]. We shall check that, when traders have the same rate of time preference, it is possible to choose the rate of decrease of the money stock so that any resulting steady market equilibrium is Pareto efficient. We shall however prove that the implementation of such a policy introduces a double indeterminacy of steady-state market equilibria. As a matter of fact, in the case of such a policy, for *every* Pareto optimal allocation of consumption goods, one can find an *infinity* of steady-state market equilibria which achieve this allocation. Moreover, if one considers the set of steady-state market equilibria associated with a given Pareto allocation of consumption goods, one finds that " real " balances are indeterminate and can be arbitrarily large. This shows that it is not legitimate to say that such a monetary policy sets traders' stationary real balances at their " optimum level ". In addition, we shall prove that, if the rate of decrease of the total money stock is too large (compared to the traders' rate of time preference), steady-state market equilibria no longer exist. One should of course interpret these results with care, for some of them may well depend on the particular form given to traders' utility functions.[3] The results do however show that the advocates of such a monetary policy should also be rather more careful when

---

[1] This is obviously a very strong assumption, which is made in order to simplify the analysis. It would be desirable to cover the case where the traders' rates of time preference depend on their consumption stream. The study of such a case, which appears difficult at first sight, was outside the scope of this paper.

[2] In this we follow the majority of the writers in the field. It is clearly a strong restriction. A complete study of the efficiency of a monetary economy should consider the *ex post* path of the economy starting from arbitrary initial conditions. A major source of inefficiency in that case would be that at any point of time traders have imperfect information about the future. Such a study was outside the scope of this paper.

[3] These results may, in particular, depend on the assumption that the traders' rate of time preference is independent of their consumption. See footnote 1 above.

stating their conclusions. Finally, we analyse in Section 4 the case where the government imposes lump sum taxes on traders as in Section 3, but also pays a constant nominal interest rate on cash balances. We show that the payment of a nominal rate of interest on money holdings cannot by itself affect the " real " magnitudes describing the steady-state market equilibria. What can affect the stationary allocation of consumption goods is the gap between the nominal interest rate and the rate of inflation (i.e., the " real " rate of interest on money) *which is created by the taxation policy*. This is almost a triviality. However, as this fact is sometimes forgotten by writers in the subject, we felt it was worth-while to emphasise it by stating it in a separate section.

The remainder of this paper is devoted to a precise proof of these statements (Sections 1 to 4). In addition, we prove in a mathematical appendix (Section 5) a result which is used throughout the paper. As our main concern is the formal treatment of the model, heuristic comments will be reduced to a minimum.

1. DEFINITIONS AND ASSUMPTIONS

The number of consumption goods available in any period is N. There are by assumption I traders, each of whom is indexed by $i = 1, ..., I$. Let us consider the ith trader at time t. His endowment of consumption goods is ω_i, a point of R^N. It is constant over time and fully anticipated by the trader. We shall assume[1]:

$(a.1)$ $\omega_i \geq 0$ *for all* i;

$(a.2)$ $\sum_i \omega_i > > 0$.

The stock of money carried over from the previous period by the ith trader is denoted $m_i(t-1) \geq 0$. At the beginning of period t, our trader may receive from the government a nominal rate of interest $r > -1$. In addition, he may have to pay a tax which, by convention, we represent by a *nonpositive* real number $a_i(t)$. The stock of cash balances which is available to the trader when the tth market opens is therefore $(1+r)m_i(t-1)+a_i(t)$.

Let $p(t)$ represent the monetary prices of the N consumption goods which prevail at time t. As we only consider positive prices, the vector $p(t)$ belongs to the set

$$P = \{p \in R^N \mid p > > 0\}.$$

Given this price system, the ith trader must choose an action $x_i(t) = (q_i(y), m_i(t)) \in R^{N+1}_+$, which describes his consumption $q_i(t) \in R^N_+$ in the current period and the money balances $m_i(t) \geq 0$ he wishes to carry over until the next period. By assumption, his choice will have to satisfy the following requirements. First,[2]

$$p(t) \cdot q_i(t) + m_i(t) = p(t) \cdot \omega_i + (1+r)m_i(t-1) + a_i(t)$$

represents his *budget constraint*. Second, we impose a *transactions constraint* on the trades which are feasible; this constraint reflects the difficulty for the sellers and buyers to get together during the marketing period. The trader's action must satisfy:

$$G_i(p(t), q_i(t)) \leq (1+r)m_i(t-1) + a_i(t).$$

Then $G_i(p(t), q_i(t))$ can be interpreted as the minimum amount of cash which is needed in order to achieve the consumption $q_i(t)$ when the price system $p(t)$ prevails. In order to simplify the analysis, we shall specify:

$$G_i(p(t), q_i(t)) = p(t) \cdot (q_i(t) - \omega_i)^+ - kp(t) \cdot (q_i(t) - \omega_i)^-$$

---

[1] The following notation is used. For any x and y in R^N, $x \geq y$ means $x_n \geq y_n$ for all n, while $x > y$ means $x \geq y$ and $x \neq y$. Finally $x > > y$ means $x_n > y_n$ for all n.
[2] For p and q in R^N, $p \cdot q$ denotes the inner product $\sum_n p_n q_n$.

201

where $(q_i(t) - \omega_i)^+$ and $(q_i(t) - \omega_i)^-$ denote respectively the trader's net purchases and net sales,[1] and k is a parameter satisfying $0 \leqq k \leqq 1$ (all the results hold with obvious notational changes, if we specify $G_i(p, q) = p \cdot (q - \omega)^+ - \sum_n k_{in} p_n (q - \omega)_n^-$). This constraint means that the trader will be unable to use a fraction $(1 - k)$ of his current sales $p(t) \cdot (q_i(t) - \omega_i)^-$ in order to finance his purchases during the same marketing period. In what follows, we shall take these transactions constraints as a characteristic datum of the economy. It will be convenient to assume:

(b) $k > 0$.

By definition, a short run market equilibrium at time t, is reached if the price system $p(t)$ equates supply and demand for all consumption goods and for nominal cash balances.

The ith trader's choice at time t in response to $p(t)$ will clearly depend on his intertemporal preferences and on his anticipations of the future.

As the trader's planning horizon is infinite, his intertemporal preferences at time t will be defined on the set Y_i of all possible consumption streams y, i.e., all countable arrays $(q_i(t + h))$, $h \geqq 0$, of elements of R_+^N. We shall assume for all i:

(c) *The i-th trader's intertemporal preferences on Y_i at time t can be represented by a utility function of the form:*

$$U_i(y) = \sum_{h=0}^{h=\infty} \delta_i^h u_i(q(t+h))$$

where the real valued function u_i is continuous, bounded, strictly concave and strictly monotone,[2] and δ_i is a parameter satisfying $0 < \delta_i < 1$. The characteristics u_i and δ_i are independent of time t.

By definition, the ith trader's rate of time preference ρ_i is implicitly given by

$$\delta_i = 1/(1 + \rho_i).$$

In order to make a choice at time t, the ith trader must forecast the equilibrium price systems $p(t + h)$, $h \geqq 1$, in subsequent periods.[3] We assume point expectations.[4] We also assume that a trader's forecast is described by a function ψ_i of current and past prices which is independent of time t. Then $\psi_i(p(t), p(t-1), p(t-2), ...)$ represents the ith trader's forecast of future price systems when current and past price systems are $p(t), p(t-1), ...$. Note that $\psi_i(p(t), p(t-1), ...)$ represents a countable array of price systems of P. We shall assume, for all i:

(d) *For any p in P and any $\alpha > 0$,*

$$\psi_i(p, \alpha^{-1}p, \alpha^{-2}p, ...) = (\alpha p, \alpha^2 p, \alpha^3 p, ...).$$

This assumption means that if relative prices and the rate of inflation were constant in the past, then traders expect these quantities to remain constant in the future. For short:

Definition. A regular trader is defined by his characteristics $(u_i, \omega_i, \delta_i, \psi_i)$ and satisfies (a.1), (c), and (d).

---

[1] For any x in R^N, x^+ denotes the vector of components max $(0, x_n)$ for all n. In addition $x^- = (-x)^+$.
[2] That is, $q > q'$ implies $u_i(q) > u_i(q')$.
[3] In what follows, the taxes an individual trader must pay will follow a regular pattern. In addition, the nominal rate of interest on money holdings will be a constant. We implicitly assume that these quantities are fully anticipated by the traders.
[4] This is not really a restriction, since we only consider steady-state market equilibria, along which relative prices and the rate of inflation are constant.

2. THE INEFFICIENCY OF A MONETARY EQUILIBRIUM UNDER LAISSEZ-FAIRE

We consider in this section the case where the total money stock is constant over time: there are no taxes to be paid in money. Our economy is thus described by the number, I, of regular traders, their characteristics $(u_i, \omega_i, \delta_i, \psi_i)$, the characteristics of the exchange process (k) and the total stock of money $M > 0$. The (regular) economy is denoted

$$E = (I, (u_i), (\omega_i), (\delta_i), (\psi_i), k, M).$$

Our objective is to study the efficiency of a stationary market equilibrium. Heuristically, such a market equilibrium is described by a price system and an allocation of consumption goods and of cash balances which are constant over time. As the price system is constant over time, assumption (d) tells us that it is fully anticipated by the traders. Formally, we shall say that $(p^*, (x_i^*))$ defines a *stationary market equilibrium*, where p^* belongs to P and $x_i^* = (q_i^*, m_i^*)$ belongs to R_+^{N+1} for all i, if:

1. $\sum_i (q_i^* - \omega_i) = 0.$

2. $\sum_i m_i^* = M.$

3. For every i, the programme $(\bar{q}_i(t), \bar{m}_i(t))$, defined by $\bar{q}_i(t) = q_i^*$ and $\bar{m}_i(t) = m_i^*$ for all $t \geqq 0$ is solution of the following problem:

$$\max_{(q(t), m(t))} \sum_{t=0}^{t=\infty} \delta_i^t u_i(q(t))$$

subject to   (i) $p^* \cdot (q(t) - \omega_i) + m(t) - m(t-1) = 0$

(ii) $G_i(p^*, q(t)) \leqq m(t-1)$

(iii) $q(t) \geqq 0$, $m(t) \geqq 0$ for all $t \geqq 0$,

where by convention, $m(-1) = m_i^*$.

(*Remark.* Since u_i is strictly monotone for every i, the equality sign in (i) can be replaced by an inequality sign $\leqq$.)

The following characterization of a stationary market equilibrium will be a key point of our argument.

Proposition 2.1. *Let* $p^* \in P$ *and* $x_i^* = (q_i^*, m_i^*) \in R_+^{N+1}$ *for all* i, *with* $\sum_i (q_i^* - \omega_i) = 0$ *and* $\sum_i m_i^* = M$. *Then* $(p^*, (x_i^*))$ *defines a stationary market equilibrium for the regular economy* $E = (I, (u_i), (\omega_i), (\delta_i), (\psi_i), k, M)$ *if and only if there exist for every* i *two real numbers* $\lambda_i > 0$ *and* π_i *such that:*

1. $p^* \cdot (q_i^* - \omega_i) = 0$

2. $G_i(p^*, q_i^*) \leqq m_i^*$ *and* $\pi_i \geqq 0$

3. $m_i^* \geqq 0$ *and* $\lambda_i \geqq \delta_i(\lambda_i + \pi_i)$

(*with complementary slackness in each pair of inequalities in 2 and 3*)

4. $\Phi_i(q; p^*, \lambda_i, \pi_i) = u_i(q) - \lambda_i p^* \cdot (q - \omega_i) - \pi_i G_i(p^*, q)$

is maximized at q_i^* *over* R_+^N.

Proof. If we apply Lemma 5.1 (with $\alpha = 1$ and $a = 0$) and Corollary 5.2 of the appendix, we see that the conditions are sufficient. Now, let $(p^*, (x_i^*))$ be a stationary market equilibrium. If we consider an index i such that $\omega_i \neq 0$, then $q_i^* \neq 0$, and we can again apply Lemma 5.1 and Corollary 5.2. This proves the existence of $\lambda_i > 0$ and π_i which satisfy 1 to 4. Now, if $\omega_i = 0$, for some i, then $q_i^* = 0$. Therefore, q_i^* maximizes $u_i(q)$ over $\{q \in R_+^N \mid p^* \cdot (q - \omega_i) \leqq 0\}$. By the Kuhn-Tucker Theorem, [10, Theorem 7.1.2], there exist $\lambda_i > 0$ such that $u_i(q) - \lambda_i p^* \cdot (q - \omega_i)$ is maximized at q_i^* over R_+^N. If we remark that one has $m_i^* = 0$ in that case, it is sufficient to take $\pi_i = 0$ in order to get the two numbers λ_i and π_i we are looking for. Q.E.D.

It is useful to give an heuristic economic interpretation of the two parameters λ_i and π_i which appear in this proposition. Let $(p^*, (x_i^*))$ be a stationary market equilibrium. It is clear from the above result that if we consider the following one period problem: max $u_i(q)$ subject to $q \in R_+^N$, $p^* \cdot (q - \omega_i) \leqq 0$ and $G_i(p^*, q) \leqq m_i^*$, then q_i^* is the optimum solution and λ_i is the " dual " variable of the budget constraint while π_i is the dual variable of the transactions constraint. Now let us imagine that the ith trader considers a small deviation from the stationary programme (q_i^*, m_i^*): he would consume a bit less in period zero and draw his cash balances from m_i^* up to $m_i^* + dm$. He would then keep his cash balances constant and equal to $m_i^* + dm$ from period 1 ad $infinitum$. His loss of current utility would be $\lambda_i dm$, while his gain of (undiscounted) utility in each period $t = 1, 2, \ldots$ would be measured by $\pi_i dm$. The corresponding total gain of $discounted$ utility would then be $((\pi_i/\rho_i) - \lambda_i)dm$. As this gain must be nonnegative, and as $dm > 0$, we get $\lambda_i \geqq \pi_i/\rho_i$. When in addition $m_i^* > 0$, one can get the reverse inequality by taking $dm < 0$. This is precisely the relationship we got in 3 of Proposition 2.1.

It appears from this discussion that the dual variable π_i of the transactions constraint in our model corresponds to the concept of the " marginal utility " of stationary cash balances which is commonly used in the literature.

We shall show in the remainder in this section that indeed in our model a stationary equilibrium is inefficient because for some traders this dual variable is $positive$.

On the other hand, Proposition 2.1 tells us that if the ith trader keeps a positive stock of money m_i^* along a stationary market equilibrium, then the corresponding dual variables satisfy $\pi_i = \rho_i \lambda_i$. It follows that when $m_i^* > 0$, one has $\pi_i > 0$ $because$ the $trader$ is $impatient$. This proposition is therefore important for it precisely establishes the link between traders' impatience and the inefficiency of a monetary equilibrium.

Finally, another (heuristic) interpretation of the variable π_i should be noted. Let $m_i^* > 0$. As $G_i(p, q)$ is homogeneous of degree one with respect to p, the variable π_i represents the marginal gain of (undiscounted) utility in periods 0, 1, ... for the ith trader if the price level $permanently$ decreased from p^* to $(1 - \varepsilon)p^*$ (where $\varepsilon > 0$ is small) and if he decided to keep unchanged his nominal money balances m_i^*. These two interpretations show that π_i is very close to the common concept of " marginal utility of real balances ".

We now show that a stationary equilibrium is in general inefficient. We recall some definitions. An allocation (q_i) of consumption goods is such that $q_i \in R_+^N$ for all i, and $\sum_i (q_i - \omega_i) = 0$. The allocation (q_i^*) $dominates$ the allocation (q_i) if $u_i(q_i^*) \geqq u_i(q_i)$ for all i, with strict inequality for some i. The allocation (q_i^*) is $Pareto$ $efficient$ if there exists no other allocation (q_i) which dominates it. Then,

Theorem 2.2. *Consider a regular economy $E = (I, (u_i), (\omega_i), (\delta_i), (\psi_i), k, M)$. Let $(p^*, (x_i^*))$, with $x_i^* = (q_i^*, m_i^*)$ for all i, be a stationary market equilibrium. Assume that $q_i^* >> 0$ and that u_i is differentiable at q_i^* for all i. Then the allocation (q_i^*) is Pareto inefficient.*

Proof. First, note that $k < 1$ necessarily holds [5, Theorem 2.4]. Second, there exists an i such that $m_i^* > 0$. As $m_i^* = (1 - k)p^* \cdot (q_i^* - \omega_i)^+$, [5, Proposition 1.2, (3.b)], q_i^* differs from ω_i. Since $p^* \cdot (q_i^* - \omega_i) = 0$, there must be two consumption goods n and l such that

$q_{in}^* > \omega_{in}$ and $\omega_{il} > q_{il}^* > 0$. From Proposition 2.1, (3) and (4) and the fact that u_i is differentiable, there exist $\lambda_i > 0$ and $\pi_i = \rho_i \lambda_i$ such that

$$\partial u_i / \partial q_{in} = (\lambda_i + \pi_i) p_n^* \quad \text{and} \quad \partial u_i / \partial q_{il} = (\lambda_i + k \pi_i) p_l^*,$$

where partial derivatives are taken at q_i^*. As $k < 1$ and $\pi_i > 0$, one gets

$$(\partial u_i / \partial q_{in}) / (\partial u_i / \partial q_{il}) > p_n^* / p_l^*.$$

Now, there must be a consumer j such that $q_{jl}^* > \omega_{jl}$. Choose λ_j and π_j which satisfy Proposition 2.1. Since u_j is differentiable, condition (4) of this proposition yields

$$\partial u_j / \partial q_{jl} = (\lambda_j + \pi_j) p_l^*.$$

Consider the consumption good n. If $q_{jn}^* > \omega_{jn}$, Proposition 2.1, (4) yields

$$\partial u_j / \partial q_{jn} = (\lambda_j + \pi_j) p_n^*.$$

If $q_{jn}^* = \omega_{jn}$, we have $\partial u_j / \partial q_{jn} \leqq (\lambda_j + \pi_j) p_n^*$. Finally, if $q_{jn}^* < \omega_{jn}$, the condition becomes $\partial u_j / \partial q_{jn} = (\lambda_j + k \pi_j) p_n^*$. As $k < 1$, $\pi_j \geqq 0$, we have in any case

$$(\partial u_j / \partial q_{jn}) / (\partial u_j / \partial q_{jl}) \leqq p_n^* / p_l^*.$$

Therefore, we find that there exist two traders i and j such that

$$(\partial u_i / \partial q_{in}) / (\partial u_i / \partial q_{il}) > (\partial u_j / \partial q_{jn}) / (\partial u_j / \partial q_{jl})$$

where partial derivatives are taken at q_i^* and q_j^* respectively. Clearly, the allocation (q_i^*) is inefficient. Q.E.D.

The above concept of efficiency involved the comparison of the allocation (q_i^*) *with all other allocations*. One may think that this is asking too much since the redistribution of endowments (ω_i) is not costless. Accordingly, an alternative approach would be to consider the distribution (ω_i) as a datum and to require that any reallocation of consumption goods must take place through the monetary exchange process as represented by the transactions constraints (this is the point of view developed by F. Hahn in [6, 7]). However, we are going to show that, if one strengthens slightly the assumptions of Theorem 2.2, a stationary market equilibrium allocation (q_i^*) is inefficient among the class of stationary allocations of consumption goods which can be reached through the market mechanism, provided that changes in the price level can be made at no cost. More precisely, if we start from a stationary market equilibrium $(p^*, (x_i^*))$, with $x_i^* = (q_i^*, m_i^*)$ for all i, we shall show that it is possible to find an allocation (q_i) which dominates (q_i^*) and a real number $0 < \beta < 1$ such that $\beta p^* \cdot (q_i - \omega_i) = 0$ and $G_i(\beta p^*, q_i) \leqq m_i^*$ for all i: *in order to be able to reach the better allocation (q_i) by the monetary exchange process, all that is required is a lower price level.*

Assume in Theorem 2.2 that there are two traders h and j and two consumption goods n and l such that $q_{hn}^* > \omega_{hn}$, $\omega_{hl} > q_{hl}^*$ and $\omega_{jn} > q_{jn}^*$, $q_{jl}^* > \omega_{jl}$. It follows that $m_h^* > 0$ and $m_j^* > 0$. Thus, if (λ_h, π_h) and (λ_j, π_j) are chosen as in Proposition 2.1, one has

$$\pi_h = \rho_h \lambda_h > 0 \quad \text{and} \quad \pi_j = \rho_j \lambda_j > 0.$$

One then shows as in the proof of Theorem 2.2 that

$$(1) \quad (\partial u_h / \partial q_{hn}) / (\partial u_h / \partial q_{hl}) > p_n^* / p_l^*$$

$$(2) \quad (\partial u_j / \partial q_{jn}) / (\partial u_j / \partial q_{jl}) < p_n^n / p_l^*.$$

Now choose a real number $\theta > 0$ and define a new allocation $(q_i(\theta))$ as follows. For $i \neq h, j$ let $q_i(\theta) = q_i^*$. For the hth trader, let $q_{hs}(\theta) = q_{hs}^*$ for $s \neq n$, l $q_{hn}(\theta) = q_{hn}^* + \theta / p_n^*$ and $q_{hl}(\theta) = q_{hl}^* - \theta / p_l^*$. For the jth trader, let $q_{js}(\theta) = q_{js}^*$ for $s \neq n$, l $q_{jn}(\theta) = q_{jn}^* - \theta / p_n^*$ and $q_{jl}(\theta) = q_{jl}^* + \theta / p_l^*$. When θ is small enough, $q_i(\theta) \in R_+^N$ for all i, $\sum_i (q_i(\theta) - \omega_i) = 0$, while

$u_h(q_h(\theta)) > u_h(q_h^*)$ and $u_j(q_j(\theta)) > u_j(q_j^*)$ both hold. Fix such a θ, and consider the stationary allocation $(q_i(\theta), m_i^*)$ of consumption goods and of cash balances. The allocation $(q_i(\theta))$ clearly dominates (q_i^*). Given the price system p^*, it seems to the individual traders that this allocation is not attainable through the market mechanism. Indeed, the budget constraints $p^*(q_i(\theta) - \omega_i) = 0$ would be satisfied for all i, but the transactions constraint would be violated for traders h and j, since $G_i(p^*, q_i(\theta)) > m_i^*$ when $i = h$ or j. On the other hand, if we consider the economy as a whole at time 0, and if we start from the initial distribution of money balances (m_i^*), it is always possible to achieve the stationary allocation $(q_i(\theta))$ in every period, taking as a datum the distribution of endowments (ω_i) and the market mechanism. All that is required is a lower price level. More precisely, it is sufficient to choose $\beta > 0$ small enough such that, if $\bar{p} = \beta p^*$, one has $\bar{p}(q_i(\theta) - \omega_i) = 0$ and

$$G_i(\bar{p}, q_i(\theta)) \leqq m_i^*$$

for all i. This is always possible since G_i is homogeneous of degree one in p.

What are the causes of this inefficiency? The above argument shows that it is the result of two factors. The first one is the role of money as an exchange intermediary in a stationary market equilibrium. The second one is the behaviour of traders: they discount the future. Indeed, the role of money as a medium of exchange is a *necessary* condition for the mere existence of a stationary monetary equilibrium in this model: one must have $k < 1$ and trade must take place (q_i^* must differ from ω_i for some i) along a stationary equilibrium $(p^*, (x_i^*))$. But the existence of constraints on transactions does not in itself prevent the achievement of a Pareto allocation of consumption goods by the market mechanism. In order to see this, let us define $\chi_i(p)$ for any p in P as the element which maximizes $u_i(q)$ subject to $q \geqq 0$, $p(q - \omega_i) \leqq 0$, and let $\mu_i(p) = G_i(p, \chi_i(p))$ be the least amount of cash the ith trader needs in order to achieve the consumption bundle $\chi_i(p)$. It is well known that under our assumptions there exists a price system $\bar{p}$ in P, with $\sum_n \bar{p}_n = 1$, such that

$$\sum_i (\chi_i(\bar{p}) - \omega_i) = 0,$$

and that the corresponding allocation $(\chi_i(\bar{p}))$ is Pareto efficient (see, e.g. G. Debreu [2, (1) of 6.3]). If we assume in addition that for every p in P, there exists an i such that $\chi_i(p) \neq \omega_i$, we are sure that for some i, $\chi_i(\bar{p}) \neq \omega_i$, hence $\mu_i(\bar{p}) > 0$. Now define β as $M/(\sum_i \mu_i(\bar{p}))$ and $p^* = \beta \bar{p}$. Then the stationary allocation $(\chi_i(p^*), \mu_i(p^*))$ can be reached through the market mechanism if we set the price system equal to p^*, for we have $\sum_i (\chi_i(p^*) - \omega_i) = 0$, $\sum_i \mu_i(p)^* = M$, $p^*(\chi_i(p^*) - \omega_i) = 0$ and $G_i(p^*, \chi_i(p^*)) = \mu_i(p^*)$ for all i.

This makes clear that the basic cause of the inefficiency in this model is the assumption that traders discount the future. This again agrees with the literature. As a corollary, one would expect that if traders were not impatient, any stationary market equilibrium would be Pareto efficient. It turns out that this fact is an immediate consequence of a result which was proved in an earlier paper [5], when we studied the *classical dichotomy*. One can say that the classical dichotomy holds in this model if for any market equilibrium $(p^*, (x_i^*))$, the relation $x_i^* = (\chi_i(p^*), \mu_i(p^*))$ is true for every trader i. It is plain from Theorem 2.2 that the dichotomy is in general invalid. However, it can be shown that under some assumptions, the dichotomy holds in the limit when the traders' rates of time preference go to zero [5, Theorem 2.5]. Therefore, the equilibrium allocation of consumption goods becomes efficient in the limit. Alternatively, one can directly assume that traders do not discount the future and that they use the "overtaking" criterion. It can then be shown that the classical dichotomy is valid [5, Theorem 3.2]. The corresponding stationary allocation is thus Pareto efficient.

3. CHANGE OF THE MONEY STOCK BY A TAXATION POLICY

We consider in this section the effect of a steady decrease of the money stock which is achieved by means of a taxation policy as in M. Friedman [3, chap. 1, p. 16]. More precisely, we assume that the economy is as before composed of I regular traders

$$(u_i, \omega_i, \delta_i, \psi_i), \quad i = 1, \dots, I.$$

The characteristics of the exchange process are described by the parameter $0 < k \leqq 1$. But the total stock of money is no longer constant: we introduce a government which levies taxes (to be paid in money) on all traders (and burns the proceeds) so that the money stock's rate of decrease is constant over time. Formally, let $M(t-1)$ be the total stock of money which was available for trade in period $t-1$; $M(t-1)$ also represents the total stock of money the traders own at the outset of period t, before any tax payment. The total value of taxes to be paid at the beginning of period t, which by convention we denote by a nonpositive real number, is by assumption described by $(\alpha - 1)M(t-1)$ where α is a given number $0 < \alpha \leqq 1$, and is constant over time. Then $M(t) = \alpha M(t-1)$ is the stock of money which is available for trade in period t. It follows that if $M > 0$ denotes the stock of money at the beginning of period 0 before any tax payment, one has $M(t) = \alpha^{t+1}M$ for all t. We assume, as in M. Friedman's paper, that every trader has to pay a fixed share of total taxes: the distribution of taxes is described by I nonnegative real numbers θ_i, satisfying $\sum_i \theta_i = 1$. The ith trader therefore has to pay at the beginning of period t

$$a_i(t) = (\alpha - 1)\theta_i M(t-1) = \alpha^t(\alpha - 1)\theta_i M \leqq 0.$$

Note that $a_i(t)$ is independent of the amount of money the ith trader owns at the beginning of period t. The whole economy is denoted $E = (I, (u_i), (\omega_i), (\delta_i), (\psi_i), (\theta_i), k, M, \alpha)$. When $\alpha = 1$, we get the economy which was studied in Section 2.

The purpose of this section is to study the steady-state market equilibria of this economy. Loosely speaking, such an equilibrium is a sequence of short run equilibria, where relative prices are constant, the price level decreases at the same rate as the money stock, while individual consumption and "real" balances are constant over time. As relative prices and the rate of deflation are constant over time, assumption (d) tells us that these quantities are fully anticipated by the traders. Formally, we shall say that $(p^*, (x_i^*))$, where p^* belongs to P and $x_i^* = (q_i^*, m_i^*)$ belongs to R_+^{N+1} for all i, defines a steady (or steady-state) market equilibrium for E if:

(1) $\sum_i (q_i^* - \omega_i) = 0$

(2) $\sum_i m_i^* = M$

(3) For every i, the programme $(\bar{q}_i(t), \bar{m}_i(t))$, $t \geqq 0$ defined by $\bar{q}_i(t) = q_i^*$ and

$$\bar{m}_i(t) = \alpha^{t+1}m_i^* \text{ for } t \geq 0$$

is solution of:

$$\max_{(q(t), m(t))} \sum_{t=0}^{t=\infty} \delta_i^t u_i(q(t))$$

subject to

(i) $\alpha^{t+1} p^* \cdot (q(t) - \omega_i) + m(t) - m(t-1) - a_i(t) = 0$

(ii) $G_i(\alpha^{t+1}p^*, q(t)) \leqq m(t-1) + a_i(t)$

(iii) $q(t) \geqq 0$, $m(t) \geqq 0$ for all $t \geqq 0$

where by convention $m(-1) = m_i^*$.

(*Remark.* Here again, since u_i is strictly monotone, the equality sign in (i) can be replaced by the inequality sign $\leq$.)

It must be noted that (3) of the above definition can be equivalently stated as follows:

(3 bis) For every i, the programme $(\bar{q}_i(t), \bar{m}_i'(t))$, $t \geq 0$, defined by $\bar{q}_i(t) = q_i^*$ and $\bar{m}_i'(t) = m_i^*$ for $t \geq 0$ is solution of:

$$\max_{(q(t)\ m'(t))} \sum_{t=0}^{t=\infty} \delta_i^t u_i(q(t))$$

subject to

(i) $p^* \cdot (q(t) - \omega_i) + m'(t) - (m'(t-1)/\alpha) - a_i' = 0$

(ii) $G_i(p^*, q(t)) \leq (m'(t-1)/\alpha) + a_i'$

(iii) $q(t) \geq 0$, $m'(t) \geq 0$ for all $t \geq 0$

where by convention $m'(-1) = m_i^*$ and $a_i' = ((\alpha-1)/\alpha)\theta_i M$.

(Divide the constraints of (3) by α^{t+1}.) It follows that for every individual, it looks as if prices were constant and as if he was paid a nominal rate of interest on money holdings equal to $(1-\alpha)/\alpha$ which is due to the existence of deflation. This fact has an important consequence. A permanent increase of the ith trader's real balances, say from $\alpha^{t+1}m_i$ to $\alpha^{t+1}(m_i+dm)$ (or in the formulation (3 bis) from m_i' to $m_i'+dm'$) allows the trader to increase his instantaneous utility u_i in every period in *two* ways. First, this gives him an additional real income $\alpha^{t+1}((1-\alpha)/\alpha)dm$ (or $((1-\alpha)/\alpha)dm'$ in the formulation (3 bis)) which appears in his budget constraint: we call this the "income effect". Second the transactions constraint is slightly relaxed: we call this the "transaction effect". We shall see that the existence of an income effect has very important implications.

Steady market equilibria which satisfy $q_i^* \neq 0$ for all i can be characterized, as in Proposition 2.1, by introducing for every trader i the "dual" variables $\lambda_i > 0$ and $\pi_i \geq 0$ of his budget and transactions constraints (for a precise statement, see Lemma 5.1 and Corollary 5.2 in the appendix). In particular, these two variables must satisfy

$$\lambda_i \geq (\delta_i/\alpha)(\lambda_i + \pi_i),$$

with equality if $m_i^* > 0$. It is possible to justify this relation heuristically by the same type of reasoning we used in the discussion of Proposition 2.1. First, consider the one period problem:

$$\max u_i(q)$$

subject to

$$p^* \cdot (q - \omega_i) \leq ((1-\alpha)/\alpha)(m_i^* - \theta_i M)$$

$$G_i(p^*, q) \leq (1/\alpha)(m_i^* - (1-\alpha)\theta_i M)$$

and

$$q \geq 0.$$

It is easily seen from Lemma 5.1 and Corollary 5.2 that q_i^* is the solution of this problem, and that λ_i and π_i are the dual variables of the budget and transactions constraints. Now, imagine that the ith trader examines a switch from his optimal steady programme of money holdings $(\alpha^{t+1}m_i^*)$ to $(\alpha^{t+1}(m_i^*+dm))$ for $t \geq 0$, initial cash balances at the beginning of period 0 being m_i^* in both cases. Then the marginal loss of utility in period 0 is $\lambda_i dm$. The undiscounted marginal gain of utility in every period $t \geq 1$ is $\lambda_i((1-\alpha)/\alpha)dm + (\pi_i/\alpha)dm$. Total discounted gain is precisely:

$$\left[\lambda_i \frac{(1-\alpha)}{\alpha} \frac{\delta_i}{1-\delta_i} + \pi_i \frac{\delta_i}{(1-\delta_i)\alpha} - \lambda_i \right] dm$$

which must be nonnegative. The first term represents the total gain of utility due to the income effect; the second term represents the total gain due to the transaction effect. Elementary calculus shows that the above expression can be written

$$[(\delta_i/\alpha)(\lambda_i + \pi_i) - \lambda_i]dm,$$

which gives the relation we were looking for.

In order to make our results comparable to those obtained by Friedman in [3], we shall focus attention on the case where all traders have the same rate of time preference ($\delta_i = \delta$ for all i), and study the relation between steady market equilibria and Pareto efficient allocations when $\alpha = \delta$.[1] If we again consider the dual variables (λ_i, π_i) associated with a steady market equilibrium, we see that *the relation $\lambda_i \geq (\lambda_i + \pi_i)$ implies $\pi_i = 0$ for all i.* By analogy with the argument of the last section, we would expect that any steady market equilibrium gives rise to a Pareto efficient allocation of consumption goods. We shall prove below that this is true.

However, we shall see that there is a fundamental indeterminacy of steady-state market equilibria. This is due to the presence of an income effect, which implies that traders may be willing to hold real balances which are *strictly greater* than the minimum needed for transactions purposes when $\alpha = \delta$. In order to see this, let $(p^*, (x_i^*))$ be a steady-state market equilibrium and let $(\alpha^{t+1}m_i^*)$ be the ith trader's corresponding programme of money holdings. Assume that $G_i(\alpha^{t+1}p^*, q_i^*) < \alpha^t m_i^* + \alpha^t(\alpha - 1)\theta_i M$. Then, it is not worthwhile to decrease " real " balances. Since a marginal decrease of " real " money holdings from $(\alpha^{t+1}m_i^*)$ to $(\alpha^{t+1}(m_i^* - dm))$ for $t \geq 0$ would allow the trader to gain $\lambda_i dm$ in period 0, but this gain would be offset by a loss of utility in subsequent periods measured by

$$\lambda_i[(1-\alpha)/\alpha][\delta/(1-\delta)]dm = \lambda_i dm,$$

which is due to the income affect. As a result, we shall see that *every* Pareto efficient allocation of consumption goods (q_i^*) can be sustained by a *continuum* of steady market equilibria. The following set of results will make this precise. We first give a characterization of steady-state market equilibria when $\alpha = \delta$.

Theorem 3.1. *Consider a regular economy $E = (I, (u_i), (\omega_i), (\delta_i), (\psi_i), (\theta_i), k, M, \alpha)$ with $\delta_i = \delta$ for all i and $\alpha = \delta$. Let $p^* \in P$ and $x_i^* = (q_i^*, m_i^*) \in R_+^{N+1}$ for all i, with*

$$\sum_i (q_i^* - \omega_i) = 0.$$

Then $(p^*, (x_i^*))$ defines a steady market equilibrium for E if and only if the following conditions hold, for all i:

(1) $p^* \cdot (q_i^* - \omega_i) = ((1-\alpha)/\alpha)(m_i^* - \theta_i M)$

(2) $m_i^* \geq (1-k)p^* \cdot (q_i^* - \omega_i)^-$

(3) q_i^* *maximizes u_i over the set $\{q \in R_+^N \mid p^* \cdot q \leq p^* \cdot q_i^*\}$.*

Proof. The conditions are necessary. Let $(p^*, (x_i^*))$ be a steady market equilibrium. Then (1) expresses the ith trader's budget constraint in every period, while (2) is equivalent to his transactions constraint. If $q_i^* = 0$, (3) trivially holds. If $q_i^* \neq 0$, one can apply Lemma 5.1 and Corollary 5.2 (with $a = (\alpha - 1)\theta_i M$): there are two numbers λ_i and π_i which satisfy the conditions of this lemma. In particular $\lambda_i \geq \lambda_i + \pi_i$ implies $\pi_i = 0$. It follows that q_i^* maximizes the function of q: $u_i(q) - \lambda_i p^* \cdot (q_i - q_i^*)$ on R_+^N. Then (3) of Theorem 3.1 holds by the Kuhn-Tucker Theorem [10, Theorem 7.1.2]. *Conversely,* let $(p^*, (x_i^*))$ satisfy the conditions of Theorem 3.1. Note that (1) implies $\sum_i m_i^* = M$. In

---

[1] It is easy to show that any steady-state market equilibrium is in general Pareto inefficient when $\alpha > \delta$, as in the previous section. This is left to the reader. All the material needed is provided by Lemma 5.1 and Corollary 5.2 of the appendix, and the reasoning used in Theorem 2.2.

order to show that $(p^*, (x_i^*))$ defines a steady market equilibrium it is sufficient to prove that for every i, there exist two numbers λ_i and π_i which satisfy all the conditions of Lemma 5.1. Now by (3) and by the Kuhn–Tucker Theorem [10, Theorem 7.1.2], we know that there exists λ_i such that q_i^* maximizes the function of q: $u_i(q) - \lambda_i p^* \cdot (q_i - \omega)$ over R_+^N. It suffices to take $\pi_i = 0$ in order to get the numbers we are looking for. Q.E.D.

We get as a Corollary:

Corollary 3.2. *Consider a regular economy E as in Theorem* 3.1. *For any steady market equilibrium* $(p^*, (x_i^*))$ *of this economy, with* $x_i^* = (q_i^*, m_i^*)$ *for all* i, *the allocation* (q_i^*) *is Pareto efficient.*

Proof. Apply (3) of Theorem 3.1 and [2, (1) of 6.3]. Q.E.D.

The following two corollaries show that the converse result is also true: for any Pareto allocation (q_i^*) of consumption goods, it is possible to find a steady-state market equilibrium which achieves this allocation. There is more: there are infinitely many steady-state equilibria corresponding to the same allocation of consumption goods.

Corollary 3.3. *Consider a regular economy E as in Theorem* 3.1 *and assume* $\theta_i > 0$ *for all* i. *Take any Pareto efficient allocation of consumption goods* (q_i^*). *Then there exist* p^* *in P such that, if* $m_i^* = \theta_i M + (\alpha/(1-\alpha))p^* \cdot (q_i^* - \omega_i)$ *for all* i, $(p^*, (q_i^*, m_i^*))$ *defines a steady market equilibrium for the economy E.*

Proof. It is well known that under our assumptions there exists a price system $\bar{p}$ in P such that q_i^* maximizes u_i over $\{q \in R_+^N \mid \bar{p} \cdot q \leqq \bar{p} \cdot q_i^*\}$ (see, e.g., [14, Ch. 4, Theorem 4] which can be easily extended to cover the case $q_i^* = 0$ for some i). Choose $\beta > 0$ close enough to zero so that, if $m_i^*(\beta) = \theta_i M + (\alpha/(1-\alpha))\beta \bar{p} \cdot (q_i^* - \omega_i)$ for all i, then

$$m_i^*(\beta) \geqq (1-k)\beta \bar{p} \cdot (q_i^* - \omega_i)^-$$

for all i. This is always possible since $\theta_i M > 0$ for all i. Then check that $(\beta \bar{p}, (q_i^*, m_i^*(\beta)))$ defines a steady-state market equilibrium by applying Theorem 3.1. Q.E.D.

Note that this result indirectly proves that there exist steady-state market equilibria, since Pareto efficient allocations (q_i^*) do exist in our economy [2, (1) of 6.2]. Note also that this existence theorem holds even for $k = 1$; on the other hand in the case of a constant money stock, stationary market equilibria do not exist [5, Theorem 2.4]! Again, this is due to the presence of an income effect.

Corollary 3.4. *Consider a regular economy E as in Theorem* 3.1. *Let* $(p^*, (x_i^*))$, *with* $x_i^* = (q_i^*, m_i^*)$ *for all* i, *be a steady market equilibrium. Let, for every* i *and every* $\beta > 0$,

$$m_i^*(\beta) = \theta_i M + (\alpha/(1-\alpha))\beta p^* \cdot (q_i^* - \omega_i)$$

and consider $\bar{\beta} = \sup \{\beta \mid m_i(\beta) \geqq (1-k)\beta p^* \cdot (q_i^* - \omega_i)^-$ *for all* $i\}$. *One has* $\bar{\beta} \geqq 1$. *Then for every* $0 < \beta < \bar{\beta}$ (*with possibly* $\beta = \bar{\beta}$ *if the latter is finite*), $(\beta p^*, (q_i^*, m_i^*(\beta)))$ *defines a steady market equilibrium for the economy. In addition,* $\bar{\beta}$ *is infinite if and only if either* (1) "$k = 1$ *and* $m_i^* = \theta_i M$ *for all* i", *or* (2) "$k \neq 1$ *and* $q_i^* = \omega_i$ *for all* i" *holds.*

The proof of this result is easily obtained by adapting the reasoning used for Corollary 3.3. This is left to the reader. Corollary 3.4 shows that if we consider all the steady-state market equilibria corresponding to a given Pareto efficient allocation of consumption goods, relative prices are determined, but the price level can be taken arbitrarily low. However, in most cases, transactions constraints impose an upper bound on this price level (the cases where there is no upper bound are those for which money is not needed in transactions in order to achieve the equilibrium allocation of consumption goods).

The following result shows that the implementation of the monetary policy which was described in this section may be very dangerous in this economy, for it may introduce great instability in the actual path followed by the economy over time. If one slightly " overshoots ", that is, if $\alpha < \delta$, then steady-state market equilibria no longer exist. Again, this is due to the presence of an income effect. In that case, when a trader is faced by steadily decreasing prices $(\alpha^{t+1} p^*)$, $t \geqq 0$, he is unwilling to keep his real balances constant: it always pays him to increase his real money holdings.

Theorem 3.5. *Consider a regular economy* $E = (I, (u_i), (\omega_i), (\delta_i), (\psi_i), (\theta_i), k, M, \alpha)$ *where* $\delta_i = \delta$ *for all* i, *and* $\alpha < \delta$. *Then no steady-state market equilibrium exists.*

Proof. Assume the contrary and consider a steady-state market equilibrium $(p^*, (x_i^*))$, with $x_i^* = (q_i^*, m_i^*)$ for all i. There must be an i such that $q_i^* \neq 0$. Therefore, Lemma 5.1 and Corollary 5.2 can be applied. It would follow that there exist $\lambda_i > 0$ and $\pi_i \geqq 0$ such that $\lambda_i \geqq (\delta/\alpha)(\lambda_i + \pi_i)$. This would imply $\pi_i < 0$, which is impossible. Q.E.D.

The reader can check for himself that none of this section's results depends on the particular form we gave to the functions $G_i(p, q)$. We need only assume that the G_i's are (1) homogeneous of degree one in prices p and (2) convex and strictly increasing in q (check that Lemma 5.1 and Corollary 5.2 of the appendix are valid under these assumptions). One should however be cautious when drawing conclusions from these results: some of them may depend on the form given to the traders' utility functions and in particular on the assumption that a trader's rate of time preference ρ_i is independent of his consumption. The study of the case where the ρ_i's depend on consumption (which appears rather difficult at first sight) was outside the scope of this paper.

4. THE LONG RUN NEUTRALITY OF INTEREST PAYMENTS ON MONEY

We assume in this section that the government pays interest on money and levies lump sum taxes on all individuals. We shall show that interest payments can have no effect on the " real " magnitudes of steady-state market equilibria.

As before, the economy is composed of I regular traders $(u_i, \omega_i, \delta_i, \psi_i)$, $i = 1, ..., I$. The exchange process is described by the parameter $0 < k \leqq 1$. Now, let $M(t-1)$ be the total stock of money which is available for trade in period $t-1$. It also represents the outstanding stock of money at the outset of period t before any interest or tax payment. We assume that the government pays a rate of interest $r > -1$ on money holdings which is constant over time, so that the value of interest payments at the beginning of period t is $rM(t-1)$. We assume on the other hand that the government levies lump sum taxes to be paid in money which are equal to $(\alpha-1)(1+r)M(t-1)$, where α is constant over time and satisfies $0 < \alpha \leqq 1$. It follows that the money stock $M(t)$ which is available for trade in period t is equal to $\alpha(1+r)M(t-1)$. If $M > 0$ denotes the total stock of money at the outset of period 0 before any interest or tax payment, then one has $M(t) = \alpha^{t+1}(1+r)^{t+1}M$. We assume as before that the distribution of taxes is fixed and characterized by I nonnegative numbers θ_i which satisfy $\sum_i \theta_i = 1$. It follows that the amount of taxes $a_i(t) \leqq 0$ the ith trader must pay at the beginning of period t is equal to $\theta_i(\alpha-1)\alpha^t(1+r)^tM$. The whole (regular) economy is denoted by $E = (I, u_i, \omega_i, \delta_i, \psi_i, k, M, \alpha, r)$. If $r = 0$, we get the type of economy we considered in the previous section. If $r = 0$ and $\alpha = 1$, the economy is the one we described in Section 2.

As before, a steady-state market equilibrium is a sequence of short run equilibria, where relative prices are constant, the price level grows (or decreases) at the same rate as the total money stock, while " real " quantities are constant. As relative prices and the rate of inflation are constant over time, assumption (d) tells us that they are fully anticipated by the traders. Formally, we shall say that $(p^*, (x_i^*))$ where p^* belongs to P and

$$x_i^* = (q_i^*, m_i^*)$$

belongs to R_+^{N+1} for all i, *defines a steady* (or *steady-state*) *market equilibrium* for the regular economy E if:

(1) $\sum_i (q_i^* - \omega_i) = 0$

(2) $\sum_i m_i^* = M$

(3) For every i, the programme $(\bar{q}_i(t), \bar{m}_i(t))$, $t \geq 0$, defined by $\bar{q}_i(t) = q_i^*$ and

$$\bar{m}_i(t) = \alpha^{t+1}(1+r)^{t+1}m_i^* \text{ for } t \geq 0$$

is solution of:

$$\max_{(q(t), m(t))} \sum_{t=0}^{t=\infty} \delta_i^t u_i(q(t))$$

subject to

(i) $\alpha^{t+1}(1+r)^{t+1}p^* \cdot (q(t)-\omega_i) + m(t) - (1+r)m(t-1) - a_i(t) = 0$

(ii) $G_i(\alpha^{t+1}(1+r)^{t+1}p^*, q(t)) \leq (1+r)m(t-1) + a_i(t)$

(iii) $q(t) \geq 0$, $m(t) \geq 0$ for all $t \geq 0$

where by convention $m(-1) = m_i^*$.

The following theorem says that the value of r has no influence on the allocation of consumption goods and of " real " balances along steady market equilibria.

Theorem 4.1. *Consider a regular economy* $E = (I, u_i, \omega_i, \delta_i, \psi_i, k, M, \alpha, r)$. *Then* $(p^*, (x_i^*))$ *defines a steady-state market equilibrium for* E *if and only if* $(p^*, (x_i^*))$ *defines a steady-state market equilibrium for* $E_0 = (I, u_i, \omega_i, \delta_i, \psi_i, k, M, \alpha, 0)$.

This result is a trivial consequence of the following remark. Consider the economy E and the ith trader. Given p^* in P and $m_i^* \geq 0$, consider a programme $(q(t), m(t))$, $t \geq 0$, which satisfies the constraints (i), (ii), (iii) which appear in the definition of a steady-state market equilibrium. Then the programme $(q(t), m'(t))$, $t \geq 0$, where $m'(t) = m(t)/(1+r)^{t+1}$ for all $t \geq 0$, satisfies the constraints:

(i) $\alpha^{t+1}p^* \cdot (q(t)-\omega_i) + m'(t) - m'(t-1) - a_i'(t) = 0$

(ii) $G_i(\alpha^{t+1}p^*, q(t)) \leq m'(t-1) + a_i'(t)$

(iii) $q(t) \geq 0$, $m'(t) \geq 0$ for all $t \geq 0$

where $m'(-1) = m_i^*$ and by definition $a_i'(t) = (\alpha-1)\alpha^t M$ for all $t \geq 0$. Note that this result depends on the assumption that G_i is homogeneous of degree one in prices, but does not depend on other properties of G_i.

The economic interpretation of this result is clear. Our traders are only interested in " real " interest payments on money balances. As the payment of a nominal rate of interest rate r on money holdings induces (in the long run) an equal increase of the rate of inflation, this leaves unchanged the " real " long run rate of interest on money holdings. Therefore, the payment of a nominal rate of interest on money balances cannot by itself influence steady-state consumption and real balances. Only taxation policy by means of lump sum taxes can do so by creating a gap between the nominal interest rate and the rate of inflation.

5. MATHEMATICAL APPENDIX

We prove in this section that the Kuhn-Tucker Theorem (or the Maximum Principle) can be applied to our problem. The methods we shall use to deal with this infinite horizon case are well known and can be found in E. Malinvaud [13], D. Gale [4], Y. Younes [20] or W. R. S. Sutherland [18, 19].

Let u be a real valued function defined on R_+^N, concave and strictly monotone. Let δ be a real number, $0 < \delta < 1$. Choose $p \in R^N$, $p > > 0$ and let $\omega \in R^N$, $\omega \geqq 0$. As in the text, for any $q \in R_+^N$, $G(p, q) = p \cdot (q - \omega)^+ - kp \cdot (q - \omega)^-$ where $k > 0$. As $G(p, q)$ can be written $p(q - \omega) + (1 - k)p(q - \omega)^-$, G is convex in q. Let α be a positive real number. Consider the following.

Problem. Given $m^* \geqq 0$, choose $(q(t), m(t)) \in R_+^{N+1}$ for $t \geqq 0$ in order to maximize $\sum_0^\infty \delta^t u(q(t))$ subject to, for all $t \geqq 0$:

(i) $\alpha^{t+1} p \cdot (q(t) - \omega) + m(t) - m(t-1) - a(t) \leqq 0$

(ii) $G(\alpha^{t+1}p, q(t)) - m(t-1) - a(t) \leqq 0$

(iii) $q(t) \geqq 0$, $m(t) \geqq 0$

where $m(-1) = m^*$ by convention, and where $a(t)$ is a sequence of given real numbers which satisfies $a(t) = \alpha^t a$ for some a.

Lemma 5.1. *Let* $q^* \in R_+^N$, $q^* \neq 0$. *Define* z *as* $((1 - \alpha)m^* + a)/\alpha$. *Then the programme defined by* $\bar{q}(t) = q^*$ *and* $\bar{m}(t) = \alpha^{t+1} m^*$ *for all* $t \geqq 0$ *is a solution of the above problem if and only if there exist two real numbers* λ *and* π *such that:*

(1) $\lambda \geqq 0$ *and* $p \cdot (q^* - \omega) - z \leqq 0$

(2) $\pi \geqq 0$ *and* $G(p, q^*) - m^* - z \leqq 0$

(3) $\lambda \geqq (\delta/\alpha)(\lambda + \pi)$ *and* $m^* \geqq 0$

with complementary slackness in each pair of inequalities, and

(4) *The function of* q, $\Phi(q; \lambda, \pi) = u(q) - \lambda p \cdot (q - \omega) - \pi G(p, q)$ *is maximized at* q^* *on* R_+^N.

Remark. The condition $q^* \neq 0$ plays the role of a qualification constraint and is needed only in the proof of the necessity of the conditions. It makes sure that the programme $q(t) = 0$, $m(t) = \bar{m}(t)$ for all t satisfies the problem constraints (i) and (ii) with a *strict* inequality sign.

Proof. (i) *The conditions are sufficient.* Consider the programme $\bar{y} = (\bar{q}(t), \bar{m}(t))$ satisfying (1), (2), (3) and (4). Consider any programme $y = (q(t), m(t))$ satisfying the constraints of the problem. Fix T and consider:

$$A = \sum_0^T \delta^t [u(\bar{q}(t)) - u(q(t))].$$

By (4),

$$A \geqq \sum_0^T \delta^t [\lambda p \cdot (\bar{q}(t) - q(t)) + \pi(G(p, \bar{q}(t)) - G(p, q(t)))].$$

By (1), (2) and the fact that y satisfies the problem's constraints,

$$A \geqq \sum_0^T (\delta^t/\alpha^{t+1})[\lambda(\bar{m}(t-1) - \bar{m}(t) + m(t) - m(t-1)) + \pi(\bar{m}(t-1) - m(t-1))].$$

By reordering and using $\bar{m}(-1) = m(-1) = m^*$, we get

$$A \geqq \left[\sum_0^{T-1} (\delta^t/\alpha^{t+1})(\bar{m}(t) - m(t))((\delta/\alpha)(\lambda + \pi) - \lambda) \right] + \delta^T/\alpha^{T+1}\lambda(m(T) - \bar{m}(T)).$$

From (3), the first term is nonnegative. Since $m(T) \geqq 0$, we get

$$A \geqq -(\delta^T/\alpha^{T+1})\lambda\bar{m}(T).$$

As $\bar{m}(T) = \alpha^{T+1}m^*$, $A \geq -\delta^T \lambda m^*$. Now let T tend to infinity. In the limit

$$\sum_0^\infty \delta^t(u(\bar{q}(t)) - u(q(t))) \geq 0.$$

This proves (i).

(ii) *The conditions are necessary.* Let $(\bar{q}(t), \bar{m}(t))$ be a solution to the problem. Fix T and consider the truncated problem: choose $(q(t), m(t))$, $t = 0, ..., T$ in order to maximize $\sum_0^T \delta^t u(q(t))$ subject to

(i) $\alpha^{t+1}p \cdot (q(t) - \omega) + m(t) - m(t-1) - a(t) \leq 0$

(ii) $G(\alpha^{t+1}p, q(t)) - m(t-1) - a(t) \leq 0$

(iii) $q(t) \geq 0$, $m(t) \geq 0$

where $m(-1) = m^*$, $m(T) = \bar{m}(T)$ by convention. Clearly, an optimal solution of this problem is given by $q(t) = q^*$, $m(t) = \alpha^{t+1}m^*$ for $t = 0, ..., T$. As $q^* \neq 0$, one can apply the Kuhn-Tucker Theorem [10, Theorem 7.1.1]: there exist numbers $\lambda_T(0)$, $\pi_T(0)$, ..., $\lambda_T(T)$, $\pi_T(T)$ such that for $t = 0, ..., T$, the following conditions hold:

(1') $\lambda_T(t) \geq 0$ and $p \cdot (q^* - \omega) - z \leq 0$ (for $t \geq 0$)

(2') $\pi_T(t) \geq 0$ and $G(p, q^*) - m^* - z \leq 0$ (for $t \geq 0$)

(3') $\lambda_T(t-1) \geq (\delta/\alpha)(\lambda_T(t) + \pi_T(t))$ and $m^* \geq 0$ (for $t \geq 1$)

with complementary slackness in each pair and

(4') $\Phi(q; \lambda_T(t), \pi_T(t))$ is maximized on R_+^N at q^* for $t \geq 0$.

Now define $\lambda_T = (1/(T+1)) \sum_0^T \lambda_T(t)$ and $\pi_T = (1/(T+1)) \sum_0^T \pi_T(t)$. Taking the average of relations (1') to (4') we get:

(1'') $\lambda_T \geq 0$ and $p \cdot (q^* - \omega) - z \leq 0$

(2'') $\pi_T \geq 0$ and $G(p, q^*) - m^* - z \leq 0$

(3'') $\lambda_T - (1/(T+1))\lambda_T(T) \leq (\delta/\alpha)[\lambda_T + \pi_T - (1/(T+1))(\lambda_T(0) + \pi_T(0))]$ and $m^* \geq 0$

with complementary slackness in each pair, and

(4'') $\Phi(q; \lambda_T, \pi_T)$ is a maximum over R_+^N at q^*.

In order to achieve the proof, it is sufficient to prove that the set $D \subset R_+^2$ of pairs (λ, π) such that $\Phi(q; \lambda, \pi)$ is maximized on R_+^N at q^* is compact. For in that case, any limit point of the sequence (λ_T, π_T) as T tends to infinity would have the properties we are looking for. Now for any (λ, π) in D, $\Phi(q^*; \lambda, \pi) \geq \Phi(0; \lambda, \pi)$, hence:

$$u(q^*) - u(0) \geq \lambda p \cdot q^* + \pi(G(p, q^*) - G(p, 0)).$$

Now, as $q^* \neq 0$, $p \cdot q^* > 0$ and $G(p, q^*) > G(p, 0)$. It follows that D is bounded. As D is clearly closed, the proof is complete. Q.E.D.

Corollary 5.2. *In Lemma 5.1, condition (1) can be replaced by:*

(1 bis) $\lambda > 0$ and $p \cdot (q^* - \omega) - z = 0$.

Proof. If $\lambda = 0$, $\pi = 0$ by (3) and from (4), $u(q^*) \geq u(q)$ for all q in R_+^N, which is impossible. Q.E.D.

REFERENCES

[1]   Clower, R. W.   " Is There an Optimal Money Supply? ", *Journal of Finance*, **25** (May 1970).

[2]   Debreu, G.   *Theory of Value* (John Wiley and Sons, New York, 1959).

[3]   Friedman, M.   *The Optimum Quantity of Money* (Aldine, Chicago, 1969).

[4]   Gale, D.   " On Optimal Development in a Multi-Sector Economy ", *Review of Economic Studies*, **34** (1967), 1-18.

[5]   Grandmont, J. M., and Younes, Y.   " On the Role of Money and the Existence of a Monetary Equilibrium ", *Review of Economic Studies*, **39** (July 1972).

[6]   Hahn, F. H.   " Equilibrium with Transaction Costs ", *Econometrica*, **39** (1971), 417-439.

[7]   Hahn, F. H.   " Professor Friedman's Views on Money ", *Economica*, **38** (1971), 61-80.

[8]   Johnson, H. G.   " Money in a Neo-Classical One-Sector Growth Model ", in *Essays in Monetary Economics* (Allen and Unwin, London, 1967).

[9]   Johnson, H. G.   " Is There an Optimal Money Supply? ", *Journal of Finance*, **25** (May 1970).

[10]   Karlin, S.   *Mathematical Methods and Theory in Games, Programming, and Economics* Vol. I (Addison-Wesley, Reading, Massachusetts, 1959).

[11]   Kolm, S. C.   " L'Economie Monétaire Normative: Sous-Liquidité et Pleine Liquidité ", *Revue d'Economie Politique*, **6**, (1971), 1005-1016.

[12]   Kolm, S. C.   " External Liquidity ", to appear in *Mathematical Methods in Finance*, G. P. Szegö (Ed.).

[13]   Malinvaud, E.   " Capital Accumulation and Efficient Allocation of Resources ", *Econometrica*, **21** (1953), 233-268. " A Corrigendum ", *Ibid.*, **30** (1962), 570-573.

[14]   Montbrial, T. de.   *Economie Théorique* (Presses Universitaires de France, Paris, 1971).

[15]   Patinkin.   *Money, Interest and Prices* (Harper and Row, New York, 2nd Ed., 1965).

[16]   Samuelson, P. A.   " What Classical and Neoclassical Monetary Theory Really Was ", *Canadian Journal of Economics*, **1** (1968), 1-15.

[17]   Samuelson, P. A.   " Nonoptimality of Money Holdings under Laissez Faire ", *Canadian Journal of Economics*, **2** (1969), 303-308.

[18]   Sutherland, W. R. S.   " On Optimal Development Programs when Future Utility is Discounted " (Doctoral dissertation, Brown University, Providence, R.I., 1967).

[19]   Sutherland, W. R. S.   " On Optimal Development in a Multi-Sectoral Economy: The Discounted Case ", *Review of Economic Studies*, **37** (1970), 585-589.

[20]   Younes, Y.   " Relation entre l'Existence d'un Programme Optimal et l'Existence d'un Programme Régulier Compétitif et Efficient ", *Cahiers du Séminaire d'Econométrie*, **10** (1968), 31-59.

Monetary and Fiscal Policies in a General Equilibrium Model

F. Gagey, G. Laroque, and S. Lollivier*

INSEE, 18 Boulevard A. Pinard,
75675 Paris Cedex 14, France

Received December 31, 1984; revised December 20, 1985

In the short run, if price expectations are inelastic, the government has full control of the nominal interest rate. While the model is purely competitive, the conclusions are similar to those of the standard IS–LM analysis. In the long run, it is argued that the proper measure of the government deficit is not the usual one. The interests lost by the money holders because of the transactions constraint must be included as an additional government income, the seignoriage tax. *Journal of Economic Literature* Classification Numbers: 021, 022, 023. © 1986 Academic Press, Inc.

This paper studies the impact of monetary policy, both in the short and in the long run, in a simplified competitive general equilibrium framework. This is, of course, not a new subject. There are a number of results in this field, none of which is fully convincing. It is in fact difficult to integrate the microeconomic demand for money in a full equilibrium model of an economy, where other durable assets are available. The various lines of approach which appear in the literature can be related to the three motives of holding money put forward by Keynes in the general theory. In the first approach, uncertainty is at the origin of the agents' diversification of assets holdings [15]. This is the speculative motive, which has lead to a celebrated study of the optimum quantity of money [3]. The second approach, linked with the precautionary motive, introduces uncertainty in the timing of transactions [1, 12]. (Note however that, in the quoted papers, there does not exist a durable asset other than money). Finally, and this is the line which is pursued here, money is held essentially for transaction purposes in an environment without uncertainty. However, we do not represent explicitly the transaction technology (e.g., as in [11, 14, 10]), but we use a generalization of the ad hoc "cash in advance" constraint proposed by Clower [2] (see also [7, 8]).

---

* We have benefited from the remarks of an anonymous referee.

Reprinted from *Journal of Economic Theory* **39** (1986), 329–357, © 1986 by Academic Press, Inc. All rights of reproduction in any form reserved.

We consider an exchange economy with overlapping generations of agents who live two periods and reproduce identically. There are I types of consumers which differ by tastes and endowments of consumption goods. At each date, there are two traders of a given type, a young one and an old one. Furthermore, a government is present in the economy at all dates. It produces public goods from consumption goods, collects taxes on the transactions of the private agents, and manages the money stock through open market operations.

At each date, competitive markets are open among *living* traders on which a non-storable consumption good and short term bonds are exchanged against money. By definition a unit of a bond is a note obligating the issuer to pay to the bearer one unit of money one period later. The price s of a unit of bond implicitly defines the nominal rate of interest r by $s = 1/(1 + r)$. The bond market operates as a perfect financial market, and the government stands for the issuer in case of bankruptcy. As explained above, the agents hold money balances for transaction purpose only, because of a Clower constraint.

What is the impact of monetary policy in the short run in such a model? We identify the short run with the temporary competitive equilibria of the economy. As is well known, the existence of such equilibria in similar contexts, and therefore the consistency of the theory, cannot be guaranteed unless the price expectations are sufficiently inelastic with respect to the current prices (see, e.g., Grandmont [5]). If price expectations are inelastic, it turns out that the government has full control of the nominal interest rate (as well as of the level of the deficit in nominal terms). An often debated issue concerns the control of the money supply. While our model is purely competitive, we reach here conclusions similar to those of the standard IS–LM analysis. When real balance effects are neglected, the monetary authorities can drive both the money supply and the price level to zero by raising the nominal interest rate to infinity. In this circumstance, the government has thus full control of the money supply in the short run, and can regulate inflation.

The short run analysis considers price expectations largely as inherited from the past. We then look at long run situations, by focusing on the stationary competitive equilibria of the economy with perfect forecasts. More precisely, we look for conditions on government policy which allow for a constant allocation of real resources over time, while nominal quantities increase at a constant rate. The crucial condition in this respect is a maximum size for the government deficit, computed without taking into account interest payments or receipts. If M is the quantity of money in circulation, the deficit should not exceed $(1-s)M$, i.e., $rM/1+r$ the interest lost by the money holders because of the transaction constraints. $(1-s)M$ can be considered as a seignoriage tax, a tax levied through monetary policy. Consequently, we point out that the proper measure of the government deficit for the study of long run situations is *not* the usual one. One should include, as an additional government income, the above seignoriage tax.

Then, we look more closely at the relationship between fiscal and monetary policies in our model in the long run. We obtain the following neutrality result. Given a stationary equilibrium associated with a positive nominal interest rate r and a rate of inflation π, it is theoretically possible to design a tax system, which, associated with the monetary policy $r' = 0$, would lead to the same real allocation, but to a lower rate of inflation π', such that $1 + \pi' = (1 + \pi)/(1 + r)$ (the real rate of interest is unchanged). As expected, regular taxes appear to be less inflationary than the seignoriage tax. In this sense, the seignoriage tax can be considered as an inflation tax. Note that this theoretical new tax system may be difficult to implement in practice. These practical difficulties could justify sometimes the use of a mixture between fiscal and monetary policies.

The paper is organized as follows. The first three sections describe respectively the general framework, the behaviour of the consumers, and the operations of the government. The results concerning the temporary equilibria and the long run equilibria are presented in the fourth and fifth sections. All the proofs are gathered in the final section.

I. THE GENERAL FRAMEWORK

We consider an overlapping generations model with consumers and a government.

There are I types of consumers who live two periods. Total population is constant. At each date, there are $2I$ agents in the economy. Each of them is indicated by an index $i = 1,..., I$ and an index $h = 1, 2$. If $h = 1$ (resp. $h = 2$), we say that the consumer is young (resp. old). The government is present in the economy at all dates. It is indicated by an index g. It produces public goods and collects taxes. Also, as a central bank, it manages the money supply through open market operations.

There is one non-storable consumption good available in each period (all the results hold for an economy with a finite number of such goods, as it is clear from the proofs given in the final section: we restrict our attention to a single good economy for convenience of notation only). At the outset of each period, each consumer owns an endowment of consumption good, which can be interpreted as his own production. This endowment depends on the type i of the consumer and on his age h. It is represented by $(\omega_{i1}, \omega_{i2})$, where ω_{ih} is a real number for all i, h. We assume that the pattern of endowments for each type i is invariant over time and is known with certainty by the consumers of type i. Furthermore, we assume:

(a.1)　$\omega_{ih} \geqslant 0$ for all i and h

(a.2)　$\sum_{i=1}^{I} \omega_{ih} > 0$ for $h = 1, 2$.

For simplicity, we assume that the preferences of the consumers over private good consumption bundles are independent of the level of public goods provided by the government (again this restriction is made for convenience only: it is inessential for the results given below). A consumer of type i has preferences on private goods which are defined on the set $Q = \{(q_{i1}, q_{i2}), q_{i1} \geqslant 0, q_{i2} \geqslant 0\}$ of feasible consumption streams over his life time. These preferences are assumed to be invariant over time. Furthermore:

(b)　*the preferences of the consumers of type i over private goods can be represented by a utility function u_i defined on Q. u_i is continuous, strictly quasi-concave, and strictly increasing in each of its arguments, on Q. Furthermore, for all (q_1, q_2) in Q, $q_2 \neq 0$,*

$$u_i(q_1, q_2) > u_i(q_1, 0).$$

The government produces a perishable public service at each date through a constant returns technology which transforms one unit of consumption good into one unit of public good.

There are two other commodities in this economy. First, fiat money is used as a unit of account and for transaction purposes (see below). It takes the form of banknotes issued by the central bank. Second, short term bonds can be issued or held by any agent in the economy at the prevailing nominal rate of interest r. Bonds are guaranteed by the government which stands for the issuer in the event of bankruptcy, so that a unit of a bond entitles with certainty its owner to receive one unit of money one period later.

At each date t, competitive spot markets, where the current consumption goods and bonds are traded against money, are organized, but there are no forward markets. Money is the numeraire. The monetary price of a bond is denoted by s, a non-negative real number. This price implicitly defines the nominal rate of interest r, though $s = 1/(1 + r)$. The government has the power to tax the trade in consumption good. The tax system is described as follows. The before tax monetary price of the consumption good is denoted p, an element of $P = \{p$ in $\mathscr{R}, p > 0\}$. The before tax money value of a net trade z (bought quantities are counted positively, sales negatively) in the consumption good is the product $v = pz$. At date t, the after tax money value of the trade z is described by a real function $V_t(v)$. We assume the following:

(c.1) V_t *is a function from $\mathcal{R}$ into $\mathcal{R}$, such that $V_t(0) = 0$. For all v in $\mathcal{R}$,*

$$V_t(v) \geqslant v.$$

(c.2) V_t *is convex and strictly increasing.*

(c.1) says that the government collects non-negative taxes on any trade: buyers pay more money and sellers receive less for the same trade than in the absence of a tax system. (c.2) implies that the marginal tax rate is positive and non-decreasing. Any linear or progressive tax either on labor income or of the VAT type fits in this framework.

Finally, in each period, money is not only used as a unit of account and for the definition of assets, but also as a means of exchange. This is formalized here in a rather ad hoc way, which hopefully can stand for more sophisticated formulation. We assume, as [2, 7, 8], that the traders are forced to keep a part of their receipts of their current sales in cash until the end of the period. Thus the demand of cash transaction purposes can be represented by a constraint which defines a minimum end of period money balance. If v is the after-tax money value of the trade in commodity during the period, we denote by $\mu(v)$ the required money holdings at the end of the period (in an economy with several goods, μ would depend on the vector of the trades on all markets).

(d.1) μ *is a non-negative convex function defined on $\mathcal{R}$. Furthermore* $\mu(0) = 0$.

(d.2) *For v in $\mathcal{R}$, $v + \mu(v)$ is a non-decreasing function of v. $v + \mu(v)$ tends to $-\infty$, when v tends to $-\infty$.*

(d.1) says that there are no economies of scale in the transaction technology: this is in conformity with Clower [2], but in disagreement with the Baumol–Tobin models. (d.2) ensures that transaction costs are not large enough to discourage any trade. It is easy to check that this formulation includes Grandmont and Younes, [7, 8] as a particular case.[1]

---

[1] The Grandmont–Younes formulation has $\mu(v) = 0$ for $v \geqslant 0$ and $\mu(v) = -(1-k)v$ for $v \leqslant 0$ with k in $(0, 1)$. Without loss of generality, we allow for a constraint bearing on the buyers, as well as non homogeneity at least in the short run (in the long run, see (e.1) below, we assume positive homogeneity). Note that, like Grandmont and Younes, we rule out in (d.2) the case considered by Clower, $k = 0$.

II. The Behaviour of the Consumers

At date t, the consumer (i, h) chooses an action $x_{ih}(t) = (q_{ih}(t), m_{ih}(t), b_{ih}(t))$, which specifies his current consumption bundle $q_{ih}(t)$ in $\bar{P}$, the (non-negative) money holdings $m_{ih}(t)$ and the (positive or negative) number of bonds which he holds at the end of period t.

A. Young Consumers ($h = 1$)

In order to choose this action, the young consumer i makes point forecasts on the market conditions of the next period, i.e., on p_{t+1}, s_{t+1}, and the tax system V_{t+1}. We shall denote these forecasts as $f^i_{t+1} = (p^{ie}_{t+1}, s^{ie}_{t+1}, V^{ie}_{t+1})$. In all the rest of the paper, we assume that p^{ie}_{t+1} belongs to P, s^{ie}_{t+1} belongs to $\bar{P}$, the closure of P, and V^{ie}_{t+1} satisfies assumptions (c). For the time being, we treat the forecast f^i_{t+1} as a parameter. In due time, we shall make more explicit its dependence on the history and the current state of the economy.

Given these expectations, the consumer's problem is to choose a consumption stream $(\bar{q}_1, \bar{q}_2)$ (we drop the index i for a moment) which maximizes $u(q_1, q_2)$ on the set of the consumption streams which he expects to be feasible, i.e., on the set of (q_1, q_2) in Q such that there exist (m_1, b_1) and (m_2, b_2) with:

(i) $V_t(p_t(q_1 - \omega_1)) + m_1 + s_t b_1 = 0$

(ii) $m_1 \geqslant \mu(V_t(p_t(q_1 - \omega_1)))$

(iii) $V^e_{t+1}(p^e_{t+1}(q_2 - \omega_2)) + m_2 + s^e_{t+1} b_2 = m_1 + b_1$

(iv) $m_2 \geqslant \mu(V^e_{t+1}(p^e_{t+1}(q_2 - \omega_2)))$

(v) $m_2 + b_2 \geqslant 0$.

(i) and (iii) are the budget constraints of periods t and $t + 1$. (ii) and (iv) are the transaction constraints which bear on the end of period money holdings. (v) is a no bankruptcy condition at the end of the life of the consumer.

In the standard case where the transaction constraint bears only on sales, the foregoing budget constraints can be interpreted as follows. If the consumer sells in his youth in order to buy in his old age, m_1 is strictly positive, meaning that, because of the transaction constraints, he can invest only a part of his receipts of the first period into bonds (while m_2 is equal to zero). On the other hand, if the consumer buys in the first period and sells in the second, m_1 is equal to zero and he has to borrow in the first period. However, because of the transaction constraints he cannot use all the proceeds of its sales before the end of the second period (m_2 is strictly positive). Therefore we give him the possibility to subscribe a new loan in period 2 for liquidity purposes. This loan is to be refunded at the end of period 2 (constraint (v) above).

Let $(\bar{m}_1, \bar{b}_1)$ be any value of (m_1, b_1) associated with a solution $(\bar{q}_1, \bar{q}_2)$ of the consumer's problem. An optimal action $\bar{x}_{i1}(t)$ is then a three dimensional vector of the form $(\bar{q}_1, \bar{m}_1, \bar{b}_1)$. The set of optimal actions of consumer $(i, 1)$ is denoted $\xi_{i1}(p_t, s_t, f^i_{t+1})$. Then one can show:

PROPOSITION II.1:   *Let* $f^i_{t+1} = (p^{ie}_{t+1}, s^{ie}_{t+1}, V^{ie}_{t+1})$. *Let* (p_t, s_t) *be in* $P \times \bar{P}$. *Then*:

(1) $\xi_{i1}(p_t, s_t, f^i_{t+1})$ *is non-empty if and only if* $s_t \neq 0$, $s_t \leqslant 1$, *and* $s^{ie}_{t+1} \leqslant 1$.

(2)   *If* $0 < s_t < 1$ *and* $s^{ie}_{t+1} \leqslant 1$, $\xi_{i1}(p_t, s_t, f^i_{t+1})$ *has a unique element* $(\bar{q}, \bar{m}, \bar{b})$. *It satisfies* $\bar{m} = \mu(V_t(p_t(\bar{q} - \omega_{i1})))$.

(3)   *If* $s_t = 1$ *and* $s^{ie}_{t+1} \leqslant 1$, *there is a unique element* $(\bar{q}, \bar{m}, \bar{b})$ *in* $\xi_{i1}(p_t, s_t, f^i_{t+1})$ *which satisfies* $\bar{m} = \mu(V_t(p_t(\bar{q} - \omega_{i1})))$. *All other elements* (q, m, b) *in* $\xi_{i1}(p_t, s_t, f^i_{t+1})$ *are of the form* $(\bar{q}, \bar{m} + \delta, \bar{b} - \delta)$, *where* δ *is an arbitrary positive real number*.

From Proposition II.1, it is clear that an equilibrium cannot be reached if $s(t) > 1$ or $s(t) = 0$, i.e., if the nominal interest rate is negative or equal to $+\infty$. We shall therefore concentrate on prices s for bonds which belong to $S = \{s \text{ in } P, s \leqslant 1\}$. Similarly, from now on, we assume that the agents' forecasts s^{ie} belong to S.

Remark II.2.   From the foregoing proposition, the optimal consumption plan of the consumer can always be associated with a money balance in the first period equal to $\mu(V_t(p_t(\bar{q}_1 - \omega_{i1})))$. Similarly, the second period money balance can be taken to be equal to $\mu(V^{ie}_{t+1}(p^{ie}_{t+1}(\bar{q}_2 - \omega_{i2})))$. Thus $(\bar{q}_1, \bar{q}_2)$ maximizes $u_i(q_1, q_2)$ on the set of (q_1, q_2) in Q such that there exist $(m_1 + b_1, m_2 + b_2)$ in $\mathscr{R} \times \mathscr{R}$ with:

(i) $V_t(p_t(q_1 - \omega_{i1})) + (1 - s_t)\mu(V_t(p_t(q_1 - \omega_{i1}))) + s_t(m_1 + b_1) = 0$

(ii) $V^{ie}_{t+1}(p^{ie}_{t+1}(q_2 - \omega_{i2})) + (1 - s^{ie}_{t+1})\mu(V^{ie}_{t+1}(p^{ie}_{t+1}(q_2 - \omega_{i2}))) + s^{ie}_{t+1}(m_2 + b_2) = m_1 + b_1$

(iii) $m_2 + b_2 \geqslant 0$.

Equivalently, if we define a *generalized tax system*

$$W_t(p_t(q - \omega), s_t) = V_t(p_t(q - \omega)) + (1 - s_t)\mu(V_t(p_t(q - \omega))),$$

the young consumer's preferred consumption plan can be obtained by maximizing $u_i(q_1, q_2)$ on the set of (q_1, q_2) in Q which satisfy

$$W_t(p_t(q_1 - \omega_{i1}), s_t) + s_t W^{ie}_{t+1}(p^{ie}_{t+1}(q_2 - \omega_{i2}), s^{ie}_{t+1}) \leqslant 0.$$

It is easy to check that, for any s in S, $W(\cdot, s)$ satisfies assumptions (c.1)–(c.2).

B. *Old Consumers* $(h = 2)$

Let $\bar{x}_{i1}(t-1) = (\bar{q}_{i1}(t-1),\ \bar{m}_{i1}(t-1),\ \bar{b}_{i1}(t-1))$ be the action which the old consumer i took when he was young. Given (p_t, s_t) in $P \times S$, his set of feasible actions at date t is the set of $x_2 = (q_2, m_2, b_2)$ with $q_2 \geqslant 0$ which satisfy:

$$V_t(p_t(q_2 - \omega_{i2})) + m_2 + s_t b_2 = \bar{m}_{i1}(t-1) + \bar{b}_{i1}(t-1)$$

$$m_2 \geqslant \mu(V_t(p_t(q_2 - \omega_{i2})))$$

$$m_2 + b_2 \geqslant 0.$$

When this set is non-empty, the demand correspondence of consumer i is the set $\xi_{i2}(p_t, s_t, \bar{x}_{i1}(t-1))$ of (q_2, m_2, b_2) which maximize $u_i(\bar{q}_{i1}(t-1), q_2)$ on this set.

When this set is empty, we say that the consumer is *bankrupt*. In this circumstance, his demand correspondence $\xi_{i2}(p_t, s_t, \bar{x}_{i1}(t-1))$ is defined as the set of (q_2, m_2, b_2) such that $q_2 = 0$, $m_2 \geqslant \mu(V_t(-p_t\omega_{i2}))$ with equality if $s_t < 1$, and $m_2 + b_2 = 0$. Thus the consumer redeems partially his debt by giving back:

$$\bar{m}_{i1}(t-1) - V_t(-p_t\omega_{i2}) - (1 - s_t)\,\mu(V_t(-p_t\omega_{i2})).$$

The rest of his debt, $\rho_i(p_t,\ s_t,\ \bar{x}_{i1}(t-1)) = \bar{b}_{i1}(t-1) + \bar{m}_{i1}(t-1) - V_t(-p_t\omega_{i2}) - (1 - s_t)\mu(V_t(-p_t\omega_{i2}))$, is taken care of by the bank, which acts as a lender of last resort.

As for the young consumer, we can show:

PROPOSITION II.3. *Let* (p_t, s_t) *be in* $P \times S$ *and* $\bar{x}_{i1}(t-1) = (\bar{q}_{i1}(t-1), \bar{m}_{i1}(t-1), \bar{b}_{i1}(t-1))$ *be in* $\bar{P} \times \bar{P} \times \mathcal{R}$. *Then:*

(1) $\xi_{i2}(p_t, s_t, \bar{x}_{i1}(t-1))$ *is non-empty and all its elements* $(\bar{q}, \bar{m}, \bar{b})$ *satisfy* $\bar{m} + \bar{b} = 0$.

(2) *There is always an element* $(\bar{q}, \bar{m}, \bar{b})$ *in* $\xi_{i2}(p_t, s_t, \bar{x}_{i1}(t-1))$ *which satisfies* $\bar{m} = \mu(V_t(p_t(\bar{q} - \omega_{i2})))$. *When* $s(t) < 1$, *this is the unique element of* $\xi_{i2}(p_t, s_t, \bar{x}_{i1}(t-1))$. *When* $s(t) = 1$, *all the elements of* $\xi_{i2}(p_t, s_t, \bar{x}_{i1}(t-1))$ *are described by* $(\bar{q}, \bar{m} + \delta, \bar{b} - \delta)$, *where* δ *is an arbitrary non negative real number.*

Finally, an argument similar to the one given for the young consumer shows that the preferred consumption of the old consumer, when he is not bankrupt, maximizes $u_i(\bar{q}_{i1}(t-1), q_2)$ on the set of $q_2 \geqslant 0$ such that:

$$W_t(p_t(q_2 - \omega_{i2}), s_t) \leqslant \bar{m}_{i1}(t-1) + \bar{b}_{i1}(t-1).$$

III. The Operations of the Government

The government collects taxes, buys goods on the market (in order to produce public services), and, as a central bank, acts as a lender of last resort in case of bankruptcies and undertakes open market operations. At time t, it takes an action $x_g(t) = (q_g(t), \; m_g(t), \; b_g(t))$, which specifies its current non-negative purchase of private good $q_g(t)$, the (positive or negative) quantity of money $m_g(t)$ called in during the period, and the stock of bonds $b_g(t)$ held at the end of the period.

At time t, the government holds a stock of assets $\bar{b}_g(t-1)$ (negative if it is in debt). Its net income $T(t)$ is equal to the taxes collected from the private sector $V_t(p_t(q_{ih} - \omega_{ih})) - p_t(q_{ih} - \omega_{ih})$ summed over all $i = 1, \ldots, I$ and $h = 1, 2$, minus its forced payments in case of bankruptcies $\sum_{i=1}^{I} \rho_i(p_t, s_t, \bar{x}_{i1}(t-1))$. Thus the government's action is subject to the following budget constraint:

$$p_t q_g + m_g + s_t b_g = T(t) + \bar{b}_g(t-1).$$

This budget constraint leaves two degrees of freedom for policy choices. We shall use two parameters to describe the government's actions: a nominal deficit target $\bar{D}$, so that $p_t q_g = \mathrm{Max}(T(t) + \bar{D}, 0)$, and the nominal interest rate $\bar{s} = s(t)$ in S, the bank supplying through open market operations the number of bonds necessary to equilibrate the market at this interest rate. Note that $(\bar{D}, \bar{s})$ stands only as a parametrization of government's policy, which may be compatible with various objectives (control of the money supply, etc., see below). Given $\bar{b}_g(t-1)$ and $T(t)$, $\bar{D}$ and $\bar{s}$ in S, the government demand correspondence $\xi_g(p_t, T(t), \bar{b}_g(t-1); \bar{s}, \bar{D})$ is the set of (q, m, b) such that $p_t q = \mathrm{Max}(T(t) + \bar{D}, 0)$ and $p_t q + m + \bar{s}b = T(t) + \bar{b}_g(t-1)$.

The definition of the deficit which is given above involves only the current government operations, and does not take into account the interest payments. To constrast it both with more common measures of the deficit and with a "generalized" deficit which is useful to interpret our results we must disaggregate our government between, say the administration with assets b_a, and the central bank with assets b_b. We have $b_g = b_a + b_b$. First, usually, the published measures of the deficit differ from $\bar{D}$ because they take into account the interest income $(1 - s_t) b_a$ (or the debt burden when b_a is negative) among the receipts of the administration. Thus they are close to $\bar{D} - (1 - s_t) b_a$. Second, in some countries (for example, in the United States), the profits of the central bank, $(1 - s_t) b_b$, are an income of the administration. In this circumstance, the published deficit becomes $\bar{D} - (1 - s_t)(b_a + b_b) = \bar{D} - (1 - s_t) b_g$.

On the other hand, our "generalized" deficit implies a modification of $\bar{D}$

GAGEY, LAROQUE, AND LOLLIVIER

in line with the generalized tax system of Remark II.2. The generalized tax income is equal to $T(t) + (1 - s_t) \sum_{ih} m_{ih}(t)$. Thus the generalized deficit is equal to $\bar{D} - (1 - s_t) \sum_{ih} m_{ih}(t)$.

The decomposition of the money stock into inside money and outside money, following Gurley and Shaw, helps to link the three quantities $\bar{D}$, $\bar{D} - (1 - s_t) b_g$, and $\bar{D} - (1 - s_t) \sum_{ih} m_{ih}(t)$. By definition, the quantity of inside money is equal to the aggregate debt of the private sector $-\sum_{ih} b_{ih}(t)$, and the quantity of outside money is the aggregate value of the monetary assets of the private sector $\sum_{ih} (m_{ih}(t) + b_{ih}(t))$. Since the bond market is in equilibrium, $b_g = -\sum_{ih} b_{ih}$. Therefore the United States measure of the deficit is equal to the current operations measure of the deficit $\bar{D}$ minus interest payments on the quantity of inside money. To get the generalized deficit, the interest on outside money must also be deducted.

IV. TEMPORARY EQUILIBRIUM

We now proceed to the study of the existence and properties of a competitive equilibrium at time t. To complete the description of the economy at the outset of period t, we have to make more precise the initial endowments of the agents and the way expectations are formed.

At the beginning of period t, a young (resp. old) consumer of type i has an initial endowment $(\omega_{i1}, 0, 0)$ (resp. $(\omega_{i2}, \bar{m}_{i1}(t-1), 0)$) of consumption good, fiat money, and new claims. The government has no initial resources, so that the total endowment of consumption good, fiat money, and new claims is

$$e(t) = \left(\sum_{i=1}^{I} (\omega_{i1} + \omega_{i2}), \sum_{i=1}^{I} \bar{m}_{i1}(t-1), 0 \right).$$

We assume here that the expectations f_{t+1}^i of the young consumers are based on past information, which is given at time t, and on the current price system (p_t, s_t).

By definition, given the actions $\bar{x}_{i1}(t-1)$, $i = 1, ..., I$ and $\bar{x}_g(t-1)$ of the agents in period $t-1$, a temporary equilibrium at time t corresponding to the government policy $(\bar{s}, \bar{D})$, $\bar{s}$ in S, $\bar{D}$ in $\mathcal{R}$, is described by a price system $(p_t, \bar{s})$ p_t in P, a set of agents' actions

$$x_{ih}(t) = (q_{ih}(t), m_{ih}(t), b_{ih}(t)), \qquad i = 1, ..., I, \quad h = 1, 2,$$
$$x_g(t) = (q_g(t), m_g(t), b_g(t)),$$

226

and a net income of the government

$$T(t) = \sum_{i,h} \left[V_t(p_t(q_{ih}(t) - \omega_{ih})) - p_t(q_{ih}(t) - \omega_{ih}) \right] + \sum_i \rho_i(p_t, s_t, \bar{x}_{i1}(t-1))$$

which satisfy:

$(\alpha.1)$ $\displaystyle\sum_{i=1}^{I} (x_{i1}(t) + x_{i2}(t)) + x_g(t) = e(t)$

$(\alpha.2)$ for all i, $i = 1,..., I$:

$x_{i1}(t)$ belongs to $\xi_{i1}(p_t, s_t, f_{t+1}^i)$,

$x_{i2}(t)$ belongs to $\xi_{i2}(p_t, s_t, \bar{x}_{i1}(t-1))$,

$x_g(t)$ belongs to $\xi_g(p_t, T(t), \bar{b}_g(t-1); \bar{s}, \bar{D})$.

We can now state an existence theorem.

THEOREM IV.1. *Assume that*

(1) *for all $i = 1,..., I$, the expectation function $f_{t+1}^i = (p_{t+1}^{ie}, s_{t+1}^{ie}, V_{t+1}^{ie})$ is such that p_{t+1}^{ie} and s_{t+1}^{ie} are continuous functions of (p_t, s_t), while V_{t+1}^{ie} is independent of (p_t, s_t);*

(2) *for all $i = 1,..., I$, the image of $P \times S$ by p_{t+1}^{ie} is contained in a compact subset of P.*

Then there exists a temporary equilibrium at time t corresponding to the policy $(\bar{s}, \bar{D})$.

Thus the government may fix arbitrarily the nominal rate of interest and the level of the deficit target. Other policies may be implemented. For example, a similar existence theorem holds for the case where the government fixes the rate of interest and the level of the generalized deficit. Can the government fix the quantity of money in circulation at a given predetermined level $\bar{M}$, $\bar{M} > 0$? The answer is not as straightforward and needs some investigation.

If the government succeeds in fixing the deficit target at $\bar{D}$ and the money in circulation $\sum_{i=1}^{I} (m_{i1}(t) + m_{i2}(t))$ at $\bar{M}$, the corresponding temporary equilibrium (equilibria) will have a nominal interest rate s_t in S. Thus the domain of values at which the government can fix the quantity of money, given $\bar{D}$, is the range of values taken by $\sum_{i=1}^{I} (m_{i1}(t) + m_{i2}(t))$ at the temporary equilibria corresponding to the government policy $(s, \bar{D})$, when s varies in S. The government controls freely the money in circulation if this range is equal to the strictly positive real line.

First, we expect this range to be an interval of the real line in a number of circumstances:

THEOREM IV.2. *Assume that for all s in S, $s < 1$, there exists a unique temporary equilibrium at time t, corresponding to the policy $(s, \bar{D})$. Then there exists a non-negative number* **m** *such that the range of the equilibrium quantity of money $\sum_{i=1}^{I} (m_{i1}(t) + m_{i2}(t))$ is* $[\mathbf{m}, +\infty)$ *or* $(\mathbf{m}, +\infty)$ *when s varies in S.*

The government has full control of the quantity of money when $\mathbf{m} = 0$. In order to reduce the money in circulation, the monetary authorities may raise the interest rate: given the current and expected prices, the current demand for consumption good decreases (or supply increases). Given inelastic expectations of future prices, the current price level has to decrease to maintain equilibrium between supply and demand. If in the limit, it tends to zero, the quantity of money necessary for transactions will also go to zero.[2] Deflation is accompanied by the bankruptcies of the agents in debt, and indeed it works, provided that there are no real balance effects to stimulate demand during the process.

THEOREM IV.3. *Suppose, in addition to the assumptions of Theorem IV.1, that:*

(1) *for all $i = 1, ..., I$, $\bar{m}_{i1}(t-1) + \bar{b}_{i1}(t-1) \leq 0$;*

(2) $\bar{D} \leq 0$.

Then when $\bar{s}$ tends to zero, at any temporary equilibrium corresponding to the policy $(\bar{s}, \bar{D})$, the price level p_t and the money stock $\sum_{i=1}^{I} (m_{i1}(t) + m_{i2}(t))$ tend to zero. Furthermore all the old debtors i, with $\bar{m}_{i1}(t-1) + \bar{b}_{i1}(t-1) < 0$, become bankrupt.

However, the above process is of course stopped by real balance effects as shown by the next proposition.

THEOREM IV.4. *Suppose, in addition to the assumptions of Theorem IV.1, that:*

(1) *either $\bar{D} > 0$, or for some i $\bar{m}_{i1}(t-1) + \bar{b}_{i1}(t-1) > 0$;*

(2) *for all $v < 0$, $\mu(v) > 0$.*

Then there exists $m > 0$, such that for any $\bar{s}$ in S, at any temporary

---

[2] This should be contrasted with the result of [6, 9]. Note that, in these works, the quantity of money in the economy is defined as the sum of the asset holdings of all the agents who save in the economy, quite a different definition from the one adopted here.

equilibrium at time t corresponding to the policy $(\bar{s}, \bar{D})$, the money stock $\sum_{i+1}^{I} (m_{i1}(t) + m_{i2}(t))$ is larger than m.

(Condition (2) of the theorem ensures that money is in fact needed for transactions: it rules out the case where μ is identically equal to zero.)

The above results describe the behaviour of the economy in the short run, when price expectations are somewhat inelastic with respect to current prices. We find that, in this circumstance, monetary policy has properties which are close to that obtained in Keynesian macroeconomic models. While, here, current prices are fully flexible, Theorems IV.3 and IV.4 show that, by raising the interest rate, the central bank can reduce the quantity of money in circulation and depress the price level. This, of course, reduces the wealth of the agents who are indebted in nominal terms, since their current resources are sold at a lower price. The only obstacle which monetary policy meets in the deflation process is the real balance effect which prevents the prive level to go to zero.

V. LONG RUN EQUILIBRIUM

The purpose of this section is to present some properties of the long run stationary equilibria along which the agents make perfect forecasts. We focus our attention on situations where all real variables remain constant and all nominal variables grow at a common rate of inflation $\theta - 1$, where θ is a strictly positive inflation factor.

For such long run equilibria to exist, we must make further assumptions on the demand of money for transactions purposes and on the evolution of government policy over time.

To keep the real cost of transactions constant over time in an inflationary environment, we assume the cash requirement for transactions to be positively homogeneous:

(e.1)   *For all $\lambda \geqslant 0$ and v in $\mathcal{R}$,*

$$\mu(\lambda v) = \lambda \mu(v).$$

Furthermore, government policy must exhibit some stationary properties to be compatible with a stationary equilibrium. Along an equilibrium with inflation factor θ, we ask that, $s_t = s$, $\bar{D}_t = \theta^t \bar{D}$ and, for all v in $\mathcal{R}$, $V_t(\theta^t v) = \theta^t V(v)$, where s, $\bar{D}$, and V stand respectively for the price of bonds, deficit and tax schedule at date 0.

By definition, given an initial price level p in P and government policy s in S, $\bar{D}$ in $\mathcal{R}$, V satisfying (c.1)–(c.2), a *stationary temporary equilibrium with perfect forecasts* (for short a *long run equilibrium*), is described by an inflation factor θ in P and a set of agents' actions

$$x_{ih}(t) = (q_{ih}, \theta^t m_{ih}, \theta^t b_{ih}), \qquad i = 1,..., I, \quad h = 1, 2,$$

$$x_g(t) = (q_g, \theta^t m_g, \theta^t b_g)$$

a tax schedule

$$V_t(v) = \theta^t V(v/\theta^t) \qquad \text{for all } v \text{ in } \mathcal{R}$$

and a net government income

$$T(t) = \sum_{i,h} [V_t(\theta^t p(q_{ih} - \omega_{ih})) - \theta^t p(q_{ih} - \omega_{ih})]$$

which satisfy:

$(\beta.1)$ $\displaystyle\sum_{i=1}^{I} (x_{i1}(t) + x_{i2}(t)) + x_g(t) = e(t);$

$(\beta.2)$ for all $i = 1,..., I$:

$x_{i1}(t)$ belongs to $\xi_{i1}(\theta^t p, s, f_{t+1}^i)$,

$x_{i2}(t)$ belongs to $\xi_{i2}(\theta^t p, s, x_{i1}(t-1))$;

$x_g(t)$ belongs to $\xi_g(\theta^t p, T(t), \theta^{t-1} b_g; s, \theta^t \bar{D})$;

$(\beta.3)$ for all $i = 1,..., I$:

$$f_{t+1}^i = (\theta^{t+1} p, s, V_{t+1}).$$

(Note that, since the agents have perfect expectations, there are no bankruptcies along a long run equilibrium, and the expression given for $T(t)$ is appropriate).

From the above definition, a long run equilibrium is fully described by $(p, s, \bar{D}, V)$, θ, $x_{ih} = (q_{ih}, m_{ih}, b_{ih})$ for all i and h and, $x_g = (q_g, m_g, b_g)$.

We proceed to study the properties of the long run equilibria $(p, s, \bar{D}, V)$, θ, (x_{ih}), x_g.

THEOREM V.1. *Assume that* $(p, s, \bar{D}, V)$, θ, (q_{ih}, m_{ih}, b_{ih}), (q_g, m_g, b_g) *define a long run equilibrium. Then, for any* $\lambda > 0$ $(\lambda p, s, \lambda \bar{D}, V_\lambda)$, θ $(q_{ih}, \lambda m_{ih}, \lambda b_{ih})$, $(q_g, \lambda m_g, \lambda b_g)$ *also define a long run equilibrium, where* V_λ *is defined by*

$$\text{for all } v \text{ in } \mathcal{R}, \qquad V_\lambda(v) = \lambda V(v/\lambda).$$

This shows that the quantity theory of money is valid in the long run in our economy, provided that the tax schedule is revised in line with the quantity of money and the price level. Thus, without any loss of generality, we take $p = 1$ in all the following. In the initial period, one unit of commodity is worth one unit of money. Consequently the deficit, tax schedule, money holdings have a direct interpretation in real terms.

Under which conditions does there exist such a long run equilibrium? We cannot expect the government to run a large target deficit: if the initial endowment is Pareto-optimal in the set of stationary allocations, the government cannot extract any commodity from the private sector in our economy.

THEOREM V.2.   *The set of long run equilibria associated with any s in S, V satisfying* (c.1)–(c.2) *and* $\bar{D} \leqslant 0$ *is non-empty. Furthermore, if there does not exist an equilibrium with* $\theta = 1/s$ *in this set, there are at least two long run equilibria, one with negative real interest rate* $(s\theta - 1 > 0)$, *one with positive real interest rate* $(s\theta - 1 < 0)$.[3]

Theorem V.2 shows that, as should have been expected, the set of stationary equilibria has similar properties as those exhibited by Gale [4] and Grandmont and Laroque [6] in overlapping generations model. The number of equilibria is typically even. It is worth emphasizing that, when the target surplus $-\bar{D}$ is large, the equilibria of Theorem V.2 correspond typically to $q_g = 0$. Public expenditure is stuck at its lower bound, and any target surplus greater than $\bar{D}$ would lead to the same long run equilibrium inflation rate and traded quantities. In other words, the target deficit $\bar{D}$ is not a fully adequate parameter to describe the long run equilibria. The equilibria associated with a real interest rate equal to zero are of particular interest.

THEOREM V.3:   *for any s in S, V satisfying* (c.1)–(c.2) *there is a unique long run equilibrium such that* $\theta = 1/s$, $m_{ih} = \mu(V(q_{ih} - \omega))$, *and* $\bar{D}_t = \theta' q_g - T(t)$. *It satisfies* $\bar{D} = (1 - s) \sum_{i=1}^{I} (m_{i1} + m_{i2})$.

Thus, in fact, when s is smaller than 1 and when there is money in the economy, the government can have a permanent deficit in the long run.

The origin of this phenomenon lies with the implicit seignoriage tax levied on the consumers through the monetary policy. This "tax" is equal to the interest earnings lost by the agents forced to hold money rather than

---

[3] One can extend Theorem V.2, replacing $\bar{D} \leqslant 0$ by $D \leqslant (1 - s) \sum_{i,h} m_{i,h}$. Since the quantity of money is endogeneous this extension may be vacuous. However in some economies it is a real extension. The proof follows the same line as in Section 6. We thank an anonymous referee for this remark.

bonds to undertake transactions. So in the long run, the most pertinent indicator of government deficit is not the current deficit, but the generalized deficit induced by both budgetary and monetary policy. When this generalized deficit is non positive a steady equilibrium does exist (note that the current deficit is larger than or equal to the generalized deficit).

Moreover, it is easy to check that, for some economies, there does *not* exist any long run equilibrium with a strictly positive generalized deficit. For instance, consider an economy with two types of agents with identical preferences $u(q_1, q_2) = q_1 q_2$ (this utility function fails to satisfy the assumption of strict monotonicity of preferences on the boundary of Q, but this is unimportant). The first (resp. second) type's endowment is $(\omega, 0)$ (resp. $(0, \omega)$). There are no taxes, and money is held by the sellers: $\mu(v) = -kv$ for $v \leqslant 0$, and $\mu(v) = 0$ for $v > 0$. Then the quantity of money in the economy in period 0 is $k\omega$, and there does *not* exist a long run equilibrium with $\bar{D} > (1-s) k\omega$.

The foregoing remark gives an upper bound to the size of the public deficit which can, irrespectively of the economy, be sustained in the long run. This bound can be seen as the maximum amount of public good which can be financed in excess of tax receipts through monetary policy. It is equal to $(1-s) \sum_{i=1}^{I} (m_{i1} + m_{i2})$, where m_{i1} and m_{i2} depend on s. This implies that in order to sustain a deficit in the long run, the nominal interest rate must be strictly positive, and one would expect as in Helpman and Sadka [13], in a second-best environment, to find an optimal government policy mixing regular taxes and the above implicit seignoriage tax.[4] The following theorem helps to clarify this issue.

THEOREM V.4. *Assume that* $(1, s, \bar{D}, V)$, θ (q_{ih}, m_{ih}, b_{ih}) (q_g, m_g, b_g) *define a long run equilibrium. Then, for any* s' *in* S $(1, s', \bar{D}', V')$, θ' $(q_{ih}, m'_{ih}, b'_{ih})$ (q_g, m'_g, b'_g) *also define a long run equilibrium, where: for all* v *in* V, $V'(v) + (1-s') \mu(V'(v)) = V(v) + (1-s) \mu(V(v))$,

$$s'\theta' = s\theta,$$

$$m'_{ih} = \mu(V'(q_{ih} - \omega_{ih}) \text{ and } m'_{ih} + b'_{ih} = m_{ih} + b_{ih} \text{ for all } i = 1, ..., I, \quad h = 1, 2,$$

$$\bar{D}' - \bar{D} = (1-s') b'_g - (1-s) b_g = (1-s') \sum_{i,h} m'_{ih} - (1-s) \sum_{i,h} m_{ih}$$

$$m'_g = (1 - 1/\theta') \sum_{i,h} m'_{ih}$$

[4] When there are no taxes, and when the public good brings no utility to the agents, it is easy to check that the long run equilibria such that $s = \theta = 1$ are Pareto efficient in the class of stationary allocations (see Grandmont and Laroque [6], Proposition 7.7]). This gives the *optimum quantity of money.* If $s \neq 1$ and money matters (i.e., there are transaction costs and there is some trade at equilibrium), the long run equilibrium is inefficient. To restore efficiency, it is necessary (while not sufficient: there may exist several equilibria with $s = 1$) to fix a zero nominal interest rate.

Theorem V.4 exhibits an important property of the steady states of the model. Take $s' = 1$, i.e., a zero interest rate, and modify the regular tax on transactions so that $V'(v) = V(v) + (1 - s) \mu(V(v))$. After this transformation, the government income collected through monetary policy (i.e., the income generated by the transactions constraint, or the seignoriage tax) is reduced to zero and this is compensated by an increase in fiscal rates. Then the allocation of real resources at equilibrium is unchanged, while the rate of inflation is reduced, as expected in a pure fiscal policy.[5]

In other words, as soon as the tax on transactions can mimic the effects of the cash constraints, the two instruments, monetary policy and fiscal policy, reduce in fact to only one, at least as far as the distribution of resources is concerned. In this circumstance, monetary policy is of no use, and the second best problem (how to finance the cost of a public good) reduces to the standard optimal taxation problem.[6]

Of course, government meets in practice various limitations in the design of the tax system. For example, tax evaders can create a black market. Or political considerations may preclude an increase in the tax rates. In these cases, monetary policy may have an independent role to play in the long run.

Remark V.5. In the long run, results of comparative statics are difficult to obtain without specific assumptions on the shape of demand functions. However, we can show the following very limited result:

The following equality, which can be derived through manipulation of the budget constraints and of the equalities between supply and demand, holds at a long run equilibrium. The actual deficit D defined by $D_t = \theta' q_g - T(t)$ is

$$D = \left(s - \frac{1}{\theta} \right) \sum_{i=1}^{I} (m_{i1} + b_{i1}) + (1 - s) \sum_{i=1}^{I} (m_{i1} + m_{i2}).$$

---

[5] Thus in the long run, contrary to what appeared in the study of the temporary equilibria, an increase in the nominal rate of interest leads to an increase in the rate of inflation. In fact the short run and long run results are perfectly compatible. In the temporary equilibrium, price expectations are inelastic, and the increase in the nominal interest rate by lowering current prices leads to an increase in the expected rate of inflation. Here, the expected rate of inflation is equal to the effective rate of inflation.

[6] Helpman and Sadka [13] reach a different conclusion [13, Proposition 5, p. 159]. This is due to their introduction of money balances in the agents' utility function which is not backed by a microeconomic argument. They find, not surprisingly, that there is an optimal mix of fiscal and monetary policies in their model, which depend on the degree of substitution between commodity and money in the utility function. We believe that our treatment of money balance is more appropriate. With this treatment, the assumptions of Helpman and Sadka's Proposition 5 are not satisfied.

Consider, as a point of reference, the equilibrium such that $\theta = s = 1$ and $D = 0$. Assume that $\sum_{i=1}^{I} (m_{i1} + b_{i1})$, the quantity of outside money, is strictly positive (resp. negative) at this equilibrium. Then if there is a sequence of equilibria with $s = 1$ and positive deficits converging to the point of reference, the equality $D = (\theta - 1) \sum_{i=1}^{I} (m_{i1} + b_{i1})$ implies by continuity that the rate of inflation will be positive (resp. negative) at these equilibria. In this very limited sense, government deficits seem to generate inflation for economies with a positive quantity of outside money. Further work is needed to investigate the dependence of the long run equilibria with respect to the size of the deficits.

VI. Proofs

All proofs are gathered here. We start with a preliminary lemma.

P1. *Given s in S, the function from $\mathcal{R}$ into $\mathcal{R}$ defined by* $W(v, s) = V(v) + (1 - s) \mu(V(v))$ *is convex, strictly increasing and tends to* $+\infty$ *with v.*

Proof. From (c.2) and (d.2) W is strictly increasing. Furthermore, since V is convex and $\mu(v) + v$ is strictly increasing, for any λ between 0 and 1 and any real numbers v_1 and v_2:

$$\mu(V(\lambda v_1 + (1 - \lambda) v_2) + V(\lambda v_1 + (1 - \lambda) v_2)$$
$$\leqslant \mu(\lambda V(v_1) + (1 - \lambda) V(v_2)) + \lambda V(v_1) + (1 - \lambda) V(v_2).$$

Since μ is convex, $\mu(\lambda V(v_1) + (1 - \lambda) V(v_2)) \leqslant \lambda \mu(V(v_1)) + (1 - \lambda) \mu(V(v_2))$, and this shows that $\mu(V(v)) + V(v)$ is convex in v. Thus, $W(v, s) = (1 - s)(\mu(V(v)) + V(v)) + sV(v)$ is convex in v, as the sum of the two convex functions. Finally, when v tends to $+\infty$, $V(v)$ tends to $+\infty$, and since $\mu(V(v)) \geqslant 0$, $W(v, s)$ tends to $+\infty$. Q.E.D.

For any (p, s) in $\bar{P} \times \bar{P}$ and any $f = (p^e, s^e, V^e)$, where (p^e, s^e) belongs to $\bar{P} \times \bar{P}$, and V^e satisfies assumptions (c.1) and (c.2), let $\chi_i(p, s, f)$ be the set of consumption streams $(\bar{q}_1, \bar{q}_2)$ which maximize $u_i(q_1, q_2)$ among the set $\gamma_i(p, s, f)$ of all (q_1, q_2) in $\bar{P} \times \bar{P}$ such that there exist two numbers $m_1 \geqslant 0$, $m_2 \geqslant 0$ with

(α) (i) $V(p(q_1 - \omega_{i1})) + sV^e(p^e(q_2 - \omega_{i2})) + (1 - s)m_1 + s(1 - s^e)$
$m_2 \leqslant 0$

(α) (ii) $m_1 \geqslant \mu(V(p(q_1 - \omega_{i1})))$

(α)(iii) $m_2 \geqslant \mu(V^e(p^e(q_2 - \omega_{i2})))$.

234

P2. *Let* $f = (p^e, s^e, V^e) \cdot \chi_i(p, s, f)$ *is empty if*

$$\text{either} \quad p = 0 \qquad \text{or} \quad p^e = 0$$

$$\text{or} \quad s = 0 \qquad \text{or} \quad s > 1 \qquad \text{or} \quad s^e > 1.$$

Proof. The proof is by contraposition. Assume that there exists $(\bar{q}_1, \bar{q}_2)$ in $\chi_i(p, s, f)$ and let $\bar{m}_1$, $\bar{m}_2$, be the corresponding associated money holdings. If $p = 0$ (resp. $p^e = 0$), $q_1' = \bar{q}_1 + 1$, $q_2' = \bar{q}_2$ (resp. $q_1' = \bar{q}_1$, $q_2' = \bar{q}_2 + 1$) is feasible and gives a higher level of utility than $(\bar{q}_1, \bar{q}_2)$, a contradiction. A similar argument holds in all other cases:

(1) If $s = 0$, $q_1' = \bar{q}_1$, $q_2' = \bar{q}_2 + 1$, $m_1' = \bar{m}_1$, $m_2' = \mu(V^e(p^e(q_2' - \omega_{i2})))$.

(2) If $s > 1$, $q_1' = \bar{q}_1 + 1$, $q_2' = \bar{q}_2$, $m_1' = \bar{m}_1 + \delta$, $m_2' = \bar{m}_2$, where δ is equal to the maximum of $\mu(V(p(q_1' - \omega_{i1})))$ and of $(V(p(q_1' - \omega_{i1})) - V(p(\bar{q}_1 - \omega_{i1})))/(s - 1)$. The case $s^e > 1$ is treated symetrically. Q.E.D.

From now on, unless it is specified otherwise, we take p and p^e in P, s and s^e in S.

P3. *For any* (p, s) *in* $\bar{P} \times \bar{P}$ *and any* $f = (p^e, s^e, V^e)$, *where* (p^e, s^e) *belongs to* $\bar{P} \times \bar{P}$, $\gamma_i(p, s, f)$ *is the set of* (q_1, q_2) *in* $\bar{P} \times \bar{P}$ *such that:*

(1) *there exist* $m_1 \geqslant 0$, $m_2 \geqslant 0$, b_1 *and* b_2 *with*

$$V(p(q_1 - \omega_{i1})) + m_1 + sb_1 = 0$$

$$m_1 \geqslant \mu(V(p(q_1 - \omega_{i1})))$$

$$V^e(p^e(q_2 - \omega_{i2})) + m_2 + s^e b_2 = m_1 + b_1$$

$$m_2 \geqslant \mu(V^e(p^e(q_2 - \omega_{i2})))$$

$$m_2 + b_2 \geqslant 0.$$

If (p, s) *and* (p^e, s^e) *belong to* $\bar{P} \times \bar{S}$, $\gamma_i(p, s, f)$ *is the set of* (q_1, q_2) *in* $\bar{P} \times \bar{P}$ *such that:*

(2) $W(p(q_1 - \omega_{i1}), s) + sW^e(p^e(q_2 - \omega_{i2}), s^e) \leqslant 0.$

Proof. (1) stems from the elimination of b_1 and b_2 through

$$sb_1 = -V(p(q_1 - \omega_{i1})) - m_1$$

$$s^e b_2 = -V^e(p^e(q_2 - \omega_{i2})) - m_2 + m_1(1 - 1/s) - V(p(q_1 - \omega_{i1}))/s.$$

(2) follows trivially through the elimination of m_1 and m_2 in the definition of $\gamma_i(p, s, f)$. Q.E.D.

P4: *For any* (p, s) *in* $P \times S$ *and any* $f = (p^e, s^e, V^e)$, *where* (p^e, s^e) *belongs to* $P \times \bar{S}$, *the set* $\chi_i(p, s, f)$ *reduces to a single point* $(\bar{q}_1, \bar{q}_2)$ *which satisfies*

$$W(p(q_1 - \omega_{i1}), s) + sW^e(p^e(q_2 - \omega_{i2}), s^e) = 0.$$

Proof. By **P3**(2), $\gamma_i(p, s, f)$ contains $(\omega_{i1}, \omega_{i2})$, and by **P1** it is closed and convex. Moreover it is bounded. In fact W is increasing, $W(p(q_1 - \omega_{i1}), s) \leqslant -sW^e(-p^e\omega_{i2}, s^e)$, and $W^e(p^e(q_2 - \omega_{i2}), s^e) \leqslant -W(-p\omega_{i1}, s)/s$. By (c.1) and (d.1), this implies $p(q_1 - \omega_{i1}) \leqslant -sW^e(-p^e\omega_{i2}, s^e)$ and $p^e(q_2 - \omega_{i2}) \leqslant -W(-p\omega_{i1}, s)/s$. Thus $\chi_i(p, s, f)$ reduces to a single point since it is obtained by maximization of a strictly quasi-concave function on a non-empty convex and compact set.

Finally, if $W(p(\bar{q}_1 - \omega_{i1}), s) + sW^e(p^e(\bar{q}_2 - \omega_{i2}), s^e)$ were strictly negative, by **P3** $(\bar{q}_1 + \varepsilon, \bar{q}_2)$ would belong to $\gamma_i(p, s, f)$ for ε positive small enough and give a higher level of utility than $(\bar{q}_1, \bar{q}_2)$, a contradiction. Q.E.D.

P5. *Proof of Proposition II.1.*

Proof. By **P3**(1), any element $(\bar{q}_1, \bar{m}_1, \bar{b}_1)$ in $\xi_{i1}(p_t, s_t, f^i_{t+1})$ is such that there exists $\bar{q}_2$ in $\bar{P}$ and $(\bar{q}_1, \bar{q}_2)$ belongs to $\chi_i(p_t, s_t, f^i_{t+1})$. Thus **P2** and **P4** prove II.1(1).

By **P3**(2) and **P4**, when (p_t, s_t) and $(p^{ie}_{t+1}, s^{ie}_{t+1})$ belong to $P \times S$, the last two components of ξ_{i1} are such that:

$$\bar{m}_1 \geqslant \mu(V(p_t(\bar{q}_1 - \omega_{i1})))$$

$$(1 - s_t)\bar{m}_1 = (1 - s_t)\mu(V(p_t(\bar{q}_1 - \omega_{i1})))$$

$$s_t\bar{b}_1 = -V(p_t(\bar{q}_1 - \omega_{i1}))) - \bar{m}_1.$$

This proves II.1(2) and II.1(3). Q.E.D.

The proof of Proposition II.3 can be derived from similar arguments. We omit it for the sake of brevity.

In all the following, we shall often consider the function $\hat{\xi}_{ih}$ defined as the unique element $(\bar{q}, \bar{m}, \bar{b})$ of ξ_{ih} such that $\bar{m} = \mu(V(p(\bar{q} - \omega_{ih})))$, $i = 1, ..., I$, $h = 1, 2$.

P6. *Let* (p^k, s^k) *be a sequence in* $P \times S$ *which converges to* $(\bar{p}, \bar{s})$ *in* $\bar{P} \times \bar{S}$, *and let* $f^k = (p^{ek}, s^{ek}, V^{ek})$ *be a sequence converging to* $\bar{f} = (\bar{p}^e, \bar{s}^e, \bar{V}^e)$. *Assume that either* (1) $\bar{p}\omega_{i1} > 0$ *or* (2) $\bar{s}\bar{p}^e\omega_{i2} > 0$. *Then any cluster point* $(\bar{q}_1, \bar{q}_2)$ *of the sequence* $(q_1^k, q_2^k) = \chi_i(p^k, s^k, f^k)$ *belongs to* $\chi^i(\bar{p}, \bar{s}, \bar{f})$.

Proof. Clearly $(\bar{q}_1, \bar{q}_2)$ belongs to $\gamma_i(\bar{p}, \bar{s}, \bar{f})$. Let (q_1, q_2) be arbitrary in this set. Choose $0 \leqslant \lambda < 1$, and define $q_h^\lambda = \lambda q_h$, $h = 1, 2$. By convexity of W and W^e (P1):

$$W(\bar{p}(q_1^\lambda - \omega_{i1}), \bar{s}) \leqslant \lambda W(\bar{p}(q_1 - \omega_{i1}), \bar{s}) + (1 - \lambda) W(-\bar{p}\omega_{i1}, \bar{s})$$

$$W^e(\bar{p}^e(q_2^\lambda - \omega_{i2}), \bar{s}^e) \leqslant \lambda W^e(\bar{p}^e(q_2 - \omega_{i2}), \bar{s}^e) + (1 - \lambda) W^e(-\bar{p}^e\omega_{i2}, \bar{s}^e).$$

From assumption (d.2), $\bar{p}\omega_{i1} > 0$ implies $V(-\bar{p}\omega_{i1})) + \mu(V(-\bar{p}\omega_{i1}, \bar{s}) < 0$, and thus $W(-\bar{p}\omega_{i1}, \bar{s}) < 0$. Similarly $\bar{p}^e\omega_{i2} > 0$ implies $W^e(-\bar{p}^e\omega_{i2}, \bar{s}^e) < 0$. Thus, if either (1) or (2) holds,

$$W(\bar{p}(q_1^\lambda - \omega_{i1}), \bar{s}) + \bar{s}W^e(\bar{p}^e(q_2^\lambda - \omega_{i2}), \bar{s}^e) < 0.$$

This implies, by **P3**(2), that for k large enough $(q_1^\lambda, q_2^\lambda)$ belongs to $\gamma_i(p^k, s^k, f^k)$, and therefore: $U_i(q_1^\lambda, q_2^\lambda) \leqslant U_i(q_1^k, q_2^k)$. Consequently, taking a subsequence converging to $(\bar{q}_1, \bar{q}_2)$: $U_i(q_1^\lambda, q_2^\lambda) \leqslant U_i(\bar{q}_1, \bar{q}_2)$. Since this is true for any $0 \leqslant \lambda \leqslant 1$, we have $U_i(\bar{q}_1, \bar{q}_2) \geqslant U_i(q_1, q_2)$ for all (q_1, q_2) in $\gamma_i(\bar{p}, \bar{s}, \bar{f})$. Thus $(\bar{q}_1, \bar{q}_2)$ belongs to $\chi_i(\bar{p}, \bar{s}, \bar{f})$.   Q.E.D.

P7. *Assume that*

(i) *for all $i = 1,..., I$, the expectation functions $f_{t+1}^i = (p_{t+1}^{ie}, s_{t+1}^{ie}, V_{t+1}^{ie})$ is such that p_{t+1}^{ie} and s_{t+1}^{ie} are continuous functions of (p_t, s_t), while V_{t+1}^{ie} is independent of (p_t, s_t);*

(ii) *for all $i = 1,..., I$, the image of $P \times S$ by p_{t+1}^{ie} is contained in a fixed compact subset of P. Then*

(1) $\xi_{i1}(p_t, s_t, f_{t+1}^i(p_t, s_t))$ *is a continuous bounded below function of (p_t, s_t) on $P \times S$;*

(2) $\|\sum_{i=1}^I \xi_{i1}(p_t, s_t, f_{t+1}^i(p_t, s_t))\|$ *tends to $+\infty$ when either*

(i) p_t *tends to 0, and s_t converges to some s in S, or*

(ii) s_t *tends to 0, and p_t converges to some p in P, or*

(iii) p_t *tends to $+\infty$.*

Proof. We first prove (1). We recall from **P3**(1) and the definition that $(\bar{q}_1, \bar{m}_1, \bar{b}_1)$ belongs to $\xi_{i1}(p_t, s_t, f_{t+1}^i(p_t, s_t))$ if and only if there exists $\bar{q}_2 \geqslant 0$ such that $(\bar{q}_1, \bar{q}_2) = \chi_i(p_t, s_t, f_{t+1}^i(p_t, s_t))$ and $\bar{m}_1 = \mu(V(p_t(\bar{q}_1 - \omega_{i1})))$, $s_t\bar{b}_1 = -V(p_t(\bar{q}_1 - \omega_{i1})) - \mu(V(p_t(\bar{q}_1 - \omega_{i1})))$.
We show that ξ_{i1} is bounded below $-\bar{q}_1$ and $\bar{m}_1$ are non-negative. To prove that $\bar{b}_1$ has a lower bound, note that by **P3**(1),

$$\bar{m}_1 + \bar{b}_1 \geqslant V_{t+1}^{ie}(p_{t+1}^{ie}(\bar{q}_2 - \omega_{i2})) \geqslant V_{t+1}^{ie}(-p_{t+1}^{ie}\omega_{i2}).$$

Since by **P7**(ii), p_{t+1}^{ie} stays in a fixed compact set, the right-hand side of the inequality is bounded below. Moreover by **P3**(2),

$$V(p_t(\bar{q}_i - \omega_{i1})) \leqslant -s_t W_{t+1}^{ie}(p_{t+1}^{ie}(\bar{q}_2 - \omega_{i2}), s_{t+1}^{ie})$$
$$\leqslant -s_t W_{t+1}^{ie}(-p_{t+1}^{ie}\omega_{i2}, s_{t+1}^{ie}).$$

Thus, again by **P7**(ii), $V(p_t(\bar{q}_1 - \omega_{i1}))$ is bounded above, and $\bar{m}_1 = \mu(V(p_t(\bar{q}_1 - \omega_{i1})))$ as well. $\bar{b}_1 \geqslant -\bar{m}_1 + V_{t+1}^{ie}(-p_{t+1}^{ie}\omega_{i2})$ is therefore bounded below.

Clearly, by **P6**, $\hat{\xi}(p_t, s_t, f_{t+1}^i(p_t, s_t))$ is continuous on $P \times S$, whenever either $\omega_{i1} > 0$ or $\omega_{i2} > 0$. When $\omega_{i1} = \omega_{i2} = 0$, $\hat{\xi}_{i1}$ is identically equal to zero. This completes the proof of (1).

(2)(i), (ii) are a consequence of **P6** and **P2**, since by (a.2) there is always an i with $\omega_{i1} > 0$ and one with $\omega_{i2} > 0$. In both cases $\|\chi_i(p_t, s_t, f_{t+1}^i(p_t, s_t))\|$ tends to $+\infty$. Let $(\bar{q}_1, \bar{q}_2) = \chi_i(p_t, s_t, f_{t+1}^i(p_t, s_t))$. When $\bar{q}_1$ tends to $+\infty$, $\|\hat{\xi}_{i1}\|$ tends also to $+\infty$ and the argument is completed. Otherwise $\|\bar{q}_2\|$ tends to $+\infty$ and $\bar{m}_1 = \mu(V(p_t(\bar{q}_1 - \omega_{i1})))$ has a limit. Therefore, (c.1) and the equality $\bar{m}_1 + \bar{b}_1 = W^e(p_{t+1}^{ie}(\bar{q}_2 - \omega_{i2}))$ imply that $\|\bar{b}_1\|$ tends to $+\infty$, and in this case too $\|\xi_{i1}\|$ tends to $+\infty$.

To prove (2)(iii), we show that when p_t tends to $+\infty$, $\|\chi_i(p_t, s_t, f_{t+1}^i(p_t, s_t))\|$ tends to $+\infty$ for some i. Assume, on the contrary, that it has a cluster point $(\bar{q}_1, \bar{q}_2)$. By **P4**, (c.1), and (d.2), this implies that $\bar{q}_1 = \omega_{i1}$. Take an agent i with $\omega_{i1} > 0$. Now, by strict monotonicity of U_i, for any $\eta > 0$, there exists $\varepsilon > 0$ such that $U_i(\omega_{i1} - \varepsilon, \bar{q}_2 + \eta) > U_i(\omega_{i1}, \bar{q}_2)$. Using (d.2), it is easy to check that $(\omega_{i1} - \varepsilon, \bar{q}_2 + \eta)$ belongs to $\gamma_i(p_t, s_t, f_{t+1}^{ie}(p_t, s_t))$ for p_t large enough. But this gives a contradiction. Q.E.D.

P8. $\sum_{i=1}^I \hat{\xi}_{i2}(p_t, s_t, \bar{x}_{i1}(t-1))$ is a continuous bounded below function of (p_t, s_t) on $P \times S$.

Proof. The argument is standard. We omit it for the sake of brevity. Q.E.D.

P9 (Walras' law). *Given D in $\mathcal{R}$ and $\bar{x}_{i1}(t-1) = (\bar{q}_{i1}, \bar{m}_{i1}, \bar{b}_{i1})$ in $\mathcal{R}^3$ for $i = 1,..., I$, let $(q_{i1}, m_{i1}, b_{i1}) = \hat{\xi}_{i1}(p, s, f^i)$ $(q_{i2}, m_{i2}, b_{i2}) = \hat{\xi}_{i2}(p, s, \bar{x}_{i1}(t-1))$ for $i = 1,..., I$, and $(q_g, m_g, b_g) = \xi_g(p, T, \bar{b}_g(t-1); s, D)$, where $T = \sum_{i,h}(V(p(q_{ih} - \omega_{ih})) - p(q_{ih} - \omega_{ih}) - \rho_i(p, s, \bar{x}_{i1}(t-1)))$. Then $[\sum_{i,h}(p(q_{ih} - \omega_{ih}) + m_{ih} + sb_{ih}) + pq_g]$ is bounded above independently of p, s, f^i, and $\bar{b}_g(t-1)$.*

Proof. Summing up the budget constraints of the consumers gives:

$$\sum_{i,h}(V(p(q_{ih} - \omega_{ih})) + m_{ih} + sb_{ih}) = \sum_i (\bar{m}_{i1} + \bar{b}_{i1} + \rho_i(p, s, \bar{x}_{i1}(t-1))).$$

Using the definition of T, this can be rewritten:

$$\sum_{i,h} (p(q_{ih} - \omega_{ih}) + m_{ih} + sb_{ih}) = \sum_i (\bar{m}_{i1} + \bar{b}_{i1}) - T.$$

Since, according to the government's behavior, $pq_g = \text{Max}(T + D, 0)$, we get

$$\sum_{i,h} (p(q_{ih} - \omega_{ih}) + m_{ih} + sb_{ih}) + pq_g = \sum_i (\bar{m}_{ih} + \bar{b}_{i1}) + \text{Max}(D, -T).$$

Since by (c.1) taxes are non-negative:

$$-T \leqslant \sum_i \rho_i(p, s, \bar{x}_{i1}(t-1))$$

and thus,

$$-T \leqslant -\sum_i \bar{b}_{i1}$$

which completes the proof.   Q.E.D.

P10. *Proof of Theorem* IV.1.

Proof. Let (P^k) be an increasing sequence of compact convex subsets of P such that $\bigcup_k P$ contains P. Now define a correspondence from P^k into itself which associates to any p_0 in P^k the set of p in P^k such that $(p - p')(\sum_{i,h}(q_{ih} - \omega_{ih}) + q_g) \geqslant 0$ for all p' in P^k, where $(q_{i1}, m_{i1}, b_{i1}) = \xi_{i1}(p_0, \bar{s}, f^i_{t+1}(p_0, \bar{s}))$, $(q_{i2}, m_{i2}, b_{i2}) = \xi_{i2}(p_0, \bar{s}, \bar{x}_{i1}(t-1))$, for all $i = 1, ..., I$ and (q_g, m_g, b_g) belongs to $\xi_g(p_0, T, \bar{b}_g(t-1); \bar{s}, \bar{D})$, with $T = \sum_{ih}(V(p_0(q_{ih} - \omega_{ih})) - p(q_{ih} - \omega_{ih}) - \rho_i(p_0, \bar{s}, \bar{x}_{i1}(t-1)))$. By **P7**(1) and the continuity of the government's behavior this gives an upper hemi-continuous convex valued correspondence from P^k into P^k. Thus it has a fixed point p^k.

Consider the associated $(q^k_{ih}, m^k_{ih}, b^k_{ih})$, $i = 1, ..., I$, $h = 1, 2$ and (q^k_g, m^k_g, b^k_g). From **P9**, $\sum_{i,h}(p^k(q^k_{ih} - \omega_{ih}) + m^k_{ih} + sb^k_{ih}) + p^k q^k_g$ has an upper bound independent of k. By construction of the sets P^k and the above correspondence, this is also true when p^k is replaced by p^1. By **P7**(1) (q_{ih}, m_{ih}, b_{ih}) is bounded below, and thus, the sequence $(q^k_{ih}, m^k_{ih}, b^k_{ih})$, q^k_g stay in a fixed compact set. We claim that (p^k) stays also in a fixed compact subset of P: otherwise one would contradict either **P7**(2)(i) or **P7**(2)(iii). Let p_t be a limit point of the sequence (p^k), $(q_{ih}(t), m_{ih}(t), b_{ih}(t))$, $i = 1, ..., I$, $h = 1, 2$ and $q_g(t)$ the corresponding quantities. By construction of the correspondence, we have

$$\sum_{i,h} (q_{ih}(t) - \omega_{ih}) + q_g(t) = 0.$$

Let $m_g(t) = \sum_i \bar{m}_{i1}(t-1) - \sum_{i,h} m_{ih}(t)$, $b_g(t) = -\sum_{i,h} b_{ih}(t)$. We have to check that $(q_g(t), m_g(t), b_g(t))$ belongs to $\xi_g(p(t), T(t), \bar{b}_g(t-1), \bar{s}, D)$, where

$$T(t) = \sum_{ih} (V(p_t(q_{ih}(t) - \omega_{ih})) - p_t(q_{ih}(t) - \omega_{ih}) + \sum_i \rho_i(p_t, s_t, \bar{x}_{i1}(t-1)),$$

i.e., that

$$p_t q_g(t) + m_g(t) + \bar{s} b_g(t) = T(t) + \bar{b}_g(t-1).$$

Summing up the budget constraints of the consumers, as in the proof of **P9** and using the definition of $T(t)$ gives

$$\sum_{i,h} (p_t(q_{ih}(t) - \omega_{ih}) + m_{ih}(t) + \bar{s} b_{ih}(t)) = \sum_i (\bar{m}_{i1}(t-1) + \bar{b}_{i1}(t-1)) - T(t)$$

which leads to the desired result since $\bar{b}_g(t-1) = -\sum_{i,h} \bar{b}_{ih}(t-1)$.   Q.E.D.

P11. Proof of Theorem IV.2.

Given s in $\mathring{S}$, let $(p, s, (q_{ih}, m_{ih}, b_{ih}), x_g, T)$ be the unique temporary equilibrium corresponding to the policy (s, D) such that for all i and h, $m_{ih} = \mu(V(p(q_{ih} - \omega_{ih})))$. We show that the equilibrium is a continuous function of s. Take a sequence s^k converging to s. If the temporary equilibria associated with s^k have a limit, then the limit point is clearly an equilibrium (conditions $(\alpha.1)$ and $(\alpha.2)$ of the definition are satisfied by continuity), and thus it is the unique equilibrium associated with s. To complete the argument, we show that there exists a compact neighbourhood of s in $\mathring{S}$ such that the temporary equilibria associated with any s' in the neighbourhood stay in a fixed compact set. Suppose on the contrary that p' goes to 0 or to $+\infty$: the definition of equilibrium would contradict **P7**(i) or (ii). Thus p stays in a compact subset of P, and the continuity of the demand functions guarantees a similar behaviour of the other components of the equilibrium.

Thus the range of the equilibrium quantity of money, when s varies in $\mathring{S}$, is a connected subset of the real line, as the image by a continuous function of a connected set. For $s = 1$, by (3) of Proposition II.1, the range of the equilibrium quantity of money is of the shape $[m, +\infty)$. Since the unique equilibrium when $s < 1$ converges to an equilibrium for $s = 1$ when s tends to 1, we get the desired result.   Q.E.D.

P12. Proof of theorem IV.3.

Let $(p, s, (q_{ih}, m_{ih}, b_{ih}), (q_g, m_g, b_g), T)$ be a temporary equilibrium. We want to see whether p converges to zero when s goes to zero.

At any temporary equilibrium, the following relationships hold:

$$V(p(q_{i1} - \omega_{i1})) + m_{i1} + sb_{i1} = 0$$

$$V(p(q_{i2} - \omega_{i2})) + (1 - s) m_{i2} = \bar{m}_{i1}(t - 1) + \bar{b}_{i1}(t - 1) + \rho_i(p, s, \bar{x}_{i1}(t - 1))$$

$$pq_g = \text{Max}\left(0, \sum_{i,h} V(p(q_{ih} - \omega_{ih})) - p(q_{ih} - \omega_{ih}) + \bar{D} - \sum_i \rho_i(p, s, \bar{x}_{i1}(t - 1))\right)$$

where ρ_i is defined as equal to zero when the consumer is not bankrupt.

Because of assumption (1) of the theorem, both $V(p(q_{i2} - \omega_{i2}))$ and $V(p(q_{i2} - \omega_{i2})) - \rho_i(p, s, \bar{x}_{i1}(t - 1))$ are non-positive for all i.

Suppose, by contraposition, that p does not converge to zero with s. From **P7**(2)(i), (iii), this implies that $\|\sum_{i=1}^{I}(q_{i1}, m_{i1}, b_{i1})\|$ goes to $+\infty$. But $\sum_{i=1}^{I} q_{i1}$ is in a fixed compact set, since it corresponds to a feasible allocation. Thus $\|\sum_{i=1}^{I}(m_{i1}, b_{i1})\|$ goes to $+\infty$, and since (m_{i1}, b_{i1}) is bounded below by **P7**(1), this implies that $\sum_{i=1}^{I} V(p(q_{i1} - \omega_{i1}))$ is strictly negative for s sufficiently close to zero.

Consider now two cases: either $q_g = 0$ or $q_g > 0$. If $q_g = 0$, we cannot be at an equilibrium, since $q_{i2} \leqslant \omega_{i2}$ for all i and $p \sum_{i=1}^{I}(q_{i1} - \omega_{i1}) \leqslant \sum_{i=1}^{I} V(p(q_{i1} - \omega_{i1})) < 0$ for s sufficiently close to zero. Now, if $q_g > 0$, using the fact that $q_g + \sum(q_{ih} - \omega_{ih}) = 0$, we get from the government budget identity:

$$\sum_{i,h} V(p(q_{ih} - \omega_{ih})) + \bar{D} - \sum_i \rho_i(p, s, \bar{x}_{i1}(t - 1)) = 0$$

again leading to a contradiction, since by assumption (2) of the theorem, $\bar{D} < 0$.

Finally, it is immediate to check that for p sufficiently small, the old consumers cannot repay their debts $\bar{m}_{i1}(t - 1) + \bar{b}_{i1}(t - 1) < 0$ with their initial endowments whose value $V(-p\omega_{i2})$ goes to zero.   Q.E.D.

P13.   *Proof of Theorem IV.4.*

In both cases, either the government, or some old consumer spends a strictly positive amount of money v on the market to buy goods. Thus, at the equilibrium, there exist other consumers who sell goods for the same value, and at least one who sell $v/2I$. Let $m = \mu(-v/2I)$, which is strictly positive.   Q.E.D.

We now proceed to the study of the long run equilibria.

P14. $(p, s, \bar{D}, V)$, θ, (x_{ih}), $i = 1, ..., I$, $h = 1, 2$, *and* x_g *describe a long equilibrium if and only if*:

(i) $(p, s, \bar{D}, V)$ and θ are such that

$$\text{Max}\left[\bar{D} + \sum_{ih} V(p(\chi_{ih}(p, s, f) - \omega_{ih}), \sum_{ih} (\chi_{ih}(p, s, f) - \omega_{ih})\right] = 0$$

where $f = (p, s, \theta V)$;

(ii) for all $i = 1, ..., I$, $h = 1, 2$:

$$q_{ih} = \chi_{ih}(p, s, f) \qquad\qquad m_{ih} \geqslant \mu(V(p(q_{ih} - \omega_{ih})))$$

$$V(p(q_{i1} - \omega_{i1})) + m_{i1} + sb_{i1} = 0 \qquad\qquad m_{i2} + b_{i2} = 0,$$

and, for the government:

$$q_g = \sum_{ih} (\omega_{ih} - q_{ih}) \qquad m_g + (1 - 1/\theta) \sum_{ih} m_{ih} = 0$$

$$b_g = \sum_{ih} b_h = 0.$$

Proof. (x_{ih}) and x_g describe the allocation resources at date $t = 0$. We start with the consumer's behaviour. From **P3**(1), $x_{i1} = (q_{i1}, m_{i1}, b_{i1})$ belongs to $\xi_{i1}(p, s, f)$ if and only if $q_{i1} = \chi_{i1}(p, s, f)$, $m_{i1} \geqslant \mu(V(p(q_{i1} - \omega_{i1})))$, and $V(p(q_{i1} - \omega_{i1})) + m_{i1} + sb_{i1} = 0$. f_1 is equal to $(\theta p, s, V_1)$. But since for all z, by definition, $V_1(\theta pz) = \theta V(pz)$, by assumption (e.1):

$$W^e(p^e(q_2 - \omega_{i2}), s) = V_1(\theta p(q_2 - \omega_{i2})) + (1 - s)\,\mu(V_1(\theta p(q_2 - \omega_{i2})))$$

$$= \theta W(p(q_2 - \omega_{i2}), s),$$

we can replace f_1 by $f = (p, v, \theta V)$ without changing the young consumer's program. In a world of perfect forecasts, old consumers act as they planned to do in their youth. A similar argument shows that $x_{i2} = (q_{i2}, m_{i2}, b_{i2})$ belongs to $\xi_{i2}(p, s, x_{i1}(t-1))$ if and only if $q_{i2} = \chi_{i2}(p, s, f)$, $m_{i2} \geqslant \mu(V(p(q_{i2} - \omega_{i2})))$, and $m_{i2} + b_{i2} = 0$.

Now the equality between supply and demand (β.1) is satisfied if and only if: $q_g = \sum_{ih}(\omega_{ih} - q_{ih})$, $\sum_{i,h} m_{ih} + m_g = (1/\theta)\sum_{i,h} m_{ih}$ and $b_g + \sum_{ih} b_{ih} = 0$.

There rests to be checked that the behaviour of the government x_g belongs to $\xi_g(p, T, b_g/\theta; s, \bar{D})$, where T is equal to $\sum_{ih}[V(p(q_{ih} - \omega_{ih})) - p(q_{ih} - \omega_{ih})]$, is satisfied if and only if (i) holds. Recall that ξ_g is defined by the two following equalities:

$$pq_g + m_g + sb_g = T + b_g/\theta$$

$$pq_g = \text{Max}(T + \bar{D}, 0).$$

The first one is satisfied by Walras' law, summing up the budget's constraints of the private sector, and using the equality between supply and demand. The second is equivalent to **P14**(i) using the fact that $q_g = \sum_{ih}(\omega_{ih} - q_{ih})$ and $q_{ih} = \chi_{ih}(p, s, f)$.   Q.E.D.

The study of the long run equilibria is therefore closely associated with the study of the solutions of the equation **P14**(i).

P15. *Given s in S and V satisfying* (c.1)–(c.2),

(1) $\sum_{ih} \chi_{ih}(1, s, (1, s, \theta V))$ *is a continuous bounded below function of* θ *on* P;

(2) $\sum_{ih} \chi_{ih}(1, s, (1, s, \theta V))$ *tends to* $+\infty$ *when either* θ *tends to zero or* θ *tends to* $+\infty$.

Proof. (1) is a direct consequence of **P6**. (2) can be shown by adapting slightly the arguments given in **P7**. The details are left to the reader.
                    Q.E.D.

P16. *Proof of Theorem* V.1.

Proof. It is immediate to check that the characterization of a long run equilibrium of **P14** is preserved during the transformation, using

$$V_\lambda((q_{ih} - \omega_{ih})) = \lambda V(q_{ih} - \omega_{ih})$$
$$\mu(\lambda V(q_{ih} - \omega_{ih}))) = \mu \lambda V(q_{ih} - \omega_{ih}).$$ Q.E.D.

P17. *Proof of Theorem* V.2.

Proof. Let $(q_{i1}, q_{i2}) = \chi_i(1, s, (1, s, \theta V))$. Given s in S, and V satisfying (c.1)–(c.2), we are looking for a θ in P which solves **P14**(i):

$$\text{Max}\left[D + \sum_{ih} V(q_{ih} - \omega_{ih}), \sum_{ih} (q_{ih} - \omega_{ih}) \right] = 0$$

(**P14**(ii) follows then immediately).

Let $\phi(\theta)$ denote the left-hand side of the above equation, when θ varies in P. From **P1**, ϕ is a continuous bounded below function on P which tends to $+\infty$ when θ tends to zero or to $+\infty$.

Now, the budget constraint of consumer i is (**P3**(2)):

$$W(q_{i1} - \omega_{i1}, s) + s\theta\, W(q_{i2} - \omega_{i2}, s) \leqslant 0$$

Since $W(q - \omega, s) \geqslant V(q - \omega) \geqslant (q - \omega)$ by (d.1) and (c.1), we obtain directly, summing over i and using $D \leqslant 0$:

$$\phi(1/s) \leqslant 0.$$

Thus if $\phi(1/s) < 0$, there are at least two equilibria, one with $\theta < 1/s$ one with $\theta > 1/s$.

Q.E.D.

P18. *Proof of Theorem V.3.*

Proof. **P14**(ii) together with the equality $D = q_g - T$, gives the unique long run equilibrium allocation, if it exists. One then has to check **P14**(i). The sum of the agents' budget constraints over the type gives:

$$\sum_{ih} V(q_{ih} - \omega_{ih}) + (1 - s) \sum_{ih} \mu(V(q_{ih} - \omega_{ih})) = 0.$$

The second term of the expression on the left is non-negative. Thus by (c.1), $\sum_{ih}(q_{ih} - \omega_{ih}) \leq 0$. We now check that **P14**(i) is satisfied, we just saw that $\sum_{ih}(q_{ih} - \omega_{ih}) < 0$. We now compute $\bar{D} + \sum_{ih} V(q_{ih} - \omega_{ih})$. Since $q_g = -\sum_{ih}(q_{ih} - \omega_{ih})$, and $T = \sum_{ih} V(q_{ih} - \omega_{ih}) - (q_{ih} - \omega_{ih})$, then $\bar{D} + \sum_{ih} V(q_{ih} - \omega_{ih}) = 0$. Finally using the agent's budget constraints $\bar{D} = (1 - s) \sum_{ih} m_{ih}$.

Q.E.D.

P19. *Proof of Theorem V.4.*

Proof. Recall that $(q_{i1}, q_{i2}) = \chi_i(1, s, (1, s, \theta V))$ is the maximum of $V_i(q_1, q_2)$ over $\gamma_i(1, s, (1, s, \theta V))$, the set of (q_1, q_2) in Q which satisfies

$$W(q_1 - \omega_{i1}, s) + s\theta \, W(q_2 - \omega_{i2}, s) \leq 0$$

where $W(v, s) = V(v) + (1 - s) \mu(V(v))$, for all v in $\mathscr{R}$.

Now, by construction, $W(v, s) = W'(v, s')$ for all v in $\mathscr{R}$, and $s\theta = s'\theta'$. Therefore $\chi_i(1, s, (1, s, \theta V)) = \chi_i(1, s', (1, s', \theta'V'))$. **P14**(ii) gives the values of m'_{ih} and b'_{ih}, $i = 1,..., I$, $h = 1, 2$, as well as m'_g and b'_g.

Finally $\bar{D}'$ can be computed through

$$= \sum_{i,h} (V'(q_{ih} - \omega_{ih}) - (q_{ih} - \omega_{ih})) + \bar{D}'$$

which yields

$$\bar{D}' - \bar{D} = \sum_{i,h} [V(q_{ih} - \omega_{ih}) - V'(q_{ih} - \omega_{ih})]$$

or

$$\bar{D}' - \bar{D} = (1 - s') \sum_{i,h} m'_{ih} - (1 - s) \sum_{i,h} m_{ih}.$$

It is immediate to check that **P14**(i) is still satisfied.

Q.E.D.

REFERENCES

1. T. BEWLEY, The optimum quantity of money, *in* "Models of Monetary Economics," (J. H. Kareken and N. Wallace, Eds.), Federal Reserve Bank of Minneapolis, Minneapolis, 1980.

2. R. W. CLOWER, A reconsideration of the microfoundations of monetary theory, *Western Econ. J.* **6** (1967), 1–8.

3. M. FRIEDMAN, "The Optimum Quantity of Money and Other Essays," Adline, Chicago, 1969.

4. D. GALE, Pure exchange equilibrium of dynamic economic models, *J. Econ. Theory* **6** (1973), 12–36.

5. J. M. GRANDMONT, On the short run equilibrium in a monetary economy, *in* "Allocation under Uncertainty, Equilibrium and optimality" (J. Drèze, Ed.), Macmillan, London, 1974.

6. J. M. GRANDMONT AND G. LAROQUE, On money and banking, *Rev. Econ. Stud.* **42** (1975), 207–236.

7. J. M. GRANDMONT AND Y. YOUNES, On the role of money and the existence of a monetary equilibrium, *Rev. Econ. Stud.* **39** (1972), 355–372.

8. J. M. GRANDMONT AND Y. YOUNES, On the efficiency of a monetary equilibrium, *Rev. Econ. Stud.* **40** (1973), 149–165.

9. J. M. GRANDMONT, "Money and value," Cambridge Univ. Press, Cambridge, 1983.

10. S. GROSSMAN AND L. WEISS, A transactions-based model of the monetary transmission mechanism, *Am. Econ. Rev.* **73** (1983), 871–880.

11. F. H. HAHN, Equilibrium with transaction costs, *Econometrica* **39** (1971), 417–439.

12. M. HELLWIG, Precautionary money holding and the payment of interest on money, Core DP 8236, Université Catholique de Louvain, 1982.

13. E. HELPMAN AND E. SADKA, Optimal financing of the government's budget: Taxes, bonds, or money?, *Am. Econ. Rev.* **69** (1979), 152–160.

14. M. KURZ, Equilibrium with transaction cost and money in a single market exchange economy, *J. Econ. Theory* **7** (1974), 418–452.

15. J. TOBIN, Liquidity preference as a behaviour towards risk, *Rev. Econ. Stud.* **2** (1985), 65–86.

CHAPTER V

Deterministic Dynamics

Econometrica, Vol. 44, No. 6 (November, 1976)

DYNAMICS OF TEMPORARY EQUILIBRIA AND EXPECTATIONS

By Gérard Fuchs and Guy Laroque

This paper is devoted to the analysis of the dynamic behavior of a sequence of temporary equilibria. The model chosen is a generalization of Samuelson's pure consumption loan model as introduced by J. M. Grandmont and G. Laroque in [5]. Three main results are given. First there is an open and dense subset $\mathcal{U}$ of economies for which, near stationary equilibria and cycles, the dynamics take the standard form of an ordinary difference equation. Then conditions are obtained so that, for an economy $\mathscr{E}$ in $\mathcal{U}$, stationary equilibria are locally asymptotically stable; these conditions are discussed in the case where there is only one good in addition to money. Last, it is proven that the qualitative behavior of trajectories of $\mathscr{E}$ near stationary equilibria and cycles is preserved under small perturbations; i.e., one has a property of local structural stability; this is true in particular with respect to changes in the individual expectations of the agents.

INTRODUCTION AND DEFINITIONS

THIS PAPER IS A FIRST STEP in the analysis of the dynamic behavior of a sequence of temporary equilibria. Its purpose is to investigate the dynamic structure of a simple model in order to derive properties of local asymptotic stability of some specific trajectories (stationary or cyclical) and to investigate, in a neighborhood of these trajectories, the sensitivity of the dynamics to small perturbations of the data, in particular individual expectations of the agents.

The underlying framework is Samuelson's pure consumption loan model [8], generalized in a temporary equilibrium context as it appears in J. M. Grandmont and G. Laroque [5]. The mathematics include the use of differential topology, through now standard techniques that can be found, for instance, in [2 or 4], and also some results derived from the theory of dynamic systems that are presented in [3].

There are $l - 1$ nonstorable goods ($h = 2, 3, \ldots, l$) and one storable one which is used to transfer value over time and which we shall call money ($h = 1$). There are I types of consumers who live two periods, so that at each time t there are two living consumers of each type i ($i = 1, \ldots, I$): one "young" labelled by ($i1$) and one "old" labelled by ($i2$). At the beginning of each period of their lives consumers receive an endowment of the $l - 1$ nonstorable goods. They trade on the spot market of the corresponding period. Young consumers can save by buying from the old ones the money these had themselves bought in the previous period; the total monetary stock remains constant.

Let us consider consumer ($i1$), born at date t. His behavior was represented in [5] by the maximization of a utility function in his consumption set, under the current budget constraint and an expected budget constraint for time $t + 1$. We shall use here a description by demand functions. At time t the action of the young consumer ($i1$) depends on the current price system p_t and on his expectation p_{t+1}^i of the price system that will prevail at time $t + 1$. We shall, as in [5], assume that this expectation depends on the current prices and on the T past observed

  Reprinted from *Econometrica* **44** (1976), 1157–1178.

price systems. Similarly, we shall describe the action at time t of the old consumer ($i2$) (who is born at time $t - 1$) by a demand function depending on his past action, i.e., on p_{t-1} and p_t^i, and on the present actual price system p_t.

The set of prices $p = (p^1, p^2, \ldots, p^l)$ we shall consider for money and nonstorable goods is $P = \mathbb{R}^+ \times S$ where

$$\mathbb{R}^+ =]0, +\infty[, \quad S = \{p \in \mathbb{R}^{l-1} \mid \sum_k p^k = 1, p^k > 0 \qquad \forall k = 2, \ldots, l\}$$

($\mathbb{R}^{l-1}$ being the space of goods).

A consumer i ($i \in I$) will be characterized by:

(i) Two demand functions:[1] $z_{i1} \in C^1(P^2, \mathbb{R}^l)$ and $z_{i2} \in C^1(P^3, \mathbb{R}^l)$, the first components of which, z_{i1}^1 and z_{i2}^1, describe demands of money of the agents, the last $l - 1$ components, z_{i1}^k and z_{i2}^k, representing *excess* demands of nonstorable goods; we ask for the following assumptions:[2]

ASSUMPTION 1: $z_{i1}^1(p_t, p_{t+1}^i) \in [0, +\infty[, \forall (p_t, p_{t+1}^i) \in P^2$.

ASSUMPTION 2 (Budget constraints): $p_t \cdot z_{i1}(p_t, p_{t+1}^i) = 0, \forall (p_t, p_{t+1}^i) \in P^2$, and $p_t \cdot z_{i2}(p_{t-1}, p_t^i, p_t) = 0, \forall (p_{t-1}, p_t^i, p_t) \in P^3$.

ASSUMPTION 3 (An old consumer spends all the money he saved when he was young): $z_{i2}^1(p_{t-1}, p_t^i, p_t) = -z_{i1}^1(p_{t-1}, p_t^i), \forall (p_{t-1}, p_t^i, p_t) \in P^3$.

ASSUMPTION 4:

$$z_{i1}^1(p, p) = (p^1)^{-1} z_{i1}^1(\hat{p}, \hat{p}),$$

$$z_{i1}^k(p, p) = z_{i1}^k(\hat{p}, \hat{p}),$$

$$z_{i2}^k(p, p, p) = z_{i2}^k(\hat{p}, \hat{p}, \hat{p}), \qquad \forall k = 2, \ldots, l, \forall p \in P,$$

where $\hat{p} = (1, p^2, \ldots, p^l)$ (*for constant consecutive price systems, demand of money is inversely proportional to its price, demand of nonstorable goods only depends on their relative prices*).

(ii) A price expectation function $\Psi_i \in C^1(P^{T+1}, \mathbb{R}^l)$ with the following assumption:

ASSUMPTION 5: $\Psi_i(P^{T+1}) \subset P$.

We shall then call D the vector space:

$$D = [C^1(P^2, \mathbb{R}^l) \times C^1(P^3, \mathbb{R}^l) \times C^1(P^{T+1}, \mathbb{R}^l)]^I;$$

---

[1] $C^1(X, Y)$ denotes the space of continuously differentiable maps from X to Y.
[2] $\cdot$ stands for scalar product in $\mathbb{R} \times \mathbb{R}^{l-1} = \mathbb{R}^l$.

B will be the subset of elements $\mathscr{B} = (z_{i1}, z_{i2}, \Psi_i)$ in D such that Assumptions 2 through 5 hold; our space agents will be for the moment the subset A' of B such that Assumption 1 holds.

We now define the excess demand function Z as the map

$$Z : B \rightarrow C^1(P^{T+2}, \mathbb{R}^l)$$

given by $(t \in \mathbb{Z}; e_t = (p_t, p_{t-1}, \ldots, p_{t-T}) \in P^{T+1}; s_t = (p_t, e_{t-1}) \in P^{T+2})$:

(1) $\qquad Z(\mathscr{B}; s_t) = \sum_i z_{i1}(p_t, \Psi_i(e_t)) + \sum_i z_{i2}(p_{t-1}, \Psi_i(e_{t-1}), p_t).$

$Z(\mathscr{B}; s_t)$ represents the vector of aggregated excess demand at time t, given the present and $T + 1$ past price systems. Thanks to Assumption 2, Z satisfies Walras law:

(2) $\qquad p_t \cdot Z(\mathscr{B}; s_t) = 0, \qquad \forall \mathscr{B}, \forall s_t$

so that we can indeed consider that Z maps B in $C^1(P^{T+2}, \mathbb{R}^{l-1})$.

Consider a series of definitions:

DEFINITION 1: A point p_t in P is a *temporary equilibrium* at time t for an element $\mathscr{B}$ in B if there exists e_{t-1} in P^{T+1} such that

(3) $\qquad Z(\mathscr{B}; p_t, e_{t-1}) = 0.$

For each $(\mathscr{B}; e_{t-1})$ the set of temporary equilibria will be labelled by $V(\mathscr{B}; e_{t-1})$.

DEFINITION 2: Given an element $\mathscr{B}$ in B a *trajectory* is an infinite sequence $\{p_t\}$ with $p_t \in P, t \in \mathbb{Z}$, such that

$$p_t \in V(\mathscr{B}; e_{t-1}) \qquad \forall t.$$

An important remark is then that, thanks to Assumption 3 and Definition 2, for $e_t \in P^{T+1}$ the quantity

(4) $\qquad M(\mathscr{B}; e_t) = \sum z_{i1}^1(p_t, \Psi_i(e_t)),$

which is the *total monetary stock* at time t, *is constant along a trajectory.*

An *economy* $\mathscr{E}$ will then be defined through the data of the characteristics of its agents—i.e., an element $\mathscr{A}$ in A'—and a monetary stock m we shall now on suppose to be strictly positive. We shall call E' the space of economies $A' \times \mathbb{R}^+$ and F the set $B \times \mathbb{R}^+$.

Given an economy $\mathscr{E} = (\mathscr{A}, m)$, or more generally an element $\mathscr{F} = (\mathscr{B}, m)$ in F, we thus see that the set of prices which will describe the possible states of the system is the subset of P^{T+1} given by

$$X(\mathscr{F}) = \{ e \in P^{T+1} | M(\mathscr{B}, e) = m \}.$$

We thus have for any $\mathscr{B}$ a sort of "stratification" of the set of trajectories, strata being characterized by a total monetary stock m.[3]

[3] In some sense, the role of m can be compared to the role of total energy in the dynamic problem of celestial mechanics.

We now add two supplementary definitions.

DEFINITION 3: If a trajectory $\{p_t\}$ defines a periodic sequence in P with period $\tau > 1$ we shall say it is a *cycle* of length τ.

For each $\mathscr{F}$ the set of cycles will be labelled by $\Gamma(\mathscr{F})$.

DEFINITION 4: If a trajectory $\{p_t\}$ is the repetition of some $\bar{p}$, it is represented in P by a fixed point we shall call a *stationary temporary equilibrium* (STE).

For each $\mathscr{F}$ the set of STE will be labelled by $W(\mathscr{F})$.

The so-called "long run" studies are concerned with the asymptotic behavior of the trajectories and their dependance on the characteristics of the economies. But very little can be said at this level of generality in our model and we shall restrict ourselves to a somewhat more precise problem: study those trajectories which, in some sense, are neighbors of stationary temporary equilibria or of cycles, concepts which, as we shall see, are not empty.

It is then quite natural to introduce additional conditions on the expectations of the agents so as to express some type of learning by experience. We shall only use here the assumption already made in [5], namely:

ASSUMPTION 6: $\Psi_i(p, \ldots, p) = p, \forall i, \forall p \in P$.

We include Assumption 6 from now on in the definition of B and A'. Other assumptions could be imagined for cycles (at least if their period τ is shorter than the memory T of the agents). They would complicate our proofs without changing their results.

Using Assumptions 3, 4, and 6, we then observe that, trying to look for STE associated with a given $\mathscr{F} = (\mathscr{B}, m)$, the first component Z^1 of Z vanishes identically while the others do not depend on the first component p^1 of p. On the other hand, belonging to $X(\mathscr{F})$ then implies:

$$(5) \qquad p^1 = m^{-1} \sum_i z_{i1}^1(\hat{p}, \hat{p})$$

(this is the property of dichotomy between nonstorable goods and money). Thus, with λ being any positive number and with $\bar{p}_\lambda = (\lambda^{-1}\bar{p}^1, \bar{p}^2, \ldots, \bar{p}^l)$, we are led to the following Remarks.

REMARK 1: *The quantity theory of money* holds in our model. Indeed, if $\bar{p} \in W(\mathscr{A}, m)$, $\bar{p}_\lambda \in W(\mathscr{A}, \lambda m)$.

REMARK 2: If we had allowed the price of money to be zero we could have been tempted to use (5) to define possibly "extended STE" $\bar{p}$ with $\bar{p}^1 = 0$ and then study *inflation paths* converging asymptotically to $\bar{p}$. However, it is clear that if one allows $\bar{p}^1$ to be zero, then demands of money surely are correspondences with no differentiability properties, which makes any local study rather difficult. Some features of inflation can be obtained though in our model, when an STE $\bar{p}$ is such that $\bar{p}^k/\bar{p}^1 \gg 0, \forall k$; in this case there may be sets of inflation paths along which monetary prices of real goods will keep growing up to very large values, but the rate of inflation then will always go asymptotically to zero.

In Section 1 we recall already known results on the nonvacuity of the correspondences of temporary equilibria and STE, introduce a topology on our set of economies, and prove some compacity properties for equilibria. Section 2 then shows there exists an open and dense subset $\mathscr{V}$ of economies such that STE (which are finite in number) and cycles (if any) have neighborhoods in which the dynamics of our problem takes the simple form of a diffeomorphism acting on a manifold. Section 3 next investigates some conditions of asymptotic stability for STE associated with elements $\mathscr{E}$ of $\mathscr{V}$. Section 4 shows that the qualitiative behavior near STE and cycles of the trajectories associated with economies $\mathscr{E}$ in an open and dense subset $\mathscr{U}$ of $\mathscr{V}$, is the same for any $\mathscr{E}'$ near enough to $\mathscr{E}$, i.e., one has a property of local structural stability (see [3]); this is true in particular with respect to changes in the individual expectations of the agents. Section 5 then contains the proofs of our propositions and theorems.

1. FIRST PROPERTIES OF EQUILIBRIA AND CYCLES

A. *The Existence Problem*

One can find in [5] sufficient conditions, in terms of utility functions and expectations, for an economy $\mathscr{E}$ to admit temporary equilibria and STE with a positive price of money. These conditions are easily translated into our formalism and lead us to the following additional assumptions:[4]

ASSUMPTION 7 (Consumption sets are bounded below): z_{i1}^k and z_{i2}^k are bounded below $\forall i, \forall k = 2, \ldots, l$.

ASSUMPTION 8 (Desirability assumption):

$$p_t \in P \to p^0 \in \mathbb{R}^+ \times \bar{S} \backslash S \Rightarrow \sum_i \sum_{k=2}^l z_{i2}^k(p_{t-1}, p_t^i, p_t) \to +\infty,$$

$$\forall (p_{t-1}, p_t^i) \in P^2.$$

ASSUMPTION 9 (Demand of money increases if its value is expected to increase):

$$p_t \in p \to p^0 \in \{0\} \times S \text{ and } (p_{t+1}^i)^1 \geqslant \alpha > 0 \Rightarrow \sum_i z_{i1}^1(p_t, p_{t+1}^i) \to +\infty,$$

$$\forall p_{t+1}^i \in P.$$

---

[4] $\bar{S}$ is the closure of S in $\mathbb{R}^{l-1}$.

ASSUMPTION 10: $p_t \in P \to p^0 \in \{0\} \times S \Rightarrow \forall i, \forall (p_{t-1}, \ldots, p_{t-T}) \in P^T$, $\exists \beta > 0$ such that $\Psi_i^1(e_t) > \beta$.

Assumption 10 expresses the assumption given in [5] that expectations do not depend "too much" on the current price system.

We then have the following theorem:

THEOREM 1: *Let $\mathscr{E}$ be an economy satisfying Assumptions 7 through 10; then* $\forall e_{t-1} \in X(\mathscr{E})$, $V(\mathscr{E}; e_{t-1})$ *is non-empty and compact valued*

Next, using the property of dichotomy, we introduce the assumptions:

ASSUMPTION 11 (Desirability assumption again):

$$q \in S \to q^0 \in \bar{S} \backslash S \Rightarrow \sum_{k=2}^{l} Z^k(\mathscr{E}; q, \ldots, q) \to +\infty.$$

ASSUMPTION 12: $\Sigma_i z_{i1}^1(p, p) > 0, \forall p \in P$.

This assumption means we consider only those economies which have the characteristic that, in the long run, there always exist potential lenders; this is the situation of Theorem 2 in [5].

We then have the following theorem:

THEOREM 2: *Let $\mathscr{E}$ be an economy satisfying Assumptions 7, 11, and 12; then* $W(\mathscr{E})$ *is nonempty and compact valued.*

Now, as to cycles, we shall not give any existence theorem. We only present in the Appendix a simple model with two goods and one type of consumer where cycles of length two do occur.

In the following, A and E will denote the subsets of A' and E' such that Assumptions 7 through 12 hold.

B. *Topology on F and E*

To describe further properties of the model we shall introduce on F and E a notion of proximity. We do this by defining a topology τ_1 on F: precisely, τ_1 is obtained from the basis of open neighborhoods $\mathscr{U}(\mathscr{F}, \eta)$ ($\forall \mathscr{F} \in F, \forall \eta > 0$) where:

$$\mathscr{U}(\mathscr{F}, \eta) = \{\mathscr{F}' = (z_{i1}', z_{i2}', \Psi_i, m) \in F \,|\, \|z_{i1}' - z_{i1}\|^1 < \eta,$$
$$\|z_{i2}' - z_{i2}\|^1 < \eta, \|\Psi_i' - \Psi_i\|^1 < \eta, |m' - m| < \eta\}.$$

($\|\cdot\|^1$ stands for the uniform C^1 norm on the appropriate space of functions; see [2] or [4].) We then equip E with the induced topology (but in the following $\mathscr{U}(\mathscr{E}, \eta)$ will still denote a neighborhood of $\mathscr{E}$ in F).

C. Compactness Properties

From our last assumptions we can also get, as in [2 or 4], a supplementary result about the location of the equilibria for neighboring economies. More precisely, we have:

PROPOSITION 1: *For any $\mathscr{E}$ in E and $\eta > 0$, there exists a compact subset $K(\mathscr{E}, \eta)$ in P such that $\forall \mathscr{F} \in \mathscr{U}(\mathscr{E}, \eta)$, $W(\mathscr{F})$ lies in $K(\mathscr{E}, \eta)$.*

No similar result holds for cycles: Assumptions 7 through 12 do not exclude the possibility that there exists an infinite sequence of them, the projections of which on S accumulate to $\bar{S} \setminus S$. It is clear, however, that the compact set of Proposition 1 can always be chosen in such a way that it contains any finite number of given cycles of $\mathscr{E}$.

2. DISCUSSION OF THE DYNAMICS

From the definitions and comments given in the Introduction we see that we have implicitly given ourselves, for each $\mathscr{F} = (\mathscr{B}, m) \in F$, a dynamic process through:

$$(6) \qquad p_t \in V(\mathscr{B}; e_{t-1}), \qquad e_{t-1} \in X(\mathscr{F}).$$

This dynamic process, however, in its general form seems to have very little attraction. It takes place on a set $X(\mathscr{F})$, the structure of which we ignore; it is given in an implicit form and if we now know that the correspondence V is never empty it may very well admit a continuum of elements; last, we have no reasonable economic assumptions to guarantee the existence of backwards solution (i.e., given $p_t, \ldots, p_{t-T}$, the existence of a p_{t-T-1} such that (3) holds); in other words, we do not know if there exists any trajectory at all outside the STE.

A first temptation is then to enforce supplementary restrictions on the space of economies so as to give V and X more precise properties (for instance, reduce V to be single valued and X to be some open set in a subspace of P^{T+1}). Our approach here will be different and probably richer: this section will prove that there exists an open and dense subset $\mathscr{V}$ of E such that, for any $\mathscr{E}$ in $\mathscr{V}$: (i) the phase space $X(\mathscr{E})$ is a C^1 submanifold of codimension 1 of P^{T+1}; and (ii) there exists a subset U in $X(\mathscr{E})$, neighborhood of all STE in $W(\mathscr{E})$ (which are finite in number) and of any finite number of cycles in $\Gamma(\mathscr{E})$, such that on U (6) is equivalent to a diffeomorphism from U in $X(\mathscr{E})$.

For elements $\mathscr{E}$ in $\mathscr{V}$ our dynamics thus takes, at least locally, the standard form of a diffeomorphism acting on a manifold (see [3]).

A. Properties of F, E, Z(·), and M(·)

As in [2 or 4] our results will rely heavily on properties of the sets F and E and of the maps $Z(\cdot)$ and $M(\cdot)$.

First, it is clear that for any $\mathcal{F} \in F$ and $\eta > 0$ the set $U(\mathcal{F}, \eta)$ is a C^1 Banach manifold (Assumptions 2 through 4, the conditions $\Sigma_{k=2}^l \Psi_i^k(\cdot) = 1, \forall i$, and Assumption 6 characterize an affine subspace D' of D; then the facts that the Ψ_i are valued in P and that m is strictly positive are open conditions) and so thus is F itself.

On the other hand, E has the obvious property, as a subset of F, that its closure is equal to the closure of its interior (this is clear from Assumptions 1 and 12 and the fact that Assumptions 7 through 11 are open conditions). This guarantees that the intersection of E with a dense subset of F is dense in F.

Let K now be any compact subset of P with a nonempty interior. We call $F(K)$ the subset of

$$[C^1(K^2, \mathbb{R}^l) \times C^1(K^3, \mathbb{R}^l) \times C^1(K^{T+1}, \mathbb{R}^l)]^l \times \mathbb{R}^+$$

such that Assumptions 2 through 6 hold, $E(K)$ the subset of $F(K)$ such that Assumption 1 and Assumptions 7 through 12 hold. With the topology $\tau_1 F(K)$ is a second countable C^1 Banach manifold (see [4]).

Given any $\mathcal{E}$ and $\eta > 0$, let j then be the map from $\mathcal{U}(\mathcal{E}, n)$ to $F(K)$ defined through the restriction of demands and expectations to prices in K. We have the following proposition:

PROPOSITION 2: *The map j is continuous and open.*

As an important corollary we have the result that $G(K) = j(\mathcal{U}(\mathcal{E}, \eta))$ is a second countable C^1 Banach manifold. We shall note $g, g', \ldots$ the elements of $G(K)$.

We then define ζ as the map from $G(K)$ to $C^1(K^{T+2}, \mathbb{R}^{l-1})$ obtained by restriction of $Z(\cdot)$ and, similarly, μ as the map from $G(K)$ to $C^1(K^{T+1}, \mathbb{R})$ obtained by restriction of $M(\cdot)$. We have:

PROPOSITION 3: $ev\zeta \in C^1(G(K) \times K^{T+2}, \mathbb{R}^{l-1})$; $ev\mu \in C^1(G(K) \times K^{T+1}, \mathbb{R})$ (given $C^1(X, Y)$ the map ev is defined through

$$ev : (f, x) \mapsto f(x) \quad \forall f \in C^1(X, Y) \quad \forall x \in X).$$

We shall now apply the standard theorems of the theory of transversal mappings (see [1, 2, or 4] for definition of transversality ($\pitchfork$) and precise formulation of those theorems).

B. Structure of $X(\mathcal{E})$

One knows that the inverse image $X(\mathcal{E})$ of the point m in $\mathbb{R}^+$ by the map $M(\mathcal{A}; \cdot)$ is a manifold whenever one has $M(\mathcal{A}; \cdot) \pitchfork m$ and then codimension is conserved. Use of any K of the second part of Proposition 3 and of theorems of openness and density of transversal mappings then leads us to the next theorem:

THEOREM 3: *There is an open and dense subset $\mathcal{V}'$ of E such that, for any $\mathcal{E}$ in $\mathcal{V}'$, $X(\mathcal{E})$ is a C^1 submanifold of codimension 1 in P^{T+1}.*

C. Statics and dynamics near STE

We now introduce the "diagonal" map $\zeta^{(1)}$ from $G(K)$ to $C^1(K, \mathbb{R}^{l-1})$ given by:

$$\zeta^{(1)}(g; p) = \zeta(g; p, \ldots, p).$$

From the dichotomy property and choosing $K = K' \times L$, with K' compact in S and L compact in $\mathbb{R}^+$, we know that, in fact, $\zeta^{(1)}(g; \cdot)$ maps K' in $\mathbb{R}^{l-2}$ where $\mathbb{R}^{l-2}$ is for instance the subspace of $\mathbb{R}^{l-1}$ orthogonal to the vector $(1, \ldots, 1)$.

Choosing then for K, the set $K(\mathscr{E}, \eta)$ of Proposition 1 we have the important remark that, given any $\mathscr{F}$ in $\mathscr{U}(\mathscr{E}, \eta)$, the projection on S of the set of STE $W(\mathscr{F})$ is identical to the set of zeros of $\zeta^{(1)}(j(\mathscr{F}); \cdot)$.

The map $\zeta^{(1)}$ is such that:

PROPOSITION 4: $ev\zeta^{(1)} \pitchfork 0$ in $\mathbb{R}^{l-2}$.

And so we are in position to get, by now standard methods, the following theorem:

THEOREM 4: *There is an open and dense subset $\mathscr{V}'_1$ of $\mathscr{V}'$ such that, for any $\mathscr{E}$ in $\mathscr{V}'_1$: (i) $W(\mathscr{E})$ is a finite set, and (ii) locally in $\mathscr{V}'_1$, the elements $\bar{p}$ of $W(\mathscr{E})$ are C^1 functions of $\mathscr{E}$ and are constant in number.*

As usual, we shall call *regular economies* the elements of $\mathscr{V}'_1$.

The idea of what comes next is then the following. Given some regular economy $\mathscr{E}$, it has a finite number of STE; since we are interested only in long run studies we can in a first approach restrict our attention to neighborhoods of these points in $X(\mathscr{E})$ and see whether or not the dynamics given by (6) take a simpler form there. More precisely, as an STE $\bar{p}$ is nothing but a special type of temporary equilibrium; one may hope that (6) can be solved more easily in p_t, given $p_{t-1}, \ldots, p_{t-T-1}$ near $\bar{p}$ and, maybe even, can also be solved in p_{t-T-1} given $p_t, \ldots, p_{t-T}$ near $\bar{p}$, also.

Using the implicit section theorem, the following result could indeed turn out to be true.

PROPOSITION 5: *There exists within the set of regular economies an open and dense subset $\mathscr{V}_1$ such that for any $\mathscr{E}$ in $\mathscr{V}_1$ and for any $\bar{p}$ in $W(\mathscr{E})$: (i) there is around each $\bar{e} = (\bar{p}, \ldots, \bar{p})$ an open neighborhood $U(\bar{e})$ in $X(\mathscr{E})$, such that the closures of all $U(\bar{e})$ are disjoints and such that, with e_{t-1} or e_t in $U(\bar{e})$, the equation $Z(\mathscr{A}; s_t) = 0$ can be solved respectively by*

$$p_t = \pi(\mathscr{E}; e_{t-1}) \quad (\text{with } \pi(\mathscr{E}; \bar{e}) = \bar{p})$$

and by

$$p_{t-T-1} = \pi'(\mathscr{E}; e_t) \quad (\text{with } \pi'(\mathscr{E}; \bar{e}) = \bar{p});$$

(ii) there is an open neighborhood $\mathscr{U}(\mathscr{E})$ of $\mathscr{E}$ in $\mathscr{V}_1$ such that the maps π and π' are both C^1 on $\mathscr{U}(\mathscr{E}) \times U(\bar{e})$.

It is worth noting that proof of Proposition 5 gives in fact a density result within the set of economies with a given monetary stock.

Proposition 5 allows us to define for any $\mathscr{E}$ in $\mathscr{V}_1$ and $\bar{p}$ in $W(\mathscr{E})$ a map $\varphi(\mathscr{E}, \bar{e}; \cdot)$ in $C^1(U(\bar{e}), X(\mathscr{E}))$ through

$$
\begin{aligned}
q_t &= \pi(\mathscr{E}; e_{t-1}), \\
(7) \qquad q_{t-1} &= p_{t-1}, \\
&\ \ \vdots \\
q_{t-T} &= p_{t-T}.
\end{aligned}
$$

We shall write $\varphi(\cdot)$ instead of $\varphi(\mathscr{E}, \bar{e}; \cdot)$ when there is no ambiguity. We then have directly the next theorem:

THEOREM 5: *For any $\mathscr{E}$ in $\mathscr{V}_1$ and $\bar{e}$ in $W(\mathscr{E})$, the map φ is a C^1 diffeomorphism from $U(\bar{e})$ to its image in $X(\mathscr{E})$ with $\bar{e}$ as a fixed point; φ defines the local dynamics of our problem.*

This is clearly the most we can do at this stage. We cannot say, for instance, that φ really defines a $\mathbb{Z}$ action on $U(\bar{e})$; stated otherwise, unless stronger assumptions are made, of stability for instance, the image of some point of $U(\bar{e})$ under repeated actions of φ will generally go outside $U(\bar{e})$ so we cannot define its trajectory too far into the future (or in the past); all we can say is some empirical statement of the form: the nearer we start from $\bar{e}$, the longer we shall stay in $U(\bar{e})$.

Before going to stability problems we, however, devote some interest to cycles also.

D. *Some Results on the Dynamics Near Cycles*

As already stated, we have no existence theorem for cycles, nor can we deduce from Assumptions 7 through 12 that all cycles (if any) lie in some compact set K. So our results here will be somewhat more partial than for STE. Our general line, however, will be quite similar, doing successively for cycles of increasing periods $\tau = 2, 3, \ldots$ what we have done for STE.

To study cycles of some given period τ for economies in some $\mathscr{U}(\mathscr{E}, \eta)$, we introduce a map $\zeta^{(\tau)}$ from $G(K)$ to $C^1(K_\tau, \mathbb{R}^{(l-1)\tau})$—where K is now any compact in P, we can, for instance, choose it large enough so it contains some known cycle Γ, and K_τ is any compact in K^τ such that it cannot contain any STE or cycle of period smaller than τ—through $(\alpha = 1, \ldots, \tau)$:

$$
(8) \qquad \zeta^{(\tau)}(g; p_\alpha) = \begin{cases} \zeta(g; p_\tau, p_{\tau-1}, \ldots) \\ \zeta(g; p_{\tau-1}, p_{\tau-2}, \ldots). \\ \zeta(g; p_1, p_\tau, \ldots) \end{cases}
$$

It is clear that elements Γ in $\Gamma(\mathcal{F})$ with $\mathcal{F} \in \mathcal{U}(\mathscr{E}, \eta)$ and $\Gamma \subset K$ with period τ are in one to one correspondence with the zeros of $\zeta^{(\tau)}(j(\mathcal{F}); \cdot)$.

Similarly to Proposition 4 we then have the following proposition:

PROPOSITION 6: $ev\zeta^{(\tau)} \pitchfork 0$.

Proposition 6 allows us to get results analogous to Theorems 4 and 5 and from it we deduce the next two theorems.

THEOREM 6: *There exists an open and dense subset $\mathscr{V}'_2$ in E such that for any $\mathscr{E}$ in $\mathscr{V}'_2$: (i) cycles any period smaller than some integer n and with prices lying in some fixed compact set are in finite number; (ii) locally in $\mathscr{V}'_2$ these cycles are C^1 functions of $\mathscr{E}$ and are constant in number.*

THEOREM 7: *There exists an open and dense subset $\mathscr{V}_2$ in $\mathscr{V}'_2$ such that for any $\mathscr{E}$ in $\mathscr{V}_2$ and Γ a cycle in $\Gamma(\mathscr{E})$, there exists a neighborhood $U(\Gamma)$ of the cycle in $X(\mathscr{E})$ in which the dynamics of our problem are given by a diffeomorphism $\varphi(\mathscr{E}, \Gamma(\mathscr{E}); \cdot)$ and φ is C^1 in some neighborhood $\mathscr{U}(\mathscr{E}) \times U(\Gamma)$.*

Note that these results in addition to Proposition 1 include Theorems 4 and 5 (an STE is a cycle of length one!).

Now we define $\mathscr{V}$ as $\mathscr{V}_1 \cap \mathscr{V}_2$, $U(\mathscr{E})$ as the union of all $U(\bar{e})$ and $U(\Gamma)$ for $\bar{p}$ in $W(\mathscr{E})$ and Γ in $\Gamma(\mathscr{E})$ in K with period smaller than n, $\varphi(\mathscr{E}; \cdot)$ or $\varphi(\cdot)$) the diffeomorphism obtained by patching together the $\varphi(\mathscr{E}, \bar{e}; \cdot)$ and $\varphi(\mathscr{E}, \Gamma; \cdot)$.

We thus see that we are, in fact, "most often" in good position to study the asymptotics of our model, at least for those states of an economy the limits of which are stationary or cyclical when time goes to infinity.

3. ASYMPTOTIC STABILITY OF STATIONARY TEMPORARY EQUILIBRIA

Given an economy $\mathscr{E}$ in $\mathscr{V}$ we are now in position to investigate a first type of question: in the regions of the phase space where it takes a satisfactory form, what are the asymptotics of our dynamics and, more precisely, when do we have local asymptotic stability?

We shall limit ourselves here to the study of what happens near STE; the difficulty with cycles comes less from a problem of method—a cycle is just a set of fixed points for some iterate map—than from a problem of interpretation of the results we obtain.

A standard sufficient condition of asymptotic stability for some STE $\bar{p} \in W(\mathscr{E})$ is that the Jacobian of $\varphi(\mathscr{E}, \bar{e}; \cdot)$ at point $\bar{e}$ has all its eigenvalues smaller than one. To avoid tedious calculations of derivatives along $X(\mathscr{E})$ we shall consider a map $\hat{\varphi}$ which coincides with φ on $X(\mathscr{E})$ (so the derivatives along $X(\mathscr{E})$ coincide, too) and has a zero derivative along some direction transversal to $X(\mathscr{E})$: thus if the Jacobian of $\hat{\varphi}$ has its eigenvalues smaller than one, so has the Jacobian of φ.

We first introduce the map $\hat{Z}(\mathscr{E}\,;\cdot)$ obtained by substituting $-m$ to

$$\sum_i z_{i2}^1(p_{t-1},\,\Psi_i(e_{t-1}),\,p_t)$$

in $Z(\mathscr{E}\,;\cdot)$; we then solve, in p_t, $\hat{Z}(\mathscr{E}\,;s_t)=0$ (this is possible because we are in $\mathscr{V}$ and the Jacobians of Z with $\hat{Z}$ with respect to p_t coincide); last, we get $\hat{\varphi}$ by substituting into π in (7) the new expression of p_t. It is clear enough that the map $\hat{\varphi}$ has all the announced properties ($\hat{Z}^1$ does not depend any more on p_{t-T-1}!).

Calling $\hat{Z}_u$ the Jacobian of the first $l-1$ components of $\hat{Z}(\mathscr{E}\,;\cdot)$ with respect to $p_u^1,\ldots,p_u^{l-1}$ ($u=t,\ldots,t-T-1$) at point $\bar{p}$ we are then led to the next theorem:

THEOREM 8: *Let $\mathscr{E}$ be an economy in $\mathscr{V}$. A sufficient condition for an STE $\bar{p}$ in $W(\mathscr{E})$ to be locally asymptotically stable for the dynamics generated by (7) is that* $\sum_{u=t-1}^{t-T-1}\|(\hat{Z}_t)^{-1}\hat{Z}_u\| < 1.$

This condition links all the price effects on demand: effects through the expectation processes and effects through the shape of the demand functions. Its detailed form can easily be given but its complexity does not allow very interesting comments.

Now in case one is interested in situations which involve only money and one nonstorable good, interpretation of Theorem 8 becomes easier and we shall devote a few more lines to this.

In such a situation $p_u^2 = 1\forall u$ and need not be mentioned any more; in the following we shall write p_u instead of p_u^1. Thus

$$\hat{Z}(\mathscr{E}\,;s_t)=\sum_i z_{i1}^1(p_t,\,\Psi_i(e_t))-m$$

and $\hat{Z}(\mathscr{E}\,;s_t)=0$ is nothing but the equation for $X(\mathscr{E})$. Then, with straightforward notations,

$$\hat{Z}_t = \sum_i (\partial_1 z_{i1}^1 + \partial_2 z_{i1}^1 \partial_1 \Psi_i),$$

$$\hat{Z}_u = \sum_i (\partial_2 z_{i1}^1 \partial_{t-u+1}\Psi_i) \qquad\qquad (u=t-1,\ldots,t-T),$$

and we have the following Corollary without difficulty.

COROLLARY 1: *In a model with only one nonstorable good and for $\mathscr{E}\in\mathscr{V}$, $\bar{p}\in W(\mathscr{E})$, then: (i) if $\partial_2 z_{i1}^1 \geqslant 0\forall i$ and $\partial_{t-u+1}\Psi_i \geqslant 0,\,\forall i,\forall u=(t-1,\ldots,t-T),\bar{p}$ is locally asymptotically stable; (ii) if $\partial_2 z_{i1}^1$ is small enough, $\forall i$, $\bar{p}$ is locally asymptotically stable; (iii) if $\partial_2 z_{i1}^1 \neq 0,\,\forall i$ and, $\forall i$, $\partial_1\Psi_i$ is sufficiently close from $-\partial_1 z_{i1}^1/\partial_2 z_{i1}^1$, then $\bar{p}$ is not locally asymptotically stable.*

This shows that, under the reasonable assumption $\partial_2 z_{i1}^1 \geqslant 0\forall i$, when the expected price is a positive combination of the previous prices, $\bar{p}$ is a stable STE. However, in the case of extrapolative expectations (i.e., $p_{t+1}^i = p_t + a^i(p_t - p_{t-1})$; $a^i > 0\forall i$), the local dynamics near $\bar{p}$ depend on the shape of the demand functions.

4. LOCAL STRUCTURAL STABILITY

Last, we turn our attention to the question of how the phase portrait (i.e., the set of trajectories) of a given economy, near its stationary equilibria or some set of cycles, depends on small perturbations in the characteristics of the economy. In particular, when does this phase portrait remain qualitatively unchanged?

In the mathematical language of dynamic systems our question more precisely is when do we have a property of "local structural stability?" We recall briefly the definition of structural stability, for a diffeomorphism φ acting on a manifold X (see [3] or [7] for more details): φ is structurally stable if it has a τ_1 neighborhood N such that for any φ' in N there exists an homeomorphism h from X to X with: $\varphi' = h^{-1} \circ \varphi \circ h$ (φ and φ' are then said to be conjugate; it is clear that then they have the same phase portrait up to the deformation generated by h).

Our situation is a little more complicated, though, since to different economies $\mathscr{E}$ we associate diffeomorphisms $\varphi(\mathscr{E})$ acting on different manifolds $X(\mathscr{E})$. However, we only work inside neighborhoods $U(\mathscr{E})$ of $W(\mathscr{E})$ and $\Gamma(\mathscr{E})$ in $X(\mathscr{E})$ and so we have without difficulty the next proposition:

PROPOSITION 7 : *For any $\mathscr{E}$ in $\mathscr{V}$ and $\mathscr{E}'$ in a small neighborhood of $\mathscr{E}$, there exists a diffeomorphism $\Psi_{\mathscr{E}\mathscr{E}'}$, of P^{T+1}, from $U(\mathscr{E})$ onto $U(\mathscr{E}')$, which is near the identity map in P^{T+1}.*[5]

So (see [3] again) we shall say in our model that an economy $\mathscr{E}$ is locally structurally stable near its STE and cycles contained in $U(\mathscr{E})$ if it has a τ_1 neighborhood N in E such that, for any $\mathscr{E}'$ in N, $\varphi(\mathscr{E})$ is conjugate on $U(\mathscr{E})$ to $\Psi_{\mathscr{E}\mathscr{E}'}^{-1} \circ \varphi(\mathscr{E}') \circ \Psi_{\mathscr{E}\mathscr{E}'}$.

Now it has been shown in [3] that the answer to our question depends crucially on two points: (i) the properties of the dynamic model itself, i.e., of the map which associates to any economy a diffeomorphism on the phase space or part of the phase space (for us, the map $\varphi(\mathscr{E} ; \cdot)$ on $U(\mathscr{E})$); and (ii) the properties of the precise diffeomorphism, i.e., of the economy $\mathscr{E}$, we wish to submit to some perturbation.

We shall in fact introduce these points together here. The basic notion we use is that of hyperbolicity: we recall that a periodic point of period τ of a diffeomorphism φ is said to be hyperbolic if the tangent map $T_x\varphi^\tau$ of the τth iteration of φ at x (i.e., in local coordinates, the Jacobian of φ^τ at x) has no eigenvalue of modulus one. One can then show the following proposition:

PROPOSITION 8: *There exists an open and dense subset of economies $\mathscr{U}$ in $\mathscr{V}$ such that $\forall \mathscr{E} \in \mathscr{U}$, STE and cycles of $\mathscr{E}$ with period smaller than any given integer n and prices in a given compact set, are hyperbolic for $\varphi(\mathscr{E})$.*

Now it is well known and rather intuitive that hyperbolic periodic points for a diffeomorphism are locally structurally stable (see, for instance, [7, p. 82]) so, for $\mathscr{E}$ in $\mathscr{U}$, $\varphi(\mathscr{E})$ admits a neighborhood N (in $C^1(U(\mathscr{E}), X(\mathscr{E}))$) of φ' which is conjugate

---

[5] The assertion that the whole of $X(\mathscr{E}')$ is diffeomorphic to $X(\mathscr{E})$ would imply differentiability assumptions of higher order.

to it. On the other hand we have seen, from Proposition 5 and Theorem 7, that $\varphi(\,\cdot\,)$ is continuous in $\mathscr{E}$. The addition of these results[6] leads us to Theorem 9:

THEOREM 9: *The open and dense set $\mathscr{U}$ is such that all its elements are economies which are locally structurally stable around their STE and their cycles of length smaller than n with prices contained in some given compact set.*

From Theorem 9 we then deduce easily the next theorem:

THEOREM 10: *For any economy $\mathscr{E}$ in $\mathscr{U}$, the behavior of the trajectories of the dynamic system generated by our model, near equilibria and a finite number of cycles, is preserved under small modifications in the total monetary stock, demand functions of the agents, and their expectations.*

This last point is, of course, of particular interest; it means that for most economies (and in particular, of course, those for which the condition of Theorem 8 is satisfied for any STE), the dynamics in the long run near limit points such as STE or cycles, are but slightly affected by changes in the agents' forecasts, at least so long as variations of these are not too large.

5. PROOFS

PROOFS OF THEOREMS 1 AND 2: The existence proofs are standard.

In the case of temporary equilibria, Assumptions 7 through 10 together with Assumption 2, imply that, for any fixed set of past price systems, the excess demand of money and nondurable goods points inwards on the boundary of $\bar{P}$

In the case of STE, thanks to the property of dichotomy and Assumption 2 again, the excess demand of nondurable goods satisfies Walras' law and is independent of the price of money. Assumption 11 ensures the existence of an equilibrium on the real markets. Then Assumption 12 guarantees that equation (5) gives a strictly positive price of money. *Q.E.D.*

PROOF OF PROPOSITION 1: Using the property of dichotomy we first have, from Assumption 11 and thanks to compacity of $\bar{S}\setminus S$, that $\forall \mathscr{E}, \forall a > 0, \exists \delta(\mathscr{E}, a) > 0$ such that

$$d(q, \bar{S}\setminus S) < \delta(\mathscr{E}, a) \Rightarrow \sum_{k=2}^{l} Z^k(\mathscr{E}; q, \ldots, q) > (l - 1)a$$

(where $q \in S$ and d is the Euclidian distance). From Assumption 6 this means $\exists k$ (which may depend on q) such that

$$\sum_i z_{i1}^k(q, q) + \sum_i z_{i2}^k(q, q, q) > a.$$

---

[6] Apparently the properties we use are somewhat different from those sought in [3] to define a structurally stable dynamic model. In fact, Proposition 8 defines some sort of local C^1 openness property for φ instead of C^0 openness; but, as we consider only neighborhoods of periodic points, this is sufficient to obtain density results for structurally stable economies.

Given any $\eta > 0$ and choosing $a = 2I\eta$ we thus see from the definition of the topology τ_1 that the prices of nonstorable goods associated with any STE of any $\mathscr{F}$ in $\mathscr{U}(\mathscr{E}, \eta)$ lie in the compact set:

$$K'(\mathscr{E}, \eta) = \{q \in S \mid d(q, \bar{S} \setminus S) \geqslant \delta(\mathscr{E}, 2I\eta)\}.$$

Then, by Assumptions 5 and 12, prices of money associated with vectors of $K'(\mathscr{E}, \eta)$ also lie in a compact subset $L(\mathscr{E}, \eta)$ of $\mathbb{R}^+$.

Proposition 1 is then proven with $K(\mathscr{E}, \eta) = L(\mathscr{E}, \eta) \times K'(\mathscr{E}, \eta)$.   *Q.E.D.*

PROOF OF PROPOSITION 2: Continuity of j is obvious because, as a restriction map, it is contracting.

Let us then consider some $j(\mathscr{F})$, with $\mathscr{F} \in \mathscr{U}(\mathscr{E}, \eta)$, and the ball $B(\eta')$ of center $j(\mathscr{F})$ and radius η' in $F(K)$. By standard extension theorems (see [2 or 4]) for η' small enough, any g in $B(\eta')$ can be extended in an element $\mathscr{F}'$ of F with $\mathscr{F}' \in \mathscr{U}(\mathscr{F}, \eta') \subset \mathscr{U}(\mathscr{F}, \eta)$ which proves openness.   *Q.E.D.*

PROOF OF PROPOSITION 3: Proposition 3 is an immediate consequence of the fact that ζ and μ are compositions of C^1 maps defined on compact subsets of some $\mathbb{R}^n$ (see [1, p. 25]).   *Q.E.D.*

PROOF OF THEOREM 3: The question is for which economies $\mathscr{E} = (\mathscr{A}, m)$ is the map $M(\mathscr{A}; \cdot)$ transversal to m.

First, using Proposition 3 for μ the openness theorem of transversal mappings tells us immediately that, for any K, the set of g in $C(K)$ such that $\mu(g; \cdot) \pitchfork m$ is open.

On the other hand, a similar result for density deserves a little more care. We can use again Proposition 3 for μ; for any K $G(K)$ and K are second countable; in addition, we get easily that $ev\mu \pitchfork m$ (this comes from the linearity dependence of $M(\cdot)$ in z_{11}^1, for instance). But then we still have a problem with dimensions: the density theorem of transversal mappings only works in the C^r sense, with $r > (l-1)(T+1) - 1$. We get τ_1 density, however, thanks to the following facts: (i) K^{T+1}, $\mathbb{R}^+$ and the point m are in fact C^∞ manifolds; (ii) C^1 demands and expectations can be approximated (in the τ_1 sense) by C^r maps; and (iii) the topology τ_1 is coarser than the C^r topology.

From Proposition 2 we thus have that, for any K, there exists an open and dense subset of E such that, on K, $\mu(j(\mathscr{E}); \cdot) = M(\mathscr{E}; \cdot) \pitchfork_K m$, which completes our proof.   *Q.E.D.*

PROOF OF PROPOSITION 4: We shall now write K and K' for $K(\mathscr{E}, \eta)$ and $K'(\mathscr{E}, \eta)$.

Let $g = (z_{i1}, z_{i2}, \Psi_i, m)$ be an element of $G(K)$ (we denote similarly elements in F and their restriction to prices in K). We choose a particular set of tangent vectors at g to $G(K)$, namely those which are defined through $(0, dz_{11}^2, \ldots, dz_{11}^l)$ where $dz_{11}^k \in C^1(K'^2, \mathbb{R}^{l-1})$ and $q \cdot dz_{11}(q, q) = 0 \; \forall q \in K'$. The vector map dz_{11} can be looked at as a small perturbation in the excess demand of nonstorable goods of the young agent of the first type; it defines a new element g' and:

$$\zeta^{(1)}(g';q) - \zeta^{(1)}(g;q) = dz_{11}(q,q), \qquad \forall q.$$

As the right-hand side can be any vector in $\mathbb{R}^{l-2}$ whatever q is, we thus have proved surjectivity of the tangent map of $ev\zeta^{(1)}$.   Q.E.D.

PROOF OF THEOREM 4: Proof of Theorem 4 is in two steps:
First, thanks to the first part of Proposition 3 and to Proposition 4, and thanks to the fact that dim $K' = l - 2$, we can apply to the maps $\zeta^{(1)}(g;\cdot)$, the theorems of openness and density of transversal mappings, and the implicit section theorem (the general argument is given in [2]). One obtains in this way an open-dense subset $\mathcal{V}'_1$ of $G(K)$ such that, for g in $\mathcal{V}'_1$, $\zeta^{(1)}(g;\cdot)$ has a finite number of zeros which are C^1 functions around g and locally constant in number.
    Then, by Proposition 2, $\mathcal{V}'_1$ is sent by j^{-1} in an open dense subset of $\mathcal{U}(\mathcal{E},\eta)$. As this can be done for any $\mathcal{E}$ and η we can build in this way an open dense set which, by intersection with $\mathcal{V}'$, will give rise to the set $\mathcal{V}'_1$. Now the first component of the elements of $W(\mathcal{E})$ is obtained by equation (5) (which tells us we are in $X(\mathcal{E})$) and clearly enjoys thus the same properties as components 2 to l.   Q.E.D.

PROOF OF PROPOSITION 5: This is the hard part of the paper. Intuitively one has to show that there is an open dense set of economies $\mathcal{E}$ such that, *at the same time*, the tangent maps of $Z(\mathcal{E};\cdot)$ along the diagonal P of P^{T+2} and along the first and the last copy of P in P^{T+2}, tangent maps taken at any point $\bar{s} = (\bar{p}, \bar{e})$ with $\bar{p} \in W(\mathcal{E})$, have full rank (respectively, $l - 2$, $l - 1$, and $l - 1$). But this time we cannot just apply transversality theorems; because our maps are now indiced both by $\mathcal{E}$ and prices we cannot prove directly that there exists $(\mathcal{E}, \bar{p}(\mathcal{E}))$ such that our conditions are satisfied. Our way out will be a constructive proof which will proceed in four steps.
    (i) Let us first take an arbitrary $\mathcal{E}$ in $\mathcal{V}'_1$. As $\#W(\mathcal{E})$ is finite, one can easily choose in P^{T+2} open neighborhoods $U'(\bar{s})$ of the $\bar{s}$, contained in a compact set R and with disjoint closures.
    We now consider a definite $\bar{p}$ and look at the two tangent maps of the first $l - 1$ components of $Z(\mathcal{E};\cdot)$ with respect to the first $l - 1$ components of p_t and p_{t-T-1}, respectively. If these tangent maps, taken at point $\bar{s}$, have not full rank $l - 1$ we then modify $\mathcal{E} = (\mathcal{A}, m)$ as follows.
    In $U'(\bar{s})$ we add to z_{11}, z_{12}, and Ψ_1 the quantities:

$$dz^1_{11}(q_1,q_2) = \gamma(\bar{p}^1)^2\left(\frac{1}{q_1^1} - \frac{1}{q_2^1}\right),$$

$$dz^k_{11}(q_1,q_2) = \gamma(q_2^k - q_1^k) \qquad\qquad (k = 2,\ldots,l-1),$$

$$dz^1_{12}(q_1,q_2,q_3) = -dz^1_1(q_1,q_2),$$

$$dz^k_{12}(q_1,q_2,q_3) = \gamma(\bar{p}^k - q_2^k) \qquad\qquad (k = 2,\ldots,l-1),$$

$$d\Psi_1(q_0,\ldots,q_T) = \gamma(q_0 - q_T),$$

where γ is any small positive number; dz'_{11} and dz'_{12} are chosen so that Assumption 2 is satisfied; we leave z_{11}, z_{12}, and Ψ_1 unchanged inside the other $U'(\bar{s})$ and outside the compact R; we then patch together the maps we have thus defined. It is clear enough that, for γ small enough, the triplet $(z'_{i1}, z'_{i2}, \Psi'_1)$ defines some element $\mathcal{B}$ in B and, moreover, by construction, that $Z(\mathcal{B}; \bar{s}) = 0$ for any $\bar{p}$ in $W(\mathcal{E})$ and that $M(\mathcal{B}, \bar{p}) = m$. Let $\mathcal{F}$ be $(\mathcal{B}, m)$.

(ii) We then claim we can choose γ small enough so that:

(a) $\mathcal{F}$ lies in any given neighborhood of $\mathcal{E}$ so $\mathcal{F}$ is regular and, by Theorem 4 and our previous remark, $W(\mathcal{F}) = W(\mathcal{E})$; and (b) the tangent maps we are interested in, with $\mathcal{E}$ replaced by $\mathcal{F}$, have rank $l - 1$. Our first assertion is trivial. Our second one is a consequence of two facts: first, with obvious notations,

$$\frac{D\,dz_{11}}{Dq_1}(\bar{e}) = \frac{D\,dz_{11}}{Dq_2}(\bar{e}) = \frac{D\,dz_{12}}{Dq_2}(\bar{e}) = -\gamma\mathbb{1} \quad \text{and}$$

$$\frac{D\,dz_{12}}{Dq_3}(\bar{e}) = 0; \quad \frac{D\,d\Psi_1}{Dq_0}(\bar{e}) = -\frac{D\,d\Psi_1}{Dq_T}(\bar{e}) = \gamma\mathbb{1};$$

then, T_1 and T_2 being any matrices with det $T_1 = 0$, we have that $T_1 + \gamma T_2 + \gamma^2\mathbb{1}$ has a nonzero determinant for $\gamma > 0$ small enough.[7]

(iii) Let us then look at the subset $\mathcal{V}_1$ of economies in $\mathcal{V}'_1$ for which the tangent maps we look at have rank $l - 1$. From what we have just shown, $\mathcal{V}_1$ is dense in $\mathcal{V}'_1$. On the other hand, $\mathcal{V}_1$ is also open in E: this comes from openness of $\mathcal{V}'_1$, continuity of equilibria (Theorem 4), joint continuity of tangent maps in $\mathcal{E}$ and prices (Proposition 3), and finiteness of the number of equilibria (Theorem 4 again).

(iv) Last, given any $\mathcal{E}$ in $\mathcal{V}_1$ we can now apply the implicit section theorem to solve the first $l - 1$ components of $Z(\mathcal{E}; s_t) = 0$, near $\bar{s}$, as well in p_t as in p_{t-T-1} and we get immediately (i) and (ii) of Proposition 5. $\qquad$ Q.E.D.

PROOF OF THEOREM 5: Theorem 5 is but a simple corollary of Proposition 5. Indeed, it is clear that $\varphi(\mathcal{E}, \bar{e}; \cdot)$ maps $U(\bar{e})$ in $X(\mathcal{E})$ and that the C^1 map defined through

$$p_{t-1} = q_{t-1},$$
$$\cdot \qquad \cdot \qquad \cdot$$
$$p_{t-T} = q_{t-T},$$
$$p_{t-T-1} = \pi'(\mathcal{E}; q_t, q_{t-1}, \dots, q_{t-T}),$$

is a right and left inverse of φ on the suitable domains. $\qquad$ Q.E.D.

---

[7] Indeed, det $(T_1 + \gamma T_2 + \gamma^2\mathbb{1})$ is a polynomial of degree 2 $(l - 1)$ in γ (because det $\mathbb{1} \neq 0$!) which is zero for $\gamma = 0$ and thus nonzero for $\gamma \neq 0$ small enough.

PROOF OF PROPOSITION 6: With similar notations as for Proposition 2 we get

$$\zeta^{(\tau)}(g';p_\alpha) - \zeta^{(\tau)}(g;p_\alpha) = \begin{cases} dz_{11}(p_1, \Psi_1(p_2,p_3,\ldots)) \\ \phantom{dz_{11}} \cdot \qquad \cdot \qquad \cdot \\ \phantom{dz_{11}} \cdot \qquad \cdot \qquad \cdot \\ dz_{11}(p_\tau, \Psi_1(p_1,p_2,\ldots)) \end{cases}$$

where dz_{11} is any map in $C^1(K^2, \mathbb{R}^{l-1})$; as the p_α are all different, the right-hand side can be any vector in $\mathbb{R}^{(l-1)\tau}$ which proves the surjectivity we look for. *Q.E.D.*

PROOFS OF THEOREMS 6 AND 7: These proofs come immediately from generalizations to $\zeta^{(\tau)}$ of the proofs given for $\zeta^{(1)}$ in Theorems 4 and 5; one has only to work in higher dimensions and keep to periods smaller than some n so as to intersect only a finite number of open dense subsets of E which is then still open dense. *Q.E.D.*

PROOF OF THEOREM 8: We shall show that the condition of Theorem 8 implies that the eigenvalues of the Jacobian at point $\bar{e}$ of the map $\hat{\phi}(\mathcal{E}, \bar{e}; \cdot)$ are of modulus strictly smaller than one.

From (7) this Jacobian is a matrix of the form:

$$\hat{J} = \begin{pmatrix} \hat{A}_1 & \hat{A}_2 & \ldots & \hat{A}_T & \hat{A}_{T+1} \\ \mathbb{1} & 0 & \ldots & 0 & 0 \\ - & - & \ldots & - & - \\ 0 & 0 & \ldots & \mathbb{1} & 0 \end{pmatrix}$$

where $\hat{A}_j = -(\hat{Z}_t)^{-1}\hat{Z}_{t-j}$ $(j = 1,\ldots, T+1)$; we shall rewrite $\hat{J} = \hat{A} + B$ with

$$\hat{A} = \begin{pmatrix} \hat{A}_1 & \hat{A}_2 & \ldots & \hat{A}_T & \hat{A}_{T+1} \\ 0 & 0 & \ldots & 0 & 0 \\ - & - & \ldots & - & - \\ 0 & 0 & \ldots & 0 & 0 \end{pmatrix}, \quad B = \begin{pmatrix} 0 & 0 & \ldots & 0 & 0 \\ \mathbb{1} & 0 & \ldots & 0 & 0 \\ - & - & \ldots & - & - \\ 0 & 0 & \ldots & \mathbb{1} & 0 \end{pmatrix}.$$

Now, to say that the eigenvalues of $\hat{J}$ are of modulus smaller than one is equivalent to saying that $\hat{J} - \mu\mathbb{1}$ is invertible for any μ with $|\mu| \geq 1$. But we have ($B - \mu\mathbb{1}$ is clearly invertible for $\mu \neq 0$):

$$\hat{J} - \mu\mathbb{1} = (\mathbb{1} + \hat{A}(B - \mu\mathbb{1})^{-1})(B - \mu\mathbb{1}),$$

so we only need a condition which guarantees that $\mathbb{1} + \hat{A}(B - \mu\mathbb{1})^{-1}$ is itself invertible. Using the identity $\mathbb{1} - \mu^{-1}B = \Sigma_0^\infty \mu^{-j}B^j$ and the fact that B is nilpotent, we then get easily that

$$\hat{A}(B - \mu\mathbb{1})^{-1} = \begin{pmatrix} -\sum\limits_{1}^{T+1} \hat{A}_j\mu^{-j} & -\sum\limits_{2}^{T+1} \hat{A}_j\mu^{-j+1} & \ldots & -\mu^{-1}\hat{A}_{T+1} \\ 0 & 0 & \ldots & 0 \\ \cdot & \cdot & \ldots & \cdot \\ 0 & 0 & \ldots & 0 \end{pmatrix}.$$

Thus, a sufficient condition for stability is:

$$\left\| \sum_{1}^{T+1} \hat{A}_j \mu^{-j} \right\| \leqslant \sum_{1}^{T+1} \|\hat{A}_j\| |\mu^{-j}| \leqslant \sum_{1}^{T+1} \|\hat{A}_j\| < 1$$

which is the condition of Theorem 8.

$Q.E.D.$

PROOF OF COROLLARY 1: For any i we have from Assumption 4:

$$\partial_1 z_{i1}^1 + \partial_2 z_{i1}^1 = -(\bar{p})^{-2} z_{i1}^1(1, 1)$$

and thus from $\hat{Z}(\mathscr{E}; \bar{s}) = 0$,

$$\sum_i (\partial_1 z_{i1}^1 + \partial_2 z_{i1}^1) = -(\bar{p})^{-1} m.$$

On the other hand, we have from Assumption 6,

$$\sum_{u=t}^{t-T} \partial_{t-u+1} \Psi_i = 1.$$

Theorem 8 then gives easily the two results (i) and (ii) of the Corollary.

Now (iii) comes from the fact the sum of the A_i is very large ($\Sigma_{t-1}^{t-T+1} \hat{Z}_u \simeq -(\bar{p})^{-1} m$) and thus so is one at least of the eigenvalues of J. $Q.E.D.$

PROOF OF PROPOSITION 7: $U(\mathscr{E})$ and $U(\mathscr{E}')$ are unions of elementary neighborhoods in $X(\mathscr{E})$ and $X(\mathscr{E}')$ of STE and cycles. Those, from Theorems 4 and 6, are in one to one correspondence if $\mathscr{E}'$ is close enough to $\mathscr{E}$. Now, as $X(\mathscr{E})$ and $X(\mathscr{E}')$ are C^1 submanifolds of P^{T+1} (because $\mathscr{E}$, being in $\mathscr{V}$, is in $\mathscr{V}'$ and $\mathscr{E}'$ is near $\mathscr{E}$) with the same codimension, the elementary neighborhoods are trivially diffeomorphic. The implicit section theorem once more then shows that $\Psi_{\mathscr{E}\mathscr{E}'}$ is near identity.

$Q.E.D.$

PROOF OF PROPOSITION 8: We have here our second difficult demonstration which proceeds in four steps. To simplify its presentation and make its line clearer we shall deal only with STE and suppose that T is equal to one: the extension to the general case is lengthy but straightforward. We shall use the same notations as for the proof of Theorem 8.

(i) The proof that $\mathscr{U}$ is an open set is easy. From Proposition 5 we have that for any $\mathscr{E}$ in $\mathscr{U}$ and $\bar{p} \in W(\mathscr{E})$, $\hat{J}$ is locally continuous around $\mathscr{E}$. On the other hand, the eigenvalues of a matrix are continuous functions of the matrix itself (see, for instance, [6]). Thus, if $\hat{J}$ has no eigenvalue of modulus 1 this will remain true for nearby $\mathscr{E}'$.

(ii) To get density we shall need two intermediary results. We first discuss here some properties of the $\hat{Z}_u$ ($u = t, t - 1, t - 2$). We have already mentioned in Section 3 that $\hat{Z}_{t-2}$ has, from its definition, its first line equal to zero (which means $\hat{J}$ always has an eigenvalue equal to zero). We call this property (P1). Then, from Assumption 4 one sees easily that the sum of the $\hat{Z}_u$ is a matrix the first column of which is a vector x with first component equal to $-m(\bar{p}^1)^{-1}$ and the others equal to zero. We call this second property (P2).

(iii) We now prove some sort of converse result. We assert that there exists an open dense subset of $\mathscr{E}$ in $\mathscr{V}$ such that the following holds: given any set of matrices Y_u neighbors of $\hat{Z}_u$ and satisfying (P1) and (P2), then there exists an $\mathscr{E}'$ near $\mathscr{E}$ such that the Y_u are equal to the associated $\hat{Z}'_u$.

We shall prove this result constructively, by perturbing our given initial $\mathscr{E}$. We first change the $l - 1$ first components of Ψ_1 by

$$d\Psi_1(q_0, q_1) = F(q_0 - q_1)$$

where F is any small $(l - 1) \times (l - 1)$ real matrix (clearly Assumption 6 remains satisfied and $d\Psi_1^l$ can be chosen so Assumption 5 is satisfied, too). Next, we change the $l - 1$ first components of z_{11} and z_{12}, locally around $\bar{p}$, by

$$dz_{11}^1(q_1, q_2) = -dz_{12}^1(q_1, q_2, q_3) = \frac{\bar{p}^1}{q_1^1} \sum_{k=2}^{l-1} \alpha_k (q_2^k - \bar{p}^k), \quad \text{and}$$

$$d\tilde{z}_{11}(q_1, q_2) = 0, \quad d\tilde{z}_{12}(q_1, q_2, q_3) = B(q_1 - \bar{p}) + C(q_3 - \bar{p}),$$

where the α_k are any small real numbers and B and C are any small $(l - 2) \times (l - 1)$ real matrices such that $B + C$ has its first column equal to zero; x being a vector in $\mathbb{R}^l$, $\tilde{x}$ is the vector $(x^2, \ldots, x^{l-1})$ in $\mathbb{R}^{l-2}$ (clearly Assumptions 3 and 4 remain satisfied, $\bar{p}$ is still an STE of the new economy, dz_{11}^l and dz_{12}^l can be chosen so Assumption 2 is satisfied).

We now show we can choose the α_k, B, and C so the new economy $\mathscr{E}'$ is such that the associated $\hat{Z}'_u$ are made equal to the Y_u. First, $Y_{t-2} = \hat{Z}_{t-2}$ allows us to calculate F up to a matrix $F' = (\beta_1 v, \ldots, \beta_{l-1} v)$ where v is a column vector orthogonal to the $(l - 1)$ last lines of $(Dz_{12}/Dq_2)(\bar{e})$ (if $(Dz_{12}/Dq_2)(\bar{e})$ is supposed to be invertible—which, from proof of Proposition 5, is an open dense situation— v is unique) and $\beta_1, \ldots, \beta_{l-1}$ are arbitrary real constants. Then $\Sigma Y_u = \Sigma \hat{Z}'_u$ fixes the α and $B + C$. Last, $Y_{t-1} + Y_{t-2} = \hat{Z}'_{t-1} + \hat{Z}'_{t-2}$ gives B and the β, at least if $(Dz_{11}/Dq_2)(e)$ is invertible, which is again an open dense condition (indeed, then $(D(z_{11} + dz_{11})/Dq_2)(\bar{e})$ will then be invertible, too, if the α are small enough; and the vector v is nonorthogonal to $(Dz_{11}^1/Dq_2)(\bar{e}) = -(Dz_{12}^1/Dq_2)(\bar{e}))$. We thus have our result.

(iv) Last, we start with an economy $\mathscr{E}$ as previously chosen and such that $\hat{J}$ admits one eigenvalue λ_0 of modulus 1. Let us consider for any small γ the matrix $\hat{J}(\gamma)$ obtained from $\hat{J}$ by replacing the $\hat{A}_j$ by $(1 + \gamma)^j \hat{A}_j$ $(j = 1, 2)$. It is first clear enough that $\hat{J}(\gamma)$ has for eigenvalues the eigenvalues of J times $1 + \gamma$: thus, for any γ smaller than some γ_0, $\hat{J}(\gamma)$ has no eigenvalue of modulus 1. But one can find matrices Y_u $(u = t, t - 1, t - 2)$ such that for any α

$$-Y_t^{-1} Y_{t-1} = (1 + \alpha)\hat{A}_1, \quad -Y_t^{-1} Y_{t-2} = (1 + \alpha)^2 \hat{A}_2,$$

and that in addition the Y_u satisfy (P1) and (P2) ((P2) allows us to fix a set of admissible Y_t; because $\mathscr{E}$ is a regular economy, $\hat{Z}_t + \hat{Z}_{t-1} + \hat{Z}_{t-2}$ is invertible and, thus, so is $\hat{Z}_t + (1 + \alpha)\hat{Z}_{t-1} + (1 + \alpha)^2 \hat{Z}_{t-2}$ for α small enough; then Y_{t-2} can be determined, using the arbitrariness of Y_t so (P1) is satisfied; last, Y_{t-1} is then fixed). But from (iii) this means there exists $\mathscr{E}'$ such that $\hat{J}(\gamma)$ is the associated $\hat{J}'$ and thus we have our density result. *Q.E.D.*

Note that here again density holds for any given monetary stock m.

PROOF OF THEOREM 9 : Theorem 9 is an immediate consequence of Proposition 8 —from the theorem of local stability of hyperbolic fixed points ([7]; see also Theorem C in [3]) and of Proposition 7—the Jacobian of any $\Psi_{\mathscr{E}\mathscr{E}'}$ for $\mathscr{E}'$ near $\mathscr{E}$ is near the identity matrix. *Q.E.D.*

PROOF OF THEOREM 10: Theorem 10 just translates in a more economic formulation the statement of Theorem 9. *Q.E.D.*

CONCLUSION

The above analysis of the dynamics of a sequence of temporary equilibria probably exhausts the results that can be obtained from the set of hypotheses we have made (it is very likely that the sufficient conditions for stability we gave in Theorem 8 can be improved, but their nature will not change). The results obtained, especially about local structural stability, are consistent with the required characteristics of a conceptually satisfactory dynamic model.

Besides some natural generalizations of the model already suggested in [5] (in particular, longer time of life of the agents...) two directions seem to open for further research in the field : (i) The first one is to give to the dynamic model some more realistic economic features, for instance by introducing several financial assets ; (ii) the second one is to search for reasonable conditions, on the characteristics of our economies on one hand, on the rules of time evolution on the other hand, so that some global analysis of the dynamics can be undertaken (if possible, something less drastic than the requirement for the temporary equilibrium correspondence to be single valued !).

One could then hope to obtain a satisfactory modelization of the role of expectations of the agents in the evolution of economic systems.

Laboratoire d'Econometrie de l'Ecole Polytechnique
and
Ecole Nationale de la Statistique et de l'Administration Economique

Manuscript received February, 1975 ; revision received January, 1976.

APPENDIX

We give here an example of economies with money, one nonstorable good, and one type of consumer (so at each time only two consumers are trading) with an infinite number of cycles.

According to notation already used in Section 3, as $p_u^2 = 1$, we write p_u instead of p_u^1. We shall only define demands and expectations for prices in a compact subset K of $\mathbb{R}^+$, to avoid all boundary

G. FUCHS AND G. LAROQUE

problems. Then an economy $\mathscr{E}$ is given through

(i) $z_1^1(p_t, p_{t+1}^e) = (p_t p_{t+1}^e)^{-\frac{1}{2}}$; $\quad z_2^1(p_{t-1}, p_t^e, p_t) = -(p_{t-1}p_t^e)^{-\frac{1}{2}}$;

$z_1^2(p_t, p_{t+1}^e) = -(p_t/p_{t+1}^e)^{\frac{1}{2}}$; $\quad z_2^2(p_{t-1}, p_t^e, p_t) = p_t(p_{t-1}p_t^e)^{-\frac{1}{2}}$ (the index e stands for "expected");

(ii) ψ any function in $C^1(K^{T+1}, K)(T \geqslant 2)$ such that

$\psi(q_1, q_2, q_1, \ldots) = q_2$, $\quad \psi(q_2, q_1, q_2, \ldots) = q_1$, $\quad \forall (q_1, q_2) \in K^2$ (agents have memory of

elementary sequences);

(iii) m any positive number with m^{-1} in the interior of K.

Clearly then, all assumptions which are not related to the boundary of $\mathbb{R}^+$ are satisfied. The elements of $V(\mathscr{E}; e_{t-1})$ are the solutions of

$m^2 p_t \psi(e_t) = 1$.

One becomes easily convinced that the positive number $\bar{p} = m^{-1}$ belongs to $W(\mathscr{E})$ and that the pairs

$\bar{q}_1 = \alpha m^{-1}$ and $\bar{q}_2 = \alpha^{-1} m^{-1}$

define cycles of length two for any $\alpha > 0, \alpha \neq 1$.

REFERENCES

[1] ABRAHAM, R., AND J. ROBBIN: *Transversal Mappings and Flows*. Reading, Mass.: Benjamin, 1967.
[2] FUCHS, G.: "Private Ownership Economies With a Finite Number of Equilibria," *Journal of Mathematical Economics*, 1 (1974), 141–158.
[3] ——: "Structural Stability for Dynamical Economic Models," *Journal of Mathematical Economics*, 2 (1975), 139–154.
[4] FUCHS, G., AND G. LAROQUE: "Continuity of Equilibria for Economies With Vanishing External Effects," *Journal of Economic Theory*, 9 (1974), 1–22.
[5] GRANDMONT, J. M., AND G. LAROQUE: "Money in the Pure Consumption Loan Model," *Journal of Economic Theory*, 6 (1973), 382–395.
[6] KATO, T.: *Perturabtion Theory for Linear Operators*. New York: Springer-Verlag, 1966.
[7] NITECKI, Z.: *Differentiable Dynamics*. Cambridge, Mass.: MIT Press, 1971.
[8] SAMUELSON, P. A.: "An Exact Consumption-Loan Model of Interest With or Without the Social Contrivance of Money," *Journal of Political Economy*, 66 (1958), 467–482.

Stability in a Simple
Pure Consumption Loan Model*

GEORG TILLMANN

*Department of Economics, University of Bonn,
53 Bonn, West Germany*

Received August 17, 1981

We consider a simple overlapping generation model with outside money and one consumption good. A class of price expectation functions is characterized such that the Stationary Market Equilibrium is globally stable. *Journal of Economic Literature* Classification Numbers: 021, 022.

I. INTRODUCTION

It is often assumed in standard models of general equilibrium that there exists a complete set of spot and forward markets and all contracts can be made at the beginning of the first period. In such a world there is no room for money. On the other hand, if one takes into account—as in Samuelson's [6] "pure consumption loan model"—that at any point of time there are newborn agents it is clear that sequential trading must occur. In these models the existence of money can be justified and the introduction seems desirable, as a resulting stationary market equilibrium is Pareto-efficient in many cases.

However, for this conclusion to be valid we have to show that traders are willing to hold money both in the short run and in the long run; in other words, we have to show existence of a short run equilibrium and a long-run equilibrium. Additionally, we have to show as Grandmont and Laroque [4, p. 383] formulate: "Moreover, one must prove that the system is stable, i.e., starting from any initial conditions, say, at time 0, the sequence of short run equilibria must converge to a stationary market equilibrium as time tends to infinity. Otherwise, the optimality of a stationary market equilibrium would be an irrelevant result."

Now, Fuchs and Laroque [2] consider the dynamics of Temporary

* I would like to thank Jean-Michel Grandmont and John Weymark for helpful comments. This article was written while I was visiting CORE, Belgium. Financial support from this institution is gratefully acknowledged.

Equilibria (TE), but from a differential-topological point of view. As a special case they have the "one good economy," too. However, to ensure existence of TE they need a tightness condition as in [4]; they start directly with demand functions and for getting positive results they have to exclude a big class of utility functions. Finally, they consider asymptotic stability only. We want to show now in a simple model—which is similar to Samuelson's [6]—with one consumption good only and money, that the unique stationary equilibrium is globally stable if we restrict the expectations in the following way: they must not be too elastic, and they must give present prices more weight than past prices. Especially, we will consider expectations which are linear combinations of present and past prices. In the first section we define the model and formulate our results; the proofs are gathered in Section II.

II. THE MODEL

We study a model similar to Samuelson's [6] "pure consumption loan model" (compare Grandmont and Laroque [4]). There are n "types" of traders who live two periods. The total population is constant. Therefore, at each date t, there are $2n$ individuals. Each of them is indicated by an index i, $i \in I$, $|I| = n$, and an index $h = 1, 2$. If $h = 1$ ($h = 2$) we shall say that the consumer is young (old). There is only one non-storable consumption good c. At the beginning of each period every agent has an endowment of this good. Of course, it depends on the type i and on the age h: it is described by $w^i = (w^{i1}, 0)$. Therefore we assume that old agents have a zero-endowment. They need money if they want to consume positive amounts of the consumption good. Money is the only store of value. The total stock $M > 0$ of money is constant over time. The only way for the young agents to get money is to trade with the old ones. (There is no bequest.)

At each date t there are only markets for current consumption and money. The prices are p_t and 1. Preferences of agent i are represented by a utility function $u^i(c_1^i, c_2^i)$. Here c_1^i, c_2^i denote consumption of today and tomorrow. We assume:

(A1) For all i, u^i is twice differentiable on $\mathbb{R}_{++}^2$, strictly concave, strictly monotone, and $u_{12}^i \geqslant 0$.

At date t, the young agent i must forecast the price that will prevail in $t + 1$. This forecast depends on past prices and the current one, p_t. For simplicity we assume that only the price p_{t-1} is taken into account.

Therefore the price expectation is a function f^i,

$$f^i: \mathbb{R}^2_{++} \to \mathbb{R}_{++}$$
$$(p_{t-1}, p_t) \to f(p_{t-1}, p_t),$$

which is independent of time t.
We assume:

(A2)　For all i:

(a) $f^i: \mathbb{R}^2_{++} \to \mathbb{R}_{++}$ is continuously differentiable;
(b) $f^i(p, p) = p$ 　　for all $p \in \mathbb{R}_{++}$.

It is now possible to make precise the traders' behavior. (In the following we omit the index i.)

Assume $(p_{t-1}, p_t) \in \mathbb{R}^2_{++}$ are given. The young consumer has to choose an action (c_1, m_1) which specifies his consumption in the current period and the money balances he wishes to hold. This choice is made as follows: If $f(p_{t-1}, p_t)$ is the price expectation, the agent maximizes his utility, that is:

$$\max_{(c_t, c_{t+1})} u(c_t, c_{t+1}) \text{ s.t. } (c_t, c_{t+1}) \geqslant 0 \qquad m_t \geqslant 0,$$
$$p_t c_t + m_t \leqslant p_t w,$$
$$f(p_{t-1}, p_t) c_{t+1} \leqslant m_t.$$

This defines the young traders' demand correspondence ξ,

$$\xi: \mathbb{R}^2_{++} \to \mathbb{R}^2_+$$
$$(p_{t-1}, p_t) \to \xi(p_{t-1}, p_t) = (c_t, m_t).$$

Let us now consider the old agent. He took an action (c_{t-1}, m_{t-1}) when he was young. His problem is to maximize:

$$\max_c u(c_{t-1}, c) \text{ s.t. } p_t c \leqslant m_{t-1}, c \geqslant 0.$$

This defines a demand correspondence $\psi(c_{t-1}, m_{t-1}, p_t)$, $\psi: \mathbb{R}^2_+ \times \mathbb{R}_{++} \to \mathbb{R}_+$.

DEFINITIONS.　A consumer i, defined by (u^i, f^i, w^i), is called C1, if (A1), (A2) and $w^{i1} > 0$ are satisfied. A C1 agent is called C2 if additionally

$$u_1(0, x) = \infty = u_2(y, 0), \qquad x, y \in \mathbb{R}_{++}.$$

An economy $(I, (u^i), (f^i), (w^i), M)$ is called C1 if it is composed of n C1 traders and $M > 0$.

Consider the C1 economy E. By definition an allocation (a_{ih}) is defined by $2n$ actions a_{ih} with $a_{i1} = (c_1^i, m_1^i)$, $a_{i2} = (c_2^i, 0)$ such that $\sum_{i \in I} (a_{i1} + a_{i2}) = (\sum_{i \in I} w^{i1}, M)$.

Let the past price p_{t-1}^* and the allocation $(a_{ih}^*(t-1))$ be given.

DEFINITIONS. $(p_t^*, a_{ih}^*(t))$ defines a Temporary Equilibrium (TE) at time t, if $(a_{ih}^*(t))$ is an allocation with $a_{i1}^*(t) \in \xi^i(p_{t-1}^*, p_t^*)$ and $a_{i2}^*(t) \in \psi^i(a_{i1}^*(t-1), p_t^*)$.

Let $W(p_{t-1}^*, a_{ih}^*(t-1))$ be the set of such temporary equilibria.

A Stationary Market Equilibrium (SME) is defined by a price p^* and an allocation (a_{ih}^*) such that $(p^*, (a_{ih}^*)) \in W(p^*, (a_{ih}^*))$. We denote the set of all SME with $W(E)$.

By definition an allocation of consumption goods (c_{ih}) is $2n$ consumption bundles $c_{ih} \in \mathbb{R}_+$ $(1 \leqslant i \leqslant n, h = 1, 2)$ such that $\sum_{i,h} c_{ih} = \sum_i w^{i1}$. We shall say that such an allocation (c_{ih}) is Pareto-efficient if there exists no other allocation (d_{ih}) such that $(d_{i1}, d_{i2}) \succsim_i (c_{i1}, c_{i2})$ for all i, and $(d_{i1}, d_{i2}) \succ_i (c_{i1}, c_{i2})$ for some i.

In the following we want to show that the institution of financial inter-mediation is consistent with the workings of decentralized markets; that is, there exist a unique short run and a unique long run equilibrium and the latter is globally stable.

Here we mean that the sequence of temporary equilibrium prices (p_t^*) converges to the stationary equilibrium price p^*. It is clear that, in general, the price p_t^* depends on p_{t-1}^* and (m_{t-1}^{*i}), the wealth distribution of the old agents. However, as there is only one consumption good this distribution is inessential for p_t^*. For every distribution aggregate demand of the old agents is M/p_t^*. Therefore in this case "dynamics is driven" only by "expectation formation" of the young consumers. But it is clear, of course, that $m^i(p_{t-1}^*, p_t^*) \to m^i(p^*, p^*)$ as $p_{t-1}^* \to p^*$, $p_t^* \to p^*$ and m^i is continuous in its arguments. However, it is possible that we begin the process with the stationary money distribution but that $p_1^* \neq p^*$ because expectations are "wrong." If time goes to infinity we come back to this stationary state.

In the n-commodity case independence of money distribution can be preserved under some restrictions: All consumers must have identical utility functions which are additive relative to the two periods, and demand for each good must be a linear function in wealth. (It is clear, of course, that this condition is only sufficient but not necessary.)

Before presenting our results we define finally:

DEFINITION. A utility function $u: \mathbb{R} \to \mathbb{R}$ has constant relative risk aversion, if

$$r := -\frac{yu''(y)}{u'(y)} \quad \text{is constant.}$$

As Pratt [5] has shown these are the functions $u_\gamma(y) = (1/\gamma)y^\gamma$, $\gamma \in (-\infty, 1)$.

PROPOSITION 1. *All agents are* C1 *and there exists at least one consumer* i_0 *who is* C2 *and fulfills*

$$\lim_{p_t \to \infty} \frac{f^{i_0}(p_{t-1}, p_t)}{p_t} = A^{i_0} < \infty,$$

$$\lim_{p_t \to \infty} f^{i_0}(p_{t-1}, p_t) > 0.$$

Then a temporary equilibrium exists. The equilibrium is unique if all agents are C2 *and the expectations fulfill*

$$0 \leqslant \frac{\partial f^i}{\partial p_t} \frac{p_t}{f^i} \leqslant 1 \qquad \forall i.$$

PROPOSITION 2. *All agents are* C1 *and at least one agent is* C2. *Then a unique stationary market equilibrium* (SME) *exists. Additionally, the* SME *is Pareto-efficient.*

PROPOSITION 3. (a) *All agents are* C2 *and their expectations fulfill*

(1) $$0 \leqslant \frac{\partial f^i}{\partial p_t} \frac{p_t}{f^i} \leqslant 1,$$

(2) (i) $$0 \leqslant \frac{\partial f^i}{\partial p_{t-1}},$$ (ii) $$\frac{\partial f^i}{\partial p_{t-1}} \leqslant \frac{\partial f^i}{\partial p_t} \qquad \forall i.$$

Then the SME *is globally stable. If all agents have additive utility functions with constant relative risk aversion* r, $r \leqslant 1$, (2ii) *can be dropped.*

(b) *Every agent is* C2.

All agents are identical with utility function $U(c_1, c_2) = u(c_1) + \alpha u(c_2)$, $\alpha > 0$, *u has constant relative risk aversion* r. *If* p *is the price in the* SME *define* β *by*

$$\beta := \frac{r}{r-1}(1 + \alpha^{1/r}) \qquad \text{and} \qquad f_1 := \frac{\partial f}{\partial p_{t-1}}(p, p).$$

If $f_1 \neq \beta$ *for every* $p_{t-1} \in U(p)$, $U(p)$ *a suitable neighborhood of* p, *there exists exactly one* TE p_t *and* $p_t = W(p_{t-1})$ *is differentiable.* p *is locally asymptotically stable (unstable) if*

$$r < 1 \quad \text{and} \quad \beta/2 < f_1 \quad (\beta/2 \geqslant f_1),$$

$$r > 1 \quad \text{and} \quad f_1 < \beta/2 \quad (\beta/2 \leqslant f_1).$$

Remarks. (1) It is clear, of course, that the SME is invariant if the f^i are modified, but (A2b) is not changed.

(2) $(\partial f/\partial p)(p/f) \leqslant 1$ implies $\lim_{p \to \infty}(f/p) < \infty$.

(3) Proposition 3 shows that the sequence of temporary equilibria converges to the SME if the price expectations are not too elastic (the elasticity is bounded by one) and if the expectation functions do not give p_{t-1} more weight than p_t. Loosely speaking, expectations must depend on present price for the most part.

A class of functions which fulfill this condition is

$$\{f \mid f(p_{t-1}, p_t) = (1 - a) p_{t-1} + a p_t, \tfrac{1}{2} \leqslant a < 1\}.$$

In the following we consider some examples: Assume all consumers are identical $(n = 1)$ with utility function $u(c_1, c_2) = \sqrt{c_1} + \sqrt{c_2}$. The SME is (p^*, c_1^*, c_2^*), $c_1^* = w/2 = c_2^*$, $p^* = 2M/w$. If $f(p_{t-1}, p_t) = (1 - a) p_{t-1} + a p_t$, $a \in (0, 1)$, we get (here p_{t-1}^*, p_t^* are the equilibrium prices in period $t - 1, t$):

EXAMPLE I.

$$p_t^* = \frac{p^*(1 + a)}{4} + \sqrt{\left(\frac{p^*(1 + a)}{4}\right)^2 + \frac{p^*}{2}(1 - a) p_{t-1}^*}.$$

EXAMPLE II. We get for $f(p_{t-1}, p_t) = p_t^2/p_{t-1}$:

$$p_t^* = \frac{p^* p_{t-1}^*}{2p_{t-1}^* - p^*}.$$

This expectation is interesting because we can get it if the consumer expects a constant inflation rate: $p_{t-1}/p_t = p_t/p_{t+1}$. Additionally consider $f(p_{t-1}, p_t) = p_t^3/p_{t-1}^2$.

EXAMPLE III. Here

$$p_{t_{1,2}}^* = \frac{p_{t-1}^{*2}}{p^*} \pm \sqrt{\left(\frac{p_{t-1}^{*2}}{p^*}\right)^2 - p_{t-1}^{*2}}.$$

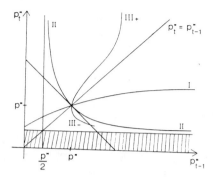

FIG. 1. Several equilibrium-price correspondences $W(p_{t-1})$.

If the expectation is linear we have stability, but not in the second case (the condition of Proposition 1 is not fulfilled; therefore an equilibrium does not exist for every p^*_{t-1}. Additionally, (2) of Proposition 3 is violated).

The behaviour is cyclical: Fix p^*_{t-1}. Then $p^*_{t+i} = p^*_{t-1}$, $p^*_{t+j} = p^*_t$; $i = 2m + 1, j = 2m, m \in N$.

In Example III, we see that an equilibrium does not always exist. But if $p^*_{t-1} > p^*$ there are two equilibria. It is interesting to see that the sequence (p^*_t) diverges $(p^*_t \to_{t \to \infty} \infty)$ if we use the "positive root III$_+$," but that in period $t + 1$ no equilibrium exists if we use "the negative root III$_-$" in period t.

If all consumers have an additive log-utility function we have adjustment in only one step.

The following example shows that assumption (2ii) (Proposition 3) is really necessary, even in the case of constant risk aversion utility functions.

Consider the case $f(p_{t-1}, p_t) = p_{t-1}$ and $u(c_1, c_2) = -c_1^{-n} - ac_2^{-n}$, $n > 0$, $a > 0$. A simple computation yields

$$\frac{dp^*_t}{dp^*_{t-1}}\bigg|_{p^*_{t-1}=p^*} = -\frac{n}{1 + (n + 1)\, a^{1/(n+1)}}.$$

Therefore,

$$\frac{dp^*_t}{dp^*_{t-1}}\bigg|_{p^*} < -1 \quad \text{if} \quad a < \left(\frac{n-1}{n+1}\right)^{n+1},$$

and

$$\frac{dp^*_t}{dp^*_{t-1}}\bigg|_{p^*} \xrightarrow{a \to 0} -n.$$

277

GEORG TILLMAN

In the SME-price p^* the derivative of the function can be made as big as you want, if a is sufficiently small.

III. PROOFS

We have to show:

LEMMA 1. *If trader i is C1, ξ^i and ψ^i are continuous functions of their arguments for every $(p_{t-1}, p_t) \in \mathbb{R}^2_{++}$, $(c^i_{t-1}, m^i_{t-1}) \in \mathbb{R}^2_+$. Additionally $\psi^i(c^i_{t-1}, m^i_{t-1}, p_t) = m^i_{t-1}/p_t$. (ξ^i, ψ^i) are differentiable if i is C2.*

Proof. The proof that (ξ, ψ) are continuous is standard. You can see at once that ψ^i is differentiable. The implicit Function Theorem ensures that ξ^i is differentiable (use that i is C2 and apply the Kuhn–Tucker method). We have (omit the i)

$$\frac{f(p_{t-1}, p_t)}{p_t} u_1\left(c_1, \frac{m_1}{f(p_{t-1}, p_t)}\right) = u_2\left(c_1, \frac{m_1}{f(p_{t-1}, p_t)}\right). \tag{1}$$

Proof of Proposition 1. To apply the usual fixed-point argument (see [3]), we have to show:

LEMMA 2. *Consider any sequence $(p^n_t)_{n \in N}$ such that either $p^n_t \to 0$ or $p^n_t \to \infty$. Then*

$$\left\| \sum_{i \in I} (\xi^i(p_{t-1}, p^n_t) + \psi^i(m^i_{t-1}, p^n_t)) \right\| \to \infty.$$

Proof. (In the following we again omit the index i_0.) Consider $p^n_t \to \infty$ and assume m^n_1 remains bounded, $m^n_1 \to M_1 < \infty$. It follows that $c^n_1 \to w$ and $c^n_2 \to c^0_2 < \infty$ as $\lim_{p_t \to \infty} f > 0$. Define

$$\tilde{c}^n_1 := c^n_1 - \frac{1}{p^n_t}, \qquad \tilde{m}^n_1 := m^n_1 + 1, \qquad \tilde{c}^n_2 := c^n_2 + \frac{1}{f(p_{t-1}, p^n_t)}.$$

For n big enough $\tilde{c}^n_1 > 0$ and $(\tilde{c}^n_1, \tilde{c}^n_2)$ is a feasible consumption plan. Now we distinguish two cases:

(1) $\lim_{p^n_t \to \infty} f(p_{t-1}, p^n_t) =: K < \infty$. We have $u(\tilde{c}^n_1, \tilde{c}^n_2) \leq u(c^n_1, c^n_2)$ and in the limit we get

$$u\left(w, c^0_2 + \frac{1}{K}\right) \leq u(w, c^0_2).$$

278

(2) $\lim_{p_t^n \to \infty} f(p_{t-1}, p_t^n) = \infty$. We have with

$$\psi_n \in \left[c_2^n, \frac{1}{f(p_{t-1}, p_t^n)} + c_2^n \right] \quad \text{and} \quad \theta_n \in \left[c_1^n - \frac{1}{p_t^n}, c_1^n \right]:$$

$$0 \geqslant u(\tilde{c}_1^n, \tilde{c}_2^n) - u(c_1^n, c_2^n)$$

$$= \frac{1}{f(p_{t-1}, p_t^n)} \left[u_2(c_1^n, \psi_n) - \frac{f(p_{t-1}, p_t^n)}{p_t^n} u_1(\theta_n, \tilde{c}_2^n) \right].$$

But $\psi_n \to_{n \to \infty} c_2^0$, $c_2^0 = 0$; therefore $u_2(c_1^n, \psi_n) \to u_2(w, 0) = \infty$,

$$\frac{f(p_{t-1}, p_t^n)}{p_t^n} u_1(\theta_n, \tilde{c}_2^n) \to A \cdot u_1(w, 0) < \infty.$$

For n big enough the difference is positive.

Consider now the case $p_t^n \to 0$. There exists at least one old agent j with $m_{t-1}^j > 0$. Because of $c_2^j = m_{t-1}^j / p_t$, $\lim_n c_2^j(p_t^n) = \infty$. Therefore there exists a TE. Define:

$$F(p_{t-1}, p_t, m_t) := f(p_{t-1}, p_t) u_1 \left(w - \frac{m_t}{p_t}, \frac{m_t}{f(p_{t-1}, p_t)} \right)$$

$$- p_t u_2 \left(w - \frac{m_t}{p_t}, \frac{m_t}{f(p_{t-1}, p_t)} \right) = 0. \tag{2}$$

(This is Eq. (1), rewritten.)

Using the Implicit Function Theorem, we compute

$$\frac{\partial m_t}{\partial p_t} = - \frac{\left(\dfrac{\partial f}{\partial p_t} u_1 - u_2 \right) + \dfrac{f m_t}{p_t^2} u_{11} - \dfrac{\partial f}{\partial p_t} \dfrac{m_t}{f} u_{12} - u_{12} \dfrac{m_t}{p_t} + \dfrac{\partial f}{\partial p_t} \dfrac{m_t p_t}{f^2} u_{22}}{- \dfrac{f}{p_t} u_{11} + 2 u_{12} - \dfrac{p_t}{f} u_{22}}.$$

Because of (1),

$$\frac{df}{\partial p_t} u_1 - u_2 = \left(\frac{\partial f}{\partial p_t} \frac{p_t}{f} - 1 \right) u_2.$$

Therefore

$$\frac{\partial m_t}{\partial p_t} > 0 \quad \text{if} \quad 0 \leqslant \frac{\partial f}{\partial p_t} \frac{p_t}{f} \leqslant 1. \tag{$*$}$$

If all agents are C2 and fulfill (∗), $\sum_{i \in I} m_1^i \neq M$ for $p \neq p_t^*$. The equilibrium is unique.

Proof of Proposition 2. Consider the C2 agent. He faces the problem $\max_{c_1, c_2} u(c_1, c_2)$ s.t. $pc_1 + pc_2 = pw$. Therefore in optimum $u_1(c_1, c_2) = u_2(c_1, c_2)$. There exists exactly one $(c_1^*, c_2^*) \gg 0$ which solves the equation. (If the agent is C1 his demand is unique, too, but not necessarily strictly positive.) As $p > 0$, $m_1 := pc_2^* > 0$. Because of the simple budget equation we always have that the markets are cleared, that is, $\sum_{i \in I} (c_1^i + c_2^i) - \sum_{i \in I} w_i = 0$. Consider now $\sum_{i=1}^{n} m_1^i$ for $\bar{p}$ fixed. This sum is positive and may be equal to δ. Then choose $p^* = (M/\delta) \bar{p}$, $m_1^{*i} = (M/\delta) m_1^i$. $(p^*, (c_1^{*i}), (m_1^{*i}))$ is a unique SME. Pareto efficiency follows at once (see [4]).

Proof of Proposition 3. (We omit the stars in the following.) We have shown in Proposition 2 that only one SME exists. Therefore the diagonal and $p_t = W(p_{t-1})$ only cut or touch in p. We want to show that $W(p_{t-1})$ is differentiable and crosses the line $p_t = 2p - p_{t-1}$ only in p, too, and does not touch in any other point and that

$$\left. \frac{dp_t}{dp_{t-1}} \right|_p \in (-1, 1).$$

Therefore $W(p_{t-1})$ must be in the interior of $A \cup B$. That is sufficient for global stability because it implies: $|p_t - p| < |p_{t-1} - p| \ \forall t, \ p_0 \neq p$.

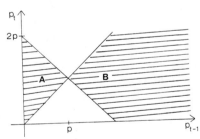

FIG. 2. Admissible for $W(p_{t-1})$ is the shaded area.

We have shown in Proposition 1 that $W(p_{t-1})$ is a function on $\mathbb{R}_+$. Using the Implicit Function Theorem we shall show that it is even differentiable (therefore continuous). In equilibrium the following equations are fulfilled, as all agents are C2:

$$F_1(p_{t-1}, p_t, m_t^1) = f^1(p_{t-1}, p_t) u_1^1 \left(w^1 - \frac{m_t^1}{p_t}, \frac{m_t^1}{f^1(p_{t-1}, p_t)} \right)$$

$$- p_t u_2^1 \left(w^1 - \frac{m_t^1}{p_t}, \frac{m_t^1}{f^1(p_{t-1}, p_t)} \right) = 0,$$

$$F_n(p_{t-1}, p_t, m_t^n) = f^n(p_{t-1}, p_t) u_1^n \left(w^n - \frac{m_t^n}{p_t}, \frac{m_t^n}{f^n(p_{t-1}, p_t)} \right)$$

$$- p_t u_2^n \left(w^n - \frac{m_t^n}{p_t}, \frac{m_t^n}{f^n(p_{t-1}, p_t)} \right) = 0.$$

$$F_{n+1}(m_t^1, m_t^2, \ldots, m_t^n) = \sum_{i=1}^{n} m_t^i - M = 0.$$

To shorten the notation we define

$$\alpha_i := u_1^i - f^i u_{12}^i \frac{m_t^i}{f^{i2}} + u_{22}^i p_t \frac{m_t^i}{f^{i2}},$$

$$\beta_i := -u_2^i + f^i u_{11}^i \frac{m_t^i}{p_t^2} - p_t u_{12}^i \frac{m_t^i}{p_t^2} < 0.$$

We get

$$\frac{\partial F_i}{\partial p_{t-1}} = \frac{\partial f^i}{\partial p_{t-1}} \alpha_i =: a_i,$$

$$\frac{\partial F_i}{\partial p_t} = \frac{\partial f^i}{\partial p_t} \alpha_i + \beta_i =: b_i,$$

$$\frac{\partial F_i}{\partial m_t^i} = -\frac{f^i}{p_t} u_{11}^i + \frac{f^i u_{12}^i}{f^i} + \frac{p_t u_{12}^i}{p_t} - \frac{p_t u_{22}^i}{f^i} =: c_i.$$

We see that $c_i > 0$, $b_i < 0$ (because of assumption (1), b_i is exactly the numerator of $\partial m_t / \partial p_t$ computed in the proof of Proposition 1), the sign of a_i may change.

Now we get the following system:

$$\begin{bmatrix} b_1 & c_1 & & & & \\ b_2 & 0 & c_2 & & \bigcirc & \\ b_3 & 0 & 0 & c_3 & & \\ \vdots & & & & \diagdown & \\ b_n & & \bigcirc & & & c_n \\ 0 & 1 & 1 & 1 & \cdots & 1 \end{bmatrix} \begin{bmatrix} dp_t \\ dm_t^1 \\ dm_t^2 \\ \vdots \\ \\ dm_t^n \end{bmatrix} = - \begin{bmatrix} a_1 \\ a_2 \\ a_3 \\ \vdots \\ a_n \\ 0 \end{bmatrix} dp_{t-1}$$

$\Leftrightarrow: A_n x = -b.$

Using induction over n, one easily shows

$$\det A_1 = b_1 < 0$$

and if $n \geqslant 2$,

$$\det A_n = (-1)^{n+1} \sum_{\substack{i=1}}^{n} b_i \prod_{\substack{j=1 \\ j \neq i}}^{n} c_j > 0, \qquad n = 2K,$$

$$< 0, \qquad n = 2K + 1, K \in \mathbb{N}.$$

A_n is non-singular for every n, $n \in \mathbb{N}$.

With Cramer's rule,

$$\frac{dp_t}{dp_{t-1}} = \frac{(-1)^n \det \tilde{A}_n}{\det A_n}.$$

($\tilde{A}_n$ results from A_n, replacing the first column of A_n by $(a_1, a_2, ..., a_n, 0)^{\mathrm{T}}$; T means transpose.) Therefore $W(p_{t-1})$ is a differentiable function. We examine the slope of the function in the SME-price p:

$$\left| \frac{dp_t}{dp_{t-1}} \right|_{p_{t-1}=p} = \frac{\left| \sum_{i=1}^{n} a_i \prod_{j \neq i} c_j \right|}{\sum_{i=1}^{n} |b_i| \prod_{j \neq i} c_j} \Bigg|_p \leqslant \frac{\sum_{i=1}^{n} |a_i| \prod_{j \neq i} c_j}{\sum_{i=1}^{n} |b_i| \prod_{j \neq i} c_j} \Bigg|_p .$$

We have shown

$$\left| \frac{dp_t}{dp_{t-1}} \right|_p < 1 \qquad \text{if} \quad |a_i| < |b_i| \text{ for all } i.$$

In $p_{t-1} = p$,

$$\frac{\partial f^i}{\partial p_{t-1}} = 1 - \frac{\partial f^i}{\partial p_t} \geqslant 0;$$

therefore we have

$$a_i = \left(1 - \frac{\partial f^i}{\partial p_t} \right) \alpha_i,$$

$$0 > b_i = \frac{\partial f^i}{\partial p_t} \alpha_i + \beta_i, \qquad \beta_i < 0.$$

We get

$$(a_i \leqslant 0): \left| \frac{a_i}{b_i} \right|_{|p} = \frac{\left(1 - \dfrac{\partial f^i}{\partial p_t} \right) |\alpha_i|}{\dfrac{\partial f^i}{\partial p_t} |\alpha_i| + |\beta_i|} \Bigg|_{|p} \leqslant \frac{\dfrac{\partial f^i}{\partial p_t} |\alpha_i|}{\dfrac{\partial f^i}{\partial p_t} |\alpha_i| + |\beta_i|} \Bigg|_{|p} < 1. \tag{1}$$

$$(\alpha_i > 0) \quad \left| \frac{a_i}{b_i} \right|_{|p} = \left| \frac{\left(1 - \frac{\partial f^i}{\partial p_t}\right)\alpha_i}{\frac{\partial f^i}{\partial p_t}\alpha_i + \beta_i} \right|_{|p} < 1$$

$$\Leftrightarrow \left(1 - \frac{\partial f^i}{\partial p_t}\right)\alpha_i \bigg|_p < -\frac{\partial f^i}{\partial p_t}\alpha_i - \beta_i \bigg|_p \Leftrightarrow (\alpha_i + \beta_i)|_p < 0. \quad (2)$$

But you can see at once that this is fulfilled in the SME, as $(f^i/p)\,u_1 = u_1 = u_2$. Therefore,

$$\left| \frac{dp_t}{dp_{t-1}} \right|_{|p} < 1.$$

Consider now (we omit any index i):

$$F(2p - p_t, p_t, m) = f(\cdot)\,u_1(\cdot) - p_t u_2(\cdot) = 0.$$

Define

$$d := -\frac{\partial f}{\partial p_{t-1}}(2p - p_t, p_t) + \frac{\partial f}{\partial p_t}(2p - p_t, p_t)$$

$$\text{and} \quad m^* := m(p).$$

We know $F(p, p, m^*) = 0$. Computing $\partial m / \partial p_t$ yields

$$\frac{\partial m}{\partial p_t} = -\frac{du_1 - u_2 + u_{11}\dfrac{fm_1}{p_t^2} - u_{12}\dfrac{m_1}{f}d - u_{12}\dfrac{m_1}{p_t} + u_{22}\dfrac{m_1}{f^2}p_t d}{-u_{11}\dfrac{f}{p_t} + 2u_{12} - \dfrac{p_t}{f}u_{22}}.$$

According to assumption (2), $d \geqslant 0$. Therefore, $\partial m / \partial p_t > 0$. But we assumed assumption (2) for all i; therefore we get

$$\sum_{i \in I} m_t^i(2p - p_t, p_t) \neq M \qquad \text{if} \quad p \neq p_t.$$

It follows that $W(p_{t-1})$ and $p_t = 2p - p_{t-1}$ have only the SME in common. It is shown that the SME is stable.

We now consider utility functions

$$U(c_1, c_2) = u(c_1) + \alpha u(c_2) \qquad \alpha > 0,$$

where u has constant relative risk aversion r. a_i simplifies to

$$a_i = \frac{\partial f^i}{\partial p_{t-1}} \left(\frac{p}{f^i} (1 - r_i) u' \left(\frac{m_t^i}{f^i} \right) \alpha \right).$$

Therefore

$$a_i > 0 \Leftrightarrow r_i < 1,$$
$$= 0 \quad r_i = 1,$$
$$< 0 \quad r_i > 1.$$

If $r_i \leqslant 1$ and for at least one i_0, $r_{i_0} < 1$, we get $dp_t/dp_{t-1} > 0$ for all $p_{t-1} > 0$.

In this case we do not need assumption (2ii) of Proposition 3. We cannot show the same result for $r_i > 1$. Without this assumption (2ii), in many cases $\lim_{p_{t-1} \to 0} W(p_{t-1}) = \infty$ (consider, for example, $r = 2$ and $f(p_{t-1}, p_t) = \sqrt{p_{t-1} p_t}$). We can show only that p_t is monotone decreasing. Therefore, if we want to admit any expectations for this special class of utility functions, we can only get positive results in the neighborhood of the SME. Some tedious calculation yields

$$\frac{dp_t}{dp_{t-1}} \bigg|_p = \frac{\dfrac{\partial f}{\partial p_{t-1}} (p, p)(1 - r)}{\dfrac{\partial f}{\partial p_{t-1}} (p, p)(1 - r) + r(1 + \alpha^{1/r})} = \frac{1}{1 - \dfrac{\beta}{f_1}}.$$

Therefore the statements of Proposition 3(b) follow at once.

IV. Conclusion

It was the aim of this paper to explore the role of expectations in a dynamic framework. The result of Proposition 3, especially that positive linear combinations of prices lead to global stability, seems to be rather robust: We have many examples with non-differentiable utility functions in which our result holds, too. Of course, it is a desirable aim to generalize the model to the n goods case. This should be the subject of further research.

References

1. J. Drèze, "Allocation under Uncertainty, Equilibrium and Optimality," Macmillan, London, 1974.
2. G. Fuchs and G. Laroque, Dynamics of temporary equilibria and expectations, *Econometrica* **44** (1976), 1157–1178.

3. J.-M. GRANDMONT, On the short run equilibrium in a monetary economy, *in* J. Drèze, "Allocation under Uncertainty, Equilibrium and Optimality," Macmillan, London, 1974.
4. J.-M. GRANDMONT AND G. LAROQUE, Money in the pure consumption loan model, *J. Econ. Theory* **6** (1973), 382–395.
5. J. PRATT, Risk-aversion in the small and in the large, *Econometrica* **32** (1964), 122–136.
6. P. A. SAMUELSON, An exact consumption-loan model of interest with or without the social contrivance of money, *J. Pol. Econ.* **66** (1978), 467–482.

Is Error Learning Behaviour Stabilizing?

GÉRARD FUCHS

Laboratoire d'Économetrie, École Polytechnique, 75230 Paris, Cedex 05, France

Received June 24, 1977; revised December 15, 1977

It is very commonly admitted that error-learning behaviour in general improves the stability of dynamical economic evolutions. We show here, in the context of Temporary General Equilibrium Theory, that such an intuition is not true, in the sense that "most often," for a large class of models, learning does not assuredly leads to more stable dynamics. The presentation of the problem then allows for a discussion of the type of hypothesis—very high levels of information or very careful behaviours—which can invalidate such a conclusion.

INTRODUCTION

In most dynamical economic models, the evolution crucially depends on the forecasts that are made by the agents for the future values of some significant parameters of the state v that describes the system of which they are part. Such a situation appears in macroeconomics, both applied and theoretical, as well as in microeconomics, for instance in the field of temporary general equilibrium theory. It is one of the main characteristics of social systems as opposed to mechanical systems. The forecasts themselves are in general built as the values of expectation functions, one for each agent, defined on some set of attainable information. The expectation function of an agent summarizes the vision, implicit or explicit, that he has formed about the economic system as a whole. Then, in general, the model under consideration admits at least one stationary state $\bar{v}$ and a key problem is to study the asymptotic stability of this state. More precisely, one is often interested in the set $G(\bar{v})$ of expectation functions which are such that, all other characteristics of the model being kept fixed, the stationary state $\bar{v}$ is an attractor (under standard assumptions of "rationality" for expectations, $\bar{v}$ itself does not change with expectations). We shall call the elements of $G(\bar{v})$ "*stabilizing expectations*".

Next, one can look at somewhat more sophisticated models which, in addition, embody the possibility for the agents of revising the expectation functions themselves and thus their "vision of the world". This revision is usually performed in relation with the acquisition of some new information and, in this spirit, a commonly considered type of rule of revision is the *"error learning rule"*: in one way or another this rule reflects the idea that the expectation function ψ^i_{t-1} of an agent i at some time $t-1$ should not be changed at time t if the forecast it has predicted turns out to be correct (of course one can extend this definition to sequences of several periods). The possibility of revising expectations leads naturally to consider now as the states of the system pairs $y = (v, \psi^i)$, i.e. the space of states takes the form $Y = V \times \Psi^I$, where V is the initial phase space, I the number of agents, Ψ some space of admissible expectation functions; and the dynamics of the system now appear in fact as dynamics on Y. Again there may be a stationary state $\bar{y}$, which will then be of the form $(\bar{v}, \bar{\psi}^i)$ where $\bar{v}$ is the same as previously (this appears as a consequence of the definition of an error learning rule) and the original problem now becomes: given a definite error learning rule which fixes the dynamics of the model, when is $\bar{v}$ a locally asymptotically stable point.

It would then seem to be a rather natural result that, given any subset G of $G(\bar{v})$ (possibly $G(\bar{v})$ itself), one could exhibit a nice set L of cleverly chosen error learning rules generating dynamics such that:

(i) Trajectories $\{y_t\}$ starting at some $y_0 = (v_0, \psi_0^i)$, where the point (ψ_0^i) belongs to G and v_0 is in some neighbourhood of $\bar{v}$ in V, are such that y_t converges to $(\bar{v}, G)$.

(ii) In addition, there exist expectations functions (ψ_0^i) with (ψ_0^i) not in G such that, still, trajectories $\{y_t\}$ starting at $y_0 = (v_0, \psi_0^i)$, with v_0 in some neighbourhood of $\bar{v}$ in V, are such that y_t converges to $(\bar{v}, G)$.

(We shall only consider here discrete time models.)

Clearly, dynamics with no revision of expectations satisfy (i). Our "intuition" thus just says that, given G, there should exist some clever ways of learning from past history which improve somewhat the situation (that is (ii)).

Now one would expect that the set L is of a significant size, i.e., in more mathematical terms , that given a reasonable topology on the set of error learning rules, L is a set with non empty interior.

We shall exhibit in this paper a class of non pathological models for which this last intuition turns out to be false; i.e., for any G in $G(\bar{v})$ and for any neighbourhood U of $\bar{v}$ in V, except for a "small set" of lerning rules, there are trajectories $\{y_t\}$ starting at $y_0 = (v_0, \psi_0^i)$ with v_0 in U and (ψ_0^i) in G such that y_t does not go to $(\bar{v}, G)$ for t going to infinity.

In other terms, "most often", it does not help the stability of the economic system that the agents use any learning process at all.

The proof of the above result also allows us to discuss precisely the nature of more restrictive hypotheses, information structures corresponding to a very high level of information or types of learning corresponding to very careful behaviours, which could lead to the opposite situation. But it then appears that those hypotheses cannot be considered as very natural or likely.

The paper is divided in five sections. Section I introduces the framework of our study which is derived from the general model for dynamics of expectations in temporary general equilibrium theory presented in [1]. Section II then specifies our question and states the Theorem which expresses our result. Section III contains the proof of this Theorem. Section IV then illustrates the previous definitions and results for the simple situation where traders, with demands deriving from logarighmic utility functions, exchange only one consumption good and money and have linear expectation functions. Discussion and comments are presented in Conclusion.

I. PRESENTATION OF THE MODEL

As we just said in the Introduction the framework of our study will be the model in temporary general equilibrium theory considered in [1]. However, as we are now interested in studying a particular question, namely: "is error learning behaviour stabilizing.·", we shall somewhat simplify the general features introduced there.

a. *First Elements of the Model*

We consider exchange economies with l goods; we do not mind here whether they are storable or not. We suppose there are I consumers living two periods, so the total population is constant to $2I$. At each date t ($t \in \mathbb{N}$) there is a market for each good which is then immediately delivered; there are no future markets. At time t the action of young agent i, ($i1$), depends on the current price system p_t and on his forecast p_{t+1}^i of the price system that will prevail at time $t + 1$; the action of old agent i, ($i2$), young at time $t - 1$, depends on his past action—and thus on p_{t-1} and p_t^i—and on the present actual price system p_t (he of course has nothing to forecast). We shall suppose that prices are normalized to the unit simplex P in $\mathbb{R}^l$.

A consumer i is characterized by two continuously differentiable excess demand functions: z_{i1} and z_{i2}, with assumption that for any p_t, p_{t-1}, p_t^i, p_{t+1}^i in P and[1] $i = 1,...,I$:

$$p_t \cdot z_{i1}(p_t, p_{t+1}^i) = 0, \qquad p_t \cdot z_{i2}(p_{t-1}, p_t^i, p_t) = 0 \tag{A}$$

(budget constraint; additional constraints on the z_i· are considered in [1] or [2] where money is explicitly introduced).

---

[1] · stands for Euclidean scalar product in $\mathbb{R}^l$.

The space A of agents is then the set of (z_{i1}, z_{i2}) such that (A) holds, equipped with the topology τ_1 of C^1 uniform convergence (uniform convergence of maps and of their first order derivatives). Given $\mathscr{A}$ in A the value of the aggregated excess demand at time t is thus:

$$Z(\mathscr{A}; p_t, p_{t-1}, p_{t+1}^i, p_t^i) \equiv \sum_i z_{i1}(p_t, p_{t+1}^i) + \sum_i z_{i2}(p_{t-1}, p_t^i, p_t). \quad (1)$$

We shall say that a price $\bar{p}$ is a *stationary temporary equilibrium* (S.T.E.) for $\mathscr{A}$ if:

$$Z(\mathscr{A}; \bar{p}, \bar{p}, \bar{p}, \bar{p}) = 0. \quad (2)$$

We shall call $W(\cdot)$ the correspondence which associates with any $\mathscr{A}$ the set of its S.T.E. One can find in [2] sufficient conditions for W to be non empty valued; we shall suppose that they are satisfied here.

Let us now go back to the forecasts. We shall suppose that, at time t, the forecast p_{t+1}^i depends on the current price system p_t and on some sequence of T passed observed price systems ($T \geqslant 1$). We set $V = P^{T+1}$ and call v_t the element $(p_t, p_{t-1}, ..., p_{t-T})$ in V. We suppose then that, at time t, the young agent i has formed an expectation function ψ_t^i which is a continuously differentiable map from V to P and claim that $p_{t+1}^i = \psi_t^i(v_t)$.

Now due to our particular aim here, and to make exposition and proofs simpler, we shall suppose that the set of expectation functions is restricted to "admissible" expectation functions, parametrized by $\alpha \in \mathbb{R}$. In other words $\psi(\cdot) \equiv \chi(\alpha, \cdot)$, where χ itself is a fixed continuously differentiable map from $\mathbb{R} \times V$ to P.

We shall suppose that, given $\mathscr{A} \in A$, the map χ is such that

$$\chi(\alpha, \bar{v}) = \bar{p} \qquad \forall \alpha \in \mathbb{R} \qquad \forall \bar{p} \in W(\mathscr{A}) \quad (3)$$

(this implies that $\psi(\bar{v}) = \bar{p}$ for all admissible expectation functions and represents some sort of "rationality" condition).

In addition we shall ask for the following technical condition to hold:

$$\alpha' \neq \alpha'' \Leftrightarrow \chi(\alpha', \cdot) \neq (\alpha'', \cdot) \quad (T)$$

(In other words our one parameter set of expectation functions is in bijection with the real line).

The following interpretation of this limitation can be given: the agents all know (or believe to know) the structural form χ of the price dynamics of the world in which they live, up to the setting of the real parameter α. The expectation function ψ_t^i of young agent i at time t is then equal to $\chi(\alpha_t^i, \cdot)$

for some $\alpha_t{}^i$ in $\mathbb{R}$. The problem of evolution of the i-th expectation function then becomes one dimensional.[2]

Considering $\chi(\cdot, \cdot)$ as fixed once for all, we can identify an economy with an element $\mathscr{A}$ of A. We then set, in the spirit of the Introduction:

DEFINITION 1. A *state* of an economy is an element $y = (v, \alpha^i)$ in $Y = V \times \mathbb{R}^l$.

We shall now consider a precise set of possible dynamics on Y, defined, at least locally around some $\bar{v}$, by a map:

$$\Phi: Y \to Y \tag{4}$$

which will describe the evolution of states after a unit time interval.

As a first part of Φ we shall naturally introduce the market clearing conditions. We thus ask that the aggregated excess demand at time t, given $\mathscr{A}$ and the successive states y_{t-1} and y_t, is equal to zero ($t \in \mathbb{N} + 1$):

$$Z(\mathscr{A}; y_t, y_{t-1}) \equiv \sum_i z_{i1}(p_t, \chi(\alpha_t{}^i, v_t)) + \sum_i z_{i2}(p_{t-1}, \chi(\alpha_{t-1}^i, v_{t-1}), p_t) = 0. \tag{5}$$

From (A) we have of course $p_t \cdot Z(\mathscr{A}; y_t, y_{t-1}) = 0$ (Walras law). Thus we can consider that the implicit equation (5) formally allows us to calculate p_t, given the previous prices and the previous and current expectations. And we know from [1] or [2] that the difficulty related to the possibility of multiple solutions can be ruled out, at least for an open dense set of $\mathscr{A}$ and locally around some chosen $\bar{p}$, where one can isolate a definite continuously differentiable price solution of (5).

We shall come back to this point in Section II.

b. *Revision of Expectations*

To complete the definition of the map Φ we are then led to make precise the way the agents revise their expectation functions. We shall suppose that this revision is done along the following line.

Let H be in $\mathbb{R}^l$ the hyperplane:[3]

$$H = \left\{ q \in \mathbb{R}^l \ \middle| \ \sum_1^l q^h = 0 \right\}.$$

We set:

---

[2] One could extend without much difficulty the results of the paper to the case where α would belong to some $\mathbb{R}^n$ or where there would be different χ_i for each agent.
[3] H can be identified with the tangent plane to P at any p.

DEFINITION 2. An *error learning rule* is a continuously differentiable map F from $\mathbb{R} \times H$ to $\mathbb{R}$ such that

$$F(\alpha, q) = \alpha \quad \text{if} \quad q = 0. \tag{B}$$

F associates with the expectation function characterized by α_1 and with the vector q—which has to be thought of as the difference between the price system of a period and the price forecast of the previous period—a new expectation function characterized by α_2; $\alpha_2 = \alpha_1$ if the error q is equal to zero.[4]

We then now suppose that each agent i is also characterized by a map F_i satisfying (B) and we consider finally as our space of economies E the set of (z_i, F_i) with assumptions (A) and (B), again equipped with the topology τ_1 of C^1 uniform convergence.

The revision process for expectations for the economy $\mathscr{E}$ in E and the agent i, given successive states y_{t-1} and y_t, is then given through ($t \in \mathbb{N} + 1$):

$$\alpha_t^i - F_i(\alpha_{t-1}^i, p_t - \chi(\alpha_{t-1}^i, v_{t-1})) = 0. \tag{6}$$

In other words, the value α_t^i which characterizes the new expectation function at time t depends on the previous value α_{t-1}^i (and thus on the previous expectation function) and on the error characterized by the difference between p_t and the price forecast made at the previous period $\chi(\alpha_{t-1}^i, v_{t-1}) = p_t^i$.

c. *Final Setting of the Model*

We are thus led to retain to define the map Φ of (4) the set of coupled Eqs. (5) and (6). In the spirit of [1] or [2] we introduce:

DEFINITION 3. The correspondence of *temporary state equilibria* $V(\cdot; \cdot)$ is defined for any economy $\mathscr{E}$ in E and any state y_{t-1} in Y as the set of states y_t in Y such that (5) and (6) are satisfied.

DEFINITION 4. Given an economy $\mathscr{E}$, a future *trajectory* is an infinite sequence $\{y_t\}$ in Y such that $y_t \in V(\mathscr{E}; y_{t-1}) \, \forall t \geqslant 1$.

DEFINITION 5. The correspondence of *stationary temporary state equilibria* (S.T.S.E.) $W_S(\cdot)$ is defined for any economy $\mathscr{E}$ in E as the set of states $\bar{y}$ in Y such that $\bar{y} \in V(\mathscr{E}; \bar{y})$.

---

[4] Definition 2 corresponds to what has been called in [1] an error learning rule of the second type with order one.

GÉRARD FUCHS

II. Dynamical Results

We are now in position to state our problem in a more precise form. Namely, given some $\mathscr{A}$ in A, given a S.T.E. $\bar{v}$ in $W(\mathscr{A})$, given G in $G(\bar{v})$, what can be said about the subset L of (F_i) considered in Introduction?

To handle this question we shall need the asymptotic results obtained in the general context of [1]. But before giving their translation in the present model, we first have to make precise what we call stabilizing expectations.

From Eq. (5) with α^i instead of α_t^i and α_{t-1}^i we see that, given $\mathscr{A}$ in A and $\bar{v}$ in $W(\mathscr{A})$, the set $G(\bar{v})$ is now equivalent to the set of (α^i) in $\mathbb{R}^I$ such that the implicit price evolution given by (5) admits $\bar{v}$ as a local attractor. Now we shall take for the definition of an attractor the fact that the Jacobian J of the implicit map $v_{t-1} \mapsto v_t$ defined through (5), taken at point $\bar{v}$, has the modulus of all its eigenvalues smaller than one,[5] which yields the definition of $G(\bar{v})$.

More concretely, let us introduce the following notations. Let Z_u be the Jacobian at point $(\bar{p},...,\bar{p})$ of the $l-1$ first components of $Z(\mathscr{A}; (v_t, \alpha^i),$ $v_{t-1}, \alpha^i))$ with respect to the $l-1$ first components of p_u (we suppose that p_l has been eliminated thanks to price normalization). Let Z_t^{-1} be the inverse matrix of Z_t. Equation (13) in [1] or Theorem 8 in [2] then give:[6]

PROPOSITION 1. *Given $\mathscr{A}$ in A a sufficient condition for (α^i) in $\mathbb{R}^I$ to be in $G(\bar{v})$ is that*

$$\sum_{u=t-1}^{t=T-1} \| Z_t^{-1} Z_u \| < 1. \tag{7}$$

Equation (7) just gives a sufficient condition for the norm of J to be smaller than one, which implies in turn that all the eigenvalues of J have modulus smaller than 1.[7]

Next we translate those dynamical results of [1] and [2] which are useful for our problem.

PROPOSITION 2. *There exists an open dense subset $\mathscr{U}$ of E such that, for $\mathscr{E} = (\mathscr{A}, F_i)$ in $\mathscr{U}$:*

(i) *$W(\mathscr{A})$ consists of a finite, locally constant, number of points, which are locally continuously differentiable functions of $\mathscr{A}$.*

---

[5] In a more mathematical language one would talk about an "hyperbolic" attractor; one knows from Proposition 8 in [2] that economies such that $\bar{v}$ is hyperbolic form an open dense set.

[6] $\| \cdot \|$ is the usual norm for linear operators between Euclidian spaces.

[7] Note that in [1] the definition retained for $G(\bar{v})$ was $\| J \| < 1$, so that our definition here is now slightly more extensive.

(ii) $W_S(\mathscr{E})$ is the set of elements $\bar{y} = (\bar{v}, \alpha^i)$ with $\bar{v} \in W(\mathscr{A})$ and (α^i) any point in $\mathbb{R}^l$.

(From Proposition 1 and Theorem 1 in [1]; in fact, as $W_S(\mathscr{E}) = W_S(\mathscr{A})$, Proposition 2 is also equivalent to Theorem 4 in [2].)

PROPOSITION 3. *There exists an open dense subset $\mathscr{V}$ of $\mathscr{U}$ such that the following holds. Let $\mathscr{E}$ be in $\mathscr{V}$, $\bar{v}$ in $W(\mathscr{A})$, G any open subset of $G(\bar{v})$; there exists a neighbourhood Q of G in Y such that for any y_0 in Q:*

(i) *there exists a unique trajectory $\{y_t\}$ starting at y_0 ; it is given by $y_t = \Phi(y_{t-1})$ where Φ is an invertible map, continuously differentiable so as its inverse;*

(ii) *the α_t^i converge to some α^i in G;*

(iii) *the v_t converge to $\bar{v}$.*

(Proposition 3 is an immediate consequence of Theorem 5 in [1].)

A good illustration of the situation described by Proposition 3 is given by Fig. 1 (the arrows indicate the direction of the time evolution).

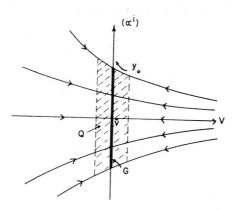

FIGURE 1.

Now the question raised in Introduction can be given the following graphic interpretation. Given any G strictly contained in $G(\bar{v})$, in case there are no learning procedures there is a cylindric neighbourhood $U \times G$ of G in Y such that all trajectories starting in $U \times G$ have constant expectations and prices convergent to $\bar{p}$ (see Fig. 2). Now we wish to see for which set L of learning rules (F_i) trajectories starting in some $U' \times G$ still converge to $(\bar{v}, G)$ and, in addition, there are initial expectations ψ_0^i outside G such that that trajectories starting at $y_0 = (v_0, \psi_0^i)$, with v_0 in U', still converge to $(\bar{v}, G)$ (as mentioned in the Introduction this clearly defines a situation where

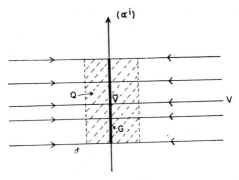

FIGURE 2

error learning improves price stability). In other words, we are interested in learning rules (F_i) for which the neighbourhood Q of Proposition 3 strictly contains some sylindric neighbourhood of the form $U' \times G$. We see that the learning rules generating the dynamics of Fig. 1 do not belong to L (consider the trajectory starting in y_0). At the opposite, learning rules generating such dynamics as defined through Fig. 3 would belong to L.

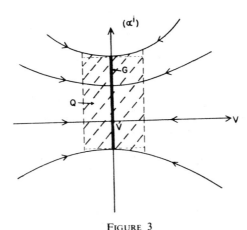

FIGURE 3

We thus see intuitively that the important point is the "angle" at which trajectories approach the boundary of G: if the approach is not orthogonal to the axis (α^i), the underlying (F_i) do not belong to L and, conversely, a necessary condition for some (F_i) to be in L is that the approach is orthogonal.

To set this intuition on some more mathematical basis, we shall introduce the following definition (see [3]).

DEFINITION 6.   Given $\mathscr{E}$ in $\mathscr{V}$ and $\bar{y}$ in $W_S(\mathscr{E})$ the *strong stable manifold* of $\bar{y}$ is the set:

$$W^{ss}(\bar{y}) = \{\, y \mid d(\Phi^t(y), \bar{y}) < c\alpha^t \forall t \in \mathbb{N}\}$$

($c > 0, 0 < \alpha < 1$, d is the Euclidian distance on Y).

In other words, $W^{ss}(\bar{y})$ is the set of y which flow exponentially fast towards $\bar{y}$. It is now well known· mathematical results that, as Φ is continuously differentiable:

(i) $W^{ss}(\bar{y})$ is a C^1 submanifold of Y, i.e. defines a smooth surface in Y so that we can speak of the tangent plane to $W^{ss}(\bar{y})$ at point $\bar{y}$: $T_{\bar{y}}W^{ss}(\bar{y})$;

(ii)   Given the Jacobian of Φ at $\bar{y}$: $T_{\bar{y}}\Phi$, the tangent plane $T_{\bar{y}}W^{ss}(\bar{y})$ is nothing but the eigenspace of $T_{\bar{y}}\Phi$ corresponding to eigenvalues with modulus smaller than 1. (See [3]).

Our problem thus is to look at the set of (F_i) such that this eigenspace is orthogonal to $\mathbb{R}^l$ in Y.

We are then led to the following result:

THEOREM.   *Let $\mathscr{A}$ be an element of A, $\bar{p}$ an element of $W(\mathscr{A})$, G a subset of $G(\bar{v})$. Let L be the subset of error learning rules (F_i) such that there exists a neighbourhood U of $\bar{v}$ in V with the properties that:*

(i) $\mathscr{E} = (\mathscr{A}, F_i)$ *is in $\mathscr{V}$;*

(ii)   *Trajectories $\{\, y_t\}$ starting at $y_0 = (v_0, \alpha_0{}^i)$ with v_0 in U and $(\alpha_0{}^i)$ in G converge to $(\bar{v}, G)$.*

(iii)   *There are trajectories $\{\, y_t\}$ starting at $y_0 = (v_0, \alpha_0{}^i)$ with v_0 in U and $\alpha_0{}^i$ outside G also converging to $(\bar{v}, G)$.*

Then L is a closed set with empty interior for the topology τ_1.

III. PROOF

Let $\mathscr{A}$ be an element of A, $\bar{y} = (\bar{v}, \bar{\alpha}^i)$ be a point in $W_S(\mathscr{A})$ with $(\bar{\alpha}^i)$ in some subset G of $G(\bar{v})$. Let $\mathscr{E} = (\mathscr{A}, F_i)$ be an economy in $\mathscr{V}$.

(a)   We shall first calculate $T_{\bar{y}}\Phi$ by differentiating (5) and (6) with respect to $y_t = (v, \alpha_t{}^i)$ and $y_{t-1} = (v_{t-1}, \alpha_{t-1}^i)$. In matrix notation we then obtain an expression of the form:

$$a\, dy_t + b\, dy_{t-1} = 0 \qquad (8)$$

and we know then that, if a is invertible, $T_{\bar{y}}\Phi$ is equal to $-a^{-1}b$ (this is just the standard implicit function theorem).

GÉRARD FUCHS

To make the explicit calculation, we shall now use the precise features of our model. First the fact that expectation functions are constrained by (3) implies that the coefficients of $d\alpha_t^i$ and $d\alpha_{t-1}^i$ in the differential of (5) are zero (the partial derivative of χ with respect to α is zero at point $\bar{v}$). Next, assumption (B) implies that $\partial_1 F_i = (DF_i/D\alpha)(\alpha^i, 0) = 1$. Using the additional notations: $\partial_2 F_i = (DF_i/Dq)(\bar{\alpha}^i, 0)$ and $\partial_j \chi_i = (D\chi/Dp_{t-j})(\bar{\alpha}^i, \bar{v})$ ($j = 1, 2,...,$ $T + 1$), the differentials of (5) and (6) thus give the explicit form of (8):

$$\sum_{u=t}^{t-T-1} Z_u \, dp_u = 0, \tag{9}$$

$$d\alpha_t^i - d\alpha_{t-1}^i - \partial_2 F_i \, dp_t + \sum_{j=1}^{T+1} \partial_2 F_i \partial_j \chi_i \, dp_{t-j} = 0. \tag{10}$$

Using the already mentioned definition of $T_{\bar{y}}\Phi$ through

$$\left(\begin{matrix} dv_t \\ d\alpha_t^i \end{matrix} \right) = T_{\bar{y}}\Phi \left(\begin{matrix} dv_{t-1} \\ d\alpha_{t-1}^i \end{matrix} \right)$$

we see from (9) and (10) that $T_{\bar{y}}\Phi$ has the structure:

$$T_{\bar{y}}\Phi = \begin{pmatrix} J & 0 \\ L & 1 \end{pmatrix}, \tag{11}$$

where:

· J is the square matrix of dimension $(l - 1)(T + 1)$ given by:

$$J = \begin{pmatrix} -Z_t^{-1}Z_{t-1} & \cdots & -Z_t^{-1}Z_{t-T} & -Z_t^{-1}Z_{t-T-1} \\ 1 & \cdots & 0 & 0 \\ \cdots & \cdots & \cdots & \cdots \\ 0 & \cdots & 1 & 0 \end{pmatrix}$$

(1 is here the identity matrix on $\mathbb{R}^{l-1}$; Z_t is invertible and thus J well defined because $(\bar{\alpha}^i)$ is in $G(\bar{v})$);

· 1 is the identity matrix on $\mathbb{R}^l$;

· L is a rectangular matrix with $(l - 1)(T + 1)$ columns and I rows, where row i is easily seen to be the succession of the vector blocks:

$$L_{ij} = -\partial_2 F_i \{ Z_t^{-1} Z_{t-j} - \partial_j \chi_i \} \tag{12}$$

for $j = 1,..., T + 1$.

(b) Now the tangent plane to $W^{ss}(\bar{y})$ is the invariant space of $T_{\bar{y}}\Phi$ corresponding to the set of eigenvalues of modulus smaller than 1. From (11) and (12) it is easily seen that for this space to be orthogonal to $\mathbb{R}^l$, all

L_{ij} must be zero. Then necessary conditions for this result to hold are that, for each i:

· either $\partial_2 F_i = 0$; but this means that $\bar{\alpha}_i$ has to be a common zero of the $l - 1$ partial derivatives of F_i with respect to q^k ($k = 1,..., l - 1$) at point $\bar{y}$; it is a well known result of differential topology (see for instance [4], Theorem 19.1) that, if $l > 2$, such conditions will not be satisfied for an open dense set of F_i and that, if $l = 2$, for an open dense set of F_i again, it will be satisfied only for isolated values of $\bar{\alpha}_i$;[8]

· or $\partial_2 F_i$ is an eigenvector corresponding to a zero eigenvalue for all the matrices:

$$M_{ij} = -Z_t^{-1} Z_{t-j} + \partial_j \chi_i$$

($j = 1,..., T + 1$), with one at least of the M_{ij} non zero; but the same argument (see [4] or note 8) shows that such a situation cannot occur for an open dense set of F_i ;

· or, last, all the M_{ij} are identically zero; but they are nothing but the first order price derivatives at $\bar{y}$ of the error term $p_t - \chi(\alpha_{t-1}^i, v_{t-1})$, where p_t is expressed in terms of y_{t-1} ; the fact that all the M_{ij} are zero thus means that, at first order, the expectation functions $\chi(\bar{\alpha}^i, \cdot)$ predict the exact evolution; we can thus assert that, at first order always, they coincide with the exact expectation function ψ_∞ obtained by solving in p_{t+1} the equation:

$$\sum_i z_{i1}(p_t, p_{t+1}) + \sum_i z_{i2}(p_{t-1}, p_t, p_t) = 0 \qquad (13)$$

(this point is detailed through Lemma 1 in [1]); now as there is at most one solution ψ_∞ of (13) around $\bar{v}$ and as χ has been supposed to satisfy the technical condition (T), this means that the situation we consider happens at most for a unique value $(\bar{\alpha}^i) = (\bar{\alpha})$.

Thus, for an open dense of (F_i) all L_{ij} cannot be zero except may be for isolated points $(\bar{\alpha}^i)$. As there are at least two agents in the economy this means that only isolated points of the boundary ∂G of G in $\mathbb{R}^l$ are such that the orthogonality condition may hold, which implies the Theorem. ∎

It may be worth while to notice that the proof above would not be altered if each individual learning rule F_i was a function not only of α_{t-1}^i but also of the α_{j-1}^t, $j \neq 1$, i.e. of the previous expectations of the other agents (see Eq. (6)): so long that $F_i((\alpha^i), 0) = \alpha^i$, the structure (11) remains unchanged.

[8] An intuition of the result can be obtained by perturbing F_i in F_i' with $F_i'(\alpha, q) = F_i(\alpha, q) + \lambda \cdot q$ where λ is a small vector in $\mathbb{R}^{l-1}$: a suitable choice of λ easily shows that, if by accident $\bar{\alpha}^i$ was a common solution of the $l - 1$ lines of $\partial_2 F_i = 0$, it would not remain a common solution of the $l - 1$ lines of $\partial_2 F_i' = 0$.

IV. An Example

a. *The Model*

We shall describe here a simple situation where traders exchange only one consumption good ($l = 2$) and money ($l = 1$), as in the example already given in [2]. We suppose that money has no direct utility and that, q_1 and q_2 being a consumption bundle for agent i when he is young and old respectively, the associated utility is given by:

$$u(q_1, q_2) = \log q_1 q_2.$$

We now choose a price normalization where the price of money is constant to 1 and where $\pi \in \mathbb{R}^+ =]0, +\infty[$ denotes the price of the consumption good in real terms.[9]

Supposing that agent i receives an endowment ω_1 when he is young and ω_2 when he is old (in term of consumption good only), a standard calculation of maximization of u under the budget constraints defined by a present price of good equal to π_t and an expected price equal to $\pi_t{}^i$, then lead to a demand of money at time t, for a young agent, equal to:[10]

$$z_{i1}^1(\pi_t, \pi_{t+1}^i) = \tfrac{1}{2}(\omega_1\pi_t - \omega_2\pi_{t+1}^i).$$

We shall suppose as in [2] that old agent i just spends the money that he had bought when he was young. If m denotes the total (and constant) stock of money in the economy $\mathscr{E}$, the aggregated excess demand for money at time t is then given by:

$$Z^1(\mathscr{E}; \pi_t, \pi_{t+1}^i) = \sum_i \tfrac{1}{2}(\omega_1\pi_t - \omega_2\pi_{t+1}^i) - m$$

(the excess demand for the consumption good can easily be obtained from Walras law).

Then, there is a unique stationary temporary equilibrium given by:

$$\bar{\pi} = \frac{2m}{I(\omega_1 - \omega_2)}$$

($\bar{\pi}$ is positive if $\omega_1 > \omega_2$: see assumption 12 in [2] for the existence of a S.T.E.).

---

[9] This normalization, for two goods, leads to a demand for money which is linear in prices.

[10] This expression is of course only valid in the region of $\mathbb{R}^2$ where it is non negative.

Next we shall suppose that our one parameter family of expectation functions is given, locally around $\bar{\pi}$, through ($\alpha \in \mathbb{R}$; $\pi, \pi' \in \mathbb{R}^+$):

$$\chi(\alpha, \pi', \pi'') = \pi' + \alpha(\pi' - \pi''). \tag{14}$$

Clearly χ maps $\mathbb{R} \times (\mathbb{R}^+)^2$ outside $\mathbb{R}^+$. But, from the specific form of χ and by continuity, the inverse image of $\mathbb{R}^+$ surely contains a neighbourhood of $\mathbb{R} \times \varDelta$ (where $\varDelta$ is in $(\mathbb{R}^+)^2$ the "diagonal" set of elements of the form (π, π)); and it is sufficient for our study to work in such a neighbourhood which contains all points $(\alpha, \bar{\pi}, \bar{\pi})$. We see that $\chi(\alpha, \bar{\pi}, \bar{\pi}) = \bar{\pi}$ and that χ also satisfies the technical condition (T) of Section I. The expectation function of young agent i at time t is then equal to $\chi(\alpha_t{}^i, \cdot)$.

A *state* of the economy is then now an element of $Y = (\mathbb{R}^+)^2 \times \mathbb{R}^I$.

The market clearing condition is (we note with primes the equations of our example which correspond to the equations without primes of the previous sections):

$$\sum_i \tfrac{1}{2}\{\omega_1 \pi_t - \omega_2[\pi_t + \alpha_t{}^i(\pi_t - \pi_{t-1})]\} - m = 0. \tag{5'}$$

As error learning rules we shall here limit ourselves to a linear class. We define for any $\lambda \in \mathbb{R}$:

$$F_\lambda(\alpha, q) = \alpha + \lambda q$$

so that, instead of being infinite dimensional, our space of error learning rule is just the real line.

The revision process for expectations, for the economy $\mathscr{E} = (z_{i1}, \lambda_i, m)$, is then given by:

$$\alpha_t{}^i - \alpha_{t-1}^i - \lambda_i[\pi_t - \pi_{t-1} - \alpha_{t-1}^i(\pi_{t-1} - \pi_{t-2})] = 0 \tag{6'}$$

and (5') and (6') together define the (implicit) dynamics we are interested in.

b. *The Results*

The interest of our simple example is that all our equations now are separately linear in π and α, so that the concepts which are introduced in Part II and III become very easy to handle.

First, the set of stabilizing expectations $G(\bar{v})$ is the set of (α^i) in $\mathbb{R}^I$ such that the price dynamics given by (5') with $(\alpha_t{}^i) = (\alpha^i)$ are convergent. This amounts to:

$$\left| \left(\sum_i \omega_2 \alpha_i \right) \left[\sum_i (\omega_1 - \omega_2(1 + \alpha^i)) \right]^{-1} \right| < 1. \tag{7'}$$

Next, given G in $G(\bar{v})$, the system (5'), (6') defines trajectories in a neighbourhood Q of G in Y (see Proposition 3) if it can be solved locally so to take the form:

$$\pi_t = \pi(\pi_{t-1}, \pi_{t-2}, \alpha_{t-1}^i),$$

$$\alpha_t^i = \alpha(\pi_{t-1}, \pi_{t-2}, \alpha_{t-1}^i)$$

(here $V = P^2$). From the precise expression of (5') and (6'), the calculation can go as follows. Inserting (6') in (5') gives an equation defining implicitly π_t in terms of π_{t-1}, π_{t-2} and α_{t-1}^i. From the implicit function theorem, this equation can be solved locally around $\bar{\pi}$ if its first order derivative with respect to π_t, taken for all $\pi. = \bar{\pi}$ is non zero. Now a short calculation shows that this derivative is equal to:

$$\sum_i \tfrac{1}{2}\{\omega_1 - \omega_2(1 + \alpha_{t-1}^i)\}$$

(for $\alpha_{t-1}^i = \bar{\alpha}^i$ this is just the quantity Z_t). From (7') it is non zero for (α_{t-1}^i) near enough of (α^i) in $G(\bar{v})$. Then one can insert this solution π_t in (6') to get α_t^i in terms of π_{t-1}, π_{t-2} and α_{t-1}^i, and so obtain the local dynamics of our problem.

Next, by differentiating (5') and (6') at point $\bar{y} = (\bar{\pi}, \bar{\pi}, \bar{\alpha}_i)$ one obtains easily:

$$\sum_i \tfrac{1}{2}\{[\omega_1 - \omega_2(1 + \bar{\alpha}_i)] \, d\pi_t + \omega_2 \bar{\alpha}_i \, d\pi_{t-1}\} = 0, \tag{9'}$$

$$d\alpha_t^i - d\alpha_{t-1}^i - \lambda_i[d\pi_t - d\pi_{t-1} - \alpha^i(d\pi_{t-1} - d\pi_{t-2})] = 0, \tag{10'}$$

By identifying with:

$$\begin{pmatrix} d\pi_t \\ d\pi_{t-1} \\ (d\alpha_t^i) \end{pmatrix} = T_{\bar{y}}\Phi \begin{pmatrix} d\pi_{t-1} \\ d\pi_{t-2} \\ (d\alpha_{t-1}^i) \end{pmatrix}$$

one gets immediately:

$$T_{\bar{y}}\Phi = \begin{pmatrix} \beta & 0 & 0 \\ 1 & 0 & 0 \\ -\lambda_i\beta - \lambda_i(1 + \bar{\alpha}_i) & \lambda_i\bar{\alpha}_i & \delta_{ij} \end{pmatrix}, \tag{11'}$$

where $\beta = -(\sum_i \omega_2 \bar{\alpha}_i)(\sum_i (\omega_1 - \omega_2(1 + \bar{\alpha}_i))^{-1}$.

Last one can see that the eigenspace corresponding to the two eigenvalues of $T_{\bar{y}}\Phi$ smaller than 1 (here β and 0)[11] is orthogonal to $\mathbb{R}^I$ if and only if, for each i:

---

[11] The appearance of a zero eigenvalue, at the difference of the general situation where $T_{\bar{y}}\Phi$ is invertible, is just a consequence of the conservation of money that we have introduced in this example (see [2]).

· either $\lambda_i = 0$, which, in the linear set up that we have chosen for error learning rules, means that there is no learning at all;

· or $\bar{\alpha}_i = 0$ and $\beta = -1$, which is not compatible with the fact that $(\bar{\alpha}_i) \in G(\bar{v})$ (see (7')).

Note that this last point, as compared with Section III, just expresses the fact that our set of admissible expectation functions (defined through (14)) does not contain the exact expectation function ψ_∞. Indeed this function, which is obtained by solving in π_{t+1} the expression:

$$\sum_i \tfrac{1}{2}(\omega_1 \pi_t - \omega_2 \pi_{t+1}) - m = 0 \qquad (13')$$

does not depend on the prices of the previous period.

V. COMMENTS AND CONCLUSION

a. *Interpretation of the Result*

To discuss the exact meaning of our Theorem and to avoid misunderstanding, one has to pay special attention to the quantity of information available to each agent.

First it is clear enough that if all agents know the exact initial state y_0 of the economy, the position of a stationary temporary equilibrium $\bar{v}$ near v_0 and the corresponding set of stabilizing expectations $G(\bar{v})$, their natural behaviour would be:

— if $(\psi_0{}^i)$ was in $G(\bar{v})$, keep their expectation functions constant without trying to improve the dynamics,

— if $(\psi_0{}^i)$ was not in $G(\bar{v})$, try, by talking together, to find a set of error learning rules (F_i) that would lead the price dynamics to flow to $\bar{v}$ (see Fig. 1).

This behaviour, which would be quite natural at least in more sophisticated models where it is known that $\bar{v}$ is an optimal point (see, for instance [5]), does not of course contradict our approach.

Indeed, the infromation available in a realistic situation is far from being as complete as we have supposed above. In a first type of situation it may be natural to suppose that v_0 is well known of all agents; but then already $\bar{v}$ will not be known in general except may be by a very special agent such as a government or a central planning agency; and, even for such an agent, $\bar{v}$ will only be approximateively known; moreover, the knowledge of all $\psi_0{}^i$ means a huge amount of information; last the set $G(\bar{v})$ seems to be even more out of the scope of possible knowledge or calculation. At the opposite one can imagine a situation where, for a while, an economy remains in a stationary state, and then is perturbed by some random exogenous shock; this time $\bar{v}$ and even $\bar{y}$ may be known from anyone; but it is now v_0 and y_0 which will be hardly predictable and thus immediately accessible.

The interpretation of our result then appears more clearly: it means that, unless a very high level of global information is attained, attempts by the agents to learn something useful by comparing their forecasts to the actual dynamics have no chance to succeed. In this sense, the result of the model agrees again with intuition. But at the same time it exhibits how limited probably are the possible outputs of dynamical learning procedures.

b. *The Exceptional Cases*

For the sake of completeness we shall end by discussing the interpretation of the conditions, introduced in the proof of our Theorem, which make the L_{ij} ($i = 1,..., I; j = 1,..., T + 1$) equal to zero.

First we have the situation where all the M_{ij} are equal to zero. This clearly covers the case where the set of admissible expectation functions contains the exact expectation function ψ_∞ and, in addition, ψ_∞ belongs to $G(\bar{v})$. Then we get the not unexpected result that in this case, whatever the learning rule is, trajectories starting at (v_0, ψ_∞) converge to $(\bar{v}, \psi_\infty)$.

Next the situation where some $\partial_2 F_i$ is a common eigenvector for a zero eigenvalue of the M_{ij} for all j has partially a similar interpretation: it implies that the price forcast for at least one good, or basket of goods, turns out to be verified (at first order at least). Then of course again the learning rule for this price can be arbitrary.

Now the last way of having the L_i equal to zero is to constrain learning rules to satisfy automatically the condition:

$$\frac{DF}{Dq}(\alpha, 0) = 0 \qquad \forall \alpha \in \mathbb{R}. \tag{15}$$

In terms of Taylor expansion this means that we only consider admissible learning rules of the form:

$$F(\alpha, q) = \alpha + Q(\alpha, q) + \cdots,$$

where Q is a quadratic form in q with coefficents depending on α. This means that learning rules are of a very special type, revealing a particular carefulness: no first order sensitivity to the error. It corresponds to the situation illustrated by Fig. 3, where the problem now becomes to study the sign of curvatures instead of the slope of tangent planes. It is clear that for the subset of learning rules defined through (15) the answer to our initial question can then become positive. But this is at the price of a condition which cannot be thought of as very natural.

c. *Directions for Further Work*

We have in this paper essentially focused our attention on some of the applications that could be given to a formalism characterized by the attempt to endogeneize completely the problem of the expectation functions. Our discussion on the information content of the models we have considered, as well here as in [1], suggests that it might prove to be interesting to reintroduce exogeneous actions.

From the beginning of our discussion here we see for instance that such question as: how should a government or a central planning agency act in order to lead agents to choose learning behaviour that guarantees or improves convergence, could now be dealt with: according to the possibilities of acting on the choice of the F_i one could imagine a central regulator that helps in the choice of F_i either with optimal first derivatives, or leading to stable manifolds with strong curvature, etc.

Such constructions, with a mixture of endogenous and exogenous evolution for expectation functions, could allow one to deal with more precise concrete situations.

REFERENCES

1. G. FUCHS, "Dynamics of Expectations in Temporary General Equilibrium Theory," Working paper, École Polytechnique No. A1500177, 1977; *J. Math. Econ.*, in press.
2. G. FUCHS AND G. LAROQUE, Dynamics of temporary equilibria and expectations, *Econometrica* **44**, No. 6 (1976), 1157.
3. J. SOTOMAYOR, Generic bifurcations of dynamical systems, *in* "Dynamical Systems" (M. M. Peixoto, Ed.), Academic Press, New York, 1973.
4. R. ABRAHAM AND J. ROBBIN, "Transversal Mappings and Flows," Benjamin, New York, 1967.
5. J. M. GRANDMONT AND G. LAROQUE, Money in the pure consumption loan model, *J. Econ. Theory* **6** (1973), 382.

CHAPTER VI

Stochastic Processes

STOCHASTIC PROCESSES OF TEMPORARY EQUILIBRIA*

Jean-Michel GRANDMONT and Werner HILDENBRAND

C.O.R.E., Heverlee, Belgium

Received April 1974

It is the aim of the paper to study within the framework of an 'overlapping generation model' the evolution of temporary equilibria. At date t, there are 'newborn' agents and 'old' agents who were born in previous periods; the old agents hold cash balances (fiat money) that they carried over from the previous period. At the beginning of period t, all agents receive a *random* endowment of consumption goods. Then the agents exchange these endowments and money on spot markets at date t (trading in future markets is not considered). Once a temporary equilibrium is reached, the economy moves to the next date. Agents who were born at date t then become old and meet agents born at period $t+1$.

It is shown that the evolution of temporary equilibria in this model leads to analyse the ergodic properties of a certain class of Markov processes with stationary transition probability.

1. Introduction

In Temporary Competitive Equilibrium analysis, one views the evolution of the economy as a sequence of equilibria. The existence of a temporary, or short-run, equilibrium at a single date in economies under uncertainty has been recently investigated in various setups by Grandmont (1970, 1971), Green (1971, 1972), Radner (1973), Sondermann (1971), Stigum (1969, 1972). Yet we do not have much information on the dynamic properties of such economies. The purpose of this paper is to make an attempt in that direction. To this end, we shall use the convenient framework of Samuelson's (1958) pure consumption loan model. The concepts and techniques herein developed should, however, be of interest in other temporary equilibrium models.

The basic feature of Samuelson's model is the existence of overlapping generations. This leads to the natural introduction of sequential trading, since there are, at any date, agents who are not yet born and thus cannot participate in current markets. We shall study the simplest version of this model. Agents are assumed to live two periods, and total population is stationary. The restriction to a life of two periods is inessential, and our analysis carries over to the case where agents live an arbitrary finite number of periods; the same number of

*The work was done in part at the Center for Operations Research and Econometrics, Louvain (Belgium) and University of California, Berkeley. The financial support from Fonds National de la Recherche Scientifique and NSF is gratefully acknowledged. We would like to thank R. Radner for many many helpful discussions and critiques.

Reprinted from *Journal of Mathematical Economics* 1 (1974), 247–278, © North-Holland Publishing Company.

periods for all agents. However, this would complicate the notations so much that it does not justify the gain in generality. Consumption goods available in each period are perishable, while money can be stored at no cost. The total stock of money is constant over time. The reader will quickly discover that we do not offer a substantial monetary theory. As a matter of fact, the good that we call 'money' could be any durable good. However, the presence of such a good is an important feature of the model – 'money' provides a link between the past and the present, and thus, contributes in an essential way to the temporal structure of the model. The evolution of the economy can be viewed as follows. At date t, there are, say, n 'old' agents who were born at the previous date; they hold cash balances that they carried over from the previous period. On the other hand, there are n newborn or 'young' agents. At the outset of period t, all agents receive a (random) endowment of consumption goods. Then the agents exchange these endowments and money on spot markets at date t (trading on future markets is not considered in this model). Once a (temporary) equilibrium is reached, the economy moves to the next date. Agents who were born at date t then become old and meet with agents born at time $t+1$. The process goes on forever.

The state of the economic system in any period is described by a price vector (including the price of money), the agents' endowments of consumption goods, their consumption and cash holdings. We shall make simplifying assumptions ensuring that the equilibrium state (if any) at date t depends only on the past state and on the agents' current endowments of consumption goods.[1] By adapting the arguments of Grandmont (1971) and Grandmont–Laroque (1973), we shall give sufficient conditions for the existence of such an equilibrium state, and shall investigate the existence of invariant (in particular, compact) subsets of the state space (section 4).

In order to simplify the analysis, we focus the attention on uncertainty about the agents' endowments of consumption goods, although uncertainty about the agents' other characteristics can be incorporated in the model. Then, it will be shown (section 5) that, if the agents' endowments follow a Markov process with stationary transition probability, the evolution of the economic system itself can be described as a Markov process. Under some continuity assumptions, the existence of an invariant probability measure on the state space of the economy will be proved.

We next (section 6) investigate the effect of the law of large numbers in this temporary equilibrium model.[2] For any sample, that is, for any realization of the process of the agents' endowments, the economy is a deterministic one, and thus, the set of its possible trajectories over time is well defined. Any such trajectory determines a sequence of equilibrium price systems. We shall show that, roughly

---

[1]If the equilibrium state at date t depends on finitely many past states, the analysis can proceed along the same lines by properly enlarging the state space.

[2]A different approach to this problem has been previously implemented by Younès (1972).

speaking, almost surely, such a sequence can be approximately considered as a sequence of equilibrium prices of a 'limit', non-random economy when the number of agents is large and if their random endowments are stochastically independent. Thus, for such a large economy, macroeconomic observables such as temporary equilibrium prices become in some sense non-random,[3] although uncertainty is not removed for individual agents.

The law of large numbers often permits conclusions to be drawn in large systems when the analysis of small ones is untractable. We give an illustration of that fact for this economy in section 7. As we said earlier, we shall now show in section 5 the existence of invariant distributions on the state space of the economy. We are unable, however, to find acceptable conditions implying the existence of invariant measures assigning probability one to a positive price of money. We show in section 7 that one can give an answer to that problem for large economies by reasoning in the 'limit' economy.

2. Definitions and assumptions

There are ℓ perishable consumption goods available in each period. The space of consumption goods is thus R^l. Fiat money can be stored at no cost from one period to the next. The commodity space is R^{l+1}.

Prices are expressed in an abstract unit of account. An accounting price system in any period is given by $p = ((\dot{p}, s)) \in R^{l+1}_+$, where $\dot{p} = (p_1, \ldots, p_l) \in R^l_+$ is the vector of prices of consumption goods, while $p_{l+1} = s \in R_+$ is the accounting price of money. If $s > 0$, one can define monetary prices of consumption goods by $p_j/s, j = 1, \ldots, \ell$. As agents are only interested in relative prices between money and goods, one can normalize prices by, for instance, $\sum_{j=1}^{l+1} p_j = 1$. We define

$$\bar{S} = \left\{ p \in R^{l+1}_+ \mid \sum_{j=1}^{l+1} p_j = 1 \right\} \qquad \text{(price simplex)},$$

$$\mathring{S} = \{ p \mid p \in \bar{S}, p \gg 0 \} \qquad \text{(prices of goods and of money are positive)},$$

$$S = \{ p = (\dot{p}, s) \mid p \in \bar{S}, \dot{p} \gg 0 \} \qquad \text{(prices of goods are positive, but the price of money may be zero)}.$$

---

[3]This approach must be contrasted with the approach used in the traditional Arrow–Debreu model, where trade must take place once for all at the beginning of all times, *before* the resolution of uncertainty [see Hildenbrand (1971) and Malinvaud (1972, 1973)]. Here prices are observed in any period *after* the resolution of uncertainty in that period. Thus our result says that *ex post* equilibrium prices become non-random for large economies. That type of result is by definition meaningless in the Arrow–Debreu model.

In any given period, an agent is indicated by a couple (i, h), where i belongs to a finite set I with n elements, $\#I = n$, and h takes the value 1 and 2 if the agent is young and old, respectively.

2.1. Endowments

In any period, the initial endowments of consumption goods received (or produced) by a young and old agent belong to the sets E_1 and E_2, respectively. These sets do not depend on the date nor on the agent's index i. Let $E = E_1 \times E_2$.

We shall assume:

(a) $E_h (h = 1, 2)$ *is a compact subset of strictly positive vectors in* R^l.

2.2. Preferences

Every agent lives two periods. Furthermore, any young agent will face a decision problem under uncertainty. Accordingly, an agent's preferences will be described by a complete preordering $\succ$ defined on the space $\mathcal{M}(Q)$ of all probability measures on $Q = R^l_+ \times R^l_+$.[4] All preferences $\succ$ considered here satisfy the *Expected Utility Hypothesis*; that is:

(b) *There is a continuous and bounded utility function* $u : Q \to R$ *such that* $[v(\lambda) = \int_Q u \, d\lambda, \; \lambda \in \mathcal{M}(Q)]$ *is an order-preserving mapping of* $(\mathcal{M}(Q), \succ)$ *into* R. *In addition, one assumes that* u *is strictly concave and strictly increasing.*

The function u is then called a *von Neumann–Morgenstern representation* of the preferences $\succ$. The preordering $\succ$ on $\mathcal{M}(Q)$ induces a preordering on Q, which will be described by the same symbol. For an exposition of the theory underlying this postulate, see, e.g., Arrow (1970).

2.3. Expectations

At any date, a young agent makes a forecast of the equilibrium price system and of his endowment of consumption goods in the next period. This forecast takes the form of a probability measure defined on $S \times E_2$, that is, an element of $\mathcal{M}(S \times E_2)$. This implies that the agent excludes from his forecast zero prices of consumption goods [indeed, equilibrium prices belonging to $\bar{S} \backslash S$ are ruled out by the monotonicity assumption on preferences made in (b)], but does not necessarily exclude a zero price of money.

---

[4]In what follows, if X is a metric space, then $\mathcal{B}(X)$ will be the σ-algebra generated by the open sets of X, while $\mathcal{M}(X)$ will denote the space of all probability measures defined on $(X, \mathcal{B}(X))$, endowed with the topology of weak convergence. For details, see Billingsley (1968, ch. 1) or Parthasarathy (1967, ch. 2).

By assumption, the agent's forecast depends only on the price system which is currently quoted and the equilibrium price system that prevailed in the preceding period. Further, this forecast may be influenced by the value taken by his current endowments of consumption goods. Thus, his *pattern of expectations* is defined by a function ψ which takes $S \times S \times E_1$ into $\mathscr{M}(S \times E_2)$. We shall assume:

(c) *The expectation function* $\psi : S \times S \times E_1 \rightarrow \mathscr{M}(S \times E_2)$ *is continuous.*

In the sequel, we shall assume, for simplicity of the exposition, that *all agents in the economy have the same preference relation* $\succ$ *and the same expectation function* ψ. This restriction is inessential. Our analysis is still valid if different characteristics $(\succ_i, \psi_i)$ are associated with different indices i in I.

Assumptions (a), (b) and (c) are taken for granted throughout the paper.

2.4. Demand

At any date, an agent, either young or old, must choose an action $x = (q, m)$, an element of the action space $X = R_+^{l+1}$, which specifies his current consumption $q \in R_+^l$ and the money $m \in R_+$ that he wants to carry over until the next period. This choice will be made in a different manner by an old agent or by a young one.

Let us first consider an *old agent* ($h = 2$) at time t, with characteristics $(\succ, \psi)$. He knows his current endowment of consumption goods, $e \in E_2$, and is faced by the current price system $p = (\dot{p}, s) \in S$. Moreover, the action $x_1 = (q_1, m_1) \in X$ that he took at date $t-1$ is a datum of his problem. Consider the set of $q_2 \in R_+^l$ that maximize $u(q_1, q_2)$ subject to

$$\dot{p} \cdot q_2 = \dot{p} \cdot e + s m_1,$$

where q_2 is unknown.

Since $\dot{p} \gg 0$, $e \gg 0$, $m_1 \geqq 0$, and since the utility u is continuous and strictly concave, this set has a unique element which is denoted $\varphi(p, e, x_1)$. Then, $\xi_2(p, e, x_1) = \big(\varphi(p, e, x_1), 0\big) \in X$ is the action chosen by the old agent. This defines the *old agent's demand function,*

$$\xi_2 : S \times E_2 \times X \rightarrow X,$$

which is independent of time t.

Now, consider a *young agent* ($h = 1$) at time t with characteristics $(\succ, \psi)$. This agent knows the price system $p(t-1) \in S$ of the previous period. He is given his current endowment of consumption goods $e_1(t) \in E_1$, and faces a price system $p(t) = \big(\dot{p}(t), s(t)\big) \in S$. His forecast is accordingly $\psi\big(p(t), p(t-1), e_1(t)\big)$, an element of $\mathscr{M}(S \times E_2)$. The agent's problem is to choose a *strategy*, that is, an action $x_1 = (q_1, m_1) \in X$ and a measurable function $q_2(\cdot)$ of $S \times E_2$ into R_+^l, subject to

(i) $\dot{p}(t) \cdot q_1 + s(t)m_1 = \dot{p}(t) \cdot e_1(t);$

(ii) $\dot{p} \cdot q_2(p, e) = \dot{p} \cdot e + sm_1,$ *for every* $p = (\dot{p}, s) \in S$
                                           and $e \in E_2$.

Any such strategy defines a random variable $q(\cdot)$ from the probability space $(S \times E_2, \mathscr{B}(S \times E_2), \psi)$ into Q by $q(p, e) = (q_1, q_2(p, e))$. That random variable in turn determines a probability measure on Q. The expected utility of this probability measure is

$$\int_{S \times E_2} u(q_1, q_2(\cdot)) \, d\psi(p(t), p(t-1), e_1(t)).$$

The agent is supposed to maximize this expression subject to (i) and (ii). To the set of optimal strategies corresponds a set of optimal actions x_1, which is denoted $\xi_1(p(t), p(t-1), e_1(t))$. This defines a *young agent's demand correspondence*,

$$\xi_1 : S \times S \times E_1 \to X,$$

which is independent of time t. As a matter of fact, we shall prove below (see section 3) that under our assumptions ξ_1 reduces to a single point whenever $p(t) \in \mathring{S}$, i.e., when the current price of money is positive.

2.5. State space

As was stated earlier, the population of the economy is stationary. Thus, at any date, there are n old agents and n young ones. We further assume that the total stock of money is constant and equal to $M > 0$. Accordingly, the state of the economy in any period is described by a price system $p \in S$, the agents' actions $x_{ih} \in X$ and endowments $e_{ih} \in E_h$ ($i \in I$, $h = 1, 2$), subject to appropriate 'balance conditions'. Formally, the *state space* Z of the economy is the set of all $z = (p, (x_{ih}), (e_{ih}))$ such that

(i) $p \in S, \quad x_{ih} \in X, \quad e_{ih} \in E_h, \qquad i \in I, h = 1, 2;$

(ii) $\sum_{i,h} (q_{ih} - e_{ih}) = 0;$

(iii) $\sum_i m_{i1} = M \quad \text{and} \quad m_{i2} = 0, \quad \text{all } i \in I.$

The state space Z is a bounded, yet not a closed, subset in Euclidean space.

2.6. Temporary equilibrium

Consider the economy at time t. The economy is composed of n young agents and n old ones with common characteristics $(\succ, \psi)$. The past state $z(t-1) = \big(p(t-1), (x_{ih}(t-1)), (e_{ih}(t-1))\big) \in Z$ as well as the current endowments of consumption goods, $e(t) = (e_{ih}(t)) \in E^n$, are given. We shall say that the current state $z(t) = \big(p(t), (x_{ih}(t)), (e_{ih}(t))\big) \in Z$ defines a *temporary equilibrium*, if $x_{i1}(t) \in \xi_1\big(p(t), p(t-1), e_{i1}(t)\big)$ and $x_{i2}(t) = \xi_2\big(p(t), e_{i2}(t), x_{i1}(t-1)\big)$ for all $i \in I$.

We shall denote by $W\big(e(t), z(t-1)\big)$ the set of corresponding temporary equilibria. When $e(t)$ and $z(t-1)$ are parametrically varied in E^n and Z, respectively, this defines a relation W of $E^n \times Z$ into Z. This relation W does not depend on the date t under consideration. It only depends on the index set I, the stock of money M, and the characteristics $(\succ, \psi)$. The main object of the two next sections is to state and prove some essential properties of this relation.

3. Properties of demand functions ξ_1 and ξ_2

We consider in this section an agent with characteristics $(\succ, \psi)$, and recall a few properties[5] of the demand function ξ_1 and ξ_2 defined in section 2.4.

The following properties of the *old agent's demand function* ξ_2 can be proved by standard arguments [see, e.g., Debreu (1959)].

(3.1) ξ_2 *is a continuous function on* $S \times E_2 \times X$.

(3.2)   *Let the sequence* (p^k, e^k, x^k) *in* $S \times E_2 \times X$ *be convergent to* (p, e, x) *such that* $p \in \bar{S} \backslash S$, *and* $p \cdot (e, m) > 0$, *where* $x = (q, m)$. *Then* $\| \xi_2(p^k, e^k, x^k) \|$ *tends to* $+\infty$.

We next consider a *young agent's demand correspondence* ξ_1. It is straightforward to check that, given $p(t) \in S$, $p(t-1) \in S$, and $e_1(t) \in E_1$, the set of optimal actions $\xi_1(p(t), p(t-1), e_1(t))$ can be obtained by the following backward dynamic programming procedure.

For any $x_1 = (q_1, m_1) \in X$, consider the associated strategy $(x_1, q_2(\cdot))$, where $q_2(p, e) = \varphi(p, e, x_1)$ for all $(p, e) \in S \times E_2$ (the function φ was defined in section 2.4 for an old agent). Define

$$v(x_1, p(t), p(t-1), e_1(t))$$
$$= \textstyle\int_{S \times E_2} u(q_1, \varphi(\cdot, \cdot, x_1)) \, d\psi(p(t), p(t-1), e_1(t)).$$

Then $\xi_1(p(t), p(t-1), e_1(t))$ is obtained by maximizing $v(x_1, p(t), p(t-1), e_1(t))$ with respect to $x_1 = (q_1, m_1)$ subject to $x_1 \in X$ and $p(t) \cdot x_1 = \dot{p}(t) \cdot e_1(t)$.

(3.3) v *is continuous on* $X \times S \times S \times E_1$.

---

[5] The material of this section is adapted from Grandmont (1971) and Grandmont–Laroque (1973).

Proof. Let $x_1 = (q_1, m_1) \in X$ and $p(t) \in S$, $p(t-1) \in S$, $e_1 \in E_1$. Consider $(q_1, \varphi(\cdot, \cdot, x_1))$, a random variable from the space $S \times E_2$, endowed with the probability measure $\psi(p(t), p(t-1), e_1)$ into Q. Let $\chi(x_1, p(t), p(t-1), e_1) \in \mathcal{M}(Q)$ be the probability distribution of this random variable. Clearly,

$$v(x_1, p(t), p(t-1), e_1) = \int_Q u \, d\chi(x_1, p(t), p(t-1), e_1).$$

Since u is continuous and bounded, it suffices to show that the mapping χ from $X \times S \times S \times E_1$ into $\mathcal{M}(Q)$ is continuous. But this immediately follows from Billingsley (1968, ch. 1, Theorem 5.5), the continuity of φ and assumption (c). Q.E.D.

It is easy to verify the following properties of v. Fix $(p(t), p(t-1), e_1)$ in $S \times S \times E_1$ and write $v(x)$ for $v(x, p(t), p(t-1), e_1)$.

(3.4)   *Consider* $x' = (q', m')$ *and* $x'' = (q'', m'')$ *in* X. *Then*

         (i) $x' \geqq x''$ *implies* $v(x') \geqq v(x'')$;

         (ii) $q' > q''$, $m' \geqq m''$ *implies* $v(x') > v(x'')$;

         (iii) $q' = q''$, $m' > m''$ *implies* $v(x') > v(x'')$ *if and only if* $\psi(p(t), p(t-1), e_1)$ *assigns a positive probability to* $\mathring{S} \times E_2$.

(3.5)   *Consider* $x' = (q', m')$ *and* $x'' = (q'', m'')$ *in* X, *such that* $x' \neq x''$. *Then, for any* $0 < \lambda < 1$, $v(\lambda x' + (1-\lambda)x'') \geqq \lambda v(x') + (1-\lambda)v(x'')$. *Inequality is strict if either* (1) $q' \neq q''$, *or* (2) $\psi(p(t), p(t-1), e_1)$ *assigns a positive probability to* $\mathring{S} \times E_2$.

Now the following properties of the relation ξ_1 of $S \times S \times E_1$ into R^{l+1} are immediate consequences[6] of (3.3)–(3.5).

(3.6)   (i) ξ_1 *has a closed graph*;

         (ii) ξ_1 *is non-empty-compact-valued, and u.h.c. on* $\mathring{S} \times S \times E_1$;

         (iii) $\xi_1(p(t), p(t-1), e_1)$ *has a unique element if* $p(t) \in \mathring{S}$;

         (iv)   *Let* $(p(t), p(t-1), e_1) \in S \times S \times E_1$ *such that* $s(t) = 0$. *Then* $\xi_1(p(t), p(t-1), e_1)$ *is non-empty if and only if* $\psi(p(t), p(t-1), e_1)$ *assigns zero probability to* $S \times E_2$. *If* $\bar{x} = (\bar{q}, \bar{m}) \in \xi_1(p(t), p(t-1), e_1)$, *then all elements in* $\xi_1(\cdot)$ *are given by* $(\bar{q}, m)$, *where* $m \geqq 0$ *is arbitrary.*

---

[6]A correspondence φ from the metric space X into the metric space Y is P-valued if $\varphi(x)$ has the property P for all $x \in X$; φ has a *closed graph* if $[x^k \in X, x^k \to x \in X, y^k \in \varphi(x^k), y^k \to y \in y]$ implies $[y \in \varphi(x)]$. The correspondence φ is upper hemicontinuous (u.h.c.) if for any open subset G of Y, the set $\{x \in X | \varphi(x) \subset G\}$ is open in X. It can be shown that the correspondence φ is compact-valued and u.h.c. if and only if $[x^k \in X, x^k \to x \in X, y^k \in \varphi(x^k)]$ implies [there is a convergent subsequence $y^{k_q} \to y \in Y$ such that $y \in \varphi(x)$].

Proof

(i) From (3.4), (ii), $\xi_1(\cdot)$ is obtained by maximizing $v(x, \cdot)$ with respect to x, subject to $x \in X$ and $p(t) \cdot x \leqq p(t) \cdot e_1$. Since, by (2.3), v is continuous, (i) follows by a standard argument.

(ii) Obvious.

(iii) Follows immediately from (3.5). Indeed, let $x' = (q', m')$ and $x'' = (q'', m'')$ be in $\xi_1(\cdot)$ when $s(t) > 0$. Then, by (3.5 – 1), $q' = q''$. But this implies $m' = m''$, since $p(t) \cdot x' = p(t) \cdot x''$ and $s(t) > 0$.

(iv) The fact that $\xi_1(p(t), p(t-1), e_1)$ is non-void when $s(t) = 0$ if and only if $\psi(p(t), p(t-1), e_1)$ assigns zero probability to $S \times E_2$ immediately follows from (3.4 – i and iii). Then, the last statement follows from (3.5 – 2).   Q.E.D.

Remark. We showed continuity of ξ_1 and ξ_2 when prices and endowments vary. Similar continuity results can be obtained when the characteristics $(\succ, \psi)$ also vary, provided that the space of agents' characteristics is properly topologized.

First, ψ is a continuous mapping from the separable metric space $S \times S \times E_1$ into the separable metric space $\mathcal{M}(S \times E_2)$. When the space ψ of such mappings is endowed with the topology of uniform convergence on compacta, it can be shown as in (3.3), that v is continuous with respect to actions, prices, endowments, and pattern of expectations ψ. Continuity properties of ξ_1 then follow as in (3.6). For details, see Christiansen (1972).

Second, $\succ$ is a continuous complete preordering on the separable metric space $\mathcal{M}(Q)$, and can therefore be identified with a closed subset of the product space $\mathcal{M}(Q) \times \mathcal{M}(Q)$. The set of these preorderings can thus be topologized by means of the Hausdorff distance, as in Debreu (1969). Then it can be shown that ξ_2 and ξ_1 are continuous with respect to preferences $\succ$ as well as with respect to the other parameters. It should be noted that the concept of closed convergence that was employed by Hildenbrand (1970, 1974) is not a topological concept here, since $\mathcal{M}(Q)$ may not be locally compact.

4. Temporary equilibrium correspondence

The relation W of $E^n \times Z$ into Z as defined in section 2.6 describes the way in which the set of current equilibria depends upon current endowments and the past state of the economy. The internal consistency of the model requires that the relation W be well defined.

Theorem 1. **The relation W of $E^n \times Z$ into Z is a compact-valued and u.h.c. correspondence.**

Proof

(1) *For every* $e^1 = (e_{ih}^1) \in E^n$ *and* $z^0 = (p^0, (x_{ih}^0), (e_{ih}^0)) \in Z$, $W(e^1, z^0)$ *is nonempty.*

This will be proved by adapting standard arguments. For any $p \in S$, consider the set $\zeta(p)$ of aggregate excess demand,

$$\zeta(p) = \sum_i [\xi_1(p, p^0, e_{i1}^1) + \{\xi_2(p, e_{i2}^1, x_{i1}^0)\} - \{(e_{i1}^1 + e_{i2}^1), M)\}].$$

We wish to find a vector p^* such that $0 \in \zeta(p^*)$. Now, from (3.1) and (3.6), ζ is a correspondence that is u.h.c. on $\mathring{S}$. Further, $\zeta(p)$ reduces to a single point when $p \in \mathring{S}$. Finally, $p \in S$, $y \in \zeta(p)$ imply $p \cdot y = 0$. Next, consider a sequence of compact, convex subsets S^k of $\mathring{S}$ such that $S^k \subset S^{k+1}$ and $\bigcup^k S^k \supset \mathring{S}$. For each k, apply Debreu's Lemma (1956). We thus get a sequence $p^k \in S^k$ and a sequence $y^k \in \zeta(p^k)$ such that $p \cdot y^k \leq 0$ for all $p \in S^k$. This implies that y^k is bounded, for y^k is bounded below and $p^1 \cdot y^k \leq 0$, with $p^1 \gg 0$, for all k. We can therefore assume without loss of generality that y^k converges to $y^* \in R^{l+1}$ and p^k converges to $p^* \in \bar{S}$. Clearly, $p^* \in S$, for otherwise, one could contradict (3.2). Since ζ has a closed graph, this implies $y^* \in \zeta(p^*)$. Finally, $p \cdot y^* \leq p^* \cdot y^* = 0$ for all $p \in S$. It follows that $y^* \leq 0$. Hence $y^* = 0 \in \zeta(p^*)$ if $p^* \in \mathring{S}$. When $p^* \in S \backslash \mathring{S}$, i.e., of $s^* = 0$, we get $q^* = 0$ and $m^* \leq 0$, where $y^* = (q^*, m^*)$. In view of (3.6 – iv), this implies $0 \in \zeta(p^*)$ in this case, too.

(2) *W is compact-valued and u.h.c.*

Since ξ_2 is continuous (3.1), and ξ_1 has a closed graph (3.6 – i), it is easy to check that W itself has a closed graph. Hence, it suffices to show: for any sequence $(e^k, z^k) \in E^n \times Z$ converging to $(e, z) \in E^n \times Z$, every sequence $\bar{z}^k \in W(e^k, z^k)$ is contained in a compact subset of Z. That means that no subsequence of $\bar{z}^k$ can converge to a z involving a zero price for some consumption good, which is an immediate consequence of (3.2). Q.E.D.

The foregoing result guarantees the existence of temporary equilibrium. However, the equilibrium price of money may be zero – an awkward situation, since we are dealing with a monetary economy. It is clear that we must make additional assumptions in order to prevent such a situation from arising. Indeed, if, at date t, all agents expect the price of money to be zero at time $t+1$ for every current price system in S, then the equilibrium price of money *must* be zero at date t. In order to avoid such a situation, we must assume that the agents assign a positive probability to the event 'the price of money will be positive at date $t+1$' even when the price of money at time t is zero. Such an assumption is acceptable, however, only if the past equilibrium price of money was itself positive. Formally, let $\check{Z} = Z \cap (\mathring{S} \times X^{2n} \times E^n)$. Then

Corollary. Assume that for every $p(t-1) \in \mathring{S}$, any $p(t) \in S \backslash \mathring{S}$ and $e_1(t) \in E_1$, $\psi(p(t), p(t-1), e_1(t))$ assigns a positive probability to $\mathring{S} \times E_2$. Then, for any $z(t-1) \in \mathring{Z}$ and $e(t) \in E^n$, one has $z(t) \in \mathring{Z}$ for all $z(t) \in W(e(t), z(t-1))$.

The proof is obvious from Theorem 1 and (3.6(iv)).

Under the assumption of this corollary, we are sure that $\mathring{Z}$ is invariant under W, that is, $z \in \mathring{Z}$ and $e \in E^n$ imply $W(e, z) \subset \mathring{Z}$. In the sequel, it will be important to know whether there are *compact* subsets K of Z that are *invariant* under W, i.e.,

$$W(E^n, K) \subset K.$$

Proposition 1. For every state $z \in Z$ there is a compact subset K of Z containing z which is invariant under W.

Proof. Assume the proposition is false. Then there exists $\bar{z} \in Z$ such that for every compact K containing $\bar{z}$ we have

$$W(E^n, K) \not\subset K,$$

i.e., there exists $(e_K, z_K) \in E^n \times K$ and there is $\bar{z}_K \in K$ such that (1) $\bar{z}_K \in W(e_K, z_K)$ and (2) $\bar{z}_K \notin K$. Hence there are sequences $(\bar{z}^k) = (\bar{e}^k, \bar{p}^k, \bar{x}_{ih}^k)$, (e^k), and (z^k) such that property (1) and (2) imply that

$$\bar{x}_{i2}^k = \xi_2(\bar{p}^k, \bar{e}_{i2}^k, \bar{x}_{i1}^k), \qquad i \in I,$$

and

$$\bar{p}^k \to p \in \bar{S} \backslash S.$$

Since $\bar{z}^k \in W(\bar{e}^k, \bar{z}^k)$ it follows that the sequence $(\bar{x}_{i2})$ is bounded, which is a contradiction to property (3.2). Q.E.D.

It should be noted that even when $\mathring{z} \in \mathring{Z}$, an *invariant compact* set K containing $\mathring{z}$ *is not in general a subset of $\mathring{Z}$*: $z \in K$ may imply a zero price of money. By slightly modifying the proof of the foregoing proposition, it would be possible to show that, given $z \in \mathring{Z}$, there is a compact subset $K(z)$ of $\mathring{Z}$ containing z that is invariant under W if the following condition is satisfied:

(A) *For every* $p(t) \in S \backslash \mathring{S}$, $p(t-1) \in S$, *and* $e_1(t) \in E_1$, $\psi(p(t), p(t-1), e_1(t))$ *assigns positive weight to* $\mathring{S} \times E_2$.

This condition, however, is far too strong from an economic point of view. It may not be unreasonable to postulate, as we did in the above corollary, that the price of money is expected to differ from zero with some positive probability when the current price of money is zero *provided that the past price of money was positive.* It is harder to accept the same postulate when *both* past and current prices of money are equal to zero. It would indeed be incompatible with a property that seems natural and that we shall take as an assumption in section 6 – if past and current prices are equal, then the traders expect the same prices in the future.

Remark. The existence of a temporary equilibrium in that class of models was originally proved in Grandmont (1971) and Grandmont–Laroque (1973) under a slightly different set of assumptions on expectations. Basically, the traders' behavior was defined in those studies only for positive prices of money. These assumptions can be translated in the present framework as follows.

Expectations are defined only on $\mathring{S} \times \mathring{S} \times E_1$ and are summarized by a mapping taking values in $\mathcal{M}(S \times E_2)$. Assumption (c) is replaced by

(c.1) $\psi : \mathring{S} \times \mathring{S} \times E_1 \to \mathcal{M}(S \times E_2)$ *is continuous.*

(c.2)   *Given* $p(t-1) \in \mathring{S}$ *and* $e_1(t) \in E_1$, *for any sequence* $p^r \in \mathring{S}$ *tending to* $p \in S \backslash \mathring{S}$,

    (i)   *the family* $\psi^r = \psi(p^r, p(t-1), e_1(t))$ *is tight in* $\mathcal{M}(S \times E_2)$;

    (ii)   *there exists* $\varepsilon > 0$ *and a compact subset* C *of* $\mathring{S}$ *such that* $\psi^r(C \times E_2) \geqq \varepsilon$ *for* r *large enough.*

[Actually this set of assumptions is more general than in the above mentioned papers, since there, expectations took values in $\mathcal{M}(\mathring{S} \times E_2)$.] It is then not difficult to show that, under (a), (b), (c.1) and (c.2), given $z(t-1) \in \mathring{Z}$ and $e(t) \in E^n$, there exists a temporary equilibrium $z(t) \in \mathring{Z}$. This result is indeed essentially equivalent to the corollary to Theorem 1, except that the continuity of expectations when the price of money varies continuously from a positive to a zero level, which was assumed in (c), is no longer postulated. Indeed, expectations may not even be defined for zero prices of money.

Under (a), (b), (c.1) and (c.2), it is thus possible to define a temporary equilibrium correspondence, taking $E^n \times \mathring{Z}$ into $\mathring{Z}$, that displays the properties stated in Theorem 1. But, given $z^* \in \mathring{Z}$, we would then be unable to assert the existence of a compact invariant subset $K(z^*)$ of $\mathring{Z}$ containing z^*, unless we are willing to accept a condition like (A).

In the text, the existence of a compact invariant subset of Z such that the restriction of W to this compact is u.h.c. crucially depends upon the continuity assumption (c). It should be emphasized that this postulate is not so innocuous. Some economists might argue, with good reason, that a change from a positive to a zero price of money involves a discontinuity that should be reflected in the agents' expectations. Given our present knowledge, however, it seems difficult to proceed without it.

5. Markov processes of temporary equilibria

We now attempt to study the dynamic behavior of the economy when the agent's endowments are random.

Uncertainty about the agents' endowments of consumption goods at subsequent dates $t = 1, 2, \ldots$ is described by random variables defined on a common probability space $(\Omega, \mathscr{F}, \nu)$. Specifically, old agents at time 1 have random endowments given by a family $(\alpha_i^0)_{i \in I}$ of random variables with values in E_2. Agents born at time $t = 1, 2, \ldots$ have random endowments described by a family $(\alpha_i^t)_{i \in I}$ of random variables with values in $E = E_1 \times E_2$. The economy is then *characterized by the index set I, the stock of money M and the agents' common characteristics* $(\succ, \psi)$, *the state* $z(0)$ *at time* 0 *and the endowments process* α_i^t,

$$\mathscr{E} = (I, \succ, \psi, (\alpha_i^t)_{i \in I}, z(0), M).$$

For each $t = 1, 2, \ldots$, we define a random variable e^t with values in E^n that describes the random endowments of the n young agents and of the n old ones at that date. Formally, let proj_h be the projection of $E = E_1 \times E_2$ onto E_h ($h = 1, 2$). Then

$$e^1 = ((\text{proj}_1 \circ \alpha_i^1, \alpha_i^0))_{ii \in I}),$$

while, for $t \geq 2$,

$$e^t = ((\text{proj}_1 \circ \alpha_i^t, \text{proj}_2 \circ \alpha_i^{t-1})_{i \in I}).$$

Then, for any given sample $\omega \in \Omega$, *a possible trajectory of the economy* is a sequence $\{z(t) \in Z, t \geq 0\}$ that satisfies

$$z(t) \in W(e^t(\omega), z(t-1)),$$

all $t \geq 1$.

In this section, however, we wish to consider only trajectories which can be viewed as a realization of a stochastic process $\{z^t, t \geq 0\}$ defined on $(\Omega, \mathscr{F}, \nu)$. The foregoing definition does not satisfy this requirement, since W may be multivalued. In order to circumvent this difficulty, we shall assume *in this section* that, at each date, a unique equilibrium is chosen by a procedure which is represented by a selection f of W, that is, a function $f: E^n \times Z \to Z$ such that $f(e, z) \in W(e, z)$ for all $(e, z) \in E^n \times Z$. Since the correspondence W is compact-valued and u.h.c., it follows from a well-known result by Kuratowski and Ryll-Nardzewski (1965) – for an easy proof see, e.g., Hildenbrand (1974, D.II, Lemma 1) – that there exists a *measurable* selection f of W. Then, in the sequel, we assume that:

(d) *f is a measurable selection of the correspondence W.*

With this assumption, the evolution of the economy is described by a stochastic process $\{z^t, t \geq 0\}$ defined on $(\Omega, \mathscr{F}, v)$ by

$$z^0(\omega) = z(0) \quad and \quad z^t(\omega) = f(e^t(\omega), z^{t-1}(\omega)),$$
$$all \ t \geq 1 \ and \ \omega \in \Omega.$$

We wish to make assumptions ensuring that the process (z^t) is a Markov process with stationary transition probabilities. Now, the state of the economy at time t is entirely determined by the state at time $t-1$ and the values of endowments of consumption goods at time t. It is thus clear that the process z^t will have the desired property if the process $\{e^t, t \geq 0\}$ [where $e^0(\omega) = e(0)$ for every $\omega \in \Omega$] is itself Markov with stationary transition probabilities. We therefore postulate:

(e) *The sequence* $\{e^0, e^1, e^2, \ldots\}$ *of endowments is a Markov process with stationary transition probability Q acting on E^n.*

Thus, for every $e \in E^n$ and $B \in \mathscr{B}(E^n)$, the number $Q(e, B) \in [0, 1]$ gives the probability that endowments belong to B at date $t+1$ if endowments are equal to e at time t. Given $e \in E^n$, $Q(e, \cdot)$ is an element of $\mathscr{M}(E^n)$; given $B \in \mathscr{B}(E^n)$, $Q(\cdot, B)$ is a measurable function of E^n into $[0, 1]$.
· For any $z = (p, x, e) \in Z$ and $B \in \mathscr{B}(Z)$, let

$$P(z, B) = Q(e, \{e' \in E^n \,|\, f(e', z) \in B\}).$$

The mapping $P: Z \times \mathscr{B}(Z) \to [0, 1]$ is a transition probability. Indeed:

Lemma 1. *Under assumptions (d) and (e),*

(1) $P(z, \cdot) \in \mathscr{M}(Z)$ *for any* $z \in Z$;

(2) $P(\cdot, B)$ *is a measurable function for any* $B \in \mathscr{B}(Z)$.

Proof

(1) Given $\bar{z} = (\bar{p}, \bar{x}, \bar{e}) \in Z$, the function $f(\cdot, \bar{z})$ is a random variable from the probability space $(E^n, \mathscr{B}(E^n), Q(\bar{e}, \cdot))$ into Z. The measure $P(\bar{z}, \cdot)$ is precisely the distribution of this random variable, that is, $P(\bar{z}, B) = Q(\bar{e}, \{e \in E^n \,|\, f(e, \bar{z}) \in B\})$.

(2) Given any $A \in \mathscr{B}(E^n) \otimes \mathscr{B}(Z)$, and $z = (p, x, e) \in Z$, consider the section $A_z = \{e \in E^n \,|\, (e, z) \in A\}$, which belongs to $\mathscr{B}(Z)$. For every set A, consider the function $z \mapsto Q(e, A_z)$. Let $\mathscr{A}$ be the class of sets A such that $z \mapsto Q(e, A_z)$ is measurable. The class $\mathscr{A}$ contains all rectangles $C \times D$ where $C \in \mathscr{B}(E^n)$, $D \in \mathscr{B}(Z)$. It is not difficult to check that $\mathscr{A}$ is closed under the operations of complementation and of finite, pairwise disjoint unions. It is a monotone class, too. Thus $\mathscr{A}$ is a σ-algebra that contains $\mathscr{B}(E^n) \otimes \mathscr{B}(Z)$.

Now, given $B \in \mathcal{B}(Z)$, let $A = \{(e, z) \in E^n \times Z \mid f(e, z) \in B\}$. Since f is measurable, $A \in \mathcal{B}(E^n \times Z)$. Since E^n and Z are separable metric spaces, $\mathcal{B}(E^n \times Z) = \mathcal{B}(E^n) \otimes \mathcal{B}(Z)$. Now, remark that $P(z, B) = Q(e, A_z)$ for all $z = (p, x, e) \in Z$. Thus $P(\cdot, B)$ is measurable.   Q.E.D.

Thus, under assumptions (d) and (e), the sequence $\{z^t, t \geq 0\}$ is a Markov process with stationary transition probability $P(\cdot, \cdot)$ acting on Z. Loosely speaking, $P(z, B)$ is the probability that the economic system moves into the set of states B at date $t+1$ if it is in the state z at time t.

It is natural to ask now whether the economic system described by the Markov process $\{z^t, t \geq 0\}$ displays some kind of stochastic stability. This question leads us to study the ergodic properties of the Markov process (z^t). Of particular interest is the question under what conditions on the economy $\mathscr{E}$ the probability distribution of the state z^t at time t tends to a limit in $\mathcal{M}(Z)$ as t tends to infinity. It should be clear that this is not a statement on trajectories. Rather, we try to make a prediction on the state of the economy at time t conditionally upon the state at $t = 0$.

It is well known that the probability distribution of the random variable z^t is given by $P^t(z(0), \cdot)$, where $P^t(\cdot, \cdot)$ denotes the tth iterate of the transition probability $P(\cdot, \cdot)$, i.e.,

$$P^t(z, B) = \int_Z P(y, B) P^{t-1}(z, \mathrm{d}y), \qquad z \in Z, \, B \in \mathcal{B}(Z), \quad t \geq 1,$$

where P^0 denotes the identity, i.e.,

$$P^0(z, B) = \begin{cases} 1, & \text{if } z \in B, \\ 0, & \text{if } z \notin B. \end{cases}$$

Our problem thus is a well-known problem in the ergodic theory for Markov processes. Obviously, without making certain assumptions on the structure of the transition probability P there is no hope of obtaining a positive answer to the above question. Any assumption on the transition probability P, however, should be derived from certain properties of the selection f and in turn these properties on the selection f should be derivable from assumptions on the defining data of the economy $\mathscr{E}$. We are not able to give in this paper a satisfactory treatment of this program. We shall come back to this point in a subsequent paper.

If the economic system is *stochastically stable* in the sense that the sequence $(P^t(z, \cdot))_{t=1, 2,...}$ converges to a measure μ^* on Z (which may depend on z), then μ^* is an *invariant measure* for the transition probability P, i.e.,

$$\mu^*(B) = \int_Z P(z, B) \mu^*(\mathrm{d}z), \qquad B \in \mathcal{B}(Z).$$

In this case, the stochastic process $(z_t, z_{t+1}, \ldots)$ converges to a *stationary* stochastic process which is defined by the invariant measure μ^* and the transition probability P. Thus, if we are interested in the long-run behavior of the economy, then it is justified to analyse directly this stationary Markov process (μ^*, P). This leads to the concept of a 'long-run statistical equilibrium' as a stationary stochastic process as it was introduced by Radner (1973, see in particular section 5.2).[7]

A first step towards a stability analysis of the Markov process $z(t)$ is the existence of an invariant measure μ^* for the transition probability P. Of particular importance is the case where the invariant measure is unique. Obviously, this can be expected only in quite special situations. We now summarize some known results on the existence of invariant measures applied to our particular situation.

The purely measure theoretic case

Assume that on the state space Z is given a probability measure $m \in \mathcal{M}(Z)$ with respect to which the transition probability P is non-singular, i.e., $m(B) = 0$ implies $P(z, B) = 0$ for m-almost every $z \in Z$. There are many such measures m. For example, let $\bar{m}$ be any probability measure on Z, e.g., $P(\bar{z}, \cdot)$, and let $Q^t(B) = \int_Z P^t(z, B)\bar{m}(dz)$. Then one can choose

$$m(B) = \sum_{t=0}^{\infty} \frac{1}{2^{t+1}} Q^t(B).$$

Then we have the following result [e.g., Foguel (1969)]:

The state space Z may be decomposed uniquely (up to m-null sets) into the disjoint union

$$Z = Z_0 \cup Z_1,$$

where

(i) $\qquad Z_0 = \bigcup_{n=1}^{\infty} S_n \quad with \quad S_n \subset S_{n+1} \quad and \quad \frac{1}{k} \sum_{t=0}^{k-1} P^t(z, S_n) \xrightarrow[k \to 8]{} 0$

uniformly in z (up to an m-null set);

---

[7]The expectation function ψ, as defined in section 2.3, was given ad hoc; expectations were not explicitly related to the uncertainty about the environment. Therefore it can well happen in our model that the price-expectation function ψ is different from the 'actual' conditional probability distribution of prices derived from the stationary process (v^*, P). A natural question is whether there exists self-fulfilling price expectations. There are, however, in our opinion several conceptual difficulties. We thank R. Radner for bringing to our attention this gap in the paper.

(ii) $P(z, Z_0) \leqq \begin{cases} 0, & if\ z \notin Z_0 \\ 1, & if\ z \in Z_0 \end{cases}$; *thus the Markov process (z^t) with transition probability P can be restricted to the subset Z_1;*

(iii)   *for the restricted process on Z_1 with transition probability $P \mid Z_1$, there exists an invariant measure $\mu \in \mathcal{M}(Z_1)$ and the measure v has the same null sets as the measure m.*

This result does not, in general, guarantee the existence of an invariant measure, since, of course, the set Z_1 may be empty. However, this general result gives some insight into what happens if there is no invariant measure. Clearly, it remains to investigate under what assumptions on the economy $\mathscr{E}$ or on the selection f the set Z_1 will be non-empty or every Z_0 will be empty.

The above result does make no use of the fact that the state space can be assumed to be a compact space (*see Proposition 1*). If we use this topological structure of Z we can apply the so-called:

Kryloff–Bogoliouboff Theory

A transition probability $P(\cdot, \cdot)$ acting on Z defines a mapping, again denoted by P, of the space of bounded measurable function h into itself,

$$(Ph)(z) = \int h(y)P(z, dy), \qquad z \in Z.$$

The Kryloff–Bogoliouboff Theory assumes that the state space is compact and that the above mapping assigns to every *continuous* function h a *continuous function Ph*. Hence we have to search for conditions on the selection f of W such that the derived transition probability P has this property.

Lemma 2.   Assume in addition to assumptions (d) and (e) that:

(1)   *The mapping $e \mapsto Q(e, \cdot)$ of E^n into $\mathcal{M}(E^n)$ is continuous.*

(2)   *The selection f is continuous, or, more generally, for every $\bar{z} = (\bar{p}, \bar{x}, \bar{e}) \in Z$, the selection f is continuous at $(e, \bar{z}) \in E^n \times Z$ for $Q(\bar{e}, \cdot) - $ almost every $e \in E^n$.*

Then every bounded continuous function h of Z into R is mapped by P into a bounded continuous function Ph.

Proof.   Let the sequence $z_n = (p_n, x_n, e_n)$ be convergent to $z = (p, x, e)$. We have to show that $(Ph)(z_n)) \to (Ph)(z)$, i.e.,

$$\int h(y)P(z_n, dy) \to \int h(y)P(z, dy).$$

Since h is by assumption a bounded continuous function we have to show that the sequence $(P(z_n, \cdot))$ converges weakly to $P(z, \cdot)$. By definition, $P(z_n, \cdot)$ is the distribution of the mapping $f(z_n, \cdot)$ defined on the probability space $(E^n, \mathscr{B}(E^n), Q(e_n, \cdot))$. Since the sequence $Q(e_n, \cdot)$ converges by assumption (1) weakly to $Q(e, \cdot)$ and since f has the continuity property specified in (2), it follows [e.g., Billingsley (1968, Theorem 5.5)] that the sequence $P(z_n, \cdot)$ converges weakly to $P(z, \cdot)$.   Q.E.D.

The Kryloff–Bogoliouboff Theory [e.g., Jacobs (1962, vol. II, p. 359)] applied to our situation then, gives the following result:

Let K be a compact subset of the state space which is invariant under W (Proposition 1). Restrict the Markov process (z^t) to the set K and assume that the assumptions of the lemma hold. Then:

(i)   *The set V of invariant probability measures for the transition probability P is non-empty, convex, and compact.*

(ii)   *There exists a subset $K_0 \subset K$ with $\mu(K_0) = 1$ for every $\mu \in V$, such that*

(a)   *for every $z \in K_0$, there exists a probability measure μ_z such that the sequence*

$$\frac{1}{k} \sum_{t=0}^{k=1} P^t(z, \cdot)$$

converges weakly to μ_z;

(b) $$\lim_k \inf \frac{1}{k} \sum_{t=0}^{k-1} P^t(z, \mathscr{U}) > 0$$

for every neighborhood $\mathscr{U}$ of $z \in K_0$ (thus, every point in K_0 is in a 'strong sense' recurrent).

(iii)   *The measure μ_z on K, defined in (a), is an ergodic invariant measure for $P(\cdot, \cdot)$ (i.e., if $B \in \mathscr{B}(K)$) is such that*

$$P(y, B) = \begin{cases} 1, & if \ y \in B, \\ 0, & if \ y \notin B, \end{cases}$$

then $\mu_z(B)$ is either 1 or 0); further, the measure μ_z is an extremal point of the set V of all invariant measures.

(iv)   *If z^* belongs to the support of the measure μ_z, then $\mu_{z^*} = \mu_z$.*

Remarks

(1) If one looks at the limit μ (if it exists) of the sequence $P^t(z(0), \cdot)$, or, more generally, at a measure μ_z [as defined above by property (a)], one would like to know something about the weight assigned by μ to a positive price of money, i.e., to $\mathring{Z}$. We know that, under economically reasonable conditions (see the corollary to Theorem 1), $P^t(z(0), \mathring{Z}) = 1$ for all $t \geq 1$ if $z(0) \in \mathring{Z}$. The measure μ can nevertheless assign probability 1 to a zero price of money. We do not know at present of acceptable conditions that would prevent such a phenomenon. Of course, a condition like (A) of section 4 would do the trick, but we already pointed out that such a condition is too restrictive. We shall see later on that one can make some progress on this question if one can appeal to the law of large numbers, so that macroeconomic observables such as equilibrium prices become (in some sense) non-random.

(2) The process $\{z^t, t \geq 0\}$ is no longer Markov if the agents' expectations at time t depend on the state of the economic system at dates $t-2, t-3, \ldots$, or, if agents live for more than two periods (for instance, an agent's preferences in the third period of his life are conditioned by his actual consumption at the previous two dates). In such cases, the set of temporary equilibria at time t depends upon the state of the economic system at dates $t-1, t-2, \ldots, t-T$, for instance. If T is fixed then the analysis can nevertheless be carried out along the same lines by properly enlarging the state space of the process.

(3) We deliberately focused the attention on uncertainty on endowments in order to simplify the analysis. Uncertainty on the agents' other characteristics $(\succ, \psi)$ can be incorporated in the model. An agent born at time t would then be given by a random variable α^t defined on $(\Omega, \mathscr{F}, \nu)$ with values in a compact subset of the space of the agents' characteristics $(\succ, \psi, e_1, e_2)$ properly topologized (see the remark at the end of section 3).

6. Large economies with individual uncertainty

In the last section we considered the endowments of every agent in every period as a random variable. Now we shall assume that in every period t the family $\{\alpha_i^t\}_{i \in I}$ of random endowments of agents born at time t are stochastically independent. The effect of this assumption on an intuitive level is obvious – the fluctuation in the sequence of temporary equilibrium prices, which are due to the randomness of the individual endowments, will be reduced and will be negligible if there are 'many' agents in the economy. The purpose of this section is to show that a large economy with stochastically independent endowments – for simplicity, for all agents of the same probability law – can be considered approximately as a large economy with deterministic endowments, where the distribution of agents' endowments in the commodity space is according to the probabilistic law of the random endowments in the original economy.

An economy $\mathscr{E}$ with random endowments is described by

$$\mathscr{E} = (I, \succ, \psi, (\alpha_i^t)_{i \in I}, M, (\alpha_i^0, x_{i1}^0)_{i \in I}, p(0)),$$

where I denotes the index set of agents; $(\succ, \psi)$ their common characteristics, preferences $\succ$ and expectation function ψ; α_i^t is the random endowment vector of consumption goods of agent i born at time t, α_i^t has values in $E = E_1 \times E_2$; M is the total stock of money; $[(\alpha^0, x_{i1}^0)_{i \in I}, p(0)] = z(0)$ describes the initial state of the economy. The past price system at time $t = 1$ is $p(0)$, an old agent i at time $t = 1$ has the random endowments α_i^0 which has values in E_2, and x_{i1}^0 describes his actions when he was young.

For every sample $\omega \in \Omega$ the endowments $\alpha_i^t(\omega) \in E$ and $\alpha_i^0(\omega) \in E_2$ are specified, and we can consider the corresponding evolution of the economy. As explained in section 5, a possible *trajectory* of the economy, given the sample $\omega \in \Omega$, is a sequence $(z(t))_{t=1,\ldots}$ such that

$$z(t+1) \in W(e^t(\omega), z(t)), \qquad t = 1, 2, \ldots .$$

Any such trajectory determines in particular a sequence $(p(t))_{t=1,\ldots}$ of equilibrium prices. The set of all such equilibrium price sequences for the economy $\mathscr{E}$ is denoted by $\Pi_{\mathscr{E}}(\omega)$. The dependence of this set $\Pi_{\mathscr{E}}(\omega)$ on the particular sample will now be analyzed for large economies.

If the economy is large, and in particular if one wants to consider a sequence of economies with an increasing number of agents, then the above description of an economy is not convenient since the index set I does not remain fixed. Instead of considering for every sample $\omega \in \Omega$, the mappings $i \mapsto \alpha_i^t(\omega)$ and $i \mapsto (\alpha_i^0(\omega), x_{i1}^0)$ we consider their distributions, that is to say, the measure $\mu^t(\omega, \cdot)$ on E and the measure $\gamma^0(\omega, \cdot)$ on $E_2 \times X$ defined by

$$\mu^t(\omega, \cdot) = \frac{1}{\#I} \sum_{i \in I} \delta_{\alpha_i^t(\omega)} ,$$

$$\gamma^0(\omega, \cdot) = \frac{1}{\#I} \sum_{i \in I} \delta_{(\alpha_i^0(\omega), x_i^0)} ,$$

where δ_y denotes the probability measure concentrated on the point y. In other words, $\mu^t(\omega, \cdot)$ is the empirical distribution of the sample $(\alpha_i^t(\omega))_{i \in I}$ and $\gamma^0(\omega, \cdot)$ is the (joint) empirical distribution of the sample $(\alpha_i^0(\omega), x^0)_{i \in I}$. Thus we replace the individualistic (microscopic) description of an economy by a description 'in distributions' (macroscopic description). The index set I is then superfluous. The number $\mu^t(\omega, B)$ gives the fraction of agents born at time t who have their endowments in the set B. The stock of money M is replaced, accordingly, by $(1/\#I)M = \overline{M}$, i.e., stock of money per head of old agents. Thus the description of an *economy in distribution* or the *macroscopic description* is given by

$$(\succ, \psi, \mu^t(\omega, \cdot), \overline{M}, \gamma^0(\omega, \cdot), p(0)).$$

The essential advantage of this description of an economy is that the randomness enters in the distribution μ^t and γ^0 but these empirical distributions will not depend very critically on the particular prevailing sample. This fact is due to the Law of Large Numbers.

The macroscopic description of an economy is sufficient if one is interested in equilibrium price sequence $(p(t))_{t=1,\dots}$. Indeed, in order to decide whether the sequence $(p(t))$ with $p(t) \gg 0$ belongs to $\Pi_{\mathscr{E}}(\omega)$, we need only to know the total excess demand in every period t, since by definition the equilibrium price system $p(t)$ is such that total excess demand with respect to $p(t)$ and the past data is zero. Therefore, we shall now show how the total demand of young and old agents in every period is determined by the distributions $\mu^t(\omega, \cdot)$ and $\gamma^0(\omega, \cdot)$. Since the sample ω is fixed, we shall drop the index ω and write for short $\mu^t(\cdot)$ and $\gamma^0(\cdot)$.

Let the past and current price systems be $p(t-1)$ and $p(t)$, respectively, and assume that $p(t-1)$ and $p(t)$ are strictly positive. Then the *mean demand of the young agents* in period t is given by

$$\frac{1}{\#I} \sum_{i \in I} \xi_1(p(t), p(t-1), \alpha_i^t(\omega)) = \int_E \xi_1(p(t), p(t-1), \operatorname{proj}_1(\cdot))\, d\mu^t.$$

[We recall that ξ_1 is a continuous *function* when $p(t) \gg 0$; see (3.6).] The mean demand of the young agents in period t is denoted by

$$\overline{\xi}_1(p(t), p(t-1), \mu^t) = \int_E \xi_1(p(t), p(t-1), \operatorname{proj}_1(\cdot))\, d\mu^t.$$

Obviously, this defines mean demand for *any* distribution μ^t.

In order to derive the mean demand of the old agents in period t, we need the joint distribution of their current endowments and past actions.

Consider the function $g : E \to E_2 \times X$ defined by

$$g(e) = (\operatorname{proj}_2(e), \xi_1(p(t), p(t-1), \operatorname{proj}_1(e))).$$

Given $p(t)$ and $p(t-1)$ strictly positive, g is a continuous function defined on the probability space $(E, \mathscr{B}(E), \mu^t)$ with values in $E_2 \times X$. Then, let γ^t be the distribution of g, i.e.,

$$\gamma^t = \mu^t \circ g^{-1} \in \mathscr{M}(E_2 \times X).$$

We remark that the measure γ^t has a compact support and satisfies

$$\int_{E_2 \times X} \operatorname{proj}_X\, d\gamma^t = (\overline{q}(t), \overline{M})$$

for some $\bar{q}(t) \in R^l_+$. Clearly, γ^t depends on the sample $\omega \in \Omega$, since the empirical distribution $\mu^t = \mu^t(\omega, \cdot)$ depends on $\omega \in \Omega$. Now, for every price system $p(t) \geqslant 0$, the *mean demand of the old agents* in period t is given by

$$\frac{1}{\#I} \sum_{i \in I} \xi_2(p(t), \alpha_i^{t-1}(\omega), x_{i1}^{t-1}) = \int_{E_2 \times X} \xi_2(p(t), \cdot, \cdot) \, \mathrm{d}\gamma^{t-1}.$$

The mean demand of the old agents in period t is denoted by

$$\bar{\xi}_2(p(t), \gamma^{t-1}) = \int_{E_2 \times X} \xi_2(p(t), \cdot, \cdot) \, \mathrm{d}\gamma^{t-1}.$$

Consequently, a sequence $(p(t))_{t=1,\ldots}$ with $p(t) \geqslant 0$ belongs to $\Pi_{\mathscr{E}}(\omega)$, i.e., is an equilibrium price sequence given the sample $\omega \in \Omega$, if

$$\bar{\xi}_1(p(t), p(t-1), \mu^t(\omega, \cdot)) + \bar{\xi}_2(p(t), \gamma^{t-1}(\omega, \cdot))$$
$$= (\bar{e}_1(t) + \bar{e}_2(t), \overline{M}),$$

where $\bar{e}_1(t)$ and $\bar{e}_2(t)$ denotes the young and old agents' mean endowments of consumption goods at time t, respectively, i.e.,

$$\bar{e}_1(t) = \int_E \mathrm{proj}_1 \, \mathrm{d}\mu^t(\omega, \cdot),$$

and

$$\bar{e}_2(t) = \int_E \mathrm{proj}_2 \, \mathrm{d}\mu^{t-1}(\omega, \cdot).$$

Since the excess demand of the young and old agents is determined by the distributions (μ^t) and (γ^t), we can define in the same way the set of equilibrium price sequences for *any* economy given in a macroscopic description $(\succ, \psi, \mu^t, M, \gamma^0, p(0))$, whether or not the distributions are derived from finite economies.

Steadily increasing sequence of economies

Having justified the macroscopic description of an economy, we shall now show that this description does not change very much if one considers the economy in different samples ω and ω' and Ω, provided the economy is large and the random endowments in every period are stochastically independent.

In order to make this precise, let $(\mathscr{E}_n)$ be a sequence of economies, where the economy $\mathscr{E}_n$ is composed at every date of n young agents and n old ones, which have the common characteristics $(\succ, \psi)$. The economy satisfies assumptions (a), (b) and (c) of section 2. The agents' index set is now $I_n = \{1, \ldots, n\}$, while the total stock of money is given by $M_n > 0$. The random endowments of consumption goods at dates $t = 1, 2, \ldots$ are described by random variables defined on a probability space $(\Omega, \mathscr{F}, P)$. Specifically, we consider for every t a sequence of random variables α_i^t, $i = 1, 2, \ldots$, with values in $E = E_1 \times E_2$ (with values in E_2 if $t = 0$). The economy $\mathscr{E}_n$ is then obtained by taking the n first elements of each sequence; as before, α_i^t represents the random endowments of consumption goods of agent i in the economy $\mathscr{E}_n$ who is born at date t.

We shall need the following assumption on endowments:

(f) *For each $t \geq 0$, the sequence of random variables (α_i^t), $i = 1, 2, \ldots$, is stochastically independent; the random variables (α_i^t) have the same distribution μ^t (an element of $\mathscr{M}(E_2)$ when $t = 0$, of $\mathscr{M}(E)$ when $t \geq 1$).*

We shall impose now conditions on the sequences of money stocks M_n and of initial states $z_n(0)$. First, we shall assume that the money stock 'per head of old agents', M_n/n, tends to a limit $M > 0$. This condition is rather natural, since we wish to deal 'in the limit' with a monetary economy. Second, look at the sequence $z_n(0) = (p_n(0), (x_{ih}^n(0))_{i \in I_n}, (e_{ih}^n(0))_{i \in I_n}) \in Z_n$. We concentrate on the case $p_n(0) \in \mathring{S}$ – which is the only meaningful case from an economic point of view – and postulate that $p_n(0)$ tends to a limit $p(0) \in \mathring{S}$. Further, we assume that the actions taken at time zero by the agents born at that date, $(x_{i1}^n(0))_{i \in I_n}$ are in fact the n first elements of a given sequence $(\bar{x}_i)$, $i = 1, 2, \ldots$, contained in a compact subset of X. Then, the associated sequence of empirical distributions,

$$\chi_n(0) = \frac{1}{n} \sum_{i=1}^{n} \delta_{\bar{x}_i} \in \mathscr{M}(X),$$

must be contained in a compact subset of $\mathscr{M}(X)$. Hence it has a convergent subsequence. We shall, in fact, assume that the sequence $\chi_n(0)$ itself converges in $\mathscr{M}(X)$. Formally, we assume that

(g) (1) $\lim_n (M_n/n) = M > 0$;

(2) $\lim_n p_n(0) = p(0) \gg 0$;

(3) *the sequence $(\bar{x}_i)$ belongs to a compact subset of X and* $\lim_n \chi_n(0) = \chi(0) \in \mathscr{M}(X)$.

We shall call the sequence $(\mathscr{E}_n)$ *steadily increasing* if, in addition to assumptions (a), (b) and (c) of section 2, it satisfies assumptions (f) and (g).

Consider now the macroscopic description of the economy $\mathscr{E}_n$ at the sample $\omega \in \Omega$, i.e.,

$$(\succ, \psi, \mu_n^t(\omega, \cdot), M_n/n, \gamma_n^0(\omega, \cdot), p_n(0)), \qquad n = 1, \ldots .$$

The well-known Glivenko–Cantelli Theorem [e.g., Parthasarathy (1967,

Theorem 7.1, p. 53)] now implies that this macroscopic description becomes independent of the particular sample $\omega \in \Omega$ if n tends to infinity.

Proposition 2. Let $(\mathscr{E}_n)$ be a steadily increasing sequence of economies. Then, for almost all sample $\omega \in \Omega$, we have

$$\mu_n^t(\omega, \cdot) \xrightarrow[n \to \infty]{} \mu^t, \qquad t = 1, \ldots,$$

and

$$\gamma_n^0(\omega, \cdot) \xrightarrow[n \to \infty]{} \mu^0 \times \chi(0).$$

Proof. Recall the underlying probability space was denoted by $(\Omega, \mathscr{F}, P)$. For each $t \geq 1$, there exists $G^t \in \mathscr{F}$, with $P(G^t) = 1$, such that $\lim_n \mu_n^t(\omega) = \mu^t$ for every $\omega \in G^t$. This follows from assumption (f) and the Glivenko–Cantelli Theorem [see, e.g., Parthasarathy (1967, Theorem 7.1)].

Next, we wish to show that almost surely in Ω, $\lim_n \gamma_n^0(\omega) = \mu^0 \times \chi(0)$. This will be proved by adapting the proof of the Glivenko–Cantelli Theorem. Consider an arbitrary real-valued function $h : E_2 \times X \to R$ that is continuous and bounded. Let for every n and ω, $g_n(\omega) = h(\alpha_n^0(\omega), \bar{x}_n)$. The sequence of real random variables (g_n) is stochastically independent and uniformly bounded. We therefore know [see, e.g., Loève (1963, section 16, II.A, p. 238)] that if

$$c_n = \frac{1}{n} \sum_{i=1}^n \int_\Omega g_i \, dP$$

tends to a finite limit c, then, almost surely in Ω, $(1/n) \sum_{i=1}^n g_i(\omega)$ tends to c. Now, clearly,

$$c_n = \int_{E_2 \times X} h \, d(\mu^0 \times \chi_n(0)).$$

Since, by assumption (g.3), $\lim_n \chi_n(0) = \chi(0)$, then $\mu^0 \times \chi_n(0)$ converges to $\gamma(0) = \mu^0 \times \chi(0)$ [Billingsley (1968, ch. 1, Theorem 3.2)]. Since h is continuous and bounded, c_n tends to

$$c = \int_{E_2 \times X} h \, d\gamma(0).$$

Now, for every n and ω,

$$\frac{1}{n} \sum_{i=1}^n g_i(\omega) = \int_{E_2 \times X} h \, d\gamma_n^0(\omega).$$

Therefore, we know that, given h, there exists $H \in \mathscr{F}$, with $P(H) = 1$, such that for all $\omega \in H$,

$$\lim_n \int_{E_2 \times X} h \, d\gamma_n^0(\omega) = \int_{E_2 \times X} h \, d\gamma(0).$$

The rest of the proof is standard. We know that, since $E_2 \times X$ is separable, there is a countable set $\{h_1, \ldots, h_k, \ldots\}$ of real-valued functions that are continuous and bounded on $E_2 \times X$, such that $\gamma_n \in \mathcal{M}(E_2 \times X)$ converges to $\gamma \in \mathcal{M}(E_2 \times X)$ if and only if

$$\int_{E_2 \times X} h_k \, d\gamma_n \to \int_{E_2 \times X} h_k \, d\gamma, \qquad \text{for all } k,$$

[e.g., Parthasarathy (1967, Theorem 6.6, p. 47)]. For each h_k, associate H_k as above, and consider $G^0 = \bigcap_{k=1}^\infty H_k$. Clearly, $P(G^0) = 1$, and for all $\omega \in G^0$, $\lim_n \gamma_n^0(\omega) = \gamma(0)$.

Then the set G, the existence of which is asserted in Proposition 2, is equal to $\bigcap_{t=0}^\infty G^t$.   Q.E.D.

Proposition 2 suggests that one associates to a steadily increasing sequence $(\mathscr{E}_n)$ a 'limit economy', $\mathscr{E}_\infty$, described by

$$\mathscr{E}_\infty = \left(\succ, \psi, \mu^t = \lim_n \mu_n^t(\omega, \cdot), M = \lim \frac{M_n}{n}, \mu^0 \times \chi(0) \right.$$

$$\left. = \lim \gamma_n^0(\omega, \cdot), p(0) = \lim_n p_n(0) \right).$$

We emphasize that to speak of a limit economy $\mathscr{E}_\infty$ is, of course, only meaningful if it is viewed in a macroscopic description. In other words, 'in the limit' it is only meaningful to speak of distributions of agents' characteristics or actions. Note also that in the limit economy $\mathscr{E}_\infty$ the endowments are nonrandom.

We are now prepared to relate the set $\Pi_{\mathscr{E}_n}(\omega, \cdot)$ of equilibrium price sequences of the economy $\mathscr{E}_n$ at the sample ω to the set $\Pi_{\mathscr{E}_\infty}$ of equilibrium price sequences of the limit economy $\mathscr{E}_\infty$. This set, of course, is independent of the sample $\omega \in \Omega$.

One can show that the set of equilibrium price sequences is an upper hemicontinuous correspondence in the distribution μ^t $(t = 1, \ldots)$ and initial state $(\gamma^0, p(0))$. We shall, however, formulate this result only in the more special case of a steadily increasing sequence.

Denote by $\mathrm{Ls}\,\Pi_{\mathscr{E}_n}(\omega)$ the set of sequences $(p(t))_{t=1,\ldots}$ with the property: there exists a subsequence $(n_k)_{k=1,\ldots}$ and for every k a sequence $(p_k(t))_{t=1,\ldots} \in \Pi_{\mathscr{E}_{n_k}}(\omega)$ such that $\lim_k p_k(t) = p(t)$ for every $t = 1, \ldots$.

Theorem 2. Let $(\mathscr{E}_n)$ be a steadily increasing sequence of economies. Assume further that for every $p(t) \in S \backslash \mathring{S}$, $p(t-1) \in \mathring{S}$ and $e_1 \in E_1$ the expectation $\psi(p(t))$,

$p(t-1), e_1)$ *assigns positive probability to* $\mathring{S} \times E_2$. *Then, for almost all* ω *in* Ω, Ls $\Pi_{\mathscr{E}_n}(\omega)$ *is a non-empty subset of* $\Pi_{\mathscr{E}_\infty}$.

Proof. It follows from Proposition 2 that there exists $G \in \mathscr{F}$ with $P(G) = 1$ such that for every $\omega \in G$, $\lim \gamma_n^0(\omega) = \gamma^0 = \mu^0 \times \chi^0$ and $\lim \mu_n^t(\omega, \cdot) = \mu^t(t = 1, \ldots)$.

From now on, fix ω in G, and consider $\Pi_n(\omega)(= \Pi_{\mathscr{E}_n}(\omega))$. We know from the corollary to Theorem 1 that $\Pi_n(\omega)$ is a non-empty subset of $(S)^N$, which, in turn, is a subset of the compact space $(\bar{S})^N$. Thus Ls $\Pi_n(\omega)$ is a non-empty subset of $(\bar{S})^N$. Choose $((p(t))_{t \geq 1})$ in this set. By definition, there exists a subsequence $((p_k(t))_{t \geq 1}) \in \Pi_k(\omega)$ which tends to $((p(t))_{t \geq 1})$ as k goes to infinity. We must show that this limit belongs to $\Pi_\infty(= \Pi_{\mathscr{E}_\infty})$.

Consider $p(t) \in \mathring{S}$, $p(t-1) \in \mathring{S}$. Let $\mu \in \mathscr{M}(E)$ and define

$$\bar{\xi}_1(p(t), p(t-1), \mu) = \int_E \xi_1(p(t), p(t-1), \text{proj}_1(\cdot)) \, d\mu.$$

For a $\gamma \in \mathscr{M}(E_2 \times X)$ with a compact support, define

$$\bar{\xi}_2(p(t), \gamma) = \int_{E_2 \times X} \xi_2(p(t), \cdot, \cdot) \, d\gamma.$$

Now, consider the measures $\gamma^t \in \mathscr{M}(E_2 \times X)(t \geq 0)$, defined by $\gamma^0 = \mu(0) \times \chi(0)$ and, for $t \geq 1$, $\gamma^t = \mu^t \circ (g^t)^{-1}$, where the function g^t from E into $E_2 \times X$ is equal to $(\text{proj}_2(\cdot), \xi_1(p(t), p(t-1), \text{proj}_1(\cdot)))$. In view of the definition of Π_∞, we must show for every $t \geq 1$, that $p(t) \in \mathring{S}$ and that

(C) $\quad \bar{\xi}_1(p(t), p(t-1), \mu^t) + \bar{\xi}_2(p(t), \gamma^{t-1}) = (\bar{e}(t), M),$

where $\bar{e}(t) = \int_E \text{proj}_1 d\mu^t + \int_E \text{proj}_2 \, d\mu^{t-1}$. For an arbitrary k, define for all $t \geq 1$,

$$\gamma_k^t(\omega) = \mu_k^t(\omega) \circ (g_k^t)^{-1} \in \mathscr{M}(E_2 \times X),$$

where the function g_k^t from E into $E_2 \times X$ is equal to $(\text{proj}_2(\cdot), \xi_1(p_k(t), p_k(t-1), \text{proj}_1(\cdot)))$. We know that for all $t \geq 1$, $p_k(t) \in \mathring{S}$. Further, the definition of a temporary equilibrium at time t for the economy $\mathscr{E}_k$ yields

(H) $\quad \bar{\xi}_1(p_k(t), p_k(t-1), \mu_k^t(\omega)) + \bar{\xi}_2(p_k(t), \gamma_k^{t-1}(\omega)) = (\bar{e}_k^t(\omega), (M_k/k)),$

where $\bar{e}_k^t(\omega) = \int_E \text{proj}_1 \, d\mu_k^t(\omega) + \int_E \text{proj}_2 \, d\mu_k^{t-1}(\omega)$. It is intuitively clear that we will get condition (C) for the limit economy $\mathscr{E}_\infty$ by letting k go to infinity in (H). In order to do that, we need to establish a few preliminary properties of the functions $\bar{\xi}_1$ and $\bar{\xi}_2$.

(6.1) $\quad \bar{\xi}_1$ *is a continuous function on* $\mathring{S} \times \mathring{S} \times \mathscr{M}(E)$.

(6.2)   *Let A be any compact of $E_2 \times X$, and C the set of probability measures $\gamma \in \mathcal{M}(E_2 \times X)$ such that $\gamma(A) = 1$. Then $\overset{\approx}{\xi}_2$ is continuous on $\overset{\circ}{S} \times C$.*

These statements immediately follow from the continuity of ξ_1 established in (2.6 – ii and iii), and of ξ_2 [see (3.1)]. It suffices to reason in each case in the range space X, and to use the same argument as in (3.5), by using Billingsley (1968, ch. 1, Theorem 5.5). This is left to the reader.

(6.3)   *Let $\gamma \in \mathcal{M}(E_2 \times X)$ and $p = (\dot{p}, s) \in \bar{S} \backslash S$. Consider a sequence (p_k, γ_k) in $\overset{\circ}{S} \times \mathcal{M}(E_2 \times X)$ tending to (p, γ), where γ_k has a compact support. Then $\|\overset{\approx}{\xi}_2(p_k, \gamma_k)\|$ tends to $+\infty$ if $\int_{E_2 \times X} \mathrm{proj}_m \, d\gamma > 0$ [where proj_m is the mapping which associates m to any $(e_2, (q, m)) \in E_2 \times X$].*

Proof.   For any $x \in X$, takes as a definition of $\|x\|$ the expression $\sum |x_j|$ (which is equal here to $\sum x_j$ since $x \geqq 0$). We know that there exists a set $B \in \mathcal{B}(E_2 \times X)$, with $\gamma(B) > 0$, such that $(e_2, x) \in B$, where $x = (q, m)$, implies $p \cdot (e_2, m) > 0$. It is easy to check by slightly adapting the argument of Hildenbrand (1970, appendix F, (3)) that it is possible to impose on this B to be γ-boundaryless. Fix once for all this B.

Consider an arbitrary real number $\lambda > 0$. For any $p \in S, e_2 \in E_2, x \in X$, define $f^\lambda(p, e_2, x) = \mathrm{Min}\,(\lambda, \|\xi_2(p, e_2, x)\|)$.

We have

$$\overset{\approx}{\xi}_2(p_k, \gamma_k) \geqq \int_{E_2 \times X} f^\lambda(p_k, \cdot, \cdot) \, d\gamma_k \geqq \int_{E_2 \times X} 1_B f^\lambda(p_k, \cdot, \cdot) \, d\gamma_k,$$

where 1_B stands for the indicator of B. Let, for any $a = (e_2, x) \in E_2 \times X$, $g_k(a) = I_B(a) f^\lambda(p_k, a)$ and $g(a) = 1_B(a)\lambda$. We know from (3.2) that for any sequence $a_k \in B$ converging to $a \in B$, one has $\lim g_k(a_k) = \lambda = g(a)$. Further, for any sequence $a_k \notin \bar{B}$ which converges to $a \notin \bar{B}$, $g_k(a_k) = 0 = g(a)$. Since B is γ-boundaryless, it follows from another application of Billingsley (1968, ch. 1, Theorem 5.5) that

$$\lim \int_{E_2 \times X} g_k \, d\gamma_k = \int_{E_2 \times X} g \, d\gamma = \lambda \gamma(B).$$

Hence

$$\lim \inf \|\overset{\approx}{\xi}_2(p_k, \gamma_k)\| \geqq \lambda \gamma(B).$$

Since this is true for every $\lambda > 0$, the result stated in (6.3) is proved.   Q.E.D.

(6.4)   *Let $p(t) \in S \backslash \overset{\circ}{S}$, $p(t-1) \in \overset{\circ}{S}$ and $\mu \in \mathcal{M}(E)$. Assume that for any $e_1 \in E_1$, $\psi(p(t), p(t-1), e_1)$ assigns positive probability to $\overset{\circ}{S} \times E_2$. Then, for any sequence $(p_k(t), p_k(t-1), \mu_k) \in \overset{\circ}{S} \times \overset{\circ}{S} \times \mathcal{M}(E)$ tending to $(p(t), p(t-1), \mu)$, $\|\overset{\approx}{\xi}_1(p_k(t), p_k(t-1), \mu_k)\|$ tends to $+\infty$.*

Proof. We know that for any sequence $e_k \in E$ tending to $e \in E$, $\|\xi_1(p_k(t),$ $p_k(t-1), \text{proj}_{E_1}(e_k))\|$ tends to $+\infty$ [see (3.6)]. Thus (6.4) can be proved by the same argument used in the proof of (6.3) (with $B = E$ here). Q.E.D.

We now have enough material to complete the proof of Theorem 2. This will be done by induction on t.

Let $t = 1$. Since $\omega \in G$, we know from Proposition 2 that $\lim_k \gamma_k^0(\omega) = \gamma^0 = \mu^0 \times \chi(0)$ and that $\lim_k \mu_k^1(\omega) = \mu^1$. Moreover, by assumption (g.3), there is a compact A^0 of $E_2 \times X$ such that $\gamma_k^0(\omega)$ assigns probability 1 to A^0, for all k. Therefore, $\lim_k \bar{e}_k^1(\omega) = \bar{e}(1)$. Further, by assumption, (M_k/k) tends to M.

Next, remark that $p(1)$ must belong to $\mathring{S}$. Indeed, one must have

$$\lim_k \int_{E_2 \times X} \text{proj}_X \, d\gamma_k^0(\omega) = \lim_k \left(q_k, \frac{M_k}{k}\right) = (q, M)$$

$$= \int_{E_2 \times X} \text{proj}_X \, d\gamma(0).$$

In addition, the sequence $\tilde{\xi}_2(p_k(1), \gamma_k^0(\omega))$ is necessarily bounded. Therefore, if $p(1) \in \bar{S} \setminus S$, one could contradict (5.3). Thus $p(1) \in S$. In the same way, one shows that $p(1)$ cannot belong to $S \setminus \mathring{S}$, for otherwise, one could contradict (6.4). Thus $p(1) \in \mathring{S}$. It then follows from the continuity of $\tilde{\xi}_1$ and $\tilde{\xi}_2$ [see (6.1) and (6.2)] that the left-hand side of (H) converges to the left-hand side of (C) when k goes to infinity, for $t = 1$.

Finally, remark that $\lim_k \gamma_k^1(\omega) = \gamma^6$ follows from the continuity of ξ_1 and Billingsley (1968, ch. 1, Theorem 5.5). Moreover, there exists clearly a compact A^1 of $E_2 \times X$ such that, for all k, $\gamma_k^1(\omega)$ assigns probability 1 to A^1. Therefore, one can prove that $p(t) \in \mathring{S}$ and that (H) yields (C) by continuity when k tends to infinity for $t = 2$, and this can be done by induction for any t.

This completes the proof of Theorem 2. Q.E.D.

Remark. The above result can be extended in several directions. First, Theorem 2 is clearly still valid when the agents' forecast depend on $p(t-2)$, $p(t-3), \ldots$ as well as on $p(t-1)$. Theorem 2 does not in general hold when the agents' forecast is influenced by past allocations and endowments if these data involve information about *individual* traders. But an analog to Theorem 2 can be proved if the agents have access only to past *empirical distributions* (represented by probability measures) of consumption, money holdings and endowments. Roughly speaking, this is so because these statistics display little randomness when the number of agents is large. Finally, we studied for the simplicity of the argument the case where the agents' endowment have the same probability law. The analysis can be extended, as in Hildenbrand (1971, section 4) to the case where the probability distributions of the agents' endowments belong to a countable set. Also, the assumption of independence in (f) can be relaxed as in Bhattacharya and Majumdar (1973), Delbaen (1971), Malinvaud (1973).

The analysis can also be easily extended to the case where agents live for more than two periods. Finally, uncertainty on the agents' characteristics $(\succ, \psi)$ can be incorporated in the model, provided that the space of characteristics $(\succ, \psi, e_1, e_2)$, properly topologized (see Remark at the end of section 3), is compact.

7. Stationarity for economies with non-random endowments

We consider in this section an economy given in macroscopic description,

$$(\succ, \psi, \mu(t)_{t=1,\dots}, M, \gamma(0), p(0)).$$

These economies have been defined in the preceding section. The limit economy $\mathscr{E}_\infty$ associated to a steadily increasing sequence is of this type.

We studied in section 5 an economy of size n, and made there assumptions implying that the evolution of this economy could be considered as a Markov process with stationary transition probability. We were able there to show the existence of an invariant probability measure but could not find acceptable conditions ensuring that there were invariant measures assigning probability 1 to a positive price of money. We wish to go back to this problem within the framework of economies $\mathscr{E}$, given in a macroscopic description, i.e.,

$$\mathscr{E} = (\succ, \psi, \mu(t), M, \gamma(0), p(0)).$$

First, it is clear that we must make a stationarity assumption on endowments:

(h) $\mu(t) = \mu \in \mathscr{M}(E)$, *for all t.*

We next introduce the concept of a *stationary equilibrium price system for $\mathscr{E}$*. For every $p \in \mathring{S}$, let $\gamma(p)$ be the measure induced on $E_2 \times X$ by the function $g : E \to E_2 \times X$ defined by $(\text{proj}_2\,(\cdot),\, \xi_1(p, p, \text{proj}_1\,(\cdot)))$, i.e., $\gamma(p) = \mu \circ g^{-1}$. By definition, a stationary equilibrium price system is an element $p^* \in \mathring{S}$ such that

$$\bar{\xi}_1(p^*, p^*, \mu) + \bar{\xi}_2(p^*, \gamma(p^*)) = (\bar{e}, M),$$

where $\bar{e} = \int_E \text{proj}_1\, d\mu + \int_E \text{proj}_2\, d\mu$. The justification of the use of this concept is provided by the following argument. Take any $((p(t))_{t \geq 1})$ in $\Pi_\mathscr{E}$. If $p(t)$ tends to, say, $p^* \in \mathring{S}$ when t goes to infinity, then, from the continuity of $\bar{\xi}_1$ and $\bar{\xi}_2$ [see (6.1) and (6.2)], p^* is a stationary equilibrium price system. The purpose of this section is to give sufficient conditions for the existence of such a price system.

First, it is natural to assume that, if, at any date, past and current prices are equal, then the traders forecast the same price system for the next period. Formally,

(i) *For any $p \in \mathring{S}$ and $e_1 \in E_1$, $\psi(p, p, e_1)$ assigns probability 1 to $\{p\} \times E_2$.*

Intuitively speaking, the existence of a stationary equilibrium price system will depend upon the young agents' willingness to save part of their current income and to hold the existing stock of money when the price system is constant in $\mathring{S}$. This is the motivation of the following assumptions:

(j) Let $\mu_1 \in \mathcal{M}(E_1)$ be the marginal distribution of μ on E_1, that is, $\mu_1 = \mu \circ (\text{proj}_1)^{-1}$. Given any $p = (\dot{p}, s) \in \mathring{S}$, there exists $B \in \mathcal{B}(E_1)$, with $\mu_1(B) > 0$, such that $\dot{p} \cdot e_1 > \dot{p} \cdot e_2$ for every $e_1' \in B$ and every $(p, e_2) \in$ supp $\psi(p, p, e_1)$.

(k) The preferences $\succ$ on $\mathcal{M}(Q)$ have a von Neumann representation such that $u(q_1, q_2) = u^*(q_1) + u^*(q_2)$ for every $(q_1, q_2) \in Q$.

Assumption (j), together with (i), implies that a positive proportion of young agents have an incentive to save when prices are constant over time. This incentive, however, will be ineffective if the agents discount the future too much. Hence, assumption (k), which says that agents are indifferent between present and future consumption.

Proposition 3. Consider the economy $\mathscr{E} = (\succ, \psi, \mu, M, \gamma(0), p(0))$ satisfying (h), (i), (j) and (k). Then there exists a stationary equilibrium price sytem $p^* \in \mathring{S}$.

The proof of this proposition can be made by adapting the argument of Grandmont–Laroque (1973, Proof of Theorem 2) which dealt with the case of a finite economy with non-random endowments. This is left to the reader.

The set of stationary equilibrium price systems by definition only depends on the characteristics $(M, \succ, \psi)$ of the economy. Consider the set of economies $\mathscr{E}$ which satisfy (h) and (i). Assume the set of preferences relations $\succ$ is topologized by means of the Hausdorff distance and that the set of patterns of expectations ψ is endowed with the topology of uniform convergence on compacta (see Remark at the end of section 3). It can then be shown by using continuity arguments that a stationary equilibrium price system still exists if the economy is close enough (in the sense of the topology) to an economy satisfying (j) and (k).

The foregoing analysis leaves open the problem of the *stability* of the economic system. Even if a stationary equilibrium price system exists, it is still possible that the price equilibrium sequence $(p(t))_{t \geq 1}$ does not tend to any limit, or tends to a price system $p \in S \backslash \mathring{S}$ involving a zero price of money as t goes to infinity.

References

Arrow, K.J., 1970, Essays in the theory of risk-bearing (North-Holland, Amsterdam).
Arrow, K.J. and F.H. Hahn, 1971, General competitive analysis (Holden Day, San Francisco, Calif.).
Bhattacharya, R.M. and M. Majumdar, 1973, Some limit theorems on random exchange economies, Journal of Economic Theory 6, 37–67.
Billingsley, P., 1968, Convergence of probability measures (Wiley, New York).
Breiman, L., 1968, Probability (Addison-Wesley, Reading, Mass.).

Christiansen, D.S., 1972, A continuity property of temporary equilibrium (Department of Economics, Stanford, Calif.).

Debreu, G., 1956, Market equilibrium, Proceedings of the National Academy of Sciences of the United States, 876–78.

Debreu, G., 1959, Theory of value (Wiley, New York).

Debreu, G., 1969, Neighboring economic agents, in: La décision (Editions du Centre National de la Recherche Scientifique, Paris).

Delbaen, F., 1971, Stochastic preferences and general equilibrium theory, to appear in: J. Drèze, ed. (1974).

Drèze, J., ed., 1974, Allocation under uncertainty, equilibrium, and optimality (Macmillan, New York) forthcoming.

Foguel, S.R., 1964, The ergodic theory of Markov processes, Mathematical Studies no. 21 (Van Nostrand, New York).

Grandmont, J.M., 1970, On the temporary competitive equilibrium, Working Paper no. 305, unpublished Ph.D. dissertation (Center for Research in Management Science, University of California, Berkeley, Calif.).

Grandmont, J.M., 1971, On the short-run equilibrium in a monetary economy, CEPREMAP DP, to appear in: J. Drèze, ed. (1974).

Grandmont, J.M. and G. Laroque, 1973, Money in the pure consumption loan model, Journal of Economic Theory.

Green, J.R., 1971, Temporary general equilibrium model in a sequential trading model with spot and futures transactions, Working Paper (Center for Operations Research and Econometrics, Catholic University of Louvain) to appear in Econometrica.

Green, J.R., 1972, Pre-existing contracts and temporary general equilibrium, Harvard Discussion Paper (Harvard University, Cambridge, Mass.).

Hildenbrand, W., 1970, On economies with many agents, Journal of Economic Theory 2, 161–188.

Hildenbrand, W., 1971, Random preferences and equilibrium analysis, Journal of Economic Theory 3, 414–429.

Hildenbrand, W., 1974, Core and equilibria in large economies, (Princeton University Press, Princeton, N.J.).

Jacobs, K., 1962, Lecture notes on ergodic theory, vols. I and III, mimeo. (Aarhus University, Aarhus).

Kuratowski, K. and C. Ryll-Nardzewski, 1965, A general theorem on selectors, Bulletin Acad. Polonaise Sci., Serie Sci. Math. 13, 397–403.

Loève, M., 1963, Probability theory, 3rd ed. (Van Nostrand, Princeton, N.J.).

Malinvaud, E., 1972, The allocation of individual risks in large markets, Journal of Economic Theory 4, 312–328.

Malinvaud, E., 1973, Markets for an exchange economy with individual risks, Econometrica 41, 383–410.

Neveu, J., 1965, Mathematical foundations of the calculus of probability (Holden-Day, San Francisco, Calif.).

Parthasarathy, K.R., 1967, Probability measures on metric spaces (Academic Press, New York).

Radner, R., 1973, Market equilibrium and uncertainty: Concepts and problems, Technical Report no. 21 (Center for Research in Management Science, University of California, Berkeley, Calif.).

Samuelson, P.A., 1958, An exact consumption loan model of interest with or without the social contrivance of money, Journal of Political Economy 66, 467–482.

Sondermann, D., 1971, Temporary competitive equilibrium under uncertainty, Working Paper (Center for Operations Research and Econometrics, Catholic University of Louvain) to appear in: J. Drèze, ed. (1974).

Stigum, B., 1969, Competitive equilibria under uncertainty, Quarterly Journal of Economics 83, 533–561.

Stigum, B., 1972, Resource allocation under uncertainty, International Economic Review 13, 431–459.

Younès, Y., 1972, Monnaie et motif de précaution dans une economie d'échanges ou les ressources des agents sont aléatoires, CEPREMAP Discussion Paper.

NEW TECHNIQUES FOR THE STUDY OF STOCHASTIC EQUILIBRIUM PROCESSES

Lawrence E. BLUME*

University of Michigan, Ann Arbor, MI 48109, USA

Received February 1979, final version accepted December 1980

This paper develops the notion of transition correspondences; the set-valued analog of transition probabilities. A generalization of the Feller property for transition probabilities is shown to imply the existence of a selection from the transition correspondence having a stationary equilibrium. These techniques are applied to the existence problem for Markov temporary equilibrium processes in place of assumptions about the existence of continuous selections from the equilibrium price correspondence.

1. Introduction

In this paper I propose a method of constructing Markov processes of temporary equilibrium states that provides a useful alternative to the usual approach [Grandmont and Hildenbrand (1974) and Blume (1977)]. In this new method I construct transition correspondences, the set-valued analog of transition probabilities. Properties such as the existence of stationary equilibria are studied by using the hemi-continuity properties of the transition correspondence rather than continuity or stability properties of some pre-chosen selection from the equilibrium correspondence. It will be seen that the required upper hemi-continuity of the transition correspondence is often more easily established than the existence of a selection from the equilibrium correspondence having the desired properties.

The usual approach to this question involves constructing a correspondence defining equilibrium states. A selection is chosen from this correspondence and used to construct a transition probability. Desirable properties for the transition probability such as the Feller property can be inferred from properties of the selection, and these properties in turn imply the existence of an invariant probability measure for the transition probability. The technique proposed in this paper avoids all difficulties concerning the existence of well-behaved selections by working directly with the equilibrium correspondence. Theorems 2.1, 3.1 and 3.2 taken together in

---

*The author is grateful for comments received from the referee, and especially grateful to Jim Jordan for finding an error in an earlier version of this paper.

effect prove the existence of a selection from the equilibrium correspondence such that the transition probability constructed from it has an invariant probability measure.

In section 2, Markov transition correspondences are defined, and sufficient conditions for the existence of an invariant measure are given. Section 3 shows how to construct Markov transition correspondences satisfying the sufficient conditions of section 2. An application of the results to stochastic equilibrium is offered in section 4.

2. Invariant probability measures

In this section I show that convex-valued upper hemi-continuous transition correspondences have fixed points. The dependence of fixed points on parameters is also studied. Let X and Z be subsets of complete, separable metric spaces, with X compact and Z closed. Let $C(X)$ denote the set of all continuous functions from X into the real line, and let D denote the unit ball in $C(X)$ (with the sup norm). Let $\sigma(X)$ denote the σ-field of Borel subsets of X, and let $M(X)$ denote the set of all probability measures on $(X, \sigma(X))$, topologized with the topology of weak convergence. Also, $\sigma(M(X))$ is the Borel σ-field on $M(X)$.

Transition probabilities are particular examples of stochastic kernels, and so I begin by defining multivalued stochastic kernels:

Definition 2.1. A *multivalued stochastic kernel* (m.s.k.) is a correspondence $K:Z \to M(X)$ with measurable graph.

This definition generalizes the stochastic kernel concept. A stochastic kernel is a function $\hat{K}:Z \times \sigma(X) \to \mathbf{R}$ such that $K(z, \cdot) \in M(X)$, $\forall z \in Z$, and $K(\cdot, A)$ is measurable for all $A \in \sigma(X)$. If an m.s.k. is singleton valued, then the measurable graph condition implies that the function $K:Z \to M(X)$ is measurable. Define $\hat{K}:Z \times \sigma(K) \to \mathbf{R}$ such that $\hat{K}(z, A) = K(z)(A)$. The maps $\lambda_A : \mu \to \mu(A)$, $\forall \mu \in M(X)$, are measurable for all $A \in \sigma(X)$, so $\hat{K}(\cdot, A)$ is measurable. Since $\hat{K}(z, \cdot) = K(z) \in M(X)$, $\hat{K}$ is a stochastic kernel.

The action of an m.s.k. K on a measurable function f is defined by applying to f measurable selections from K. If $g:Z \to M(X)$ is a measurable selection from K, I will write $g \sim K$.

Definition 2.2. If $f:X \to \mathbf{R}$ is measurable, then $\int f(x)K(z, dx) = \beta_f(z) = \{\int f(x)g(z, dx); g \sim K\}$.

If K were a stochastic kernel and f a bounded measurable real-valued function, then $\beta_f(Z)$ would be a bounded measurable real-valued function. An analogous property holds for m.s.k.'s.

Proposition 2.1. If K is an m.s.k. and f a bounded measurable real-valued function, then β_f is a correspondence with $(\sigma(Z) \times \sigma(R))$ analytic graph.

Proof. The map $\mu \to \int f \, d\mu$ is measurable. The conclusion follows from Hildenbrand (1974, D.II.3, proposition 2). Q.E.D.

The Feller property for stochastic kernels states that if $f \in C(X)$, then $\beta_f \in C(Z)$. This property is a key sufficient condition for the existence of invariant probability measures for transition probabilities. An analogous property for m.s.k.'s plays the same role in the study of multivalued transition probabilities:

Definition 2.3. An m.s.k. K has the *multivalued Feller property* if for all $f \in C(X)$, $\beta_f : Z \to R$ is upper hemi-continuous (u.h.c.).

The Feller property for stochastic kernels implies that the map $K : Z \to M(X)$ is continuous. This result generalizes.

Proposition 2.2. An m.s.k. K has the multivalued Feller property, iff K is upper hemi-continuous.

Proof. Let I denote the interval $[-1, 1]$. The map $\lambda : M(X) \to \Pi_{f \in D} I$ defined such that $\lambda(\mu)_f = \int f \, d\mu$ is continuous with respect to the product topology and is a homeomorphism of $M(X)$ onto $\lambda(M(X))$. Thus it suffices to show that $\lambda \cdot K : Z \to \Pi_{f \in D} I$ is u.h.c.

It suffices to show that $\{z \in Z : \lambda \cdot K(z) \subset A\}$ is open for all A in some sub-base of $\Pi_{f \in D} I$. Consider the sub-base of sets of the form $A'_f = \Pi_{f \in D} B(f)$ where $B_f = I$ if $f \neq f'$, and B'_f is open in I. Then $\{z : \lambda \cdot K(z) \subset A'_f\} = \{z : \beta_f(z) \subset B'_f\}$ which is open since β_f is u.h.c.

Conversely, if K is u.h.c., then β_f has closed graph. Since f is bounded, range β_f is compact and so β_f is u.h.c. Q.E.D.

Stochastic kernels also act upon probability measures. If K is a stochastic kernel, then $\int K(z, A) \, d\mu = \nu(A)$ defines a probability measure ν. A similar action can be defined for m.s.k.'s.

Definition 2.4. If $\mu \in M(X)$ then $\gamma(\mu)(A) = \int K(z)(A) \, d\mu = \{\int g(z)(A) \, d\mu ; g \sim K\}$.

Note that $\gamma(\mu) \subset M(X)$, and $\gamma(\mu) \neq \phi$ since, from the Aumann selection theorem, there exists an (a.e.μ) selection g from K.

The Feller property for stochastic kernels implies that γ is a continuous function. This result also generalizes.

Proposition 2.3. If an m.s.k. K has the multivalued Feller property, then $\gamma:M(Z)\to M(X)$ is u.h.c.

Proof. The idea is the same as that in Proposition 2.2. It suffices to show that $\lambda\cdot\gamma$ is u.h.c. The set

$$\{\mu:\lambda\cdot\gamma(\mu)\subset A_f\}=\{\mu:\textstyle\int_x f(x)\int_z g(z,dx)d\mu\subset B_f,\forall f\in D,g\sim K\}$$
$$=\{\mu:\textstyle\int_x f'(x)\int_z g(z,dx)d\mu\subset B'_f,\forall g\sim K\}$$
$$=\{\mu:\textstyle\int_z\int_x f'(x)g(z,dx)d\mu\in B'^f,\forall g\sim K\}$$
$$=\{\mu:\textstyle\int_z\beta_f(z)d\mu\subset B'_f\}.$$

Thus it suffices to show that for all $f\in D$, the correspondence $\mu\to\int\beta_f(z)d\mu$ is u.h.c. Since $\beta_f:Z\to I$, I need only show that this correspondence has closed graph. Let $\mu_n\to\mu_0$, and applying Skohorod's theorem, there exists a probability space (S,Σ,ν) and measurable maps h_n, h_0 such that $\mu_n=\nu\cdot h_n^{-1}$, $\mu_0=\nu\cdot h_0$, and $h_n\to h$ a.e.ν. From Hildenbrand (1974, D.II.4, theorem 5) conclude that $\int\beta_f d\mu_n=\int\beta_f\cdot h_n d\nu_0$ for $n\geq 0$. Then his D.II.4, theorem 6, implies that $\int\beta_f d\mu$ has closed graph. Q.E.D.

So far, the definition of the domain of the stochastic kernel has been general. Now I want to explicitly consider multivalued transition probabilities. In applications I might want to study a parametric class of multivalued transition probabilities and see how the invariant measures depend on the parameter.

Definition 2.5. A parametric multivalued transition probability (p.m.t.p.) is a multivalued stochastic kernel $K:X\times Z\to M(X)$.

The main result of this paper is the following theorem:

Theorem 2.1. Let K be a convex valued p.m.t.p. satisfying the multivalued Feller property. Then for all $\nu\in M(Z)$ there exists $\mu\in M(X)$ such that $\mu\in\gamma(\mu\times\nu)$. Furthermore, the correspondence $\nu\to\{\mu:\mu\in\gamma(\mu\times\nu)\}$ is u.h.c.

Neglecting the parameters, this theorem says that, under the given hypotheses, there exists a selection $g\sim K$ and a $\mu\in M(X)$ such that for all $A\in\sigma(X)$, $\mu(A)=\int g(x)(A)d\mu$. A transition probability having an invariant probability can be selected from K. The selection g need not satisfy the Feller property, and in fact no selection satisfying it may exist.

Proof. Fix ν. The map $\mu\to\mu\times\nu$ is continuous, so from Proposition 2.3, the correspondence $\mu\to\gamma(\mu\times\nu)$ is non-empty and u.h.c. If K is convex-valued, then so is $\gamma(\mu\times\nu)$. For let $\delta,\delta'\in\gamma(\mu\times\nu)$. Then there exists $g,g'\sim K$ such that $\delta(\cdot)=\int g(x,z)(\cdot)d(\mu\times\nu)$, $\delta'(\cdot)=\int g'(x,z)(\cdot)d(\mu\times\nu)$. Then $\alpha\delta+(1-\alpha)\delta'(\cdot)=\int\alpha g+(1-\alpha)g'(\cdot)d(\mu\times\nu)$, and $\alpha g+(1-\alpha)g'\sim K$. $M(X)$ is convex and compact, and so Ky Fan's fixed point theorem implies the existence of $\mu\in\gamma(\mu\times\nu)$. Since γ is u.h.c. and $(\mu,\nu)\to\mu\times\nu$ is continuous, the fixed point correspondence is u.h.c. Q.E.D.

3. Identifying convex-valued p.m.t.p.'s with the multivalued Feller property

Multivalued stochastic kernels amenable to the analysis of section 2 arise in a variety of economic settings. In this section I identify an important source of these kernels — those arising as distributions of a correspondence with respect to a transition probability. As before, let X be compact and Z closed. Furthermore, let E be a compact subset of a complete separable metric space.

Assumption 3.1. Let $\phi : X \times Z \times E \rightarrow X$ be a non-empty valued u.h.c. correspondence.

Assumption 3.2. Let $\psi : X \rightarrow M(E)$ be a map with the following two properties:

(i) ψ is continuous,
(ii) $\mu \in$ range ψ implies that μ is atomless.

Definition 3.1. Let $K(x,z) = \psi(x) \cdot \phi^{-1} = \{\mu \in M(X) : \mu = \psi(x) \cdot g^{-1}(\cdot, x, z)$ for some $g \sim \phi \}$.

The main results of this section are:

Theorem 3.1. If ϕ satisfies Assumption 3.1 and ψ satisfies Assumption 3.2.i, then K has the multivalued Feller property.

Theorem 3.2. If ϕ satisfies Assumption 3.1 and ψ satisfies Assumption 3.2.i, ii, then K is convex valued.

Thus if Assumptions 3.1 and 3.2 are satisfied, the hypotheses of Theorem 2.1 are satisfied.

Proof of Theorem 3.1. Since X is compact, it suffices to show that $K : X \times Z \rightarrow M(X)$ has closed graph. So, let $\{(x_n, y_n)\}_{n=1}^{\infty}$ be a sequence with limit (x_0, y_0). Skorohod's theorem says that there exists a probability space (Ω, a, λ) and measurable functions $f_n : \Omega \rightarrow E$, $n \geq 0$ such that $f_n \rightarrow f_0$ a.e. λ and $\psi(x_n) = \lambda \cdot f_n^{-1}$. Without loss of generality a negligible set can be removed from Ω so that convergence is sure in the topology of pointwise convergence on E^{Ω}. Thus, let $F = \bigcup_{n=0}^{\infty} \{f_n\}$. Then $F \subset E^{\Omega}$ is compact. Let $Y = \bigcup_{n=0}^{\infty} \{(x_n, z_n)\}$ and $Y(w) = \bigcup_{n=0}^{\infty} \{(x_n, z_n, f_n(w))\}$. These sets are compact in $X \times Z$ and $X \times Z \times E$, respectively.

Let $G_n = \{g : E \rightarrow X, g \sim \phi(x_n, z_n, \cdot)\}$ for $n = 0, 1, \ldots$. Then since ϕ is u.h.c. and $Z \times E$ is compact, $\phi(Z \times E)$ is compact, and so $\bigcup_{n=0}^{\infty} G_n$ is compact in X^E. Let $H = \bigcup_{n=0}^{\infty} G_n \cdot f_n$. Thus, $h \in H$ iff for some n there exists a $g \in G_n$ such that $g_n \cdot f_n = h$.

Lemma 3.1. H is compact.

Proof of Lemma. It suffices to show that (a) H is pointwise closed, and (b) $\Pi_w(H) = \{h(w): h \in H\}$ is compact in X.

(a) Let $\{h_\alpha, \alpha \in \Lambda\}$ be a net in H with limit h. Then $h_\alpha = g_\alpha \cdot f_\alpha$, where $g_\alpha \in G_n$ for some n and $f_\alpha = f_n$. Since F is compact, the net $\{f_\alpha, \alpha \in \Lambda\}$ has a convergent subnet $\{f_\beta, \beta \in \Lambda'\}$ with limit $f \in F$. Then there exists a $g: E \to X$ such that the diagram

$$f$$
$$\Omega \to E$$
$$h \searrow \;\; \swarrow g$$
$$X$$

comments. Since $f = f_n$ for some n, it suffices to show that $g \in G_n$.

Consider the net $\{(x_\beta, z_\beta, f_\beta, h_\beta), \beta \in \Lambda'\}$ where $(x_\beta, z_\beta) = (x_n, z_n)$ iff $h_\beta = g_n \cdot f_n$. Since Y is compact there exists a subnet $\{(x_\alpha, z_\alpha, f_\alpha, h_\alpha), \alpha \in \Lambda''\}$ with limit (x_n, y_n, f_n, h). For each w, $(x_\alpha, y_\alpha, f_\alpha(w), h_\alpha(w)) \in \mathrm{Gr}\,\phi|_{Z \times E}$. Since ϕ is u.h.c. and $Z \times E$ is compact, $\mathrm{Gr}\,\phi|_{Z \times E}$ is compact. Hence, for all w, $(x_n, z_n, f_n(w), h(w)) \in \mathrm{Gr}\,\phi|_{Z \times E}$. Now $f_n(\Omega)$ and its complement are analytic sets (hence measurable). Define $g|_{f_n}(\Omega)$ such that $g(f_n(w)) = h(w)$. Define $g|_{f_n}(\Omega)_c$ to be an arbitrary measurable selection from $\phi(x_n, z_n, \cdot)|_{f_n}(\Omega)_c$. Then g so defined is a function in G_n, and $h = g \cdot f_n$, as was to be shown.

(b) Choose $w \cdot \Omega$. Then $\Pi_w(H) = \bigcup_{n=0}^{\infty} \{g_n(f_n(w)): g_n \in G_n\} = \phi(Z(w))$ which is compact since $Z(w)$ is compact and ϕ is u.h.c. This proves the lemma.

To complete the proof of the theorem, it suffices to show that $K(Z)$ is compact. But $K(Z) = \{\lambda \cdot h^{-1}: h^{-1} \in H\}$ which is compact since H is compact. Q.E.D.

Proof of Theorem 3.2. Let $v \in M(E)$ be atomless. It suffices to show that $v \cdot \phi^{-1}$ is convex. I need some intermediate propositions.

Lemma 3.2. Let $\{X_1, \ldots, X_n\}$ be a finite, measurable partition of X. Then the set $\{\mu(X_1), \ldots, \mu(X_n); \mu \in v \cdot \phi^{-1}\}$ is convex.

Proof of Lemma 3.2. Let $g_1, g_2 \sim \phi$. Let $a_i = (v \cdot g_i^{-1}(X_1), \ldots, v \cdot g_i^{-1}(X_n))$ for $i = 1, 2$. We need to find for each α, $0 \leq \alpha \leq 1$, a measurable function $g \sim \phi$ such that $a = (v \cdot g^{-1}(X_1), \ldots, v \cdot g^{-1}(X_n)) = \alpha a_1 + (1-\alpha)a_2$.

Let $E^{ij} = g_i^{-1}(X_i)$ for $j = 1, 2$, $i = 1, \ldots, n$. Let $E_{kl} = g_1^{-1}(X_k) \cap g_2^{-1}(X_l)$. Then $\{E_{k,l}\}_{k,l=1}^n$ is a measurable partition of E. Also, $\bigcup_k E_{kl} = E^{l,2}$, $\bigcup_l E_{kl} = E^{k,1}$, Finally, $v \cdot g_j^{-1}(X_i) = v(E^{ij})$.

Since v is atomless, there exists for all α, $0 \leq \alpha \leq 1$, sets $R_{kl} \subset E_{kl}$ such that $v(R_{kl}) = \alpha v(E_{kl})$. Then the sets $\{R_{k,l}, E_{k,l} \backslash R_{k,l}\}_{k,l=1}^n$ form a measurable partition of E. Define g as follows:

$$g(e) = g_1(e), \quad e \in \bigcup_{k,l} R_{k,l},$$

$$= g_2(e), \quad e \in \bigcup_{k,l} (E_{k,l} \backslash R_{k,l}), \qquad k, l = 1, \ldots, n.$$

Evidently g is measurable, and $g \sim \phi$. Furthermore, $g^{-1}(X_k) = (\bigcup_l R_{kl}) \cup (\bigcup_l E_{lk} \backslash R_{lk})$. Thus

$$v \cdot g^{-1}(X_k) = \sum_l v(R_{kl}) + \sum_l v(E_{lk} \backslash R_{lk})$$

$$= \alpha \sum_l v(E_{kl}) + \alpha(1-\alpha) \sum_l v(E_{lk})$$

$$= \alpha v(E^{k1}) + (1-\alpha) v(E^{k2})$$

$$= \alpha v \cdot g_1^{-1}(X_k) + (1-\alpha) v \cdot g_2^{-1}(X_k).$$

Since this holds for all k, the Proposition is proved.   Q.E.D.

An immediate consequence of Lemma 3.2 is:

Lemma 3.3. Let $\{X_1, \ldots, X_n\}$ be a measurable partition of X, and let $f_1, \ldots, f_k$ be k functions such that $f_i(\ ) = c_{ij}$ for $x \in X_j$. Then the set $\{\int f_1 d\mu, \ldots, \int f_k d\mu; \ \mu \in v \cdot \phi^{-1}\}$ is convex.

Proof of Lemma 3.3. We have $\int f_i d\mu = \sum_j c_{ij} \mu(X_j)$. The result then follows from Lemma 3.2.   Q.E.D.

Lemma 3.4. Let $h_1, \ldots, h_k$ be k functions founded and continuous from X into R. Then $\{\int_1 d\mu, \ldots, \int h_k d\mu; \ \mu \in v \cdot \phi^{-1}\}$ is convex.

Proof of Lemma 3.4. There exists a sequence of functions $\{(f_1^n, \ldots, f_k^n)\}_{n=1}^\infty$, each set of functions $(f_1^n, \ldots, f_k^n)$ constant on members of a partition $\{X_1^n, \ldots, X_n^n\}$ of X, and such that $f_i^n \to h_i$ uniformly. Let $A_n = \{\int f_1^n d\mu, \ldots, \int f_k^n d\mu; \ \mu \in v \cdot \phi^{-1}\}$. From Theorem 3.1 each A_n is closed. Let $A = \lim_k A_k$. Thus $a \in A$ iff there is a sequence $\{\mu_n\} \subset v \cdot \phi^{-1}$, $a = \lim_n (\int f_1^n d\mu_n, \ldots, \int f_k^n d\mu_n)$. Since $v \cdot \phi^{-1}$ is compact, there is a subsequence $\{\mu_m\} \subset \{\mu_n\}$, $\mu_m \to \mu \in v \cdot \phi^{-1}$. For each i, $\| \int f_i^m d\mu_m - \int h_i d\mu \| \leq \int \| f_i^m - h_i \| d\mu_m + \| \int h_i d\mu_m - \int h_i d\mu \|$. Each term converges to 0, and so $\lim_m \int f_i^m d\mu_m = \int h_i d\mu$. Thus $a \in A$ iff a

$= (\int h_i d\mu, \ldots, \int h_k d\mu)$ for some $\mu \in v \cdot \phi^{-1}$. Since each A_k is closed and convex (Theorem 3.1 and Lemma 3.3), A is convex. Q.E.D.

Let $\{h_i\}_{i=1}^{\infty}$ be a dense set of continuous functions from X into the unit interval I. Let $R_n(\phi) = \{(\int h_1 d\mu, \ldots, \int h_n d\mu); \; \mu \in v \cdot \phi^{-1}\} \times I \times I \times \ldots$. Then $R_n(\phi)$ is convex subset of the Hilbert cube. Let $R(\phi) = \{(\int h_1 d\mu, \ldots);$ $\mu \in v \cdot \phi^{-1}\}$. Then $R(\phi) = \bigcap_n R_n(\phi)$, and so $R(\phi)$ is a convex subset of the Hilbert cube. Define the map $\lambda : M(X) \to \prod_{i=1}^{\infty} I$ by $\lambda(\mu) = (\int h_1 d\mu, \ldots)$. This map is continuous, linear, and invertible. Thus $v \cdot \phi^{-1} = \lambda^{-1}(R(\phi))$, and so $v \cdot \phi^{-1}$ is convex. Q.E.D.

This concludes the proof of Theorem 3.2.

4. Applications

In this section I give an application of the techniques presented in sections 2 and 3 to stochastic equilibrium analysis.

In the usual temporary equilibrium framework [Grandmont (1977)] there is a compact subset $D \subset R^m$ of endogenous variables and a compact subset $E \subset R^n$ of exogenous variables. The state space for the Markov equilibrium process is $X = E \times D$. The evolution of the stochastic equilibrium process is determined by an upper hemi-continuous correspondence $\phi : E \times X \to X$ and by a transition probability $\psi : E \times \sigma(E) \to [0, 1]$. The correspondence ϕ is the equilibrium correspondence, and $\phi(x_{t-1}, e_t)$ is the set of all possible equilibrium states x_t that can occur at time t if the state at time $t-1$ was x_{t-1} and exogenous random variable e_t is realized at time t. The transition probability ψ describes the Markovian evolution of the exogenous random variable.

The tradition approach has been to choose a measurable selection $f \sim \phi$, and to describe the evolution of equilibrium states by the transition probability

$$K_f(x, \cdot) = \psi(x) \cdot f^{-1}(x, \cdot).$$

The problem to be addressed is the existence of a stationary distribution of states. Does there exist a selection f from ϕ such that K_f admits an invariant distribution? This question was first addressed by Grandmont and Hildenbrand (1974), who showed that if ψ has the Feller property and the selection f is continuous, K_f satisfies the Feller property, and thus admits an invariant distribution. However, the existence of a continuous selection — tantamount to the uniqueness of equilibrium in each state — is not often satisfied. Theorems 3.1, 3.2 and 2.1 together imply that, under the additional assumption that for all $x \in X$, $\psi(x)$ is atomless, there always exists a selection $f \sim \phi$ such that K_f admits an invariant probability.

The results of the previous section can also be used to solve a problem considered by several authors: Blume (1977), Easley (1978), and Knieps (1977). The problem is the existence of weakly rational expectations.[1]

Recall that the state space is $X = E \times D$, where D is the set of endogenous variables. The endogenous variables are of two types: those that are actions of individual agents, and those that are jointly determined by the actions of the agents (such as prices). Each agent is determining his optimal action by observing current jointly determined and some current exogenous variables, and by solving a dynamic programming problem. To solve this problem, agents need to have some expectations about those variables they observe. Let there be n agents, and let S_i be the set of variables that the ith agent observes. We assume that agents do not have beliefs about the dynamic evolution of the s_{it}, and so the expectations of the ith agent can be represented by probability distributions $\mu_i \in M(S_i)$, the set of probability distributions on S_i. Thus the term 'weakly' in the title of the problem. However, it does seem plausible that in a stationary equilibrium, agents should know the true marginal distribution of s_i from the invariant probability measure. Thus the word 'rational'. Our problem, then, is to find a stationary equilibrium where agents have the correct marginal distribution of the observed variables as their expectations.

This can be studied as a fixed point problem. Give $M(S_i)$ the topology of weak convergence. Then let $M = \prod_{i=1}^{n} M(S_i)$, $v \in M$ is a vector $(v_1, \ldots, v_n)$ of probabilities on the S_i. We derive an equilibrium correspondence $\phi : X \times E \times M \to X$, and, because the world is simple, ϕ is upper hemi-continuous. See Blume (1977), Easley (1978) or Knieps (1977) for details. If we assume that ψ has atomless range, then $K(x, v)$ is compact, convex and non-empty valued, and upper hemi-continuous (Theorem 3.2).

Let $\rho : M(X) \to M$ be the map such that $\rho(\mu)$ is the vector of marginal distributions of μ on $S_1, \ldots, S^n$, respectively. The map ρ is continuous, and so the correspondence $K(x, \rho(\mu)) : X \times M(X) \to M(X)$ is upper hemi-continuous, etc. Now define $\Lambda : M(X) \times M(X) \to M(X)$ such that $\Lambda(\mu, \mu') = \int K(X, \rho(\mu')) \mu(\mathrm{d}x)$. Then Λ is upper hemi-continuous, convex and compact and non-empty valued. In particular, its restriction to the diagonal of $M(X) \times M(X)$ enjoys these properties. By identifying $M(X)$ with the diagonal of $M(X) \times M(X)$ we have a correspondence $\bar{\Lambda} : M(X) \to M(X)$ which satisfies all the conditions of Ky Fan's Fixed Point Theorem. Thus, there exists a $\mu \in M(X)$ such that $\mu \in \int K(x, \rho(\mu)) \mu(\mathrm{d}x)$. In other words, μ is a stationary equilibrium in which each agent knows the correct one-period distribution of his observable variables.

In earlier work, Blume (1977), Easley (1978) and Knieps (1977) all had to choose a continuous $f \sim \phi$. Here we have demonstrated the existence of a

---

[1] So named by Easley.

selection $h \sim \phi$ such that the transition probability constructed from it admits a weakly rational expectations equilibrium. The cost of weakening the requirements on selections from ϕ is only the stronger requirement on ψ. In fact, the development of these techniques was motivated by a study by the author of rational expectations when agents are aware of the dynamic structure of the economy [Blume (1979)]. In this case, where transition probabilities on the S_i must be considered, it is clear that non-trivial examples admitting continuous selections exist.

References

Blume, L., 1977, The stationarity of Markov processes of temporary equilibrium, IBER/CRMS working paper 252 (University of Califor⁻ia, Berkeley, CA).

Blume, L., 1979, Consistent expectations, .ʃnpublished paper (University of Michigan, Ann Arbor, MI).

Easley, D., 1978, The formation of expectations in an uncertain environment, Unpublished Ph.D. thesis (Northwestern University, Chicago, IL).

Grandmont, J.M., 1977, Temporary general equilibrium, Econometrica 45, no. 3, 535–572.

Grandmont, J.M. and W. Hildenbrand, 1974, Stochastic processes of temporary equilibrium, Journal of Mathematical Economics 1, no. 3, 247–277.

Hildenbrand, W., 1974, Core and equilibria of a large economy (Princeton, NJ).

Knieps, G., 1977, Unpublished Ph.D. thesis (University of Bonn, Bonn).

Markov Rational Expectations Equilibria in an Overlapping Generations Model

STEPHEN E. SPEAR AND SANJAY SRIVASTAVA

Graduate School of Industrial Administration,
Carnegie–Mellon University, Pittsburgh, Pennsylvania 15213

Received January 12, 1984; revised June 7, 1985

In this paper, we analyze rational expectations equilibrium paths in a stochastic overlapping generations model. The work presented here builds on results of S. E. Spear (*J. Econ. Theory* **35** (1985), 251–275), where it is shown that in a model with multiple goods and time non-separable preferences, a stochastic steady state equilibrium will generically fail to exist. A stochastic steady state is defined as an equilibrium in which the stochastic process of endogenously determined variables is measure isomorphic to the exogenous process driving the model. In this paper, we establish the existence of non-steady state equilibria and provide a characterization of their stochastic properties. *Journal of Economic Literature* Classification Numbers: 021, 022, 023. © 1986 Academic Press, Inc.

I. INTRODUCTION

In this paper, we study the problem of existence of equilibrium in a general stochastic overlapping generations (henceforth OLG) model, and provide a characterization of the dynamic properties of the equilibrium.

Since its introduction in 1958 by Samuelson [18], the OLG framework has been applied extensively in the analysis of a variety of dynamic economic problems. These include problems in monetary economics (see, for example, the survey by McCallum [15]), public finance (Diamond [7]), finance (Huberman [13]), capital theory (Cass and Yaari [4]), business cycle theory (Lucas [14]), and general equilibrium theory (Balasko and Shell [2]).

In studies concerned with dynamics in explicitly stochastic models (e.g., Lucas [14]), the type of equilibrium typically studied is a "measure isomorphic" steady state equilibrium. Such an equilibrium is defined as follows. Suppose that the stochastic process governing the exogenous variables of the model (e.g., the process on endowments) is a kth-order Markov process. If the equilibrium distribution of the endogenous variables (e.g., prices and allocations) is a time invariant measurable function of the exogenous variables alone, then the distribution of the endogenous variables is "measure isomorphic" to that of the exogenous variables. In particular, the endogenous variables will follow a kth-order Markov process. Such an equilibrium is studied, for example, in Lucas [14].

In a recent paper, Spear [19] has shown that in an OLG model with time non-separable preferences, stochastic endowments, and at least two commodities in every period, such a measure isomorphic equilibrium will generically fail to exist. However, a rational expectations equilibrium does exist. Taken together, these results imply that the equilibrium distribution of the endogenous variables must be of higher order than that of the exogenous variables. In other words, the endogenous variables must exhibit higher-order serial dependence than the exogenous variables. A question then arises about the smallest degree of serial dependence that can be supported in equilibrium, and a study of this question is precisely the topic of this paper. We show in a two-period lived model, if the exogenous process is zero-order Markov, then there exists a first-order Markovian equilibrium. A second important question that arises concerns the statistical properties of the model, and, in particular, the question of whether the equilibrium stochastic process is ergodic. This issue is of critical importance in any potential study of the empirical implications of the model.

In Spear and Srivastava [20], we prove the existence of a Markov equilibrium for the case of a finitely supported stochastic process on endowments. With a finitely supported process on endowments, the tree of realization possibilities at any finite time has a finite number of paths, and this makes it possible to apply the results of Balasko and Shell [2] to prove the existence of an equilibrium. The Markovian characterization of equilibrium is then obtained by expanding the state space to include lagged prices and allocations, and using the structure of the overlapping generations model to map entire histories onto the augmented state space.

With a continuous process on endowments, the existence of equilibrium can also be demonstrated by adapting the proof of Balasko and Shell [2], but the Markovian characterization of equilibrium is not at all apparent in this approach. Further, it does not appear to be straightforward to approximate the continuous distribution with a sequence of finitely supported distributions and to make a limiting argument. It is also unclear whether the Markovian characterization of equilibrium will survive such a limiting result.

For these reasons, we take a different approach toward proving the existence of a Markov equilibrium in the continuous case by looking directly for the existence of a joint probability distribution on prices and allocations. Our analysis makes heavy use of the results obtained by

Balasko [1] on the graph of the (Walrasian) equilibrium correspondence and of results obtained by Grandmont and Hildenbrand [12] on temporary equilibria.

The method behind the proof is familiar: we start with an arbitrary joint probability measure, and work through the temporary equilibrium system to obtain an induced joint measure. A fixed point of this mapping yields a rational expectations equilibrium. The analysis is complicated by the possibility of a zero price of money. This is handled in a way similar to that used in temporary equilibrium theory by extending arguments established for the interior of the price space to its boundary.

In Section II, we provide a description of our model. Section III examines the structure of equilibrium, and indicates how we adapt the results of Balasko [1] to our case. Section IV contains the main result on the existence of an equilibrium that takes the form of a first-order Markov process on prices, allocations and endowments.

Having established existence, we turn, in Section V, to an analysis of the stochastic behavior of the equilibrium process. We study the particular case of a model in which the endowment distribution is finitely supported by verifying that the so-called Doeblin condition holds. This condition requires that there not exist an absorbing set of zero measure which is invariant. The case where the endowment distribution is non-atomic has been studied by Grandmont and Hildenbrand [11] in the context of a temporary equilibrium economy. Their framework corresponds to the rational expectations equilibrium whose existence we establish in the Appendix. For this case, the key result is that the equilibrium transition probability measure depends continuously on conditioning variables. Since this condition implies the Doeblin condition, all of the results of Section V will hold for this case as well.

II. THE MODEL

The model we employ is a standard overlapping generations model with uncertainty. Time is discrete and indexed by t, $t = 0, 1, \ldots$. In every period N agents are born, each of whom lives for two periods. Thus, at any time $t \geq 1$, there are $2N$ agents present in the economy. One group, born at $t - 1$ is called old; the other group, born at t, is called young. At $t = 0$, we have a single group of N agents who will live through period 1.

In every period, there are l completely perishable physical commodities and one costlessly storable asset called money. The commodity space is thus $\mathbb{R}^{l+1}$. Uncertainty enters the model through the endowments of the young, which we assume evolve over time as a stochastic process of independently and identically distributed random vectors. Old agents receive a fixed, non-stochastic endowment.

We assume that consumption goods endowments are strictly positive for both young and old; these endowments are denoted

$$\hat{\omega}_{ij} \in \mathbb{R}^l_{++}, \qquad i = 1, 2; \qquad j = 1,..., N$$

where the subscript $i = 1$ denotes a young agent, and $i = 2$ denotes an old agent. We assume further that all endowments of consumption goods lie in a compact subset of the positive orthant,

$$\hat{\omega}_{ij} \in \hat{\Omega}_{ij} \subset \mathbb{R}^l_{++}, \qquad i = 1, 2; \qquad j = 1,..., N.$$

Young agents receive no endowment of money; thus, the total endowment of a young agent is

$$\omega_{1j} = [\hat{\omega}_{1j}, 0] \in \hat{\Omega}_{1j} \times \mathbb{R}, \qquad j = 1,..., N.$$

Money endowments of the old are the amounts carried forward from the previous period; thus, the total endowment of an old agent in any period $t \geqslant 1$ is

$$\omega'_{2j} = [\hat{\omega}_{2j}, \bar{m}_j^{t-1}] \in \hat{\Omega}_{2j} \times \mathbb{R} = \Omega'_{2j}, \qquad j = 1,..., N.$$

Agents born in period zero receive a fixed money endowment $\bar{m}_j, j = 1,..., N$ with $0 < \bar{m}_j \leqslant \bar{m}$ for all j, and

$$\bar{m} = \sum_{j=1}^{N} \bar{m}_j < \infty.$$

Thus, an old agent's endowment set may be taken to be

$$\Omega_{2j} = \hat{\Omega}_{2j} \times [0, \bar{m}] \subset \mathbb{R}^l_{++} \times \mathbb{R}_+, \qquad j = 1,..., N.$$

Similarly, a young agent's endowments can be taken as elements of the compact set

$$\Omega_{1j} \times \hat{\Omega}_{1j} \times [0, \bar{m}].$$

Finally, let

$$\Omega_i = \underset{1}{\overset{N}{\mathsf{X}}} \, \Omega_{ij}, \qquad i = 1, 2$$

$$\hat{\Omega}_i = \underset{1}{\overset{N}{\mathsf{X}}} \, \hat{\Omega}_{ij}, \qquad i = 1, 2$$

$$\Omega = \Omega_1 \times \Omega_2.$$

To model the stochastic nature of endowments, let $\mathscr{B}$ denote the Borel σ-algebra of Ω; then $[\Omega, \mathscr{B}]$ is a measurable space. Let μ_1 be the joint probability measure on Ω_1 which determines the endowments of the young. We let μ_2 be the degenerate measure on Ω_2 defined by

$$\mu_2(A) = 1 \quad \text{if } [\hat{\omega}_{2i},..., \hat{\omega}_{2N}] \in A$$
$$= 0 \quad \text{otherwise}$$

where $\hat{\omega}_2 \in \hat{\Omega}_2$ is the non-stochastic endowment of the old, and $A \in \mathscr{B}$. We let $\mu = \mu_1 \times \mu_2$. The measure μ and the assumption that the endowments of the young are i.i.d. over time completely characterize the endowment process.

To complete the discussion of endowments, we assume that agents born in period zero have some endowments

$$[\hat{\omega}_{0j}, \bar{m}_j] \text{ at } t = 0,$$

and

$$[\hat{\omega}_{2j}, \bar{m}_j] \text{ at } t = 1, \quad \text{for} \quad j = 1,..., N.$$

To simplify matters, we assume that the endowments at $t = 0$ are chosen so that no trade within period zero occurs.

Allocations are denoted $x_{ij}^t = [\hat{x}_{ij}^t, m_{ij}^t]$, where

$\hat{x}_{ij}^t$ = allocation of consumption goods to the jth type i agent in period t,

and

m_{ij}^t = money allocation to the jth type i agent at t, for $i = 1, 2$ and $j = 1,..., N$.

Agents have preferences over consumption goods given by time invariant utility functions

$$u_j: \mathbb{R}^{2l}_{++} \to \mathbb{R}.$$

These utility functions are assumed to be continuous, strictly concave, monotonic, and satisfy the boundary condition that all upper contour sets are uniformly bounded below, i.e., there exists a vector $\hat{y}_j \leqslant 0$, $\hat{y}_j \in \mathbb{R}^{2l}$ such that

$$\hat{y}_j \ll \text{cls}\{(\hat{x}_1, \hat{x}_2) \in \mathbb{R}^{2l}_{++} \mid u_j[\hat{x}_1, \hat{x}_2] \geqslant c\}$$

for all c in the range of u_j.

Agents living after $t = 0$ may trade on one period spot markets at prices $p^t = [\hat{p}^t, p^t_m]$, where $\hat{p}^t$ is an l-vector of consumption goods prices and p^t_m is the price of money. Prices are normalized to lie in the unit simplex of $\mathbb{R}^{l+1}_+$,

$$\Delta = \{ p \in \mathbb{R}^{l+1}_+ \mid u \cdot \hat{p} + p_m = 1, i = [1,..., 1] \}$$

The rational expectations hypothesis is embodied in the assumption that prices are perfectly foreseen, i.e., agents know the distributions of relevant future prices.

Market demands arise as solutions to agents' constrained utility maximizations. A typical young agent's decision problem can be analyzed using standard dynamic programming techniques. Let ν^t denote the distribution on future prices and endowments a young agent in period t expects to prevail in period $t+1$. (For convenience, we ignore the distinction between members of the same generation here.) In the first stage of the optimization, the young agent takes his first-period allocation as given and solves

$$\max_{\hat{x}^t_2{}^{+1}} u[\hat{x}^t_i, \hat{x}^t_2{}^{+1}] \tag{2.1a}$$

subject to

$$\hat{p}^{t+1} \cdot \hat{x}^{t+1}_2 \leqslant \hat{p}^{t+1} \cdot \hat{\omega}_2 + p^{t+1}_m m^t_1.$$

(It is obvious that $m^{t+1}_2 = 0$ for a maximum.)

This yields a demand function

$$\hat{x}^{t+1}_2[x^t_1, p^{t+1}, \hat{\omega}_2]$$

with the usual properties. This demand functions induces a measure on $\hat{x}^{t+1}_2$ allocations via the measure ν^t. In the second stage, the young agent solves

$$\max_{x^t_1} \mathrm{Eu}[\hat{x}^t_i, \cdot] \tag{2.1b}$$

subject to

$$\hat{p}^t \cdot \hat{x}^t_1 + p^t_m m^t_1 \leqslant \hat{p}^t \cdot \hat{\omega}^t_1 \text{ and } m^t_1 \geqslant 0$$

where $\hat{\omega}^t_1 \in \hat{\Omega}_1$ and the expectation is taken with respect to the induced measure on $\hat{x}^{t+1}_2$. It will be convenient for the subsequent analysis to let

$$V[x^t_1] = \mathrm{Eu}[\hat{x}^t_1, \hat{x}^{t+1}_2(x^t_1, \cdot)].$$

The solutions to the optimization problem laid out above have been studied extensively in the literature on temporary general equilibrium theory (for a comprehensive treatment, see Grandmont [10], and Grandmont and Hildenbrand [11]), where it is shown that (2.1b) yields a demand correspondence

$$x_1^t = \zeta_1^t [p_1^t, v^t, \omega_1^t].$$

If v^t is such that the probability of $p_m^{t+1} > 0$ is positive, then ζ_1^t will be single-valued. It can also be shown that, under this assumption, the expected utility function $V[x_1^t]$ is continuous, monotonic, strictly concave, and satisfies the required boundary condition imposed above. Hence, the demand function will exhibit all of the usual properties associated with static utility maximization over a space of consumption goods. In particular, money can be treated as a commodity like any other. If v^t assigns zero probability to $p_m^{t+1} > 0$, then $p_m^t = 0$ and any money holdings will be optimal. We note that since we are working with the assumption of perfect foresight (at the level of distributions), it follows that in equilibrium, either $p_m^t = 0$ or $p_m^t > 0$ for all t. Thus, in developing our results, we can focus on these two cases separately. We will, therefore, develop our results under the assumption that the price of money is strictly positive for all t, up to the point where we show existence of equilibrium. The case of zero money price may be handled using the same techniques by reinterpreting notation to eliminate the money markets. The two cases will be considered jointly again in the section on existence of equilibrium.

To complete the specification of the model, we need to define what we mean by equilibrium. The simplest possible type of equilibrium one might hope to show existence for is one in which the stochastic process of equilibrium prices and allocations is measure isomorphic to the endowment process. For the overlapping generations model, equilibria of this type can be shown to exist if $l = 1$ (i.e., one consumption good per period). Recent work by Peled [16] shows that such an equilibrium is optimal. Unfortunately, if $l > 1$, Spear [19] has shown that at least for C^2 utility functions, steady state equilibria generically fail to exist (i.e., for an open and dense set of utility functions).

Intuitively, this non-existence result holds when there is diversity in the commodities available because time non-separabilities in preferences introduce lags in demand behavior. In the single good model, the budget constraint trivializes old agents' consumption decisions, and, in effect, makes the lags inoperative. If $l > 1$, this choice is no longer trivial, the lags are operative in equilibrium, and the equilibrium stochastic process exhibits serial dependence. Since our assumptions on preferences include the class examined by Spear, the non-existence result leads us to search for what can be characterized as a Markov equilibrium.

The assumption of rational expectations imposes the restriction that agent's beliefs about future realizations be the true distributions of the relevant variables. This consistency requirement can be imposed in several ways, and we focus on two polar cases. From the optimization problem of the young (2.1b) we note that the only future variables to be forecasted are next period's prices. Thus, one notion of a correct expectation, which we call a fulfilled expectation, is to require that young agents forecast future prices in terms of a distribution on prices which, in equilibrium, is the true distribution of prices. With fulfilled expectations, the consistency requirement is then imposed on the *marginal* distribution of prices, as in (2) and (3) of the following definition.

DEFINITION 1. A fulfilled expectations equilibrium (FEE) is a stationary (i.e., time-invariant) probability measure η^* defined on prices p^t, endowments ω^t, and one-period lagged allocations of young agents

$$x_1^{t-1} = [x_{11}^{t-1}, ..., x_{1N}^{t-1}]$$

such that given x_1^{t-1},

(1) $\sum_{j=1}^{N} [\tilde{x}_{1j}^t + \tilde{x}_{2j}^t] = \sum_{j=1}^{N} [\tilde{\omega}_{1j}^t + \omega_{2j}]$ (where $\tilde{\ }$ denotes the random allocations induced by randomness of endowments).

(2) Agents' demands solve problem (2.1) with expectations of future prices given by the marginal probability v^* on prices obtained from η^* by integrating out the allocation variables.

(3) The equilibrium distribution of $[\omega^t, x_1^{t-1}, p^t]$ is η^*.

(4) Conditions (1)–(3) hold for $t = 1, 2, ...,$ with $x_{1j}^0 = \omega_{0j}$, for $j = 1, ..., N$.

While the price expectations in Definition 1 are self-fulfilling, agents will typically have more information than that embodied in Definition 1. For instance, given that generically the equilibrium distribution of prices will depend on current variables, it is rational for the agents to employ a conditional distribution on future prices. This leads to the next definition, which is the usual definition of a rational expectations equilibrium.

DEFINITION 2. A rational expectations equilibrium (REE) is a stationary (i.e., time-invariant) probability measure η^* defined on prices p^t, endowments ω^t, and one-period lagged prices p^{t-1} such that given p^{t-1},

(1) $\sum_{j=1}^{N} [\tilde{x}_{1j}^{t} + \tilde{x}_{2j}^{t}] = \sum_{j=1}^{N} [\tilde{\omega}_{1j}^{t} + \omega_{2j}]$ (where $\sim$ denotes the random allocations induced by randomness of endowments).

(2) Agents' demands solve problem (2.1) with expectations of future prices given by the conditional probability v^* on prices at $t+1$ given prices and endowments at time t, obtained from η^* by taking a Radon–Nikodym derivative with respect to the marginal distribution on time t prices and endowments.

(3) The equilibrium distribution of $[\omega', x_1^{t-1}, p']$ is η^*.

(4) Conditions (1)–(3) hold for $t = 1, 2,...,$ with $x_{1j}^{0} = \omega_{0j}$, for $j = 1,..., N$.

Here, the conditioning variables are current prices and endowments.

If the distribution on endowments is finitely supported, the existence of a Markov rational expectations equilibrium is proved in Spear and Srivastava [20]. With a continuous distribution on endowments, however, the techniques applied in that paper do not easily yield the existence of a Markov equilibrium. Here, we will demonstrate the existence of a REE when the endowment distribution is non-atomic. We will also prove the existence of a FEE for a general distribution on endowments. Since we employ the same techniques in either case, and the exposition for the case of a FEE is somewhat easier, the remainder of the text is devoted to the existence of a FEE. The modifications required to establish the existence of a REE are given in the Appendix.

To complete this section, we introduce some notation which will be helpful in developing our subsequent results. If W is a measurable space, we will denote the space of probability measures on W by $\mathcal{M}(W)$. If Y is another measurable space and the mapping $g: W \to Y$ is measurable, then we define the induced map $g_*: \mathcal{M}(W) \to \mathcal{M}(Y)$ by $v = g_*[\eta] = \eta g^{-1}$ for $\eta \in \mathcal{M}(W)$. The spaces $\mathcal{M}(Y)$ are endowed with the weak topology, so that if $\eta_j \in \mathcal{M}(Y)$, for $j = 1, 2,...,$ then $\eta_j \to \eta$ if and only if for every bounded continuous function $f: Y \to \mathbb{R}$,

$$\int_Y f \, d\eta_j \to \int_Y f \, d\eta.$$

III. STRUCTURE OF EQUILIBRIUM

In order to maintain the greatest degree of generality in our assumptions about the measure defining the endowment process, we will make use of some well-known results on the structure of the graph of the equilibrium price correspondence. These results were first obtained under very general assumptions on preferences and consumption sets in a beautiful paper by Balasko [1], which builds on earlier results of Debreu [6].

To state Balasko's results, we consider a static pure exchange economy with a finite number, l, of commodities and a finite number, m, of agents. Let $\Omega_0 \subset \mathbb{R}^{lm}$ be the set of agents' initial endowments; Ω_0 is assumed to be open and convex. Let $S \subset \Delta$ be an open, connected subset of admissible prices in the l-simplex Δ. Agents have demand functions

$$f_i : S \times (a_i, b_i) \to \mathbb{R}^l$$

where the interval (a_i, b_i) contains all $w_i = p \cdot \omega_i$ for ω_i in agent i's endowment set. Each f_i is assumed to be continuous and to satisfy Walras' Law, $p \cdot f_i[p, w_i] = w_i$. Furthermore, it is assumed that the image of the mapping defined by

$$\bigoplus_i f_i(p, w_i) = [(f_1(p, w_1), \ldots, f_m(p, w_m))]$$

is contained in Ω_0. Define mappings

$$\varphi : S \times \Omega_0 \to S \times \mathbb{R} \times [\mathbb{R}^l]^{m-1}$$

and

$$\psi : S \times \mathbb{R} \times [\mathbb{R}^l]^{m-1} \to S \times \mathbb{R}^{lm}$$

by

$$\varphi[p, \omega_1, \ldots, \omega_m] = [p, p \cdot \omega_1, \omega_2, \ldots, \omega_m]$$

and

$$\psi[p, w_1, \omega_2, \ldots, \omega_m] = [p, f_1(p, w_1) + \sum_{j=2}^{m} [f_j(p, p \cdot \omega_j) - \omega_j], \omega_2, \ldots, \omega_m].$$

Finally, let

$$E = \left\{ (p, \omega_1, \ldots, \omega_m) \in S \times \Omega_0 \mid \sum_{j=1}^{m} [f_j(p, p \cdot \omega_j) - \omega_j] = 0 \right\};$$

E is the equilibrium set, i.e., the graph of the equilibrium price correspondence.

The basic result we require is the following.

THEOREM (Balasko). *If Ω_0 is bounded below, then E is homeomorphic to $S \times \mathbb{R}^{lm-(l-1)}$.*

The homeomorphism is actually given by the map ψ above. The inverse of ψ is $\tilde{\varphi} = \varphi|_E$. Letting id denote the identity map, one can easily check that

$$\psi \circ \tilde{\varphi} = \mathrm{id}_E$$

and that

$$\tilde{\varphi} \circ \psi = \mathrm{id}_B, \qquad B = S \times \mathbb{R} \times \mathbb{R}^{l(m-1)}.$$

We wish to apply Balasko's results to the temporary equilibrium system obtained by giving young agents in period t some fixed (homogeneous) expectation of future prices, denoted $v_0 \in \mathcal{M}(\Delta)$. We maintain the assumption that v_0 puts positive weight on $p_m > 0$ in period $t + 1$. We then obtain a static general equilibrium system consisting of $2N$ agents. Young agents are characterized by endowments in the set Ω_{1j}, and preferences given by the expected utility function

$$V_j(x_{1j}^t) = \mathrm{Eu}_j[\hat{x}_{1j}^t, \tilde{x}_2] \qquad \text{for} \quad j = 1,..., N.$$

Old agents are characterized by endowments in the set Ω_{2j}, and preferences given by the utility function

$$W_j(x_{2j}^t) = u_j[x_{1j}^{t-1}, x_{2j}^t]$$

for $j = 1,..., N$. The lagged allocations $x_1^{t-1} = [x_{11}^{t-1},...,)x_{1N}^{t-1}]$ are assumed fixed. For the remainder of this section, we suppress the temporal notation.

To apply Balasko's result to this system, we must ensure that the assumptions on consumption sets and demand functions are satisfied. It simplifies the analysis if we assume that the utility functions u_j have upper contour sets bounded below by $0 \in \mathbb{R}^{2l}$ (i.e., all indifference surfaces lie in $\mathbb{R}^{2l}_{++}$). The more general case specified in Section II is handled in the same way, but at some cost in notational convenience. With this assumption, the V_j and W_j utilities will have all upper contour sets for consumption goods in the positive orthant of $\mathbb{R}^l$. Denote demand functions by

$$x_{ij}[p, w_{ij}] \qquad \text{for} \quad i = 1, 2 \text{ and } j = 1,..., N,$$

where

$$w_{ij} = p \cdot \hat{\omega}_{ij} + p_m \bar{m}_{ij} = p \cdot \omega_{ij}, \qquad i = 1, 2; \, j = 1,..., N.$$

Under the assumptions on V_j, $\hat{x}_{1j}$ will be strictly positive as long as $w_{1j} > 0$. Similarly, $\hat{x}_{2j}$ will be strictly positive with positive wealth. Young agents' money demands will be non-negative while old agents' money demands will always be zero.

Since young agents also receive money endowments $m_{1j} = 0$, we have

$$[x_{11}(p, w_{11}),..., x_{2N}(p, w_{2N})] \in \mathbb{R}_+^{2N(l+1)} - \{0\}$$

for every $p \in \Delta$ and

$$w_{ij} \in \{w \in \mathbb{R}_+ \mid w = p \cdot \omega_{ij} \text{ for } \mathbb{R}_+^{l+1} - \{0\}, p \in \Delta\}$$

for $i = 1, 2$ and $j = 1,..., N$.

Balasko's results, however, require that the "enveloping" consumption sets be open, and $\mathbb{R}_+^{l+1} - \{0\}$ is not. We can, however, extend the consumption sets to open sets containing $\mathbb{R}_+^{l+1} - \{0\}$ by an appropriate choice of the admissible price set S, based on the fact that given compactness of endowment sets Ω_{ij} and the positive money price expectation of the young, equilibrium prices will be bounded away from zero. Define

$$\bar{\Omega}_A = \left\{ \omega \in \mathbb{R}_+^{l+1} \mid \omega = \sum_{i,j} \omega_{ij} \text{ for } \omega_{ij} \in \Omega_{ij} \right\}$$

and let

$$\Omega_A = \overset{N}{\underset{1}{\times}} \bar{\Omega}_A$$

$$x_1^t = \sum_j x_{1j}^t[p^t, \omega_{1j}^t]$$

and

$$x_2^t = \sum_j x_{2j}^t[p^t, \omega_{2j}^t].$$

We then have the following result.

LEMMA 3.1. *There exists a compact set $K \subset \text{int } \Delta$ such that for every $[x_1^{t-1}, \omega_1, \omega_2] \in \Omega_A \times \Omega_1 \times \Omega_2$, if $p^t \notin K$ then $x_1^t + x_2^t \notin \Omega_A$.*

Proof. (This result and the proof is adapted from Grandmont and Hildenbrand [11, Proposition 1].)

Suppose the result were not true; then it would have to be the case that for every compact $K \subset \text{int } \Delta$, there would exist

$$[x_1^{t-1}, \omega_1, \omega_2] \in \Omega_A \times \Omega_1 \times \Omega_2$$

such that

$$x_1^t + x_2^t \in \bar{\Omega}_A$$

with

$$p^t \in K.$$

But this implies that a sequence $p' \to \partial \Delta$ leaves aggregate demand bounded, which is a contradiction. ∎

We note that

(1) the time-invariance of utilities and endowments (given the expectations of the young) imply that K is independent of t;

(2) since the value of money depends on v_0, the bound on money prices also depends on v_0; and

(3) bounds on consumption goods prices which are independent of v_0 can be obtained by using the fact that if $p_k \to 0$ for some $k = 1, ..., l$, then $x_{2j} \to \infty$ for any j.

Now, fix $\varepsilon > 0$ such that $p_i \geq \varepsilon$ for all i and let Δ_ε be the ε-trimmed price simplex, i.e.,

$$\Delta_\varepsilon = \{ p \in \Delta \mid p_i > \varepsilon, i = 1, ..., l \}.$$

For sufficiently small ε, $\Delta_\varepsilon \neq \varnothing$. For $\varepsilon_0 > 0$, let

$$S(\varepsilon_0) = \{ p \in \Delta_\varepsilon \mid p_m > \varepsilon_0 \}, \text{ where } \varepsilon_0 \text{ is chosen so that } S(\varepsilon_0) \neq \varnothing$$

and let

$$\bar{S}(\varepsilon_0) = \text{cls } S(\varepsilon_0).$$

Lemma 3.1 then tells us that if $v_0 \in \mathcal{M}[\bar{S}(\varepsilon_0)]$, then the temporary equilibrium price of money is bounded away from zero. In fact, we can find an $\varepsilon_1 > 0$ such that for all $v_0 \in \mathcal{M}[\bar{S}(\varepsilon_0)]$, the price of money is greater than ε_1. Let

$$S(\varepsilon_1) = \{ p \in \Delta_\varepsilon \mid p_m > \varepsilon_1 \}.$$

We take $S(\varepsilon_1)$ as the set of admissible prices for $v_0 \in \mathcal{M}[\bar{S}(\varepsilon_0)]$. To extend consumption sets, define the open cone (see Figure 1)

$$\Lambda(\varepsilon_1) = \{ \omega \in \mathbb{R}^{l+1} \mid p \cdot \omega > 0 \text{ for } p \in S(\varepsilon_1) \}$$

Clearly, $\mathbb{R}^{l+1}_+ - \{0\} \subset \Lambda(\varepsilon_1)$, and if $\omega_{ij} \in \Lambda(\varepsilon_1)$, then $w_{ij} > 0$ so that

$$x_{ij} \in \mathbb{R}^{l+1}_+ - \{0\}.$$

Since the demand functions are continuous, Balasko's results may now be applied. Let $\gamma \in \mathbb{R}^{l+1}_{++}$ be a vector such that for every $\omega \in \bar{\Omega}_A$, $\omega \ll \gamma$. Let

$$\Gamma = \{ \omega \in \mathbb{R}^{l+1} \mid \omega \ll \gamma \}, \qquad \Omega'(\varepsilon_1) = \Lambda(\varepsilon_1) \cap \Gamma, \qquad \text{and} \qquad \Omega(\varepsilon_1) = \overset{2N}{\underset{1}{\times}} \Omega'(\varepsilon_1).$$

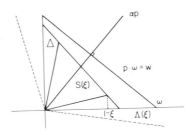

FIG. 1. Modification of the commodity space.

The set $\Omega(\varepsilon_1)$ is open, convex, and contains all possible $2N$-tuples of demands. Thus the equilibrium set for any $v_0 \in \mathcal{M}(\bar{S}(\varepsilon_0))$ is well-defined and Balasko's results yield the following (not necessarily commutative) diagram of mappings (for convenience we denote $S(\varepsilon_1)$ by S_1, $\Omega(\varepsilon_1)$ by Ω_1, etc.):

$$
\begin{array}{ccc}
S_1 \times R_+ \times (\Omega_1') & \xrightarrow{\;\psi\;} & E \subset \Delta \times \Omega_1 \\
{\scriptstyle\varphi}\big\uparrow & & \big\downarrow{\scriptstyle \mathrm{pr}_\Omega} \\
S_1 \times \Omega_1 & \xrightarrow[\;\mathrm{pr}_\Omega\;]{} & \Omega_1
\end{array}
$$

The maps φ and ψ are as defined above; pr_Ω denoted orthogonal projection on Ω_1. Let $h = \mathrm{pr}_\Omega \circ \psi \circ \varphi \colon S_1 \times \Omega_1 \to \Omega_1$. We note that h is continuous on $S_1 \times \Omega_1$, and on $\mathcal{M}[S_0]$. Continuity on $\mathcal{M}[S_0]$ follows from the fact that demand functions of young agents depend continuously on v_0 through the expected utility, and the map ψ depends continuously on the demand functions.

Now, extend h to $\bar{S}_1 \times \bar{\Omega}_1$ by continuity. Since continuous mappings are measurable, the diagram above yields the following induced diagram on the space of probability measures.

$$
\begin{array}{ccc}
\mathcal{M}[\bar{S}_1 \times R_+ \times (\bar{\Omega}_1')^{2N-1}] & \xrightarrow{\;\psi_*\;} & \mathcal{M}(\bar{E}) \\
{\scriptstyle\varphi_*}\big\uparrow & & \big\downarrow{\scriptstyle \mathrm{pr}_*} \\
\mathcal{M}[\bar{S}_1 \times \bar{\Omega}_1] & \xrightarrow[\;\mathrm{pr}_*\;]{} & \mathcal{M}[\bar{\Omega}_1]
\end{array}
$$

Let $h_* = \mathrm{pr}_* \circ \psi_* \circ \varphi_*$; h_* is easily shown to be continuous (in the weak topology). Now, consider measures $\eta \in M[\bar{S}_1 \times \bar{\Omega}_1]$. We say that $v = \eta[\cdot, \Omega_1]$ is a consistent temporary equilibrium for expectation v_0 if

$$
h_*[\eta] = \mathrm{pr}_*[\eta] = \mu.
$$

We define a correspondence

$$\Phi: \mathcal{M}[\bar{S}_0] \rightrightarrows \mathcal{M}[\bar{S}_1]$$

by

$$\Phi[v_0] = \{v = \eta[\cdot, \bar{\Omega}_1] \in \mathcal{M}[\bar{S}_1] \mid h_*[\eta; v_0] = \mathrm{pr}_*(\eta) = \mu\}.$$

The properties of Φ are given by the following result.

LEMMA 3.2. Φ is non-empty-, closed-, and convex-valued. Φ is upper hemi-continuous in v_0.

Proof. Non-emptiness is implied by the existence of temporary equilibria: let F be a measurable selection of the temporary equilibrium price correspondence (defined by projecting the inverse correspondence

$$\mathrm{pr}_\Omega^{-1}: \Omega \to E$$

onto Δ), and let $G(\omega) = [F(\omega), \omega]$. Define

$$\eta = \mu G^{-1}.$$

Then $h_*[\eta] = \mu$ and $v = \eta[\cdot, \bar{\Omega}_1] \in \Phi(v_0)$. This kind of construction is carried out in Grandmont and Hildenbrand [11]; a proof of the existence of a measurable selection can be found in Hildenbrand [12].

Closed-valuedness and upper hemi-continuity of Φ are simple consequences of the continuity of h_* in v and v_0.

To show that Φ is convex-valued, suppose v, $v' \in \Phi(v_0)$ and let $v = \eta[\cdot, \bar{\Omega}_1]$, and $v' = \eta'[\cdot, \bar{\Omega}_1]$. Consider $\eta^\lambda = \lambda\eta + (1 - \lambda)\eta'$ for $\lambda \in [0, 1]$. Then for every $f \in C[\Omega_1, \mathbb{R}]$,

$$\int_{\Omega_1} f \, dh_*(\eta^\lambda) = \int_{\Omega_1} f \, d[\lambda\eta + (1 - \lambda)\eta'] \, h^{-1}$$

$$= \int_{h^{-1}(\Omega_1)} f \circ h \, d[\lambda\eta + (1 - \lambda)\eta']$$

$$= \lambda \int_{h^{-1}(\Omega_1)} f \circ h \, d\eta + (1 - \lambda) \int_{h^{-1}(\Omega_1)} f \circ h \, d\eta'$$

$$= \lambda \int_{\Omega_1} f \, dh_*(\eta) + (1 - \lambda) \int_{\Omega_1} f \, dh_*(\eta') = \int_{\Omega_1} f \, d\mu.$$

Hence, $h_*(\eta^\lambda) = \mu$ and $v^\lambda = \lambda v + [1 - \lambda] v' \in \Phi(v_0)$. ∎

363

To complete our discussion of the correspondence Φ, we note that while the arguments of Φ are elements of $\mathcal{M}(\varDelta)$, the values of Φ should be interpreted as conditional probability measures since they depend on x_1^{t-1}. Since this interpretation is important for the proof of existence of equilibrium, we need to show that $v_1 \in \Phi(v_0)$ is in fact a conditional probability by showing that it is a measurable function of x_1^{t-1}. To show this, we let $v_1 = \eta_1(\cdot, \Omega_1)$ and fix $B \subset S$. Let $\hat{B}(x_1^{t-1}) = [B \times \Omega_1] \cap E(v_0, x_1^{t-1})$ so that $v(B|x_1^{t-1}) = \eta_1(\hat{B}[x_1^{t-1}])$.

Because the demand functions depend continuously on x_1^{t-1}, E depends continuously on x_1^{t-1}. Since E is the graph of an upper-hemi-continuous correspondence, it follows that $\hat{B}$ is upper-hemi-continuous in x_1^{t-1}. (This can also be shown directly as in Grandmont and Hildenbrand by showing that the equilibrium price correspondence defined in terms of the state variables (ω^t, x_1^{t-1}) is upper-hemi-continuous.) Next, define the correspondence of consistent temporary equilibrium measures

$$\mathcal{N}(x_1^{t-1}) = \{\eta \in \mathcal{M}[E(v_0; x_1^{t-1})] | h_* \eta = pr_* \eta = \mu\}.$$

A simple convergence argument based on the fact that $E(v_0, x_1^{t-1})$ depends continuously on x_1^{t-1} shows that $\mathcal{N}$ is uhc. The existence of a temporary equilibrium ensures that $\mathcal{N}$ is non-empty valued. Evaluating the measures $\eta \in \mathcal{N}$ at $\hat{B}(x_1^{t-1})$ then yields a correspondence

$$\hat{N}(x_1^{t-1}): \Omega_A \rightrightarrows \mathbb{R}$$

defined by

$$\hat{\mathcal{N}}(x_1^{t-1}) = \{\eta[\hat{B}(x_1^{t-1}), x_1^{t-1}] | \eta \in \mathcal{N}(x_1^{t-1})\}.$$

This correspondence is uhc, so there exists a measurable selection from the correspondence. This selection then yields the desired conditional probability function

$$v_1[B|x_1^{t-1}] = \eta_1[\hat{B}(x_1^{t-1}), x_1^{t-1}].$$

IV. Existence of Equilibrium

Our strategy for proving existence of a Markov equilibrium focuses on the correspondence Φ. In this section, we show that Φ can be extended to a compact subset of $\mathcal{M}(\varDelta)$ in such a way that Φ maps this subset to itself. We then derive an associated correspondence Ψ defined on a compact subset of $\mathcal{M}[\varDelta \times \Omega_A \times \Omega_1]$ mapping into this subset. Application of Glicksburg's fixed point theorem then yields an equilibrium.

To begin the analysis, we recall that the equilibrium structures examined in Section 2, and hence the correspondence Φ, depend on lagged allocations of current old,

$$x_1^{t-1} = [x_{11}^{t-1}, ..., x_{1N}^{t-1}] \in \Omega_A$$

through old agents' utility functions and money holdings. Lemma 3.2 tells us that the properties of Φ hold pointwise for $x_1^{t-1} \in \Omega_A$. Lemma 3.1 tells us that the bounds on prices, while depending (via the price of money) on v_0, are uniform with respect to x_1^{t-1}. We can, therefore, define a sequence of sets $S(\varepsilon_n)$ by induction.

(a) $S(\varepsilon_0)$ is defined as in Section 2.
(b) Given $S(\varepsilon_{n-1})$, let

$$K_n[x_1^{t-1}] = \operatorname{supp} \Phi[\mathcal{M}(S(\varepsilon_{n-1})); x_1^{t-1}]$$

and

$$K_n = \bigcup_{x_1^{t-1} \in \Omega_A^N} K_n[x_1^{t-1}].$$

Then let

$$\varepsilon_n = \inf_{j=1,...,l+1} \{ p_j \mid p \in K_n \}, \qquad \text{where} \quad p_{l+1} = p_m.$$

(c) Now, define

$$S(\varepsilon_n) = \{ p \in \Delta \mid p_j > \varepsilon_n \text{ for } j = 1, ..., l+1 \}.$$

Lemma 3.1 guarantees that $\varepsilon_n > 0$. If there is an n such that $\bar{S}(\varepsilon_n) \subset \bar{S}(\varepsilon_{\bar{n}})$ for all $n > \bar{n}$, then Φ maps $\mathcal{M}[\bar{S}(\varepsilon_{\bar{n}})]$ into itself. If there is no such n, then we can assume without loss of generality that the sequence $\{\varepsilon_n\}_{n=0}^{\infty}$ is decreasing, so that the sequence of sets $\bar{S}(\varepsilon_n)$, $n = 0, 1, ...$ is increasing. Since every $\bar{S}(\varepsilon_n) \subset \bar{\Delta}$, we have an increasing sequence of compact sets. The limit set exists and we denote its closure by $\bar{S}_\infty$. Since the correspondence Φ is well-defined for every $v \in \mathcal{M}\lceil S(\varepsilon_n) \rceil$, it is defined and has the properties indicated in Lemma 3.2 on $\mathcal{M}[\lim_{n \to \infty} \bar{S}(\varepsilon_n)]$. If $\bar{S}_\infty$ includes a zero money price, let

$$\partial \mathcal{M}[\bar{S}_\infty] \subset \mathcal{M}[\bar{S}_\infty]$$

denote measures assigning probability one to zero money price. For $\bar{v} \in \partial \mathcal{M}[\bar{S}_\infty]$, there exists a sequence of $v_n \in \mathcal{M}[\bar{S}(\varepsilon_n)]$ converging to $\bar{v}$ such that $\Phi(v_n)$ is well-behaved. Defining

$$\Phi(\bar{v}) = \Phi(\lim v_n)$$

and using the properties of Φ given in Lemma 3.2 (particularly the upper hemi-continuity), one can easily show that $\Phi(\bar{v})$ is well-defined and has the same properties as it does on each of the $M[\bar{S}(\varepsilon_n)]$. Intuitively, this result turns on the fact that, although money holdings are indeterminate when money is worthless, these holding can be made determinate by assigning the limit of the holding of young agents' equilibrium money demands as the value of money goes to zero to be the demands when money is worthless.

Let $\bar{S}$ be either $S(\varepsilon_n)$ if convergence occurs in finite n, or $\bar{S}_\infty$ otherwise. In either case, we have

$$\Phi(\mathscr{M}[\bar{S}]) \subset \mathscr{M}[\bar{S}]$$

for every $x_1^{t-1} \in \Omega_A$.

Our next task is to use Φ to determine a correspondence

$$\Psi: \mathscr{M}[\bar{S} \times \Omega_A \times \Omega_1] \rightrightarrows \mathscr{M}[\bar{S} \times \Omega_A \times \Omega_1].$$

Define a mapping

$$r: \mathscr{M}[\bar{S} \times \Omega_A \times \Omega_1] \to \mathscr{M}[\bar{S}] \times \mathscr{M}[\Omega_A \times \Omega_1]$$

by

$$r[\eta] = [\nu, \rho]$$

where the measure $\eta \in \mathscr{M}[\bar{S} \times \Omega_A \times \Omega_1]$, $\nu \in \mathscr{M}[\bar{S}]$ and $\rho \in \mathscr{M}[\Omega_A \times \Omega_1]$. The measures (ν, ρ) are the respective marginals of η.

Let $q: \mathscr{M}(\bar{S}) \times \mathscr{M}[\Omega_A \times \Omega_1] \to \mathscr{M}[\bar{S} \times \Omega_A \times \Omega_1]$ be defined by

$$q(\pi_y, \rho) = \eta'$$

where

$$\eta'[P, X] = \int_X \pi_y[P \mid x] \, d\rho(x).$$

Here, $\pi_y \in \mathscr{M}[S]$ is a conditional probability depending on x_1^{t-1} and is assumed measurable with respect to this variable (see the comment at the end of the previous section). Clearly, both r and q are weakly continuous.

Define the correspondence $\Psi: \mathscr{M}[\bar{S} \times \Omega_A \times \Omega_1] \rightrightarrows \mathscr{M}[\bar{S} \times \Omega_A \times \Omega_1]$ by

$$\Psi = q \circ [\Phi \times \mathrm{id}] \circ r$$

We have the following result.

THEOREM 4.1. *The correspondence Ψ has a fixed point.*

Proof. The space $\mathscr{M}[\bar{S} \times \Omega_A \times \Omega_1]$ is convex and compact (in the weak topology). The correspondence Ψ is non-empty-, closed-, and convex-valued, and upper hemi-continuous. These properties follow from the fact that r and q are continuous, and Φ has the relevant properties. Thus,

Glicksburg's fixed point theorem [9] is applicable and there exists a measure η^* such that $\eta^* \in \Psi(\eta^*)$. The fixed point

$$\eta^* \in \mathscr{M}[\bar{S} \times \Omega_A \times \Omega_1]$$

is a Markov equilibrium of the system. ∎

The fixed point of the Ψ correspondence defined in this way will be a fulfilled expectations equilibrium. As noted in our definition of equilibrium, the same technique can be used to establish existence of a rational expectations equilibrium under the assumption that the endowment distribution is non-atomic. The modifications necessary for showing this are indicated in the Appendix.

V. Stochastic Properties of the Equilibrium Sequences

In this section, we undertake an analysis of the stochastic properties of the REE by considering cases where standard results in the statistical literature can be applied to the model. The first step in applying these results requires that we show that the equilibrium process is not completely transient. This can be done by showing that the so-called Doeblin condition (stated below) is satisfied. As noted in the Introduction, this analysis will be carried out for the case of a finitely supported endowment distribution. The results developed here carry over to the case where the transition probability depends continuously on the conditioning variables (since these measures satisfy the Doeblin condition). This condition will hold, for example, if the measure μ is non-atomic. Since this case was treated in Grandmont and Hildenbrand [11], we focus on the finite support case in developing the results of this section. To keep notation simple, we assume that the endowments of the young are drawn independently from the set $\{\omega^\alpha, \omega^\beta\}$, and we denote by π^s the probability of ω^s. We denote by the vector

$$y_t = \{x^t, p^t, p_m^t)$$

the equilibrium allocations and prices at time t. Where necessary we denote by σ_t the t-tuple of event histories $(s_1,...,s_t)$ up to time t, so that realizations of $\tilde{y}$ can be written as $y_t = y(\sigma_t)$. The basic state space we will be considering is the compact subset of $\mathbb{R}_+^{2(l+1)} \times \mathbb{R}_+$ containing all of the equilibrium prices and the equilibrium prices and allocations, which we denote by K. (That K may be taken compact is a consequence of our assumptions on endowments and the price normalization convention.) Where measure theoretic considerations come into play, we understand the space to be a measurable space $[K, B(K)]$, where $B(K)$ is the Borel σ-field induced by the (relatively) open subsets of K. We denote the Markov equilibrium transition measure derived in the previous section

$$P(B \mid y) = v^*[B \mid y] \tag{5.1}$$

where the measure v^* is as in Section IV. We make this change in notation to correspond to that found in the statistical literature. Restating the result of Section IV, we have the following.

PROPOSITION 5.1. *The conditional probability measure* (5.1) *generates a first-order, homogeneous Markov process on* K. ∎

Our next goal is to demonstrate that the process satisfies so-called Doeblin condition:

(D)   There is measure ψ on K with $\psi(K) > 0$ and an integer $n \geqslant 1$ such that if $A \in B(K)$ and $\psi(A) \leqslant \varepsilon$, then for every y_t, $P^n(A \mid y_t) \leqslant 1 - \varepsilon$.

The iterate of the transition probability function is defined recursively by

$$P^n(A \mid y) = \int_K P(A \mid z) \, P^{n-1}(dz \mid y).$$

When condition (D) is satisfied, the Markov process will be non-pathological and all of the results in the substantial literature on such processes can be invoked.

Note that condition (D) can be equivalently stated as:

(D′)   There is a measure ψ on K with $\psi(K) > 0$ and it is not the case $\forall \varepsilon > 0$, $\forall n > 1$, if $A \in B(K)$ and $\psi(A) < \varepsilon$, then for some y_t, $P^n(A \mid y_t) > 1 - \varepsilon$.

In this form, condition (D) requires that the measure ψ be such that no set A of zero ψ-measure is absorbing at y and invariant. (A set is absorbing at a point y if $P(A \mid y) = 1$; it is invariant if for any $y \in A$, $P(A \mid y \in A) = 1$.) Thus, for condition (D) not to hold, there would have to exist a set of measure zero which the process could enter with positive probability and never leave. We will derive a measure on K for the set of equilibrium values of the process and show that this measure cannot have such sets. We assume the initial conditions are fixed at $y_0 \in K$; this amounts to specifying the characteristics of the initial old agents alive at period zero. We define a sequence of measures by considering iterates of the transition function,

$$\psi_n(B) = P(B \mid y_0) \tag{5.2}$$

with

$$\psi_1(B) = P(B \mid y_0) = 0 \qquad \text{if } B \cap \{y(\alpha), y(\beta)\} = \varnothing$$

$$= \pi^s \qquad \text{if } B \cap \{ y(\alpha), y(\beta) \} = y(s), s \in S$$

$$= 1 \qquad \text{otherwise}$$

and where $y(s) = y(\sigma_1)$.

By compactness, the sequence of measures $\{\psi_n\}$ is tight (see, e.g., Billingsley [3]). By Theorem 29.3 of Billingley [3], then, there is a subsequence $\{\psi n_j\}$ which converges to a measure ψ on K. This will be the measure we work with. Now, suppose there is a set A which is invariant and such that $\psi(A) = 0$. Then

$$\psi_{n_j}(A) \to 0 \qquad \text{as} \quad n_j \to \infty.$$

If for some n_k, $\psi_{n_k}(A) > 0$, then there must exist an n_j and n_{j+1} such that

$$\psi_{n_{j+1}}(A) < \psi_{n_j}(A).$$

Using the definition of the ψ_{n_j} and of the iterates of the transition probability, we have

$$P^{n_{j+1}}(A \mid y_0) = \int_K P^{n_{j+1} - n_j}(A \mid z) P^{n_j}(dz \mid y_0)$$

$$= \int_{K-A} P^{n_{j+1} - n_j}(A \mid z) P^{n_j}(dz \mid y_0)$$

$$+ \int_A P^{n_{j+1} - n_j}(A \mid z) P^{n_j}(dz \mid y_0).$$

Since A is invariant, when $z \in A$, $P^{n_{j+1} - n_j}(A \mid z) = 1$. Hence, the second term on the right is

$$\int_A P^{n_j}(dz \mid y_0) = P^{n_j}(A \mid y_0).$$

Thus,

$$P^{n_{j+1}}(A \mid y_0) - P^{n_j}(A \mid y_0) = \int_{K-A} P^{n_{j+1} - n_j}(A \mid z) P^{n_j}(dz \mid y_0).$$

The right-hand side of this expression must be ≥ 0. Hence, it cannot be that $\psi_{n_{j+1}}(A) < \psi_{n_j}(A)$. So, we must have $\psi_{n_k}(A) = 0$ for all k. Now, let n be any of the n_k. We have

$$0 = P^n(A \mid y_0) = \int_K P(A \mid z) P^{n-1}(dz \mid y_0).$$

The condition $P^n(A \mid y_0) = 0$ implies that $y(\sigma_n) \notin A$ for any $\sigma_n \in S \equiv \{\alpha, \beta\}^n$, since P^n is a discrete measure. Suppose some $y(\sigma_{n-1}) \in A$. Then, for $z = y(\sigma_{n-1})$, $P(A \mid z) = 1$ since A is invariant. But then

$$\int_K P(A \mid z) P^{n-1}(dz \mid y_0) > 0$$

which is a contradiction. Hence $y(\sigma_{n-1}) \notin A$ for any $\sigma_{n-1} \in S^{n-1}$, and $P^{n-1}(A \mid y_0) = 0$. Continuing in this way, we find $y(\sigma_j) \notin A$ for any $j \leqslant n$. Since this argument is valid for every n_j, we conclude that for every n, $P^n(A \mid y_0) = 0$ and $y(\sigma_n) \notin A$, $\sigma_n \in S^n$. It follows $P(A \mid y_0) = 0$ so A cannot be absorbing at any y_t. Hence, we have following result.

PROPOSITION 5.2. *The equilibrium Markov process satisfies the Doeblin condition* (D). ∎

With condition (D) satisfied, several results in Doob [8] becomes available. Of particular importance is the following.

PROPOSITION 5.3. *There exists an invariant measure μ on K for the equilibrium process.*

Comment. The measure μ is invariant if for $E \in B(K)$

$$\mu(E) = \int_K P(E \mid z)\, \mu(dz).$$

Proof. Doob [8, Theorem V.5.7]. ∎

We note in passing that if the invariant measure μ is taken as a starting measure, then the equilibrium process will be strictly stationary and can be extended to a process defined for $-\infty < t < \infty$ (see Doob [8, p. 456]).

Under the Doeblin condition, we are also assured that the equilibrium process is well-behaved asymptotically. This is the thrust of the following two results.

PROPOSITION 5.4. *There is a unique decomposition of K into a finite number of disjoint ergodic sets, each of which has positive μ-measure.*

Proof. Doob [8, Theorem V.5.6]. ∎

The ergodic sets are the non-null minimal invariant sets of the process. Minimal invariant sets contain no invariant sets of smaller μ-measure. Clearly, once the process enters an ergodic set, it remains there.

PROPOSITION 5.5. *With probability one, the process will enter an ergodic set in finite time.*

Proof. Doob [8, Theorem V.5.6]. ∎

Using Doob's discussion preceding the statement of his Theorem V.5.7, one associates with each ergodic set an invariant measure. Letting K_j, $j = 1, ..., r$, be an enumeration of the ergodic sets, we denote the invariant measures on K_j by ρ_j. Then $\rho_j(K) = 1$, $\rho_j(K) = 0$ if $i \neq j$. We also have the usual result that

$$\rho_j(A) = \lim_{n \to \infty} \frac{1}{n} \sum_{j=1} P^j(A \mid y)$$

for $A \in K_j$, $y \in K_j$.

For the following, when we write ρ without a subscript, it is understood that the statement or result applies to any argodic set.

Define the space

$$L_2^X(\rho_j) = \{\text{square } \rho_j\text{-integrable mappings from } K_j \text{ into } X\}.$$

The space X will usually be either K or $\mathbb{R}$. The following result is well-known.

PROPOSITION 5.6.   *For each $f \in L_2^{\mathbb{R}}(\rho)$, the limit*

$$\bar{f} = \lim_{n \to \infty} \frac{1}{n} \sum_{j=1}^{n} f[y_{t+j}]$$

exists and is independent of t with probability 1. The $\{y_{t+j}\}$, $j = 1, 2,...,$ are sample realizations of the process. Furthermore,

$$\bar{f} = \int_K f(z) \, \rho(dz)$$

Proof.   Doob [8, Theorem V.6.1]. ∎

COROLLARY 5.7.   *The equilibrium process is recurrent. If $E \in B(K)$, and $\mu(E) > 0$, then*

$$P_{y_t}\left[\sum_{j=1} \chi_E(y_{t+j}) = \infty\right] = 1 \qquad \forall y_t \in E$$

where $P_{y_t}[\cdot]$ is the probability of the event $[\cdot]$ when the process starts at an equilibrium $y_t \in E$, and where χ_E is the characteristic function of E.

Proof. $\mu(E) > 0 \Rightarrow E$ is not transient, so E contains ergodic subsets E_j such that $\rho_j(E) > 0$, and $E = \bigcup_j E_j \pmod 0$.

If $y_t \in E_K$, take $f = \chi_{E_K}$ in the previous proposition to conclude that the process hits E_K infinitely often. Then, use the fact that

$$\chi_E = \sum_j \chi_{E_j}. \quad ∎$$

Now, define for $A \in B(K_j)$ the random variable

$$S_A = \inf\{n > 0 \mid y_{t+n} \in A \text{ if } y_t \in A\}.$$

S_A is the first-return time of the sample sequence $\{y_{t+j}\}$, $j = 1, 2,...,$ for a return to the set A.

PROPOSITION 5.8. *If $\rho_j(A) > 0$, then*

$$P[S_A < \infty \mid y] = 1 \qquad \textit{for any equilibrium } y \in A.$$

Proof. Revuz [17, Proposition 3.1.2 and Corollary 3.1.11]. ∎

Comment. This proposition states the well-known fact that for a discrete Markov chain, recurrent sets are positively recurrent, that is, with probability one, the return to A occurs in finite time.

The recurrence result taken in conjunction with the denumerability of the ergodic equilibria makes possible the following inference on the stability of monetary equilibria, when such equilibria exist.

PROPOSITION 5.9. *On an ergodic set, either $p_{mt} = 0$ for all t, or there exists $\varepsilon > 0$ such that $\infty > \limsup p_{mt} > \varepsilon$, where p_{mt} is the period t price of money.*

Proof. If at any time τ, $p_{m\tau} = 0$, then $p_{mt} = 0$ for all $t \geqslant \tau$; otherwise, some young agent would wish to hold unlimited quantities of money (a feasible demand when the price of money is zero).

Suppose for some t, $p_{mt} > 0$. If, along any sample path, the $\lim_{t \to \infty} p_{mt} = 0$, then for sufficiently large T, it must be that $p_{mt} > p_{m(t+1)}$ for $t > T$.

But this implies that for $t > T$, the y_t realizations cannot recur, a contradiction. That $p_{mt} < \infty$ is obvious. ∎

To complete our analysis of the structure of the equilibrium Markov chain, we cite the following well-known result on the sub-ergodic decomposition of the state space.

PROPOSITION 5.10. *For each ergodic component E_j, $j = 1, 2, ..., m$, there is an integer $d_j \geqslant 1$ and a unique decomposition of E_j into d_j disjoint subsets C_{ij}, $i = 1, ..., d$ which may be ordered so that*

$$P[C_{ij} \mid y \in C_{kj}] = \begin{cases} 1 & \textit{if } k = i - 1 \textit{ for } i = 2, ..., d_j \\ 0 & \textit{otherwise} \end{cases}$$

and

$$P[C_{ij} \mid y \in C_{dj}] = 1$$

The C_{ij} are cyclic classes.

Proof. Chung [5, Theorem I.3.4]. ∎

The question of whether (or when) $d_j = 1$ is, at present, unanswered. The problem of determining the periodicity of the chain appears quite difficult since direct verification via the definition of d_j as the greatest common factor of the set of integers

$$N(i) = \{n > 0 \mid P_0^n(i \mid i > 0\}$$

requires detailed knowledge of when certain equilibrium transitions are forbidden. We can, for example, show that if $\omega_1^\alpha \gg \omega_1^\beta$, then if $y_t = y_{\hat{t}}$, $s_t = s_{\hat{t}}$. Beyond this, we know very little.

Approaching the problem through a difference equation (as in Spear and Srivstava [20]) has also proven difficult since our results are in the form of existence theorems which provide no characterizations of the properties of the difference system.

APPENDIX

In this Appendix, we indicate how the existence proof of the text must be modified in order to demonstrate existence of a conditional rational expectations equilibrium in which agents' forecasts of future prices are conditioned on current information.

As we noted in the text, the existence proof for this case requires a strengthening of our assumptions on the stochastic process on endowments. We will make the particular assumption that the measure μ on endowments is non-atomic, together with the assumption that agents' preferences are smooth. We will indicate below how the assumption on preferences can be relaxed. In order to keep this exposition brief, we will also make the simplifying assumption that there is no money in the economy (or equivalently, that $p_m = 0$ for all t).

To begin the analysis, we make the following definitions:

1. $z^t = (p', \omega')$ are the state variables.

2. $Z = \Delta \times \Omega$ is the state space.

3. $\hat{\mathcal{M}}(\Delta \times Z) \subset \mathcal{M}(\Delta \times Z)$ is the space of probability measures on $\Delta \times \Omega$ having Radon–Nikodym derivatives with respect to z which depend continuously on z in the sense that for any set $B \subset \Delta$, $\mathrm{prob}(B|z)$ is continuous in z. One can show easily that $\hat{\mathcal{M}}(\Delta \times Z)$ is closed in $\mathcal{M}(\Delta \times Z)$.

By way of notation, we denote measures in $\hat{\mathcal{M}}(\Delta \times Z)$ by η. Radon–Nikodym derivatives of these measures taken with respect to z will be denoted $v(\cdot|z)$. We will let $S \subset \Delta$ denote the admissable price set.

We now assume that young agents' expectations of future prices are given by measures v formed from measures $\eta \in \hat{\mathcal{M}}(\Delta \times Z)$. This assumption can be justified by noting that since current equilibrium allocations enter in the determination of future prices, young agents may wish to condition their forecasts on current demands. This, in turn, is equivalent to conditioning on current prices and endowments. When the expectation v depends continuously on (p, ω), the resulting demand functions are continuous, and a temporary equilibrium will exist. In particular, all of Balasko's results on the properties of the temporary equilibrium manifold will hold. Of particular importance is the fact that the manifold $E(v; z^{t-1}) \subset S \times \Omega$ will move continuously in z^{t-1}. Finally, we let $S \subset \varDelta$ be the admissable price set. As shown in the text, when money is not present in the economy, S can be defined independently of the expectation v. We note that the existence result presented here can be extended to the case when money is present in the economy using the same arguments as in the text.

Now, we reinterpret the mapping h defined in the text by replacing the space of allocations with Z. As before, h takes $S \times \Omega$ into Ω. Fix z^{t-1} and consider measures $\zeta \in \mathcal{M}(S \times \Omega)$. We say that $v(\cdot | z^{t-1}) = \zeta(\cdot, \Omega)$ is a consistent temporary equilibrium for the expectation generated by $\eta_0 \in \hat{\mathcal{M}}(S \times Z)$ if

$$h_*[\zeta; \eta_0] = pr_*[\zeta] = \mu.$$

We define a correspondence

$$\Phi : \hat{\mathcal{M}}(S \times Z) \rightrightarrows \mathcal{M}(S) \times Z$$

by

$$\Phi(\eta_0) = \{ v = \zeta(\cdot, \Omega) \in \mathcal{M}(S) \times Z \mid h_*[\zeta; \eta_0] = pr_*[\zeta] = \mu \}.$$

The properties of this correspondence are the same as those of the related correspondence in the text and can be established formally by the same arguments as those presented in Lemma 3.2.

Under the non-atomicity assumption on μ and the assumption that agents' have smooth preferences, we show that the measure $v(\cdot | z^{t-1})$ is continuous in z^{t-1}. First, since the temporary equilibrium correspondence is uhc and its graph moves continuously as z^{t-1} varies, the correspondence $pr^{-1}(\text{supp } \mu) \subset E(\eta_0)$ is uhc. Since this set contains supp $\zeta(z^{t-1})$, this correspondence is also uhc. Hence, if $\{z_n^{t-1}\}$ is any sequence converging to z^{t-1}, the sequence of sets supp $\zeta(z_n^{t-1})$ either converges to supp $\zeta(z^{t-1})$, or the equilibrium price correspondence "explodes" and supp $\zeta(z^{t-1}) \supset \lim_{n \to \infty}$ supp(z_n^{t-1}).

Under the smoothness assumption, this implies that

$$\text{supp } \zeta(z^{t-1}) = \lim_{n \to \infty} \text{supp}(z_n^{t-1}) \cup D(z^{t-1})$$

where $D(z^{t-1})$ is a set of critical economies in the support of ζ. Since the associated critical ω's have Lebesgue measure zero, while μ is absolutely continuous with respect to Lebesgue measure, it follows that $\zeta(B, \Omega; z^{t-1})$ depends continuously on z^{t-1}.

To relax the smoothness assumption on preferences, note that all that is really required for continuity is that critical economies in the support of ζ have μ-measure zero. Formally, if $D(z^{t-1})$ is a set of discontinuity points of the set

$$pr_\Omega^{-1}(\Omega) \cap E(\eta_0, z^{t-1})$$

then we require that $pr_\Omega(D(z^{t-1}))$ have μ-measure zero. A similar condition can be found in Grandmont and Hildenbrand's analysis of the ergodicity of the temporary equilibrium stochastic process.

This result shows that the image of Φ consists of temporary equilibrium measures on prices which depend continuously on the state variables z^{t-1}. Hence, we may define the correspondence

$$\Psi: \hat{\mathcal{M}}(Z \times Z) \rightrightarrows \hat{\mathcal{M}}(Z \times Z)$$

by mapping $\eta_0 \in \hat{\mathcal{M}}(Z \times Z)$ into (ν_0, ρ_0) (where ν_0 is the measure on prices conditional on z, and ρ_0 is the marginal on (ω', z^{t-1})) by operating on ν_0 with Φ to get the set of ν_1's, which we compound with ρ_0 to define η_1. The rest of the proof is identical to that of the text.

References

1. Y. Balasko, Some results on uniqueness and on stability of equilibrium in general equilibrium theory, *J. Math. Econ.* **2** (1975), 95–118.
2. Y. Balasko and K. Shell, The overlapping generations model I: The case of pure exchange without money, *J. Econ. Theory* **23** (1980), 307–322.
3. P. Billingsley, "Probability and Measure," Wiley, New York, 1979.
4. D. Cass and M. Yaari, Individual saving, aggregate capital accumulation and efficient growth, *in* "Essays on the Theory of Optimal Economic Growth" (K. Shell, Ed.), MIT Press, Cambridge, Mass., 1967.
5. K. L. Chung, "Markov Chains with Stationary Transition Probabilities," Springer-Verlag, Berlin, 1960.
6. G. Debreu, Economies with a finite set of equilibria, *Econometrica* **38** (1970) 387–392.
7. P. Diamond, National debt in a neoclassical growth model, *Amer. Econ. Rev.* **55** (1965), 1126–1150.
8. J. S. Doob, "Stochastic Processes," Wiley, New York, 1953.
9. I. Glicksberg, A further generalization of the Kakutani fixed point theorem with application to Nash equilibrium points, *Proc. Amer. Math. Soc.* (1952).
10. J. M. Grandmont, Temporary general equilibrium theory, *Econometrica* **45** (1977), 535–572.
11. J. M. Grandmont and W. Hildenbrand, Stochastic processes of temporary equilibria, *J. Math. Econ.* **4** (1974), 247–277.
12. W. Hildenbrand, "Core and Equilibria of a Large Economy," Princeton Univ. Press, Princeton, N.J., 1974.

13. G. HUBERMAN, Capital asset pricing in an overlapping generations model, *J. Econ. Theory* **33** (1984), 232–248.
14. R. LUCAS, Expectations and the neutrality of money, *J. Econ. Theory* **4** (1972), 103–124.
15. B. MCCALLUM, "The Role of Overlapping Generations Models in Monetary Economics," Carnegie–Rochester Conference Series on Public Policy, Vol. 18, pp. 9–44, 1983.
16. D. PELED, Stationary pareto optimality of stochastic asset equilibria with overlapping generations, *J. Econ. Theory* **34** (1984), 396–403.
17. D. REVUZ, "Markov Chains," North-Holland, Amsterdam, 1975.
18. P. SAMUELSON, An exact consumption loans model of interest with or without the social contrivance of money, *J. Pol. Econ.* **66** 1958, 467–482.
19. S. SPEAR, Rational expectations in the overlapping generations model, *J. Econ. Theory* **35**(1985), 251–275.
20. S. SPEAR AND S. SRIVASTAVA, "Equilibrium Dynamics in a Stochastic Overlapping Generations Model," Carnegie–Mellon University Working Paper, 1983.

Corrigenda

Volume **31**, Number 1 (1983), in the article "Rational Demand and Expenditures Patterns under Habit Formation," by Marcel Boyer, pp. 27–53: Chung Yong-Bang has pointed out to me that expressions (10) and (11) of my paper (p. 36) are incorrect. The correct expressions are

$$
\begin{aligned}
u_{it}(\mathbf{x}_t; \mathbf{x}_{t-1}) + \beta u_{it}(\mathbf{x}_{t+1}; \mathbf{x}_t) \\
+ \beta^2 V_{w_{t+2}} [\alpha(f_{w_{t+1}} + (1-\delta))(-\alpha p_i)] - \lambda_1 p_i \\
- \lambda_2 f_{w_{t+1}} \alpha p_i \leqslant 0
\end{aligned} \tag{10}
$$

$$
\beta u_{i,t+1} + \beta^2 V_{w_{t+2}} (-\alpha p_i) + \beta^2 V_{i,t+1} - \lambda_2 p_i \leqslant 0. \tag{11}
$$

The expressions appearing in the original are a mix-up between those above and those derived for a slightly different model which was deleted from the final manuscript. The remainder of the paper is unaffected by the changes.

Volume **38**, Number 1 (1986), in the article "Markov Rational Expectations Equilibria in an Overlapping Generations Model," by Stephen E. Spear and Sanjay Srivastava, pp. 35–62:

1. Because of typographical errors in the manuscript of [3], the definition of a rational expectations equilibrium (REE) given by Definition 2 is not correct. Definition 2 should read

DEFINITION 2. *A rational expectations equilibrium* (REE) *is a stationary* (*i.e., time-invariant*) *probability measure* η^* *defined on prices* p^t, *endowments* ω^t, *one-period lagged prices* p^{t-1}, *and endowments* ω^{t-1} *such that given* $[p^{t-1}, \omega^{t-1}]$

$$
(1) \quad \sum_{j=1}^{N} [\tilde{x}_{1j}^t + \tilde{x}_{2j}^t] = \sum_{j=1}^{N} [\tilde{\omega}_{1j}^t + \omega_{2j}] \quad (where \quad \tilde{} \quad denotes \ the \ random
$$

allocations induced by randomness of endowments).

(2) *Agents' demands solve problem* (2.1) *with expectations of future prices given by the conditional probability* v^* *on prices at* $t+1$ *given prices and endowments at time* t, *obtained from* η^* *by taking a Radon–Nikodym derivative with respect to the marginal distribution on time* t *prices and endowments.*

(3) *The equilibrium distribution of* $[\,p^{t-1}, \omega^{t-1}, p^t, \omega^t\,]$ *is* η^*.

(4) *Conditions* (1)–(3) *hold for* $t = 1, 2, ...,$ *with* $x^0_{1j} = \omega_{0j}$, *for* $j = 1, ..., N$.

2. In [3], we established the existence of a stationary rational expectations equilibrium (SREE). The existence proof yielded a joint probability measure η on equilibrium $(p_{t-1}, \omega_{t-1}, p_t, \omega_t)$ (all notation as in [3]), and a corresponding stationary (i.e., time invariant) transition probability function $\hat{\eta}(A | p_{t-1}, \omega_{t-1})$. In Section 4 of the paper, we attempted to show that this stationary transition function is associated with an invariant measure when the endowment distribution has finite support. Several people have pointed out to us that this proof is incomplete.[1] While we established that there cannot exist invariant, absorbing sets of zero measure, this is not sufficient for the existence of an invariant measure for the equilibrium stochastic process.

A sufficient condition for the existence of an invariant measure is that the (nominal) perfect foresight dynamics around a non-stochastic steady state equilibrium $(\bar{p}, \bar{\omega})$ be contracting, and that the steady state equilibrium be regular. Under these conditions, which are satisfied for an open set of economies (see Kehoe and Levine[1]), if the support of the endowment distribution is a sufficiently small compact set near $\bar{\omega}$ and this distribution is weakly close to the degenerate distribution at $\bar{\omega}$, then the transition probability function $\hat{\eta}$ is continuous in the conditioning variables. The contractiveness condition further implies that the state space may be assumed to be compact, so that the transition probability function satisfies the condition of Rosenblatt [2, Theorem 1, p. 101], which is sufficient to ensure the existence of an invariant measure.

REFERENCES

1. T. J. KEHOE AND D. LEVINE, Regularity in overlapping generations exchange economies, *J. Math. Econ.* **13** (1984), 69–94.

---

[1] We are indebted to David Levine for first bringing this to our attention.

2. M. ROSENBLATT, "Markov Process," Graduate Texts in Mathematics, Springer-Verlag, New York, 1971.
3. S. SPEAR AND S. SRIVASTAVA, Markov rational expectations equilibria in an overlapping generations model, *J. Econ. Theor.* **38** (1986), 35–62.

CHAPTER VII

Quantity Rationing

Neo-Keynesian Disequilibrium Theory in a Monetary Economy [1,2]

JEAN-PASCAL BENASSY

CEPREMAP, Paris

1. INTRODUCTION

(1.1) *Presentation*

Most concepts of conventional (or neo-classical) economics hold rigorously only in general equilibrium, which precludes the study of Keynesian or Marxian Economics, or a satisfactory integration with macro-economic theory since all of these are essentially concerned with disequilibrium states, where transactions take place at non-Walrasian prices. It is our purpose in this paper to present concepts and tools permitting study of the functioning and properties of a decentralized monetary economy [3] at disequilibrium prices, in line with the work of Clower [9] [10] and Leijonhufvud [30] [31].[4]

The usual concept of demand is no longer valid as soon as we do not assume instantaneous adjustment of prices to their equilibrium values; if economic agents behave rationally, it must be replaced by a new concept, that of effective demand, introduced by Clower [9] taking into account quantity constraints as well as prices (the prototype of which is the consumption function). Further, interaction between individuals on the different markets gives rise not only to price adjustments (as in the standard Walrasian model), but to quantity adjustments very similar to the traditional dynamic multiplier, as described by Leijonhufvud [30] (the "income constrained process").

A number of authors have successfully used this approach to describe macro-economic phenomena within the framework of simple equilibrium models (Barro-Grossman [2] [3], Glustoff [15], Grossman [21] [22], Solow-Stiglitz [36]).

However, these simplified formulations can handle no more than one or two goods in disequilibrium, and we would like here to reformulate the above concepts in the usual framework of General Equilibrium analysis.[5]

So in what follows we shall study a general exchange economy "A la Debreu" with money in disequilibrium (production can be incorporated in the analysis without difficulty: Benassy [4] [7]). In this framework we shall formalize the effective demand concept, define Keynesian equilibria and prove their existence. We shall also prove an important result of Keynesian analysis: at non-Walrasian prices, multiplier effects associated with the monetary structure of exchange are responsible for the " inefficiency " of many Keynesian

[1] *First version received February 1974; final version accepted September* 1974 (*Eds.*).

[2] This paper is based on some chapters of an unpublished Ph.D. thesis [4] for which Gerard Debreu and Bent Hansen were the most patient and helpful advisers. Several people kindly read and commented this paper: R. Clower, F. Hahn, S. C. Kolm, G. Laroque, P. Malgrange, Y. Younes. I am greatly indebted to J. M. Grandmont, whose perceptive comments brought numerous changes in the exposition. I also wish to thank the editors of the *Review of Economic Studies* and a referee for their helpful suggestions. All remaining errors and obscurities are evidently mine.

[3] Analysis of non-monetary economies in disequilibrium is somewhat different, and presented in another paper (Benassy [6]).

[4] Concepts similar in spirit to those presented by Clower and Leijonhufvud are also found in the work by Hansen [24] and Patinkin [34] (Ch. 13).

[5] General Equilibrium under price rigidity has been studied with different approaches by Dreze [14], Grandmont-Laroque [18], Younes [37], [38]. We shall see, however, that our tatonnement equilibrium concept has similarities with those presented by Drèze, Grandmont-Laroque.

Reprinted from *The Review of Economic Studies* **42** (1975), 503–523.

equilibria. Finally, we shall show the very important role played by expectations in this analysis.

To keep the analysis simple, prices will be assumed fixed throughout the period of analysis: this is the "extreme Keynesian" assumption that quantities react infinitely faster than prices, found for example in Hicks' [27] "fix-price" method.[1]

(1.2) The Institutional Framework

Our analysis will hold in a pure money economy "A la Clower" [10] where money is the sole medium of exchange: "money buys goods and goods buy money; but goods do not buy goods". Consequently, if there are l goods ($h = 1 \dots l$) plus money (index m), there will be l markets on which money will be exchanged against each good. This will allow us to speak of the market, or the demand, for good h, meaning the market, or the demand, of good h against money. As was noted by Clower [11], this assimilation of goods and markets is possible only in a monetary economy. An individual i will visit these l markets successively, and express on market h a net demand for good h against money $\tilde{z}_{ih}$.

We can now sketch the functioning of the economy: agents express demands and supplies on a particular market; then the process of exchange takes place, in which each agent realizes a transaction (being eventually rationed) and perceives quantity constraints on his exchange. Then as a function of perceived constraints, he will express new demands on the subsequent markets . . . and so on.

So we see that the "natural" formulation of our model is one of sequential trading. Such a non-tatonnement model is sketched in the appendix. However, in this sequential framework the exposition very quickly becomes too cumbersome. Thus in the main body of the text we shall study a symmetrized tatonnement version, where effective demands are formulated *simultaneously* (though separately) on the l markets. Though different in this respect, the two models have in common a number of features which distinguish them from the traditional Walrasian approach.

(1.3) A Non-Walrasian Approach

The first new feature, which we already mentioned above, is evidently the introduction of quantity signals into demand functions, in addition to prices. As this will be a main theme of our study, we do not pursue it here. Another novelty comes from the fact that, in our l-market framework, demands are expressed *separately* on each market. Since these demands will generally not be satisfied, we see that *individual rationality does not imply that an individual's expressed demands $\tilde{z}_{ih}$ satisfy his budget constraint* (though his transactions must). *A fortiori*, Walras' law will not be satisfied by effective demands. That this is indeed empirically verified has been noted by many writers (e.g. Kornai [29]).

Conversely, since we want to describe "realistic" models in which transactions can actually take place, we shall require that realized transactions *identically* sum-up to zero on each market,[2] while this is only a property of the equilibrium point in conventional models.

All these modifications are clearly an important step towards realism, and join a long tradition which through Clower [9] and Hansen [24] goes back to Keynes [28], and even Marx [32] [33].

(1.4) Summary of the Study

Outlining briefly what follows, we shall see successively how transactions are realized on markets in disequilibrium and how individuals perceive their trading possibilities during this process (Section 2). We will then indicate how an individual expresses his effective demand as a function of these possibilities (Section 3). We shall then describe the tatonnement process, and prove the existence of equilibria for rigid prices; K-equilibria, close in

---

1 However, the same concepts and tools may be used fruitfully to study the case where prices can vary (Benassy [4], [7]).

2 Which we will write below $\sum_{i=1}^{n} \tilde{z}_{ih} \equiv 0$ where $\tilde{z}_{ih}$ is transaction of trader i on market h.

essence to the traditional Keynesian equilibrium (Section 4). Their properties will be studied, notably the inefficiency of "multiplier" equilibria (Section 5), which will be illustrated through a short numerical example (Section 6). Throughout, money is assumed to have an indirect utility as a store of value. We shall provide a theory of this utility in disequilibrium, and show at the same time the important role of expectations in the analysis (Section 7).

As noted above, the analysis is throughout carried in terms of a tatonnement process. The Appendix will describe a non-tatonnement sequential trading model (corresponding broadly to the topics treated in Sections 3 and 4).

2. MARKETS IN DISEQUILIBRIUM

(2.1) *Rationing and Actual Transactions*

Consider a market h on which the agents have expressed demands $\tilde{z}_{ih}$ ($i = 1 \ldots n$). In general, aggregate excess demand will differ from zero:

$$\tilde{Z}_h = \sum_{i=1}^{n} \tilde{z}_{ih} \neq 0.$$

On the other hand, since we wish to describe an actual exchange process, actual transactions $\bar{z}_{ih}$ must sum identically to zero, i.e.

$$\sum_{i=1}^{n} \bar{z}_{ih} \equiv 0.$$

A rationing scheme is thus necessary in order to go from effective demands $\tilde{z}_{ih}$ to actual transactions $\bar{z}_{ih}$. We shall assume

$$\bar{z}_{ih} = F_{ih}(\tilde{z}_{1h}, \ldots, \tilde{z}_{nh})$$

with:

$$\sum_{i=1}^{n} F_{ih}(\tilde{z}_{1h}, \ldots, \tilde{z}_{nh}) \equiv 0.$$

The exact form of the rationing functions evidently depends upon the exchange process on market h. We shall make a number of reasonable hypotheses on these functions[1]:

(i) One cannot force any agent to exchange more than he wants ("voluntary exchange").

(ii) Individuals on the "short" side (i.e. suppliers if there is excess demand, demanders if there is excess supply) can realize their demands ("frictionless market").

Mathematically, the two above conditions are written respectively:

(i) $|\bar{z}_{ih}| \leq |\tilde{z}_{ih}|$ and $\bar{z}_{ih} \cdot \tilde{z}_{ih} \geq 0$

(ii) $\tilde{Z}_h \cdot \tilde{z}_{ih} \leq 0 \Rightarrow \bar{z}_{ih} = \tilde{z}_{ih}$.

Finally, we shall also assume, which is not very restrictive, that actual transactions depend continuously on effective demands.

(iii) All F_{ih} functions are continuous in their arguments.

These conditions are satisfied for a great number of rationing schemes, and real mechanisms can take many different forms, all consistent with our assumptions: queuing or rationing tickets on goods markets, priority systems (by seniority, skills, ... etc.) on labour markets, proportional rationing on bonds and equity markets, etc.

[1] These conditions have been emphasized by Clower [8] [9], Barro-Grossman [2] and particularly Grossman [21].

2L—42/4

(2.2) Exchange Possibilities in Disequilibrium

As we shall see later, a most important element in determining the demands of agents will be the constraints they perceive on their exchange possibilities on the different markets. Voluntary exchange implies that on a market h the set of transactions perceived as possible will form an interval:

$$\tilde{z}_{ih}^s \leqq z_{ih} \leqq \tilde{z}_{ih}^d \quad \text{with} \quad \tilde{z}_{ih}^s \leqq 0 \leqq \tilde{z}_{ih}^d.$$

I.e. if a transaction is perceived as possible, any transaction of the same sign and lesser magnitude must also be perceived as possible.

From now on, in order to simplify notation, we shall make the assumption that goods are "specialized" for each individual (i.e. always supplied or demanded). We shall call D_i the set of goods demanded by i ($z_{ih} \geqq 0$), S_i the set of goods supplied ($z_{ih} \leqq 0$). So we need only specify one number $\tilde{z}_{ih}$, which is the maximum quantity that individual i can transact on market h as perceived by him.

Evidently:

$$\tilde{z}_{ih} \geqq 0 \quad h \in D_i$$

$$\tilde{z}_{ih} \leqq 0 \quad h \in S_i.$$

We now turn to the determination of this perceived constraint.

(2.3) Perceived Constraints on a Market

Consider now a market h on which agents have expressed demands $\tilde{z}_{ih}$ ($i = 1 \ldots n$) and realized transactions $\bar{z}_{ih}$. During the exchange process agent i will have perceived a constraint $\tilde{z}_{ih}$ on his possible transactions. In estimating this constraint, he takes into account all information he may have; in particular, he will be influenced by the demands expressed by other agents, and we shall write:

$$\tilde{z}_{ih} = G_{ih}(\tilde{z}_{1h}, \ldots, \tilde{z}_{nh}).$$

The fact of including all $\tilde{z}_{ih}$'s as arguments of G_{ih} does not mean that each individual knows the demands of all others, but rather that whatever information he has is a function of these demands. For example, each individual knows at least the transactions he realizes:

$$\bar{z}_{ih} = F_{ih}(\tilde{z}_{1h}, \ldots, \tilde{z}_{nh}).$$

The perceived constraint functions G_{ih} should normally have the following properties:

(α) If the agent is on the long side, and actually constrained to trade less than he wishes, it is natural to take his realized transaction as the perceived constraint, since he actually experiences the constraint. In this case the perceived constraint is *objective*:

$$|\bar{z}_{ih}| < |\tilde{z}_{ih}| \Rightarrow \tilde{z}_{ih} = \bar{z}_{ih}.$$

(β) On the other hand, if the agent can fulfil his demand, he may perceive *subjectively* some possibilities for more trade in the same direction[1]

$$\bar{z}_{ih} = \tilde{z}_{ih} \Rightarrow (\tilde{z}_{ih} - \tilde{z}_{ih}). \tilde{z}_{ih} \geqq 0$$

and generally he will indeed believe he can trade *strictly* more in the same direction.

(γ) This will be the case in particular if he was on the "short" side:

$$\tilde{z}_{ih}. \tilde{Z}_h < 0 \Rightarrow (\tilde{z}_{ih} - \bar{z}_{ih}). \tilde{z}_{ih} > 0.$$

To these natural properties we shall add the hypothesis that perceived constraints vary continuously with effective demands, i.e. that the functions G_{ih} *are continuous* in their arguments. Note that this hypothesis implies that the individual has, at least when he

---

[1] However, even if the perceived constraint is subjective, it should be a function only of signals objectively received by the individual.

is not constrained, a level of information superior to his " minimal " information (which consists of his demand $\tilde{z}_{ih}$ and his transaction $\bar{z}_{ih}$). As one can see in examples, this property will usually be verified for decentralized processes, since an unconstrained individual will actually meet other agents who will offer him exchanges of greater magnitude than his own demand (or supply).

An example

Consider a market (we drop the subscript h) with one supplier ($\tilde{z}_s < 0$) and n demanders ($\tilde{z}_i > 0$). There is for the demanders a priority system, or a queue. We take, for simplicity, the priority order to be the natural ranking from 1 to n.

When demander i meets the supplier, he is faced with the supply remaining after those before him have expressed their demands and carried out their transactions, i.e.

$$\tilde{z}_s + \sum_{i' < i} \bar{z}_{i'} = \min \{0, \tilde{z}_s + \sum_{i' < i} \tilde{z}_{i'}\}.$$

This quantity (with a change of sign because of the sign conventions) is the most natural expression for i's perceived constraint, i.e.

$$\bar{z}_i = \max \{0, -\tilde{z}_s - \sum_{i' < i} \tilde{z}_{i'}\}.$$

And his transaction will be naturally

$$\bar{z}_i = \min \{\tilde{z}_i, \max [0, -\tilde{z}_s - \sum_{i' < i} \tilde{z}_{i'}]\}.$$

In this example, as well as in the general formulation, the close interrelatedness between the rationing schemes (F_{ih}) and the perceived constraints (G_{ih}) appears quite clearly. This is most natural since the two are complementary aspects of the same exchange process.

(2.4) *Remarks on the " Specialization " Assumption*

While the assumption of " specialized " goods is realistic in many cases (labour, consumption goods, ...) it is easily seen that it implies mathematically quite strong assumptions on endowments, namely:

$$h \in D_i \Rightarrow \omega_{ih} = 0$$

$$h \in S_i \Rightarrow \begin{cases} \text{either } \omega_{ih} > 0 \quad \text{and} \quad h \in D_j \quad j \neq i \\ \text{or the consumption set is bounded above by } \omega_{ih}. \end{cases}$$

For more general cases, we would have to specify, as noted above, two perceived constraints, one on demand and another on supply

$$\bar{z}_{ih}^d = G_{ih}^d(\tilde{z}_{1h}, ..., \tilde{z}_{nh})$$

$$\bar{z}_{ih}^s = G_{ih}^s(\tilde{z}_{1h}, ..., \tilde{z}_{nh}).$$

The whole theory carries through without difficulty provided the two functions are continuous, and the perceived constraint which has the same sign as the effective demand possesses the properties as above.

We now revert to the " specialized " case, for its notational simplicity.

3. EFFECTIVE DEMANDS

(3.1) *Definition*

We can now give the expression for the demand $\tilde{z}_{ih}$ that trader i will express on market h, his effective demand for good h. Following Clower [9] and Leijonhufvud [30], we shall call effective demand for good h the exchange the agent wishes to realize on market h to maximize his utility, *taking into account the exchanges he perceives as feasible on the other markets* (while the neoclassical demand function implicitly assumes that the individual can realize whatever exchange he wants on the other markets).

Before giving a formal definition, let us describe agent i. Let $\omega_i \in R^l_+$, $x_i \in R^l_+$, $z_i \in R^l$ be vectors of endowments, final consumption and net transactions respectively, $\bar{M}_i \geqq 0$ initial holdings of money, $M_i \geqq 0$ the quantity of money held at the end of the planning period.

The ith consumer has a utility function $U_i(x_i, M_i) = U_i(\omega_i + z_i, M_i)$ continuous and concave in its arguments (money has an indirect utility as a store of value which will be derived in the last section).

$p \in R^l_+$ is the price vector of non-monetary goods. The price of money is 1.

Let $\bar{z}_{ih'}$ be his perceived constraint on market h' (notice these are constraints on exchanges, and thus on flows. If there are stocks in the problem, constraints only operate on their rates of change).

The net effective demand for good h, $\tilde{z}_{ih}$, will be the component h of the optimum vector of the following programme:

$$\text{maximize } U_i(\omega_i + z_i, M_i)$$

subject to

$$pz_i + M_i \leqq \bar{M}_i$$

$$\omega_i + z_i \geqq 0 \qquad M_i \geqq 0$$

$$z_{ih'} \leqq \bar{z}_{ih'} \qquad h' \in D_i \quad h' \neq h$$

$$z_{ih'} \geqq \bar{z}_{ih'} \qquad h' \in S_i \quad h' \neq h.$$

We call this last set $\gamma_{ih}(p, \bar{z}_i)$.

What the individual does is compute an optimal exchange plan, taking into account the constraints he perceives on the *other* markets, and then announces the trade he wishes to realize on market h. A point we should re-emphasize is that this effective demand $\tilde{z}_{ih}$ is made against money, i.e. the agent offers an amount of money $p_h \cdot \tilde{z}_{ih}$. None of the real quantities he really wishes to offer (i.e. the other components of the optimizing vector) is transmitted to the market.

(3.2) *Examples*

Clearly, the inclusion of quantity rationing signals in the demand functions, in addition to prices, is a good step towards realism, and as a result many well-known relations in macro-economic theory can be given a theoretical foundation within the framework of effective demand functions. This would be impossible in a fully neo-classical analysis. We give here two of the best-known examples:

(i) The consumption function, as pointed out by Clower [9], is the constrained demand function of individuals who cannot succeed in selling all the labour they would like to sell; their income becomes a binding constraint and enters as an argument of the demand for goods. Actually, not only realized income should be taken into account (as in the " naive " consumption function), but future constraints as well: cf. the life cycle theories of consumption.

(ii) The accelerator, as shown by Grossman [22], is the investment demand of a firm which cannot sell its notional output (i.e. profit maximizing output). Sold output becomes a constraint (and not a choice variable), and it will enter investment demand together with price variables. Here, as shown by examples in Grossman [22], the importance of forecasted constraints is crucial.

4. NEO-KEYNESIAN EQUILIBRIUM

(4.1) *Definition*

As noted earlier, prices are fixed and responses to discrepancies between supply and demand are quantity movements over the period of analysis. Thus we have a process of quantity adjustments, in which agents revise their effective demands in light of the constraints they perceive. If we start from a set of effective demands $(\tilde{z}_{ih})$, they generate a set of perceived constraints $\bar{z}_{ih}$, hence a new set of effective demands that will in general differ from the original ones. Intuitively, an equilibrium will be reached when these two sets of effective demands coincide. More formally, a K-equilibrium will be a set of effective demands $\tilde{z}_{ih}$, perceived constraints $\bar{z}_{ih}$ and realized transactions $\bar{z}_{ih}$ such that:

(a) $\tilde{z}_{ih} = G_{ih}(\tilde{z}_{1h}, ..., \tilde{z}_{nh})$

(b) $\tilde{z}_{ih}$ is obtained by maximization of $U_i(\omega_i + z_i, M_i)$ over the set $\gamma_{ih}(p, \bar{z}_i)$

(c) $\bar{z}_{ih} = F_{ih}(\tilde{z}_{1h}, ..., \tilde{z}_{nh})$.

It is easy (and may be more intuitive) to see that a K-equilibrium can be obtained as a fixed point of the following recursive tatonnement process.

Assume at time $t-1$ individuals have expressed effective demands $\tilde{z}_{ih}(t-1)$ on the different markets.

From these result perceived constraints $\bar{z}_{ih}(t-1)$. On the basis of these perceived constraints, the individual will determine a new set of effective demands $\tilde{z}_{ih}(t)$ by the following programmes:

$$\text{maximize } U_i(\omega_i + z_i, M_i)$$

subject to

$$pz_i + M_i \leq \bar{M}_i$$

$$\omega_i + z_i \geq 0 \qquad M_i \geq 0$$

$$z_{ih'} \leq \bar{z}_{ih'}(t-1) \qquad h' \in D_i \quad h' \neq h$$

$$z_{ih'} \geq \bar{z}_{ih'}(t-1) \qquad h \in S_i \quad h' \neq h.$$

(4.2) *Rationality of the K-equilibrium Concept*

From the way our K-equilibrium has been defined, it is clear that the set of transactions $\bar{z}_{ih}$ are consistent on each market, since by construction:

$$\sum_{i=1}^{n} \bar{z}_{ih} \equiv 0 \quad \forall h.$$

However, a question which comes to mind is whether at equilibrium realized transactions are acceptable to traders, i.e. whether they maximize utility subject to all the constraints they perceive. And indeed, it is easy to verify (by *reductio ad absurdum*) that the vector of transactions $\bar{z}_i$ of a trader i maximizes his utility, subject to all constraints $\bar{z}_{ih}$[1], i.e. in mathematical terms:

$$\bar{z}_i \text{ maximizes } U_i(\omega_i + z_i, M_i)$$

subject to

$$pz_i + M_i \leq \bar{M}_i$$

$$\omega_i + z_i \geq 0 \qquad M_i \geq 0$$

$$z_{ih} \leq \bar{z}_{ih} \qquad h \in D_i$$

$$z_{ih} \geq \bar{z}_{ih} \qquad h \in S_i.$$

[1] Characterized in this way, our K-equilibria are formally similar to equilibria with rationing proposed by Dreze [14] with some modifications (Grandmont-Laroque [18]): these are indeed defined as a set of feasible transactions maximizing the utility of each agent under quantity constraints (analogous to the z_{ih}) such that demand and supply are not rationed at the same time. I wish to thank J. M. Grandmont for pointing out clearly this similarity to me.

(4.3) *The Existence of a K-equilibrium*

A K-equilibrium will exist if the mapping

$$\{\tilde{z}_{ih}(t-1)\} \rightarrow \{\tilde{z}_{ih}(t)\}$$

is an upper semicontinuous mapping with convex values from a compact convex set into itself.

(a) *Determination of the compact*

An agent cannot supply more of good h than he has:

$$\tilde{z}_{ih} \geqq -\omega_{ih}.$$

On the other hand, he cannot demand more than he is able to pay for:

$$\tilde{z}_{ih} \leqq \frac{p.\omega_i + \overline{M}_i}{p_h},$$

which is finite if $p_h > 0$ for all h.

Each effective demand belongs to a closed compact interval:

$$-\omega_{ih} \leqq \tilde{z}_{ih} \leqq \frac{p.\omega_i + \overline{M}_i}{p_h}.$$

The product of these intervals is the compact convex set we are looking for.

(b) *Upper-hemicontinuity and convexity*

The set $\gamma_{ih}(p, \tilde{z}_i(t-1))$ on which the individual maximizes his utility function is convex and depends continuously upon the demand $\tilde{z}_{ih}(t-1)$. As the utility function is itself continuous and concave, the mapping will be u.h.c. with convex values.   QED

5. EFFICIENCY PROPERTIES OF K-EQUILIBRIUM

(5.1) *The Criterion*

One of the most appealing features of the concept of general equilibrium is that, under very weak assumptions, it corresponds to a Pareto-optimal state (Debreu [12]). Here, as can be easily guessed, there is no great hope that our K-equilibria will be Pareto-optimal in the usual sense (unless the price system happens to be the General Equilibrium one). Thus, we shall adopt an amended criterion for efficiency: a state will be efficient if, at the *given set of prices*, no trades involving *pairs of goods* can strictly improve the utility of all traders involved.[1]

The intuitive reason for this criterion is evidently the comparison with an *indirect* barter economy, where such pairwise trades are allowed. But, even with this very enlarged notion of efficiency, we will see that K-equilibria may very well be inefficient.

Before that, let us indicate shortly under which conditions such exchanges would be possible.

An agent i will wish to demand good h against good h' at the given set of prices, which we shall denote $h(P_i)h'$, if and only if:

$$\frac{1}{p_h} \frac{\partial U_i}{\partial z_{ih}} - \frac{1}{p_{h'}} \frac{\partial U_i}{\partial z_{ih'}} > 0$$

$$\omega_{ih'} + z_{ih'} > 0.$$

---

[1] This criterion, and the associated conditions on marginal utilities are found in Arrow-Hahn [1] (Ch. 13, section 3). They have been used by Y. Younes in a study on the optimality of monetary exchange [38].

A chain of exchanges involving pairs of goods and improving the utility of *all traders involved* (we shall call them Pareto improving trades, or chains), will exist if one finds goods $h_1 \ldots h_k$ and traders $i_1 \ldots i_k$ such that:

$$h_1(P_{i1})h_2, \ h_2(P_{i2})h_3, \ \ldots, \ h_k(P_{ik})h_1.$$

We consider here indirect barter exchanges, since in a " realistic " economy, the absence of double coincidence of wants would make direct barter exchanges insignificant (i.e. trades limited to two goods and two traders). Clearly the more disaggregated the economy, the longer will be the necessary exchange chains.

A K-equilibrium will be efficient if no such Pareto-improving chain of exchanges exists.

(5.2) *Properties of a K-equilibrium*

To determine the properties we seek, let us write the programme giving the transactions vector $\bar{z}_i$ of an agent i: as we saw above, $\bar{z}_i$ is solution of:

$$\text{maximize } U_i(\omega_i + z_i, M_i)$$

subject to

$$\omega_i + z_i \geqq 0 \qquad M_i \geqq 0$$

$$pz_i + M_i \leqq \overline{M}_i$$

$$z_{ih} \leqq \bar{z}_{ih} \qquad h \in D_i$$

$$z_{ih} \geqq \bar{z}_{ih} \qquad h \in S_i.$$

The Kuhn-tucker conditions for this programme can be written:

$$\frac{\partial U_i}{\partial M_i} \leqq \lambda_{im} \quad \text{with equality if} \quad M_i > 0$$

$$\frac{\partial U_i}{\partial z_{ih}} \leqq \lambda_{im} p_h + \delta_{ih} \quad \text{with equality if} \quad x_{ih} > 0.$$

$\lambda_{im} \geqq 0$ can be interpreted as the exchange value of money
δ_{ih} is an index of rationing for agent i on market h:

$\delta_{ih} > 0$ if i is constrained in his demand of $h(0 \leqq \bar{z}_{ih} < \tilde{z}_{ih})$

$\delta_{ih} < 0$ if i is constrained in his supply of $h(\tilde{z}_{ih} < \bar{z}_{ih} \leqq 0)$

$\delta_{ih} = 0$ if i is not constrained on market $h(\bar{z}_{ih} = \tilde{z}_{ih})$.

The above conditions on rationing schemes imply that the δ_{ih} *have the same sign for all agents* on market h (by convention we take $\delta_{im} = 0$).

If we define

$$\mu_{ih} = \frac{\delta_{ih}}{p_h} \ ^1$$

and we use the definition in the preceding section, we see that:

$$h(P_i)h' \Rightarrow \mu_{ih} - \mu_{ih'} > 0.$$

But the sign property on the δ_{ih} implies that the quantity $\mu_{ih} - \mu_{ih'}$ will have the same sign *for all agents* for the following pairs of goods:

(i) pairs in which one good is money
(ii) pairs in which one good is in excess demand ($\tilde{Z}_h \geqq 0$), the other in excess supply ($\tilde{Z}_h \leqq 0$).

---

[1] This quantity (divided by λ_{im}) is similar (except for the indices) to the μ_i's in Arrow-Hahn [1].

Thus no exchange chain, *direct or indirect*, improving strictly the utility of exchangers, can include one of the above pairs. But, and this is the fundamental result, the above criterion has no reason to apply for pairs of goods whose excess demands are non-zero, and of the same sign. Thus if we consider sets of goods all in excess demand (or all in excess supply), there will very likely be Pareto improving exchanges. In this case (which is most likely to occur if there are many goods and prices do not clear the markets) the K-equilibrium will be inefficient.

Sometimes, the inefficiency comes from a bad rationing scheme which inefficiently allocates rationed goods among the rationed consumers (this occurs for example if traders in a Pareto improving chain either buy or sell the two goods they desire to exchange against each other). This case is not very interesting.

(5.3) *Inefficiency and Multiplier Effects*

A much more interesting situation arises if, in a particular chain, each trader buys one of the two goods he would like to exchange in the chain, and sells the other (in which case he is constrained in only one of the two goods). This makes possible a circular transmission of disturbances affecting the level of transactions in each market (multiplication).

More specifically, we shall say that there is a multiplier effect if we can find a chain of k traders $(i_1 \ldots i_k)$ and k goods $(h_1 \ldots h_k)$ all in excess demand (or all in excess supply) such that:

$$i_1 \text{ is } \begin{cases} \text{constrained in good } h_1 \\ \text{unconstrained in good } h_2 \end{cases}$$

$$i_2 \text{ is } \begin{cases} \text{constrained in good } h_2 \\ \text{unconstrained in good } h_3 \end{cases}$$

$$\ldots\ldots\ldots\ldots$$

$$i_k \text{ is } \begin{cases} \text{constrained in good } h_k \\ \text{unconstrained in good } h_1. \end{cases}$$

The corresponding state is evidently inefficient.

In this case, an initial disturbance (for example, an aggravation of disequilibrium in the first market) will be transmitted with the same sign to all markets in the chain, and will ultimately come back to the first market, launching a new wave of disturbances (a mechanism similar to the traditional multiplier or multiplier-accelerator).

Generally, many such chains will be found. Multiplier effects will evidently be observed most acutely in cases of generalized excess demand or supply, since excess demands have the same sign for all goods. The best-known example of these inefficient states is the deflationary Keynesian case: an increase in employment would increase both firms' profits and individuals' utilities. But, unfortunately, the market does not provide any signal for the existence of such a profitable trade.

(5.4) *The Cause of Inefficiency*

As we have seen in the preceding paragraphs, there is more to the inefficiency properties of Keynesian equilibria than the inefficiency associated with non-flexible prices. But clearly there is also an informational and signalling problem, since transactors will often fail to realize trades which are both possible and profitable to everybody.

This informational failure is clearly due to the particular nature of effective demands in a monetary economy, and specifically to the fact that information on desired real counterparts is not transmitted.[1] The dissociation of purchases and sales which money permits certainly brings increased flexibility, but does not permit all desired exchanges.

As Leijonhufvud [30], p. 90, says, giving the example of Keynesian deflation: " The workers looking for jobs ask for *money*, not for commodities. Their notional demand for

---

[1] In mathematical terms, only $\tilde{z}_{ih}$, the hth component of each optimizing vector, is transmitted, not the remainder of the vector. This point goes back to Keynes [28] (Cf. the beginning of chapter 16.) It has been elaborated brilliantly by Clower [9] [11] and Leijonhufvud [30] [31].

commodities is *not communicated* to producers; not being able to perceive this potential demand for their products, producers will not be willing to absorb the excess supply of labor. . . . "

But the ultimate cause of inefficiency should be looked for elsewhere, in the extreme complexity of the indirect barter exchanges which would be necessary without money in our highly specialized economies: " The fact that there exists a potential barter bargain of goods for labor services that would be mutually agreeable to producers *as a group* and labor *as a group* is irrelevant to the motion of the system. The individual steel-producer cannot pay a newly hired worker by handing over to him his physical product (nor will the worker try to feed his family on a ton-and-a-half of cold rolled sheet a week). The lack of any ' mutual coincidence of wants ' between pairs of individual employers and employees is what dictates the use of a means of payment in the first place " ([30], p. 90).

6. AN EXAMPLE

We shall give here a very simplified example, designed to show numerically the inefficiency property of " multiplier equilibria ".

(6.1) *The Economy*

Consider the simplest monetary economy with three goods (1, 2, 3) and two agents (A, B). Both have the same utility functions.

$$U_A = \log x_{A1} + \log x_{A2} + \log x_{A3}$$

$$U_B = \log x_{B1} + \log x_{B2} + \log x_{B3},$$

but different endowments

$$\omega_A = (2, 0, 1)$$

$$\omega_B = (0, 2, 1).^1$$

Good 3 is taken as money. Prices will be ($p_1, p_2, 1$).

According to the values of p_1, p_2, we can distinguish four regions (Table I), separated by the lines $p_1 = 1$, $p_2 = 1$, according to the signs of effective demands (note that these regions differ from the ones given by Walrasian demands).[2]

TABLE I

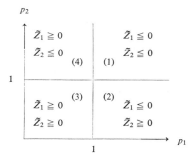

¹ Intuitively one may think of goods 1, 2, 3 as consumption goods, labour and money respectively. Agent A would represent aggregate firms, agent B aggregate consumers. For a more explicit treatment of firms and consumers, see Barro-Grossman [2] [3], Benassy [4] [5].
² The complete calculations of transactions and excess demands (for which I acknowledge the help of P. Malgrange) are a bit long and have been omitted. As an example we show how to compute transactions in the region of general excess supply (1).

From the results of (2.2), we know that exchange will be efficient in regions (2) and (4), since the aggregate effective demands are of opposite sign. On the other hand " multiplier " effects will occur in regions (1) and (3). As an illustration, we shall show what happens in region (1) (general excess supply).

(6.2) *Computation of Equilibrium Transactions (Region* (1))
Since there is excess supply in both markets transactions are determined by the demand side, i.e.

$$A\text{'s demand for good 2}: \tilde{z}_{A2} = \bar{z}_{A2} \equiv -\bar{z}_{B2}$$

$$B\text{'s demand for good 1}: \tilde{z}_{B1} = \bar{z}_{B1} \equiv -\bar{z}_{A1}.$$

A's effective demand for good 2 is given by:

$$\max \log(2 + z_{A1}) + \log z_{A2} + \log(1 + z_{A3})$$

subject to

$$p_1 z_{A1} + p_2 z_{A2} + z_{A3} = 0$$

$$z_{A1} \geq \bar{z}_{A1}.$$

We know that A's supply of 1 is constrained, so that the last constraint is binding, which yields:

$$p_2 \bar{z}_{A2} = \tfrac{1}{2}(1 - p_1 \bar{z}_{A1}) = \tfrac{1}{2}(1 - p_1 \bar{z}_{A1}).$$

We see that A's propensity to consume (out of money holdings and sales of good 1) is one-half.

Symmetrically, B is constrained in his sales of good 2 ($\bar{z}_{B2} = \bar{z}_{B2}$), and his demand for good 1 is:

$$p_1 \bar{z}_{B1} = \tfrac{1}{2}(1 - p_2 \bar{z}_{B2}) = \tfrac{1}{2}(1 - p_2 \bar{z}_{B2}).$$

We can easily solve the above system, and obtain realized transactions:

$$-\bar{z}_{A1} \equiv \bar{z}_{B1} = \frac{1}{p_1}$$

$$-\bar{z}_{B2} \equiv \bar{z}_{A2} = \frac{1}{p_2}$$

and final holdings are:

$$A: \left(2 - \frac{1}{p_1}, \frac{1}{p_2}, 1\right)$$

$$B: \left(\frac{1}{p_1}, 2 - \frac{1}{p_2}, 1\right).$$

(6.3) *Inefficiency*
Since aggregate excess demands are both negative in the interior of region (1), we would expect, according to the analysis of Section 5, Pareto improving trades involving goods 1 and 2 to be possible. This is easy to check by computing the propensities to exchange good 1 against good 2 at equilibrium:

$$\frac{1}{p_2}\frac{\partial U_A}{\partial z_{A2}} - \frac{1}{p_1}\frac{\partial U_A}{\partial z_{A1}} = \frac{2(p_1 - 1)}{2p_1 - 1} > 0$$

$$\frac{1}{p_1}\frac{\partial U_B}{\partial z_{B1}} - \frac{1}{p_2}\frac{\partial U_B}{\partial z_{B2}} = \frac{2(p_2 - 1)}{2p_2 - 1} > 0.$$

We see that A and B would both gain in exchanging 1 against 2 directly. However, with good 3 as money, there is no way they can communicate to each other these desires for trade.

Clearly, the opening of market (1 : 2) would restore efficiency. This can be checked without computation on the " diagonal " ($p_1 = p_2 = p$), where A and B would exchange *directly* one unit of 1 against one unit of 2, reaching in this way the " General Equilibrium " allocation:

$$x_A = (1, 1, 1) \quad x_B = (1, 1, 1).$$

A brief note before leaving this example: in this case, a direct barter exchange was enough to restore efficiency. Clearly this is due to the highly aggregated character of the economy. In general, much more indirect trades would be necessary as was noted by Leijonhufvud (see his quotation above).

7. EXPECTATIONS, THE INDIRECT UTILITY OF MONEY AND TEMPORARY KEYNESIAN EQUILIBRIUM

In the preceding sections we assumed *a priori* the utility of money as a store of value, which allowed us to ignore the linking between present and future periods through accumulation, as well as the role of future expectations in current equilibria, though these are evidently important themes of Keynesian analysis.

We now turn to an economy where expectations (about future prices and constraints) are uncertain (which is more realistic than certain expectations), and money links successive periods as the only store of value.

We shall make formally explicit the manner in which expectations determine the indirect utility, and how the resulting K-equilibrium will be affected (as before, to simplify, prices will be fixed in the first period).

(7.1) *The Economy*

We consider a two-period exchange economy. There are n agents, $i = 1 \ldots n$. Each one has a utility function over his two-period consumption streams of the Von Neumann-Morgenstern type:

$$U_i(\omega_{i1} + z_{i1}, \omega_{i2} + z_{i2}).$$

As we wish to concentrate on " market uncertainty " rather than " individual uncertainty ", we shall assume future endowments ω_{i2} known with certainty. Each individual will choose his actions so as to maximize his expected utility given his expectations.

Expectations

Each individual has to forecast prices for the second period p_2 as well as perceived constraints on the goods he will trade $\bar{z}_{i2}$. These parameters are not forecast with certainty but the individual holds a subjective probability distribution on them. This distribution depends on all information available to the individual in period 1 (past and present prices, past and present perceived constraints, other information variables, ...). Since the " past " as well as the prices in period 1 are given and we especially wish to emphasize the importance of current perceived constraints, we shall make the probability distribution depend explicitly upon the agent's first period perceived constraints:

$$\Psi_i(p_2, \bar{z}_{i2} \mid \bar{z}_{i1}).$$

This probability distribution will be assumed to depend continuously upon its argument $\bar{z}_{i1}$ (the set of today's perceived constraints).

(7.2) *The Indirect Utility of Money*

We are interested in deriving the actions of each agent in the first period, i.e. his effective demands for goods (and desired holding of money). The most direct way of doing this would be to compare the expected utilities of all actions. We shall use a more manageable criterion, an " indirect utility function " (including in particular money as an argument) which " summarizes " the consequences of each action.[1]

Since this indirect utility is derived in an essential way from anticipated events and decisions in period two, we study these first.

(a) The second-period problem

Consider an individual who has consumed $\omega_{i1} + \bar{z}_{i1}$ in the first period and has accumulated a quantity of money M_i. If he faces a price system p_2, constraints $\bar{z}_{i2}$ in the second period, his second-period consumption bundle will be the one maximizing his utility subject to the budget equation and the constraints on all markets (since the individual has no demand to express on future markets, we need only to know his expected transactions, which are given by the following programme):

$$\text{maximize } U_i(\omega_{i1} + \bar{z}_{i1}, \ \omega_{i2} + z_{i2})$$

subject to

$$\sum_{h=1}^{l} p_{h2} z_{ih2} \leqq M_i$$

$$\omega_{i2} + z_{i2} \geqq 0$$

$$z_{ih2} \leqq \bar{z}_{ih2} \qquad h \in D_{i2}$$

$$z_{ih2} \geqq \bar{z}_{ih2} \qquad h \in S_{i2}.$$

We call this last set $\gamma_{i2}(p_2, \bar{z}_{i2}, M_i)$.

For each anticipated $(p_2, \bar{z}_{i2})$ this results in an optimal expected vector of consumption $\omega_{i2} + z_{i2}^*$:

$$z_{i2}^* = z_{i2}^*(\omega_{i1} + \bar{z}_{i1}, p_2, \bar{z}_{i2}, M_i).$$

Also an optimal level of utility:

$$U_i^*(\omega_{i1} + \bar{z}_{i1}, M_i, p_2, \bar{z}_{i2}) = U_i(\omega_{i1} + \bar{z}_{i1}, \ \omega_{i2} + z_{i2}^*).$$

As written, this maximal utility evidently depends on money holdings and second-period anticipated prices and constraints.

(b) The indirect utility function

So for each first-period action $(\omega_{i1} + z_{i1}, M_i)$ and each expectation $(p_2, \bar{z}_{i2})$,the individual can determine his level of utility (given his best action in the second period):

$$U_i^*(\omega_{i1} + z_{i1}, M_i, p_2, \bar{z}_{i2}).$$

So, the expected utility of an action as viewed from the first period, is simply the expectation of the above utility with respect to the probability beliefs of the individual.

$$\int_{p_2, \bar{z}_{i2}} U_i^*(\omega_{i1} + z_{i1}, M_i, p_2, \bar{z}_{i2}) d\Psi_i(p_2, \bar{z}_{i2} \mid \bar{z}_{i1}) = V_i(\omega_{i1} + z_{i1}, M_i \mid \bar{z}_{i1}).$$

This is the indirect utility function. Money is now one of the arguments, together with first-period consumption.

It is important to note that this indirect utility function also depends upon anticipated prices and constraints, and thus upon today's perceived constraints.[2] This dependence is likely to increase the instability of multipliers. For example, unemployment today will

---

[1] We use the same methods as developed in the context of the Hicksian temporary equilibrium [26] by Grandmont [16].

[2] We see that the indirect utility function we have used throughout implicitly implies " fixed expectations " (i.e. Ψ_i independent of $\bar{z}_{i1}$).

cause anticipations of future restrictions on selling of labour, and increase the indirect utility of money (" precautionary motive ") so that savings will be relatively greater with unemployment (thus reinforcing the deflationary tendencies). Conversely, if there has been inflation and constraints on purchases, the indirect utility of money will be very low, and people will try to get rid of it (" flight from money "). This will accentuate the inflationary demand for goods.

(7.3) Temporary K-equilibrium

With the help of the indirect utility function, we can now derive effective demands in the first period, in much the same way as they were in Section 3.

Equilibrium is also defined almost identically: a temporary K-equilibrium will be a set of $\tilde{z}_{ih}, \bar{z}_{ih}, \bar{\bar{z}}_{ih}$ such that[1]:

    (i) $\tilde{z}_{ih}$ results from the maximization of $V_i(\omega_i + z_i, M_i \mid \bar{z}_i)$ over the set $\gamma_{ih}(p, \bar{z}_i)$

    (ii) $\bar{z}_{ih} = G_{ih}(\tilde{z}_{1h}, ..., \tilde{z}_{nh})$

    (iii) $\bar{\bar{z}}_{ih} = F_{ih}(\tilde{z}_{1h}, ..., \tilde{z}_{nh})$.

It is again helpful to see it as a fixed point of the following recursive tatonnement process: at time $t-1$ individuals have expressed effective demands $\tilde{z}_{ih}(t-1)$, from which result perceived constraints

$$\bar{z}_{ih}(t-1) = G_{ih}(\tilde{z}_{1h}(t-1), ..., \tilde{z}_{nh}(t-1)).$$

Effective demands in the following " round " $\tilde{z}_{ih}(t)$ will result from these perceived constraints through the following programmes:

$$\text{maximize } V_i(\omega_i + z_i, M_i \mid \bar{z}_i(t-1))$$

subject to

$$pz_i + M_i \leqq \bar{M}_i$$

$$\omega_i + z_i \geqq 0 \qquad M_i \geqq 0$$

$$z_{ih'} \leqq \bar{z}_{ih'}(t-1) \quad h' \in D_i \quad h' \neq h$$

$$z_{ih'} \geqq \bar{z}_{ih'}(t-1) \quad h' \in S_i \quad h' \neq h.$$

(7.4) Existence of a Temporary K-Equilibrium

Clearly, a temporary K-equilibrium will exist if the mapping $\tilde{z}_{ih}(t-1) \rightarrow \tilde{z}_{ih}(t)$ just defined above has a fixed point. From Section 4 on K-equilibrium, we know that such a fixed point will exist if the indirect utility functions $V_i(\omega_{i1} + z_{i1}, M_i \mid \bar{z}_{i1})$ are continuous in $(z_{i1}, M_i, \bar{z}_{i1})$ and concave in (z_{i1}, M_i).

For that we need some more assumptions on utilities and expectations:

    (i) $U_i(\omega_{i1} + z_{i1}, \omega_{i2} + z_{i2})$ is continuous and concave in its arguments.

    (ii) The mapping $\Psi_i(p_2, \bar{z}_{i2} \mid \bar{z}_{i1})$ from the set of first-period constraints to the set of probability measures over second-period prices and constraints is continuous with respect to the topology of weak convergence of probability measures.[2]

    (iii) No price is expected to be zero in the second period (the support of the corresponding probability measure belongs to the interior of the positive orthant).

We can now prove the above properties for each V_i.

---

[1] We omit subscript 1 since everything pertains to the first period.
[2] For some discussion of this assumption of " continuity of expectations ", see Grandmont [16].

(a) *Concavity*

Consider two couples (dropping the subscript i): (x'_1, M') and (x''_1, M'') and a given $\lambda \in [0, 1]$. Let:

$$x_1 = \lambda x'_1 + (1-\lambda)x''_1$$

$$M = \lambda M' + (1-\lambda)M''.$$

We wish to show that:

$$V_i(x_1, M \mid \bar{z}_1) \geqq \lambda V_i(x'_1, M' \mid \bar{z}_1) + (1-\lambda)V_i(x''_1, M'' \mid \bar{z}_1)$$

(α) First fix $(p_2, \bar{z}_2)$.

We have:

$$U_i^*(x'_1, M', p_2, \bar{z}_2) = U_i(x'_1, x'^*_2)$$

$$U_i^*(x''_1, M'', p_2, \bar{z}_2) = U_i(x''_1, x''^*_2).$$

As is easily checked,

$$\lambda x'^*_2 + (1-\lambda)x''^*_2 \in \gamma_{i2}(p_2, \bar{z}_2, M).$$

Hence

$$U_i^*(x_1, M, p_2, \bar{z}_2) \geqq U_i(x_1, \lambda x'^*_2 + (1-\lambda)x''^*_2) \geqq \lambda U_i^*(x'_1, x'^*_2) + (1-\lambda)U_i(x''_1, x''^*_2)$$

(the last inequality following from the concavity of U_i).

(β) Hence we have shown: for each $(p_2, \bar{z}_2)$

$$U_i^*(x_1, M, p_2, \bar{z}_2) \geqq \lambda U_i^*(x'_1, M', p_2, \bar{z}_2) + (1-\lambda)U_i^*(x''_1, M'', p_2, \bar{z}_2)$$

taking the expectation of both sides with respect to the probability distribution $\Psi_i(p_2, \bar{z}_2 \mid \bar{z}_1)$ we obtain the desired result.   QED

(b) *Continuity*

With second-period prices strictly positive, the set

$$\gamma_{i2}(p_2, \bar{z}_{i2}, M_i)$$

is continuous in its arguments.[1]

Thus, by the theorem of the maximum, the functions

$$U_i^*(\omega_{i1} + z_{i1}, M_i, p_2, \bar{z}_{i2})$$

are continuous in their arguments.

Since, in addition, expectations

$$\Psi_i(p_2, \bar{z}_{i2} \mid \bar{z}_{i1})$$

are continuous, continuity of the function V_i in its arguments follows from Theorem A-3, Section 5, of Grandmont [17].

So all V_i's satisfy the concavity and continuity assumptions, and a temporary K-equilibrium exists.   QED

8. CONCLUSION

As we saw, the formal use of the concepts of effective demand and quantity adjustment considerably enriches traditional neo-classical theory since with them we can describe a decentralized economy functioning at disequilibrium prices. Phenomena like involuntary unemployment, multiplier effects, etc., appear, which make this approach particularly well adapted for an integration of micro- and macro-economic theories.

[1] See Benassy [4], appendix, where the proof, too long to appear here, was taken from an early unpublished version of Dreze [14].

The equilibrium concept obtained, K-equilibrium, generalizes the traditional notion of Keynesian equilibrium; in particular it contains Walrasian or monopolistic equilibria as special cases.[1]

We also find in our model a particularly important result of Keynesian analysis[2]: in a *monetary* economy *in disequilibrium*, signals transmitted under the form of effective demands by the agents give a false idea of the actual exchange possibilities in the economy. The result is the existence of some equilibria (notably " multiplier " equilibria) where the level of trade and economic activity is " artificially " depressed, even taking into account the " wrong " exchange rates.

Further, we see that in contrast to the usual price adjustments, quantity adjustments have rather disequilibrating effects, especially if we take quantity expectations into account. These expectations themselves play a very important role in the determination of K-equilibria, which we " summarized " in the indirect utility of money (and it is easily seen that the same methods would apply for any other stock or store of value). Here an explicitly dynamic stock-flow analysis would be particularly desirable, and should be a subject for future research.

APPENDIX

As is the case for tatonnement processes, the ones presented in the text can describe observable states of the economy at equilibrium points only (i.e. in our K-equilibria). This is due to the fact that we treated all markets symmetrically, notably from the point of view of information (as we shall see, everything happens somehow as if each market was the first to be visited).

On the other hand, if we wish to follow the movement of the system through time (i.e. describe a non-tatonnement process), we must take into account the fact that in reality markets are visited sequentially. As it would be too cumbersome for our purposes to formalize the choice of the order of visit of markets by individuals, we shall assume that this order is given *a priori*.

(A.1) *The Institutional Framework*

As before, the analysis will hold in a monetary economy with l markets where each non-monetary good ($h = 1 \dots l$) is exchanged against money. Since we are in a non-tatonnement model, time will consist in a sequence of trading periods, or " market days ", indexed by t, during which transactions do actually take place on these l markets.

At the beginning of a period t, each trader i receives a constant endowment of non-monetary goods (ω_i) and carries the quantity of money he held at the end of the previous period:

$$\overline{M}_i(t) = \overline{M}_i(t-1) - \sum_{h=1}^{l} p_h \overline{z}_{ih}(t-1).$$

Then each trader visits the l markets in an *a priori* given order. To simplify the notation, we shall take the ordering of the goods and the order of visits be the same, i.e.:

$$h' > h \Leftrightarrow \text{Market } h' \text{ is visited after market } h$$

$$h' < h \Leftrightarrow \text{Market } h' \text{ is visited before market } h.$$

On each market h trader i expresses an effective demand $\tilde{z}_{ih}(t)$.

The exchange process on a particular market h yields transactions and perceived constraints in exactly the same way as described in Section 2:

$$\overline{z}_{ih}(t) = F_{ih}(\tilde{z}_{1h}(t), \dots, \tilde{z}_{nh}(t))$$

$$\overline{z}_{ih}(t) = G_{ih}(\tilde{z}_{1h}(t), \dots, \tilde{z}_{nh}(t)).$$

[1] See Benassy [4] [7].
[2] Cf. Keynes [28] (Ch. 16), Clower [9] [11], Leijonhufvud [30] [31].

We now turn to the determination of effective demands on each of these markets.

(A.2) *Effective Demands*

Our definition of effective demand must now take into account the sequentiality of markets, and the corresponding accumulation of information. The effective demand of trader i on market h is the exchange determined by maximizing his utility, *taking into account exchanges already realized in past markets, and expected constraints on future exchanges.*

Assume individual i has already realized transactions $\bar{z}_{ih'}(t)$ on markets visited before $h(h' < h)$, and expects constraints $\bar{z}_{ih'}^e(t)$ on markets he will visit afterwards $(h' > h)$. According to our definition, effective demand $\tilde{z}_{ih}(t)$ will be the hth component of the optimum vector of the following programme:

$$\text{maximize } U_i(\omega_i + z_i, M_i)$$

subject to

$$pz_i + M_i \leq \bar{M}_i(t) \qquad \qquad \text{...(1)}$$

$$\omega_i + z_i \geq 0 \qquad \qquad M_i \geq 0 \qquad \qquad \text{...(2)}$$

$$z_{ih'} = \bar{z}_{ih'}(t) \qquad \qquad h' < h \qquad \qquad \text{...(3)}$$

$$z_{ih'} \leq \bar{z}_{ih'}^e(t) \qquad \qquad h' > h \quad h' \in D_i \qquad \text{...(4)}$$

$$z_{ih'} \geq \bar{z}_{ih'}^e(t) \qquad \qquad h' > h \quad h' \in S_i \qquad \text{...(4')}$$

$$M_{ih'} \geq 0 \;^1 \qquad \qquad h' \geq h. \qquad \qquad \text{...(5)}$$

Three main differences may be noted as compared with the tatonnement version of effective demand seen in Section 3.

(*a*) First, we notice the appearance of transactions constraints (5), which express that the individual never plans to hold a negative quantity of money after a transaction. This type of constraint, of the same nature as Clower's [10] well-known expenditure constraint, appears as soon as the hypothesis of simultaneous exchange on all markets is abandoned.[2]

(*b*) The constraints on future markets taken into account in constraints (4) and (4'), the $\bar{z}_{ih'}^e(t)$ are expected, or *ex-ante* constraints. They should not be confused with the $\bar{z}_{ih'}(t)$, or *ex-post* constraints, which arise once the market has been held and effective demands expressed, as described in Section 2:

$$\bar{z}_{ih'}(t) = G_{ih'}(\tilde{z}_{1h'}(t), \ldots, \tilde{z}_{nh'}(t)).$$

In the tatonnement models we could somehow collapse the two concepts, since at a K-equilibrium ex-ante and ex-post constraints are the same. In the non-tatonnement process, we need specify more precisely how the ex-ante constraints are formed through expectations.[3]

(*c*) Finally, we see that the individual actually uses the information obtained on past markets by taking into account realized transactions (and constraints) on these markets instead of expected, or ex-ante constraints.

So we see that the symmetrized effective demand definition, which took into account only ex-ante constraints, was expressed as if each market was the first to be visited.

---

[1] With

$$M_{ih'} = \bar{M}_i(t) - \sum_{h'' \leq h'} p_{h''} z_{ih''}$$

$M_{ih'}$ is the amount of money held by i after transacting on market h'.
[2] For a formal treatment of this constraint in a general equilibrium framework, see for example Grandmont-Younes [19] [20].
[3] These points have been emphasized by Leijonhufvud [31].

(A.3) *The Non-Tatonnement Process and Equilibrium*

We are now almost ready to describe the non-tatonnement exchange process in time, i.e. to specify the effective demands at time t, $\tilde{z}_{ih}(t)$, provided we know the effective demands expressed in previous periods $\tilde{z}_{ih}(\tau)(\tau < t)$.

We still have to specify how the ex-ante constraints are formed, i.e. the expectations pattern for trading constraints. Let us start with a very simple and common pattern:

$$\bar{z}^e_{ih}(t) = \bar{z}_{ih}(t-1).$$

The ex-ante constraint for period t is expected to be the same as the one observed ex-post in $t-1$.[1]

Holdings of money and effective demands will be determined sequentially by the following recursive relations:

$$\bar{M}_i(t) = \bar{M}_i(t-1) - \sum_{h=1}^{l} p_h \bar{z}_{ih}(t-1).$$

$\tilde{z}_{ih}(t)$ is the hth component of the optimum vector of the programme:

$$\text{maximize } U_i(\omega_i + z_i, M_i)$$

subject to

$$pz_i + M_i \leq \bar{M}_i(t) \qquad \qquad \ldots(1)$$

$$\omega_i + z_i \geq 0 \qquad M_i \geq 0 \qquad \ldots(2)$$

$$z_{ih'} = \bar{z}_{ih'}(t) \qquad h' < h \qquad \ldots(3)$$

$$z_{ih'} \leq \bar{z}_{ih'}(t-1) \qquad h' > h \quad h' \in D_i \qquad \ldots(4)$$

$$z_{ih'} \geq \bar{z}_{ih'}(t-1) \qquad h' > h \quad h' \in S_i \qquad \ldots(4')$$

$$M_{ih'} \geq 0. \qquad h' \geq h \qquad \ldots(5)$$

We see that demands will be determined first on market $h = 1$, then $h = 2 \ldots h = l$ (because of constraints (3)). We recognise in this process a generalization of the well-known Keynesian dynamic multiplier:

$$C_t = cY_{t-1}$$

$$Y_t = C_t + \bar{I}_t.$$

An equilibrium will be a self-reproducing state of this recursive process (and the system will actually converge towards it if it is stable).[2]

As is easy to verify, at equilibrium the vector of transactions $\bar{z}_i$ and the holdings of money $\bar{M}_i$ are the solutions of the following programme:

$$\text{maximize } U_i(\omega_i + z_i, M_i)$$

subject to

$$pz_i + M_i \leq \bar{M}_i$$

$$\omega_i + z_i \geq 0 \qquad M_i \geq 0$$

$$z_{ih} \leq \bar{z}_{ih} \qquad h \in D_i$$

$$z_{ih} \geq \bar{z}_{ih} \qquad h \in S_i$$

$$M_{ih'} \geq 0. \qquad \forall h'$$

[1] Without much change in the analysis, we can use more general expectations patterns like
$$\bar{z}^e_{ih}(t) = \phi_{ih}[\bar{z}_{ih}(t-1), \ldots, \bar{z}_{ih}(t-T)],$$
which will yield permanent-income type effects in the dynamic process. Equilibria obtained will be the same provided that
$$\phi_{ih}[\alpha, \ldots, \alpha] = \alpha.$$

[2] The existence proof is similar to the one in Section 4, and is thus omitted.

2M—42/4

so that all what we said in Section 5 on the *inefficiency* properties of some K-equilibria (notably multiplier equilibria) still holds. However, the deviation amplifying mechanisms of multiplier and " spillover " effects, which are the basis of this inefficiency, can be much better seen in this explicitly dynamic context.

REFERENCES

[1] Arrow, K. J. and Hahn, F. H. *General Competitive Analysis* (Holden Day, San Francisco, 1971).

[2] Barro, R. J. and Grossman, H. I. " A General Disequilibrium Model of Income and Employment ", *American Economic Review* (March 1971).

[3] Barro, R. J. and Grossman, H. I. " Suppressed Inflation and the Supply Multiplier ", *Review of Economic Studies* (January 1974).

[4] Benassy, J. P. " Disequilibrium Theory ", unpublished Ph.D. Thesis, Working paper No. 185, CRMS UC Berkeley (June 1973).

[5] Benassy, J. P. " Théorie Néokeynésienne du Déséquilibre dans une Économie Monétaire ", CEPREMAP Discussion Paper, to appear in *Cahiers du séminaire d'Econométrie CNRS* (1974).

[6] Benassy, J. P. " Disequilibrium Exchange in Barter and Monetary Economies ", CEPREMAP Discussion Paper, February 1974, to appear in *Economic Inquiry*.

[7] Benassy, J. P. " The Disequilibrium Approach to Monopolistic Price Setting and General Monopolistic Equilibrium ", CEPREMAP Discussion Paper, March 1974.

[8] Clower, R. W. " Keynes and the Classics: A Dynamical Perspective ", *Quarterly Journal of Economics* (May 1960).

[9] Clower, R. W. " The Keynesian Counterrevolution: A Theoretical Appraisal ", in [23].

[10] Clower, R. W. " A Reconsideration of the Micro-foundations of Monetary Theory ", *Western Economic Journal* (December 1967).

[11] Clower, R. W. " Theoretical Foundations of Monetary Policy " in *Monetary Theory and Monetary Policy in 1970's*, edited by Clayton, Gilbert and Sedgwick (Oxford University Press, 1971).

[12] Debreu, G. *Theory of Value* (Wiley, New York, 1959).

[13] Dreze, J. (Ed.). *Allocation under Uncertainty, Equilibrium and Optimality* (Macmillan, 1973).

[14] Dreze, J. " Existence of an Equilibrium under Price Rigidity and Quantity Rationing ", CORE Discussion Paper, University of Louvain, August 1973.

[15] Glustoff, E. " On the Existence of a Keynesian Equilibrium ", *Review of Economic Studies* (1968).

[16] Grandmont, J. M. " Short-run Equilibrium Analysis in a Monetary Economy ", CEPREMAP Discussion Paper, February 1971, to appear in [13].

[17] Grandmont, J. M. " Continuity Properties of a Von Neumann-Morgenstern Utility ", *Journal of Economic Theory* (February 1972).

[18] Grandmont, J. M. and Laroque, G. " Equilibres Temporaires Keynésiens ", CEPREMAP Discussion Paper, November 1973.

[19] Grandmont, J. M. and Younes, Y. " On the Role of Money and the Existence of a Monetary Equilibrium ", *Review of Economic Studies* (July 1972).

[20] Grandmont, J. M. and Younes, Y. " On the Efficiency of a Monetary Equilibrium ", *Review of Economic Studies* (April 1973).

[21] Grossman, H. I. " Money, Interest and Prices in Market Disequilibrium ", *Journal of Political Economy* (September 1971).

[22] Grossman, H. I. " A Choice-theoretic Model of an Income Investment Accelerator ", *American Economic Review* (September 1972).

[23] Hahn, F. H. and Brechling, F. P. R. (Eds.), *The Theory of Interest Rates*, Proceedings of an IEA Conference (Macmillan, London, 1965).

[24] Hansen, B. *A Study in the Theory of Inflation* (Allen and Unwin, London, 1951).

[25] Hansen, B. *A Survey of General Equilibrium Systems* (McGraw-Hill, New York, 1970).

[26] Hicks, J. R. *Value and Capital*, second edition (Oxford University Press, London, 1946).

[27] Hicks, J. R. *Capital and Growth* (Oxford University Press, 1965).

[28] Keynes, J. M. *The General Theory of Employment, Interest and Money* (Macmillan, London, 1936).

[29] Kornai, J. *Anti-equilibrium: On Economic Systems Theory and the Tasks of Research* (North Holland, Amsterdam, 1971).

[30] Leijonhufvud, A. *On Keynesian Economics and the Economics of Keynes* (Oxford University Press, London, 1968).

[31] Leijonhufvud, A. " Effective Demand Failures ", *Swedish Journal of Economics* (March 1973).

[32] Marx, K. *Capital: A Critique of Political Economy* (Charles H. Kerr and Company, Chicago, 1909).

[33] Marx, K. *Theories of Surplus Value* (International Publishers, New York, 1952).

[34] Patinkin, D. *Money, Interest and Prices*, second edition (Harper and Row, New York, 1965).

[35] Robinson, J. *An Essay on Marxian Economics* (Macmillan, London, 1942).

[36] Solow, R. M. and Stiglitz, J. E. " Output, Employment and Wages in the Short Run ", *Quarterly Journal of Economics* (November 1968).

[37] Younes, Y. " Sur une Notion d'équilibre Utilisable dans le Cas où les Agents Économiques ne sont pas Assurés de la Compatibilité de leurs Plans ", Contribution to the Seminaire Roy-Malinvaud, January 1970.

[38] Younes, Y. " On the Role of Money in the Process of Exchange and the Existence of a non-Walrasian Equilibrium ", MSSB Working Paper, Berkeley, July 1973.

Equilibrium with Quantity Rationing and Recontracting*

JEAN-MICHEL GRANDMONT,[†] GUY LAROQUE,[‡] AND YVES YOUNÈS[†]

[†]CEPREMAP, 142 rue du Chevaleret, 75013 Paris, Equipe de Recherche Associée au CNRS N⁰ 507, France; [‡]INSEE, 18 Boulevard Adolphe Pinard, 75675 Paris Cedex 14, France

Received December 2, 1975; revised July 12, 1978

1. INTRODUCTION

A number of recent works rely on a description of the allocation of resources in an economy where prices are fixed at a value which may not achieve equilibrium of supply and demand in the classical sense. They all rest upon a concept of equilibrium at fixed prices which appears to be related to a number of important issues in economic theory. At the microeconomic level, this approach stems from the study of non-tâtonnement processes where transactions take place in each period at the prevailing prices while prices adjust from period to period [18]. In an economy with public goods, an analysis carried out in a similar framework leads to a characterization of the set of Lindhal equilibria [10]. At the macroeconomic level, the concept of equilibrium at fixed prices seems especially fruitful: It makes it possible to obtain within the same model, by varying the characteristic data of the economy, situations of Keynesian unemployment, stagflation, and repressed inflation [4, 5, 6, 7, 8, 14, 21, 29]. It also provides a tool to describe the functioning of centrally planned economies where prices are administered by the planning agency [26]. And, finally, it paves the way to a reconciliation between macro and micro theory, since, when transactions are not restricted any more to a single price system but may take place at any price, the model gives back the traditional competitive equilibrium (see particularly [22, 23]).

Many of these studies use the Hicksian fixprice method. That is, it is assumed that prices are temporary fixed and that the market clears during the period under consideration by means of quantity signals perceived by the agents (quantity rationing). Moreover, it is often postulated that money is the only medium of exchange so that one can imagine that the economy is composed of separate trading posts, where the traders exchange each com-

* This work was partially supported by National Science Foundation Grant SOC74-11446 at the Institute for Mathematical Studies in the Social Sciences, Stanford University. The work of Grandmont has also been partly supported by the University of Bonn. Department of Economics, during a visit in the spring quarter, 1975. The work of Laroque has been partially supported by a Ford Foundation Grant 6890114.

modity against money at the ruling prices. Finally, the rules obeyed by a rationing scheme in these studies are simple. If at the ruling prices, the demand and sypply currently expressed by the agents on a given market are compatible, then everybody should realize his plan. If there is an excess demand, then all sellers should realize their plans, while some buyers must be rationed, i.e., compelled to buy less than they intended. One speaks often in this case of a "sellers' market."

The basic features of this equilibrium concept are by now well established, although there may be variations among the authors in the way to present it [7, 8, 13, 28, 30].

Yet its exact status does not seem to be clearly perceived by all workers in the field. The ambiguity comes from the fact that these models are intended to describe "disequilibrium" states where there may be an excess supply or demand on some market, by contrast with the Walrasian model where all markets clear. In any given period, however, the final allocation is clearly the result of a *tâtonnement* on quantities. On reason comes from the assumption that the agents on the "short side" of a market always realize their plans (e.g., the sellers when there is an excess demand). When there are several buyers and sellers this assumption appears to involve a sizeable and costless exchange of information among traders, so that eventually no seller is left with an unsold commodity in the case of an excess demand. Another reason is that there is a simultaneous adjustment on the various markets. Consequently, the allocation reached on some market is influenced by the existence and the extent of a disequilibrium on others (spillover effects). In any case, the final allocation defined by the axioms postulated in the fixprice method appears to be result of an equilibrating process on quantities within the period under consideration.

The purpose of this study is to get a deeper understanding of the exact nature of this equilibrating process by using the theory of games. A simple example may help to justify the need for such a study. Consider an exchange economy with two commodities $h = 0, 1$ (commodity 0 being money), and two consumers i and j. If we look at the Edgeworth box drawn in Fig. 1, w is the initial allocation, and the line AB represents all admissible exchanges at the ruling price system p. In the picture, there is an excess demand for commodity 1, consumer i being the supplier and consumer j the demander. The rules described in this section lead to a final allocation represented by D_i: there, consumer j is constrained by the supply of consumer i. Yet the process leading to such an allocation is far from clear. It is indeed easy to understand why allocations described by points of AB outside the segment D_iD_j are unlikely to be observed. For instance, at any allocation represented by a point of AB on the left of D_i, both traders can improve their situation by moving along AB towards D_i. But any allocation represented by a point of D_iD_j in Fig. 1a, of D_iC in Fig. 1a, would appear to be "stable" in the sense that any

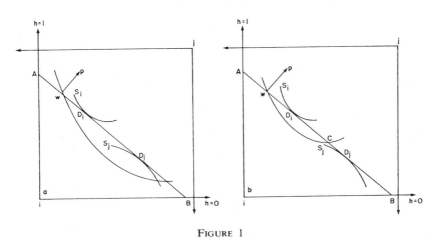

FIGURE 1

move from it while staying on *AB*, would hurt one of the traders and therefore would be opposed by him.

This heuristic discussion shows that the equilibrium concept leading to a final allocation like D_i, involves some kind of bargaining among traders which makes the sellers somewhat more powerful than the buyers when there is an excess demand on some market. The purpose of this paper is indeed to make this bargaining process clearer. A first result in that direction was already obtained by Younès [28, 30] and later on by Malinvaud and Younès [22, 23]. Their analysis, applied to the case of the fixprice method, shows that allocations like D_i are obtained if one postulates a recontracting process obeying the following axioms:

1. When recontracting, the traders take the ruling price system as given.

2. When recontracting, the traders can only exchange a single commodity against money.

3. The final allocation must be efficient commodity by commodity given the price system.

4. Nobody can be forced to exchange more than he wishes.

In the present study, we keep the first three axioms, and derive the fourth one from more basic considerations. Our starting point is that bargaining takes place among *coalitions* of traders. We assume that, when trying to improve upon a proposed allocation, a coalition will take into account, in a way that we make precise, the possible reactions of the traders who are left out of the coalition (compare with the definition of a bargaining set by Aumann and Maschler [3]). Our basic result is that allocations where the agents on the short side of a market realize their plans are the only ones which are stable—in the sense that no coalition can improve upon it—in large economies.

It is perhaps worthwhile to end this informal description of our analysis by emphasizing an important limitation of our study. In all our paper, the price system is fixed exogeneously and we consider only bargaining processes which take place at the ruling prices. However, since a fixprice allocation is not in general a full Pareto optimum, it would in general be profitable to the agents to change prices during the bargaining process. A more satisfactory theory would be to design bargaining processes taking place without any price limitation which would yield endogeneously determined price systems and corresponding fixprice allocations as stable outcomes. It is hoped that the present study will be a useful first step in this direction.

The paper is organized as follows. In Section 2 we describe our assumptions and the concept of equilibrium which is used in this work. We study in Section 3 the efficiency properties of this concept, and investigate in Section 4 the connection in large economies between equilibrium allocations and the set of allocations which cannot be improved upon by some coalition. All proofs, as well as some auxiliary results which are of independent interest, are gathered in Section 5.

2. DISEQUILIBRIUM ALLOCATIONS

We consider an exchange economy with $l + 1$ commodities indicated by $h = 0, 1,..., l$. Commodity 0 plays a particular role in the analysis and is called money. There are m consumers indicated by $i = 1,..., m$. Each consumer owns an endowment $w_i \in R_+^{l+1}$ which he wishes to trade with the others. The set of feasible net trades z for the ith consumer is a subset Z_i of R^{l+1}. Consumer i has preferences among feasible net trades given by a complete preordering $\succsim_i$ on Z_i. The following assumptions are made throughout the paper:

ASSUMPTION 1. Z_i is convex.

ASSUMPTION 2. The preferences $\succsim_i$ are strictly convex.

The price system is fixed and equal to a vector $p = (p_0, p_1,..., p_l)$ in R^{l+1}, all components of which are positive and such that $p_0 = 1$. A trade z is said to be *admissible* if $z_z \in Z_i$ and $p \cdot z = 0$. The result of the trading process is an *admissible allocation* which is described by a collection or admissible net trades (z_i) such that $\sum_{i=1}^{m} z_i = 0$.

Since adjustments on the markets do not take place by price movements but by quantity movements, clearing of the markets is brought about by *quantity constraints* $(\underline{z}_i, \bar{z}_i)$ perceived by the agents that set lower and upper bounds on the net trades that they are allowed to make. An important assumption of the model is the fact that the traders do not perceive constraints in the case of commodity 0. Thus $\underline{z}_i$ and $\bar{z}_i$ are vectors of R^l that satisfy $\underline{z}_i \leqslant \bar{z}_i$. A particular *interpretation* of the model is that there are separate markets, or trading posts, one for each commodity $h \neq 0$, where the traders exchange commodity h for money at the ruling prices. The traders however trade simultaneously on all markets. For every $h \neq 0$, let $t(h)$ be a vector (in R^{l+1}) representing an exchange of one unit of commodity h for $-p_h$ units of money: $t_0(h) = -p_h$, $t_h(h) = 1$ and $t_k(h) = 0$ for $k \neq 0, h$. Then any trade z_i such that $p \cdot z_i = 0$ can be written $z_i = \sum_{h=1}^{l} z_{ih} t(h)$, and conversely. Then z_{ih} can be interpreted as the intensity of the ith consumer's transaction of commodity h against money, and the constraints $\underline{z}_{ih} \leqslant z_{ih} \leqslant \bar{z}_{ih}$, $h \neq 0$, can be interpreted as constraints on these intensities. Given such a signal $(\underline{z}_i, \bar{z}_i)$, the set of feasible trades satisfying the budget constraint $p \cdot z = 0$ and the quantitative constraints $\underline{z}_{ih} \leqslant z_h \leqslant \bar{z}_{ih}$, $h \neq 0$, is denoted γ_i.

Let a *disequilibrium allocation* be described by an admissible allocation (z_i^*) and by quantity signals $(\underline{z}_i, \bar{z}_i)$ such that for every i, z_i^* maximizes the ith consumer's preferences on the set γ_i. Clearly, such a definition does not involve any restriction at all, since every admissible allocation (z_i^*) can be described in that way by choosing $\underline{z}_{ih} = z_{ih}^* = \bar{z}_{ih}$ for every $h \neq 0$. By contrast, the concept of a Keynesian allocation involves much more stringent conditions which we review now.

To describe whether, at a disequilibrium allocation, the ith consumer perceives binding constraints on the market for commodity h, we introduce the set γ_i^h which is obtained from γ_i by dropping the constraints associated with that commodity. That is, γ_i^h is the set of net trades $z_i \in Z_i$ which satisfy $p \cdot z_i = 0$ and $\underline{z}_{ik} \leqslant z_{ik} \leqslant \bar{z}_{ik}$, $k \neq 0, h$. The consumer is actually constrained in commodity h if there is a net trade z_i in γ_i^h such that $z_i \succ_i z_i^*$.

DEFINITION 1. A *K-allocation* is a disequilibrium allocation $(z_i^*, \underline{z}_i, \bar{z}_i)$ such that for every $h \neq 0$, either $0 \leqslant z_{ih}^* < \bar{z}_{ih}$ for all i and $z_i \in \gamma_i^h$ such that $z_i \succ_i z_i^*$, or $\underline{z}_{ih} < z_{ih}^* \leqslant 0$ for all i and $z_i \in \gamma_i^h$ such that $z_i \succ_i z_i^*$.

A K-allocation displays the following properties. If z_i^* maximizes the ith consumer's preferences on γ_i^h for all i, there is no excess demand or supply for commodity h and everybody realize his plan on that market. On the other hand if, for instance, $0 \leqslant z_{ih}^* < \bar{z}_{ih}$ whenever $z_i \in \gamma_i^h$ and $z_i \succ_i z_i^*$, there is an excess demand for commodity h and all sellers realize their plans, while some buyers are compelled to buy less of commodity h than they would like.

We study in Section 3 disequilibrium allocations which satisfy les stringent requirements than a K-allocation. Specifically, we consider the following condition:

$$(z_{ih} - z_{ih}^*)(z_{jh} - z_{jh}^*) > 0 \quad \text{whenever } z_i \in \gamma_i^h, z_j \in \gamma_j^h \text{ and } z_i \succ_i z_i^*,$$

$$z_j \succ_j z_j^*. \tag{H}$$

This condition means that the traders who perceive binding constraints for some commodity h should all be constrained in the same direction. We say that a disequilibrium allocation satisfies the *Hahn–Negishi* condition if (H) holds for every h, because such a requirement was first discussed in the context of *non tâtonnement* models.

An example may clarify the meaning of these conditions. Consider the exchange economy with two commodities ($l = 1$), and two consumers i and j which was pictured in Fig. 1. There, w is the initial allocation, and the set of admissible allocations is represented by the segment AB. The set of admissible allocations which satisfy the Hahn–Negishi condition (H) is represented by the closed segment $D_i D_j$. There exists a unique K-allocation which is represented by the point D_i.

Remark. The foregoing definition of a K-allocation does not specify how shortages are distributed among the agents. Benassy [7, 8] has proved the existence of a K-allocation corresponding to an arbitrary rationing scheme, using a concept of effective demand as in [11, 15].

3. EFFICIENCY

It is natural to ask whether a K-allocation displays any efficiency property. It is first clear that, if we wish a K-allocation to be efficient in the Pareto sense, we have to restrict ourselves to trades that satisfy the budget constraint $p \cdot z = 0$, i.e., to admissible trades. The following typical example [8, 23, 29] shows, however, that a K-allocation need not be Pareto optimal among the class of admissible allocations if we allow the consumers, when recontracting, to trade simultaneously on all markets.

Consider an exchange economy with three commodities ($l = 2$), and two consumers i and j. Assume that there exists a K-allocation (z_i^*, z_j^*), where there is an excess effective supply of commodity 1 as well as of commodity 2, and where consumer i is a net demander of commodity 1 and a net supplier of commodity 2, while the situation is reversed for consumer j. The situation so described is similar, although the analogy must not be pushed too far, to Keynesian unemployment, where there is an excess supply both on the labor market and on the market for output. At the K-allocation, the only *binding* constraint that consumer i perceives is a constraint $z_{i2} < 0$ on his supply of commodity 2, where $z_{i2} = z_{i2}^* = -z_{j2}^*$. Then z_i^* is the result of the maximization of the preferences $\succsim_i$ subject to $p \cdot z = 0$ and $z_2 \geq z_{i2}$. If the preferences $\succsim_i$ are representable by a continuously differentiable utility function U_i, and if z_i^* is interior to $Z_i = -\{w_i\} + R_+^{l+1}$, a straightforward manipulation of the Kuhn–Tucker conditions yields the two relations $U'_{i1} - p_1 U'_{i0} = 0$ and $U'_{i2} - p_2 U'_{i0} < 0$, where the partial derivatives are taken at z_i^*. Similarly, one gets for consumer j, $U'_{j1} - p_1 U'_{j0} < 0$ and $U'_{j2} - p_2 U'_{j0} = 0$. It is now clear that the two agents can both improve their position by trading simultaneously on all markets. Indeed, consider the new admissible allocation (z_i, z_j), where $z_i - z_i^* = a_1 t^1 + a_2 t^2$, with $t^1 = (-p_1, 1, 0)$, $t^2 = (-p_2, 0, 1)$, $a_1 > 0$ and $a_2 < 0$ being "small" numbers. Then

$$U_i(z_i) - U_i(z_i^*) \simeq a_1(U'_{i1} - p_1 U'_{i0}) + a_2(U'_{i2} - p_2 U'_{i0}) > 0,$$

$$U_j(z_j) - U_j(z_j^*) \simeq -a_1(U'_{j1} - p_1 U'_{j0}) - a_2(U'_{j2} - p_2 U'_{j0}) > 0.$$

When a_1 and a_2 are different from zero, the trade $z_i - z_i^* = -(z_j - z_j^*)$ involves in general an exchange of all commodities. Suppose now that the traders must exchange only a pair of commodities when trying to improve their position, starting from the given K-allocation. If we allow them to exchange directly commodity 1 for commodity 2, this corresponds to the case $a_1 p_1 + a_2 p_2 = 0$, and then both traders can be made better off. On the other hand, if the traders are restricted to monetary exchanges (either $a_1 = 0$ or $a_2 = 0$), then a trader cannot improve his position without making the other worse off.

This example suggests that we have to restrict the recontracting process to take place on a single market at a time.

DEFINITION 2. A disequilibrium allocation $(z_i^*, z_i, \bar{z}_i)$ is efficient market by market if there is no commodity $h \neq 0$, and no collection of admissible trades $z_i \in \gamma_i^h$, $i = 1,..., m$, such that $\sum_{i=1}^m z_{ih} = 0$ and $z_i \succsim_i z_i^*$ for all i, with strict preference for some i.

Note that the consumers, when they recontract by exchanging commodity h among themselves, ignore the quantitative constraints associated with that commodity, but plan to modify their transactions in the other commodities $k \neq h$, subject to the constraints perceived for these commodities.

If we go back to the example described in Fig. 1, we see that the set of efficient allocations (in our restricted sense) coincide to the closed segment $D_i D_j$. Indeed, for any point between A and D_i, for instance, it is possible to improve the situation of both consumers by moving along the line AB towards D_i. A similar statement is true for any point between D_j and B. But this is no longer possible if we start from points in the segment $D_i D_j$, for if we wanted to improve the situation of the traders, we would have then to leave the set of admissible allocations which is described by the segment AB.

We saw in Section 2 that the set of admissible allocations which satisfy the Hahn–Negishi condition was represented too by the closed segment $D_i D_j$. The following proposition states that this is a general result.

PROPOSITION 1. *A disequilibrium allocation is efficient market by market if and only if it satisfies the Hahn–Negishi condition.*

4. RECONTRACTING

We showed in the previous section that the Hahn–Negishi condition (H) characterized disequilibrium allocations that were efficient market by market. We now investigate the connection between K-allocations, and the set of disequilibrium allocations that cannot be improved upon, or "blocked," by coalitions. Our goal is to find a notion of blocking such that these two sets tend to coincide when the number of agents is large, and when each of them is negligible compared to the size of the economy.

By analogy with the traditional study of the core, and in view of the restrictions that we imposed on the recontracting process in the previous section, one might be tempted to say that a disequilibrium allocation $(z_i^*, \underline{z}_i, \bar{z}_i)$ is stable if there is no coalition S of consumers, no commodity $h \neq 0$, and no collection of admissible net trades $z_i \in \gamma_i^h$, $i \in S$ such that (i) $\sum_{i \in S} z_{ih} = 0$, and (ii) $z_i \succsim_i z_i^*$ for all i in S, with strict preference for some member of S. One would then study the relationships between the set of stable disequilibrium allocations, and the set of K-allocations. The following example shows however that, with such a definition, a K-allocation would not in general be stable. Indeed, in many cases, there would be no stable disequilibrium allocation.

Consider an economy with two commodities $(l = 1)$, three consumers. Assume that in the absence of any perceived quantitative signal, consumer 1 is willing to supply, say, 20 units of commodity 1, while each other consumer wishes to demand 30 units of commodity 1. There is an excess demand of commodity 1. A K-allocation is thus described by an allocation where consumer 1 delivers 20 units of commodity 1 to the other agents, while consumers 2 and 3 receive, respectively, z_2 and z_3 units of commodity 1, where $(z_2, z_3) \geqslant 0$ and $z_2 + z_3 = 20$. There are many such allocations, but no one of them is stable if we adopt the definition presented so far. For if, say, $z_2 < 20$, then consumer 1 and 2 can redistribute their endowments among themselves so as to make consumer 2 better off without making consumer 1 worse off. The origin of this phenomenon is the fact that we have allowed so far to much competition among the traders who are actually rationed at a K-allocation (here consumers 2 and 3). The phenomenon can be avoided by requiring that a coalition, when recontracting, must improve the position of *every* member of the coalition. We would not need, however, this additional requirement for the universal coalition (the set of all consumers) since the phenomenon cannot occur in such a case. One thus might be tempted to say that a disequilibrium allocation $(z_i^*, \underline{z}_i, \bar{z}_i)$ is stable if it is efficient market by market, and if there is no coalition S, no commodity $h \neq 0$, and no collection of admissible trades $z_i \in \gamma_i^h$, $i \in S$, such that $\sum_{i \in S} z_{ih} = 0$ and $z_i \succ_i z_i^*$ for all members of S. We see later on that with such a definition, a K-allocation is always stable. But we also prove that the set of stable allocations can then be much larger than the set of K-allocations even in large economies (see Section 5). At this stage of the argument we restrict ourselves to showing these points by looking at an example.

Let us go back to the example described in Fig. 1, and assume for the sake of simplicity that there is a continuum of agents of types i and j. We already saw in Section 3 that the allocations represented by points of AB outside the segment D_iD_j were not efficient. Consider now an allocation described by a point P of the segment D_iD_j which differs from D_i and D_j. Let $\tilde{z}_{i1} < 0$ and $\tilde{z}_{j1} > 0$ be the Walrasian supply and demand of the consumers of types i and j, respectively. There exist $\alpha_i > 0$, $\alpha_j > 0$ with $\alpha_i + \alpha_j = 1$ such that $\alpha_i\tilde{z}_{i1} + \alpha_j\tilde{z}_{j1} = 0$. If we consider a coalition S composed of a proportion α_i of consumers of type i and a proportion α_j of consumers of type j, it is possible for every member of S to achieve his most preferred trade and therefore to improve his position compared to the allocation represented by P. On the other hand, if we consider the K-allocation represented by D_i, then no coalition can improve the position of all its members for such a coalition should be exclusively composed of consumers of type j. A similar reasoning shows that the allocation described by D_j would be stable with the definition presented so far, as long as the trade wD_j does not make the traders of type j worse off compared to their initial endowment. Therefore, with the definition presented so far, the set of stable allocations is described by the points D_i and D_j in the case of Figure 1a, and reduces to the K-allocation D_i in Figure 1b.

If we wish to eliminate the allocations like D_j where, on some market h, all the buyers do realize their plans although there is an excess demand, we clearly have to allow more coalitions to recontract out than were permitted in the last definition. In doing so, we have to present a concept which captures the idea that, when there is an excess demand on some market, the sellers are somewhat more powerful than the buyers. It turns out that it is possible to achieve this goal by borrowing some features of the definition of a bargaining set.

Consider a disequilibrium allocation. Let A be the set of agents and let S be a coalition of consumers who wish to recontract out on some market h. The coalition S may need the help of some disjoint subset of traders T in order to achieve its goal. That is, the coalition S wishes to propose a collection of net trades z_i which belong to γ_i^h for all i in $S \cup T$, such that $\sum_{i \in S \cup T} z_{ih} = 0$, $z_i >_i z_i^*$ for all i in S and $z_i \sim_i z_i^*$ for all i in T. We saw at the beginning of this section that a K-allocation is not in general stable if we allow such coalitions to always block. It seems however natural to assume that this coalition will indeed propose the new allocation (z_i) and block if no member of T is likely to face an equivalent, or better proposal made by the complementary coalition $U = A\backslash(S \cup T)$. This will be the case if U is empty, which means that an allocation which is not efficient market by market is blocked, of if T is empty, which corresponds to the second definition of blocking that we considered. In all other cases, the allocation will be blocked by S if for every $V = U \cup T'$, where T' is an arbitrary nonempty subset of T, there is no collection of trades z_i' which belong to γ_i^h for all i in V such that $\sum_{i \in V} z_{ih}' = 0$ and $z_i' \gtrsim_i z_i^*$ for all members of V.

If we go back to the example described in Fig. 1, we find that this concept of blocking seems to succeed in capturing the asymmetry between sellers and buyers when there is an excess demand. Let us assume again for simplicity that there is a continuum of players of each type i and j. At the allocation represented by D_j, all sellers of commodity 1 are compelled to sell more than they intended. But they can all achieve their most preferred trade wD_i by exchanging with only a part of the set of the buyers, say T. The buyers who are left out cannot make an equivalent proposal to the members of T. The allocation represented by D_j is blocked. On the other hand, at the K-allocation described by D_i, the buyers are forced to buy less than they intended. It is true that a part S of the buyers can achieve the planned trade wD_j by exchanging with all the sellers. But in that case, the buyers who are left out can make an equivalent proposal to part of the sellers.

DEFINITION 3. The coalition S blocks the disequilibrium allocation $(z_i^*, \underline{z}_i, \bar{z}_i)$ if, for some $h \neq 0$,

(α) there exists a (possibly empty) set of traders T, disjoint from S, and a collection of net trades $z_i \in \gamma_i^h, i \in S \cup T$, such that $\sum_{i \in S \cup T} z_{ih} = 0$, $z_i \succ_i z_i^*$ for all i in S, and $z_i \sim_i z_i^*$ for all i in T;

(β) whenever $U = A \backslash (S \cup T)$ is nonempty, for every $V = U \cup T'$, where T' is some nonempty subset of T, there is no collection of net trades $z_i' \in \gamma_i^h, i \in V$, such that $\sum_{i \in V} z_{ih}' = 0$ and $z_i' \gtrsim_i z_i^*$ for all members of V.

A disequilibrium allocation is stable if there is no blocking coalition.

We wish to show now that with this definition the set of stable allocations and the set of K-allocation tend to coincide when the number of agents is large and when each of them is negligible compared to the market. To prove this claim, we use the procedure of replicating the economy [12]. The economy $\mathfrak{E}^r$ is composed of mr consumers indicated by $a = (i, q)$, with $i = 1,..., m$ and $q = 1,..., r$. Two consumers corresponding to the same index i have the same preferences $\gtrsim_i$ and the same endowments w_i. We say then that they belong to the same type i. The rth replica of a disequilibrium allocation $(z_i^*, \underline{z}_i, \bar{z}_i)$ of the original economy is clearly a disequilibrium allocation of the replica economy $\mathfrak{E}^r$. The same is true for replicas of K-allocations. These replicated allocations are denoted by the same symbol $(z_i^*, \underline{z}_i, \bar{z}_i)$. Then,

THEOREM 1. *A disequilibrium allocation which is stable for all r is a K-allocation.*

Is it true that a K-allocation is stable for every replicated economy $\mathfrak{E}^r$, or at least when r is large enough? The following example shows that this conjecture is false. Consider an exchange economy with two goods ($l = 1$) and three types of consumers. Assume that, at the ruling prices, consumers of type 1 wish to sell 20 units of commodity 1, while consumers of types 2 and 3 would like to buy 10 and 15 units of that commodity, respectively. At any K-allocation, consumer 1 actually delivers 20 units of commodity 1 to the others, while consumers 2 and 3 receive z_2^* and z_3^* units of that commodity, with $z_2^* + z_3^* = 20$, $5 \leqslant z_2^* \leqslant 10$ and $10 \leqslant z_3^* \leqslant 15$. Take any such allocation in the replicated economy $\mathfrak{E}^r$, where r is "large," and assume that $5 < z_2^* < 10$, $10 < z_3^* < 15$. We claim that this allocation can be blocked. Indeed, consider the coalition S in $\mathfrak{E}^r$ composed of all buyers of type 3, and of all buyers of type 2 except one, and let T be the set of all sellers. By exchanging with the set T, all members of S can get what they bought at the K-allocation, plus a bonus equal to $z_2^*/(2r - 1)$, which is small enough to make all of them better off when r is large. To prevent the formation of the coalition, the buyer of type 2 who was left out must propose to a member of T to buy 20 units of commodity 1. If such a purchase makes him worse off compared to what he got at the K-allocation, (β) of Definition 3 is satisfied, and S blocks. The phenomenon will occur for any large but finite r.

The example suggests, however, that the phenomenon cannot occur if we have a *continuum* of consumers of each type. For in that case, any coalition S of the type that we described would have to exclude a *positive proportion* of consumers of type 2. These consumers can always make a counterproposal to a small enough proportion of sellers. Therefore, we may conjecture from the example that, if we reason in an abstract economy with a continuum of consumers, a K-allocation is stable. We see that this conjecture is true (see the remark below at the end of Section 5). Such a result, however, would not be very comforting if we were unable to prove some stability property of a K-allocation in finite economies. The example and the remark about economies with a continuum of consumers suggest that we might succeed if we postulate that, in a replicated economy $\mathfrak{E}^r$, a blocking coalition S must contain at most δr consumers of each type, where $\delta < 1$. This is the motivation for the following definition.

DEFINITION 4. Given $0 < \delta \leqslant 1$, a disequilibrium allocation is δ-stable in the replicated economy $\mathfrak{E}^r$ if there does not exist a blocking coalition S which contains at most δr consumers of each type.

Then,

THEOREM 2. *Given $0 < \delta < 1$, and a K-allocation, there exists $\bar{r}$ such that it is δ-stable for all $r \geqslant \bar{r}$.*

As a matter of fact, Theorem 1 is still valid when one replaces the word "stable" by "δ-stable." Therefore we have the following characterization of *K*-allocations in finite economies:

COROLLARY. *Given* $0 < \delta < 1$, *a disequilibrium allocation is a K-allocation if and only if there exists $\bar{r}$ such that it is δ-stable for all $r \geq \bar{r}$.*

Remark. Definition 3 can be restated in the following equivalent way. *S* is said to block a disequilibrium allocation if for some $h \neq 0$, (α') there exists a possibly empty set of traders *T* disjoint from *S* and a collection of net trades z_i in $\gamma_i{}^h$ such that $\sum_{i \in S \cup T} z_{ih} = 0$, $z_i \succ_i z_i^*$ in *S* and $z_i \succsim_i z_i^*$ in *T*, and (β') whenever $U = A \backslash (S \cup T)$ is nonempty for every $V = U \cup T'$, where T' is a nonempty subset of *T*, there is no collection of z_i' in $\gamma_i{}^h$ such that $\sum_{i \in V} z_{ih}' = 0$, $z_i' \succsim_i z_i^*$ in *U* and $z_i' \succsim_i z_i$ in *T'*. The reader will immediately verify that a disequilibrium allocation is blocked in the sense of this definition if and only if it is blocked in the sense of Definition 3.

Either definition can be reintrepreted by using the language of the definition of a Bargaining Set [3]. Whenever there exist *S* and *T* such that (α) or (α') is satisfied, we can say that $S \cup T$ has an objection against the complementary coalition *U*. Then (β) or (β') can be interpreted as saying that *U* has no justified counterobjection. Our concept, however, departs from the usual definition of a bargaining set in one very important respect: *The complementary coalition U is not allowed to make a counterobjection to any member of S.* The equivalent of the definition of the bargaining set in our context would be obtained by replacing in (β'), "*T'* is a subset of *T*" by "*T'* is a subset of $S \cup T$". This obviously would give more power to the complementary coalition *U* to make a counterobjection, and one would expect that the set of stable allocations would then be much larger than the set of *K*-allocations, even in large economies. As a matter of fact, in the example described in Fig. 1a, when there is a continuum of traders of each type, it can be shown that, with this new definition, the set of stable allocation is described by the closed segment $D_1 X$, where *X* is the point of $D_i D_j$ satisfying $1/(wX) = \text{Max}(1/(wD_j), 1/(wD_i) - 1/(wD_j))$. The concept of a bargaining set was therefore not suited to our purpose.

5. PROOFS

PROPOSITION 1. *A disequilibrium allocation* $(z_i^*, z_i, \bar{z}_i)$ *is efficient market by market if and only if it satisfies, for all $h \neq 0$:*

$$(z_{ih} - z_{ih}^*)(z_{jh} - z_{jh}^*) > 0 \quad \text{whenever } z_i \in \gamma_i{}^h, z_j \in \gamma_j{}^h,$$

$$\text{and } z_i \succ_i z_i^*, z_j \succ_j z_j^*. \tag{H}$$

Proof. Note that if $z_i \in \gamma_i{}^h$, $z_i \succ_i z_i^*$, then $z_{ih} \neq z_{ih}^*$, otherwise, z_i^* would not maximize the preferences $\succsim_i$ on γ_i.

Let us first show that if there exist $z_i \in \gamma_i{}^h$, $z_j \in \gamma_j{}^h$ such that $z_i \succ_i z_i^*$, $z_j \succ_j z_j^*$ and $(z_{ih} - z_{ih}^*)(z_{jh} - z_{jh}^*) < 0$, for some i, j, h, then $(z_i^*, \underline{z}_i, \bar{z}_i)$ cannot be efficient market by market. Indeed, there exist λ_i and λ_j in $(0, 1)$ such that $\lambda_i(z_{ih} - z_{ih}^*) + \lambda_j(z_{jh} - z_{jh}^*) = 0$. Let $z_a' = z_a^*$ for all $a \neq i, j$, $z_i' = \lambda_i z_i + (1 - \lambda_i) z_i^*$ and $z_j' = \lambda_j z_j + (1 - \lambda_j) z_j^*$. We have $z_a' \in \gamma_a{}^h$ for all a, $\sum_{a=1}^m z_{ah}' = 0$, $z_i' \succ z_i^*$ and $z_j' \succ_j z_j^*$ because the preferences are convex. Thus $(z_i, \underline{z}_i, \bar{z}_i)$ cannot be efficient market by market.

Conversely, let us prove that if a disequilibrium allocation is not efficient market by market, then $(z_{ih} - z_{ih}^*)(z_{jh} - z_{jh}^*) < 0$ for some h and some $z_i \in \gamma_i{}^h$, $z_j \in \gamma_j{}^h$ with $z_i \succ_i z_i^*$ and $z_j \succ_j z_j^*$. Now, there exist h and $z_a \in \gamma_a{}^h$ for all a such that $\sum_{a=1}^m z_{ah} = 0$, $z_a \succsim_a z_a^*$ for all a and $z_i \succ_i z_i^*$ for some i. One has surely $z_{ih} \neq z_{ih}^*$. Thus, since $\sum_{a=1}^m (z_{ah} - z_{ah}^*) = 0$, there exists j such that $(z_{ih} - z_{ih}^*)(z_{jh} - z_{jh}^*) < 0$. Because the preferences are strictly convex, any $z_i' \in (z_j, z_j^*)$ satisfies $z_j' \in \gamma_j{}^h$, $z_j' \succ_j z_j^*$ and $(z_{ih} - z_{ih}^*)(z_{jh}' - z_{jh}^*) < 0$.
$\qquad\qquad\qquad\qquad\qquad\qquad\qquad\qquad\qquad\qquad\qquad$ Q.E.D.

We introduce now a set of disequilibrium allocations which is larger than the set of K-allocations. At a K-allocation, if there is an excess demand on some market h, all the sellers realize their plans, while some buyers are compelled to buy less than they would like. The following definition keeps open the possibility that, in such a case, all buyers realize their plans, while some sellers are compelled to sell more than they wish.

DEFINITION 5. A disequilibrium allocation $(z^*, \underline{z}_i, \bar{z}_i)$ is an R-allocation if, for all $h \neq 0$:

(1) $(z_{ih} - z_{ih}^*)(z_{jh} - z_{jh}^*) > 0$ whenever $z_i \in \gamma_i{}^h$, $z_j \in \gamma_j{}^h$ and $z_i \succ_i z_i^*$, $z_j \succ_j z_j^*$;

(2) either $z_{ih} > 0$ for all i and $z_i \in \gamma_i{}^h$ such that $z_i \succ_i z_i^*$, or $z_{ih} < 0$ for all i and $z_i \in \gamma_i{}^h$ such that $z_i \succ_i z_i^*$.

Condition (1) is the Hahn–Negishi condition. Condition (2) states that only side of the market for commodity h may be constrained. If we look again at the example described in Fig. 1, we see that the set of allocations satisfying (1) and (2) is represented by the points D_i and D_j in Fig. 1a, and reduces to the point D_i in Fig. 1b. In the general case, a K-allocation is always an R-allocation, while the converse is not necessarily true.

We wish also to work temporarily with a weaker concept of stability than was given in Definition 4.

DEFINITION 6. A disequilibrium allocation $(z_i^*, \underline{z}_i, \bar{z}_i)$ is weakly stable if it is efficient market by market and if there is no coalition S, no commodity

h, and no collection of net trades $z_i \in \gamma_i{}^h$, $i \in S$ such that $\sum_{i \in S} z_{ih} = 0$ and $z_i \succ_i z_i^*$ for all members of S.

We indicated in Section 4 that the set of R-allocations and the set of weakly stable allocations tended to coincide in large economies. The following result makes this statement precise.

PROPOSITION 2. *A disequilibrium allocation is an R-allocation if and only if it is weakly stable in all replicated economies.*

Proof. Let us first show that an R-allocation is weakly stable for all r. It suffices to do so for the original economy.

Proposition 1 shows that this R-allocation is efficient market by market. Let us suppose now that there exist a coalition S, a commodity h, and a collection of net trades $z_i \in \gamma_i{}^h$, $i \in S$, such that $\sum_{i \in S} z_{ih} = 0$ and $z_i \succ_i z_i^*$ for every member of S. Condition (2) implies that, say, $z_{ih} > 0$ for all i in S. But this would imply $\sum_{i \in S} z_{ih} > 0$. We get a contradiction, which proves that an R-allocation is weakly stable.

Conversely, consider an allocation which is weakly stable for all r. Proposition 1 tells us that (1) holds. On the other hand, since the disequilibrium allocation cannot be improved upon by one-member coalitions, $z_i \succ_i z_i^*$, $z_i \in \gamma_i{}^h$ implies $z_{ih} \neq 0$. It remains to show that (2) holds. Suppose that it does not. Then, for some h, there exist $z_i \in \gamma_i{}^h$, $z_i \succ_i z_i^*$ and $z_j \in \gamma_j{}^h$, $z_j \succ_j z_j^*$ such that $z_{ih} > 0$ and $z_{jh} < 0$. Hence, there are $\alpha_i > 0$, $\alpha_j > 0$ with $\alpha_i + \alpha_j = 1$ such that $\alpha_i z_{ih} + \alpha_j z_{jh} = 0$. From (1), we know that $(z_{ih} - z_{ih}^*)$ and $(z_{jh} - z_{jh}^*)$ have the same sign. Suppose that they are both negative (the other case is treated in a similar way). Define $n_i{}^r$ as the largest integer less than or equal to $r\alpha_i$ and $n_j{}^r$ as the smallest integer greater than or equal to $r\alpha_j$. Let

$$ z_{ih}^r = \left(\frac{r\alpha_i}{n_i{}^r} \right) z_{ih} \quad \text{and} \quad z_{jh}^r = \left(\frac{r\alpha_j}{n_j{}^r} \right) z_{jh} . $$

For r large enough, one has $z_{ih} \leqslant z_{ih}^r < z_{ih}^*$ and $z_{jh} \leqslant z_{jh}^r < z_{jh}^*$. In addition,

$$ n_i{}^r z_{ih}^r + n_j{}^r z_{jh}^r = r(\alpha_i z_{ih} + \alpha_j z_{jh}) = 0. $$

Fix such an r. Let z_i' (resp. z_j') be the convex combination of z_i (resp. z_j) and of z_i^* (resp. z_j^*) such that $z_{ih}' = z_{ih}^r$ (resp. $z_{jh}' = z_{jh}^r$). We have $z_i' \in \gamma_i{}^h$ and $z_i' \succ_i z_i^*$, and the same thing for j. Therefore, in the rth replica, the coalition composed of $n_i{}^r$ consumers of type i and of $n_j{}^r$ consumers of type j can do better for all its members. This leads to a contradiction. Therefore (2) holds, which completes the proof of the proposition. Q.E.D.

We proceed now to the proofs of Theorems 1 and 2. They are independent of Proposition 2.

THEOREM 1. *A disequilibrium allocation which is stable for all r is a K-allocation.*

Proof. Consider a disequilibrium allocation which is stable for all r. It must be efficient market by market. Consider an arbitrary $h \neq 0$, and pick $\tilde{z}_i$ in γ_i^h such that $\tilde{z}_i >_i z_i^*$ for all types i who are constrained in commodity h. We know that $\tilde{z}_{ih} - z_{ih}^*$ has the same sign for all these types. Suppose that $\tilde{z}_{ih} - z_{ih}^* > 0$ for all types who are constrained (the other case where $\tilde{z}_{ih} - z_{ih}^* < 0$ is treated in a similar fashion). If the disequilibrium allocation fails to satisfy the definition of a K-allocation on market h, there must exist a nonempty set S^* of types of consumers who are constrained with $z_{ih}^* < 0$ for all i in S^*. Since $\sum_{i=1}^{m} z_{ih}^* = 0$, this implies:

$$\sum_{z_{ih}^*>0} z_{ih}^* = - \sum_{z_{ih}^*<0} z_{ih}^* \geqslant - \sum_{i \in S^*} z_{ih}^* > - \sum_{i \in S^*} \tilde{z}_{ih}.$$

Therefore, if r is large enough, one can find an integer $n_r < r$ such that

$$-r \sum_{i \in S^*} z_{ih}^* > n_r \sum_{z_{ih}^*>0} z_{ih}^* > -r \sum_{i \in S^*} \tilde{z}_{ih}. \tag{5.1}$$

Fix such an r and n_r. Let S be the coalition of all members $a = (i, q)$ of the rth replica such that $i \in S^*$. We claim that S can block the disequilibrium allocation. Let T be an arbitrary set of consumers $a = (i, q)$ composed of n_r agents of each type i such that $z_{ih}^* > 0$. For every $a = (i, q)$ in T let $z_a = z_i^*$. For every $a = (i, q)$ in S, let $z_a = \lambda z_i^* + (1 - \lambda) \tilde{z}_i$, where λ is chosen so that $\sum_{a \in S \cup T} z_{ah} = 0$. It is readily checked that $0 < \lambda < 1$, because of (5.1). Thus $z_a \in \gamma_i^h$ for every $a = (i, q)$ in $S \cup T$, $\sum_{a \in S \cup T} z_{ah} = 0$, $z_a >_i z_i^*$ for all $a = (i, q)$ in S and $z_a = z_i^*$ for all $a = (i, q)$ in T.

Let A^r be the set of agents in the rth replica. Then $U = A^r \backslash (S \cup T)$ is certainly nonempty. Consider an arbitrary coalition V which is the union of U and of some nonempty subset T' of T.

Consider an arbitrary collection of net trades z_a', $a \in V$ such that $z_a' \in \gamma_a^h$ and $z_a' \succsim_a z_a^*$ for all a in V (with the convention $z_a^* = z_i^*$ for all $a = (i, q)$ in V). We have

$$\sum_{a \in V} z_{ah}' \geqslant \sum_{a \in V} z_{ah}^* > \sum_{a \in U} z_{ah}^*.$$

But $\sum_{a \in U} z_a^* + \sum_{a \in S \cup T} z_a^* = 0$, and the first part of (5.1) means that $\sum_{a \in S \cup T} z_h^* < 0$. Therefore, $\sum_{a \in V} z_{ah}' > 0$. This means that S blocks, a contradiction to the assumption that the disequilibrium allocation is stable for all r. Therefore, the disequilibrium allocation is a K-allocation. Q.E.D.

Remark that the foregoing proof shows that a disequilibrium allocation which is stable for infinitely many r is a K-allocation. Also, it is obviously possible to choose the blocking coalition S in such a way that it contains at most δr members of each type, where $0 < \delta \leqslant 1$.

THEOREM 2. *Given $0 < \delta < 1$ and a K-allocation, there exists $\bar{r}$ such that it is δ-stable for all $r \geqslant \bar{r}$.*

Proof. Let $0 < \delta < 1$, and consider a K-allocation $(z_i^*, \underline{z}_i, \bar{z}_i)$. For every $h \neq 0$, let S_h^* be the set of types i of consumers who are actually constrained in commodity h. If S_h^* is empty, let $\bar{r}_h = 1$. If S_h^* is not empty, choose for each i in S^* an arbitrary vector ζ_i^h in γ_i^h such that $\zeta_i^h >_i z_i^*$, and let $\hat{z}_{ih}$ be the hth component of ζ_i^h. Define $B_h = |\sum_{i \in S_h^*} (\hat{z}_{ih} - z_{ih}^*)| > 0$. Let A_h be the maximum of $|z_{ih}^*|$ over all i such that $i \notin S_h^*$ whenever there are such i, and 0 otherwise. Then define $\bar{r}_h$ as the smallest integer greater than or equal to $A_h/(B_h(1 - \delta))$. Let $\bar{r}$ be the maximum of all $\bar{r}_h$, $h \neq 0$. We claim that the K-allocation is δ-stable for all $r \geqslant \bar{r}$.

Choose such an r, and let A^r be the set of all consumers in the rth replica. Consider an $h \neq 0$, let S be a nonempty subset of A^r which contains at most δr consumers of each type, and let T be another (possibly empty) subset of A^r which is disjoint from S. Assume that there exist $z_a \in \gamma_i^h$ for every $a = (i, q)$ in $S \cup T$ such that $\sum_{a \in S \cup T} z_{ah} = 0$, $z_a >_i z_i^*$ for all $a = (i, q)$ in S and $z_a \sim_i z_i^*$ for all $a = (i, q)$ in T. Since a K-allocation is efficient market by market, the complementary coalition $U = A^r \backslash (S \cup T)$ is nonempty. We wish to show that U can make an equivalent or better proposal to a nonempty subset T' of T.

Since h is fixed, we write from now on S^* for S_h^*. First it is clear that $i \in S^*$ for every member $a = (i, q)$ of S. For every i in S^*, let s_i be the number of consumers of type i who belong to S. We have $0 \leqslant s_i \leqslant \delta r$. To fix the ideas, assume that $z_{ih}' > z_{ih}^* \geqslant 0$ for all i in S^* and all $z_i' \in \gamma_i^h$ with $z_i' >_i z_i^*$ (the other case where $0 \geqslant z_{ih}^* > z_{ih}^i$ for all such i and z_i' can be treated in a similar way). Let us partition T into $T_1 = \{a = (i, q) \in T \mid i \in S^*\}$ and $T_2 = \{a = (i, q) \in T \mid i \notin S^*\}$. We claim that U can make an equivalent or better proposal to a subset T' of T which is the union of T_1 and of a nonempty subset T_2' of T_2.

Indeed, let us suppose for a moment that we have found a nonempty subset T_2' of T_2 such that, if $T' = T_1 \cup T_2'$ and $V = U \cup T'$,

$$\sum_{a \in V} z_{ah}^* \leqslant 0 \leqslant \sum_{a \in V} z_{ah}^* + \sum_{i \in S^*} (r - s_i)(\hat{z}_{ih} - z_{ih}^*) \qquad (5.2)$$

with the convention $z_a^* = z_i^*$ whenever $a = (i, q)$. Then, there exists λ in $[0, 1]$ such that

$$\sum_{a \in V} z_{ah}^* + \lambda \sum_{i \in S^*} (r - s_i)(\hat{z}_{ih} - z_{ih}^*) = 0. \qquad (5.3)$$

But define z_a' for every a in V as follows. For all $a = (i, q)$ in V, let $z_a' = z_i^*$

whenever $i \notin S^*$, and $z'_a = (1 - \lambda) z_i^* + \lambda \tilde{\zeta}_i^h$ whenever $i \in S^*$. We have $z'_a \succsim_i z_i^*$ for all $a = (i, q)$ in V, and (5.3) is equivalent to $\sum_{a \in V} z'_{ah} = 0$. Therefore S could not block.

To complete the proof, we have to show that there exists a nonempty subset T'_2 of T_2 such that (5.2) holds. To simplify the notations, let $V_1 = U \cup T_1$. First, remark that $z_{ah}^* \geqslant 0$ for all a in S implies

$$\sum_{a \in V_1} z_{ah}^* + \sum_{a \in T_2} z_{ah}^* \leqslant \sum_{a \in A^r} z_{ah}^* = 0.$$

On the other hand, $z_{ah}^* \geqslant 0$ for all a in T_1, $z_{ah} \geqslant z_{ah}^*$ for all a in T and $z_{ah} > z_{ah}^*$ for all a in S imply

$$\sum_{a \in V_1} z_{ah}^* \geqslant - \sum_{a \in SUT} z_{ah}^* > - \sum_{a \in SUT} z_{ah} = 0.$$

We have therefore shown that

$$\sum_{a \in V_1} z_{ah}^* + \sum_{a \in T_2} z_{ah}^* \leqslant 0 < \sum_{a \in V_1} z_{ah}^* \tag{5.4}$$

which proves in particular that $\sum_{a \in T_2} z_{ah}^* < 0$.

The argument is virtually complete now. From (5.4), there must exist a nonempty subset T'_2 of T_2 and an agent $\alpha \in T'_2$ with $z_{ah}^* < 0$ such that, if $V = V_1 \cup T'_2$.

$$\sum_{a \in V} z_{ah}^* \leqslant 0 < \left(\sum_{a \in V} z_{ah}^* \right) - z_{\alpha h}^*.$$

But from the choice of $\bar{r}$, and the fact that $s_i \leqslant \delta r$ for all $i \in S^*$, we have

$$| z_{\alpha h}^* | \leqslant A_h \leqslant r(1 - \delta) B_h \leqslant \sum_{i \in S^*} (r - s_i)(\tilde{z}_{ih} - z_{ih}^*)$$

which yields (5.2), as announced. The proof is complete.   Q.E.D.

Remark. Consider an economy with a continuum of agents, as in [2]. Let the set of consumers A be the unit interval $[0, 1]$. The class $\mathfrak{a}$ of possible coalitions is represented by the Borel subsets of A. If μ is the Lebesgue measure on A, then for every $S \in \mathfrak{a}$, $\mu(S)$ is the proportion of consumers who belong to S. Assume that every agent a in A has preferences $\succsim_a$ defined on a set of net trades Z_a which satisfy assumptions (1) and (2) of Section 1. In addition, assume that the set $\{(a, x, y) \mid x \succsim_a y\}$ is measurable.

All definitions can be easily reworded in this context. Then it is straight-forward to translate the proofs of the propositions to get the following fact.

A disequilibrium allocation is an R-allocation if and only if it is weakly stable.

The nice thing is the fact that Theorems 1 and 2 become:

A disequilibrium allocation is K-allocation if and only if it is stable.

The "if" part is easy to prove by a simple rewording of the proof of Theorem 1. The proof of the fact that a K-allocation is stable goes along the same lines as that of Theorem 2, and is indeed much simpler. We sketch the argument. Suppose that there exist $h \neq 0$, a coalition S with $\mu(S) > 0$, another coalition T disjoint from S, and a measurable function $z(\cdot)$ such that $z(a) \in \gamma^h(a)$ a.e. in $S \cup T$, $\int_{S \cup T} z_h(a) = 0$, $z(a) \succ_a z^*(a)$ a.e. in S, and $z(c) \sim_a z^*(a)$ a.e. in T. One can focus the attention on the case where $z_h(a) > z_h^*(a) \geqslant 0$ a.e. in S. If $T_2 = \{a \in T \mid z_h^*(a) < 0\}$ and $U = A \backslash (S \cup T)$, one can show by the same reasoning used in the proof of Theorem 2 to prove (5.4) that

$$0 < \int_U z_h^*(a) \leqslant - \int_{T_2} z_h^*(a).$$

Now, since μ is atomless, there exists a Borel subset T' of T_2 such that

$$0 < \int_U z_h^*(a) = - \int_{T'} z_h^*(a).$$

Obviously $\mu(T') > 0$. It suffices to take $V = U \cup T'$ and $z'(a) = z^*(a)$ for all a in V to show that S cannot block.

ACKNOWLEDGMENTS

We wish to thank Jean-Pascal Benassy and Roger Guesnerie of CEPREMAP and Werner Hildenbrand of the University of Bonn for very stimulating conversations. An earlier version of this paper was presented at the Summer Seminar of the IMSSS at Stanford, in 1975. We are grateful to all participants, and especially to Ken Arrow, Frank Hahn, Walter Heller, Roy Radner, and Ross Starr for their comments and suggestions.

REFERENCES

1. K. J. ARROW, Towards a theory of price adjustment, *in* "The Allocation of Economic Resources" (A. Abramovitz, Ed.), Stanford Univ. Press, Stanford, Calif., 1959.
2. R. J. AUMANN, Markets with a continuum of traders, *Econometrica* 32 (1964), 39–50.
3. R. J. AUMANN AND M. MASCHLER, The bargaining set for cooperative games, *in* "Advances in Game Theory," (M. Dresher, L. S. Shapley, A. W. Tucker, Eds.), Annals of Mathematical Studies, Vol. 52, Princeton Univ. Press, Princeton, N. J., 1964.
4. R. J. BARRO AND H. I. GROSSMAN, A general disequilibrium model of income and employment, *Amer. Econ. Rev.* 61 (1971), 82–93.
5. R. J. BARRO AND H. I. GROSSMAN, Suppressed inflation and the supply multiplier, *Rev. Econ. Stud.* 41 (1974), 87–104.
6. R. J. BARRO AND H. I. GROSSMAN, "Money, Employment and Inflation," Cambridge Univ. Press, London, 1976.

7. J. P. BENASSY, Disequilibrium theory, unpublished Ph.D. thesis, CRMS Working Paper No. 185, University of California at Berkeley, 1973.
8. J. P. BENASSY, Neokeynesian disequilibrium theory in a monetary economy, *Rev. Econ. Stud.* **42** (1975), 503–523.
9. J. P. BENASSY, The disequilibrium approach to monopolistic price setting and general monopolistic equilibrium, *Rev. Econ. Stud.* **43** (1976), 69–81.
10. P. CHAMPSAUR, "Rationing and Lindhal Equilibria," ENSAE, Paris, 1977.
11. R. W. CLOWER, The Keynesian counterrevolution: A theoretical appraisal, *in* "The Theory of Interest Rates" (F. H. Hahn and F. P. Brechling, Eds.), Macmillan, New York, 1965.
12. G. DEBREU AND H. SCARF, A limit theorem on the core of an economy, *Int. Econ. Rev.* **4** (1963), 235–246.
13. J. DREZE, Existence of an exchange equilibrium under price rigidities, *Int. Econ. Rev.* **16** (1975), 301–320.
14. J. M. GRANDMONT AND G. LAROQUE, On Keynesian temporary equilibria, *Rev. Econ. Stud.* **43** (1976), 53–67.
15. H. I. GROSSMAN, Money, interest and prices in market disequilibrium, *J. Polit. Econ.* **79** (1971), 943–961.
16. H. I. GROSSMAN, A choice-theoretic model of an income investment accelerator, *Amer. Econ. Rev.* **62** (1972), 630–641.
17. F. H. HAHN, On non Walrasian equilibria, *Rev. Econ. Stud.* **45** (1978), 1–17.
18. F. H. HAHN AND T. NEGISHI, A theorem on non tatonnement stability, *Econometrica* **30** (1962), 463–469.
19. J. HICKS, "Value and Capital," Oxford Univ. Press, London, 1939.
20. A. LEIJONHUFVUD, "On Keynesian Economics and the Economics of Keynes," Oxford Univ. Press, London, 1968.
21. E. MALINVAUD, "The Theory of Unemployment Reconsidered," Blackwell, Oxford, 1977.
22. E. MALINVAUD AND Y. YOUNÈS, "Une Nouvelle Formulation Générale pour l'Étude des Fondements Microéconomiques de la Macroéconomie," INSEE and CEPREMAP, Paris, 1974.
23. E. MALINVAUD AND Y. YOUNÈS, A new formulation for the microeconomic foundations of macroeconomics, Paper presented at an IEA Conference on the Microeconomic Foundations of Macroeconomics, S'Agaro, Spain, July 1975.
24. T. NEGISHI, Existence of an Underemployment Equilibrium *in* "Equilibrium and Disequilibrium in Economic Theory" (G. Schwödiauer, Ed.), proceedings of a conference held in Vienna, Reidel, Boston, 1978.
25. D. PATINKIN, "Money, Interest and Prices," 2nd ed., Harper & Row, New York, 1965.
26. R PORTES, Macroeconomic equilibrium and disequilibrium in centrally planned economies, D. P. No. 45, Birbeck College, London, 1976.
27. R. M. SOLOW AND J. E. STIGLITZ, Output, employment and wages in the short run, *Quart. J. Econ.* (1968).
28. Y. YOUNÈS, "Sur une Notion d'Équilibre Utilisable dans le Cas où les Agents Économiques ne sont pas Assurés de la Compatibilité de leurs Plans," CEPREMAP, Paris, 1970.
29. Y. YOUNÈS, "Sur les Notions d'Équilibre et de Déséquilibre Utilisées dans les Modèles Décrivant l'Évolution d'une Économie Capitaliste," CEPREMAP, Paris, 1970.
30. Y. YOUNÈS, On the role of money in the process of exchange and the existence of a non Walrasian equilibrium, *Rev. Econ. Stud.* **42** (1975), 489–501.

On Non-Walrasian Equilibria

FRANK HAHN

Cambridge University

1. INTRODUCTION

I shall call an economy non-Walrasian whenever the trading possibilities of agents cannot be described as the set of trades which at given prices make the value of purchases no greater than the value of sales.

There are many reasons for being interested in non-Walrasian economies. My own immediate reason comes from an attempt to study more precisely the meaning one might give to the old proposition that the division of labour depends on the extent of the market. In the usual Walrasian context it is not easy to define " the extent of the market ". But there are of course many other reasons amongst which the desirability of studying " Keynesian " propositions in the context of General Equilibrium analysis ranks high. If non-Walrasian models are rejected on whatever grounds, then so it would seem must properly formulated Keynesian models. This is not because of difficulties of reconciling unemployment with equilibrium, it is not at all obvious that Keynes' theory requires it, but rather because as long as market opportunities are described only in the Walrasian way no distinction can be drawn between demand and effective demand (Clower [4] and Leijonhufvud [9]). But this distinction seems so central to the Keynesian theory that it seems impossible to proceed without it. There are also sound reasons for arguing that one must abandon the Walrasian hypothesis that agents treat prices parametrically if one is to make sense of Keynesian doctrines.

To all of this one must add that the Walrasian procedure runs into both logical and empirical difficulties. The former arise when one wishes to study an economy out of equilibrium. Then not only does the Walrasian theory provide no logical way in which actual agents could change prices (Arrow [1]) but the theory also runs into trouble should there be constant returns to scale (Arrow and Hahn [2]). The empirical difficulties are not only that for many actual firms a perfect competition postulate is plainly wrong and incapable of yielding explanations of such phenomena as advertising but also that it is wrong for almost all agents. Thus it is not possible to explain the wide requirement of collateral when borrowing or the wide support for unemployment insurance.

The central difficulty in studying non-Walrasian economies, which to some extent it shares with Walrasian sequence economies, is the distinction between the trading possibilities as perceived by an agent and the " true " trading possibilities. This difficulty is recognized for instance when we distinguish between expectations and rational expectations but it is rather more severe in the non-Walrasian case. For instance in a Walrasian sequence economy with single valued price expectations we say that the expectations are rational when they are confirmed by the sequence of equilibrium prices. Compare this with the non-Walrasian case studied by Negishi [11]. The trading possibilities as perceived by some agents included a conjectural demand curve for the goods sold by them. In an equilibrium of the economy they sell what at the going price and the conjectured demand curve is most profitable. There will be no further experience suggesting that their conjectures should be revised. But the demand curve which is conjectured may not be the " true " demand curve, if indeed the latter can be defined. Here the circumstance that the market signals that the agent has not made a mistake does not ensure that he is in fact not mistaken. The difficulty then is that these Negishi-like equilibria will be " boot-strap "

A—45/1

Reprinted from *The Review of Economic Studies* **45** (1978), 1–8.

equilibria, that is dependent on unexplained conjectures of agents, and that there will be many of them depending on what the conjectures of agents actually are. It is the ad-hoc element in the theory which of course also occurs in the study of short-period Walrasian equilibria, which in the usual model we try to avoid by studying rational expectations. In the non-Walrasian context it is not always clear what rational expectations are and even when it is we may find that we finish with an implausibly exacting concept of equilibrium. To this must be added the rather obvious point that the existence of rational non-Walrasian equilibria is by no means easy to establish.

Although there is much recent literature on this topic it cannot be claimed that we are very close to the kind of understanding which we have gained of the Walrasian economy. What follows is essentially an attempt to gain some insight into the main difficulties in the hope that this will be of use in the eventual construction of more general models.

I begin Section 2 with the extreme case studied by Drèze [6] and by Grandmont and Laroque [7]. Here it is supposed that prices are fixed and that agents are rationed. One considers certain quantity-constrained equilibria which one can think of as resulting from non-tâtonnement. The equilibria one wants to show to exist have two features: only one side of the market is restrained by rationing (Hahn and Negishi [8]), and some trade occurs. I call such equilibria orderly and non-trivial. The existence of an orderly and non-trivial equilibrium for this case has already been provided by Drèze and others. So why do it again? Here are the answers:

(i) The proof is different and very natural since it uses implicit prices for rations. It is also very simple.

(ii) Orderly and non-trivial equilibria may be Pareto-inefficient relative to the requirement that each agent satisfies his budget constraint (Arrow and Hahn [2], Younès [15]). The method of proof allows one to understand this better. In particular it shows that quantity constraints give rise to an essential externality. This understanding is underlined by showing that there would exist rationing schemes (by means of coupons) at fixed money prices, in which the externality would be overcome.

In Section 3 I relax the fixed price assumption. I replace it by allowing agents to have conjectures of how a given perceived ration might be relaxed by their willingness to offer a different price. The idea here is closely related to the pioneering work of Negishi [11], although it is different. *In particular I do not wish to make imperfect competition intrinsic to the model. The conjectures I consider always permit a Walrasian equilibrium. What I show is that there are also non-Walrasian equilibria.* This seems to me of some interest since it shows that an economy can settle into a quantity-constrained equilibrium even when prices are not fixed *a priori* and in particular a Walrasian equilibrium is available. This section is related to Benassy [3] and to Malinvaud and Younès [10].

But neither of these authors showed that the Walrasian equilibrium was also a possible equilibrium for their economy. This is what makes Section 3 of interest. For once agents change prices (and not the auctioneer), an economy, which with given conjectures has a competitive equilibrium, may " get stuck " in a non-Walrasian one. If one starts with monopolistic competition this is not the case. There are some objections to this result which depends on the class of conjectures I have chosen. The objections will be discussed in their proper place (see Section 3).

However, it may be thought that a fundamental objection is the arbitrariness of conjectures, an objection which I have already touched upon. As a first reply I would suggest that it is not obvious that one is justified in treating preferences as given and quite unjustified in treating conjectures as given. Certainly almost any feasible allocation can be a Walrasian equilibrium for some preferences and certainly we do not believe that we emerge from the womb with formed preferences or that the latter are independent of economic experiences. We treat preferences as exogenous for the very good reason that we have no good and manageable theory of an economy in which they are treated as endogenous. In any case I would not be alarmed if conjectures, at least in the short period, are taken as formed by history. One would have to look at what conjectures they are for applications; but the theory would still be useful.

But one must keep on trying. So in Section 4 I examine a notion of rational conjectures (evidently I am here inspired by rational expectations). I show that for a class of conjectures no rational conjectural equilibrium exists.

An editor of this journal believes that there may be a relationship between the negative result of Section 4 and the negative results of the literature on incentive compatibility. He is almost certainly right. On the other hand his further suggestion that one could sail into " positive " waters by considering a large economy is less helpful. If agents are of measure zero, then one cannot make them responsible for price adjustments.

2. FIXED PRICES

In this section I consider an economy in which agents receive both price and quantity signals which they treat parametrically. One asks: do there exist quantity signals, given a fixed price signal, which are compatible with an equilibrium? To give this question some interest we shall look for a *non-trivial* and *orderly* equilibrium. By non-trivial we mean that some trade is permitted and occurs. By orderly we mean that in any one market in equilibrium quantity signals either restrain demand or supply but not both.

The notation is as follows. There is a finite number, A, of agents indexed by a, and a finite number, l, of goods, indexed by i. The agent's consumption set is R_+^l and $x_a \in R_+^l$ is a consumption, $e_a \in R_{++}^l$ an endowment. One defines $t_a \in R^l$ by

$$t_a = x_a - e_a$$

and calls it a trade of a. The agent receives signals $\sigma_a \in R_+^{3l}$ where

$$\sigma_a = (p, b_a, s_a)$$

and $p \gg 0$ is a price vector and b_a, s_a are quantity signals restricting the purchases and sales of a. The precise interpretation is given by a's trading correspondence: $T_a : R_+^{3l} \to R^l$, where

$$T_a(\sigma_a) = \{t_a \mid pt_a \leqq 0, \ b_a \geqq t_a, \ s_a \geqq -t_a\}.$$

To keep matters simple I shall use

Assumption 2.1. For all a, preferences on R_+^l are representable by a Cobb-Douglas utility function.

This could easily be replaced by more usual postulates on the convexity and continuity of preferences. Its merit here is that it allows one to simplify as follows:

(i) For b_{ai} finite, b_{ai} will be a " biting " constraint as $p_i \to 0$.

(ii) When the agent has maximized utility on

$$F_a(p, b_a, s_a) = T_a(p, b_a, s_a) \cap \{t_a \mid e_a + t_a \in R_+^l\}$$

a unique choice $t_a(\sigma_a)$ results.

(iii) There will be a unique $p^* \gg 0$ in the simplex $\Delta \subset R_+^l$ for which there exist (b_a^*, s_a^*), each a, such that each a gives the quantity constraints zero shadow prices and $\Sigma t_a(p^*, t_a^*, s_a^*) = 0$. (So p^* is a unique Walrasian equilibrium.)

Now let $t(\sigma) = \Sigma t_a(\sigma_a)$, where $\sigma = (p, b_1, \dots, b_a, s_1, \dots, s_a)$. Then

Definition 2.1. σ^0 is a *non-Walrasian equilibrium* if (i) $p^0 \neq p^*$ and (ii) $t(\sigma^0) = 0$.

Let α_{ai} be the shadow price of the constraint $b_{ai} \geq t_{ai}$ and β_{ai} the shadow price of the constraint $s_{ai} \geq -t_a$. Then

Definition 2.2. σ^0 is a *non-trivial* and *orderly* non-Walrasian equilibrium if Definition 2.1 (i)-(ii) are satisfied and

(i) $t_a(\sigma^0) \neq 0$ some a (i.e. equilibrium is non-trivial).

(ii) For all i: either $\alpha_{ai} = 0$, all a, or $\beta_{ai} = 0$, all a (i.e. equilibrium is orderly).

A non-trivial equilibrium may not exist (Theorem XIII.1, Arrow and Hahn [2]) even when the trivial equilibrium is Pareto-inefficient relatively to $pt_a = 0$, all a. So one will need some assumption.

I shall use the following:

Definition 2.3. Let $A(i)$ be the set of agents who are not quantity constrained in market i, when $p \gg 0$. The economy satisfies *strong tradeability* if there exists $\varepsilon > 0$ such that

$$\Sigma_{A(i)}|t_{ai}| \geq \varepsilon \qquad \text{all } i.$$

This assumption is somewhat strong. I discuss in the Appendix the consequence of using a weaker version. One now has

Theorem 2.1. *Let* $p \neq p^*$, $p \gg 0$ *and let the strong tradeability condition be satisfied. Then there exists* σ^0 *with* $p^0 = p$ *which is a non-trivial orderly non-Walrasian equilibrium.*

To establish this I consider an interesting fictional economy. In that economy a central agency sells rights to buy and to sell for a special currency. Let $v_i \geq 0$, $w_i \geq 0$, respectively denote the prices of the right to buy and to sell one unit of good i denominated in the special currency. Each is allocated λm_a units of the currency $0 \leq \lambda \leq 1$, $m_a > 0$. The trading set of agent a is, when $v = (v_1, ..., v_l)$, $w = (w_1, ..., w_l)$:

$$T_a^0(p, v, w, \lambda) = \{t_a \mid pt_a \leq 0, \ b_a \geq t_a, \ s_a \geq -t_a \ \text{ with } \ vb_a + ws_a \leq \lambda m_a\}.$$

The set of feasible choices, in view of Assumption 2.1, can be written

$$F_a^0(p, v, w, \lambda) = T_a^0(p, v, w, \lambda) \cap \{t_a + e_a \gg 0\}.$$

The strategy is to show that the fictional economy has an equilibrium and thence that this equilibrium corresponds to an orderly non-trivial Drèze equilibrium.

To this end let $G \subset R_+^l$ where

$$G = \{g \mid \Sigma |g_i| \leq 1, g_1 \equiv 0\}$$

and define the map from G to R_+^{l+1} by

$$v_i(g) = \max(0, g_i), \ w_i(g) = \max(0, -g_i), \ \lambda(g) = \max(\varepsilon^1, 1 - \Sigma |g_i|)$$

where $\varepsilon^1 = \varepsilon/m$, ε given from strong tradeability and $m = \Sigma m_a$.

The feasible set is now written as $F_a^0(p, g)$. It is continuous on G. Let $t_a(p, g)$ be the " best " trade at (g). It is unique and continuous.

Now some budget arithmetic. For $t_a \in F_a^0$ one has

$$\lambda m_a \geq v(g)b_a + w(g)s_a \geq v(g)t_a^+ - w(g)t_a^- = g \cdot t_a + w(g)t_a^+ - v(g)t_a^-. \qquad ...(2.1)$$

Here $t_a^+ = \{\max(0, t_{ai})\}$, $t_a^- = \{\min(0, t_{ai})\}$, two l-vectors. Suppose $g_i < 0$. Then $w_i = -g_i$ and $-g_i t_{ai}^+$ is the amount of fictional currency suppliers of good i need if they are to be able to meet the demand for i by a. Similarly if $g_i > 0$, $-g_i t_{ai}^-$ is the amount of fictional currency required by demanders of good i if they are to be able to take up a's supply. So if

$$R(p, g) = w(g)\Sigma t_a^+(p, g) - v(g)\Sigma t_a^-(p, g)$$

then $R(\cdot)$ measures the fictional currency requirement if markets are to clear. Notice that

$$R(p, g) \geq \varepsilon^1 m \quad \text{for all } g \in G \quad \text{with} \quad \Sigma |g_i| = 1. \qquad ...(2.2)$$

For if say $g_i > 0$ then $-g_i \Sigma t_{ai}^-(p, g) = |g_i| \Sigma_{A(i)} |t_{ai}|$ so that (2.1) follows at once. On the other hand if

$$\mu_a(p, g) = v(g)t_a^+(p, g) - w(g)t_a^-(p, g)$$

then $\mu_a(\cdot)$ is the minimum amount of fictional currency required to finance the given trades. Of course $\mu_a(p, g) \leqq \lambda m_a$. Then if

$$M(p, g) = \Sigma_a \mu_a(p, g)$$

we obtain from summing (2.1) over agents and rearranging

$$Z(p, g) \equiv M(p, g) - R(p, g) = g . t(p, g).$$

We can now use the well known method of Debreu [5] to show the existence of g^0 such that

$$Z(p, g^0) = g^0 t(p, g^0) \geqq g . t(p, g^0) \quad \text{all } g \in G. \qquad \ldots(2.3)$$

Suppose $t(p, g^0) \neq 0$. Then since

$$g^0 t(p, g^0) \leqq \Sigma |g_i^0| |t_r(p, g^0)|$$

where $|t_r(p, g^0)| \geqq |t_i(p, g^0)|$ all i, it follows from 2.3 that $\Sigma |g_i^0| = 1$ and so from (2.2) *and strong tradeability* that $R(p, g^0) \geqq \lambda(g^0)m \geqq \Sigma \mu_a(p, g^0)$. Also $\lambda(g^0) = \varepsilon^1$ so $Z(p, g^0) \leqq 0$. But then in (2.3) setting $g_i = \pm 1$ we obtain

$$0 \geqq |t_i(p, g^0)| \quad \text{all } i$$

a contradiction. Hence $t(p, g^0) = 0$. Summing up

Lemma 2.1. *Under the conditions of Theorem 2.1 there exists* (v^0, w^0, λ^0) *such that* $t^0(p, v^0, w^0, \lambda^0) \equiv \Sigma_a t_a^0(p, v^0, w^0, \lambda^0) = 0$, *i.e. the fictional economy has an equilibrium.*

Lemma 2.2. *The equilibrium of the fictional economy is orderly and non-trivial.*

Proof. (i) It is orderly since one of $(v_i(g^0), w_i(g^0))$ is zero each i.

(ii) By strong tradeability.

Lemma 2.3. *The actual economy shares at least one equilibrium with the fictional economy.*

Proof. In the actual economy let

$$b_{ai}^0 = +\infty \quad \text{if} \quad g_i^0 \leqq 0 \quad \text{and} \quad = \max(0, t_{ai}^0(p, g^0)) \quad \text{otherwise}$$

$$s_{ai}^0 = +\infty \quad \text{if} \quad g_i^0 \geqq 0 \quad \text{and} \quad = \max(0, -t_{ai}^0(p, g^0)) \quad \text{otherwise}.$$

Then certainly $t_a^0(p, g^0) \in T_a(p, b_a^0, s_a^0)$. On the other hand if $t_a \in T_a(p, b_a^0, s_a^0)$ then $t_a \in T_a^0(p, g^0)$ which suffices for the proof.

These three Lemmas prove Theorem 2.1. ‖

It should be emphasized that this theorem proves the existence of an orderly non-trivial equilibrium and that the rationing scheme of the fictional economy is to be regarded as no more than a mathematical device. It plays the same role as do, say, personalized prices in the theory of general equilibrium where public goods are paid by taxes. If one is interested in showing that in general there may be many orderly non-trivial equilibria then one modifies the fictional economy by letting agents receive different amounts of the fictional currency. This was noted by a referee who is interested in showing that there are many such equilibria. In an earlier version of this proof I proceeded differently and as it turned out mistakenly.[1] However, one mistake had a lesson which I now discuss.

One is interested in whether there are rationing schemes such that the resulting fixed price equilibria are Pareto-efficient relative to each agent a being constrained by $p.t_a \leqq 0$.

In the economy so far considered, agents receive the signal (p, b_a, s_a) and they are constrained by $t_a \leq b_a$, $-t_a \leq s_a$. The agent then receives no signal which would tell him that if he, say, bought more in a market in which he has no biting quantity constraint, he might, by enabling some other agent to trade more, relax a biting constraint in some other market. In equilibrium there may then be Pareto-improving trades at fixed prices which are not revealed by the signals.

So let me begin by formulating the notion of an orderly non-Walrasian equilibrium more generally. Let $R_a \subset R^l$ be thought of as a's rationing constraint. So if

$$B_a(p) = \{t_a \mid p \cdot t_a \leq 0, \ t_a + e_a \in R^l_+\},$$

the agents' choice must be in $R_a \cap B_a(p)$.

Definition 2.4. For $p \neq p^*, R_a^0, R_b^0 \ldots, t_a^0, t_b^0 \ldots$ is a *generalized non-Walrasian equilibrium* if (i) t_a^0 is not dominated in a's preferences on $R_a^0 \cap B_a(p)$, all a, (ii) $\Sigma t_a^0 = 0$.

Again it is of interest to restrict the class of admissible equilibrium rationing constraints:

Definition 2.5. A generalized non-Walrasian equilibrium is *orderly* if for every i with $t_{ai}^0 \neq 0$, some a:

(i) *either*, all t_a, with $(t_{ai} \geq t_{ai}^0, \ t_{ak}(k \neq i)) \in R_a^0$, all a

(ii) *or* all t_a, with $(t_{ai} \leq t_{ai}^0, \ t_{ak} = t_{ak}^0 (k \neq i)) \in R_a^0$, (all a).

So orderliness requires that for any good traded in equilibrium the rationing constraint should either not restrict purchases or not restrict sales for any a.

Proposition 2.2. *There exists a rationing scheme for which the orderly non-Walrasian equilibrium is Pareto-efficient relative to the constraints $p \cdot t_a = 0$, all a.*

Proof (a) Let $\bar{G} = \{\bar{g} \in R^{l-1} \times R_+ \mid \Sigma |\bar{g}_i| = 1, \bar{g}_1 \geq 0\}$ and define

$$R_a(\bar{g}) = \{t_a \mid \bar{g} \cdot t_a \leq 0\}, \quad \text{all } a.$$

A generalized non-Walrasian equilibrium (if it exists) is now $\bar{g}^0$ (i.e. $R_a(\bar{g}^0) = R_a^0$) and t_a^0, t_b^0 etc such that $\Sigma t_a^0 = 0$ and $t_a >_a t_a^0$ implies $t_a \notin R_a(\bar{g}^0) \cap B_a(p)$, all a. Such an equilibrium is orderly since $\bar{g}_i > 0$ does not restrict sales of i in any $R_a(\bar{g}^0)$ and $\bar{g}_i < 0$ does not restrict any a.

(b) Let $\hat{\imath} \in XR^l$ denote a trade allocation $(t_a, t_b \ldots)$. Suppose that $\hat{\imath}$ is Pareto-superior to $\hat{\imath}^0$ under the constraint $t_a \in B_a(p)$, all a. Let A_0 be the subset of agents for whom $\bar{g}^0 t_a < 0$. Then for $a \in A_0$, t_a^0 is optimal in $B_a(p)$. Hence given Assumption 2.1 which ensures $p \cdot t_a^0 = 0$, all a, if $t_a \neq t_a^0$ (some $a \in A_0$) it must be true that $p \cdot t_a > 0$. So we need only consider $\hat{\imath}$ which are Pareto superior to $\hat{\imath}^0$ under the budget constraints and for which

$$t_a = \bar{\imath}_a^0, \quad \text{all } a \in A_0.$$

(c) Let A' be the complement of A_0 in the set of agents. Then we now have

$$\bar{g}^0 t_a \geq 0 \text{ all } a \in A', \quad \bar{g}^0 t_a > 0, \text{ some } a \in A'.$$

whence

$$\bar{g}^0 \Sigma_{A'} (t_a - t_a^0) > 0.$$

Hence $\bar{g}_i^0 \Sigma_{A'} (t_{ai} - t_{ai}^0) > 0$, some i. If $\bar{g}_i^0 > 0$ one has together with (b): $t_i > 0$ so $\hat{\imath}$ is not feasible. If $\bar{g}_i^0 < 0$ the same argument gives $t_i < 0$. But $p \cdot t = 0$ whence there must be j with $t_j > 0$ so once again $\hat{\imath}$ is not feasible. Hence $\hat{\imath}$ is Pareto-efficient relative to the constraints $B_a(p)$. ‖

An interpretation of the rationing scheme is as follows. Under this scheme an agent buying one unit of good i has to pay $v_i \geqq 0$ units of a coupon. However, by buying he is supplying one unit of the right to sell good i for which he receives $w_i \geqq 0$ units of a coupon. The net coupon cost of buying one unit of good i is thus $v_i - w_i$. The analogous map in Lemma 2.1 gives us $\bar{g}_i$. It should be noticed that this scheme signals the externalities involved in quantity constraints. For instance suppose $\bar{g}_i < 0$. Then in deciding how much of i to buy agent a, if he is a buyer of i, will take account of the fact that his purchase will increase his coupon income and thereby improve his ability to buy rights to buy or sell other goods.

Lastly one wants to know whether an equilibrium for the rationing scheme exists. Since for all $\bar{g} \in \bar{G}$, $B_a(p) \cap R_a(\bar{g})$ has a non-empty interior, theory, together with Assumption 2.1, gives us all the continuity we require. Together with $\bar{g}t(p, \bar{g}) \leqq 0$ where $t(p, \bar{g}) = \Sigma t_a(p, \bar{g})$ and $t_a(p, \bar{g})$ is the optimum choice of agent a at $(p, \bar{g})$ this allows the good old Debreu method to do the rest.

It is of course obvious that there will be many other equilibria of the kind here discussed which are not Pareto-efficient in the above sense. Indeed, if one continues to put a short-period interpretation on the model with fixed prices then it is not at all clear that the equilibria will be orderly leave alone Pareto-efficient. For it takes time and information to find such equilibria. So none of the above is very interesting as such under this interpretation. But there is another possible interpretation: prices are fixed because no agent wishes to change them in spite of being " rationed ". It is to this far more interesting case to which I now turn.

3. CONJECTURES

In this section I consider the implication of the fact that an agent whose transactions are constrained at p must abandon the postulate that he can trade whatever he wishes to at p (Arrow [1]). It is then difficult to continue with the postulate that the agent treats all signals parametrically. In the spirit of Negishi [11] I shall therefore suppose that agents conjecture a relationship between the prices they offer and the quantity signals which they receive. My programme differs from Negishi's as follows. *I do not assume that the economy is intrinsically one of monopolistic competition.* The economy to be studied always has a Walrasian equilibrium. I shall show that it also has non-Walrasian equilibria. Hence the " price flexibility " implied by the conjectures does not ensure a competitive equilibrium.

The class of conjectures which I consider is restricted in the following way. Firstly I suppose that agents who do not encounter a quantity constraint take the price at which they must trade as given. Secondly it is supposed that agents who are quantity constrained in a market conjecture that they must raise price in order to be allowed to buy more than they are buying and that they must lower price in order to be allowed to sell more than they are selling. In view of a referee's comments and an important observation of Maskin's it is worth while emphasizing the following:

(1) The formulation is designed in order to avoid straightforward monopolistic competition. An agent believes he can affect price only when he has had a signal that he is not a perfect competitor, i.e. experiences a quantity constraint. This signal is endogenous to the economy. All this is done in order to consider economies which always do have Walrasian equilibria. A referee asked me to relate this to the literature. Well, it is not the model Negishi [11] considered. I have not found it in Benassy. The kink which my formulation gives rise to has recently been used by Negishi [12] in a different context. Since I had not seen it when I wrote this and since Negishi is concerned with a special case that is all I can say on the matter.

(2) On the other hand Maskin has made an important point when he points out to me that I have cooked the story in favour of the result I am looking for, viz. the possibility of non-Walrasian equilibria when Walrasian ones are available. This I do by not allowing

an agent to consider that he could trade at prices other than the ones ruling when he notices that other agents are constrained. Most vividly: why when labour is rationed and employers are not rationed in the labour market, do not employers respond to the observation that labour is rationed, by lowering price? There may be an answer to this . . . agents cannot observe the constraints on other agents but at best only their constrained trades; e.g. unemployment statistics are not published. But it may also be that my present hypotheses can only be sensibly maintained by introducing further features, such as informational imperfections into the story. I hope to examine this on a future occasion.

I now turn to the more formal account.

Interpret b_{ai} as the signal received by a that he cannot buy more of good i than that at the given price. Interpret s_{ai} analogously. Let

$$\zeta_{ai} = \max(0, t_{ai} - b_{ai}), \quad \zeta_a \in R_+^l$$

$$\xi_{ai} = \min(0, t_{ai} + s_{ai}), \quad \xi_a \in R_-^l.$$

Definition 3.1. $C_a: R_+^l \times R_-^l \times \Delta \to R_+^l$ is called the *conjecture* of a. It shows, given p, the price vector at which a believes he must trade as a function of (ζ_a, ξ_a) the excess of his trade over the amount indicated by the quantity signals.

I shall stipulate:

Assumption 3.1. (i) C_a is a continuous function and for given s_a, b_a, $C_a(\cdot)t_a$ is a convex function in t_a.

(ii) $C_{ai}(p, \zeta_{ai}, \xi_{ai}) = p_i$ when $\zeta_{ai} = \xi_{ai} = 0$.

(iii) $C_{ai}(\cdot)$ is an increasing function of ζ_{ai} and ξ_{ai} for $p_i > 0$.

The set of feasible choices under the conjecture is F_a^c where

$$F_a^c(p, b_a, s_a) = \{t_a \mid C_a(p, \zeta_a, \xi_a)t_a \leq 0\} \cap \{t_a \mid e_a + t_a \geq 0\}. \qquad \ldots(3.1)$$

By Assumption 3.1 this is a convex set since $C_a(\cdot)t_a$ is a convex function in t_a. The agent chooses his best trade in (3.1). By Assumption 2.1, he chooses a unique $t_a^c(p, b_a, s_a)$ satisfying

$$C_a(p, \zeta_a, \xi_a)t_a^c(p, b_a, s_a) = 0. \qquad \ldots(3.2)$$

Now define $\hat{c}_a(p, b_a, s_a) \in R_+^l$ as having components

$$\hat{c}_{ai}(p, b_a, s_a) = C_{ai}(p, \max(0, t_{ai}^c(p, b_a, c_a) - b_{ai}), \min(0, t_{ai}^c(p, b_a, s_a) + s_{ai})).$$

Then $\hat{c}_{ai}(\cdot)$ is the price for good i at which a offers to trade. One has

$$\hat{c}_{ai}(p, b_a, s_a) > 0, \quad \text{for all } i, \quad p \in \Delta, \quad b_a \geq 0, \quad s_a \geq 0. \qquad \ldots(3.3)$$

The reason for (3.3) is clear: By Assumption 2.1 the optimum trade at a zero price for i must be an unbounded purchase of good i. If that is restrained by b_{ai} then $\zeta_{ai} > 0$ and so via Assumption 3.1 (iii) one has (3.3). (It is assumed here that C_{ai} is differentiable at $p_i = 0$.)

An equilibrium of an economy now requires two conditions to be fulfilled: markets must clear and agents must accept current prices as optimal. Formally

Definition 3.2. $(p^0, \hat{b}, \hat{s})$ with $p^0 \in \Delta$, $\hat{b}^0 \in \times_A R_+^l$, $\hat{s}^0 \in \times_A R_+^l$ is a *conjectural equilibrium* if:

(i) $t^c(p^0, \hat{b}^0, \hat{s}^0) = \Sigma_a t_a^c(p^0, b_a^0, s_a^0) = 0.$

(ii) $\hat{c}_a(p^0, b_a^0, s_a^0) = p^0$ all a.

The motivation is clear. If (ii) but not (i) then the quantity signals cannot be what they are. If (i) but not (ii) agents will offer prices other than what they are. It will be clear that the Walrasian equilibrium with $b_{ai}^* \geqq t_i(p^*)$, $s_{ai}^* + t_i(p^*) \geqq 0$, all a and i, is also a conjectural equilibrium. I show, that with two additional assumptions, there are other conjectural equilibria. Since the Walrasian equilibrium is unique this suffices for the main contention that " conjectural price flexibility " is consistent with non-Walrasian conjectural equilibrium.

In what follows write

$$t_i^+ = \Sigma_a \max (0, t_{ai}), \quad t_i^- = \Sigma_a \min (0, t_{ai})$$

and for notational ease the superscript c is omitted. I shall use

Assumption 3.2. There is ε in the open interval $(0, 1)$ and $r \in R_{++}^A$ with $\Sigma r_a = 1$ such that when $p_1 > 0$

(i) $t_1(p, \hat{b}, \hat{s}) < 0$ and

(ii) $\Sigma \zeta_{a1}(p, b_a, s_a) \leqq \varepsilon' t_1^+ (p, \hat{b}, \hat{s}), \quad 0 < \varepsilon' \leqq \varepsilon$

then also:

$$\Sigma_a r_a \hat{c}_{a1}(p, b_a, s_a) < p_1. \qquad \qquad ...(3.4)$$

The interpretation is as follows: if at $(p, \hat{b}, \hat{s})$ good 1 is in excess supply then if the " short-fall " in desired purchases is small relatively to the total desired purchases a weighted average of the offered prices for market 1 is less than the prevailing price. This postulate is not very restrictive. I also use

Assumption 3.3. For $p \gg 0$, $p \in \Delta$ and all $\hat{b}$, $\hat{s}$ which are admissible $t_{ai}(p, b_a, s_a) > 0$, some a, each i.

This stipulates that at all the specified signals every good has a buyer. It is somewhat stronger than Assumption 3.2 but one can live with it. We now have:

Theorem 3.1. *Given Assumptions 2.1, 3.1–3.3 there exists a non-Walrasian conjectural equilibrium, when one good is not rationed.*

Before giving the formal proof it will be convenient to give a preliminary discussion. For this purpose let B_a and S_a be two large compact cubes in R_+^l and $B = \bigtimes_A B_a$, $S = \bigtimes_A S_a$. I shall construct a continuous map $\theta = \theta^p \times \theta^b \times \theta^s : \Delta \times B \times S \to \Delta \times B \times S$. As in earlier sections let $\sigma = (p, \hat{b}, \hat{s})$.

(i) θ^p: $\Delta \times B \times S \to \Delta$ is given by

$$\theta_i^p = \frac{\hat{c}_i^*(\sigma)}{c_0(\sigma)} \quad i = 1...l, \qquad \qquad ...(3.5)$$

where $\hat{c}_i^* = (1/A)\Sigma \hat{c}_{ai}$ for $i \neq 1$, $\hat{c}_1^* = \Sigma r_a \hat{c}_{a1}$, $c_0 = \Sigma_{i=1} \hat{c}_i^*$. From (3.3) one has $\theta^p \gg 0$ and $\theta^p \in \Delta$.

(ii) $\theta^s : \Delta \times B \times S \to S$ is given by

$$
\left.
\begin{aligned}
\theta_{ai}^s &= \frac{t_{ai}^-(\sigma)}{\mu_i(\sigma)} \quad i = 1...l-1, \text{ all } a \\
\theta_{al}^s &= k \qquad \text{all } a, \text{ where } k \text{ is very large}
\end{aligned}
\right\} \qquad ...(3.6)
$$

where

$$\mu_i(\sigma) = \frac{t_i^-(\sigma) - m}{t_i^+(\sigma) + m}, \quad m > 0$$

so

$$
\left.
\begin{aligned}
t_i &< 0 \Leftrightarrow -\mu_i > 1 \\
t_i &> 0 \Leftrightarrow -\mu_i < 1.
\end{aligned}
\right\} \qquad ...(3.7)
$$

Summing (3.2) over a and using (3.3) confirms that $-\mu_i$ is bounded above and below for all σ in the domain. Since for each a t_{ai}^- is bounded below by finite endowment one has $\theta^s \in S$ if S is chosen large enough.

(iii) θ^b: $\Delta \times B \times S \to B$ is given by

$$
\left.
\begin{array}{ll}
\theta_{ai}^b = -\mu_i(\sigma)t_{ai}^+(\sigma), & \text{all } a \text{ and all } i \neq 1 \text{ and } i \neq l \\
\theta_{al}^b = k, & \text{all } a \text{ and } k \text{ very large} \\
\theta_{a1}^b = -\lambda(p)\mu_1(\sigma)t_{a1}^+(\sigma), & \text{all } a
\end{array}
\right\} \qquad \ldots(3.8)
$$

where

$$
\lambda(p) = 1 - \varepsilon + \min\,(\varepsilon,\, d(p, p^*)). \qquad \ldots(3.9)
$$

In (3.9) ε is given by Assumption 3.2 and $d(p, p^*)$ is the Euclidean distance in Δ of p from the unique Walrasian equilibrium p^*. From (3.9),

$$
0 < \lambda(p) \leq 1 \quad \text{all } p \in \Delta. \qquad \ldots(3.10)
$$

By routine argument $\theta^b \in B$ if B is chosen large enough.

Proof of Theorem 3.1. Let σ^0 be a fixed point of the map θ just given.

(a) $c_0(\sigma^0) = 1$. Since good l is not rationed one has by Assumption 3.1

$$
p_l^0 = \hat{c}_l^*(\sigma^0).
$$

(b) It follows from (a) that

$$
p_i^0 = \hat{c}_i^*(\sigma^0) \quad \text{all } i.
$$

Hence, for $i \neq 1, l$, one has $t_i(\sigma^0) = 0$. For suppose, say $t_i(\sigma^0) > 0$. Then by (3.8)

$$
b_{ai}^0 \leq t_{ai}^+(\sigma^0), \quad \text{all } a
$$

with strict inequality, some a. But then by Assumption 3.1: $p_i^0 < \hat{c}_i^*(\sigma^0)$.

(c) By the same argument $t_1(\sigma^0) > 0$ is impossible since $\lambda(p^0) \leq 1$. So suppose $t_1(\sigma^0) < 0$ but $p_1^0 = \hat{c}_1^*(\sigma^0)$. Then for some a one must have by Assumption 3.3

$$
b_{a1}^0 < t_{a1}^+(\sigma^0), \quad \text{i.e. } \lambda(p^0) < 1. \qquad \ldots(3.11)
$$

By (3.8)

$$
t_{a1}^+(\sigma^0) - b_{a1}^0 = (1 + \mu_1(\sigma^0)\lambda(p^0))t_{a1}^+(\sigma^0) \leq (1 - \lambda(p^0))t_{a1}^+(\sigma^0).
$$

But

$$
\lambda(p^0) = (1 - (\varepsilon - d(p^0, p^*))) = 1 - \varepsilon'
$$

so

$$
t_{a1}^+(\sigma^0) - b_{a1}^0 \leq \varepsilon' t_{a1}^+(\sigma^0).
$$

This must be true for all a constrained in their buying. So the conditions of Assumption 3.2 are satisfied whence

$$
p_1^0 > \hat{c}_1^*(\sigma^0) \qquad \ldots(3.12)
$$

a contradiction.

(d) So by (3.2) $t_i(\sigma^0) = 0$, all i. But then certainly $\lambda(p^0) = 1$ since otherwise (3.11) holds for some a and so (3.12). But then from the definition of λ, $d(p^0, p^*) \geq \varepsilon$. $\parallel$

I have now shown that an economy can get stuck in a non-Walrasian equilibrium even when prices are free to vary. Price setting is now part of a story of rationally acting agents. This involves conjectures and one must ask where they come from, or at least, whether they must be restricted in some way. Before I turn to this there is a piece of tidying up yet to be done in the present account. For I have not demanded of the conjectural non-Walrasian equilibrium that only one side of each market should be constrained.

For each good i define $\sigma(i, b)$ as having the components of σ except that b_{ai} is replaced by a large positive scalar k_b each a. Similarly $\sigma(i, s)$ has the components of σ except that s_{ai} is replaced by a large positive scalar k_r, each a. Then one writes $t_a(\sigma(i, b))$ as the best choice in $F_a^c(\sigma(i, b))$ and $t_a(\sigma(i, s))$ as the best choice in $F_a^c(\sigma(i, s))$. Suppose

$$t_{ai}^+(\sigma(i, b)) < t_{ai}^+(\sigma).$$

Then from the definitions $t_a(\sigma(i, b)) \in F^c(\sigma)$ which contradicts the definition of $t_a(\sigma)$ as the unique choice in $F^c(\sigma)$. So in general

$$t_{ai}^+(\sigma(i, b)) \geqq t_{ai}^+(\sigma), \quad t_{ai}^-(\sigma(i, s)) \leqq t_{ai}^-(\sigma), \quad \text{all } a \text{ and } i. \qquad \ldots(3.13)$$

Now alter the map of the proof of Theorem 3.1 as follows

(i) In (3.6) for each $i \neq l$ replace $\mu_i(\sigma)^{-1}$ by

$$r_i^s(\sigma) = \frac{t_i^+(\sigma(i, b)) + m}{t_i^-(\sigma) - m}.$$

(ii) In (3.8) for each $i \neq 1$, l replace $\mu_i(\sigma)$ by

$$r_i^b(\sigma) = \frac{t_i^-(\sigma(i, s)) - m}{t_i^+(\sigma) + m}.$$

Otherwise make no change in the map which remains continuous and has a fixed point which I again write as σ^0. I sketch a proof that σ^0 is an equilibrium on the lines of the previous proof.

(a') As in (a).

(b') Suppose $t_i(\sigma^0) < 0$, for some $i \neq 1$, l. In view of (3.13) this gives $-r_i^b(\sigma^0) > 1$ and so $b_{ai}^0 - t_{ai}^+(\sigma^0) > 0$ all a which must mean

$$t_{ai}^+(\sigma^0) = t_{ai}^+(\sigma^0(i, b)), \quad \text{all } a$$

and so $-r_i^s(\sigma^0) < 1$ from which $s_{ai}^0 + t_{ai}^-(\sigma^0) = 0$, all a, with strict inequality, some a. Hence one deduces $c_0(\sigma^0) < 1$. One deals with $t_i(\sigma^0) > 0$ analogously.

(d') Proceed as in (d).

But now notice

(e) For all $i \neq 1$: $\min [-r_i^s(\sigma^0), -r_i^b(\sigma^0)] \geqq 1$. If the strict inequality holds then neither side of the market is restricted. If say $-r_i^s(\sigma^0) = 1$ then in view of $t_i(\sigma^0) = 0$ and (3.13): $t_i^+(\sigma^0(i, b)) = t_i^+(\sigma^0)$ and so while sellers may be restricted, buyers are not. Symmetrically $-r_i^b(\sigma^0) = 1$ implies that sellers are not restricted.

One now has

Theorem 3.2. *Given the assumption of Theorem 3.1 there exists a non-Walrasian conjectural equilibrium where in $(l-1)$ markets at most one side of the market is quantity constrained.*

4. RATIONAL AND REASONABLE CONJECTURES

The objection to a conjectural equilibrium is the arbitrariness of the conjecture. It should be emphasized that the traditional perfectly competitive Walrasian economy with a finite number of participants is open to the same objection. For it is an equilibrium relative to the conjecture that an agent can trade what he wishes to at given prices which is only correct for the equilibrium trade. Similarly in the conjectural non-Walrasian equilibrium which I have discussed: the equilibrium prices confirm the equilibrium conjecture. Put crudely: the conjectured demand curve coincides with the " actual " demand curve which one can consider.

When one attempts to tie down permissible conjectures it is natural to think first of the requirement that they be " correct ". For instance one is familiar with the reason for considering rational expectations in Walrasian sequence models (Radner [13]). But here matters are harder. For in the Walrasian case agents observe discrepancies between their conjectures and outcomes while in the present case agents may be in a situation where they trade what they wish at the terms they expect and yet their wishes may be based on conjectures the falsity of which they could only discover by varying their trades. That is experiment rather than observation would be required to verify conjectures (see Rothschild [14]).

These are much deeper waters for general equilibrium theory and I go only a small way in a number of small steps.

I start with some definitions.

Definition 4.1. Call $\sigma^0(t_a)$ a conjectural equilibrium relative to t_a, an arbitrary trade vector of agent a, if

    (i) For all $a' \neq a$: $p^0(t_a) = C_{a'}(\sigma^0(t_a))$

    (ii) $t_a + \Sigma_{a' \neq a} t_{a'}(\sigma^0(t_a)) \underset{\text{def}}{=} t(\sigma^0(t_a), t_a) = 0$

    (iii) $b_a^0(t_a) \geq t_a^+$ and $s_a^0(t_a) + t_a^- \geq 0$.

Notice that by (i): $p^0(t_a)\Sigma_{a' \neq a} t_{a'}(\sigma^0(t_a)) = 0$, whence from (ii) and (iii) if a's conjectures satisfy Assumption 3.1,

$$t_a \in F_a^c(\sigma^0(t_a)).$$

It seems that it would be useful to give a verbal account of Definition 4.1 so here it is. Consider an agent a who fixes his trade at t_a and do not just now worry about his budget constraint. We shall be interested to know whether t_a is consistent with some conjectural equilibrium of the economy. Since, however, t_a has been taken as given such an equilibrium cannot also insist on a being in conjectural equilibrium. Hence a conjectural equilibrium relative to t_a is a price vector $p^0(t_a)$ and a set of rations to all agents such that (i) all agents other than a are in conjectural equilibrium, (ii) the net trade of the economy excluding a makes t_a possible and (iii) the rations allocated to a are consistent with the given t_a. Hence if this equilibrium exists the arbitrary t_a is consistent with an equilibrium of all agents other than a, and t_a can be carried out in such an equilibrium. Arithmetic then ensures that t_a also satisfies the budget constraint for a at $p(t_a)$.

Now it seems a first sensible step to suppose that if no conjectural equilibrium exists relative to t_a that t_a cannot be carried out. This of course is not a proposition but an assumption. I refer to t_a as *equilibrium infeasible* if no conjectural equilibrium relative to t_a exists. I now try

Definition 4.2. Let σ^0 be a conjectural equilibrium and let

$$\tau_a(\sigma^0) = \{t_a \mid t_a >_a t_a(\sigma^0)\}.$$

Then C_a is called a *rational conjecture* for a at σ^0 if all $t_a \in \tau_a(\sigma^0)$ are equilibrium infeasible. One calls σ^0 a *rational conjectural equilibrium* if the conjectures of all agents are rational for σ^0.

Once again I put this into words. For a conjectural equilibrium to be rational there should be no other conjectural equilibrium in which all agents other than a given one are in conjectural equilibrium and markets clear with the given agent's trade being higher in his preferences. It is perhaps worth noting why this somewhat complicated concept is used.

Some authors, e.g. D. Gale in his Cambridge Thesis, postulate at given prices a rationing mechanism which is a map from the trade of all agents to the rations for each agent. One can, in this context, then ask of an equilibrium that given this mechanism, and given the trades of all other agents, no agent should be able to choose a preferred trade. This then is a straightforward Nash requirement. I, however, want to consider a situation where an agent by changing a price may change his ration. The mechanism here is hard to specify. For that reason, and also because I want to take the conjectures rather than the trades of other agents as given, I look simply whether there is an equilibrium where $t_a >_a t_a^0$, all agents other than a being in conjectural equilibrium.

If conjectures are rational for σ^0 then one might argue that experiments will confirm them although this would be a rather weak argument since one would require experiments on the part of one agent only. In particular of course a rational conjectural equilibrium does not imply that there is no equilibrium, when two agents attempt arbitrary trades, preferred to those at σ^0. The reverse argument is also rather weak: if σ^0 is not a rational equilibrium it does not follow that agents' conjectures are likely to change. In spite of these arguments the notion is sufficiently interesting to study a little further.

Consider the following case where $A(a)$ is the set of agents excluding a.

Assumption 4.1. It is possible to choose an a such that for every market i there are at least two agents a', $a'' \in A(a)$ with

$$t_{a'i}(\sigma)t_{a''i}(\sigma)<0, \quad \text{for all } \sigma \text{ with } p\gg0, \ \hat{b} \in B, \ \hat{s} \in S.$$

This assumption of " variety " among agents does not seem very strong. It has, however, the unpleasant consequence that the class of conjectures satisfying Assumption 3.1 is incompatible with the existence of rational conjectural equilibrium.

To establish this take agent a of Assumption 4.1 and let

$$\bar{t}_a \in \tau_a(\sigma^0), \ |\bar{t}_a-t_a(\sigma^0)| \leq \varepsilon.$$

If u_a is a's utility function write $u_a(\bar{t}_a) = \bar{u}_a$. Define

$$t^a(\sigma) = \Sigma_{A(a)}t_{a'}(\sigma)$$

and

$$\tilde{t}_a(\sigma) \text{ solves: } \min_{u_a(t_a) \geq \bar{u}_a} W(\Sigma_i \,|\, t_i^a(\sigma)+t_{ai} \,|), \qquad \qquad \ldots(4.1)$$

where W is a strictly convex increasing function. Hence given the concavity of u_v, (4.1) defines $\tilde{t}_a(\sigma)$ uniquely. Given the continuity of $t^a(\sigma)$ one has $\tilde{t}_a(\sigma)$ continuous over the domain. Lastly let

$$\tilde{t}(\sigma) = t^a(\sigma)+\tilde{t}_a(\sigma).$$

Theorem 4.1. *Given Assumption* 4.1 *there exists no rational conjectural equilibrium for the class of conjectures satisfying Assumption* 3.1.

Proof. Let $B(a) = \mathsf{X}_{A(a)} B_{a'}$, $S(a) = \mathsf{X}_{A(a)} S_{a'}$ and $\bar{\theta}: \Delta \times B(a) \times S(a)$ into itself where $\bar{\theta}$ is defined as follows.

(a) For all $a' \in A(a)$, $\bar{\theta}_{a'}^s$ is the mapping (3.6) where $\tilde{\mu}_i(\sigma)$ replaces $\mu_i(\sigma)$. Here $\tilde{\mu}_i(\sigma)$ is derived from $\mu_i(\sigma)$ by replacing $t_i^-(\sigma)$ and $t_i^+(\sigma)$ by $\tilde{t}_i^-(\sigma)$ and $\tilde{t}_i^+(\sigma)$.

(b) For all $a' \in A(a)$ let (3.8) be the map of $\bar{\theta}_{a'}^b$, except (i) that $\tilde{\mu}_i(\sigma)$ replaces $\mu_i(\sigma)$ and (ii) $\tilde{\lambda}(p) \equiv 1$, all p, replaces $\lambda(p)$. (We are not now specially concerned with non-Walrasian equilibria.)

(c) The map $\bar{\theta}^p$ is given by

$$\bar{\theta}_i^p = \frac{\hat{c}_i^*(\sigma, a)}{c_0(\sigma, a)}, \quad i = 1\ldots l \qquad \qquad \ldots(4.2)$$

where

$$\hat{c}_i^*(\sigma, a) = \frac{1}{A-1} \Sigma_{A(a)}\hat{c}_{a'i}(\sigma), \quad i = 1\ldots l,$$

$$c_0(\sigma, a) = \Sigma_i\hat{c}_i^*(\sigma, a).$$

(d) The map certainly has the fixed point property. Let $\sigma^0(a)$ be such a fixed point.

(i) $\tilde{\imath}(\sigma^0(a)) = 0$. Suppose not and $\tilde{\imath}_i(\sigma^0(a)) > 0$. Then by Assumption 4.1 $t_{a'i}(\sigma^0(a)) < 0$, all $a' \in A(a)$, is not possible. Hence by (b): $b^0_{a'i}(a) < t^+_{a'i}(\sigma^0(a))$ some $a' \in A(a)$ and by (c): $s^0_{a'i}(\sigma^0(a)) + t^-_{a'i}(\sigma^0(a)) \geqq 0$ all $a' \in A(a)$. Hence by Assumption 3.1

$$p^0_i(a) < \hat{c}^*_i(\sigma^0(a), a), \qquad \qquad ...(4.3)$$

whence $c_0(\sigma^0(a), a) > 1$. But this now implies that (4.3) holds for all $i = 1...l$ and so by Assumption 3.1 again

$$\tilde{\imath}(\sigma^0(a)) \gg 0. \qquad \qquad ...(4.4)$$

(ii) But now since

$$\Sigma c_{a'i}(\sigma^0(a)) t_{a'i}(\sigma^0(a)) > p^0(a) t_{a'}(\sigma^0(a))$$

and (3.2) one has

$$p^0(a) t^a(\sigma^0(a)) < 0$$

and $p^0(a) \gg 0$ by Assumption 2.1. Hence for at least one i

$$t^a_i(\sigma^0(a)) < 0.$$

But then by (4.1) it must be that

$$\tilde{\imath}_i(\sigma^0(a)) = 0$$

since if not then $W(\cdot)$ has not been minimized under the given constraint. Hence (4.4) is impossible. The case $\tilde{\imath}_i(\sigma^0(a)) < 0$ some i is treated symmetrically.

(iii) By (a) and (b), (i) implies

$$p^0_i(a) = c_{a'i}(\sigma^0(a)), \quad \text{all } a' \text{ and } i.$$

Hence we have shown that the fixed point is a conjectural equilibrium. But by construction $\tilde{\imath}_a(\sigma^0(a))$ is attainable and

$$\tilde{\imath}_a(\sigma^0(a)) >_a t_a(\sigma^0).$$

Even so the class of conjectures considered is small; but I believe sensible for a decentralized economy. By sensible I mean two things: (a) a small agent must not be expected to have " general equilibrium theories " embodied in his conjectures. Thus he believes that the change in his budget situation consequent upon his wishing " to break a ration " in any one market can be conjectured with reference to events in only that market. (b) an agent does not have " perverse " conjectures, i.e. he does not believe that getting a larger purchase allocation of good i goes with a lower price of that good or that getting a larger sale allocation goes with a higher price of that good. This " separability " of conjectures and their lack of perverseness I consider sensible on the grounds that postulating conjectures violating these conditions would result in models even more remote from the world than the present one.

On the other hand the result of Theorem 4.1 may simply be that our definition of rational is too demanding and in particular bound to conflict with what I have just called sensible conjectures. It must now also be noted that the requirement of rationality places no weight on the *action* of agents. To put it starkly there may indeed at σ^0 exist an equilibrium relative to t_a with $t_a \in \tau_a(\sigma^0)$ but there may still be no action of agent a which would ensure him t_a. In general the action open to an agent is a change in the price at which he offers to trade in some market. Whether such an action leads to a preferred equilibrium will not only depend on the existence of the latter but on the dynamic behaviour of the economy. Indeed, I now believe that the latter is crucial in narrowing down the conjectures to those which are likely to persist. But I cannot at present contribute to this problem.

The following two further remarks may be made.

Let us say that an agent has *competitive conjectures* if, for all a and i

$$c_{ai} = p_i \text{ identically in } p, b_{ai}, s_{ai}.$$

Evidently the Walrasian p^* is the only conjectural equilibrium. On present assumptions it is unique. Now suppose there to be a continuum of agents. Then it is intuitive that p^* will be the equilibrium of the economy whatever t_a. For agent a is of measure zero. But then $p^*t_a > 0$ for all t_a preferred to t_a^* and the Walrasian equilibrium is a rational conjectural equilibrium. I do not give a formal account of this result since it does not belong to the study of economies in which price adjustments are to be, at least in principle, deducible from the rational action of agents.

The second remark concerns the relationship between rational and " correct " conjectures. If conjectures are correct then one supposes that the agent correctly conjectures the prices at which a given trade could be carried out. But this causes some difficulties. At σ^0, $t_a \in \tau_a(\sigma^0)$ implies $pt_a > 0$ where p are the prices conjectured by a for trade t_a. But then at these conjectured prices no equilibrium relative to t_a exists. There is thus no correct conjecture for such trades. So let us restrict " correct " to refer to price conjectures for trades relative to which equilibria exist. The difficulty is now changed to that deriving from the non-uniqueness of such equilibria. One is therefore driven to a yet weaker formulation: conjectures are not incorrect when for every t_a relative to which an equilibrium exists, the conjecture p belongs to the set of equilibrium prices. But then conjectures which are not incorrect are rational. For suppose an equilibrium relative to t_a exists with $t_a <_a t_a^0$. So the conjectured p is not such an equilibrium. Then the conjecture is incorrect but it does not preclude it from being rational. For the agent may still be perfectly right in the general conjecture that $t_a >_a t_a^0$ is not available.

As I have already noted the requirement of rationality, as I have defined it, is in view of Theorem 4.1, not only too strong but perhaps also misguided. I conclude this section therefore with an alternative which is more appealing but for which I have no theorems.

Let me now choose good l as numeraire by putting $p_l \equiv 1$. I continue to write p for the price vector it being understood that $p \notin \Delta$. Consider σ^0 a conjectural equilibrium. Let p_a be a price vector announced by a where p_a differs from p^0 in at *most* one coordinate, say the rth. So agents other than a receive the price signals (p^0, p_a). Let $p(a, r)$ be a price vector with $p_r = p_{ar}$. Lastly let $P(a, r)$ represent the set of $p(a, r)$ consistent with an equilibrium of the economy when agent a chooses his trades which are best for him under his conjecture for $i \neq r$ and for $p_r = p_{ar}$ whatever his trades or rations. Then

Definition 4.4. Agent a's rth conjecture will be said to be *reasonable* at σ^0 if for all p_a different from p^0 only in the rth coordinate

either (i) $P(a, r)$ is empty.

or (ii) There is no conjectural equilibrium σ, with $p \in P(a, r)$ for which agent a's optimal choice is higher in his preference than is t_a^0.

or (iii) The response mechanism of the economy from the initial condition (σ^0, p_a) leads to an equilibrium inferior in a's preference to t_a^0.

It will be seen that I have included a number of ideas under the heading reasonable. I believe (iii) to be the most interesting but it is also the most difficult. The definition excludes strategic considerations. Indeed, it is Nash-like in taking the conjectures of agents other than a as given. But I have nothing of a formal nature to report on reasonable conjectures.

APPENDIX TO SECTION 2

In this appendix I consider a weaker tradeability assumption. It will have the consequence that I can no longer ensure that one can confine attention to the case $\lambda > 0$, i.e.

where agents have positive coupon wealth. But when $\lambda = 0$ the feasible set of an agent is not continuous and so the Debreu fixed point argument would fail there.

Definition 2.3*: Let $\mu_{ai}(e_a)$ be a's marginal rate of substitution, at e_a, between good i and good one minus the price of good i in terms of good one. Then the economy satisfies *tradeability* if there are agents a and b such that

$$\mu_{ai}(e_a)\mu_{bi}(e_a) < 0 \quad \text{some } i.$$

If an economy satisfying tradeability has an orderly equilibrium it must be non-trivial. For by orderliness either $\mu_{ai}(e_a) \geqq 0$ all a or $\mu_{ai}(e_a) \leqq 0$ all a each i.

Now let $v_i(q)$, $w_i(q)$ be defined as in the text but fix $\lambda > 0$ arbitrarily. The Debreu-map has a fixed point q^λ, t^λ:

$$\lambda m \geqq z(p, q^\lambda, \lambda) \geqq q^\lambda t^\lambda \geqq qt^\lambda \quad \text{all } q.$$

A problem arises if $z(p, q^\lambda, \lambda) > 0$ all $\lambda > 0$ which I now assume to be the case. Note that $z(\cdot)$ is not continuous at $\lambda = 0$. But if we take $\lambda \to 0$ we may take a convergent subsequence q^λ such that $v_i(q^\lambda) = 0$ all λ *or* $w_i(q^\lambda) = 0$ all λ. Along this subsequence let $q^\lambda \to \bar{q}$, $t^\lambda \to \bar{t}$. It is clear that $\bar{t} = 0$. On the other hand $\bar{t}$ need not be $\lim_{\lambda \to 0} t(p, q^\lambda, \lambda)$ because of lack of continuity.

However consider the *actual* economy where

$$\bar{b}_{ai} = \bar{t}_{ai}^+, \quad \bar{s}_{ai} = \infty \text{ for } \bar{q}_i > 0, \quad \bar{b}_{ai} = \infty, \quad \bar{s}_{ai} = \bar{t}_{ai}^- \text{ for } \bar{q}_i < 0.$$

If agent a faced this quantity constraint $\bar{t}_a$ would be his choice. For if not there would be $t_a >_a \bar{t}_a$ where we may take t_a interior to his set of feasible trades given the quantity constraints. But then for λ small, $t_a >_a t^\lambda$ a contradiction. Hence the quantity rations $(\bar{b}_a, \bar{s}_a)$ all a gives a Drèze equilibrium at p. It is of course orderly and non-trivial.

This proof which is due to Douglas Gale shows that there are Drèze equilibria which cannot be mimicked by a coupon economy or better that the coupon economy is not well defined at zero coupon wealth.

First version received February 1976; *final version accepted October* 1976 (*Eds.*).

This work was supported by National Science Foundation Grant SOC74-11446 at the Institute for Mathematical Studies in the Social Sciences, Stanford University. I have benefited from discussions with Robert Aumann, Kenneth Arrow, Jean-Michel Grandmont, and Roger Witcomb. My greatest debt is to Douglas Gale, Oliver Hart and Eric Maskin, who spotted mistakes in an earlier version. Douglas Gale also supplied the argument of the appendix and Oliver Hart convinced me that it was necessary to proceed as there indicated. The muddled mind indicated by the mistakes which were spotted must leave a suspicion that there are others.

NOTE

    1. Eric Maskin discovered one mistake and a referee the other.

REFERENCES

[1] Arrow, K. J. " Towards a Theory of Price Adjustment ", in *The Allocation of Economic Resources*, Abramovitz, A. (ed.) (Stanford University Press, 1959).

[2] Arrow, K. J. and Hahn, F. H. *General Competitive Analysis* (Holden Day, 1971).

[3] Benassy, J. P. " The Disequilibrium Approach to Monopolistic Price Setting and General Monopolistic Equilibrium ", *Review of Economic Studies*, **43** (February 1976).

[4] Clower, R. W. " The Keynesian Counterrevolution: A Theoretical Appraisal ", in *The Theory of Interest Rates*, Hahn, F. H. and Brechling, F. P. R. (eds.) (Macmillan, 1965).

[5] Debreu, G. *Theory of Value* (John Wiley and Sons, 1959).

[6] Drèze, J. " Existence of Exchange Equilibrium under Price Rigidities ", Core No. 7326, *International Economic Review*, **16** (1975).

[7] Grandmont, J. and Laroque, G. " On Temporary Keynesian Equilibria ", *Review of Economic Studies*, **43** (February 1976).

[8] Hahn, F. H. and Negishi, T. " A Theorem on Non-Tâtonnement Stability ", *Econometrica* (1962).

[9] Leijonhufvud, A. *On Keynesian Economics and the Economics of Keynes* (Oxford University Press, 1960).

[10] Malinvaud, E. and Younès, Y. " A New Formulation for the Microeconomic Foundations of Macroeconomics ", *S'Agaro* (July 1975).

[11] Negishi, T.   " Monopolistic Competition and General Equilibrium ", *Review of Economic Studies*, **28** (1960).
[12] Negishi, T.   " Unemployment Equilibrium ", Mimeo (1974).
[13] Radner, R.   " Existence of Equilibrium of Plans, Prices and Price Expectations in a Sequence of Markets ", *Econometrica* (1972).
[14] Rothschild, M.   " A Two-armed-bandit Theory of Market Pricing ", *Journal of Economic Theory* (1974).
[15] Younès, Y.   " On the Role of Money in the Process of Exchange and the Existence of a Non-Walrasian Equilibrium ", *Review of Economic Studies*, **42** (1975).

B—45/1

439

A Note on Conjectural Equilibria

DOUGLAS GALE

University of Cambridge

This note is a gloss on a paper by F. Hahn (1978). There is nothing really new here except the method of proving the two main results: existence of a non-Walrasian conjectural equilibrium and impossibility of rational conjectural equilibrium (in Hahn's sense). A great deal of use is made of the fact that competitive behaviour is a special case of conjectural behaviour and this helps draw out the connection between conjectural equilibria and W-equilibria.

1. A SIMPLE ECONOMIC MODEL

A *pure exchange economy* consists of a finite number m of traders, indexed by $i = 1, ..., m$. Each agent i is described by a set of possible *net trades* $X_i \subset R^l$ and a utility u_i (i.e. a continuous, real-valued function) defined on X_i. Let $L = \{r \in R^l \mid r_h \geq 0, h = 1, ..., l\}$ and $P = \{r \in R^l \mid r_h > 0, h = 1, ..., l\}$. Every economy $\mathscr{E} = \{(X_i, u_i)\}$ considered in the sequel is assumed to satisfy the following two conditions:

(I) u_i is strictly monotonic and strictly quasi-concave for $i = 1, ..., m$;

(II) X_i is closed, convex, bounded below and contains the origin of R^l in its interior for $i = 1, ..., m$.

Condition (I) is not necessary (local non-satiability would do) but it saves space. For any $p \in L$, let

$$\Gamma_i(p) = \{x_i \in X_i \mid p \cdot x_i \leq 0\}$$

and

$$x_i(p) = \{x_i \in \Gamma_i(p) \mid u_i(x_i) = \sup u_i(\Gamma_i(p))\}.$$

The following facts are well known:

(i) $x_i(p)$ contains at most one point and hence can be treated as defining a function over P.

(ii) At any point $p \in P$, $p \cdot x_i(p) = 0$.

(iii) $\mathscr{E}$ has at least one W-equilibrium, that is a point $p^* \in P$ such that $\Sigma_i x_i(p^*) = 0$.

Whenever a reference is made to " an economy $\mathscr{E}$ " it is understood to mean an economy satisfying (I) and (II) and hence (i)-(iii).

2. CONJECTURAL EQUILIBRIUM

In a conjectural economy each agent $i = 1, ..., m$ has a conjecture C_i. An agent i is assumed to receive a pair $(b_i, s_i) \in L \times L$ of quantity signals and a price signal $p \in P$. A typical signal (p, s_i, b_i) is denoted by $\sigma_i \in \Sigma = P \times L \times L$. If an agent receives a signal σ_i he conjectures that, for any $x_i \in R^l$, if he wishes to achieve the final net trades x_i then he must trade at the prices $C_i(\sigma_i, x_i) \in P$. Formally, a *conjecture* is a function $C_i : \Sigma \times R^l \to P$ satisfying the following conditions:

(C.1) C_i is continuous and for fixed $\sigma_i \in \Sigma$,

$C_i(\sigma_i, x_i) \cdot x_i$ defines a convex function of x_i;

C—45/1

Reprinted from *The Review of Economic Studies* **45**
(1978), 33–38.

(C.2) For each $h = 1, ..., l$, C_{ih} has the form

$C_{ih}(\sigma_i, x_i) = \hat{C}_{ih}(p, \zeta_{ih}, \xi_{ih})$, where $\zeta_{ih} = (x_{ih}^+ - b_{ih})^+$ and $\xi_{ih} = -(x_{ih}^- - s_{ih})^+$;

(C.3) For each $h = 1, ..., l$, $\hat{C}_{ih}(p, 0, 0) = p_h$ and

$\hat{C}_{ih}$ is increasing in ζ_{ih} and ξ_{ih}.

For each agent $i = 1, ..., m$, given a conjecture C_i and his other characteristics one can define a budget set correspondence $\Gamma_i \colon \Sigma \to X_i$ by putting

$$\Gamma_i(\sigma_i) = \{x_i \in X_i \mid C_i(\sigma_i, x_i) \cdot x_i \leq 0\}.$$

For any economy $\mathscr{E}$ and m-tuple of conjectures $\{C_i\}$ a *conjectural equilibrium* is an m-tuple $\{x_i^*\}$ of final net trades and an m-tuple $\{\sigma_i^*\}$ of signals such that

(E.1) $\sum_{i=1}^{i=m} x_i^* = 0$.

(E.2) For each $i = 1, ..., m$, $x_i^* \in \Gamma_i(\sigma_i^*)$ and for any $x_i \in \Gamma_i(\sigma_i^*)$, $u_i(x_i) \leq u_i(x_i^*)$.

(E.3) For each $i = 1, ..., m$, $\sigma_i^* = (p^*, b_i^*, s_i^*) \in \Sigma$ and $p^* = C_i(\sigma_i^*, x_i^*)$.

To show that a conjectural economy has a conjectural equilibrium, it is sufficient to show that it has a W-equilibrium but this is not very interesting. What would be required to show that it had a non-Walrasian equilibrium? The following proposition, whose proof is fairly obvious, suggests an answer.

Proposition 1. *If $C_i(\sigma_i, \cdot)$ is differentiable for all $\sigma_i \in \Sigma$, then any conjectural equilibrium of $(\mathscr{E}, C_1, ..., C_m)$, in which at most one side of each market is constrained, is a W-equilibrium.*

In a conjectural equilibrium, $-s_{ih}^* \leq x_{ih}^* \leq b_{ih}^*$ and by hypothesis $-s_{ih}^* < b_{ih}^*$ so the conjecture is flat for x_{ih} in the non-degenerate interval $[-s_{ih}^*, b_{ih}^*]$. Then differentiability implies that

$$\left. \frac{\partial C_{ih}}{\partial x_{ih}} \right|_{x_{ih} = x_{ih}^*} = 0.$$

In order for a non-Walrasian equilibrium to occur, there must be a " kink " in one of the conjectures. For a given $\sigma_i \in \Sigma$, $C_i(\sigma_i, x_i) \cdot x_i$ defines a convex function of x_i by (C.1), and so from (C.2), $C_{ih}(\sigma_i, x_i)x_{ih}$ is a function of x_{ih} alone, for fixed values of σ_i, and is convex in x_{ih}. Consequently it possesses right- and left-hand derivatives for x_{ih} everywhere and derivatives almost everywhere, and being a function of a single variable (when σ_i is fixed) it is continuously differentiable when it is differentiable. Here a conjecture is " kinked " if and only if it is non-differentiable, i.e. if the right- and left-hand derivatives are unequal.

Let p^* be an isolated W-equilibrium and suppose that for some agent i and commodity h, say $i = h = 1$, $x_{11}(p^*)$ is positive. Let all quantity signals other than b_{11} be very large, so they are never effective, and write $\sigma^* = (p^*, b_{11}^*)$, where $b_{11}^* = x_{11}(p^*)$. C_{11} has a " kink " at $(\sigma^*, x_1(p^*))$ only if

$$\left(\frac{\partial C_{11}}{\partial x_{11}} \right)^+_{x_{11} = b_{11}^*} > \left(\frac{\partial C_{11}}{\partial x_{11}} \right)^-_{x_{11} = b_{11}^*} = 0,$$

where $(\cdot)^+$ and $(\cdot)^-$ indicate right- and left-hand derivatives, respectively. On the other hand, if $x_1(p^*) \in \text{int } X_1$, and u_1 is continuously differentiable near $x_1(p^*)$, then

$$\lambda_1^* p_1^* = \left. \frac{\partial u_1}{\partial x_{11}} \right|_{x_1 = x_1(p^*)}$$

It is easy to see that an increase in b_{11} does not affect agent 1's behaviour and a small decrease will cause x_1 to change continuously. But since C_{11} is continuously differentiable *around* $x_{11} = b_{11}$ if $x_{11} > b_{11}$ it must be true that, at that point,

$$\frac{\partial u_1}{\partial x_{11}} = \lambda_1 \left(p_1^* + \frac{\partial C_{11}}{\partial x_{11}} \right),$$

which is impossible for b_{11} sufficiently close to b_{11}^*, since under the assumptions made, each of these terms moves continuously. The same argument extends to changes in p around p^* if it is assumed that where C_{11} is differentiable in x_{11} that derivative is continuous with respect to $\sigma = (p, b_{11})$. In short, if u_1 is smooth and C_{11} has enough smoothness apart from the kink, then around σ^*, b_{11} acts like a Dreze-type quantity constraint. Formally,

if u_1 is smooth in some neighbourhood of $x_1(p^*) \in$ int X_1 and if $\partial C_{11}(\sigma, x_1)/\partial x_{11}$ exists and is continuous with respect to (σ, x_1) in some neighbourhood of $(\sigma^*, x_1(p^*))$, except where $b_{11} = x_{11}$ then for every $\sigma = (p, b_{11})$ in some neighbourhood of $\sigma^* = (p^*, b_{11}^*)$ the optimum value of x_{11} is less than or equal to b_{11}.

This result at least suggests the kind of role the kink plays in the model; rather than extend the result, the conclusion is taken as the basis of a definition (below).

An agent i is said to have a *competitive conjecture* C_i^* if $C_i^*(\sigma_i, x_i) = p$ for all $\sigma_i = (p, b_i, s_i) \in \Sigma$ and $x_i \in R^l$. From the conjectural economy $\{\mathscr{E}, C_1, ..., C_m\}$ one can derive a much simpler economy $(\mathscr{E}, C_1^*, ..., C_m^*)$ in which C_i^* is a competitive conjecture if $i = 2, ..., m$ and

$$C_{1h}^*(\sigma_i, x_i) = p_h \quad (h = 2, ..., l)$$

$$C_{11}^*(\sigma_i, x_i) = \max \{p_1, C_{11}(\sigma_i, x_i)\}$$

for all $\sigma_i = (p, b_i, s_i) \in \Sigma$ and $x_i \in R^l$.

For all agents except agent 1, the original conjecture is replaced by the competitive conjecture, i.e. the belief that the agent can trade as much as he wants at the signalled prices. The first agent makes the same assumption except in respect of the first market. On that market he makes the original conjecture on the demand side and makes the competitive conjecture on the supply side. All quantity signals except b_{11} are irrelevant now. Let $\Gamma_1^*(\sigma)$ denote the set of feasible net trades relative to the signal $\sigma = (p, b_{11}) \in P \times R_+$ and the conjecture C_1^*.

Proposition 2. *Let $x_1^*: P \times R_+ \to X_1$ be defined by $u_1(x_1^*(\sigma)) = \sup u_1(\Gamma_1^*(\sigma))$ and $x_1^*(\sigma) \in \Gamma_1^*(\sigma)$ for each $\sigma \in P \times R_+$. x_1^* is a well-defined, continuous function, and $C_1^*(\sigma) \cdot x_1^*(\sigma) = 0$.*

The proof is entirely routine.

Definition. Let $\sigma^* \in P \times R_+$ be a signal $\sigma^* = (p^*, b_{11}^*)$, where p^* is a W-equilibrium and $b_{11}^* = x_{11}(p^*) > 0$. C_1^* is said to have a " kink " if there exists a $\delta > 0$ such that $\| \sigma - \sigma^* \| < \delta$ implies $x_{11}^*(\sigma) \leq b_{11}$.

The choice of agent 1 and commodity 1 is obviously immaterial.

It has already been stated that if $f: P \to R^l$ is the market excess demand function of an economy $\mathscr{E}$ satisfying (I) and (II) then for some $p^* \in P$, $f(p^*) = 0$. Without loss of generality f can be regarded as mapping Δ, the interior of the l-dimensional simplex, into R^l. Then the folllowing result is immediate.

Proposition 3. *If there is a unique $p^* \in \Delta$ such that $f(p^*) = 0$, if $g: \Delta \to R^l$ is continuous and $p \cdot g(p) = 0$ for all $p \in \Delta$ and there exists a very small, open neighbourhood N of p^* such that $p \notin N$ implies $f(p) = g(p)$, then for some $p^{**} \in N$, $g(p^{**}) = 0$.*

This suggests the following strategy. Make b_{11} a function of p, say $b_{11}(p)$, such that b_{11} is ineffective if $p \notin N$. Then $\sigma = \sigma(p) = (p, b_{11}(p))$ and x_1^* is a function of p such that $x_1^*(\sigma(p)) = x_1(p)$ if $p \notin N$. If b_{11} is only slightly effective when $p \notin N$, the " kink " ensures $x_{11}^*(\sigma(p)) \leqq b_{11}(p)$ and this implies $C_1^*(\sigma(p)) = p$ for all $p \in \Delta$ as required by (E.3). Also, $C_1^*(\sigma(p)) \cdot x_1^*(\sigma(p)) = 0$ (Proposition 2) implies $p \cdot x_1^*(\sigma(p)) = 0$ for all $p \in \Delta$. Proposition 3 does the rest.

Theorem 1. *If $\mathscr{E}$ satisfies* (I) *and* (II) *and possesses a unique W-equilibrium $p^* \in P$, where $x_{11}(p^*)>0$ and if C_1^* has a " kink " at $\sigma^*(p^*, x_{11}(p^*))$, then $\{\mathscr{E}; C_1, ..., C_m\}$ has a non-Walrasian conjectural equilibrium in which at most one side of any market is constrained.*

Proof. Since $x_{11}(p^*)>0$ there is an open neighbourhood N of p^* in Δ such that $p \in N$ implies $x_{11}(p) \geqq \varepsilon>0$ for some ε. Choose N so that $\overline{N}\subset\Delta$. Because of the " kink " there exists $\delta>0$ and a neighbourhood N^1 of p^* such that: (1) $N^1\subset N$. (2) If $p \in N^1$ and $\| b_{11}-b_{11}^* \| \leqq 2\delta$ then $x_{11}^*(\sigma) \leqq b_{11}$ (where $b_{11}^* = x_{11}(p^*)$). (3) If

$$p \in N^1, \| x_{11}(p)-x_{11}(p^*)\| \leqq \delta$$

(because $x_{11}(\cdot)$ is continuous). If $\| b_{11}-x_{11}(p)\| \leqq \delta$ and $p \in N^1$, then $\| b_{11}-b_{11}^* \| \leqq \delta$ and so $x_{11}(\sigma) \leqq b_{11}$.

Let $\lambda: \Delta\rightarrow[0, 1]$ be a continuous function such that: (1) $p \notin N^1$ implies $\lambda(p) = 1$. (2) $p \in N^1$ implies $\lambda(p)<1$ and $\|(1-\lambda(p))x_{11}(p)\|<\delta$. Then putting $b_{11}(p) = \lambda(p)x_{11}(p)$ for all $p \in \Delta$ the preceding discussion implies $x_{11}^*(p, b_{11}(p)) \leqq b_{11}(p)$ for all $p \in \Delta$. Define f and g by $f(p) = \Sigma_i x_i(p)$ and $g(p) = x_1^*(p, b_{11}(p))+ \sum_{i=2}^{i=m} x_i(p)$.

Then Proposition 3 implies the existence of $p^{**} \in N$ such that $g(p^{**}) = 0$. The required equilibrium is $\sigma^* = (p^{**}, b_{11}(p^{**}))$.

Corollary 1. *The conjectural equilibrium is Pareto efficient relative to the budget constraints $p^{**} \cdot x_i = 0$, $i = 1, ..., m$.*

Proof. Obvious, because agents $i = 2, ..., m$ are perfect competitors.

3. RATIONAL CONJECTURES

The following definitions are found in Hahn (1978). If $x_i^* \in X_i$, for some fixed $i = 1, ..., m$ and $\sigma^* = (\sigma_1^*, ..., \sigma_m^*) \in \Sigma^m$, and for $j \neq i$, x_j^* is most preferred in $\Gamma_j(\sigma_j^*)$ then $\{\sigma^*, x_1^*, ..., x_m^*\}$ is called a *conjectural equilibrium relative to x_i^* for agent i* if and only if:

(Ex 1) $\sigma_j^* = (p^*, b_j^*, s_j^*)$ and $p^* = C_j(\sigma_j^*, x_j^*)$ for $j \neq i$;

(Ex 2) $\sum_{i=1}^{i=m} x_i^* = 0$;

(Ex 3) $\sigma_i^* = (p^*, b_i^*, s_i^*)$ and $-s_i^* \leqq x_i^* \leqq b_i^*$.

Although (Ex 1) to (Ex 3) imply that $x_i^* \in \Gamma_i(\sigma_i^*)$, x_i^* is not necessarily most preferred.

If $x_i^* \in X_i$, then x_i^* is said to be *equilibrium feasible* for agent i if there exists a conjectural equilibrium relative to x_i^* for agent i. Otherwise it is called equilibrium infeasible. A conjectural equilibrium $\{x_i\}, \{\sigma_i\}$ is called a *rational conjectural equilibrium* if and only if for each agent $i = 1, ..., m$, if x_i^* is possible for i and preferred to $x_i(\sigma)$, then x_i^* is equilibrium infeasible for i. Hahn proves that under certain conditions $\mathscr{E}$ has no rational conjectural equilibria. A much simpler and more general proof is available, however.

Notice first of all that it is only necessary to consider W-equilibria ($\mathscr{E}$ has at least one such). If p^* is a W-equilibrium and σ another conjectural equilibrium (possibly also Walrasian) then at least one agent must be worse off at σ than at p^* (otherwise the strict quasi-concavity of preferences would imply that the W-equilibrium was not Pareto efficient). Hence, σ is not " rational ". In particular, if there is more than one W-equilibrium, then they rule out one another as possible rational conjectural equilibria. There is no loss of generality, then, in assuming $\mathscr{E}$ has a unique W-equilibrium.

If $x_i^* \in X_i$ for some agent i, then a special case of a conjectural equilibrium relative to x_i for agent i is a *competitive equilibrium relative to* x_i^* *for agent i*, that is, a price system $p \in P$ such that

(CEx 1) $$x_i^* = -\Sigma_{j \neq i} x_j(p).$$

Now the expression on the right-hand side of (i) is simply a parametric form of the Marshallian offer curve. If by sliding along the offer curve in the vicinity of p^* an agent can make himself better off than he is at the W-equilibrium, then p^* is not a rational conjectural equilibrium. This is generally possible unless p^* is a no-trade equilibrium (that is, unless the original endowments are a Pareto-efficient allocation). A simple formal proof requires one additional assumption.

(III) For each $i = 1, ..., m$, u_i (resp. $x_i(\cdot)$) is continuously differentiable over some small neighbourhood of $x_i(p^*)$ (resp. p^*) and $x_i(p^*)$ belongs to the interior of X_i.

Choose N, a neighbourhood of p^*, so that the conditions of (III) are satisfied for $p \in N$ and so that for any $p \in N$

$$x(p, i) \in X_i \quad (i = 1, ..., m)$$

where

$$x(p, i) \equiv -\Sigma_{j \neq 1} x_j(p).$$

A necessary condition for p^* to be a rational conjectural equilibrium is that for each $p \in N$ and $i = 1, ..., m$

$$u_i(x(p, i)) \leqq u_i(x_i(p^*)) = u_i(x(p^*, i)).$$

That is, $p = p^*$ is a local maximizer of $u_i(x(p, i))$ for each $i = 1, ..., m$. By (III), for $i = 1, ..., m$

$$\nabla u_i \cdot \frac{\partial x(p, i)}{\partial p_h}\bigg|_{p = p_h} = 0 \quad \text{for } h = 1, ..., l;$$

(*)   i.e. $$p^* \cdot \frac{\partial x(p^*, i)}{\partial p_h} = 0 \quad \text{for } h = 1, ..., l.$$

Since $x(p, i) - x(p, j) \equiv x_j(p) - x_i(p)$, (*) implies

$$p^* \cdot \frac{\partial x_j(p^*)}{\partial p_h} = p^* \cdot \frac{\partial x_i(p^*)}{\partial p_h}$$

but from the budget constraint this implies

$$x_{jh}(p^*) = x_{ih}(p^*)$$

for $h = 1, ..., l$ and $i, j = 1, ..., m$. Hence,

Theorem 2. *If $\mathscr{E}$ satisfies (I)-(III) and either (i) $\mathscr{E}$ has more than W-equilibrium or (ii) the allocation* $(x_1, ..., x_m) = 0$ *is inefficient, then* $\{\mathscr{E}, C_1, ..., C_m\}$ *has no rational conjectural equilibria.*

Hahn makes an assumption which he calls *variety*. For all $\sigma \in \Sigma^m$ and each $h = 1, ..., l$ there are agents $i, j \neq 1$ such that $x_{ih}(\sigma) x_{jh}(\sigma) < 0$. This implies that $x_i(p^*) \neq 0$ for some $i = 1, ..., m$, of course.

4. CONCLUSION

There is no guarantee that a conjectural equilibrium, even if it is non-Walrasian, is very different from the W-equilibrium. By choosing the neighbourhood N in Proposition 3 smaller and smaller one generates an infinite number of conjectural equilibria, approaching arbitrarily close to the W-equilibrium. But choosing N larger accomplishes nothing.

If a net trade is a point on some agents' offer curve then there is a conjectural equilibrium relative to that net trade. Thus, each offer curve represents a whole family of conjectural equilibria relative to some trade. It is not surprising that no conjectural equilibrium dominates all of them. To require a conjectural equilibrium to be " rational " is perhaps asking too much.

First version received February 1977; *final version accepted May* 1977 (*Eds.*).

I am greatly indebted to Oliver Hart for helpful discussions and in particular for pointing out that it is only necessary to show that the W-equilibrium is not a rational conjectural equilibrium. Frank Hahn, Peter Hammond and an anonymous referee made helpful suggestions about the exposition.

REFERENCE

Hahn, F. (1978). " On Non-Walrasian Equilibria ", *Review of Economic Studies*, **45**, (This issue).

A MODEL OF IMPERFECT COMPETITION WITH KEYNESIAN FEATURES*

OLIVER HART

The recent literature on "the reappraisal of Keynes" has viewed Keynesian equilibria as arising when prices are fixed and effective demands and supplies are equilibrated through the adjustment of quantities. One problem with this approach is that it lacks a theory of price determination—in particular, of why prices are fixed. In the present paper, we show that a number of Keynesian features arise in a model in which prices are fully flexible, but where agents have some monopoly power. One advantage of this approach is that it provides a theory of the determination of both prices and quantities.

I. INTRODUCTION

In the last few years, a considerable amount of work has been done under the general heading of "the reappraisal of Keynesian economics." This work has taken as its starting point Clower's observation (see Clower [1965]) that, away from a Walrasian equilibrium, effective demands and supplies rather than their notional counterparts will govern the behavior of the economic system. This has led a number of economists to study "Non-Walrasian equilibria" in which prices are fixed and effective demands and supplies are equilibrated through the adjustment of quantities and rationing (for a survey of this work, see Grandmont [1977]).

While this reappraisal has undoubtedly led to more rigorously formulated Keynesian models than existed previously, the fixed-price approach would seem to have a major shortcoming. In particular, it lacks a theory of how prices are determined. More specifically, the fixed price approach does not explain why, if prices are at non-Walrasian levels, it does not pay a rationed seller (respectively, buyer) to reduce (respectively, increase) his price by a small amount in order to increase sales (respectively, purchases). In other words, the fixed price approach does not explain how a non-Walrasian equilibrium can be sustained once one allows agents to change prices.

One way around this difficulty is to drop the commonly made assumption that agents are perfect competitors, i.e., that they face

* I am very grateful to Frank Hahn for numerous helpful discussions. I have also benefited from the comments of Philip Dybvig, Sandy Grossman, Louis Makowski, Roy Radner, Bob Rowthorn, Steve Ross, and seminar participants at Johns Hopkins University and the University of Pennsylvania. Finally, I would like to thank an editor and two anonymous referees for helpful suggestions. All errors are, of course, my own. Research support from NSF Grant SOC 790/430 is gratefully acknowledged.

Reprinted from *The Quarterly Review of Economics* **97** (1982), 109–138. © by the President and Fellow of Harvard College. Reprinted by permission of John Wiley & Sons, Inc.

perfectly elastic demand or supply curves.[1] This is the approach adopted here. We shall show that the equilibrium of an economy in which prices are fully flexible, but where agents are imperfectly competitive, exhibits a number of non-Walrasian or Keynesian features. In such an economy, an agent who would like, say, to sell more at the going price than he is able to may not find it in his interest to reduce price because the consequent increase in demand may not offset the loss in his revenue.

The imperfect competition that we analyze in this paper will be of a particular variety. Specifically, we shall assume that each agent is negligible relative to the aggregate economy, but we shall permit some agents to be of significant size relative to the particular markets in which they operate. Thus, the imperfect competition that we shall deal with is close to monopolistic competition in the sense of Chamberlin [1933], although product differentiation will not be emphasized in our analysis. In the model that we study, workers (through the formation of syndicates or unions) have monopoly power in the labor market, and firms have monopoly power in the product market (there is no bilateral monopoly). Workers and firms are assumed to set wages and prices optimally, given the demand curves facing them. The position of these demand curves will turn out to depend on the level of per capita income in the economy. Given our assumption that each agent is negligible relative to the aggregate economy, per capita income is a variable that no agent by himself can affect. Thus, each agent takes this variable as given. Per capita income is, however, determined endogenously in equilibrium as a consequence of the optimizing activities of agents. We shall show that an imperfectly competitive economy of this type exhibits the following Keynesian features: (1) in equilibrium, the economy will in general operate at too low a level of activity, and there will be underemployment; (2) an exogenous increase in demand for current consumption will increase employment and output, the latter by more than the initial increase in demand, i.e., there is a multiplier greater than unity; (3) changes in demand, which in the Walrasian model cause price changes but not output changes, may under imperfect competition lead to output changes and no price changes; (4) there is a role for a simple balanced budget fiscal policy to increase employment.

This paper is not the first attempt to develop a model of imper-

---

1. This is not the only approach. Other possibilities are to suppose that prices do not change in response to excess demand or supply for long-term contracting reasons (see, e.g., Azariadis [1975]) or because prices are a screening device (see, e.g., Weiss [1980]).

fect competition with Keynesian features.[2] One important difference between the present approach and most previous approaches is that we shall assume that agents maximize utility or profit, knowing the objective demand curves facing them, where these demand curves are, in the case of firms (respectively, workers), based on the Cournot-Nash assumption that other firms' production plans (respectively, other workers' supplies of labor) are fixed. One advantage of the Cournot-Nash approach is that it makes the amount of monopoly power possessed by each agent endogenous to the model. If an agent is small relative to his market, he will have little monopoly power and will behave approximately competitively; while, if the agent is large, he will have substantial monopoly power, and there will be a significant deviation from the competitive outcome. Thus, in particular, the Cournot-Nash approach permits us to view the competitive outcome (more precisely, an approximately competitive outcome) as arising in situations where agents set prices optimally (as opposed to taking prices as given), but where each agent is very small relative to his market. (Our approach is therefore consistent with a number of recent papers on noncooperative approaches to perfect competition; see the *JET* symposium [1980].)[3]

Unfortunately, as is well-known by now, the Cournot-Nash assumption introduces a serious nonexistence problem (see Roberts and Sonnenschein [1977]). We avoid this by considering a particularly simple model, and by making a number of strong assumptions about demand functions. There is no doubt, however, that generalizing the model significantly could be hard. For this reason, the analysis presented here should be considered more as an extended example than as a general model.

The paper is organized as follows. The basic model is presented in Sections II–III. In Section IV the multiplier and the role of fiscal policy are examined. In Section V a number of extensions to the model are considered. Finally, concluding remarks appear in Section VI.

2. Other contributions in this area include Benassy [1976, 1978], Grandmont-Laroque [1976], Hahn [1978], and Negishi [1978].

3. Most of the previous contributions that model Keynesian phenomena in terms of imperfect competition assume—in the spirit of Negishi [1960]—that agents act on the basis of conjectured or perceived demand curves, which may not in any sense be the true ones (an exception to this is Hahn [1978]). The conjectural approach, in contrast to the Cournot-Nash approach, does not distinguish between small and large economies. In particular, a highly monopolistic outcome can be sustained in a large economy if agents are given appropriate conjectures and a competitive outcome can be sustained in a small economy with different conjectures.

II. THE MODEL

We now develop a simple general equilibrium model of imperfect competition with Keynesian features. As noted in the introduction, a feature of the model is that all agents are negligible relative to the aggregate economy, but some agents are significant relative to the markets they operate in. In particular, workers have some monopoly power in labor markets, while firms have some monopoly power in product markets.

We shall assume that the aggregate economy consists of N "identical" firms and mN "identical" consumers, where N is a large number (the reason for the quotation marks will become clear later). There will be assumed to be three goods: labor, a produced good, and a nonproduced good (it is natural to think of the nonproduced good as being an asset such as money, but such an interpretation may be misleading; see the remarks in Section VI). Each consumer has an endowment of labor, given by T, an endowment of the nonproduced good, given by $\bar{k}$, and initial shareholdings in the various firms. Consumers supply labor to the firms, which use it to produce the produced good. This good is consumed by consumers, who also consume the nonproduced good. The economy is assumed to last only one period, and so there is no saving or investment.

In order to develop an appropriate model of imperfect competition, we shall assume that, for trading purposes, the economy is divided up into a large number of different labor and output markets (as we shall see below, the number of output markets will generally exceed the number of labor markets). Each market will be assumed to be a small version of the aggregate economy in the sense that the ratio of firms to consumers is $1:m$. It is assumed that agents are assigned to the various markets and cannot move between them (this is the sense in which they are not really identical). In addition, there is no trading across markets.

Consider first the product markets. We assume that these are identical and that each contains $1/\Theta$ firms and m/Θ consumers (where $1 > \Theta > 0$). We allow for the possibility that each firm is of significant size relative to its market (in particular, $1/\Theta$ can be small), but we assume that individual consumers are negligible relative to the market (i.e., m is large). As a result, firms have some monopoly power in the output market, while consumers have none.

In contrast, in the case of the labor markets, it will be assumed that consumers (or workers) have monopoly power, while firms do not. All labor markets will be assumed to be identical and to contain q

firms and mq consumers. In order to formalize the idea that workers have monopoly power, we assume that they form unions or syndicates. Each labor market will be assumed to have $1/\rho$ identical syndicates (where $1 > \rho > 0$), where each syndicate has $mq\rho$ members. We shall take q to be large (this justifies the assumption that firms have no monopoly power), but allow $1/\rho$ to be small (this justifies the assumption that syndicates have monopoly power).

In what follows, we take m to be fixed, and consider how the equilibrium of the economy depends on Θ and ρ (the equilibrium of the economy will turn out to be independent of N and q). Note that Θ, ρ are measures of how monopolistic the typical product market and labor market are. In particular, as we shall see, the limiting cases $\Theta = 0$, $\rho = 0$ correspond to perfect competition in these markets.

We shall make the following additional assumptions:

A1. Any two firms in the same product market are also in the same labor market.

A2. The consumers from any given labor market are distributed uniformly across the different product markets, i.e., there are $mq/N\Theta$ consumers from a given labor market in each product market.

A3. Each consumer owns a fraction $1/mN$ of every firm.

An implication of A1 is that the number of labor markets is less than or equal to the number of product markets. The reasons for assuming A1–A3 will become clear shortly.

The division of the economy into many subeconomies, or markets, may seem artificial. One way to think of this is that there are actually many different qualities or types of goods and labor in the economy, rather than just one type, and that different markets represent different types. If consumers and firms have differing tastes, endowments, and technologies, it is then quite natural for them to locate in different markets. (We do not, however, model the choice of which market to be in.) What is really important for our purposes is that the assumption that there are many markets allows us to capture the idea that individual agents are negligible relative to the aggregate economy, but are significant relative to the particular markets they operate in.

We shall assume that firms act as Cournot-Nash oligopolists in the product market; i.e., each firm chooses its output to maximize profits, taking as given the outputs of other firms in its market. An important implication of A2–A3 is that no firm can influence the income (or wealth) of consumers in its market. Hence firms take the income of consumers as exogenous. In addition, since individual firms are small relative to their respective labor markets, their activities have no influence on the wage rate they face. Hence firms also take wages as given. Finally, firms are assumed to know the true demand curves facing them (these will be described below).

Syndicates are also assumed to act as Cournot-Nash oligopolists in the labor market. For most of the paper, we shall suppose that syndicate members obtain neither utility nor disutility out of work. Given this, we shall assume that each syndicate chooses its supply of labor to maximize total wage receipts, taking as given the supplies of other syndicates in its market. We shall assume that members of a syndicate are treated symmetrically in the sense that if the supply of labor by a particular syndicate is L, then each member supplies labor equal to $L/mq\rho$ (thus each member is underemployed to the extent of $T - L/mq\rho$—in our analysis, there will be underemployment, but no unemployment). Since syndicate membership is fixed, it follows that maximizing total wage receipts is equivalent to maximizing wages per member.[4] In making their supply decision, syndicates are assumed to recognize that a reduction in labor supply will drive up the wage rate, and that this in turn will influence the Cournot-Nash equilibrium in the product market that their firms operate in, and hence the demand for labor.

In order to complete the model, it remains to specify agents' tastes and production possibilities. Each firm will be assumed to have a production function of the form $L = C(Y)$, where L is labor and Y is output. In order to simplify matters, we shall assume that $L = aY^{\alpha}$, where $a > 0$; i.e., the elasticity of output with respect to labor is constant. We also assume that $\alpha \geq 1$; i.e., there are nonincreasing returns to scale (this assumption can be relaxed, however; see Section V). Each consumer will be assumed to have a utility function $U(k,y)$, where k is consumption of the nonproduced good and y is consumption of the produced good. For most of the paper we shall assume that there is no disutility of work (however, see Section V). We make the following assumptions about U:

---

4. An alternative justification can also be given for maximizing wage income. Suppose that each worker is either fully employed or fully unemployed. Suppose also that when the wage is set, workers do not know which category they will be in. Then, if each worker is risk neutral, workers will want syndicates to maximize $(L/mq\rho)wT$, i.e., to maximize wL. Note that in this case we get unemployment rather than just underemployment.

A4. U is nondecreasing in k and y, and is increasing in k and y when $k,y > 0$.[5]

A5. U is continuous, homothetic, and strictly quasi-concave.

A6. U is differentiable if $k > 0$, $y > 0$, and $\partial U(0,y)/\partial k$ is defined and equal to infinity for all $y > 0$.

The homotheticity of U makes it easy to compute the demand for the produced good in a particular product market. Let I be the total income (or wealth), i.e., wages plus profits plus value of the endowment of the nonproduced good, of all the consumers in this market. Then total demand in the market is simply the solution to

$$\max U(k,y) \quad \text{subject to} \quad k + py \le I,$$
$$k,y \ge 0,$$

where p is the price of the produced good, and the price of the nonproduced good is normalized to be 1.

We may write the solution to the above problem as $y = h(p)I$. Clearly h is nonincreasing in p (all goods are normal under homothetic preferences). Let $\bar{p} = \inf\{p > 0 \mid h(p) = 0\}$, where we set $\bar{p} = \infty$ if $h(p) > 0$ for all $p > 0$. In other words, $\bar{p}$ is the lowest price at which demand for the produced good becomes zero. We shall assume that h is twice differentiable for $0 < p < \bar{p}$, differentiable to the left at $p = \bar{p}$ if $\bar{p} < \infty$, and that $h' < 0$ for all $0 < p < \bar{p}$. The following additional properties of $h(p)$, which will turn out to be useful, are implied by the assumption of utility-maximizing behavior:

(1) $$ph(p) < 1 \quad \text{for all } p > 0;$$

(2) $$\lim_{p \to 0} h(p) = \infty, \quad \lim_{p \to \infty} h(p) = 0;$$

(3) $$\frac{h(p)}{1 - ph(p)}$$

is decreasing in p for $0 < p < \bar{p}$, and hence $h'(p) + h^2(p) \le 0$ for all $0 < p < \bar{p}$.

Equation (1) follows from A6 and the fact that expenditure on the produced good cannot exceed income. The second part of (2) follows from the same consideration. The first part of (2) is a consequence of A4. Finally, (3) follows from A6 and the fact that, since

---

5. I.e., $U(k',y') \ge U(k,y)$ if $k' \ge k$, $y' \ge y$; $U(k',y) > U(k,y)$ if $k' > k > 0$, $y > 0$; $U(k,y') > U(k,y)$ if $y' > y > 0$, $k > 0$.

preferences are homothetic, $y/k = h(p)/(1 - ph(p))$ is a nonincreasing function of the price ratio p.

III. The Determination of Equilibrium

We now compute the equilibrium of the economy. In what follows we shall confine our attention to symmetric equilibria in which income, prices, etc. in each market are the same.

Equilibrium in a Typical Product Market

Consider a typical product market. By A2 and A3, the income of consumers in this market comes (almost) entirely from wages and profits earned in other markets, and from endowment of the non-produced good. Therefore, no firm has any influence on the income in its product market.[6] As above, denote this income by I. Then firms face a demand curve given by $h(p)I$, where I is exogenous. By assumption, each firm maximizes profit, taking the *outputs* of other firms in its market and the wage rate as given. Let Y be the output of a typical firm and Y' the total output of all other firms in the market. Then, if $w > 0$ is the wage rate, the equilibrium price p must maximize

(4) $$p\{h(p)I - Y'\} - wC(h(p)I - Y').$$

For if this expression is higher at $\tilde{p} \neq p$, then by selecting the output level $(h(\tilde{p})I - Y')$, the typical firm can increase its profits under the Cournot-Nash assumption. Equation (4) yields the first-order condition,

(5) $$[ph'(p) + h(p)]I - Y' \geq wC'(h(p)I - Y')h'(p)I,$$

with equality if $Y + Y' = h(p)I > 0$, i.e., if $p < \overline{p}$.

Since the left-hand side of (5) is decreasing in Y' and the right-hand side is nondecreasing in Y' (recall that $h' < 0$), there cannot be two different Y's satisfying (5). This shows that every Cournot-Nash equilibrium is symmetric: all firms choose the same output. Hence, since there are $1/\Theta$ firms, $Y = \Theta h(p)I$, and $Y' = (1 - \Theta)h(p)I$. Therefore, (5) simplifies to

(6) $$p\left(1 + \frac{\Theta}{\eta(p)}\right) \leq wC'(\Theta h(p)I) = wa\Theta^{\alpha-1}h(p)^{\alpha-1}I^{\alpha-1}$$

6. Furthermore, if a firm changes its production plan, this will have a negligible influence on income in any other market, and hence there is no reason to expect agents in other markets to react. I am grateful to Philip Dybvig and Steve Ross for pointing out that an earlier version of A2 and A3 was not strong enough to ensure this.

with equality

$$\text{if } p < \bar{p},$$

where

$$\eta(p) \equiv \frac{h'(p)p}{h(p)} < 0$$

is the price elasticity of demand.

Equation (6) is simply the formula marginal revenue equals marginal cost for each firm. The condition can also be expressed in quantities rather than prices. Let $f \equiv h^{-1}$ be the inverse of the demand function h. Then, $Y = \Theta h(p)I$ implies that $p = f(Y/\Theta I)$, and so, using the fact that $f' = 1/h'$, we may rewrite (6) as

(7)
$$f\left(\frac{Y}{\Theta I}\right) + \Theta \left[\frac{Y}{\Theta I} f'\left(\frac{Y}{\Theta I}\right)\right] = wC'(Y)$$

as long as the output of each firm, $Y > 0$.

Equation (6) (or (7)) is a necessary condition for a Cournot-Nash equilibrium to be achieved at price p (or output Y), but it is not generally sufficient because it guarantees only that each firm's profits are at a stationary point. We now make an assumption which ensures that (6) (or (7)) is necessary and sufficient. In particular, we assume that marginal revenue is decreasing in output or increasing in price.

A7.
$$\gamma(p) \equiv p\left(1 + \frac{\Theta}{\eta(p)}\right)$$

is an increasing function of p for p satisfying $0 < p < \bar{p}$. In addition, $\gamma(p) > 0$ for $0 < p < \bar{p}$.

We make this assumption for the purely pragmatic reason that, in its absence, the analysis becomes much more complicated. See Section V, Remark D.[7]

LEMMA 1. Assume A1–A7. Then, given $w > 0$, $I > 0$, there is a unique solution to (6), which we denote $p(w,I)$. Furthermore, there is a Cournot-Nash equilibrium in which the price of the produced

---

7. Note that the first part of A7 will certainly be satisfied if Θ is small; i.e., if the product market is approximately perfectly competitive. It will also be satisfied if $|\eta(p)|$ is nondecreasing in p. It follows that the first part of A7 holds for the cases where $U(k,y)$ is Cobb-Douglas or C.E.S. For general utility functions $U(k,y)$ and arbitrary Θ, however, the first part of A7 may not be satisifed. The second part of A7 is made for simplicity and can easily be relaxed.

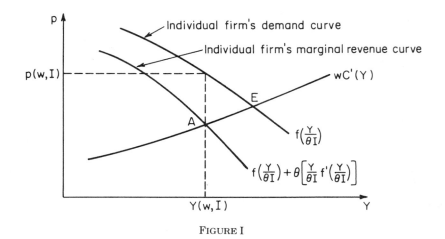

Individual firm's demand curve

Individual firm's marginal revenue curve

$wC'(Y)$

$p(w,I)$

E

A

$f\left(\frac{Y}{\theta I}\right)$

$f\left(\frac{Y}{\theta I}\right) + \theta\left[\frac{Y}{\theta I} f'\left(\frac{Y}{\theta I}\right)\right]$

$Y(w,I)$

FIGURE I

good is $p(w,I)$ and each firm supplies $Y(w,I) = \Theta h(p(w,I))$ $I(Y(w,I)$ is the unique solution to (7)). Finally, if $h(p\ (w,\ I)) > 0$, this Cournot-Nash equilibrium is unique.

Proof. See Appendix.

The Cournot-Nash equilibrium is illustrated in Figure I at A. It is clear from the diagram that each firm underproduces relative to the Walrasian equilibrium E. It is also clear that if we increase the size of a typical product market, while keeping per capita income constant—that is, if we reduce Θ and increase I so that ΘI remains constant—then the marginal revenue curve in Figure I moves upward, $Y(w,I)$ increases, and $p(w,I)$ decreases. Thus, a reduction in Θ corresponds to a reduction in monopoly power. In the limit as $\Theta \rightarrow 0$ (ΘI constant) A converges to E, so that perfect competition arises as a special case of the model where $\Theta = 0$.

Equilibrium in a Typical Labor Market

We have shown how equilibrium is determined in the product market for a fixed w and I. We turn now to a consideration of equilibrium in the labor market.

By Assumption A1, each labor market contains the firms from $q\Theta$ different product markets. Given the wage rate w in a particular labor market, a Cournot-Nash equilibrium in each of these product markets will be determined according to (6). The demand for labor at wage w in a labor market is therefore given by

(8) $L(w,I) = qC(\Theta h(p(w,I))I).$

It is easy to see that A7 implies that $p(w,I)$ is increasing in w (see also Figure I). Therefore, the demand for labor is a *decreasing* function of the wage rate, for each I.

As noted previously, we assume that there are $1/\rho$ identical syndicates in each labor market and that each syndicate makes the Cournot-Nash assumption that the total supply of labor by other syndicates is fixed. In addition, by A2 and A3, no syndicate has any influence on the income in the product markets in which the firms it works for operate, and so I is also taken as fixed. Each syndicate maximizes wage receipts,

$$(9) \qquad w\tilde{L}(w,\dots),$$

where $\tilde{L}(w,\dots)$ is the demand curve it faces. In view of the Cournot-Nash assumption, $\tilde{L}(w,\dots) = L(w,I) - L'$, where L' is the supply of all other syndicates in the particular labor market. Since $L(w,I)$ is decreasing in w, the choice for syndicates is between high wages and low employment and low wages and high employment.

A parallel argument to that of equations (4)–(6) yields the first-order condition,

$$(10) \qquad \left(w\left(1 + \frac{\rho}{\epsilon(w,I)}\right)\right) \geq 0,$$

with equality if there is underemployment, i.e., if

$$L(w,I) < mqT,$$

where

$$(11) \qquad \epsilon(w,I) = \frac{\partial L(w,I)}{\partial w} \frac{w}{L(w,I)}$$

is the elasticity of demand for labor with respect to the wage. Equation (10) is simply the condition that marginal revenue equals marginal cost for syndicates. In the absence of disutility of work, the marginal cost of providing labor is zero up to full employment and infinite thereafter.

Again (10) can be expressed in terms of quantities rather than prices. Invert (8) to write the wage rate in a typical labor market as $w = g((L/q),I)$, where L is total labor supply by all syndicates. Let $l = L/mq$ be the labor supply of each individual worker. Then we can rewrite (10) as

$$(12) \qquad g(ml,I) + \rho ml \frac{\partial g}{\partial(ml)}(ml,I) \geq 0$$

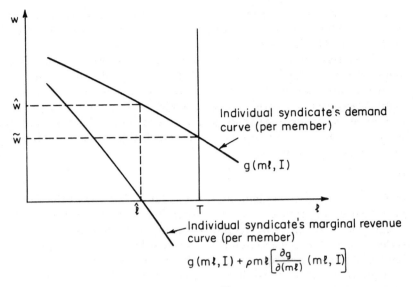

FIGURE II

with equality if $l < T$. Condition (12) is illustrated in Figure II. The solution to (12) is at $l = \hat{l}$ and the corresponding wage is $w = \hat{w}$.

As in the case of the product market, (10) (or (12)) is a necessary but not sufficient condition for Cournot-Nash equilibrium in the labor market. Below, we make an assumption which ensures that (10) (or (12)) is necessary and sufficient. This assumption says essentially that the left-hand side of (12) is decreasing in l. Given this, it is clear from Figure II that a decrease in ρ, i.e., a reduction in monopoly power in the labor market, moves the marginal revenue curve up and hence increases $\hat{l}$ and reduces $\hat{w}$. It is also clear that as $\rho \to 0$, the marginal revenue curve eventually cuts the l axis to the right of $l = T$, in which case the solution to (12) is $l = T$, $w = \tilde{w}$. In other words, when the labor market is close to being perfectly competitive, Cournot-Nash equilibrium in the labor market will involve full employment (competition between syndicates will bid down the wage until any underemployment is eliminated). However, when ρ is not close to zero, the equilibrium will generally be at a point $l < T$ and will involve underemployment.

Returning to (10), we may use (6) and (8) to express the elasticity of demand for labor, $\epsilon(w,I)$, in terms of the elasticity of demand for output $\eta(p)$. Define $z(p) = (d\gamma(p)/dp)(p/\gamma(p))$, where $\gamma(p)$ is as in

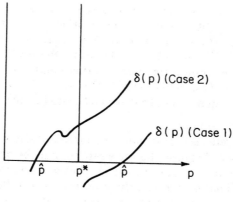

FIGURE III

A7. In the Appendix, it is shown that, if $p(w,I) < \bar{p}$,

$$(13) \qquad \epsilon(w,I) = \alpha \bigg/ \left[\frac{z(p(w,I))}{\eta(p(w,I))} - (\alpha - 1) \right].$$

Therefore, using the fact that $w = 0$ is not optimal for a syndicate, we may rewrite (10) as

$$(14) \qquad \delta(p) \equiv \left(1 + \frac{\rho}{\alpha} \left[\frac{z(p)}{\eta(p)} - (\alpha - 1) \right] \right) = 1 + \frac{\rho}{\epsilon(w,I)} \geq 0,$$

with equality if there is underemployment.[8]

We now make an assumption which ensures that (14) is a sufficient as well as necessary condition for Cournot-Nash equilibrium in the labor market. The assumption is a slightly weaker version of decreasing marginal revenue for syndicates.

A8. If $\delta(p') = 0$ for some $0 < p' < \bar{p}$, then $\delta(p) > 0$ for $\bar{p} > p > p'$ and $\delta(p) < 0$ for $0 < p < p'$.

Assumption A8 implies that, if $\delta(p) = 0$ has a solution in the range $0 < p < \bar{p}$, then the solution is unique. Denote this solution by $\hat{p}$. If no solution exists, set $\hat{p} = 0$.[9] The $\delta(p)$ curve is illustrated in Figure III.

8. Equation (13) implies, as is to be expected, that the demand for labor will be more elastic the higher is the elasticity of demand for output or the less responsive is marginal revenue to price. It is interesting to note that simplified versions of (13) may be found in Pigou [1933].

9. A8 will be satisfied if the labor market is approximately competitive. Of more interest from our point of view is the fact that it will be satisfied if the product market is perfectly competitive and $|\eta(p)|$ is increasing in p.

LEMMA 2. Assume A1–A8. Then, given I, there is a unique Cournot-Nash equilibrium in the labor market, denoted by $p(I), w(I)$. This equilibrium will satisfy $p(I) = \hat{p}$, i.e., $\delta(p(I)) = 0$, as long as $(1/m)C(\Theta h(\hat{p})I) < T$. In this case, there will be underemployment in equilibrium. On the other hand, if $(1/m)C(\Theta h(\hat{p})I) > T$, then $p(I)$ satisfies $(1/m)C(\Theta h(p)I) = T$, and there will be full employment. In both cases $w(I)$ satisfies (6) with equality.

Proof. See Appendix.

Lemma 2 tells us that if there is underemployment in equilibrium, syndicates will choose the wage rate so that the price of the produced good in output markets is $\hat{p}$; i.e., they will set w so that $\gamma(\hat{p}) = wC'(\Theta h(\hat{p})I)$. That is, it is as if the syndicates controlled the price of the produced good directly. On the other hand, if at price $\hat{p}$ there is overemployment of labor, the syndicates raise the wage until full employment is established.

Determination of an Overall Imperfectly Competitive Equilibrium (ICE)

So far, we have taken I to be exogenous. We now proceed to the determination of an overall equilibrium for the economy in which I is endogenous. The demand function for the produced good is $h(p)I$. Therefore, from the budget constraint, we know that each consumer demands y and k in the ratio,

(15) $$y/k = h(p)/(1 - ph(p)).$$

Hence, in equilibrium,

(16) $$Y/m\overline{k} = h(p)/(1 - ph(p)),$$

where Y is the output of each firm and $\overline{k}$ is the per capita endowment of the nonproduced good. The right-hand side of (16) is decreasing in p (see (3)). Let p^* be the unique solution of

(17) $$\frac{1}{m} C \left(\frac{h(p)m\overline{k}}{1 - ph(p)} \right) = T.$$

Then p^* is that price for the produced good relative to the nonproduced good which generates the level of demand consistent with full employment. If $p > p^*$, there will be underemployment. On the other hand, $p < p^*$ is infeasible.

We know from Lemma 2 that the imperfectly competitive equilibrium must be one of two types. Either there is underemployment, in which case $\delta(p) = 0$ and $p = \hat{p}$, or there is full employment in which case $p = p^*$. The two possibilities are illustrated in Figure

III (drawn according to A8). If $\delta(p^*) < 0$, then $\hat{p} > p^*$, and the equilibrium occurs at $\hat{p}$ (Case 1). Since

$$\frac{1}{m} C\left(\frac{h(\hat{p})m\overline{k}}{1 - \hat{p}h(\hat{p})}\right),$$

there will be underemployment. (In Case 1, $p = p^*$ is not a possible equilibrium, since (14) is violated at p^*.) On the other hand, if $\delta(p^*) \geq 0$, then $\hat{p} \leq p^*$, the equilibrium occurs at p^* and there will be a full employment (Case 2). (In Case 2, $p = \hat{p}$ would imply overemployment.)

PROPOSITION 1. Assume A1–A8. Let p^*, $\hat{p}$ be the solutions to (17), and $\delta(p) = 0$, respectively (if there is no solution to $\delta(p) = 0$, set $\hat{p} = 0$). Define $\bar{p} = \max(\hat{p}, p^*)$. Then there is a unique imperfectly competitive equilibrium (ICE) for the economy, given as follows: the price of the produced good is $\bar{p}$; each firm produces $\tilde{Y} = m\overline{k}(h(\bar{p})/(1 - \bar{p}h(\bar{p})))$ units of output; each consumer supplies $\tilde{l} = (1/m)C(h(\bar{p})m\overline{k}/(1 - \bar{p}h(\bar{p}))) \lambda$ units of labor; the wage rate $\tilde{w}$ satisfies $\gamma(\bar{p}) = \tilde{w}C'(\tilde{Y})$; income in each product market is given by $\tilde{I} = (\tilde{Y}/\Theta h(\bar{p}))$ and per capita income by $(\tilde{Y}/mh(\bar{p}))$. If $\hat{p} \leq p^*$, there is full employment in equilibrium. On the other hand, if $\hat{p} > p^*$, each worker is underemployed by the amount $T - (1/m)C(h(\hat{p})m\overline{k}/(1 - \hat{p}h(\hat{p})))$.

Proof. See Appendix.

As we have emphasized above, in order to get underemployment in equilibrium in our model, it is necessary for the labor market to be noncompetitive; i.e., ρ cannot be zero (or close to zero). For if $\rho = 0$, then $\delta(p) \equiv 1$, so that $0 = \hat{p} < p^*$. On other hand, underemployment is quite consistent with a competitive product market, i.e., with $\Theta = 0$. In fact, if the product market is competitive, $z(p) = 1$, and so $\delta(p) = 0$ if and only if

(18) $$\eta(p) = \frac{1}{\alpha - 1 - (\alpha/\rho)}.$$

As long as this equation does have a solution, underemployment will occur in an ICE if T is sufficiently large.[10]

10. Is this underemployment voluntary or involuntary? It is voluntary in the sense that it would disappear if workers chose not to exercise their monopoly power. On the other hand, it is involuntary in the sense that workers would be willing to work more at the going wage; i.e., the wage exceeds the reservation wage (the latter is zero). For the purpose of this analysis, the distinction between voluntary and involuntary underemployment does not seem of great importance. Of greater interest are the determinants of the equilibrium level of underemployment. Note that (18) will not have a solution if consumers' demand functions exhibit a constant elasticity of demand (unless this elasticity just happens to equal $1/(\alpha - 1 - (\alpha/\rho))$. A constant elasticity of demand everywhere, however, is inconsistent with (1) and (2), unless the constant equals -1, i.e., U is Cobb-Douglas. In the Cobb-Douglas case, (18) has no solution (since $\rho < 1$), and so our model predicts full employment.

Returning to the general case where the product market is imperfectly competitive, we may use the formula for $\delta(p)$ in (14) to derive simple comparative statics properties of an ICE. Clearly, an increase in ρ reduces $\delta(p)$ for each p (since $\epsilon(w,I) < 0$). It follows from Figure III that $\hat{p}$ rises as ρ increases. Hence, by (3), as one might expect, an increase in monopoly power in labor markets, i.e., an increase in ρ, raises the equilibrium level of underemployment, $T - (1/m)C(h(\hat{p})m\bar{k}/(1 - \hat{p}h(\hat{p})))$. The effect of a change in monopoly power in product markets is not so clearcut, however, since Θ affects γ and z in a complicated way.

Note that an ICE coincides with the usual Walrasian equilibrium in the special case $\Theta = \rho = 0$.

Finally, it is worth reviewing our assumption that firms maximize profits and that syndicates maximize wage receipts. Are these reasonable objectives given that the economy is imperfectly competitive? The answer is that they are in view of A2 and A3. For A2 implies that only a negligible fraction of workers purchase output in a market served by the firm they work for (when N is large). As a result, for a majority of workers, the beneficial effects of an increase in wages will dominate any adverse effects on output prices. Similarly, A3 implies that, when N is large, a negligible fraction of workers' incomes comes from holding shares in the firms they work for. As a result, for the majority of workers, the beneficial effects of an increase in wages will dominate any adverse effect on profits. Finally, A3 implies that a negligible fraction of a firm's owners purchase output in a market served by the firm. As a result, for the majority of shareholders, the beneficial effects of an increase in profits will dominate any adverse effect on output prices. Thus, A2 and A3 together ensure that the maximization of wage receipts is in the interest of (almost all) syndicate members and that the maximization of profits is in the interest of (almost all) firms' owners.[11]

IV. The Multiplier

In this section we consider how the imperfectly competitive equilibrium (ICE) of the last section is affected by changes in demand

11. It is also worth reconsidering at this point our assumption that consumers cannot move between markets. Since prices turn out to be the same in all markets in an ICE, the reader may wonder whether this assumption is important. The answer is that it is. For while it is true that in equilibrium consumers would not wish to move, out of equilibrium they might want to. In particular, if a firm in some product market expands and as a result the price in this market falls, this will make consumers want to move from other markets. Thus, if movement is possible, the demand curve facing an individual firm will be considerably more elastic than if, as assumed, movement is not possible.

conditions. We shall find that the imperfectly competitive model of Sections II–III exhibits a number of Keynesian features.

Suppose that demand for the produced good increases for either of the following reasons: (1) the per capita endowment of the non-produced good $\overline{k}$ increases, or (2) consumers' tastes change in such a way that the demand function for the produced good becomes $\lambda h(p)I$ for all p, where $\lambda > 1$.[12] In both cases the elasticity of demand $\eta(p)$ is not affected, and hence neither is $\gamma(p)$ nor $\delta(p)$. It follows that $\hat{p}$ stays the same. Therefore, if the economy is initially in underemployment equilibrium, i.e., $\bar{p} = \hat{p} > p^*$, then a small increase in $\overline{k}$ or λ will not affect the equilibrium price of the produced good $\bar{p}$. Output and employment will both rise, however, since equilibrium output is given by

(19) $$\tilde{Y} = \lambda h(\bar{p})m\overline{k}/(1 - \lambda \bar{p}h(\bar{p})),$$

which is an increasing function of both $\overline{k}$ and λ. Note that if demand continues to increase, then eventually full employment will be reached, and from then on an increase in demand will not affect output but will simply lead to a higher price for the produced good (relative to the nonproduced good). This is because increases in demand increase p^*, and so we eventually switch to the regime $\bar{p} = p^* > \hat{p}$.

Of particular interest is the fact that increases in demand have a multiplier effect on output. Suppose that we start off in an underemployment equilibrium with $p = \hat{p}$. Let $\lambda = 1$, and write $\sigma = mh(\hat{p})\overline{k}$. Here σ is that part of the demand for the produced good which comes from endowment income. Then, from (19) we have

(20) $$\frac{d\tilde{Y}}{d\sigma} = \frac{1}{1 - \hat{p}h(\hat{p})}.$$

That is, an increase in $\overline{k}$ that initially raises demand for the produced good by one (i.e., $mh(\hat{p})d\overline{k} = d\sigma = 1$) has the final effect of increasing output by $1/(1 - \hat{p}h(\hat{p}))$. Since $\hat{p}h(\hat{p})$ is the marginal propensity to consume (in money terms), the multiplier here is just the traditional Keynesian one: the reciprocal of one minus the marginal propensity to consume.

On the other hand, consider again an underemployment equilibrium and suppose now that λ, rather than $\overline{k}$, increases. Then

---

12. It is straightforward to show that there exists a homothetic utility function $U_\lambda(k,y)$ which generates the demand function $\lambda h(p)I$ as long as $\lambda ph(p) < 1$, and $h'(p) + \lambda h^2(p) < 0$ for all p. The latter condition ensures that the Slutsky matrix is negative semidefinite.

$$(21) \qquad \left. \frac{d\tilde{Y}}{d\lambda} \right|_{\lambda=1} = \frac{\tilde{Y}}{1 - \hat{p}h(\hat{p})} > \tilde{Y}.$$

Again the final increase in $\tilde{Y}$ exceeds the initial increase in demand; i.e., the multiplier exceeds one.

The usual dynamic story that goes with the multiplier can also be told here. An initial increase in demand leads to expansion by firms and hence to greater employment. The price of the produced good does not change, since syndicates adjust the wage to maintain $\delta(p)$ $= 0$. Consumers' incomes rise as a result of the expansion, and a fraction of this increase $(\hat{p}h(\hat{p}))$ is spent on greater consumption of the produced good. There is a further expansion, and so on. Of course, since we have no theory of dynamics, this is as usual no more than a story.

What determines the size of the multiplier? Consider again the case where demand increases as a result of a change in $\bar{k}$. Then the multiplier is $1/(1 - \hat{p}h(\hat{p}))$. We have seen above that a decrease in ρ leads to a decrease in $\hat{p}$. In general, this can either increase or decrease $\hat{p}h(\hat{p})$. If the product market is perfectly competitive, however, it follows from (18) that $\eta(\hat{p}) + 1 > 0$ and so a decrease in $\hat{p}$ decreases $\hat{p}h(\hat{p})$ and decreases the multiplier. In other words, if the product market is competitive, a reduction in monopoly power in the labor market reduces the multiplier. (Note that if ρ becomes small enough, we switch to the full employment regime, and the multiplier becomes zero.) The effects of a change in Θ on the multiplier do not seem to be clearcut.

It is possible to develop something close to the traditional Keynesian national income analysis for the model presented here. What corresponds in our model to national income is output of the produced good per firm Y. The demand for the produced good by a typical group of m consumers is given by

$$(22) \qquad c = h(p)(mi),$$

where i is per capita income (or wealth). Now $mi = w(ml) + (pY - w(ml)) + m\bar{k} = pY + m\bar{k}$. Therefore, we can rewrite (22) as

$$(23) \qquad c = h(p)(pY + m\bar{k}) = ph(p)Y + mh(p)\bar{k}.$$

If there is underemployment in equilibrium, $p = \hat{p}$. Substituting $\sigma = mh(\hat{p})\bar{k}$ and $\tau = \hat{p}h(\hat{p})$, we obtain

$$(24) \qquad c = \sigma + \tau Y,$$

which is of course the traditional linear consumption function, where

τ is the marginal propensity to consume. The equilibrium condition (since there is no investment) is

$$(25) \qquad Y = c = \sigma + \tau Y;$$

i.e.,

$$(26) \qquad Y = \sigma/(1 - \tau),$$

which is, of course, just equation (19) with $\lambda = 1$.

It is instructive to compare the effects of changes in demand in the imperfectly competitive model of Sections II–III with those in the usual Walrasian model. Suppose that $\tilde{k}$ is stochastic, and hence so is $\tilde{\sigma} = mh(\hat{p})\tilde{k}$. Then if $C(\tilde{\sigma}/(1 - \tau))$ never exceeds mT, p will remain constant at $\hat{p}$, and changes in demand in the imperfectly competitive model will lead to fluctuations in output and employment but to no fluctuations in output price. In contrast, in the Walrasian model, which occurs when $\Theta = \rho = 0$, there will always be full employment. Hence output and employment will be constant, and fluctuations in demand will simply cause fluctuations in the price of the produced good (p will vary so as to satisfy (17)). This last conclusion is true even if the product market is imperfectly competitive, as long as the labor market is perfectly competitive. We see then that the presence of imperfect competition can lead to greater fluctuations in output and smaller fluctuations in price than in the usual Walrasian model.

It should also be noted that there is a role for a simple balanced budget fiscal policy in this model. Suppose that the economy is experiencing underemployment. Then the government can stimulate demand by taxing consumers' incomes and spending these incomes in such a way as to increase demand for the produced good relative to the nonproduced good. In particular, suppose that the government taxes in a lump sum fashion all the income I of consumers, spends this income according to the demand function $\lambda h(p)I$, and gives the goods that it purchases to consumers. (As long as resale of the produced good by consumers can be prevented, crowding out will then not occur.) Then, in view of the results above, this will increase output and employment without changing output price until full employment is reached.[13] It should be noted that the fiscal policy which we are considering here differs from traditional fiscal policy in that both the marginal propensity to consume τ, and the average propensity to

---

13. An alternative policy that the government might adopt to increase demand for the produced good is to subsidize consumption through the use of commodity subsidies.

consume are affected by the government's activities. Traditional fiscal policy, which affects only the average propensity to consume, will alter the price elasticity of demand $\eta(p)$ and hence will affect p even at an underemployment equilibrium.

It is worth considering finally how changes in demand affect the wage rate. We have observed that, if we start at an underemployment equilibrium, a small increase in $\bar{k}$ or λ will not change $\hat{p}$. Rewriting (6) as $\gamma(\hat{p}) = wC'(Y)$, and using the fact that Y increases with demand, we see that w falls when demand increases if there are decreasing returns to scale and stays constant if there are constant returns. The idea that increases in demand may lead to reductions in the wage may seem strange at first sight. It is, however, analogous to the result that, in the textbook Keynesian model with fixed money wages and a competitive product market, an increase in demand leads to lower *real* wages if the marginal product of labor is declining. Note that this feature of the model will disappear if we assume that there are increasing returns in production—a case that fits well into the framework of imperfect competition. Then $\gamma(p) = wC'(Y)$ implies that w and Y move together if p stays constant.[14]

V. COMMENTS AND EXTENSIONS OF THE BASIC MODEL

A. *Introducing Disutility of Labor*

The model described above makes the strong assumption that there is no disutility of work. We now sketch how this assumption can be relaxed (a detailed exposition may be found in Hart [1980]). Suppose that each consumer's utility function is $U(k,y) - d(L)$, where L is labor and d is increasing in L on $[0,T]$. Assume also that U is homogeneous of degree one in k,y. Then the utility of a worker who supplies L units of labor at a wage w can be written as

$$(27) \qquad V(p)(wL + \pi + \bar{k}) - d(L),$$

where $V(p) \equiv \max\{U(k,y) | k + py \le 1), k \ge 0, y \ge 0\}$, π is the worker's income from profits, and p is the price of the produced good in the output market visited by the worker. A2 and A3 imply that the workers in a particular syndicate have no influence over p or π. Therefore, each syndicate's objective, given that it faces the demand curve $\tilde{L}(w, \ldots)$, is to choose w to maximize

---

14. If the increasing returns are mild enough, then Lemma 1 will continue to hold. With strongly increasing returns, however, it seems that a Cournot-Nash equilibrium may not exist in the product market.

$$(28) \qquad V(p)\frac{w\tilde{L}(w,\dots)}{qm\rho} - d\left(\frac{\tilde{L}(w,\dots)}{qm\rho}\right).$$

Arguing as in Section III and using the fact that $p(w,I) = p$ in a symmetric equilibrium yields

$$(29) \qquad V(p)\gamma(p)\delta(p) = d'((1/m)C(\Theta h(p)I))C'(\Theta h(p)I)$$

as a necessary condition for equilibrium. Under an appropriate generalization of A8, this condition is also sufficient.

We also know, however, that in equilibrium

$$(30) \qquad Y = \Theta h(p)I = (h(p)m\bar{k})/(1 - ph(p)),$$

where Y is the output of each firm. Using (30) to solve for I and substituting in (29) gives us a single equation in p as our condition for equilibrium. Once this has been solved for p, we may find the equilibrium output of each firm from (30).

The model with disutility of labor differs from the previous model in a number of ways. First, there may be multiple imperfectly competitive equilibria (even under the generalized version of A8), i.e., (29) and (30) may have several solutions.[15] Each of these solutions can be shown to have the property that the level of employment is below the Walrasian, i.e., socially optimal, level. Second, the level of employment will be suboptimal even if the labor market is competitive, as long as the product market is noncompetitive. In this case, workers equate the marginal disutility of work with the marginal utility of the real wage; however, imperfect competition in the product market makes the latter too low from a social point of view. As we have noted previously, in the no-disutility-of-work case, there is full employment; i.e., the level of employment is optimal, whenever the labor market is competitive.

Third, increases in demand due to changes in $\bar{k}$ or λ will tend to increase output price p and the level of output and employment together, rather than just affecting output when there is underemployment and price when there is full employment. This reduces the size of the multiplier when there is underemployment.

Finally, it is worth noting that the case where there is disutility of work can also be interpreted as a case where there is an alternative activity to working in the unionized sector. For example, suppose that every individual has a plot of land on which he can work. Suppose that

15. Multiple equilibria may also occur in the model of Sections II and III in the absence of A7 and A8. (Without A7 and A8, however, there is no guarantee that an ICE will exist at all; see remark D of this section.)

the individual divides his time between working in the unionized sector and on his plot. Assume that the individual's utility function can be written as $U(k,y) + G(T - L)$, where G is consumption of the (nonmarketed) crop. Then, if we write $G(T - L) = -d(L)$, we have the same model as described above. Now imperfect competition in the unionized sector causes a misallocation between the unionized and home production sectors rather than underemployment per se. (We can, equally well, interpret the underemployment in the model of Sections II and III as a misallocation between the unionized sector and the "leisure sector.")

B. Allowing the Income Distribution to Affect Demand

In the model of Sections II and III a decrease in money wages leads to a decrease in p and hence to an increase in the equilibrium output of the produced good, given by $h(p)m\bar{k}/(1 - ph(p))$, and in employment. It is sometimes argued by Keynesians, however, that an overall decrease in wages may *decrease* output and employment. This possibility can be incorporated into our model by allowing demand to depend not only on aggregate income I, but also on the distribution of income.[16]

We shall give an example to illustrate this. Suppose that $C(Y) = Y$, i.e., $a = \alpha = 1$. Let us drop the assumption that all consumers are identical and assume instead that the population of consumers is divided into two groups: workers who can supply labor, but do not own shares in firms, and capitalists who cannot supply labor but who own all the firms. To make matters very simple, we shall suppose that workers consume the produced good according to the demand function $h(p)I_w$, where I_w is workers' income, and that capitalists consume only the nonproduced good.

Under these conditions, market demand for the produced good is given by

$$(31) \qquad\qquad h(p)I_w.$$

Hence the analysis of Sections II–III applies, with I_w replacing I. In particular, the elasticity of demand is the same, for each value of p, as previously.

Let β be the fraction of consumers who are workers. Then, if we assume that the endowment of the nonproduced good is distributed evenly across all consumers, the condition for equilibrium in the product market is

16. As in, for example, Kaldor [1956].

(32) $$Y = h(p)I_w = h(p)(w(\beta ml) + \beta m\bar{k}).$$

However, since (6) holds with equality, and $C'(Y) = 1$,

(33) $$w = \gamma(p).$$

Substituting this into (32), and using the fact that $Y = C(Y) = \beta ml$, we get that equilibrium output of each firm is

(34) $$[h(p)/(1 - h(p)\gamma(p))]\beta m\bar{k}.$$

As before, p will satisfy $\delta(p) = 0$ at an underemployment equilibrium.

Assume that initially we are at an ICE. Suppose now that money wages fall in all labor markets. Then in view of (33) and A7, p will decrease. Hence, by (34), Y will decrease as long as

(35) $$\frac{d}{dp}\left[\frac{h(p)}{1 - h(p)\gamma(p)}\right] > 0;$$

i.e., as long as

(36) $$h'(p) + h^2(p)\gamma'(p) > 0.$$

Equation (36) will certainly be satisfied if $\gamma'(p)$ is large enough, i.e., as long as marginal revenue is increasing sufficiently rapidly in p at the ICE. Condition (36) ensures that a decrease in w does not decrease p so much as to cause the "normal demand" effect; i.e., the increase in demand due to the fact that the produced good is cheaper relative to the nonproduced good, to offset the decrease in demand caused by the shift in income distribution to the capitalists.

We see then that a decrease in money wages throughout the economy can *decrease* employment. However, if money wages continue to fall, then eventually employment will rise. This follows from the fact that (a) $p \to 0$ as $w \to 0$ (see (33) and Result 1(3) in the Appendix) and (b) $h(p) \to \infty$ as $p \to 0$ (see (2)). In other words, eventually the "normal demand" effect dominates.

Note that (36) will not be satisfied if the product market is competitive, for then $\gamma(p) = p$, and (36) is inconsistent with (3). Hence, we obtain the perhaps surprising result that a decrease in wages can lead to a decrease in output and employment only if the product market is imperfectly competitive. Note also that while we have obtained conditions for workers as a whole to face an upward-sloping demand curve for labor, this does not alter the fact that each syndicate faces a downward-sloping demand curve. The point is that no individual syndicate can affect the distribution of income, and therefore for an individual syndicate the "normal demand" effect always dominates. Only a general decrease in wages can change the distribution of income in such a way as to decrease the demand for labor.

C. The Role of the Nonproduced Good

The nonproduced good plays a central role in our model. On the one hand, there is a close relationship between the quantity of it available and the equilibrium activity level, represented by Y. On the other hand, "depressions" occur when demand shifts from the produced good to the nonproduced good. It is important to realize, however, that similar results can be obtained if we replace the nonproduced good by another produced good. Suppose, for example, that k is produced according to the cost function $L = D(k)$, where L is labor. Assume that production of k takes place under competitive conditions—both in labor and product markets. Then in equilibrium labor that is withheld from the unionized sector to keep the wage there high will be diverted to the production of k. Thus, there will be no underemployment—only a misallocation between sectors. (This is similar to the case discussed in subsection A above.)

Suppose now that there is a shift in demand from Y to k. Output of Y will fall, and output of k will rise. However, the relative magnitudes of these changes may be quite different. In particular, if $D'(k)$ is steeply sloped in the relevant range, then an increase in demand will bring about a large increase in the price of k and only a small increase in the quantity. Thus, in a very real sense the increase in production of k may not match the decrease in production of Y, and the shift in demand will cause the overall activity level of the economy to decline. (The case of the nonproduced good is simply the special case where $D(k) = 0$ for $0 \leq k \leq mN\bar{k}, D(k) = \infty$ otherwise.)

D. Relaxing the Assumptions

In order to carry out the analysis, we have made a number of strong assumptions. The most important of these are A1–A3. A1–A3 decompose the economy in such a way that, in spite of the existence of imperfect competition, there is a clear division between the variables each agent can affect and those it cannot affect. As a consequence, imperfectly competitive agents face, under the Cournot-Nash assumption, well-defined demand curves and have simple well-defined objective functions. In the absence of something like A1–A3, it becomes much harder to talk about the "true" demand curve facing an imperfectly competitive agent since, in principle, the agent's actions have repercussions for, and hence may set off reactions from, every other agent in the economy. It is also much harder under these conditions to define an appropriate objective function for an imperfect competitor.

We have also assumed—without any justification from consumer theory—A7 and A8. In the absence of A7 and A8, unfortunately, the analysis becomes considerably more complicated. In particular, it does not seem possible to establish the existence of an ICE. The theorems by McManus [1962] and Roberts and Sonnenschein [1976] on existence of Cournot-Nash equilibria in the absence of diminishing marginal revenue do not seem to be applicable here.

It is possible that allowing different prices in different output markets would smooth things sufficiently to permit us to establish the existence of a nonsymmetric ICE. There seems little doubt, however, that analyzing the properties of such an ICE—even if it could be shown to exist—would be a complicated task.

Given the difficulties of dropping A7 and A8, it would also seem hard to relax the assumption that consumers have homothetic preferences in k and y; and the assumption that $C(Y) = aY^\alpha$. Without homothetic preferences and the assumption that $C(Y) = aY^\alpha$, $\gamma(p)$ and $\delta(p)$ will depend on quantities like L and Y as well as on p. Under these conditions, A7 and A8 may become so strong as to be never satisfied over the whole range.

VI. CONCLUSIONS

In this paper we have argued that a number of features of Keynesian economics can be captured by a model which departs from the classical Walrasian model by assuming that agents are imperfect competitors rather than perfect competitors. In particular, we have shown that, under certain assumptions, (1) an imperfectly competitive economy will operate at too low a level of activity; i.e., it will be depressed, and there will be underemployment; (2) an increase in demand for current consumption will lead to an increase in output—moreover, this will take place without any change in output price and the increase in output will exceed the initial increase in demand, i.e., the multiplier exceeds 1; (3) a balanced budget fiscal policy can be used to stimulate the economy.

For most of our analysis, the crucial assumption has been the existence of imperfect competition in the labor market—it is this that is responsible for the existence of underemployment in our basic model. In extensions of the basic model, however, the existence of imperfect competition in the product market also has interesting implications. For example, it can imply that workers as a whole face an upward-sloping demand curve for labor if capitalists and workers have different propensities to consume.

While the model presented here covers some of the same ground as the standard fixed price model, it differs from the fixed price model in the following respects. First, whereas the fixed price model yields an infinite number of equilibria (for each initial price vector and each exogenously specified rationing scheme there is at least one equilibrium), the imperfectly competitive model will in general yield a small number of equilibria; in the case considered here, just one. Second, the Walrasian equilibrium is never an imperfectly competitive equilibrium (unless $\Theta = \rho = 0$), whereas it is always an equilibrium in the fixed price model.

Under imperfect competition, as under fixed prices, an agent's actions will depend not only on prices, but also on realized transactions, i.e., quantities. As Clower [1965] has emphasized, this seems to be a crucial feature of any Keynesian model. Under imperfect competition, the quantity constraints arise from the fact that, at any price, there is a limit to the demand for the agent's product. A consequence of this is that in an imperfectly competitive equilibrium an agent will generally want to buy or sell more at the going price. It is inappropriate, however, to describe this as "rationing" or to associate it with the nonclearing of markets. Rather it is simply an indication of the fact that an imperfectly competitive agent is not a price-taker.

In the model we have presented, demand "failures" or depressions arise because, at equilibrium prices, demand for the produced good is too low relative to that for the nonproduced good. This raises an important question about what might correspond to the nonproduced good in reality. Possible candidates are land, old masters, etc. These are straightforward. Another possible candidate for the nonproduced good is money. This is more complicated. In the static model presented here there is no reason for agents to hold money. In a model with time, cash balances might enter the (indirect) utility function as a proxy for future consumption. Note, however, that k will then correspond to real, rather than nominal, cash balances (where the deflator is the price of future consumption). Thus, there is no reason to think that a change in the nominal supply of money will lead to a change in k.[17] In any case, the incorporation of time and money into the model is a topic for further research.

---

17. To put it somewhat differently, imperfect competition by itself cannot explain the nonneutrality of money, since the marginal revenue equals marginal cost conditions are conditions about relative and not absolute prices.

While the imperfectly competitive model considered here does have Keynesian features, it is a big step from this to the conclusion that the model captures a significant part of the ideas of Keynes or of Keynesians. Leijonhufvud [1968] has argued forcefully that Keynes believed that unemployment and depressions were a consequence of the failure of the market system to provide the right signals and could not be traced simply to the existence of large agents, such as unions or monopolists. In this respect, the model presented here may be closer to the ideas of such "pre-Keynesians" as Pigou (see Pigou [1933]) than to those of Keynes himself. Note, however, that in the model of this paper, the imperfectly competitive agents are significant only at the "local" level, i.e., in their own markets. Each agent is negligible relative to the whole economy. In this sense, the model may not be so far removed from the atomistic world that Keynes had in mind.

It should also be noted that the imperfectly competitive equilibrium which we have studied in this paper applies equally to the short run and the long run. One consequence of this is that our model would not seem to be consistent with the view that Keynesian demand failures arise only in the short run, and that in the long run the economy will achieve full employment. Rather, the imperfectly competitive model suggests that demand failures can be permanent. In this respect, the model may have a greater affinity to the work of Harrod [1939], and to that of Kalecki [1954] and of some of the Marxian underconsumptionists, than it does to some neo-Keynesian thinking.

APPENDIX

RESULT 1. (1) $\lim_{p \to \bar{p}} \sup \gamma(p) > 0$; (2) $\lim_{p \to \bar{p}} \sup \gamma(p) = \infty$ if $\bar{p} = \infty$; (3) $\lim_{p \to 0} \inf \gamma(p) = 0$.

Proof. Assume that $\lim_{p \to \bar{p}} \sup \gamma(p) \le 0$. Then $\lim_{p \to \bar{p}} \sup (1 + \Theta/\eta(p)) \le 0$. Choose ϵ to be a positive number less than $1 - \Theta$. Then for $p \ge$ some p', $p' < \bar{p}$,

(1') $$1 + \Theta/\eta(p) \le \epsilon,$$

i.e.,

(2') $$h'(p)/h(p) \ge - \Theta/p(1 - \epsilon).$$

Integrating this from p' to p, we get

(3') $$\log \frac{h(p)}{h'(p)} \ge - \frac{\Theta}{1 - \epsilon} \log \frac{p}{p'}.$$

Therefore,

(4') $$h(p) \ge \frac{h(p')}{(p')^{-\Theta/(1-\epsilon)}} p^{-\Theta/(1-\epsilon)},$$

473

from which it follows that

$$(5') \qquad ph(p) \geq \frac{h(p')}{(p')^{-\Theta/(1-\epsilon)}} p^{(1-(\Theta/(1-\epsilon)))}.$$

If $\overline{p} < \infty$, then $h(\overline{p}) = 0$, which contradicts (4'). If $\overline{p} = \infty$, then (5') is not consistent with the fact that $ph(p) < 1$ for all p (recall that $\epsilon < (1 - \Theta)$). This proves (1) and that

$$\lim_{p \to \overline{p}} \sup \left(1 + \frac{\Theta}{\eta(p)} \right) > 0.$$

Condition (2) follows from this immediately. To prove (3), one uses a similar argument to that given above to show that

$$\lim_{p \to 0} \inf \left(1 + \frac{\Theta}{\eta(p)} \right) = \infty$$

is inconsistent with the fact that $\lim_{p \to 0} h(p) = \infty$. Therefore,

$$\lim_{p \to 0} \inf \left(1 + \frac{\Theta}{\eta(p)} \right) < \infty,$$

which, together with the second part of (A7), implies (3).

Proof of Lemma 1. It is worth noting that Lemma 1 is not proved by showing that firms' profit functions are concave. It appears that A7 is not strong enough to ensure concavity and yet is strong enough to ensure existence. We prove existence of $p(w,I)$ first. If $\overline{p} < \infty$ and (6) holds at $\overline{p}$, then $p(w,I) = \overline{p}$. Suppose now that $\overline{p} < \infty$ and (6) is violated at $\overline{p}$. By Result 1, $\lim_{p \to 0} \inf \gamma(p) = 0 < \lim_{p \to 0} C'(\Theta h(p)I)$. Hence by continuity there exists $0 < p < \overline{p}$ such that (6) holds with equality. The remaining case is $\overline{p} = \infty$. But then $\lim_{p \to \infty} \sup \gamma(p) = \infty > \lim_{p \to \infty} C'(\Theta h(p)I)$. Again, by continuity, there exists $0 < p < \overline{p}$ such that (6) holds with equality. This establishes the existence of $p(w,I)$. Uniqueness follows from the fact that the left-hand side of (6) is increasing in p and the right-hand side is nonincreasing in p.

To show that $p(w,I)$ is a Cournot-Nash equilibrium is trivial in the case where (6) holds with inequality. Hence assume equality. Since (6) holds with equality at $p(w,I)$, (5) holds with equality where $Y' = (1 - \Theta)h(p)I$. Suppose that (4) is not maximized; i.e., there exists p' at which a typical firm's profits are higher. Consider first the case where $p' > \tilde{p} = p(w,I)$. Then there must be a $p' \geq p \geq \tilde{p}$, at which

$$(6') \qquad \frac{d}{dp} \{p[h(p)I - Y'] - wC(h(p)I - Y')\} > 0.$$

But this means that

$$(7') \qquad [ph'(p) + h(p)]I - (1 - \Theta)h(\tilde{p})I$$
$$- wC'(h(p)I - (1 - \Theta)h(\tilde{p})I)h'(p)I > 0,$$

i.e.,

$$(8') \qquad [p - wC'(h(p)I - (1 - \Theta)h(\tilde{p})I)]h'(p)$$
$$+ h(p) > h(\tilde{p}) - \Theta h(\tilde{p}).$$

However, by (A7) and (6) and the fact that there are nonincreasing returns to scale,

$$(9') \quad p\left(1 + \frac{\Theta}{\eta(p)}\right) \geq \bar{p}\left(1 + \frac{\Theta}{\eta(\bar{p})}\right) = wC'(\Theta h(\bar{p})I)$$

$$\geq wC'(h(p)I - (1 - \Theta)h(\bar{p})I).$$

Hence

$$(10') \quad p - wC'(h(p)I - (1 - \Theta)h(\bar{p})I) \geq -\Theta p/\eta(p).$$

Substituting into (8'), we obtain

$$(11') \quad -\Theta p h'(p)/\eta(p) + h(p) > h(\bar{p}) - \Theta h(\bar{p});$$

i.e.,

$$(12') \quad h(p)(1 - \Theta) > h(\bar{p})(1 - \Theta),$$

which contradicts $p \geq \bar{p}$.

A similar argument works for the case $p' < \bar{p}$. This proves that there is a Cournot-Nash equilibrium at $p = \bar{p}$. The uniqueness of equilibrium follows from the fact that (6), which is a necessary condition for existence, has a unique solution. (Note that uniqueness does not obtain if $h(p,w)I = 0$, since then any increase in p will leave the equilibrium unchanged.)

Q.E.D.

RESULT 2.

$$\epsilon(w,I) = \alpha \bigg/ \left(\frac{z(p(w,I))}{\eta(p(w,I))} - (\alpha - 1)\right).$$

Proof. Write $p(w,I) = p$. Then

$$(13') \quad \log L(w,I) = \text{const} + \log C(\Theta h(p(w,I))I),$$

which, on differentiation with respect to $\log w$, yields

$$(14') \quad \epsilon(w,I) = \alpha\eta(p)\frac{w}{p}\frac{\partial p}{\partial w}.$$

Now

$$(15') \quad \log \gamma(p) = \log w + (\alpha - 1)\log h(p) + \text{const}.$$

Differentiating (15') with respect to $\log p$ yields

$$(16') \quad \frac{w}{p}\frac{\partial p}{\partial w} = [z(p) + (1 - \alpha)\eta(p)]^{-1}.$$

Combining (14') with (16') yields the desired result.

RESULT 3. $\lim_{p \to \bar{p}} \sup \delta(p) > 0$.

Proof. We use an argument similar to that of Lemma 1 to show that $(1 + (\rho/\epsilon(w,I))) \leq \omega < (1 - \rho)$ is inconsistent with the fact that $wL(w,I) = wqC(\Theta h(p)I) \leq qp\Theta h(p)I \leq q\Theta I$.

Proof of Lemma 2. It follows from Result 3 that either $\delta(p) > 0$ for all $0 < p < \overline{p}$ or $\delta(p) = 0$ has a unique solution $\hat{p}$ (uniqueness is implied by A8). In the former case, the unique solution of (14) is $p(I)$

475

$= p^*(I)$, where $(1/m)C(\Theta h(p^*(I))I) = T$. In the latter case, A8 implies that the unique solution of (14) is $p(I) = \max(\hat{p},p^*(I))$. That the solution to (14) is a Cournot-Nash equilibrium follows from an argument similar to that used in the proof of Lemma 1.

Proof of Proposition 1. From Lemma 2, if an ICE exists, $p = \max(\hat{p},p^*(I))$. But $p = p^*(I)$ implies full employment; i.e., $p = p^*$. Hence any ICE satisfies $\tilde{p} = \max(\hat{p},p^*)$. To prove the existence of an ICE, set $\tilde{I} = (1/\Theta)(m\bar{k}/(1 - \tilde{p}h(\tilde{p})))$, where $\tilde{p} = \max(\hat{p},p^*)$, and apply Lemma 2.

CHURCHILL COLLEGE, CAMBRIDGE

REFERENCES

Azariadis, C., "Implicit Contracts and Underemployment Equilibria," *Journal of Political Economy*, LXXXIII (1975), 1183–1202.
Benassy, J. P., "The Disequilibrium Approach to Monopolistic Price Setting and General Monopolistic Equilibrium," *Review of Economic Studies*, XLIII (1976), 69–81.
——, "A Neo-Keynesian Model of Price and Quantity Determination in Disequilibrium," in *Equilibrium and Disequilibrium in Economic Theory*, G. Schwodiauer, ed., Proceedings of a Conference held in Vienna, Austria (1978).
Chamberlin, E. H., *The Theory of Monopolistic Competition* (Cambridge, MA: Harvard University Press, 1933).
Clower, R. W., "The Keynesian Counterrevolution: A Theoretical Appraisal," in *The Theory of Interest Rates*, Hahn and Brechling, eds. (London: Macmillan, 1965).
Grandmont, J. M., "Temporary General Equilibrium Theory," *Econometrica*, XLIII (1977), 535–72.
——, and G. Laroque, "On Keynesian Temporary Equilibria," *Review of Economic Studies*, XLIII (1976), 53–67.
Hahn, F. H., "On Non-Walrasian Equilibria," *Review of Economic Studies*, XLV (1978), 1–17.
Hart, O., "A Model of Imperfect Competition with Keynesian Features," Economic Theory Discussion Paper, University of Cambridge, 1980.
Harrod, R., "An Essay in Dynamic Theory," *Economic Journal*, XLVIV (1939), 14–33.
Kaldor, N., "Alternative Theories of Distribution," *Review of Economic Studies*, XXIII (1956), 83–100.
Kalecki, M., *Theory of Economic Dynamics: An Essay on Cyclical and Long-Run Changes in a Capitalist Economy* (London: Allen and Unwin, 1954).
Leijonhufvud, A., *On Keynesian Economics and the Economics of Keynes* (London: Oxford University Press, 1968).
McManus, M., "Numbers and Size in Cournot Oligopoly," *Yorkshire Bulletin*, XIV (1962), 14–22.
Negishi, T., "Monopolistic Competition and General Equilibrium," *Review of Economic Studies*, XXVIII (1960), 196–201.
——, "Existence of an Underemployment Equilibrium," in *Equilibrium and Disequilibrium in Economic Theory*, G. Schwodiauer, ed., Proceedings of a Conference held in Vienna, Austria (1978).
Pigou, A. C., *The Theory of Unemployment* (London: Macmillan, 1933).
Roberts, J., and H. Sonnenschein, "On the Existence of Cournot Equilibrium Without Concave Profit Functions," *Journal of Economic Theory*, XIII (1976), 112–17.
——, and ——, "On the Foundations of the Theory of Monopolistic Competition," *Econometrica*, XLV (1979), 101–14.
Symposium in Journal of Economic Theory on Noncooperative Approaches to Competitive Equilibrium (April 1980).
Weiss, A., "Job Queues and Layoffs in Labor Markets with Flexible Wages," *Journal of Political Economy*, LXXXVIII (1980), 526–38.

ECONOMIC THEORY, ECONOMETRICS, AND MATHEMATICAL ECONOMICS

Edited by Karl Shell, Cornell University

Recent titles

Haim Levy and Marshall Sarnat, editors, *Financial Decision Making under Uncertainty*

Yasuo Murata, *Mathematics for Stability and Optimization of Economic Systems*

Alan S. Blinder and Philip Friedman, editors, *Natural Resources, Uncertainty, and General Equilibrium Systems: Essays in Memory of Rafael Lusky*

Jerry S. Kelly, *Arrow Impossibility Theorems*

Peter Diamond and Michael Rothschild, editors, *Uncertainty in Economics: Readings and Exercises*

Fritz Machlup, *Methodology of Economics and Other Social Sciences*

Robert H. Frank and Richard T. Freeman, *Distributional Consequences of Direct Foreign Investment*

Elhanan Helpman and Assaf Razin, *A Theory of International Trade under Uncertainty*

Edmund S. Phelps, *Studies in Macroeconomic Theory. Volume 1: Employment and Inflation. Volume 2: Redistribution and Growth*

Marc Nerlove, David M. Grether, and Jose L. Carvalho, *Analysis of Economic Time Series: A Synthesis*

Jerry Green and Jose Alexander Scheinkman, editors, *General Equilibrium, Growth and Trade: Essays in Honor of Lionel McKenzie*

Michael J. Boskin, editor, *Economics and Human Welfare: Essays in Honor of Tibor Scitovsky*

Carlos Daganzo, *Multinomial Probit: The Theory and Its Application to Demand Forecasting*

L.R. Klein, M. Nerlove, and S.C. Tsiang, editors, *Quantitative Economics and Development: Essays in Memory of Ta-Chung Liu*

Giorgio P. Szego, *Portfolio Theory: With Application to Bank Asset Management*

M. June Flanders and Assaf Razin, editors, *Development in an Inflationary World*

Thomas G. Cowing and Rodney E. Stevenson, editors, *Productivity Measurement in Regulated Industries*

Robert J. Barro, editor, *Money, Expectations, and Business Cycles: Essays in Macroeconomics*

Ryuzo Sato, *Theory of Technical Change and Economic Invariance: Application of Lie Groups*

Iosif A. Krass and Shawkat M. Hammoudeh, *The Theory of Positional Games: With Applications in Economics*

Giorgio Szego, editor, *New Quantitative Techniques for Economic Analysis*

John M. Letiche, editor, *International Economic Policies and Their Theoretical Foundation: A Source Book*

Murray C. Kemp, editor, *Production Sets*

Andreu Mas-Colell, editor, *Noncooperative Approaches to the Theory of Perfect Competition*

Jean-Pascal Benassy, *The Economics of Market Disequilibrium*

Tatsuro Ichiishi, *Game Theory for Economic Analysis*

David P. Baron, *The Export-Import Bank: An Economic Analysis*

Real P. Lavergne, *The Political Economy of U.S. Tariffs: An Empirical Analysis*

Halbert White, *Asymptotic Theory for Econometricians*

Thomas G. Cowing and Daniel L. McFadden, *Macroeconomic Modeling and Policy Analysis: Studies in Residential Energy Demand*

Svend Hylleberg, *Seasonality in Regression*

Jean-Pascal Benassy, *Macroeconomics: An Introduction to the Non-Walrasian Approach*

C.W.J. Granger and Paul Newbold, *Forecasting Economic Time Series, Second Edition*

Marc Nerlove, Assaf Razin, and Efraim Sadka, *Household and Economy: Welfare Economics of Endogenous Fertility*

Jean-Michel Grandmont, editor, *Nonlinear Economic Dynamics*

Thomas Sargent, *Macroeconomic Theory, Second Edition*

Yves Balasko, *Foundations of the Theory of General Equilibrium*

Jean-Michel Grandmont, editor, *Temporary Equilibrium: Selected Readings*

Index

Abraham, R., 270, 303
Akerlof, G., 68, 70
Alexeev, M., 70
Allais, M., 99, 173, 179, 182, 197
Allard, M., 71
Arbitrage, 12, 69, 115, 138, 156
Archibald, G.C., 182, 197
Arrow, K., ix, 3, 5, 10, 12, 23, 36, 37, 99, 140, 143, 154, 170, 179, 197, 309, 310, 336, 390, 391, 402, 421, 423, 424, 426, 429, 438
Artus, P., 70, 71
d'Aspremont, C., 69, 71
Assets markets, *see* Capital markets
Aumann, R., 69, 71, 189, 197, 404, 421
d'Autume, A., 70, 71
Azam, J.P., 70, 71
Azariadis, C., xviii, xxiii, 68, 71, 448, 476

Balasko, Y., 69, 71, 349, 350, 351, 358, 375
Balch, M., 37
Bankruptcy, 13, 15, 143, 218, 222, 228, 230
Bargaining set, 406, 415
Barrère, A., 71
Barro, R.J., 5, 25, 28, 29, 37, 55, 71, 383, 385, 393, 402, 421
Bartlett, W., 71
Baumol, W., 221
Bénard, J., vii
Bénassy, J.P., xxii, xxiii, 3, 5, 25, 28, 31, 32, 33, 37, 66, 69, 70, 71, 72, 383, 384, 393, 398, 399, 402, 405, 422, 424, 429, 438, 449, 476
Benhabib, J., xviii, xxiii
Berge, C., 112
Bernouilli, P., 99
Bertsekas, D., 143, 144, 145, 154
Bewley, T., 69, 72, 245

Bhattacharya, R.M., 334, 336
Billingsley, P., 7, 37, 112, 310, 314, 330, 333, 334, 336, 369, 375
Blackwell, D., 99, 111, 112
Blad, M.C., 72
Blanchard, O., 72
Bliss, C., 37, 72
Blocking coalition, 413
Blume, L.E., xxii, 69, 72, 339, 347, 348
Böhm, V., 31, 37, 69, 70, 72
de Boissieu, C., 72
Bonds, 70, 218, 222
Borrowing, 116, 139, 217
Bowen, R., 99
Braverman, E.M., 73
Bray, M., 46, 73
Brechling, F.P.R., 39, 179, 197, 403
Breiman, L., 179, 336
Bronsard, C., 71
Brock, W., 111, 112

Cagan, P., 173, 179
Capital markets, 12, 69, 115, 137, 156
Cash-in-advance constraint, 69, 183, 201, 217, 221, 400
Cass, D., 349, 375
Central bank, 16, 217, 225
Chae, S., 69, 73
Chamberlin, E.H., 448, 476
Champsaur, P., 46, 73, 422
Charemza, W., 70, 73
Cheffert, J.M., 70, 73
Chetty, V.K., 7, 37, 73
Christiansen, D.S., 7, 10, 37, 73, 112, 315, 337
Chung, K., 112, 372, 375
Cigno, A., 73
Classical dichotomy, 182, 187, 189, 190, 206

Classical homogeneity postulates, 173, 182
Clower, R.W., xxi, xxiii, 3, 4, 22, 24, 27, 37, 47, 73, 181, 197, 199, 215, 217, 245, 383, 384, 385, 387, 388, 392, 399, 400, 402, 422, 438, 447, 472, 476
Clower constraint, see Cash-in-advance constraint
Collateral, 134
Common expectations, see Overlapping expectations
Compact expectations, 174, 185, 227, 272, 318
Conjectural equilibrium, 431, 441
Conjectures, see Perceived demand (supply) curves
Constrained demand, 26
Consumption function, 58, 383
Continuous convergence, 97, 171
Cooper, R., 73
Coordination failures, see Effective demand failures
Cornwall, R., 99
Cournot-Nash equilibrium, 449, 454, 456
Credit, 16, 69, 217
Cuddington, J.T., 70, 73
Cycles, xx, 46, 249, 252, 253, 258, 270

Danforth, J., 111, 112
Danthine, J.P., 70, 73
Dasgupta, D., 7, 37, 73
Day, R., xviii, xxiii,
Debreu, G., ix, 3, 5, 11, 12, 14, 23, 37, 99, 115, 133, 134, 135, 138, 142, 154, 168, 169, 177, 179, 197, 215, 309, 315, 337, 358, 375, 383, 390, 402, 422, 438
De Canio, S., 46, 73
Decision making, 6, 87, 101
Decision rule, continuity of optimal, 6, 101
Dehez, P., 69, 70, 74
Delbaen, F., 9, 37, 334, 337
Diamond, P., 69, 74, 349, 375
Diewert, W.E., 3, 23, 37, 74
Disequilibrium theory, 383, 404, 423, 441, 447
Dixit, A., 70, 74
Doeblin condition, 351
Doob, J.S., 370, 371, 375
Dos Santos Ferreira, R., 69, 71
Drandakis, E., 5, 37, 165, 179
Drazen, A., 70, 74

Drèze, J., 3, 5, 25, 26, 27, 31, 32, 37, 38, 69, 70, 71, 74, 165, 284, 337, 383, 389, 393, 402, 422, 424, 438, 443

Easley, D., 347, 348
Eckalbar, J.C., 74
Eckwert, B., 82
Effective demand, 29, 383, 387, 409, 423, 447
  failures, 48–53, 68, 392, 409, 472
  and Walras' law, 384
Efficiency wages, 68
Eichberger, J., 69, 70, 74
Equicontinuity, 97
Error learning, 286, 291
Expectation function, xvi, 6, 42, 93, 102, 117, 140, 166, 185, 227, 250, 273, 286, 289, 311, 395
  and statistical estimation, xix
    classical, 9
    Bayesian, 10
  extrapolating properties of, 42, 45, 173, 185, 202, 252, 270
Expected utility, 7, 13, 17, 119, 141, 167, 170, 310, 396
  continuity of, 87, 171, 313, 397
  homogeneity of, 167, 172

Fan, K., 161, 347
Feller property, 341, 346
Fiscal policy, 201, 207, 217, 225, 233, 448, 465
Fishburn, P.C., 99
Fisher, F.M., 69, 75
Fitoussi, J.P., 70, 74, 75
Fitzroy, F.R., 38
Fleurbaey, M., 75
Foguel, S.R., 322, 337
Foley, D., 111, 112, 134, 135
Fourgeaud, C., viii, 46, 70, 75
Frictionless market, 385
Friedman, M., xxi, xxiii, 22, 38, 165, 173, 179, 181, 182, 197, 199, 200, 209, 215, 245
Frydman, R., 46, 75
Fuchs, G., xix, xxi, xxii, 36, 38, 43, 45, 46, 75, 249, 270, 271, 284, 286, 303
Futia, C.A., 75
Futures markets, 12, 115, 156

Gagey, F., xxi, 69, 75, 217
Gale, David, 38, 177, 179, 212, 215, 231, 245
Gale, Douglas, xxii, 4, 23, 24, 36, 38, 69,
    75, 76, 434, 441
Gary-Bobo, R.J., 69, 76
Gelpi, R.M., 70, 76
Gérard-Varet, L.-A., 69, 71, 76
Girshick, M.A., 99
Glicksberg, I., 367, 375
Glivenko–Cantelli theorem, 329
Glustoff, E., 5, 25, 32, 38, 383, 402
Gourieroux, C., 46, 75, 76
Government deficit, 217, 225, 231
Green, J.R., xxi, 3, 12, 14, 15, 16, 24, 36,
    37, 38, 69, 70, 77, 105, 112, 115, 135,
    139, 143, 155, 156, 158, 159, 161, 307,
    337
Greenberg, J., 69, 77
Grodal, B., 99
Grossman, H.I., 5, 25, 28, 29, 37, 38, 55,
    71, 383, 385, 388, 393, 403, 421, 422
Grossman, S., 245
Guesnerie, R., xviii, xxiii, 77

Haga, H., 70, 77
Hahn, F.H., xxii, 3, 4, 5, 16, 22, 24, 33, 37,
    38, 39, 69, 77, 116, 134, 135, 143, 154,
    165, 173, 179, 181, 183, 197, 205, 215,
    245, 336, 390, 391, 403, 422, 423, 424,
    426, 438, 441, 444, 446, 449, 476
Hahn–Negishi condition, 409, 410
Halmos, P.R., 99
Hammond, P., xxi, 69, 77, 156, 158, 160,
    161
Hansen, B., 383, 384, 403
Harrod, R., 473, 476
Hart, O.D., xxi, xxii, 15, 39, 69, 77, 137,
    155, 156, 157, 158, 160, 161, 446, 447,
    476
Heller, W.P., 3, 31, 39, 53, 67, 69, 77, 78
Hellwig, M.F., 69, 76, 78, 112, 245
Helpman, E., 39, 232, 233, 245
Hénin, P.Y., 70, 78
Herkenroth, U., 39
Herstein, I.N., 99
Hicks, J., xiii, xxiii, 4, 10, 24, 39, 47, 78,
    165, 179, 384, 403, 422
Hildenbrand, K., 78
Hildenbrand, W., xxii, 35, 36, 38, 39, 78,
    96, 161, 189, 197, 307, 309, 315, 319,

333, 334, 337, 339, 341, 342, 346, 348,
    351, 367, 375
Honkapohja, S., 69, 70, 78
Hool, B., 20, 22, 39, 69, 70, 78, 79
Household production, 105
Howard, D.H., 70, 79
Huberman, G., 349, 376

Implicit contracts, 68, 448
Increasing returns, 466
Indeterminacy of stationary equilibria, 200,
    209–210
Indirect utility function, 8, 49, 56, 92, 119,
    141
    money in the, 8, 167, 313, 395
Inefficiency of laissez faire, 199, 203
Inelastic expectations, xvii, 165, 174, 181,
    185, 217, 218, 227, 228, 254, 272, 275
Inflation tax, 207, 219
Informational discontinuity, 106
Inside money, 226
Invariant compact set, 308, 317
Invariant probability measure, 321–324, 340,
    342, 346, 370
Inventories, 70
Investment, 70
Involuntary underemployment, 461
IS-LM, 47, 70, 217
Ito, T., 70, 78, 79
Iwai, K., 33, 39
Ize, A., 79

Jacobs, K., 324, 337
Jaskold-Gabszewicz, J., 74
Jensen, M.C., 138, 155
Johansson, P.O., 70, 73, 79
John, A., 73
Johnson, H.G., 199, 215
Jordan, J.S., xxi, 7, 9, 10, 39, 79, 101, 112
Jordan, R., 76

Kahn, C., 68, 69, 79
Kaldor, N., 468, 476
Kalecki, M., 473, 476
Kareken, J.H., xxiii, 79
Karlin, S., 215
Kato, T., 270
Keiding, H., 69, 79
Kelley, J.L., 99

Kenally, G.F., 70, 79
Kennan, J., 111, 112
Keynes, J.M., 39, 384, 392, 399, 403
Keynesian multiplier, 47, 57, 64, 383, 392, 448, 462
  and unanticipated policy moves, 65
Kihlstrom, R., 36, 39
Kinked demand (supply) curve, 429, 442, 444
Kirman, A.P., 22, 38, 76
Knieps, G., 69, 79, 347, 348
Kolm, S.C., 199, 215
Kornai, J., 70, 79, 384, 403
Kryloff–Bogoliouboff theory, 323
Kuhn, H.W., 155
Kuhn–Tucker theorem, *see* Maximum principle
Kuratowski, K., 99, 319, 337
Kurz, M., 22, 39, 69, 79, 245

van der Laan, G.H., 69, 79
Laffont, J.J., 39, 46, 70, 76, 77, 79
Lambert, J.P., 70, 80
Large economies with individual uncertainty, 325
Laroque, G., xxi, xxii, xxiii, 3, 16, 18, 19, 20, 21, 23, 24, 32, 33, 36, 38, 43, 45, 46, 66, 69, 70, 71, 75, 76, 80, 217, 231, 232, 245, 249, 270, 271, 272, 284, 285, 303, 308, 313, 336, 337, 383, 388, 402, 404, 422, 424, 438, 449, 476
Laussel, D., 80
Law of large numbers, 308, 325
Law of supply and demand, 11
Ledyard, J.O., 16, 39, 101
Learning, xviii, 41–45, 249, 271, 286, 290–291
  under uncertainty, 46
Leijohnhufvud, A., 5, 24, 27, 39, 47, 80, 383, 387, 392, 399, 400, 403, 422, 438, 473, 476
Leland, H.E., 153, 155, 157, 161
Lenclud, B., 70, 75
Levine, J.P., 31, 37, 72
Lindahl, E., xiii, xxiii
Lindhal equilibrium, 404
Lintner, J., 137, 155
Lipsey, R.G., 182
Liquidity trap, 16, 20
Loeve, M., 179, 330, 337

Lofgren, K.G., 70, 73, 79, 80
Lollivier, S., xxi, 69, 75, 217
Lottery, 87
Lubrans, M., 70, 80
Lucas, R.E., Jr., xv, xxi, xxiii, 55, 69, 80, 349, 350, 376
Lump sum taxes, 207

Madden, P.J., 69, 80
Majumdar, M., 10, 37, 73, 112, 334
Malgrange, P., 80, 393
Malinvaud, E., xxiii, 25, 32, 39, 47, 55, 69, 70, 80, 81, 183, 198, 212, 215, 309, 334, 337, 405, 422, 424, 438
Market by market efficiency, 410
Market equilibrium lemma, 11, 178
Markov stochastic equilibrium, 34, 307, 318, 322, 339, 346
  with self-fulfilling expectations, 35, 69, 322, 347, 349
Marois, W., 78
Marschak, J., 99
Marx, K., 384, 403
Mas-Colell, A., 161
Maschler, M., 405, 421
Maskin, E., 69, 72, 81, 429
Maximum principle, 212
McCallum, B., 349, 376
McFadden, D., 37
McKenzie, L., ix, 177, 179
McManus, M., 471, 476
Mertens, J.F., 99
Michael, E., 112
Michel, G., 70, 71
Michel, P., 70, 71, 75, 78, 81
Milne, F., 161
Milnor, J., 99
Mirman, L.J., 36, 39, 111, 112
Modigliani, F., 70, 74
Monetary policy, 18, 217, 225, 231, 233
Money, as a store of value, 165, 249, 271, 286, 349
  as a medium of exchange, 181, 200, 217
Money demand, transaction motive, 197, 217
  precautionary and speculative motives, 197, 217, 397
Monfort, A., 46, 76
de Montbrial, T., 135, 215
Montet, C., 80
Mookherjee, D., 68, 69, 79

Morgenstern, O., 99
Morishima, M., 5, 23, 39
Mossin, J., 137, 155
Muellbauer, J., 63, 70, 81
Muller, H.H., 69, 72, 74, 77, 81
Multiplier effect, *see* Spillover effect

Nataf, A., vii
Neary, J.P., 69, 70, 81
Negishi, T., xxii, xxiii, xxiv, 24, 25, 33, 39, 66, 69, 70, 81, 422, 423, 424, 429, 438, 439, 449, 476
von Neumann, J., 99
Neveu, J., 337
Nikaido, H., 99, 177, 179, 198
Nitecki, Z., 270
Nonatomic distribution, 343, 351
Nontâtonnement, 24, 384, 399, 404, 409, 424
Norman, M.F., 35, 40
Notional demand, *see* Walrasian demand

Open market operations, 16, 218, 225
Optimum quantity of money, 181, 196, 199, 207, 232
Optimum taxation policy, 201, 207
Orderly equilibrium, 426
Outside money, 165, 181, 199, 226, 249, 271, 286, 307
Overlapping expectations, 12, 15, 126, 138, 144, 146, 153, 156, 159
Overlapping generations, 219, 231, 249, 271, 286, 307, 349
Overtaking criterion, 190, 206
Owen, R.F., 81

Parguez, A., 73
Parthasarthy, K., 7, 40, 99, 112, 135, 141, 155, 170, 174, 310, 329, 330, 331, 337
Patinkin, D., xxi, xxiv, 4, 5, 16, 19, 21, 24, 40, 47, 81, 165, 172, 175, 179, 181, 198, 199, 215, 383, 403, 422
Pegging the interest rate, 18, 225
the money supply, 227
Peled, D., 376
Perceived demand (supply) curve, 66, 423, 429, 449
rational, 424, 433, 444, 449
reasonable, 437
Perceived quantity constraint, 386, 407, 472

Perpetuity, 16
Person, T., 81
Peytrignet, M., 70, 73
Picard, P., xxiii, xxiv, 70, 75, 81
Pigou, A., 459, 473, 476
Point expectations, 117, 121, 166, 184, 222, 250, 273, 289
Polemarchakis, H., 40, 69, 72, 80
Polterovitch, V.M., 69, 81, 82
Portes, R., 63, 70, 81, 82, 422
Portfolio choices, 137, 156
Postlewaite, A., 69, 72
Pradel, J., 46, 75
Pratt, J., 275, 285
Public goods, 220, 404

Quandt, R.E., 70, 73, 82
Quantity rationing, equilibrium, 25, 46, 383, 389, 397, 404, 423, 441, 447
in the sense of Drèze, 26
in the sense of Benassy, 30, 383, 389
efficiency of, 32, 52, 390, 409
and macroeconomics, 55, 70, 383
and imperfect competition, 66, 399, 423, 447
and public economics, 69, 404
in open economies, 70
and planned economies, 70, 404
and econometrics, 70
Quantity theory of money, 19, 182, 188, 189, 190, 231, 252
Quasi-equilibrium, 189

Radner, R., 4, 9, 10, 23, 36, 40, 116, 135, 165, 179, 180, 307, 322, 337, 434, 439
Ranga Rao, R., 99
Rational expectations, *see* Self-fulfilling expectations
Rationing scheme, 28, 385, 405, 428
Recontracting process, 55, 404, 411
Replicated economy, 413
Repressed inflation, 25, 57, 404
Revision of expectations, xix, 290–291
Revuz, D., 372, 376
Richelle, Y., 71, 82
Robbin, J., 270, 303
Roberts, J., 449, 471, 476
Roberts, K., 69, 77, 81
Robinson, J., 403

Rockafellar, R.T., 144, 155
Rotschild, M., 434, 439
Roy, R., viii
Ryll-Nardzewski, C., 99, 319, 337

Sachs, J., 72
Sadka, E., 232, 233, 245
Samuelson, P.A., 40, 172, 180, 182, 189, 198, 199, 215, 270, 271, 272, 285, 307, 337, 349, 376
Sargent, T.J., xv, xxiii
Savage, L.J., 99
Savin, N.E., 46, 73
Scarf, H., 422
Schittko, U.K., 82
Schulz, W., 69, 82
Schweizer, U., 69, 81
Schwödiauer, G., 40, 82
Second best, 231
Securities, short term, 105, 115, 218
Seignoriage tax, 217, 231, 232
Selection, measurable, 319, 346
  continuous, 319, 339, 346
Self-fulfilling expectations, xiv, xvi, 35, 188, 199, 218, 229, 322, 347, 349, 356
  convergence to, xix, 41–46, 249, 259, 271
Shah, A., 82
Sharpe, W.F., 137, 155
Shell, K., 349, 350, 375
Short sales, 115, 137
Silvestre, J., 69, 82
Simonovits, A., 82
Sneessens, H.R., 70, 80, 82
Solow, R., 47, 82, 383, 403, 422
Sondermann, D., 9, 23, 40, 82, 115, 124, 135, 307, 337
Sonnenschein, H., 449, 471, 476
Sontheimer, K.C., 183, 198
Sotomayor, J., 303
Spear, S., xxii, 69, 82, 349, 350, 357, 373, 376
Spillover effect, 392, 405
Srivastava, S., xxii, 69, 82, 349, 350, 357, 373, 376
Stability of stationary state, 41–45, 197, 249, 259, 271, 275
  of cycles, 46, 249, 258
Stabilizing expectations, 286
Stahl, D.O. II, 69, 70, 83
Starr, R.M., 3, 31, 39, 69, 78, 188, 189, 198

Starrett, D., 22, 40
Static expectations, 167, 172, 175
Stationary monetary equilibrium, 181, 188, 203, 218, 229, 249, 252, 271, 289, 335
  constrained inefficiency of, 181, 196, 199, 204, 232
Stationary stochastic equilibrium, 34, 307, 318, 322, 339, 346
  with self-fulfilling expectations, 35, 69, 322, 347, 349
Steigum, E., 83
Stiglitz, J., 47, 68, 70, 71, 81, 82, 83, 383, 403, 422
Stigum, B., 5, 10, 16, 23, 40, 101, 105, 111, 112, 165, 167, 180, 307, 337
Stochastic kernel, see Transition correspondence
Stochastic stability, 321
Strom, S., 83
Structural stability, 249, 261
Superneutrality of nominal interest payments, 201, 211
Sutherland, W.R.S., 212, 215
Svensson, L.E.O., 40, 69, 81, 83
Svensson, L.G., 69, 73
Syndicate, 452

Tatonnement, on quantities, 405
Theodorescu, I., 35, 40
Tight expectations, see Compact expectations
Tillmann, G., xxii, 46, 83, 271
Tirole, J., 69, 81
Tobin, J., 170, 180, 221, 245
Townsend, R., 111, 112
Transactions constraint, see Cash-in-advance constraint
Transition, probability, 320
  correspondence, 339

Underconsumption, 57
Unemployment, Classical, 25, 47, 57, 61, 404
  Keynesian, 25, 47, 57, 59, 392, 404, 448
Unit elastic expectations, 19, 167, 276

Value added tax, 221
Value maximization, 105
Varian, H.R., 83
Veendorp, E.C.H., 83

Verhulst, M.J., viii
Villa, P., 80
Vind, K., 99
Voluntary exchange, 29, 54, 384, 406

Wages as a screening device, 448
Wallace, N., xxiii, 79
Walrasian demand, 50, 423
Weak convergence, 7, 87, 121, 141, 170, 310, 340, 397
Weddepohl, C., 69, 83, 84
Weibull, J.W., 69, 79, 83, 84
Weinrich, G., 69, 71, 84
Weiss, A., 448, 476
Weiss, L., 245
Werin, L., 83
Werner, J., 69, 84

Whitt, W., 112
Wickens, M., 46, 84
Winter, D., 70, 82
Woodford, M., 46, 84

Yaari, M., 349, 375
Yellen, J., 68, 70, 84
Younès, Y., xxi, xxii, 3, 5, 16, 20, 21, 22, 25, 32, 38, 40, 54, 55, 69, 70, 76, 81, 84, 181, 199, 212, 215, 221, 245, 308, 337, 383, 390, 400, 403, 404, 405, 422, 424, 438, 439
Yu, S.W., 37

Zagame, P., 73
Zeeman, C., 72
Zylberberg, A., 78, 84